PENGUIN BOOKS

The Guardian Book of Cricket

Matthew Engel was born in Northampton in 1951 and reported his first cricket match for the *Northampton Chronicle and Echo* in 1972. After a spell with Reuters he joined the staff of the *Guardian* in 1979 and covered some fifty different sports, from soccer to tiddlywinks, before becoming the newspaper's full-time cricket correspondent in 1983. He has also contributed articles to *Wisden* and *Wisden Cricket Monthly* and is the author of *Ashes '85*. He was named sports writer of the year for 1985 by Granada Television's *What the Papers Say*.

THE GUARDIAN
BOOK OF
CRICKET

EDITED BY MATTHEW ENGEL

PENGUIN BOOKS

PENGUIN BOOKS

Published by the Penguin Group
27 Wrights Lane, London w8 5TZ, England
Viking Penguin Inc., 40 West 23rd Street, New York, New York 10010, USA
Penguin Books Australia Ltd, Ringwood, Victoria, Australia
Penguin Books Canada Ltd, 2801 John Street, Markham, Ontario, Canada L3R 1B4
Penguin Books (NZ) Ltd, 182–190 Wairau Road, Auckland 10, New Zealand

Penguin Books Ltd, Registered Offices: Harmondsworth, Middlesex, England

First published by Pavilion Books/Michael Joseph 1986
Published in Penguin Books 1986
Reprinted 1988

Made and printed in Great Britain by
Richard Clay Ltd, Bungay, Suffolk

CONTENTS

INTRODUCTION

This book is intended as a celebration, of a great game, a great newspaper and what we like to think of as the very special connection between the two. *The Guardian* has been published, first as a local weekly, then as a bi-weekly, then as a daily and finally as a national newspaper, competing, contending and often outclassing its rivals, for 165 years, since 1821. For the past 160 it has reported cricket in a manner that has reflected the changing nature of the paper, the game and the age. *The Guardian* has probably published a billion words on cricket; what follows is a very personal selection.

Since I took over as cricket correspondent in 1983, people have often enquired whether I felt daunted by the mantle of Cardus and Arlott. The answer, frankly, is that I feel far more daunted by the day-to-day business of competing with my rivals from *The Times* and *Daily Telegraph* (both former *Guardian* writers and represented here) and the rest than to worry about the past. It was only when I began to research this volume that the full weight of history began to hit me; it is not just Cardus and Arlott, as I hope this volume will show.

The Manchester Guardian began, nicely in time for summer, on 5 May 1821, the response of a group of Mancunian radicals to the horrors of the Peterloo massacre two years earlier (an over-simplification, but this is a sports book), which was also the day Napoleon died – though the paper never really got round to reporting that, understandably, since St Helena was some way outside the circulation area. The first edition (circulation: 1,000; price: a viciously expensive sevenpence owing to stamp duty) pronounced itself to be an enemy of 'scurrility and slander, on either side', reported a thunderstorm at Liverpool and a ghost at Truro but no sport. The second issue, however, contained the card for Chester Races, including the Dee Stakes. The 43,435th issue in May 1986 did the same.

Jeremiah Garnett, partner of the paper's founder John Edward Taylor, was keen on field sports and, above all, fishing. And through the 1820s the new weekly began to include regular, if patchy, references to all kinds of pastimes, frivolous and sometimes frightening. Issue number four mentioned a 67-round fight in Ely between Thomas Hill and James Macann, after which Macann died; and two weeks later there was a brief report, under the heading PUGILISM, of the contest between Hickman 'the gas-man' and Oliver: 'Oliver was so dreadfully beaten as to be in a state of complete stupor at the close of the combat, whilst the *gas-man* received so little injury, that he played several games of billiards at Croydon on his way to London.' The next week there was a round-by-round account of the fight occupying three-quarters of a column: '. . . Oliver's *phizog* was again screwed into divers unseemly shapes . . .'

In the early years, there was much boxing and racing, along with occasional references to archery, pedestrianism and even cock-fighting. The first cricket report I could find was in 1826 (see page 137). This was tucked away between the STEAM-PACKET INTELLIGENCE and the ST. LEGER BETTING and under a piece about London fashion: '. . . the most approved colours are yellow, rose colour, lavender, ethereal blue, apricot and straw-colour.' By the 1830s SPORTING INTELLIGENCE rated a more-or-less regular heading of its own, though cricket was often recorded under LOCAL AND PROVINCIAL INTELLIGENCE. 'This most amusing game' it was called in 1833, a year when Manchester beat Rochdale by six notches 'in the presence of a vast concourse of spectators.'

The paper was a bi-weekly now and was acquiring the look it was to keep for much of the century. Above the letters there would be NOTICES TO CORRESPONDENTS, often very tart: 'G. H. has made a modest request, which, however, we have no intention to comply with;' and 'The correspondent who adopts the signature A Female Protestant, if a female at all, which we doubt, must be a silly old woman.' There would sometimes be news on the front of the four-page paper, though that seems largely due to a shortage of adverts.

In 1840, amidst a vigorous correspondence about how far north the nightingale sings and ads for Bullock's Turkey, Rhubarb and Camomile Pills, there was a scorecard showing how a local player called Hampson had taken ten wickets in an innings, a victory for Manchester over Liverpool by an innings and 29 notches and what appears to be *The Guardian*'s first foray into the groin-strain style of cricket journalism: Barnett Esq of the 5th Dragoon Guards played for the Victoria club instead of Mr. Aspinwall, 'whose fingers were much hurt a few days since.' Much of the Local and Provincial Intelligence was far more painful:

AWFULLY SUDDEN DEATH

ROBBERY BY A CHARWOMAN

THROAT CUTTING AT BURY

THE LATE DIABOLICAL ATTEMPT AT MURDER, AT LUDLOW

Most of the cricket reports of the 1830s were brief, irregular and much obsessed with the assemblage of ladies, regimental bands and betting, thus beginning the *Guardian* tradition of cheerful irrelevance.

In the 1840s and 50s they became a little more businesslike. In 1850, when sport and sports reporting was starting to be transformed by new transport and communications (the result of the Craven Stakes was received by electric telegraph) there is a sound technical account of the game between Manchester and All-England, and the first, though hardly the last, signs of criticism of Lancastrian fielding: 'their balls were not picked up or stopped with the neatness, certainty or quickness desirable.'

In 1851, amidst much discussion about whether iron bedsteads are dangerous in thunderstorms, there is the first hint of *Guardian* classicism entering cricket reporting:

ELEVEN OF ALL-ENGLAND v. 22 OF THE BROUGHTON CLUB

. . . Now caught, now run out, now bowled, now stumped – all so well done, so cleverly done, yet withal so rigorously, so unmercifully, that it were but to think of the story of those mythical gods of old, entering into the lists against mortals, and when all but themselves had thought the race won, suddenly revealed their divine origins, by the test of their superhuman exertions.

There were also signs of another perennial: Lancastrian inferiority. In advance of the match, the writer prophesied gloomily: 'Manchester, although it may have made progress as a town in the art and mystery of cricket, is as yet, notwithstanding all its advantages, but second rate. It is we fear unable to take the stand our neighbouring county has recently nobly taken.' Quite right, too. Yorkshire had beaten All-England at Sheffield. Broughton, needing 42 to win with 17 wickets standing, had lost by 21. Not just mortals v. superhumans either, perhaps . . . 'A good dinner,' remarked the correspondent in a more down-to-earth moment, 'is not always followed by superior cricket playing.'

That same year came the first criticism of a decision:

MANCHESTER v. SHREWSBURY

. . . When Mr. Barlow received a ball he played forward with a steady full-faced bat; the ball went off the bat and hit the back of his leg, when the bowler appealed, and the Shrewsbury umpire gave him out leg before wicket. Many who were on the ground state the decision to have been erroneous; and we believe had such an occurrence taken place at Lord's, very serious notice would have been taken of it . . .

And in 1852 the first major cock-up:

ERRATUM

We have received a note from the secretary of the Hulme Embden Club denying that the match between them and the Hulme Brunswick, which we inserted in our number of the 21st ult., was ever played. All we can say is, that the return was sent to us, but on whose authority we cannot now discover.

In 1855 newspaper stamp duty was abolished and *The Guardian* transformed itself into a daily to compete with the rival *Examiner*. For a long while it had been growing fatter and fitter; now it was back to the original four pages, except on Saturday, the best advertising day, and it could no longer remain aloof from adverts from racing tipsters: 'The winner of the Derby is at 200 to 1. From some extraordinary information just received I can send you the absolute winner for 18 stamps. – Address S. Bray, Post-office, Congleton, Cheshire.'

There would be a dozen or more reports of Saturday cricket matches played around Manchester appearing on summer Tuesdays. And in 1858 yet another regular theme was established, rotten catering.

Sir, – As an admirer of cricket, I generally attend the annual match at Broughton, and beg, through your medium, to direct the attention of the Committee to the class of refreshments supplied on 'the sixpenny side' of the ground last year. The so-called porter that was sold was really wretched stuff, and the faces of the consumers reminded me of the royal pump room at Harrogate: in fact it was not fit to drink, and I trust this year we shall be able to enjoy the glass, even if a little more is to be paid for it – I beg to annex my address, and remain, sir, yours respectfully,
One Who Does Not Like Fourpenny

And, next day, in those happy times when the postal system worked and cricket administrators took notice of *The Guardian*, there came an assurance that this year there would be a new caterer.

Cricket continued to do well in *The Manchester Guardian* of the 1860s, though not much else did. Friedrich Engels ('a military correspondent') would pronounce on Schleswig-Holstein and the like, but the coverage of the American Civil War was indifferent and there were times when the racing seemed to be taking over the whole paper. 'In 1862,' the *Guardian*'s historian David Ayerst noted with disgust, 'there were twelve long articles on the previous year's two-year-olds.' A. P. Wadsworth, a later editor, described the *M.G.* of the time as 'a bad paper . . . also, alas, extremely profitable.'

But the seeds of a glorious future were being sown in improbable ground. In 1867 C. P. Scott, a second year undergraduate, was offered the editor's job on the strength of being the owner's cousin. Five years later he took charge, a reign that was to last for almost half a century and shape the paper's destiny for ever.

Besides being a great journalist and radical, Scott was not without a certain late Victorian muscularity: he cycled back from the office to Fallowfield until he was past eighty. And his paper began to reflect that. Sport was becoming modern and national; county cricket was becoming properly organised; W.G. (C.P. by another name, I sometimes think) stalked the land. And *The Guardian* reported this, often at impressive length and depth. Soccer was some way behind. In 1880 there was a plaintive letter: 'Coming from the South I am surprised at the almost total absence in Manchester of the Association game. Doubtless many of your readers who are old Association men, or who would be football players but do not care for the rough handplay and handling of the Rugby game, would be glad to assist in the formation of a club . . .' Manchester City was formed that same year, United followed five years later.

Meanwhile, Scott put horse racing in its place. He did not suddenly abolish the racing service out of religious conviction; it just withered. The big occasions were given their deserts, or more: 'He who would fitly describe the Oaks of 1885 should be a poet of the Aeschylean or tragic order who can sing of dust.' The story goes that in the end the runners and riders were left out in error one night, no one complained and so the service was not restored. It was 1970 before *The Guardian* established a full, modern racing desk, perhaps the last step on the road to being a genuine national newspaper.

But Lancashire cricket began to occupy, if not quite a central position, then at least an honoured corner of the pages of *The Guardian*. There was great joy over Lancashire's triumphs of 1881. Cricket was thriving. Our London correspondent condemned the management at The Oval for not recognising that crowds had multiplied by 10 or 15 times within the past 20 years. 'Under the blazing sun of today,' he reported from the 1884 Test against Australia, 'the miseries which The Oval spectator had to undergo were intolerable . . . many could catch only occasional glimpses of the play, and those who paid five shillings for admission to the stands found they had nothing but a rough plank without a back to sit on, and that there was no awning overhead.' In 1883, there was the first example I discovered of the 'this would never have happened in my time' line of thought. A correspondent sighed for the Yorkshire bowlers of the 1850s, Freeman and Emmett. 'Truly there were giants in those days.'

Ah, 1883! There was a cure for all the world's ills then: Beecham's Pills 'worth a guinea a box'; Keating's Powder – bugs, fleas, beetles, moths are easily destroyed by Keating's Powder, which is perfectly unrivalled; Cockle's Antibiotic Pills. And the great certainties of late Victorian and Edwardian England ran through *The Guardian*'s cricket reports, which were often splendidly written and even more often splendidly Lancashire chauvinist.

Attacks on Crossland and Mold, the two Lancashire bowlers with dubious actions, were fended off as though cotton itself was under attack: 'We never had the slightest doubt that Crossland's pace had quite as much to do with the outcry against him as his alleged unfairness,' and the idea that Test cricket might take precedence over county matches came under righteous if not entirely unprejudiced fire after England beat Australia in 1890:

> A match between England and Australia is of no importance whatever in comparison with an inter-county contest, and it would be small consolation for the authorities at Bramall Lane or Old Trafford to find that they had lost a county match by permitting some of their best men to assist the Surrey or Marylebone Club in gathering in a large amount of money. County cricket is the backbone of the game, and its claims must have precedence.

It would be lovely to get away with an argument like that in these Test-mad days; but it may have been relevant in 1890 that for the first time no Lancashire player had been included in the England team.

Sadly, it has proved impossible to discover who these anonymous correspondents were, though it seems probable that at least some of the cricket in the 1890s was written by John Atkins, subsequently one of the best Boer war correspondents and author of *The Relief of Ladysmith*.

We think of these years now as the Golden Age, but it did not always seem that way at the time, certainly not to *The Guardian*'s writers. 'It was the most uninteresting Oxford and Cambridge match seen for years – perhaps even the most uninteresting ever seen,' wrote a correspondent of the 1893 University match, in which the participants included Fry, Ranji, two Palairets, F. S. Jackson, Douglas and Leveson-Gower.

And there was a dreadfully depressed letter to the editor in 1894 from one Samuel Hosegood of Swinton:

> Sir, – The present deplorable position of Lancashire is one that must give considerable pain to all who look with pride on her past cricket history. Never has she been so low down in the scale, and not a few are wondering how long such a state of things is to continue . . .

The *M.G.* flourished, though, seeing off its rival *The Manchester Examiner* shortly after *The Examiner* failed to report the Tay Bridge accident . . . 'the sub-editors having all joined a cab home shortly after the first tidings arrived. The editor thought the excuse not an unreasonable one, seeing that it had certainly been snowing hard.'

Throughout the Edwardian era cricket was given generous space in C. P. Scott's columns, and once the Balkan question and Asquith's government had been considered there was often room for a short leader on Lancashire's doings, even after quite routine results. In 1914, in popular imagination the last year of the endless and carefree Edwardian summer, there was much introverted discussion about the future of the game. 'Is golf destroying cricket?' asked one contributor in June, and this discussion went on amidst reports of suffragette outrages, the Irish question, a doctor in Peru grafting a baboon gland on to a cretinous girl, the death of Joseph Chamberlain and the tango, the Channel Tunnel (honest), Southport Council's decision to stop blotting out betting news from papers in the public library and an outbreak of ptomaine poisoning at Todmorden.

The assassination of the Archduke Franz Ferdinand on 28 June did not disturb the Lancashire players travelling from Gloucester to Edgbaston. It was reported as an important item of foreign news, but no one even remotely guessed at the consequences that would unfold. When war fever did erupt (while Lancashire were playing Gloucestershire again) *The Guardian* tried to stay aloof. As so often, it was in a minority; history proved it right.

If there was a golden age as far as the *M.G.* was concerned, it began after the war when a young man who had been serving as reporter, drama critic and Scott's personal assistant fell ill with a pulmonary condition and, by way of convalescence, went at the news editor's suggestion for a few days in the sun at Old Trafford. And Neville Cardus, 'Cricketer' as he was bylined after 1920, began to give the discerning readers of Manchester the best and most enjoyable cricket reports the world has ever seen. The mark Cardus left on journalism can be gauged by the arguments that still go on about his merits. There is no doubt that licence often drifted into fantasy and, in old age, into repetitiveness. But what emerges from a study of the files is a great deal of unexpected trenchancy, and in the early years above all an extraordinary springtime freshness, which must have been even more vivid at the time compared to the hack-stuff that was appearing in most newspapers. I can only hope it comes over in this selection, and commend in particular the Cardus account of Lancashire at Dover in 1926, all three days of which have been included, as the perfect example of cricket reporting as idyll. One can but try and think of it when struggling to convey the import of the latest drug revelations.

The 'Cricketer' era exactly spanned the inter-war period; in 1940, feeling redundant in a Manchester shorn by war of both good cricket and good concerts, Cardus sailed to Australia and did a stint as music critic of the *Sydney Morning Herald*. He wrote about cricket on and off for *The Guardian* until his death in 1975, aged eighty-five. He was called back to cover the Ashes series of 1953 and would often add think-pieces on Test matches to back up the main correspondent, but never again did the job on a day-by-day basis.

Cardus's successor, when war ended and a cricket correspondent was actually required, was Terence Prittie, who held the job only briefly before being appointed Berlin correspondent, though he retained a lifelong interest in cricket. Prittie was followed by Denys Rowbotham who, apart from a short gap in the early 50s, was in charge of the paper's cricket for more than 20 years, until his sad and sudden early death in 1968.

Rowbotham was a rather Olympian writer of great cricketing depth and integrity (much loved by his colleagues); he knew what he liked and what he did not, and I have included his account of the 1966 Gillette final as an example of the old world rubbing uncomfortably against the new. The world was changing, the game was changing and *The Manchester Guardian* was changing.

The 1940s were really no time to be a daily cricket writer. Newsprint rationing was severe, and six-page papers offered little space for a writer like Rowbotham to flourish. But in the 50s the situation gradually eased. In 1952 (the year when the young John Woodcock – later to join *The Times* and become successive *Guardian* cricket writers' most formidable and durable rival – covered the Tests) news made it to page one instead of advertising. In February 1952 even the death of George VI could not disturb the timeless clutter of classified ads on the front of the paper; in July 1953 Cardus's account of Watson and Bailey's defiance in the Second Test, headlined MIRACLE OF FAITH AT LORD'S, was the main story, ahead even of RUSSIA REJECTS WEST'S DEMANDS ON BERLIN. That same day an English holidaymaker in Copenhagen fainted in 86 degrees, was taken to hospital and found to be wearing an overcoat, jacket, trousers, woollen waistcoat, cloth waistcoat, shirt, woollen vest and long wool underpants. Old habits, as I say, were dying hard.

Two months earlier, full bylines had appeared on the sports pages instead of the quasi-anonymity of initials and confusing phrases like 'Our Cricket Correspondent', 'A Cricket Correspondent' and 'Our Special Correspondent'. In *The Guardian* of the 50s there are the first signs of the modern, national paper it was to become – London printing began, the editor moved down south taking the paper's centre of gravity with him and Manchester was dropped from the title, though there was still plenty of room for much old-fashioned Mancunian eccentricity.

In 1950, a year when the main obsessions seem to have been Korea, nylon shirts and Compton's knee, a letter-writer claimed that if the magazines *Magnet, Gem, Boys' Friend* and *Union Jack* were still published, there would be much less juvenile delinquency: ten years later, as *The Guardian* moved away from its northern roots and the country headed towards the 60s, the paper seemed to have leaped forward an eon or two.

Sport and cricket in particular remained more firmly in the past. There was good cricket writing in the paper, but the editor Alastair Hetherington was more interested in other departments, the sports pages were cramped and looked dated, and the game itself was going though one of its most depressing periods. Cricket seemed to be an increasingly marginal feature of the thinking newspaper reader's life.

And *The Guardian* itself was fighting hard to survive.

The turning point probably came in 1968, a turbulent year in politics and cricket. After Denys Rowbotham died, John Arlott was appointed cricket correspondent and at once had a classic *Guardian* issue to get hold of: the D'Oliveira affair. The era of Yorkshire dominance came to an end, as Brian Chapman (see page 145) perceptively foreshadowed. And John Samuel became sports editor (the fifth since 1931, after Evelyn Montague, his brother Larry, Bill Taylor and David Gray), a post he was to hold until Mike Averis took over in May 1986.

And it seems to me that soon after 1968 *Guardian* cricket writing may have entered a second golden age. There was some vintage stuff in the paper in the early 70s: Arlott in his pomp, Cardus firmly back in the fold for his last years, wit and craftsmanship from Eric Todd and Brian Chapman, the young Blofeld and the first brilliant flashes of Keating. After Cardus died, Ian Peebles, for all too short a period before his own death, contributed a series of quite scintillating essays. The paper had a good war during Packer, just as it did during D'Oliveira – and bodyline.

When Arlott retired to Alderney in 1980 to take over the emeritus essay-writing role Paul Fitzpatrick, a fine writer, succeeded him before becoming the first, though I dare say not the last, *Guardian* correspondent to discover that the life of a full-time cricket journalist on the non-stop money-making merry-go-round of the post-Packer era was not quite the paid holiday that outsiders imagined, especially for a family man.

Paul became the northern correspondent, mixing cricket with his beloved rugby league, and I took over the main job; like fortunate newspapermen through the ages, I was just around – sitting on the sub-editors' desk in London and pining for green fields – at the right moment.

Is there a pattern in all this? *The Guardian* has managed to be successful in the modern era while still, under Peter Preston, giving its writers an intellectual freedom that you sign away in exchange for the pay cheque just about everywhere else in the business. I think C. P. Scott would be proud. On cricket, we moderns have tried to maintain the writing tradition and remain as faithful to the county whence we sprang as a national paper possibly can. By instinct rather than design, the *Guardian* view is not necessarily the Lord's view.

I hope all of this comes over in this selection as well as is feasible when a billion words have to be boiled down to 150,000 or so. Limited co-operation from one copyright holder has meant that the book could not go ahead exactly as envisaged. Otherwise, the choice was mine. I owe special thanks for help and support to Colin Webb and Steve Dobell of Pavilion, John Samuel, Ian Ridley, Ken Murphy, Frank Singleton, David Frith; to John Claughton and Vic Marks for Latin scholarship; and to the librarian, staff and lunch-ladies at the Cambridge University Library, where much of the research was done; and also to everyone who kindly allowed their work to be reproduced.

In 1900, a *Guardian* reviewer wrote plaintively: 'Of the making of cricket books there is no end. Many of them are pretty bad, and not worth a place on one's shelves.' I trust this may be considered an exception. If there are more than a few mistakes in it, I am sorry; *The Guardian* has a thoroughly undeserved reputation in these matters, but I know regular readers would be disappointed if there were none at all.

Matthew Engel
London, June 1986

NOTE: For the most part, I have tried to let the articles speak for themselves, as they were written. Where it seems most relevant, scores and, more sparingly, footnotes have been added.

SPRING

NEVILLE CARDUS   APRIL 19 1920

At this time of year the rebirth of cricket is being observed the country over with all the appropriate rites. Men are taking up their old boots and knocking last September's turf out of the spikes, now sweet brown powder, fragrant to the memory. They are busy whitening these same old boots again – no true cricketer ever buys a new pair until he is compelled – with a small sponge and a tin of blanco, taking pains to go over the buckskin without smearing the soles.

The yellow bat comes from the shelf; it is fondled lovingly, and that slightly splintered edge is regarded concernedly. It was done in getting a fast one from Smith on the on side. Couldn't have been a really good shot, now we come to think of it! One ought really to get the ball in the middle of the bat. Still, it was a good enough shot for a country-house game, and all boundaries look alike on the scorecard.

The groundsman is out tending his pitch, his eye as keen for the fine shades as any Whistler over a nocturne. Hear him startle a barbarian of a fellow who is actually crossing the ground on a bicycle, and the turf wet! He puts two fingers over his nether lip and makes a noise whose peculiarly piercing quality can be heard a mile away. Fellow on bicycle ignominiously swerves to the path, trying to look as if he had already been going in that direction anyway. The men are fixing the nets at the far corner of the enclosure, and somebody is already waking the echoes of the pavilion as he walks along the platform of wooden laths.

What a strange charm there is in the hollow echoes of a cricket pavilion! And what a ritual lies in the opening of a cricket pavilion after a winter of solitude and quiet! It must, of course, be a place devoted wholly to cricket, where no alien footballers come in midwinter to disturb its silences. The lock is stiff, and rightly so, for sacrilege would be committed by any abrupt disturbance of this murmurous sanctuary. Inside, you get the familiar odour, an odour which might be supposed to come from the essence of a hundred bygone mellow days.

On the forms are those dirty-grey pads, with the buckle off the right-legged one. The very deuce to get it on, when you are next man in all of a sudden and you can see, from the shady interior, through the square, glassless window, the other man coming from the wicket out of the warm sunshine! And from the hooks on the wall there is hanging that very shirt, sleeves hopelessly inside out, which you left last back-end, and there it has been all through the gloom and chill of winter.

It is a reminder that one often plays cricket for the last time at the end of a summer without knowing it is the last time. Of course that way of taking leave of the greatest of games for ever so many long, dreary months is all wrong. A good cricketer ought to finish a season consciously performing a valedictory ceremony. He should feel the pathos of the farewells as the September sun falls lower and lower in the sky and the shadows lengthen on the calm grass. The declining moments should exude bitter-sweet pain. The grey early autumn mists rising around the quiet ground should strike one as the harbinger of the end, and with the last over the pageant of the dead season should pass rather sadly before the mind's eye. How exquisite, if one felt all this, would be the solemnity of the final drawing of stumps and the homeward walk to the pavilion! One would then murmur to oneself, drawing out to the full the fine sentimentality of the scene and the occasion, *Haec olim meminisse juvabit!*[1]

Happy is it that one is in no danger of missing a jot of the sense of the event when one begins a new season. Let it be a balmy April day, and how can we fail to catch the joy which comes as we feel the air filling out our flannels, making us luxuriously loose at the neck, and passing over the body with a gentle caress? Good Lord, we must ask ourselves, what lives do we lead in the winter? How absurd now seems the best Melton overcoat in the world, and the softest of silk scarves! This is the sweet o' the year.

The occasion has its pains and penalties, none the less. A batsman sends his willow out like a flail, and hits quite a yard over a miserable half-volley. Heaven help me, he might well ask himself, why do they make bats so impossibly heavy? How, in the name of justice, do they expect a mere mortal to hit a ball so outrageously small? Yet once upon a time, the distraught man tells himself, he was known to hit it – aye, even to the boundary! Will he ever accomplish the feat again?

So, too, does the bowler have his moments of misgiving, as he strains his creaking joints into activity after the winter's period of coma. The problem with him is to get the ball even halfway down the pitch, and he is thinking of writing an indignant letter to the papers asking the MCC to go in for a projectile whose specific gravity might conceivably be within human power to control with dignity.

Then comes that morning after the first practice. What cricketer does not know it? You wake up feeling there is an uncommonly large amount of you in bed, all ribs. It is as though somebody had gone over you in the night with a hard brick. At breakfast an occasion arises for laughter. You are not equal to it. Your state is, in Mr. Pecksniff's phrase, 'chronic'. Yet, how marked off from the rest of mankind you feel when you take your seat in the tramcar. You have been through a rigorous spring cleaning. You are now a being definitely of thew and sinew. The man next to you is in the way of being a worm. For you are full of fresh air and rich red blood.

He is just a colloid, in an overcoat, and probably he is asthmatical. How can you be expected to pity him, feeling as you do, as hard as nails? There is the season before you, too, and yesterday's misgivings are gone. You are determined to leave last season's average a long way behind. If only you can resist the ball on the off that goes away . . .

Yes, it is indeed the sweet o' the year for cricketers – the world just green, fresh grass and sunshine, and jolly companions in white.

[1] 'Someday it will be pleasant to remember even this.'

GREAT DAYS

OUR LONDON CORRESPONDENCE   SEPTEMBER 7 1880

For a period extending, I believe, over a month and thirty hours our London pavements have not been wet with rain. This afternoon the longest drought we have known in the South for somewhat more than ten years has been broken by a welcome fall of rain. London is 'very empty' – that is, about as empty as this great capital is ever known to be. Mr. Gladstone has in his lifetime proved many things, but this year he has successfully demonstrated that the session of Parliament and the London season have no necessary connection. For some weeks past Rotten Row has been a desert, with perhaps one or two of the lingering members of Parliament upon it. That symptom of 'the dead season', the repairing of the clubs, is in full display. The Devonshire is the guest of the Reform, and the 2,800 members of these two Liberal clubs are represented by fewer than a dozen; the Athenæum is closed; the Oxford and Cambridge is undergoing repair; so is the United Service. In fact, 'everybody' is out of town . . .

FROM OUR SPECIAL CORRESPONDENT AT THE OVAL   SEPTEMBER 7 1880

England v. Australia, the inaugural home Test

The match between the Australian Eleven and an Eleven of All England, which commenced yesterday on Kennington Oval, is without doubt the most interesting that has been played for many years, if indeed it has ever been surpassed in interest. For some months past very general regret has been expressed in cricketing circles at the apparent certainty that Spofforth and his companions would return to Australia without having been met in fair fight by an eleven really representing the cricketing strength of the mother country. The treatment which an English eleven received in Australia induced a hostile feeling against the Colonial team, and in addition to this feeling there was the knowledge that the Eleven had come over here on a purely commercial speculation. Their object was to make money, and they have followed out their

21

programme with the utmost pertinacity and success. But whilst they were making money – and, in fact, as an indispensable adjunct to making it, they were exhibiting very fine cricket, although their achievements were mainly at the expense of inferior teams – they had several opportunities of showing that they were able to hold their own against players of the highest class.

It was, therefore, very gratifying to find that at the eleventh hour the difficulties in the way of a match of first-class importance had been overcome. Lord Harris, who had the best right to complain of the treatment he and his team received in Australia, waived all objections on that score, and his Lordship was selected as the captain of the English Eleven. The 'three Graces' also consented to play, and the rest of the team was selected from Nottinghamshire, Lancashire, Surrey, Middlesex and Kent. At the first glance the team seems to be a really 'representative' one, but strong as it is there can be no doubt that it would have been immensely improved if Mr. Hornby, the famous Lancashire amateur, and George Ulyett, the crack batsman of Yorkshire, a fine bowler and a splendid 'fielder', had been included in it. It was understood, however, that Mr. Hornby and Ulyett refused to play, and in their absence it is difficult to see where the eleven could have been improved. An accident which recently deprived Spofforth of the use of his right hand necessarily also deprived the match of some of its interest, notwithstanding that there are many who maintain that Palmer is an equally good bowler. The last-named member of the Australian team has been very destructive this season and we believe has the better record of the two.

The match was regarded with immense interest in London, and in the course of the day there could not have been less than 30,000 spectators on the Oval. The preparations for their accommodation were miserably inadequate, and many thousands of the visitors never saw a ball bowled during the day. The spectators crowded the grand stand, they climbed on the fences, up the trees, and on to the roofs of the permanent buildings on the ground, and endeavoured from the precarious elevation of piles of bricks, broken chairs, old sofas, or dilapidated boxes, to gain some knowledge of what was passing in the roped arena. Outside the ring there promenaded thousands of visitors, who, as we have said, never by accident caught a glimpse of the play, and who satisfied their curiosity upon the scraps of information that were doled out to them by the more fortunate. It may be of interest in passing to state that the 'gate money' was divided between the Australians and the Surrey Club, the latter paying the expenses of advertising, &c. The Colonial team will therefore have no reason to regret their visit to the Oval as far as their pecuniary interests are concerned.

Precisely at half-past eleven England, having won the toss, decided, of course, to go in on the splendid wicket. The champion and his brother, Mr. E. M. Grace, were received with cordial applause as they appeared at the wicket. A still warmer compliment had been paid to the

Colonial team when Murdoch led them out. Boyle and Palmer started the bowling, and after a few moments had elapsed it became clear to all who were familiar with 'W.G.'s' play that he was in his very best form and bent on making a heavy score. Mr. E. M. Grace also played with unusual care, and refused to be tempted out of his ground by the most cunning devices of the bowlers. The bowling and fielding of the Australians fully maintained their high reputation. Blackham was especially active behind the wicket, whilst Alexander, Bonnor, and Bannerman in the field did wonders. Despite, however, the excellence of the attack, the two batsmen could not be separated, and the score mounted at the rate of a run per minute until, with 41 up, the first of a long series of bowling changes occurred, Alexander replacing Boyle. The change was of no avail, and Bannerman replaced Palmer, but without working any change in the batsmen. The champion's play was magnificent, and showed that he possessed, in undiminished excellence, that complete mastery of the bat which has earned him that proud title. His drives were especially a treat to witness – hard and always well down on the ground. The separation of the pair was at last effected by Bannerman, who sent one down which Mr. E. M. Grace played easily into the hands of Alexander at cover point. The retiring batsmen had made 36 in excellent style. One wicket for 91 runs – an excellent beginning. Mr. A. P. Lucas, the best bat in the Surrey eleven, next gave a magnificent exposition of a style of cricket entirely different from that shown by Mr. W. G. Grace. The free and graceful play of the bat in his hands, his extraordinary power of getting 'on the top' of the ball, and his quickness and dexterity in stopping 'shooters', served as powerful reminders of Daft and Caffyn in their best days. The Australian bowling was hit all over the field, and at five minutes past one the telegraph showed 100. At eight minutes to two 150 went up, and at two o'clock, when the Australians retired to recruit their energies at the luncheon table, the score was 167, of which Dr. Grace had made 82 and Mr. Lucas 41.

On the resumption of play runs were got at the same rapid rate. Nothing that the Australians could do was of the least avail against the splendid batsmen, and at ten minutes past three a two and a four by Mr. Lucas sent up the 200, amidst enthusiastic cheering. In a few minutes after this outburst Mr. Lucas had the misfortune to play a ball hard on to his left foot, and it rebounded from thence on to his wicket, dislodging the bails. Barnes, the hope of Nottinghamshire, succeeded, and showed some excellent cricket until he unfortunately put a ball on to his wicket. With three wickets down for 269 runs, Lord Harris came in, but soon lost the company of the champion, whose bails were removed by a plain-looking ball from Palmer after he had scored 152 by the finest batting which he has displayed for two years.

A veteran cricketer, who bears a name renowned in the annals of the game, has pronounced Dr. W. G. Grace to be the best cricketer whom England has ever produced, and all who witnessed his play yesterday will, we believe, agree that the eulogium is not an extravagant one. Included in his innings were 12 fours, 10 threes, and 14 twos. Lord Harris and Mr. Penn played brilliant cricket, the Kent captain making nine in one over from Alexander. The telegraph showed 300 at a quarter to five. It would be useless to detail the numerous changes in the Australian bowling, but it is the merest justice to the team to state that their fielding showed scarcely any signs of deterioration. Soon after 320 had been hoisted Mr. Penn was clean bowled by Bannerman, and Mr. A. G. Steel joined Lord Harris. Rain had fallen slightly for an hour, and the wicket played rather treacherously, but the run getting went on rapidly, and the batsmen repeatedly drove the ball to the boundary. At length, after putting on 52 runs in splendid style, Lord Harris was easily caught by Bonnor; and Mr. Steel, hesitating somewhat at a ball from Groube, drove the ball too high and was finely caught by Boyle. Mr. G. F. Grace, whose inclusion in the eleven had been objected to by many, was the only one who failed to score. When play ceased at six o'clock England had scored 410 runs for eight wickets – an almost unprecedented performance, and one especially gratifying when we take into account the excellence of the fielding.

England 420 (W. G. Grace 152, A. P. Lucas 55, Lord Harris 52) and 57 for 5; Australia 149 (F. Morley 5 for 56) and 327 (W. L. Murdoch 153 not out). England won by five wickets.

JULY 25 1898

Gentlemen v. Players, W.G.'s 50th birthday

The week which is past has been in a cricketing sense the greatest week of all the year. We have had Mr. Grace's jubilee match at Lord's, a match which finished in so gloriously exciting a fashion four minutes before time on Wednesday night. That game in itself would lend distinction to any season, and it will certainly live in cricket annals as a memorable encounter – memorable because of the man to whom it was, as it were, dedicated, and memorable, too, because of the play itself. Many cricketers, we are sure, would have given a good deal to see the play during those three hours on Wednesday. No one doubted when the Gentlemen began their second innings that the match would be a draw.

Though batting on a worn wicket, it seemed certain that the chosen of our English batsmen could defend themselves for so short a space of time. Grace, much bruised about the hand with the knocks he received in the first innings, and with a lame foot in the bargain, sent in his young braves in front of him. He surely never dreamt of such a series of disasters as happened. Stoddart fell early on, but Jackson and MacLaren played for a while in capital form, and runs came quickly to the bat. The Lancashire captain – we trust yet to see him in that position this season, though its period now is well advanced – was out in an unfortunate way just when things looked well with him. And now Jackson went, and the wounded Grace in his tent must have begun to feel just a trifle uneasy.

It was clear that J. T. Hearne, who knows the Lord's ground as no other bowler, had found just that broken bit of turf whereon to place his ball which is at once the joy of the man who attacks and the dismay of him who defends. Townsend did fairly well before he succumbed to the most successful bowler of our day, but Sammy Woods could only make nine and Captain Wynyard four. Lockwood took Mason for a duck and Dixon fell to Haigh for four. Now came forth a great figure to stem the tide of disaster. Grace, who had not thought of going in, limped down the pavilion steps and took his place at the wicket, and there was that look about him which said, clear as words, that if only one of two remaining partners could keep up his wicket he himself would stay the hour. But the first of the two quickly departed, and now only Kortright was left. Kortright did well where greater batsmen had failed, Grace was stern and safe, steady as a rock, paying small regard to runs, which it was rather a pain to make, and which there was no object in making, while Kortright played in that quicker way which is the only one possible to him.

Kortright it was on whom the bowlers chiefly exercised their cunning. Half-past six was sounded, and there was yet one half-hour left. The minutes crept on, the batsmen stood their ground, and the excited spectator, seeing the fingers of the clock getting very near to the seven, were full of hope that this gallant stand of the old player and the young would prove successful. It was not to be, however, for Kortright was caught just four minutes before the call of time, Mr. Grace carrying out his bat after a heroic effort to save the game for his side.

Such an occasion as the jubilee of Mr. Grace could not, of course, be allowed to pass without a dinner, which all, or nearly all, the great cricketers of the country attended. Some interesting things were said at the dinner by Sir Richard Webster and Mr. Grace himself – things personal to the hero of the occasion. Sir Richard Webster referred to the kindness of the Champion to young colts, whether they were on his side or against him. This was a proper thing to say. It is really true that Grace does like to encourage the budding player, but there are bounds beyond which he does not carry his courtesy. He mentioned, without sign of regret, the case of a young Surrey colt put on to bowl against him for the first time in an M.C.C. match at Lord's. The first ball he played quietly back. But the two next went into the nursery, somwhere by the old Armoury, while the fourth and fifth he lifted into the pavilion. The colt was not heard of again. 'If you call that giving advice to a young cricketer, well——,' but here Mr. Grace had perforce to stop, for not even his voice could sound above the laughter.

Again, when the colt comes into bat it will generally be found (as he genially admitted in his speech) that Grace tries a change of bowling.

He, in fact, goes on himself. Sammy Woods calls the colts 'rabbits'. The victims are warned against trying to hit that nice easy ball to square leg, but they invariably fall into the trap. Grace as a bowler is a fearful and wonderful being in the eyes of the young batsman. It used to be sometimes whispered, we say not with what truth, that in the old days of Gloucestershire cricket when members of the team would occasionally suggest to W.G. that a change of bowling might not be a very bad thing he would at once fall in with their views, only to put himself on at the other end. But every bowler who is also a captain is liable to this charge, and is probably guilty of it.

OUR SPECIAL CORRESPONDENT AT THE OVAL   AUGUST 14 1902

England v. Australia

LONDON, WEDNESDAY NIGHT
One may well doubt if ever an international game with so many astonishing changes has been played. To begin with, the Australians lost all their best men cheaply, and thanks to the tail brought the total up to 324. On the following day, on a ruined wicket, England also collapsed in the beginning and saved the situation by determined hitting; but they were still in a deficit of 140 odd. Even in the next innings, when the Australians more or less collapsed for 121, a victory seemed almost impossible when the first three wickets fell for 10 and the first five for 49. Then came Jessop's inspired innings, in itself one of the most astonishing feats seen for a long time in first-class cricket, and a succession of partnerships utterly surprising after the beginning. The making of the last 15 when the last pair were in was attended by such excitement as is rarely seen. It is not of much advantage to apportion credit, but Yorkshiremen may reasonably feel proud. Jackson stopped the panic, Hirst got many wickets and played two quite invaluable innings, and to him and Rhodes was left the facing of the final crisis. The fielding of the Australians throughout was a treat to see, and they were loudly cheered again and again. Trumble's performance in bowling unchanged through two long innings must be hard to parallel, and he scarcely sent down a bad-length ball.

It was with a good deal of satisfaction that the absence of rain on Tuesday night was welcomed. A continual drying of the wicket was an absolute essential if the English team were to make a bid for victory. A sprinkle of rain came this morning, but it was not enough to do an iota of harm to the wicket. The sun kept making efforts to break through the haze, and the light was as good as could be expected in such a summer as this. In the unexpected hope of a good finish a large crowd had collected to see the first ball bowled. Those who missed the first over missed one of the many excitements of this most eventful game in cricket statistics. In his first over Lockwood, bowling, as before, from the Vauxhall end, hit Armstrong's wicket. The burst of cheering indicated the relief. Armstrong had played on Tuesday as well as any one, easily and with a good deal of power. A partnership between him and Trumble was a thing to be afraid of. Kelly, an inartistic but dangerous hitter, came in last wicket, but did not survive very long. He put his leg in front of a straight one from Lockwood without scoring. It was a promising beginning. In the few overs that had been bowled there was no sign that the wicket was playing badly, though it had not increased in pace as much as might have been expected.

In the circumstances 263 did not seem an impossible score to make. Certainly the wicket was better than when the English team were batting before. If argument goes for anything in cricket, there was at any rate a chance of adding 80 to the first score. The weather report was 'fair and warmer,' but 'glorious uncertainty' is not confined to cricket. The sprinkle of so-called heat-drops of the morning began to turn to a downright shower in the interval, and after half an hour's cricket it became necessary to suspend the game. The shower, together with the results of the first few minutes' play, had put an end, in the opinion, perhaps, of everyone on the ground, to England's chances. The same two bowlers began. Trumble, ambling up to the wicket in his usual gentle, inoffensive way as if he meant no harm to anyone, began with an uneventful over from the pavilion end. Saunders took the second over at the Vauxhall end, and bowled one of the best overs he ever sent down. MacLaren, playing forward to his third ball, edged it, and the ball rolled over to the wicket. Tyldesley, who came in next, was absolutely beaten by the first ball, and was bowled 'all over his wicket' with the next. Hayward made a single, which was converted into two by an overthrow, from a mishit in the slips off the last ball. This was not the end. In his third over Palairet, who alone had looked at all comfortable, was clean bowled by a good-length ball that broke back. Three of the best wickets had fallen for 10, and as a result of the morning's play five wickets had fallen for 17 runs. There was no getting over the inference that a recovery of the wicket was an unrealised hope and a recovery of the situation almost impossible. But among present cricketers Jessop is perhaps the most likely to upset any calculation.

An improvement came over the game directly he and Jackson got together. It was clear, in spite of the early collapse, in spite of the fact that five of the best batsmen in England had fallen for 48 runs, that the wicket, after all, was not so bad. In the light of the afternoon's play one can only account for Saunders's success in the most generous way. He had bowled a succession of exceptionally difficult balls. One factor in his success is no doubt the oddity of his run. He is almost entirely concealed by the umpire until the last moment, and seeing that the oddity of this trick was rendered harmless on Tuesday by the umpire standing ten yards or so back it is odd that the same was not done again. Up to luncheon Jackson and Jessop did nothing very startling, though Jessop gave some hint of the fury of hitting that was going to possess him. Once he had driven Trumble on to the roof of the pavilion, and he hit a boundary off the next ball, but such incidents paled before the batting after lunch. At the fall of the fifth wicket one heard amateur critics grumbling at the Selection Committee. 'Schoolboys would play better,' it was said, and in going through the team Jessop's name was chiefly noted as an instance of folly in selection.

From luncheon to the end of play there was no more criticism. In the excitement of the game nobody did anything but follow the play, and probably scarcely one of the 20,000 people missed a ball. Certainly those who would otherwise have been engaged in selling cards, chocolate, and cheap verse did not miss a ball. It would be difficult to say too much of the fury of Jessop's hitting, but it was never wild. He once cut Trumble for five, and made his runs by a great variety of strokes. But as his innings progressed he came round more and more frequently to the favourite stroke, the audacious pulling of straight balls. The crowd could scarcely contain itself, and when he outdid all his previous efforts by hitting four consecutive fours off the irresistible Saunders to the square-leg boundary the crowd looked like a white poplar tree in a storm. Everyone stood up and waved something, a hat or a handkerchief or a hand, and the 'buses passing down the flanking road pulled up to see the cause of the excitement. Jessop reached 40 when Jackson was 41. He had made 73 when Jackson was at 46. But Jackson had been playing most sound and attractive cricket, and he had been the first to stop the succession of collapses. Curiously, he scored more slowly as time went on, and when he wanted only three to complete his fifty stopped scoring altogether for a long time. He stopped at 49 for ten minutes. To the general disappointment, he was caught and bowled by Trumble off a bumping ball before the one was got. He had been missed just before, but it was a fine innings, and did as much as anything to restore the confidence of the team. When he left a victory was still a remote contingency.

Both Hirst and Jessop kept up the rapid scoring. Indeed Hirst began by making runs as fast as Jessop. Up to this point there had been no change of bowling. Now Armstrong, bowling slow leg-breaking balls with just half the fieldsmen on the boundary, displaced Saunders. Hirst was very severe on him, but Jessop found a difficulty in timing the slow balls. However, by help of some enormous drives off Trumble, one of which went clean over the pavilion for six, he soon reached his hundred, and the cheering became still more furious. But the end of his great innings was near, and after mishitting one of Armstrong's slows he placed another gently into the hands of short leg. Lockwood came in and poked about nervously for a little and was out lbw to Trumble, who was now bowling round the wicket. Forty-nine runs were still wanted, and the excitement began to culminate. Lilley and Hirst played carefully but not nervously, till Lilley, in driving Trumble, was caught at mid-off. The intensity of the excitement of the next quarter of an hour is a thing impossible to impart. There is nothing comparable to the tension of a great many thousand people all absolutely absorbed in every detail of the game.

Fifteen runs were wanted when Rhodes came in, and a north-countryman whispered that all was right now two Yorkshiremen were together. He was right. Rhodes looked as calm and unmoved as when he takes those few quiet steps to the wicket. But everyone else showed the nervousness of the position. Hirst was continually busy with the pitch, and before every ball took a breathing space and twirled his bat in preparation. Darling shifted the field almost every ball, and when Rhodes was batting some of them crept very near in. Short-leg came so close that he made an attempt to catch Rhodes almost off his bat. Rhodes began luckily with a four through the slips off Noble. After this every run was a single – except one overthrow – many of them made off Trumble past short-leg. Almost every member of the crowd was keeping a record of the game aloud. If a momentary mistake had been made on the score-board there would have been a concerted yell. Both players showed nerve. Rhodes was calm, and Hirst ran out valiantly to Trumble, but could not get more than a single. At last, with three to win, Hirst put Noble away between short-leg and mid-on. There was a chance of two runs, but the second would have been a near thing, and Noble's over finished with still two to make. Trumble, who had bowled unchanged through the whole innings, was still on at the pavilion end, and he had not yet sent down a single loose ball. Hirst again went to meet the ball, made another single, and a great shout went up. The match at least could not be lost. One member of the crowd, a clergyman, thought it was won, and started running across the ground at full pace towards the pavilion. He was so excited that he did not notice his mistake till he was well out in the field and a policeman was in chase. The making of the last run was left to Rhodes. As if he were playing at a net, he hit out at Trumble and drove him to long-on. Whether it was a single or a four no one waited to see. The whole crowd rushed on to the ground and made for the pavilion in pursuit of the players. The noise and turmoil and prolonged cheering were the witness of the best finish – considering the utter unexpectedness of the victory – recorded in international matches. It surpassed the Manchester game in excitement, and it is difficult to say more.

Australia 324 (H. Trumble 64 not out, M. A. Noble 52, G. H. Hirst 5 for 77) and 121 (W. H. Lockwood 5 for 45); England 183 (Trumble 8 for 65) and 263 for 9 (G. L. Jessop 104, Hirst 58 not out, J. V. Saunders 4 for 105, Trumble 4 for 108). England won by one wicket.

A CORRESPONDENT AT OLD TRAFFORD   MAY 29 1912

Australia v. South Africa, Triangular Tournament

The Test match which came to a close at Old Trafford yesterday in the most surprisingly dramatic fashion supplied one of those historic finishes which never pass out of a spectator's memory, and which those who left early in the afternoon, bored by the even, uneventful course of the play, will never forgive themselves for having missed. Up to a point the game proceeded from stage to stage with a slow deliberation that was almost depressing. Then, about the middle of the afternoon, the character of the play changed in a flash, and from this point onwards excitement, followed upon excitement until the match ended almost on the stroke of half-past six in a crushing victory for the Australians by an innings and 88 runs.

The turning point in the game stands out with unusual sharpness. The South Africans, after a long and stubborn struggle, had got within 34 of the number of runs required to save the follow-on. Only seven wickets were down, Faulkner (122) and Beaumont (31) seemed well set, the bowling appeared to be falling away, and the tension was sensibly relaxing. Then Matthews intervened with dramatic effect. A single which Faulkner made off him carried his score one beyond Bardsley's 121 on the previous day, an incident which the spectators recognised with generous applause, and brought his partner, Beaumont, opposite the bowler. Matthews beat the batsman with a breaking ball which hit the off bail. Pegler, who succeeded him, missed the next ball and was given out leg before wicket. The last batsman, Ward, similarly missed the succeeding ball, and was also given out leg before wicket. In this startling way Matthews finished off the innings with the 'hat trick', a feat never before accomplished in a Test match between Australia and South Africa, and only once before accomplished in Test cricket in England. The previous case was that of J. T. Hearne, who, playing for England against Australia at Leeds in 1899, with successive balls bowled Hill, got Gregory caught by MacLaren, and got Noble caught by Ranjitsinhji, both catches in the slips. This match, it may be recalled, was the one in which Briggs made his last appearance, the excitement bringing on a seizure from which he never recovered.

Matthews's 'hat trick', which finished off the South Africans first innings, would have been a sufficient distinction for any bowler on his first appearance in Test cricket in England. But a little later the rare achievement was repeated, as the result of two particularly clever catches by the bowler himself. Going in a second time the South Africans' fifth wicket fell at 70 runs. At the same total Taylor, who had scored 21, was bowled by Matthews. Schwarz, the next batsman, playing forward to the first ball, received a slow one, returned it softly a little wide towards the bowler, and Matthews springing towards it sideways caught it low down with the right hand. Ward, the South

African wicket-keeper, took Schwarz's place, and it was clear that Matthews intended to go for the third wicket from the fastidious care with which he brought in his fielders around the batsman. Ward played his first ball exactly as Schwarz had done, and cocked it up. The ball, however, was hit so gently that for an instant no one thought of a catch. Then one saw a nimble little figure flying up the pitch and making a frantic dive with both hands for the ball. Matthews went tumbling over, and it was not until he had flung the ball wildly in the air that the onlookers could believe he had made the catch. His colleagues showered their congratulations upon him, and the crowd, when they had recovered from their astonishment, gave him a splendid cheer. Four wickets thus fell with the total standing at 70. Kelleway secured the ninth at 78, and the last at 95, a minute or two short of the time for drawing stumps.

Australia 448 (W. Bardsley 121, C. Kelleway 114, S. J. Pegler 6 for 105); South Africa 265 (G. A. Faulkner 122 not out, W. J. Whitty 5 for 55) and 95 (Kelleway 5 for 33). Australia won by an innings and 88 runs.

Matthews's six hat-trick victims were his only wickets of the match. They also represented a rare triumph that summer for Australia, who disliked the experimental triangular format (an attitude they were to change when they revived it 65 years later), were racked by internal disputes and were thoroughly outplayed by England. But after the First War, Armstrong's Australians proved invincible, winning eight consecutive Test matches and losing to no one, until one day in Sussex . . .

NEVILLE CARDUS AT EASTBOURNE   AUGUST 31 1921

An England XI v. The Australians

From the pains which entered the body of English cricket at Trent Bridge in May the good Lord has at long last delivered us. This afternoon, on the sunny Saffrons cricket field, the Australians' colours have been hauled down: the mighty men that authentic England elevens have found unconquerable in ten successive Test matches have been beaten, beaten by a fictitious England eleven under the leadership of our greatest cricket captain, and, moreover, beaten by a side that was routed in a first innings for forty-three paltry runs. Who on Saturday could have got the faintest glimpse of such an end to the game even in the wildest flight of fancy? All cricketers know well the infinite changefulness of the great game, but to overthrow the might of Australia from no better base than a first innings total of 43 – why, the miraculous is here, black magic, the very imps of mischief. There were the most thrilling fluctuations in the day's play: now the game was safe in Armstrong's keeping, now it slipped from his grasp, now, by a

31

desperate motion of the will, Armstrong clutches it again, and then, as, indeed, it looked his for good, out it slipped and MacLaren and his men stuck greedily to it.

At the morning's outset[1] Bardsley and Carter played the bowling comfortably. Gibson was seemingly harmless, and from his first three overs 16 runs came. Would other English captains have taken Gibson off after so bad a beginning? MacLaren did not – and true, he had no great amount of bowling at hand to embarrass him. But MacLaren has had faith in Gibson throughout the summer, and today the young University cricketer was to justify, as Barnes and Dean once justified, the insight of the master. With Australia's score 52 Gibson clean bowled Bardsley by a glorious ball that pitched on the off stump and hit the leg. Falcon then bowled a fast short one to Carter, who cut it powerfully. In the Test matches such a stroke from an Australian invariably went to the boundary. Today young Claude Ashton was in the slips; he saw the ball as a swallow sees a fly, darted forward, and caught the ball magnificently. Now the outlook for Australia was darkening, but soon the confidence of Macartney's and Andrews's cricket made slight sunshine for Armstrong. And with the total 73 Falcon bowled Macartney, who produced a weird stroke with a cross bat. Pellew and Andrews added just 30 for the fifth Australian wicket, which fell when Hubert Ashton brilliantly caught Pellew at slip. So to lunch with no man's appetite keen for food. Australia needed now 87, with five wickets in hand.

Half an hour's play after the interval, and surely the victory was Armstrong's entirely. Andrews and Ryder scored 34 runs in this short space, and, worst of all for MacLaren's prospects, they hit Falcon's bowling all over the field. The score was 140 for five when MacLaren asked Faulkner to bowl in place of Falcon. The move was made at the last moment, still at the right moment. Gibson broke the Ryder-Andrews partnership at last, but it was Faulkner, in his third over, that placed the Australians completely against the wall by upsetting Andrews's off stump with an excellent ball which whipped across the wicket from leg. Andrews was eighth out at 153, with but forty-three wanted now for his side's victory. He was in such fine form that had he endured another fifteen minutes, especially against Falcon, he would most certainly have won the match. Armstrong was the last hope of his team now. Was it just MacLaren's good luck, or was it MacLaren's superb knowledge of cricketers that ordained that Faulkner should be bowling when Armstrong came to the wicket? For Armstrong never has been able to cope with Faulkner. Today he was sorely troubled by the South African's googly. He used all his cunning to avoid Faulkner, but he had to face the music at last. And Faulkner pitched him a ball whizzing with spin on the leg stump. Armstrong lost it hopelessly, and the ball would have hit the off wicket but for Armstrong's obstructing pad. Faulkner split the skies with a jubilant 'How's that?' and Armstrong had to go. Macdonald and Mailey added nine more or less nondescript runs for the last wicket, which fell to Gibson, and rightly so. He bowled beautifully without a rest throughout the Australian innings. He has a ball which is a good imitation of Barnes's famous ball, the one that pitches on the leg stump and swings away to the off. He stuck to his task gallantly, and never allowed the crisis to upset him. In the very throes of the crisis Faulkner exploited his finger-spin audaciously.

At the finish, Armstrong in a speech to the jubilant crowd said his men had been beaten by the better side. It is certain that England in the Test matches could not show the superb fielding, the skilful and intelligent bowling of this side of MacLaren's. The fielding indeed was up to Australian standards. The crowd roared for MacLaren at the close, but MacLaren was rather overcome with emotion, and through a deputy announced this was his farewell to cricket. A beautiful farewell it has been, putting the crown on his greatness. Not in his heyday did he give us finer captaincy than he has given us in this match. It was plain this afternoon that his very presence in the field gave his men hope and courage.

Let nobody get the impression that the Australians flung this game away through a casual attitude towards it. Possibly there was just half an hour of negligent batsmanship when the Australians went in against a total of 43. But from the fall of Collins's wicket on Saturday Armstrong had his men strung taut enough. And this afternoon Armstrong's face as he witnessed the breaking of Andrews's wicket – which was a certain omen of the end – had a profoundly sombre expression. Gone the old affability! Where were his quips and oddities now?

The main causes of the Australian defeat today, as it seemed to the writer, were fielding just as brilliant as the Australians' own, captaincy that puts every fieldsman in the proper place, and clever spin bowling. As one watched the Ashtons, fleet of foot, sure of grasp, one thought of the heavy, plodding wanderings of England's Test-match outfielders. And as one saw MacLaren move his men here and there by the most deliberate, yet the gentlest waves of the hand – gestures telling of a perfectly composed mind – one thought of Douglas's volubility as he strove to obtain a tactful disposition of his forces. There was, indeed, a tincture of bitterness in the sweet as one watched the match today proceed to its superb consummation.

The bowling of Gibson and Faulkner in the Australian second innings was just of that kind Australian batsmen have never really mastered. Barnes could put even Trumper and Hill at his mercy by the ball that broke away from the bat after pitching somewhere near the leg and middle stumps. Both Gibson and Faulkner exploited this dangerous ball this afternoon and by excellent fortune they both managed also a capital length. The Australians did not again find Falcon troublesome, though he bowled not a bit below his Saturday's form. Fast and fast-medium bowling, right arm, that comes more or less straight through is the stuff Australian batsmen thrive on. They waxed fat on Howell, Douglas, Jupp and Parkin (when he bowled fast). To these bowlers they would play forward confidently. Even the slow-medium off-break rarely troubles an Australian batsman. He, commonly, is good at leg-side play and can get back to the wicket and force the ball away in the spin's direction. The ball that pitches on the wicket and breaks away they have never mastered. One might add, what batsmen have? This delivery demands the most discreet use of the 'two-eyed stance', of back play, supported judiciously by the pads. And though the Australians can play back cleverly enough on slow wickets, back play is not so much in the blood of them that they can play back easily on a fast wicket.

The finger spin used by Faulkner and Gibson today is to be tackled safely only by the perfect back-play technique employed, say, by Taylor, the South African, against Barnes a year or two ago. Armstrong's struggles with Faulkner today were pathetic; he merely lunged at the ball when it was in the air, lost it as it spun, then desperately changed his stance at the last minute. Bardsley played forward beautifully to the ball that bowled him, and had it come through straight he would have hit it. The ball spun several inches on pitching and Bardsley had no pads there as a second line of defence. A lot of abuse has been hurled at the 'two-eyed stance' this summer, and rightly, since too often has it been exploited against fast bowling. But, as this afternoon's Australian batsmanship has shown, there is not much hope against a ball spinning away at a good length if one uses the old-time lunge forward.

But the impressions of this glorious match likely to last longest are of MacLaren. One will see him, white-haired and beautifully calm, standing in the slips beckoning a man to a more judicious place in the field. One will see him plucking at his trousers' knees in the old way, hitching them up before he slightly bends into the classic slip position. One will see him moving across the pitch at the over's end, taking now and then one of his bowlers by the arm and giving him a word of encouragement and advice. And if these impressions should fade in a while, surely one will never forget his walk to the pavilion at the game's end, the crowd pressing round him and cheering – MacLaren with his sweater over his shoulders, his face almost lost in the folds of it, looking down on the grass as he moves for good from the cricket field seemingly but half aware of the praise-giving about him, seemingly thinking of other times.

[1] Australia were 25 for one at the start of the last day, needing another 171 for victory.

England XI 43 (W. W. Armstrong 5 for 15, E. A. Macdonald 5 for 21) and 326 (G. A. Faulkner 153, Macdonald 6 for 98); Australians 174 (W. Bardsley 70, M. Falcon 6 for 67, Faulkner 4 for 50) and 167 (C. H. Gibson 6 for 64). England XI won by 28 runs.

This was perhaps the finest hour for both Cardus and MacLaren. Cardus was 32 and had only been writing on cricket for three summers but he had the story to himself; the other main cricket writers were watching Middlesex play Surrey for the Championship at Lord's. MacLaren was three months short of his fiftieth birthday. His team, all amateurs, included not one of the thirty players who had tried and failed on England's behalf to beat Australia that summer.

NEVILLE CARDUS AT WORCESTER   MAY 2 1938

Worcestershire v. Australians

For the third time in succession Bradman has opened an Australian cricket season in England with a double century against Worcestershire. He was generally expected to achieve the performance, granted that he himself felt in the mood. The Worcestershire captain, indeed, sensibly resigned himself to it and decided to get it over as quickly and as painlessly as may be, for having won the toss on a thoroughly easy wicket he asked the Australians to bat first, an invitation which was unanimously accepted. The Worcestershire captain's resignation apparently achieved a philosophy so profound that he declined the new ball at 200. Probably he was right; a new ball costs money, and Worcestershire is not a wealthy club and every little counts.

Bradman seldom promised to get out; when he missed a quick-rising out-swinger from Crisp, with his score at twenty-three, and when in the same over a ball struck him on the pads, we were merely rendered surprised, not hopeful. The last innings I saw Bradman play before this ·one was at Perth, Western Australia, in March; it was done with a bat seemingly all edge. On Saturday the great machine worked as precisely as ever it has worked. Our bowlers must now face the worst – Bradman is today, compared with the Bradman of other years, not quite so easy to get out. In other words, he is beginning really to see the ball. This latest innings by him had a plan and an executive skill which were terrifying. He spent two hours and a quarter on his first fifty; then he scored another fifty in half an hour, and another fifty in thirty-five minutes. The awful point is that when he was making a hundred in an hour he concealed the pace, deceived all of us except the alert scorers. He did not barnstorm; not until he passed 200 did his bat swing or hook at all violently. He scored a hundred in an hour with restraint. He played late on the whole, and his touch was so certain that we could almost feel that the blade of his bat was endowed with sight, and also was prehensile. Now and again, true, he reached forward in a way not common for Bradman, who is a backfoot player if ever there was one. The accuracy of his timing, as he forced the ball to leg or square, made one spectator at least catch breath – yes, Bradman can still stir in us astonishment at his powers.

I suppose no man has ever been more of a master of his job than Bradman is a master of his job. He is as good as a batsman as Bach was as a composer. Yet no; he lacks felicity – that effortless touch of nature which makes the difference between a thing that grows and a thing that is constructed. A Bradman innings is designed – it does not fall on him 'by grace'. There is usually the hint of severe watchfulness, even of suspicion. An innings by a Woolley just happens, like the bloom on the peach on the sun-stained wall. This is not to deny Bradman style and a kind of beauty; people speak nonsense when they say that Bradman does not ever move the aesthetic senses. A constructed thing can be beautiful, if it cannot be spontaneous. The flight of a bird and the flight of an aeroplane mark the difference between an innings by a Woolley and one by a Bradman. And in a war the aeroplane has the grandest eagle beaten.

A large crowd assembled on the pretty Worcester ground to see Bradman and the others. There were some eleven thousand of them, and everybody breathed on everybody else's neck, and pushed and trod and elbowed. The congestion was acute; it spoiled the graciousness of the place. There were scaffoldings for the camera men, and a stand for the battalions of the press. For Worcester cricket the occasion was momentous. At the entrances to the ground the gatemen were on their guard; a policeman with a spike in his hat walked on the field during the interval obviously looking for a case. There was little lunch to be had by the mass of the people, but in spite of a clean, cold day we became soiled as the hours wore on, and sticky. Only the Cathedral kept aloof from the spirit of the age.

Worcestershire bowled well for a long time. Crisp, the South African, defeated Brown at once, lbw. Bradman came to the wicket at a quarter to twelve. He subjected the attack to austere scrutiny; for nearly an hour Fingleton was the more interesting batsman. He contrives to lend strength and freedom to strokes which are not announced by the short, cramped lift of his bat. He drove Perks to the off by means of a sudden thrust; he saw a shorter ball swiftly, and he back-cut it strong as an axe. He is clearly a cricketer who senses a ball's flight. Here is another hard nut to crack. Perks, who, according to his fate and custom, bowled ably and unluckily, once found out Fingleton's weakness, which is an involuntary flick at the out-swinger. Fingleton seemed settled for the day until a half-volley provoked him to excitement; he was caught at cover after an innings of eighty-five minutes – every second bodeful of no good to our bowlers.

McCabe put lightness of touch into the Australian innings; he is never the labourer. His defences have been strengthened more by experience than by application of principles. He is a natural batsman, with strokes which he makes as instinctively as he walks or breathes. The hook is most times a dynamic hit and, as its name denotes, a little awkward. McCabe can hook lissomely; he gives to the stroke a curve, so to say – rounds off the angles. Perks deserved McCabe's wicket, for he took it with a good honest length ball.

Badcock was not at his best. He began vaguely. I could not recognise the fierce little swordsman I had seen in Australia. He groped. He played empirically, and missed many balls, and looked apologetic. But one hit, off the back foot, told the truth, nobody but a fine batsman could have made it. He would not be put down by his mistakes; Australian cricketers seldom respond to the suggestions of circumstances that they should get out. They only get out when they do get out. Badcock did nothing in particular for an hour, and did it badly. Then he proceeded towards his fifty. The innings was a rough study for a finished work to come. He helped Bradman to score 277 for the fourth wicket.

Bradman's innings acquired preposterous immensity. The ruthlessness of it all! First a long critical inspection of the opposition, each bowler weighed in the balance as though by codified law. (Once or twice a quick out-swinger from Crisp disturbed him; possibly the seat of error is here.) Then, as soon as he had put everybody into a class – and worn them out by keeping them in suspense – he made fools of their pretensions to skill. He would not for hours even batter them – no, a contemptuous flick here, a sardonic cut there, a provoking drive on either side of the wicket. Later in the day the innings became a Juggernaut, and the field a shambles. Perhaps he was trying to get out but just could not. He missed true aim some three or four times in four hours and fifty minutes, and he hit thirty-three fours. I could not decide on what principle he struck these boundaries. I mean, I could not work out the periodic law at the bottom of them. Apparently he could have hit a four from every other ball sent to him after lunch.

There were ices for sale on the ground all day, probably made on the premises while you waited. The match is, of course, dead already as a match; the only interest now is how quickly O'Reilly will clear up the mess and leave the Worcestershire field to its proper green peacefulness.

Australians 541 (D. G. Bradman 258, C. L. Badcock 67, R. J. Crisp 4 for 170, R. T. D. Perks 4 for 147); Worcestershire 268 (E. Cooper 61, Hon. C. J. Lyttelton 50, L. O'B. Fleetwood-Smith 8 for 98) and 196 (C. H. Bull 69). Australians won by an innings and 77 runs.

DENYS ROWBOTHAM AT LORD'S   JUNE 30 1950

England v. West Indies, Second Test

Ten minutes after lunch here the West Indies won their second Test with England by 326 runs. It was not only a splendid and richly deserved victory but also a historic one, for the West Indies had not previously beaten England in England.

When Worrell had Wardle lbw and England's last wicket had fallen the enthusiasm of the West Indians' supporters knew no bounds. As each wicket had fallen this morning they had leapt from their seats, embraced each other in an ecstasy, and danced and sung to the accompaniment of their guitars until they felt Goddard needed their advice once more on exactly how he should dismiss the next batsman. Now victory had come at last. Arms and hats were flung in a frenzy to high heavens, all was a hoarse, wild cheering, and several of their members raced over the green grass to try and bear their loved heroes to the pavilion. The team was too quick for them, but they still could pay their last tribute. They assembled in front of the pavilion, their guitar master took their head, and, chanting their excited triumph, they half danced, half jog-trotted round the field to their original shrine of worship at the nursery end. Imagination boggles at what may be happening in the West Indies.

Any hopes that England might resist gallantly against overwhelming odds for another day were dispelled early in the morning. Valentine and Ramadhin found an exact length at once, and again it was apparent how difficult the latter is to play if his spin cannot be crushed at its pitch or if the batsman is persuaded to move back to a well-pitched ball. Washbrook was beaten repeatedly by the unexpected turn of Ramadhin's spin and was saved several times only by his pads when he played back. For an hour, too, Ramadhin varied his pace and flight as tantalisingly as he has done in the match. He deceived Washbrook with a slower, higher-flighted ball as cunningly as any old master could have done, and when Washbrook found its length too short for the forward push he had begun, the speed of its spin from the leg-side beat his last desperate chopped shot, it seemed, by tenths of a second.

Twenty-five minutes later at twenty past twelve a similar slower ball proved too much for Evans, who checked the sweep he was about to make and so scooped the ball simply to Rae at half-deep backward square leg. Valentine next had Yardley caught at first slip by shortening his length progressively through five successive balls from a full-toss to one which no forward shot could reach, and all seemed likely to be over before lunch. That it was not was due chiefly to two things – the determined, down-the-line defending of Wardle and Jenkins, and the fact that Ramadhin seems unable to command even an approximate accuracy of length and direction either over or round the wicket against a left-handed batsman.

That England should have lost this match in particular is not, perhaps, of special concern. The manner of her losing it is somewhat more disconcerting, for she was beaten essentially in two days, which logically are two aspects of one problem. Her spin attack, which probably would have dealt summarily with most county sides, was first mastered and in the second innings beaten into subjection after a most promising beginning by batsmen who know how to use their feet and are not afraid to use them. Her batsmen were beaten partly by a young bowler who has discovered a new trick – that of bowling an off break and leg break with an almost identical action without resort to the googly, but even more by a persistent accuracy which seems unlikely now to be destroyed unless England's batsmen can learn and be willing to use their feet as quickly and as challengingly as do their opponents.

The source of England's troubles in this match is not hard to discover. County bowling generally is so erratic that batsmen do not have to seek runs. Even half-volleys need not always be detected, because the long hops, full-tosses and leg-side balls are so frequent. English batsmen do not have to use their feet creatively and dangerously to score, therefore they lose the habit of using them at all. Complementarily, England's best bowlers do not have to fear attacking footwork and so are allowed a wide margin in which they can execute successful variations of flight, pace and length. The West Indian batsmen and bowlers in their respective ways have narrowed the margin of a good length. They are forcing England backwards towards more classical conceptions of accuracy. They are compelling England's batsmen to make runs, not to wait for them; her bowlers to take wickets, not to expect them as the necessary consequence of spin and swing unrelated to absolute control. England could undergo no finer discipline before her Australian tour.

West Indies 326 (A. F. Rae 106, E. Weekes 63, F. M. Worrell 52, R. O. Jenkins 5 for 116) and 425 for 6 dec. (C. L. Walcott 168 not out, G. E. Gomez 70, Weekes 63, Jenkins 4 for 174); England 151 (S. Ramadhin 5 for 66, A. L. Valentine 4 for 48) and 274 (C. Washbrook 114, Ramadhin 6 for 86). West Indies won by 326 runs.

JOHN WOODCOCK AT OLD TRAFFORD   JULY 21 1952

England v. India, Third Test

Extraordinary events occurred at Old Trafford on Saturday. Twice India was routed during the day – such a thing has not happened to any side in a Test match since 1894 – and by twenty minutes past five England had won by an innings and 207 runs. These are the stark facts and for some four and a half hours England was made to look like a supreme cricket team. Let no one decry her performance, for with the bat, with the ball, and in the field, it was not only inspiring but encouraging, too. On the day, however, the opposition was dreadfully poor and much of India's batting lacked that paramount quality of courage. Indeed, it is not unfair to say that it was morbid, heartless and without spirit.

When one hears of such happenings in a day's play the mind, at once searching for the reason, becomes centred on the pitch. Generally the game has been played on an appalling surface on which effective batsmanship was virtually impossible. On Saturday this was not the case. True, the wicket was lively and, by virtue of the occasional ball which pranced viciously on pitching, it bestowed the greater share of its bounties on the bowler. But at the same time it was not much worse than it had been during England's innings, and the one cause of the collapse above all others was the fast bowling of Trueman and the sheer trepidation, amounting at times to unconditional surrender, which it inflicted upon some of India's batsmen. The essential and match-winning complement of speed is good catching, and not a chance was dropped and many were brilliantly held.

One must not, as a result of this victory and the manner in which it has been obtained, become too sanguine about our prospects against Australia next summer. The very standard of Indian cricket, with its home on perfect wickets, means that much of the performance is irrelevant in such a context. But certain beacons of brightest hope stand out that perhaps have not been there in recent years. The first of these clearly is Trueman, for his achievements alone warrant such a position. He is becoming very fast, and he has gained in accuracy Test by Test. The raw material is there for something really good, and, moreover, he is keen and full of spirit.

So much happened in such a short time on Saturday that it is not possible to record it all. The brief facts, however, should paint the picture well enough. The weather was again surly and boisterous and for the third successive day rain held up the start of play. Ten minutes late of the proper time Evans and Bedser continued England's innings and in the 35 minutes before the declaration England added 55 runs. This phase belonged entirely to Evans, who has an extraordinary flair for imprinting his sparkling presence on a Test match. Three times India had paid dearly for letting him get in and his 71 in as many minutes on Saturday was a superb and impertinent piece of attacking batsmanship.

India then went in for the first time at 25 minutes past twelve and after a large part of two days in the field she knew well enough what to expect from the wicket. Mankad began with a four through the covers off Bedser and one had visions of Lord's all over again, but in the same over he glanced authentically to leg and Lock just behind square some five yards from the bat held a glorious low catch. It was the acme of control, co-ordination and balance, and Lock had soon made his presence felt. The psychological effect of losing Mankad so early had an enormous effect on India and Trueman with the wind astern and all fielders crowded like vultures round the bat now hurled himself into his task. He was not bowling short and he was bowling mostly straight but only Hazare, a poor lone figure through much of the innings, Adhikari, Manjrekar and Sen stood firm with a stout heart. The others backed away to square leg or went berserk, afraid to stand and defend their wickets. It is hard to imagine a worse innings by a number five batsman in a Test match than that played by Umrigar, who ironically enough gave such a strong and brilliant display on the same ground only a fortnight ago.

Trueman's historic figures were eight for 31; 58 was the total, the lowest ever made in a Test match at Old Trafford, and at twenty to three India came again to the slaughter. The second innings lasted for 138 minutes, and although the resistance was worthier an irresistible pressure had taken charge of events. Trueman was tiring, but, with the wicket drying out and becoming more treacherous, Bedser took charge. Lock, too, made the most of his heaven-sent chance, the fielding remained faultless, and Hutton again captained the side with ruthless skill and efficiency. The final scenes were of friendly antagonism and the end came with England, winners of the rubber, received like heroes. Oh for such a happy tale twelve months from now!

England 347 for 9 dec. (L. Hutton 104, T. G. Evans 71, P. B. H. May 69); India 58 (F. S. Trueman 8 for 31) and 82 (A. V. Bedser 5 for 27, G. A. R. Lock 4 for 36). England won by an innings and 207 runs.

Happy indeed. England regained the Ashes in 1953 after nineteen years.

DENYS ROWBOTHAM AT OLD TRAFFORD   AUGUST 1 1956

England v. Australia, Fourth Test

A superb piece of bowling by J. C. Laker not only brought England victory by an innings and 170 runs in the fourth Test match at Old Trafford yesterday (and continued custody of the 'Ashes') but created several remarkable records at the same time.

First, by taking Australia's eight remaining wickets Laker became the first bowler ever to take all ten in one innings in a Test match. These ten wickets, added to his nine in the first innings, also gave him more wickets in a single Test match than any other bowler has obtained in cricket's history. Seventeen of his nineteen wickets were taken in succession, which may also be a record. His aggregate of 51 wickets from five matches against the Australians this season seems unlikely also ever to have been beaten.

Significant records rarely are broken unless the performance is worthy. But a record which derives from an aggregate may be achieved luckily, with the willing connivance of a partner, or with a performance at the crucial moment below the record-breaker's best. More than once, one suspects, ten wickets in an innings have been taken because the bowler at the other end has 'soft-pedalled' for the last few overs or minutes. Yesterday, however, Laker's records were achieved in the highest tradition. To the end of the day at half-past five Lock used every stratagem to take even one wicket which would have quickened England's victory. Field placings, even after the ninth wicket had fallen, were adjusted subtly to enable him to take it had Johnson made only a single error. So that when Laker finally had Maddocks leg-before and the crowd burst into rounds and rounds of cheering he knew that the proudest distinctions had never been gained more genuinely.

Laker's performance becomes still more outstanding when it is emphasised, as it must be, that yesterday's wicket was never strictly sticky. Until about a quarter of an hour before lunch the ball turned slightly but exasperatingly slowly and never with a hint of bite or nip. Then the wicket still was a mud patch. Within 45 minutes of the start at 11.40 in fact Laker was replaced by Oakman, and fifteen minutes later Lock gave way to Statham. The soft surface helped an accurate Statham no more than it had Laker and Lock. Craig and McDonald had only to keep their heads, make no palpable misjudgment, and sustain a watchful concentration to survive without hint of obvious difficulty. They were able to cut and hook anything short with impunity.

All the time a strong wind was drying a wet wicket as amiably as one can well be dried. At 1.10, however, when Laker replaced Bailey at the City end, the sun came out and shone brightly, if not hotly, until roughly an hour after lunch. Within ten minutes Laker had made a ball pop, and before lunch he was turning the ball markedly more sharply and quickly. Clearly after lunch it would soon be obvious whether Australia was to save or lose the match.

The answer came more quickly than one had expected. May promptly changed Lock to the City and Laker to the more dangerous Stretford end. Twice in Laker's first over McDonald was in trouble; twice in Lock's first over balls jumped nastily. And fifteen minutes after lunch Craig was out. Laker made an off-break turn sharply from a full-length richly flighted; Craig played a half-cock, missed, and was leg-before. Ten minutes later Mackay pushed forward to flighted spin he did not smother and Oakman took the catch in the gully. For fifteen minutes after three brisk forward shots, Miller's efforts to pad off Laker hinted now of genuflection, now of outright prostration in prayer. But forward again Laker finally made him reach and this time Miller seemed so keen to make his bat irrevocably dead that he played over the slight off-break or top spinner with which Laker bowled him. Archer's dismissal was much simpler: he played half back in front of his pads and turned Laker's second off-break neatly to Oakman at short leg.

So Australia was 130 for six. That 80 minutes later, at tea, it was 180, still for six wickets, was the result of two splendid pieces of sustained concentration by McDonald and Benaud, who more than the rest of Australia's batsmen really seemed to have learned something of English turning wickets. In the morning McDonald's normal Australian methods probably would have allowed him to survive. But four things were most noticeable: his judgment was exact and showed no mark of anxiety or panic; he was playing forward only when certain he could smother the ball at its pitch; when he did play forward he deadened his bat properly with the left arm thrust forward; and he was beginning to play back English style, side-on. The difference these things made to his play was enormous. Always when Laker was bowling to McDonald the ball seemed to be turning and lifting less spitefully.

Benaud apparently had been watching and when Benaud joined McDonald at 2.55 p.m. he copied his methods from the start. And from then until 4.15 it seemed that neither batsman could be lured forward fatally. So determined was Benaud to play back that more than once Laker all but drove him on to his stumps. He did not, however, and first Lock and then Laker were rested before May brought back both at the ends from which they started in the morning.

From the Stretford end, Lock, for whom nothing seemed to go right, could find no more control than from the City end. Throughout the day he seemed to be trying to bowl too fast and to win from a digging in, which usually meant shortness, too much pop and too much turn. Laker could beat McDonald with spin only once from the City end and at tea (at least on paper) Australia still had the slenderest of chances.

Not once, however, had either Benaud or McDonald been able to relax his concentration for a moment. Before tea they were grooved in application. The break would be refreshment for England. For Australia it would mean that much more difficult thing afterwards – reapplication. So it proved. To Laker's second off-break after tea – now from the Stretford end once again – McDonald played half back, the ball flew from the edge, and Oakman held the catch at short leg. So the breakthrough had been made. And now it was that Laker reaped the full rewards of his persistence.

Laker, indeed, has done more. He has done what always must excite the imagination. He has exemplified, in a single day, all the classical conceptions of the art of slow bowling: strict control first of length and then direction; the imparting of dangerous spin by technique superbly applied; the variation of spin with the ball that runs straight through to sow doubt as well as prompt error in the batsman; the subtle changes of flight, length and pace that will induce fatal errors of judgment; and, lastly, the cool appraisal of each batsman's temperament and resource.

Back and farther back in ever richer arches of flight he drove the still cool and stubborn Benaud. Once he all but beat him with a really fast ball. Then a succession of easier, slower deliveries. Then a fully flighted ball, but pushed through quickly, this time to the length of a full half-volley. Back once more played Benaud, this time side-on fatally, for he was bowled before his shot was completed. So at five o'clock it was 198 for eight and England all but home. Laker now is tiring and Lindwall pushed forward and actually gets away with snicks and edges through the leg trap. Another ball curves tantalisingly in rich flight: this time Lindwall's forward shot just fails to smother it, the ball spins, and Lock at close fine leg is hugging the catch delightedly. A last effort by Lock, and now Laker has changed his pace and flight again; Maddocks, too, has played back to a half-volley, the Ashes are England's, and Laker has achieved the performance of a lifetime.

S. F. Barnes, who took seventeen for 159 runs against South Africa at Johannesburg in 1913-14 had the best Test match performance before Laker's. Wilfred Rhodes and the late Hedley Verity with, respectively, fifteen for 124 at Melbourne in 1903-4, and fifteen for 104 at Lord's in 1934, were until yesterday England's best performers against Australia. All three would have recognised Laker's as bowling of their vintage.

This was the first time since 1905 that a Test match at Old Trafford against Australia had reached a definite result, and it was also the first time since 1905 that England had won two matches in a series in this country.

England 459 (Rev. D. S. Sheppard 113, P. E. Richardson 104, M. C. Cowdrey 80, I. W. Johnson 4 for 151); Australia 84 (J. C. Laker 9 for 37) and 205 (C. C. McDonald 89, Laker 10 for 53). England won by an innings and 170 runs.

DENYS ROWBOTHAM AT LORD'S JUNE 26 1963

England v. West Indies, Second Test

Yesterday, the second Test match at Lord's ended in a draw as exciting as anyone could wish. With England six runs behind for nine wickets, it required the formal appearance of Cowdrey as non-striker to allow Allen to save the match for England by stopping Hall's last two deliveries after a great innings of 70 by Close had brought England within 15 of their target. When play ultimately started, ten minutes after lunch, few English supporters could have hoped for so much.

From Close's (and England's) point of view, the only disappointment was the manner of his departure. Titmus and Trueman had been dismissed by successive balls from Hall, and England, then 203 for seven, needed 31 in the last 44 minutes. This was a more formidable task in terms of time than it seemed, because the West Indian fast bowlers were averaging only 14 overs an hour and little in the way of forceful stroke-play could be expected of Allen. That it proved, after all but four hours' magnificent batting, just too much for Close's judgment is only to admit that mortals are fallible.

That there could be disappointment was tribute to Close, who through the 20 minutes before Titmus's going had developed masterfully in both the power and range of his stroke-play. It was the period during which Gibbs bowled three of his day's meagre ration of five overs. With 52 then needed in 65 minutes, Close sensed his opportunity and took it.

He swung Hall to long leg for four. As Worrell spread his fields ever deeper, Close and Titmus scampered singles for stunned defensive shots and the neatest deflections. Gibbs dropped just short and Close late-cut him for four. He over-pitched and Close swept him for four. Between times, he had reached his 50 by hooking a bumper off Hall, and, when Titmus was out, 21 runs had come in only 20 minutes.

It needed only the tail's survival and a maintenance of Close's disciplined aggression and England would have won almost comfortably. Did Trueman's going, feeling for a lifting, just short one, unnerve

Close? When, after glancing Griffith, he advanced down the wicket to Hall, one drew breath and wondered. Yet he steadied and achieved singles with firm pushes and a late cut before sweeping Griffith majestically, if soaringly near long leg, for four.

He hooked Hall still more brilliantly for another four and only 17 runs were needed now in 25 minutes. Allen had settled and the task seemed within England's capacity. Horror of horrors, when, without seeming need, Close began to advance down the wicket once more. A leg bye off Griffith should have warned him. Yet the intrepid fellow advanced yet again, edged a sweep, and was caught at the wicket.

Close had aimed at a million and missed by a unit. Certainly, his task yesterday was more formidable than on Monday. Then he had to face only one over from a Hall immediately chastened after injuring Cowdrey. Griffith and Gibbs were taxing but manageable. Barrington, moreover, was in superb form and, when Close joined him, was confidently attacking.

Yesterday Hall was again at his fastest, and though pitching less consistently short and rather less straight, was still banging the ball down on the bare patch just short of a length from which it lifted at its most acute and most unpredictable angles. Griffith was livelier and steadier than on Monday. And Barrington was so far from himself that he looked somewhat like a man suffering delayed shock.

Not for 45 minutes, indeed, did Barrington score a run. His defence off the back foot was jumpy, he seemed, overnight, to have lost the confidence to play forward, and when he tried to drive it was plain that his timing, too, was awry. When he was caught at the wicket off a reaching, edged late-cut to Griffith after 50 minutes it was surprising only that he had lasted so long.

Parks looked cool and business-like as in the first innings. He defended soundly and, in scoring 17 of 28 runs in 40 minutes, he made handsome drives through the covers and past point and pushed forward firmly to the on-side. Yet he was out to a ghastly back shot, across the line off very nearly a half-volley, and only Titmus in his mood of the first innings remained to assure Close.

Thus Close was under maximum pressure for over three hours. His first object was to concede nothing. Yet by well-placed pushes and wristy deflections he scored nine to Barrington's five of England's first 14 runs. Time, hereabouts, did not matter and he defended, splendidly upright, back and forward, to all the fiery bolts Hall thundered at him, while Parks waited for and drove Griffith's few half-volleys.

He kept his bat out of trouble either side of the wicket and he withdrew it and took on his pads or body every ball which kicked viciously from Hall. His mature composure then reorientated itself in the progressively developing stroke-play which brought him 31 runs during the hour Titmus was with him. Not many more disciplined innings have been played under comparable stresses for England, and had Titmus not finally succumbed to a lifting ball off the patch with which

Close coped to the last, Close probably would have advanced England triumphantly to victory.

There remained the last exciting 20 minutes. Hall, after bowling unchanged for three hours, or Griffith, after only five overs fewer, had to find a ball straight, fast and of length good enough to dismiss Allen or Shackleton. The breath was held with every delivery, yet with each the feeling grew that they would no more find it than the two batsmen score 15 runs through fields spread deep except for a slip.

Only Allen's running for a bye as the fourth ball of Hall's last over passed to the wicketkeeper, while Shackleton remained statuesque after his vain swish, gave the West Indians their own chance from Hall's last two deliveries. Allen withstood them and ensured another great challenge at Edgbaston. Whether Worrell should have tried spin in mid-afternoon could be debated for the rest of the summer. He pinned his faith in his two fast bowlers for 33 overs, and they failed him only by a hair's breadth.

West Indies 301 (R. B. Kanhai 73, J. S. Solomon 56, F. S Trueman 6 for 100) and 229 (B. F. Butcher 133, Trueman 5 for 52, D. Shackleton 4 for 72); England 297 (K. F. Barrington 80, E. R. Dexter 70, F. J. Titmus 52 not out, C. C. Griffith 5 for 91) and 228 for 9 (D. B. Close 70, Barrington 60, W. W. Hall 4 for 93). Match drawn.

BRIAN CHAPMAN IN SYDNEY   FEBRUARY 18 1971

Australia v. England, Seventh Test

A soldiers' general led England to victory in the final Test by 62 runs, today, and regained the Ashes after 12 years. Ray Illingworth was chaired by his men, and carried triumphantly to the dressing-room.

Whatever carping critics may say from the sidelines, this highly competent cricketer has led his team well, and never better than in the deciding 95 minutes this morning. Even though England soon gained the upper hand, and never relaxed their grip, there was always the chance that one batsman or another would break loose in that tail-end batting, and would give us a fright. A margin of 100 runs, with five wickets left, which was the position at the start, leaves little room to spare for manoeuvre. England made no mistakes, and the Australian batting appeared frail indeed.

Illingworth said afterwards that, throughout the tour, his players had given him one hundred per cent support, and that was no idle platitude. He was asked what victory pep talk he gave them before taking the field. He replied: 'I just said: "Come on, let's go." That was all that was necessary.'

His opponent, Ian Chappell, who should make an attractive leader in England in 1972, paid England a fitting tribute when he said: 'They have faced a lot of hardships, they are a strong, professional side, and they have put up a fine fighting performance.'

Even without Boycott, and deprived for the run-in of Snow, England were strong enough to recover from a poor start and win convincingly. The game sustained a high pitch of tension right through, even though the quality of cricket was not outstanding. In spite of that, Illingworth declared: 'Five Tests is a happy medium. If anyone pushes for seven they want shooting.' He also thought that 75 per cent of the up-country matches should be scrapped, now that supporters can travel easily and conveniently to the big games.

One would agree that many of these one-day affairs are due for demolition. They are not all well supported, and players seem to sustain an undue proportion of injury upon rougher surfaces. Both captains agreed, too, that the concept of the Ashes is outdated, and each series should be contested in its own right.

Illingworth himself took the all-important wicket of Greg Chappell this morning, and finished with three for 39, figures which suggest he has hitherto been too parsimonious in employing his own spinning skill.

Australia's policy was based on caution that led to the extremity of defeat; stay and the runs will come is always a doubtful tactic, and sterner aggression would have served them better. The first break-through was contrived by Underwood, when Marsh was shaping a stroke of utmost crudity which bore faint resemblance to a drive. Rowan no-balled Underwood three times for over-stepping, and perhaps the bowler was put out of his stride, for he permitted Chappell the liberty of a four through the covers. The ball from which Chappell was stumped was variously described, in the enthusiasm of the moment, as a floater, or one that spun a bit, or one that had extra bounce. Illingworth modestly described it as just a straight ball. It was the one that finally placed the Ashes under lock and key.

O'Keeffe briefly sketched a plan of attack, twice lofting Illingworth to the on for four. The captain replied with an inspired change – he brought on D'Oliveira, who, in his first over, had O'Keeffe caught at square leg, and next ball found the edge of Lillee's bat for a catch at second slip.

Jenner prodded at Underwood via bat and pad, and next moment Fletcher, at slip, was flinging the ball high in the air. He, like most of the others, has passed through times of stress and tribulation, but this was the moment that made it all worth while. Australians, as they gathered for congratulatory or consoling drinks in the pavilion, admitted that England were the better side, and that they would have suffered injustice had Australia escaped in the final encounter.

In the end it had scarcely been hard pounding, but each of the faithful band of Englishmen who have followed MCC round Australia could joyfully say: 'I would not have been elsewhere for thousands.'

It was a pity that one English critic, who perhaps found Illingworth's triumph hard to applaud, chose to introduce a recriminatory note at the press conference. Had Illingworth apologised for Saturday's behaviour?

'Certainly not,' he replied. But he had received an apology for the crowd's outburst from Alan Davidson, the former Test star, now president of New South Wales Cricket Association.

Let the snipers snipe as they will, this was Illingworth's match, and his part will be remembered and acknowledged in gratitude.

England 184 and 302 (B. W. Luckhurst 59, J. H. Edrich 57); Australia 264 (G. S. Chappell 65, I. R. Redpath 59) and 160 (K. R. Stackpole 67). England won by 62 runs.

HENRY BLOFELD AT MELBOURNE   MARCH 18 1977

Australia v. England, Centenary Test

For a long time in Melbourne yesterday, it looked as if England might score the 463 they needed to beat Australia in the Centenary Test Match, which would have been more than any side have ever scored in the fourth innings of a Test to win.

England reached 279 for two and, though Randall played a wonderful innings of 174 in his first Test against Australia, they were eventually bowled out for 417, which gave Australia victory by 45 runs – by a remarkable and happy coincidence, the same margin as it was in that first Test match between the sides of Lillywhite and Gregory.

A truly magnificent game came to an end in the second over of the last hour, when Knott was lbw, trying to turn Lillee to leg. For five days, the match had fluctuated one way and then the other in the best traditions of Anglo-Australian Test cricket.

There is no doubt that Australia deserved to win, for they had, in Lillee, the most dangerous cricketer on either side. It was he who regained the initiative so splendidly for them on the second day. He finished with 11 for 165 in what will be his last Test match until, at least, India start their series in Australia in November.

When it mattered, too, Australia played rather the more efficient cricket, though the difference between the two sides was not nearly as pronounced as it has been in the last three years, when Thomson and Lillee were bowling together. From the evidence of this match, and particularly from the way the Australians batted, England will have an excellent chance of winning back the Ashes this summer in England.

When the last day started, Australia had to bowl 13 more overs before they could take the new ball. Lillee bowled two in which he was no more than fast-medium. Having announced, just before play began, that he was unavailable to tour England because of his back injury, Lillee may have slowed up to prove his point; anyway, he was a different bowler from the first innings. After those two overs, O'Keeffe and Chappell shared the bowling until the new ball.

Randall's 100 came without any fuss. First, he swept O'Keeffe fine for four and, after surviving a half-hearted appeal for a catch off bat and pad at short-leg, he then square-cut him for three. He then late-cut Lillee wide of second slip for four and finally turned him to long leg for a single. When he took off his cap and waved his bat to the crowd, his boyish enthusiasm endeared him to everyone.

Almost at once, he started to play a celebratory hook at Lillee, changed his mind in mid-stroke and was hit on the side of the head. But, after a couple of minutes on the ground, he was bouncing around again as good as new.

Every now and then, Amiss would come down the wicket to calm down Randall as, on one occasion, he fell, avoiding a bouncer from Lillee. Finding himself on the ground, he completed a somersault before standing up again and seemed about to do an encore. When Amiss turned O'Keeffe to square leg for four, the 100 stand had come in 131 minutes, and every Englishman on the ground was doing frantic calculations.

A target of 463 had seemed impossibly far away, but a target of 247 with eight wickets and five hours left looked a different matter. Amiss's courageous 50 came just before the new ball, and 46 runs had come off 13 overs with the old one.

Lillee, of course, took the new ball. His first ball was short, Randall played at it outside the off stump and survived a loud appeal for a catch behind. Lillee had a predictable conversation with him and Randall, to his credit, at least, held his own in the exchanges and, muttering and shrugging, Lillee made his way back to his mark. It was not the least of Randall's achievements that, unlike so many recent England batsmen, he never let himself be brow-beaten by Lillee.

In the second over with the new ball, Randall played a cover drive off Walker that cannot often have been bettered at Melbourne in Test matches over the past 100 years. Lillee was now bowling faster, but caused no problems. Randall coolly let the short stuff go by, past or over the stumps and, for once, Amiss did likewise. They put on 76 in the two hours before lunch and, at 267 for two, England needed 196 in four hours. It began to seem tantalisingly close.

Australia found themselves severely handicapped because Gilmour had lost all control with his bowling and Chappell did not dare to use him. After his long spell on Wednesday, Walker was obviously tired and, after lunch, Lillee bowled off his short run, which Randall found much to his liking. In the second over after the interval he drove Lillee past extra cover and cut and hooked him thunderously for 10 runs in an over.

Chappell also used himself and, while Lillee was proving expensive, the Australian captain shut one end up in an admirable fashion. In his second over, he cut one back into Amiss, which did not get up, and hit the middle and off stumps. Amiss had stayed grimly with Randall for 230 minutes for 64 and had helped him add 166 in this time. His was a tremendous effort, for he was, perhaps, under greater personal pressure than anyone.

Randall, meanwhile, was batting with a permanent smile, thoroughly enjoying himself. He played some wonderful shots off the back foot against Lillee, but, when he had reached 146, Randall played him off his toes and Cosier dropped a catch up to his left at square leg, which he should have held. Unfortunately, Fletcher did not follow Amiss's example. After scoring just a single, he pushed at Lillee without getting behind the line, as he has done so often, and was caught behind. This must surely have been his last Test innings.

Greig drove Lillee's next ball powerfully to the extra cover boundary and repeated the stroke later in the over, leaving no one in any doubt that he was interested only in victory. Lillee's first four overs after lunch had cost 41 runs, while Chappell's first five cost only seven runs. There was nearly a run-out when Randall backed up too far and, in trying to get back, was run into by Chappell, who threw at the wicket with Randall out of his ground, but missed. It would have been a tricky decision for the umpire if he had hit the stumps.

The next alarm came when Randall played at Walker outside the off stump and was given out caught behind. But Marsh seemed to indicate that the ball had pitched before reaching him, the square leg umpire confirmed this and Randall was recalled. He was 161 at the time and as chirpy as ever.

Chappell and Walker now quietened down the scoring rate considerably, and Chappell's was a fine spell for an occasional bowler. In the afternoon, his figures were 10-6-13-1. Eventually, he brought back O'Keeffe and, in his first over of the spell, Randall was out. He prodded forward and Cosier, diving in from square short leg, held a fine left-handed catch.

Randall had batted 448 minutes for 174 and had hit 21 fours. He came in grinning and waved his hands to the crowd before walking into the pavilion past the Queen, who was sitting there before being introduced to the players during the tea interval. To his great delight, Randall was made man of the match.

With five wickets standing, England now needed 117 in 130 minutes. Greig continued to hit the ball hard, but was sixth out at 369, when he pushed O'Keefe's googly to Cosier, at forward short leg, who held on at the second attempt.

Before long, Old slashed at the ball and was caught at slip, Lever was soon lbw to a googly, Underwood was yorked swinging across Lillee, and, finally, Knott was lbw at the start of the last hour of what had been not only a remarkable occasion, but also a magnificent game watched by 250,000. The year 2077 will have something to live up to.

Australia 138 and 419 for 9 dec. (R.W. Marsh 110 not out, I. C. Davis 68, K. D. Walters 66, D. W. Hookes 56, C. M. Old 4 for 104); England 95 (D. K. Lillee 6 for 26, M. H. N. Walker 4 for 54) and 417 (D. W. Randall 174, D. L. Amiss 64, Lillee 5 for 139). Australia won by 45 runs.

England v. Australia, Fourth Test

Geoffrey Boycott scored the 100th century of his career in helping England to 252 for four against Australia in the fourth Test at Headingley yesterday. His mind was set so firmly on that objective that no one, not even the Australian team, could bar his way.

He is only the 18th cricketer to score 100 hundreds, and the first to complete them in a Test match. All Yorkshire knew he would do it, so they came in their thousands, and long before play began the dense, patient crowds in their long crocodiles to the turnstiles ensured that the gates would be closed.

They sat devotedly – almost devoutly – thickly massed all day under blazing sun, and as Boycott moved through the 80s they began to applaud every scoring stroke. When he drove Chappell straight for the conclusive four a mindless mob deprived the moment of its due dignity. The police were slow to act but when the invaders had been removed the remainder of the crowd gave Boycott their proud salute.

It was a virtually chanceless innings, although Marsh probably touched a leg-side snick off Walker when Boycott had made 22; and the Australians appealed, not quite convincingly, for a catch off his forearm, and more seriously for a leg-side catch by Marsh. The refusal of the last appeal by an Australian umpire, Alley, prompted a sharp comment from Bright to the umpire; the matter was quickly and effectively dealt with by Chappell.

This Boycott is the committed cricketer, a lonely perfectionist moved to the heart at coming to such a high peak of performance before his own people – and against the Australians – and doing so with an innings typical of a technique which probably has come nearer than that of any other batsman to the elimination of error. It is sad that English Test teams should have been deprived of such consummate skill for the past three years.

England's 252 for four wickets took them towards the safety of the draw which would be sufficient to give them the Ashes. Woolmer and Greig made useful contributions; but the day was Boycott's.

In the preliminaries Woolmer was passed fit and England made one change from their team at Trent Bridge, Roope coming in with Miller as 12th man. Australia switched spinners, Bright for O'Keefe.

The pitch was firm, with enough grass to bind it firmly. The ball moved off the seam in the morning when Thomson and Walker flogged occasional lift from it. For the rest, though, it was a true, easy paced batsman's wicket and the ball raced across the outfield – especially downhill to the grandstand – as if over ice.

When Brearley won the toss he had no hesitation about batting; and he himself was out to the third ball of the innings. Generally in this series he has handled Thomson shrewdly and soundly. Now, though, he played an indeterminate stroke outside the off stump and edged the ball to Marsh.

The start of nought for one wicket spurred Thomson and Walker to a sustained hostile spell in which Boycott and Woolmer aimed little higher than survival; content to punish the rare loose ball but otherwise respectfully cautious. Woolmer several times played fluently through the covers, while most of Boycott's opportunities came on the leg side.

Gradually Boycott's intense concentration was reflected in growing certainty of stroke. He was little concerned with anything but meticulous certainty: poring over each stroke; weighing it against the bad ball; alert, flexible in decision until the last possible moment.

He and Woolmer with a steady 82 for the second wicket refounded the innings and took the edge from the Australian seam bowling, which was sharp enough for Chappell to maintain a five-man close field for the first half of the day. A quarter of an hour after lunch Thomson pitched compellingly near to the line of Woolmer's off stump, slight outswing found the edge and Chappell made the catch securely at slip.

There was a brief, joyous interlude of Randall making the strokes of a happy cricketer, with a full, generous swing of the bat. For almost half an hour he made the method men seem too sad. Once he sent Thomson for four with a positive late cut, not the steer, dab or run of the present day but a hugely generous blow from the face of the bat. Then, going forward to Pascoe, he was manifestly lbw.

Greig, who obviously feels that he now has few worries in an innings for England, cut some risky curves round the bowling before producing a series of handsome blows interspersed with uncertainties to make 43 out of 96 with Boycott for the fourth wicket.

Boycott, driven on by determination, now was moving with all the certainty of an express train. Roope, in contrast, had some unnerving moments against Walker, whose splendid late afternoon spell was ill rewarded.

As Boycott sighted his ambition close ahead he began to walk into the bowling, pushing it away with a bat which seemed all unmissable middle. Urged on by the crowd he scored steadily in singles and twos until the final four, a stroke of utter command. Long after play ended a crowd before the pavilion chanted, called for, and celebrated him.

England 436 (G. Boycott 191, A. P. E. Knott 57, L. S. Pascoe 4 for 91, J. R. Thomson 4 for 113); Australia 103 (I. T. Botham 5 for 21, M. Hendrick 4 for 41) and 248 (R. W. Marsh 63, Hendrick 4 for 54). England won by an innings and 85 runs.

To the editor   AUGUST 17 1977

Sir, – Much as I admire both men I
cannot accept that John Arlott's comparison of Geoffrey Boycott with an express
train is on quite the right lines.

F. E. Leese.

Oxford.

PAUL FITZPATRICK AT HEADINGLEY   JULY 22 1981

England v. Australia, Third Test

Not since the golden age of cricket have England won a Test to compare
with the one they won by 18 runs against Australia at Headingley
yesterday.

Not since A. E. Stoddart led his side to victory by 10 runs in Sydney
in 1894, the only previous instance of a Test side following on and
winning the game, has an English cricket public been given quite such
cause for celebration.

This third Cornhill Test will be remembered for many things – chiefly
for the soaring performances of Ian Botham, and the marvellous bowling
yesterday of Bob Willis – but perhaps the thing that will give it an
imperishable place in cricket history alongside the tied Test of Brisbane
1960 was the utter improbability of the victory.

England, it will be remembered, scored 174 to Australia's first
innings 401 for nine declared; and at one stage on Monday they were
still 92 runs short of making Australia bat again with only three second
innings wickets standing.

To be at Headingley yesterday was to be part of a drama as gripping
as anything the fertile mind of Wilkie Collins could have dreamed of. It
was impossible to take the eye away from a single delivery; every run
that edged Australia towards their target of 130 heightened the anxiety
of an absorbed crowd; every wicket England captured added another
heartbeat of tension until by the time that Willis uprooted Bright's
middle stump to end the game most nerves could have stood no more.

Only Test cricket could have produced such a fascinating plot as this;
no other game could have allowed such an unlikely and outrageous
swing of fortune as England experienced. Only a drama that is allowed
to unfold over five days could permit such a twist in the plot so wild as to
be almost unthinkable.

After three and a half days of largely dull preamble, England were
finished, ready, it seemed, to subside to an innings defeat; ready,
humiliatingly, to go 2-0 down in a series only three matches old. Kim
Hughes already had visions of himself as the latest proud owner of the

Ashes. With three matches still to go his dream is now a long way from realisation.

The man who did most to fling logic the full length of the Kirkstall Lane was Ian Botham, with an innings that was the modern embodiment of Jessop. That blistering, sustained attack on the Australian bowling turned the game upside down on Monday afternoon, but in spite of its magnificence it seemed at best an heroic gesture. If England were to have the slightest hope of winning, another 50 or 60 runs would be needed yesterday and with only Willis left to support Botham that seemed unlikely.

Botham struck another four, his 27th of an unforgettable innings of 149, but Willis was not able to keep him company for much longer yesterday. A push forward at Alderman, an outside edge, a catch to second slip and Willis's resistance had ended, leaving Australia to score a modest 130 runs to win . . . a target to be treated with respect but not one surely to perturb unduly pragmatic Australians.

The Headingley crowd had seen the rebirth of Botham. They now saw Bob Willis peel away the years and give a display of pace bowling culled from his youth, before the days of suspect, creaking knees. No one has tried harder for his country over the years.

His performance surpassed anything that he has produced in Test cricket previously. Throughout his spell he found movement, bounce, life and pace; too much pace for eight Australians. No Englishman has ever returned a more impressive set of figures at Headingley – eight for 43, an analysis to give Willis a glow of pride when he is 'old and grey and full of sleep and nodding by the fire'.

Willis is a laconic chap, except, it seems, when he is asked on the television to give his views on the English press. He weighs questions carefully, delays the answer until you think he is not going to answer at all, and then usually produces some telling or humorous comment.

Did he think he would ever play Test cricket again when he left the West Indies in February for repair to a troublesome knee? 'I never thought I'd play cricket again, let alone Test cricket,' he replied. What motivates him? 'I want to keep playing for England. That sounds phoney, I know, but it's the truth.' Who could doubt that yesterday?

The Warwickshire captain is used to reading his obituary notice in the columns of national newspapers. If England had lost this game he might have expected to see it there again. But his desire to keep playing for England will now be fulfilled for a few more Tests yet.

Young pace bowlers with aspiration to an England place – the Allotts, Hugheses and Newmans – will have to look elsewhere for a possible opening. This vacancy is definitely filled. As Brearley said: 'I didn't think Willis could still bowl like that. He surpassed himself.'

Ron Allsopp tried and failed to produce a wicket at Trent Bridge that was fair to both batsmen and bowlers but would produce exciting cricket; Keith Boyce adopted a similar policy at Headingley and he, too, failed.

Everyone was agreed, Willis even, that the wicket was loaded in favour of the bowlers. 'If you hit the cracks,' Willis said, 'the ball either squatted or went vertical.' But although here was a track that no batsman could trust there were, as Dyson, Hughes and Yallop, Botham and Dilley had proved, surely 130 runs in it.

There was really no one else to whom Brearley could have given the new ball. It had to be Botham. His rich vein had to be tapped as long as possible and sure enough Botham raised English spirits by having Wood, who struck the first two balls from the Somerset all-rounder for four, caught at the wicket in the third over.

There followed a similar phase of cricket to the Australian first innings when Dyson, again looking technically sound and temperamentally assured, and Chappell, carefully, stoically gave the innings its spine.

But no sooner had a backbone been established than it was snapped by a furious spell of bowling that brought Willis three wickets in 11 balls without a run scored off him. England for the first time could entertain the audacious thought of win while Australia must have suffered their first serious misgivings.

An awkward, lifting delivery to the outside edge of Chappell's bat gave Taylor the second of the four catches which brought him the world-record number of dismissals. Hughes, never comfortable, could not keep down a rising delivery that caught the throat of his bat and brought Botham to a fine, tumbling catch at third slip.

Yallop, also unable to angle his bat enough over another ball of chest height, was caught alertly by Gatting at short leg. At 58 for four, Australia must have felt for the first time like unwilling victims in a plot they had no power to resist.

Border, getting an inside edge to a delivery from Old that uprooted his leg stump, became the third Australian batsman successively to collect a duck and when the obdurate Dyson, after two hours' solid resistance, fell trying to hook Willis, Australia were 68 for six and sliding fast. With Willis pounding in from the Kirkstall Lane end, a bounce in his step and bent on destruction, there was no respite either.

Marsh might so easily have done for Australia what Botham on a much grander scale had achieved for England. He is a batsman who could have put the game back into Australian hands with a few powerful swings of his woodcutter's arms.

Swing he did but only high down to fine leg, where Dilley, glancing down swiftly to make sure his feet were firmly inside the boundary line, judged a difficult catch to perfection.

Lawson, a promising batsman but still young, had neither the nerve nor the experience for the occasion and prodded fatally at Willis. Only two wickets remained and now 55 runs were still needed and England, it seemed, astonishingly, would win with something to spare.

The margin in the end, however, was a mere 18 runs, and English followers could have stood nothing closer. Bright is a sound bat, Lillee is experienced, and between them – Lillee by unorthodox but perfectly justifiable methods, Bright by more legitimate means – whittled away the deficit until Lillee tried to hook Willis to the midwicket area but succeeded only in looping the ball up to mid-on, where Gatting took his second outstanding catch of the innings.

Botham was brought back and watched Old drop Alderman twice in an over before Willis, fittingly Willis, ripped out Bright's middle stump.

Australia 401 for 9 dec. (J. Dyson 102, K. J. Hughes 89, G. N. Yallop 58, I. T. Botham 6 for 95) and 111 (R. G. D. Willis 8 for 43); England 174 (Botham 50, D. K. Lillee 4 for 49) and 356 (Botham 149 not out, G. R. Dilley 56, T. M. Alderman 6 for 135). England won by 18 runs.

To the editor   SEPTEMBER 4 1981

Sir, – On Friday I watched J. M. Brearley directing his fieldsmen very carefully. He then looked up at the sun and made a gesture which seemed to indicate that it should move a little squarer. Who is this man? – Yours sincerely,
                    S. A. Nicholas.
Longlevens, Gloucester.

Grim Days

Twenty of Rochdale v. United All-England XI

Within an hour after the close of the grand cricket match between the Eleven of England and twenty of Rochdale, on Saturday evening, a shocking accident occurred on the railway, which produced a very painful sensation in Rochdale, and which terminated in the death of Mr. Thomas Hunt, the well-known cricketer.

Gentlemen who reside in the neighbourhood of Oldham Road, Rochdale, have made it a very common practice, with a view to shorten the distance, to get upon the Lancashire and Yorkshire Railway, at Milkstone, and to walk thence to the pavilion on the cricket ground, which abuts upon the line. Mr. Hunt, at the close of the game, was requested to stop in Rochdale, in order to attend a banquet at a quarter past seven o'clock, to be held at the Wellington Hotel. He refused, saying that it would cost him less to go home, and, after packing up his cricketing materials, he engaged a man, named John Wild, to carry them to the Rochdale Station. Unfortunately, without any leave whatever, the example of walking on the line had increased very much during the match, and large numbers entered the cricket ground on Saturday that way. Mr. Hunt and the man Wild determined to walk upon it to the station. Wild went a short distance before Mr. Hunt, and the latter incautiously picked his road between the up rails; and when he had gone a distance of about 200 yards, and had nearly reached the houses at Milkstone, Wild heard the whistling of an engine, and turned round to look what it was. It was a train due at Rochdale Station from Manchester at 6.50. He saw the danger in which Mr. Hunt was, but was too far off to render him the slightest assistance. He appeared to be in a complete state of bewilderment and unable to discover a place of safety. He turned round quickly, and in a moment was caught by the buffer of the engine, which threw him down on the rails. Both his legs and his left hand were across the rails, and in that position the train passed over him, cutting off both legs across the calves, except a few shreds of skin and flesh, and smashing all the fingers of his left hand, over which the wheels seem to have gone in a slanting direction.

57

Some of the passengers, attracted no doubt by the gay appearance of the cricket field, were looking out, and saw a man on the line, and lustily called out. The driver did all that he could to stop his train, but was unable to do so until the accident had occurred. A number of people from the adjoining house jumped on the line to render assistance. The train went forward to the station to apprise the officials of the accident, and the people procured a labourers' truck close by, lifted the unfortunate man upon it, and conveyed him to the station, under the directions of Mr. Cross, the station master. Mr. Hunt was then removed to the Fleece Inn, adjoining the station. Mr. Cross instantly telegraphed for Dr. Harrison, of Manchester, the Company's surgeon, but he had left for Huddersfield. Mr. Ogden, surgeon, was then called in, and he sent for Mr. Bowers, and in a short time after, Messrs. Sellars, Coventry, and Wood (assistant to Mr. Lawton) arrived, and rendered all the assistance they could to the unfortunate man. No hemorrhage of any moment took place. The rough manner in which the limbs were mutilated caused the vessels to contract. Shortly before nine o'clock Mr. Sellars announced that Mr. Hunt was dying. Mr. Cross had telegraphed for his wife, who was expected to meet him at the Manchester Station. Dr. Molesworth, the vicar, was sent for to administer consolation to the dying man. The latter arrived just when the spark of life had fled, and Mr. Hunt's wife came by the train which leaves Manchester at 8.15 p.m. and was five minutes too late to see him alive.

It has been reported that Mr. Hunt was intoxicated at the time; but this is not true; he had had a glass or two, and boasted, before leaving the ground, that he had spent very little during the match. He appears to have lost all self-possession, and the shock to his system by the accident produced almost immediate delirium, which continued till within a few minutes of his death, when he became sensible, but his voice was very feeble. He called for his friend James Clegg, who had never left him from the time the accident occurred. In person Mr. Hunt was remarkably good-looking, being somewhat portly. He was much admired on the field during the match by the spectators. He was born at Chesterfield, in the year 1819. By trade he was a coachmaker; but for the last 14 years he has been a professional cricketer, and a great portion of that time in the service of the Manchester Club, by whom he was much respected. He has generally played with the United All-England Eleven, and in his time has been considered the best single-wicket player in England. In the match at Rochdale (the score of which is given in another column) Hunt was one of the professional players 'given' to the Rochdale Club, and acted as its wicket keeper. He leaves behind him four children – a daughter about 17 years of age by his first wife, and three children by his present wife, the eldest of whom is about nine years of age.

The accident spread a gloom over the proceedings at the Wellington Hotel, where about 70 gentlemen dined; the Mayor, R. T. Heape, Esq.

presiding. The moment his death was announced to the meeting the Mayor suggested the propriety of terminating the proceedings, and of commencing a subscription for his wife and children. This course was immediately adopted, and £33. 18s. were put down in a few minutes. Mr. Councillor S. Taylor agreed to be the treasurer for the Rochdale fund, and the professionals present – Parr, Cæsar, Reynolds, Sherman, Clarke, Jackson, Stephenson, Diver, Mortlock, and Miller – all put down handsome subscriptions, expressing a hope that other professionals would follow their example.

JULY 14 1863

One Legged v. One Armed

Yesterday, an amusing and interesting cricket match was played on the ground of the Manchester Clifford Cricket Club, at Old Trafford, between eleven one-handed men and eleven crippled of one leg. The idea of a game which requires so much physical energy and activity being played by men deficient of the very limbs most called into requisition was novel, and almost a burlesque on human deprivation and infirmity; but the skill and agility displayed by the men were surprising, and gave much amusement to the thousands of persons who were attracted to the sport. The men are, generally speaking, young and intelligent, and went through their work with much zeal and liveliness. The one-armed men had, of course, a decided advantage in fielding, but the one-legged stuck well to their stumps. A man named Langston made some splendid play on the one-armed side, and Lettford showed himself famous in arms, though wanting two legs, and both were loudly cheered.

One Legs 138 and 133; One Arms 118 (Langston 56) and 132 (Langston 77 not out). One Legs won by 21 runs.

JULY 26 1884

Lancashire v. Gloucestershire

The play in this match was resumed yesterday morning about a quarter past twelve, the weather at the time being very dull and threatening; and when one over had been bowled a thunderstorm put a stop to further proceedings for half an hour. The play on starting again was monotonous, and the Lancashire innings finished for 23 runs in excess of the Gloucester essay. A few overs were bowled before the luncheon interval, and after resumption the match was brought to an abrupt termination on account of news being received of the death of the mother of the Drs. Grace. A rumour to the effect that some such event might occur was in circulation early in the morning; but the telegraph gave news of a reassuring character and play proceeded; a relapse, however, must have occurred, and soon after three o'clock Mr. Hornby was advised by wire of the mournful intelligence which he was desired to convey to the Messrs. Grace. What a painful task this was to him can be readily imagined, and as soon as this had been done the news was imparted to the spectators, who at once left the field, the deepest sympathy being expressed with the Messrs. Grace on their bereavement . . .

To the editor   AUGUST 1 1884

Sir, – Referring to the Lancashire–Gloucestershire contest alluded to in your 'Cricket Notes', one pleasing feature of the otherwise melancholy termination of this match might be noticed. Some hundreds of Lancashire working men, attracted by a keen love of our national game, and who had no doubt with some difficulty spared the means for their journey and admission to the ground, on being informed that the game would be stopped in consequence of the sad loss which had befallen the Messrs. Grace left the field without a murmur of discontent or disappointment. Praise of conduct such as this would be almost insulting, but at any rate it proves that rough Lancashire folk may be outwardly, yet from the very humblest they yield to none in showing ready sympathy with others' troubles. – Yours, &c.,

S. H. Swire.

JULY 24 1907

Middlesex v. Lancashire

Although no rain fell in London yesterday the rainfall of the previous twenty-four hours had so saturated the Lord's wicket that no further progress was made in the match between Lancashire and Middlesex, not a ball being bowled. It was a most irritating day for all concerned. The sky was overcast but no rain fell, while the outfield, which is less heavily and much less frequently rolled than the 'pitch', was quite firm. In the absence of sun and wind, however, the pitch hardly dried at all, and presented all day a glutinous look peculiar to the ground. Under the circumstances play was out of the question, for neither the batsmen nor the bowlers could have secured a proper footing. Why people should have been admitted with the ground unfit for play and with but little prospect of play being practicable is best known to the Lord's authorities. In any case upwards of a thousand persons paid for admission. These endured with commendable patience the weary wait before lunch in the hope that play would begin after the midday meal. When it became obvious that there was no intention of making a start the spectators became indignant, and for the rest of the afternoon made a series of angry demonstrations in front of the pavilion.

At first the spectators were content to gather in groups and discuss their wrongs. But a leader is usually forthcoming under such circumstances. In the present instance he appeared in the person of a rather excited gentleman, who, after addressing the crowd, led them in a loud-voiced chorus of 'We want play', which was repeated at intervals. He also delivered several speeches in front of the pavilion, and seemed to have the crowd under his control. Mr. Lacey, the M.C.C. secretary, appeared to be in doubt as to what course to take, but eventually he went out amongst the crowd and informed them that they would receive checks admitting to the ground to-day in the event of no play taking place. This pacified the crowd for a time. When, however, the umpires went out for a final inspection and drew the stumps, this tacit intimation that play had been abandoned for the day led to a demonstration without parallel at Lord's. The umpires, on their way back to the pavilion with the stumps, were followed by a hooting and yelling mob. The umpires were escorted by only two policemen. No violence was offered to them, but they were hooted and abused as the arbiters who had decided against play. Once the umpires had reached the pavilion the crowd turned and stampeded over the pitch, the protecting ropes being ignored, while the groundsmen, in the absence of police, were unable to prevent the more unconscionable section of the crowd from venting their wrath on the offending wicket.

So seriously was the wicket damaged by the crowd that after the ground had been cleared the Lancashire captain handed the following statement to the press: 'Owing to the pitch having been deliberately torn up by the public, I, as captain of the Lancashire eleven, cannot see my way to continue the game, the groundsman bearing me out that the wicket could not again be put right. The match is accordingly abandoned.' Whether MacLaren took the right or the wrong course must remain a matter of opinion, but it is beyond dispute that the authorities at headquarters contributed to this most unhappy 'sensation' by taking money at the gates when well aware that play was very improbable. At the Oval money is not taken and the gates are not opened unless there is some prospect of play being clearly practicable.

This is the only prudent plan. It may be urged that when people are admitted on the understanding that play is not guaranteed and no money will be returned they accept the risk wilfully. At the same time, human nature is such that people, even when admitted on this understanding, are apt to think they have been 'wronged' when no play takes place. After the match had been abandoned the following official statement was issued: 'The return passes which were issued to-day at Lord's, in view of the disappointment experienced by spectators, will be available for any one day of a Middlesex match to the end of this season. – F. E. LACEY, Secretary M.C.C.'

JUNE 12 1914

Nottinghamshire v. Lancashire

There is a certain tradition of leisureliness about Notts cricket, and the batsmen who met Lancashire at Trent Bridge yesterday in the return match most worthily maintained it. Playing in glorious weather on a pitch which, if rather damp at the outset, was never really difficult, they occupied the whole day in scoring 225 runs for nine wickets. Spread over the period of play this represents an average rate of about forty an hour, but for the first two hours – that is, up to luncheon – the rate per hour was exactly 22½ runs. There were the spectators around the rails out to see a little cricket, the green turf and the flannelled players making a pleasant picture in the sunshine, and there was Gunn at one end and Hardstaff at the other solemnly placing their bats as far down the pitch as they could reach to be hit by the ball. Over after over it went on for a solid two hours. Gunn did it as artistically, perhaps, as anyone could have done it, but even the most classical style of blocking soon begins to pall on one. At the end of the first hour they had scored 23 runs, and at the end of the second 45, so that they were most consistent in the pace. Hardstaff, when he was bowled after batting for an hour and a quarter, had scored nine, and Gunn, when he went in to luncheon after two hours' play, had made 27. And the only incidents had been the dismissal of two other batsmen besides Hardstaff. The batsmen treated each ball as if it had been a bomb, which might go off if it were hit too hard. Huddleston had what must have been a unique experience. Previous to luncheon he bowled 84 balls, and the only run scored was a single off the 72nd! And even Bullough, a colt bowling for the county for the first time, was treated as if he had been a Spofforth. It might have been a memorial service.

To the editor   APRIL 30 1915

Sir, – Now that what should have been the cricket season has begun many of your readers must be looking with regret at their unused paraphernalia. We could find splendid scope down here for such things as spare bats, balls, pads and so on. There is plenty of flat ground round the camp and we want to find our men some recreation after the day's work is done (we start at 6.30 a.m.!)

So if any readers have any material handy they would be doing a real kindness by sending it on to me here. – Yours &c.,

W. S. Cunliffe.

Captain O.C.C. Co.
19th Service Battalion,
Manchester Regiment, Belton Park,
Grantham.

AUGUST 26 1915

Lancashire v. Yorkshire

A brave attempt was made yesterday at Haslingden to forget that we had been a year at war and to play a Lancashire and Yorkshire match as if nothing had happened to break the sequence of these famous meetings. And in part it succeeded. The match brought together some three thousand spectators, and the funds for equipping and maintaining a convalescent home at Alexandria for wounded soldiers of the East Lancashire Division will be a few hundred pounds better off. Some of the old county cricket atmosphere was reproduced, and people who had not met on the cricket field since the fateful August Bank Holiday week of 1914 pleasantly surprised one another with greetings, and speculated when, if ever, the old days would return. It was not, of course, quite cricket as usual, with men in khaki around the ring – some busily disposing of programmes and others bearing ugly evidence of contact with German shot and gas – but there was a quietly cheerful tone about the whole affair, and at the close everyone agreed that it had been well worth while.

To this satisfactory result the choice of the Haslingden ground for the purposes of the match and the brilliant summer weather were the main contributors. To those who were visiting the place for the first time the picturesque setting of the match must have come as a delightful surprise. For the large circle of turf, looking remarkably fresh after the recent rains, seemed to occupy a little island plateau set in the midst of encircling hills, and with the whole country bathed in sunshine one might have imagined oneself far away in the Highlands instead of in industrial Lancashire. And the cricket was just exciting enough pleasantly to occupy one's attention and to justify a half-holiday in the open.

The match itself was not taken too seriously. It developed none of those palpitating moments that most followers of Lancashire and Yorkshire games can recall. But there were some pleasant patches in the game, and occasionally some very good hitting. And in keeping with the spirit of the occasion it ended in a draw, Lancashire declaring at 210 for six wickets and the Yorkshire score standing at 173 for five when play ceased. J. T. Tyldesley captained the Lancashire side and G. H. Hirst the Yorkshire side. The teams were made up partly of county players and partly of men playing in the Lancashire Leagues. Hirst and Haigh are now clean-shaven persons, and to those who remember them in pre-war days the change of fashion has worked wonders with the well-known features.

NEVILLE CARDUS AT OLD TRAFFORD   AUGUST 31 1939

Surrey v. Lancashire[1]

Old Trafford yesterday enjoyed the unexpected boon of some fleeting hours of cricket in warm, mellow sunshine. Slow play did not and could not occur; each grain that fell in the hour-glass was counted and seen as pure gold. In the pavilion the old gentlemen watched philosophically, and now and again they discussed Hitler, but always with a reservation that the talk could at once be directed to matters of the moment, such as the bowling of a good ball, the performance of a good stroke, a swift piece of fielding, or the general condition of one's lumbago. Out in the sunshine the crowd contained a few small boys left over from the holidays. We shall realise, if the crisis is averted, how happily we have lived in the past; shall, indeed, we feel a single irritation or anxiety in life again?

Surrey batted first on a pitch a little moist from the morning dew, and Gregory was neatly caught off Pollard with only nineteen runs scored. The Lancashire attack observed the first principle of length, and not until a quarter-past twelve did we hear the grand sound of a strong drive, one by Fishlock off Nutter, a beautiful hit to the off. Fishlock played confidently and handsomely; Whitfield also let us see a clean, open method, a product of the Oval wicket; he, too, drove Nutter to the off, and in the same over cut him square to the same spot on the pavilion rails hallowed of old by J. T. Tyldesley. Surrey reached fifty in as many minutes.

Another glorious off drive off Phillipson made Fishlock 52 in sixty-five minutes; his cricket was a model of easily controlled power; there was nothing in it of the suggestion which even good left-handers give us of a certain contrariness somewhere. Roberts kept the runs down, and before lunch his persistence was rewarded. But, first of all, Whitfield was caught in the 'gully' at 107, then Fishlock, who now looked good for the day, touched a ball from Roberts which undoubtedly turned; the chance went to Pollard, the only slip, and after four or five agonising attempts Pollard held the ball. Fishlock deserved to escape and score a century.

The Lancashire bowling and fielding remained steady in spite of the fact that the team did not arrive home from Dover until four o'clock yesterday morning. An indeterminate period between Squires and Parker was broken by a square-leg hit by Squires (from a no-ball), and by a delicious late cut by Squires, off Wilkinson, who bowled again at 141. A brilliant flash of fielding by Pollard in the slips relieved the pleasant monotony of the moment; Pollard leaped and stopped a sharp cut by Squires as the ball sped upward from the ground.

After another drowsy interim, Squires wakened himself up by means of another resolute stroke, a cover drive off Nutter. Wilkinson found the wicket too slow for his uses, and we should remember, when we regard his disappointing season this year, that he has seldom had the luck to bowl on a pitch of any pace with some dust on the top. By comfortable and sound methods Squires and Parker added 99, and little or nothing could apparently disturb the even tenor of the partnership. At last Squires touched an outswinger from Phillipson at 208, and Paynter held a slip catch. Squires hit seven boundaries in his thoroughly organised innings. Parker, though he scarcely made the most of his reach, put a firm bat to the ball, and at tea Surrey were 225 for four.

Whittaker assisted in another useful if anonymous stand, and Surrey arrived at 253 for five. The new ball restored hope to the Lancashire attack. Pollard especially bowled hard, well, and loyally, and received justice and nothing less when in one over he overwhelmed Whittaker and Garland-Wells. After all, there is something in a new ball – it is not all shibboleth and my grandmother. Also there is much in untiring vigour and determination; Pollard gave a splendid exhibition of these two rare human qualities, an exhibition which almost stimulated moral glow and approbation. Surrey's fifth wicket fell at 253, and Parker, not out sixty, survived to impede Lancashire's sudden advance at a moment when the bowlers and fieldsmen must have been feeling tired and insecure at the knees. On the whole Lancashire emerged from the long day not without a certain relief and satisfaction. And as the sunshine of the evening fell on the field most of us felt that the world had somehow grown a little less stupid than at breakfast, when the barrage of the newspapers challenged our nerve and philosophy. A day on a cricket field can be extremely sanative.

[1] This was a home match for Surrey, but the Oval was unavailable owing to the crisis.

Surrey 350 for 8 dec. (J. F. Parker 79, L. B. Fishlock 70, H. S. Squires 64, R. Pollard 4 for 72) and 212 (Parker 77 not out, Pollard 6 for 65); Lancashire 211 (N. Oldfield 91, E. A. Watts 5 for 60). Match abandoned after two days owing to imminence of war.

NEVILLE CARDUS WALKING OUT OF LORD'S   JULY 30 1969

England v. New Zealand, First Test

I could not have believed, a few summers ago, that the day was at hand on which I'd be leaving Lord's on a sunny day, after watching a Test match there for only an hour or so. I departed from Lord's last Saturday, bored to limpness, because I had seen Boycott and Edrich compile, or secrete, 100 runs from 56 overs, bowled by game, enthusiastic, inexperienced New Zealand cricketers. What would Boycott and Edrich have done confronted by Lindwall and Miller, Ramadhin and Valentine, Hall and Griffith?

In a full day, England, in a winning position versus a team not stronger all round than, say, Leicestershire, produced fewer than 300. Yet, on television, someone described the innings of Edrich as 'brilliant'. Had he, as he made this public pronouncement, forgotten Bill Edrich, who one day, on a spiteful 'green' pitch, flayed his spin within an inch of its life?

The poor, hard-worked TV commentators, those of them once upon a time Test match cricketers, did their best to gloss over the England batsmen's terribly tedius anonymity. Trevor Bailey referred to New Zealand's left-arm bowler, Howarth – he said he was 'operating' – as if he were a Verity come back to revisit the glimpses of the moon. (Mr. Bailey usually refers to a bowler as 'operating' – probably, I am inclined to suggest, armed with an anaesthetic.)

All sorts of excuses for the England batsmen's sterility are put forward by the television commentators. Mr. Laker informs us periodically that the ball is turning 'appreciably'. The commentaries go on like a chanted rubric. Motz is 'coming up' to bowl; Edrich 'plays him hard to mid-off, where so-and-so picks up – no run.' Hardly a hint of humour or irony on television: the radio chatterers are much brighter; *they* are free to take their eyes from the static, somnambulistic scene, and talk of irrelevant, and refreshingly irrelevant, things.

The prodding and 'tickling round the corner' persists every day on most first-class cricket fields in this country. And every day we hear the same justification for strokelessness; the ball is 'doing' something 'off the seam', the wicket is 'green', or 'the ball is not coming off the bat'. I was brought up to believe that some physical propulsion, on the batsman's part, is needed to project a ball from the bat. The bowling, so we are told *ad nauseam*, is just short of a length; Bradman himself would, at his best, be 'kept quiet'. If you can believe all these 'scientific arrogances' you can believe anything.

Do the seam-short-of-a-length-devices check or 'keep quiet' the scoring strokes of overseas batsmen such as Goldstein, Richards, Ackerman, Pollock or Younis Ahmed? Does it paralyse Marner? None of these stroke players are half the equals of Bradman, Hammond, Compton, McCabe, each of whom would have watered at the mouth at the sight last Saturday of the attack (a technical term) of New Zealand's Taylor, Hadlee, Motz and Pollard. Howarth is undoubtedly a promising slowish left-arm bowler but, bless us, he was free to toss them up with no fieldsman behind his arm in the deep.

I remember a description of Charles Parker's spin on a dusty Cheltenham pitch, given to me by 'young' Joe Hardstaff, whose very presence at the wicket at Lord's on Saturday would have seemed to bring Derby breeding to a company of carthorses. He was then young, and he went in to bat for Nottinghamshire number six or so 'in the order'. He received the last ball of an over from Parker, which pitched on his leg stump then fizzed viciously across, just missing the off stump. So Hardstaff walked down the pitch to talk to George Gunn. 'I can't play this kind of bowling, Mr. Gunn,' he said, whereat George said: 'That's all right, son, just watch me for a little while.' And for half an hour Hardstaff had not to cope with another ball spun by Parker. Gunn kept him away from Parker.

JOHN SAMUEL AT WESTON-SUPER-MARE   AUGUST 8 1970

Somerset v. Worcestershire

The finest day so far at the Weston-super-Mare Festival yesterday was also the sorriest. Somerset, indeed, can have had few worse in their chequered, but usually cheerful, history. First a demonstrator stopped play for five minutes in protest against Somerset's decision to bat out time and not set Worcestershire a target; another demonstrator then walked to and fro in front of a sight screen; the dressing-rooms and players' cars were besieged at the end with protesting spectators; and two senior committee members went into the press box to dissociate themselves from the actions of their captain, Brian Langford, and to promise 'drastic further action'.

The outline of the situation was that with the close at six o'clock including the extra half-hour, Somerset, the bottom club in the three-day County Championship, continued batting after tea with a lead of 196 having made no attempt to score quick runs. Equally obviously, Tom Graveney, Worcestershire's captain, had made things no easier by keeping on his most accurate bowlers. Both teams, it seems, bore in mind a morning of hot sun on a drying wicket when Worcestershire were all out for 132, conceding a first innings lead of 51, and the caution which that engendered lasted through the day, to the annoyance of most in the largish holiday crowd.

They were restive before tea then broke into slow hand-clapping as Hill and Taylor walked to the wicket after the interval. There were shouts of 'What about the public?' as they continued to play the bowling cautiously. After 10 minutes a man walked slowly out to the centre of the sunlit Clarence Park ground, took a large and obviously juicy pear out of his tea bag and threw it on to the pitch.

One of the umpires, J. Arnold, a former Hampshire player, signalled for the man to be removed but no policeman was about. The man walked over to Graveney, making his last appearance on a West Country ground, to make a further protest. Graveney took him gently by the arm and walked him over to an official who had emerged from the pavilion.

The man, a 31-year-old Birmingham holiday maker, who described himself as a life-long Warwickshire supporter, said afterwards that the decision to bat on after tea had been the last straw. 'As I threw the pear I told them "Get on with that!" ' Soon afterwards the other man began his slow beat across the sight screen.

Graveney supported Langford, saying the pitch had been awkward and that Somerset had never been in a position to declare. As the bottom club, Somerset had nothing to lose and Worcestershire little to gain.

The captains could have waived the tea interval. Worcestershire could so easily have been set 200 runs in two hours. This is what the last day public is owed.

JOHN ARLOTT AT BOURNEMOUTH   SEPTEMBER 4 1974

Hampshire v. Yorkshire

Hampshire conceded the County Championship to Worcestershire at 3.45 yesterday at Bournemouth. That was when the umpires abandoned Hampshire's match with Yorkshire without a ball being bowled – for added irony, the only Championship game of the season to so end.

The President of the Immortals – or the lesser person with arbitrary control over the English weather – played Hampshire like a small fish on a strong line to the last moment. A gale during the night stood the covers on their ends, blew down marquees and overturned huts but did not quite rule out the possibility of play: indeed the strong wind proved an effective drying agent.

The captains did not agree between themselves as to the possibility of play – no prizes are offered for identifying the differing points of view – so the decision reverted to the umpires. After a conscientiously frequent series of inspections they said, at half past two, that the match might commence at 3 p.m. if no more rain fell. Captain Hampshire – not the Hampshire captain – won the toss but, before he could even announce his decision a violent storm drove them both into the pavilion and ended the game.

Richard Gilliat's first words after the decision was reached were of congratulations to Worcestershire. He was courteous in success last year; even more impressively so now, in defeat. He even forebore – as surely, few men in his position could have done – to point out that, when the two counties met in early August at Portsmouth, Hampshire had won by an innings and 44 runs.

'Had it been possible to play and we had been asked to bat first I would have gambled all the way, trying for about 120 runs quickly and giving Yorkshire a challenge they could hardly reject,' he said. 'Anyway very good luck to Worcestershire; but the final irony is when you lead from May onwards until the last match and then that gets washed out on all three days, well, that's the end.'

Gilliat remembered to emphasise the spirit and performance of his own side which he thought, especially through the addition of Roberts, was stronger than the 1973 Championship winning team. Hampshire will look forward with some confidence to next summer for their players, with the exception of the old hand, Peter Sainsbury, are all of an age to improve. Worcestershire are rather longer in the tooth and may now be at their peak.

They heard the news from Bournemouth throughout the day during their match at Chelmsford. A 'hot line' functioned almost by the minute, and reports and rumours rapidly spread. At first it was hoped to resume the match against Essex after an early lunch, but a drenching at noon ruled that out. Except for the issues at stake, there is little doubt the umpires would have abandoned play immediately. It took very little time to do so once it was certain that Worcestershire were champions.

Norman Gifford, their captain, contended that Worcestershire had performed 'fantastically well' to keep in touch with Hampshire. After the bad defeat by Hampshire, he said, his players had pulled themselves up off the floor and in their next three matches dropped only one point. He commiserated with Hampshire over the wretched luck with the weather, but added: 'We have had to play very well to wipe out the points deficit and get even within range of the title.' Basil D'Oliveira also sympathised with Hampshire – 'but at the same time you have to remember that we have won 11 games, which is more than they have done.'

So the Championship passes to another of the rising powers. Between the wars Worcestershire were an even lesser force than Hampshire, but in the past 14 years the two have won the championship five times between them.

Essex v. Kent

The England selectors were not alone in going for Snow in June. The elements, not to be outdone, put on a passable imitation of a blizzard which, abetted by sleet, made play impossible before lunch at Colchester yesterday. The snow-flakes were so thick for a time that one correspondent reported he had lost his way between the pavilion and the Press tent. The bar had not then been opened.

By 3 p.m. the wicket, or was it the piste, was judged playable and by the end Kent had scored 132 for four off 58 overs in reply to the Essex total of 302. Nobody really complained when icy rain returned to cut off the final hour of play. All through, the conditions were so unpleasant that the luckiest fellows were those required to chase round the boundaries. The rest, whether batsmen or fielders, could only warm up by continual callisthenics.

The wicket took its share in the general malevolence. Both Turner and Lever made the ball lift and Ealham was immediately caught at the wicket with the score 34 for three. Woolmer was joined rather surprisingly by Denness; surprising because he was limping from a tendon injury received during his innings of 72 not out the previous day.

It was obvious that, stroke-wise, his fluency would be restricted and that, run-wise, twos would become singles. But Denness was determined to overcome all afflictions, personal or meteorological. He stayed two hours for his 50 not out, and found opportunity to force the ball to the boundary three times – an off drive, a square cut and a pull.

His pivot, it is not unkind to say, was cramped; the analogy is that of a golfer punching short irons to the green. His driver stayed in the bag. Woolmer played his resolute part in a stand of 43 until East seized a splendid catch in the square leg region.

If anyone could set light to the afternoon it was Asif, who offered a quiver full of handsome arrows from his bow with 28 not out. Lever, with his zest and liveliness, and East with his accuracy prevented undue displays of bravado. I recall an occasion when ice had to be chipped off the pitch at Derby. Yesterday Colchester seemed even colder.

Essex 302 for 9 (G. A. Gooch 100, B. E. A. Edmeades 63, B. R. Hardie 58) and 66 for 7 dec.; Kent 181 for 4 dec. (M. H. Denness 70 not out, Asif Iqbal 53 not out) and 154 (Asif 94, S. Turner 5 for 59). Essex won by 33 runs.

Worcestershire v. Somerset

A cricket match that never was ended yesterday with Somerset conceding a Benson and Hedges Cup game to reach the quarter finals ahead of their opponents Worcestershire on a technicality.

The 10 minute game was described by all but the Somerset team as 'not cricket'. One man banged on the car windows as Brian Rose, the Somerset captain, left the ground; two Somerset supporters said they would change their minds about becoming county members; and Worcestershire refunded the entrance money to the hundred or so spectators who included a party of schoolchildren on a day out to improve their education.

Somerset had found a loophole in the rules which say that when teams finish level on points in the qualifying groups, the one with the superior rate of wicket taking goes through. That was the position (akin to goal difference in football) that Somerset found themselves in yesterday after play had been abandoned on Wednesday and Rose elected to bat after winning the toss.

He faced one over before declaring the score at one run, conceded for a no ball by Van Holder, for no wickets. Worcestershire scored the two runs needed to win the game in 10 deliveries.

Rose who was heckled as he drove away from the ground, said that the decision to declare was taken with the approval of the entire Somerset side. 'In a normal match we could have been overtaken by Worcestershire and Glamorgan,' he said. 'I had no alternative.'

He did not make the rules and if anybody had any complaint they should put it to the organisers. 'My duty is to Somerset,' he said. Others thought he and Somerset had a wider duty. The Worcestershire chairman, Mr. Geoffrey Lampard, said that the incident was against the spirit of the game. 'There is no way I or the Worcestershire captain would have condoned this from our county side,' he said.

The Benson and Hedges man on the spot Mr. Mike Pegler said it was disappointing but that the company had made it a policy not to interfere with the game itself; it was a matter for the Test and County Cricket Board. The board takes an annual look at the rules and could want an amendment, which would have the support of those who made long journeys to Worcester.

Mr. Dennis Smythe of Crediton made a 300 mile round trip with a friend and their reaction was that they had changed their minds about becoming Somerset members. A schoolteacher from Wotton-under-Edge, in Gloucestershire, said that he had brought a party of boys from Rosehill School, for the game. 'The kind of lesson we have seen today is one which no boy ought to be taught,' Mr. Austin said.

The secretary of the TCCB, Mr. Donald Carr, said: 'Somerset's action is totally contrary to the spirit of the competition. There is bound to be an inquiry at the end of the season. You cannot change the rules in mid-season.'

Glamorgan, the other team to suffer by Somerset's decision, were again washed out at Watford yesterday. Their captain, Robin Hobbs, would make no comment on the action but said: 'We know what we have got to do now to reach the next stage.' The adjudicator at Worcester, Charles Barnett, nominated no one for the Man of the Match award because it would be 'improper'.

Somerset 1 for 0 dec.; Worcestershire 2 for 0. Worcestershire won by 10 wickets. Somerset were disqualified from the competition a week later, and the rules were subsequently changed.

FRANK KEATING AT LORD'S   SEPTEMBER 1 1980

England v. Australia, Centenary Test

At tea-time the band played that tiddley-om theme tune from Monty Python's Flying Circus. Honestly it did. The Royal Marines Band it was and they were conducted by a precise and very well-turned-out chap called Hoskins, which is a very Pythonesque sort of name. So was the day.

A monumental cock-up. Lord's and all of cricket should be totally ashamed of itself. Someone should resign. No one will, of course. Their judgement of priorities is unbelievable. Apparently, last year an MCC member, nervously fingering his yellow-and-red tie, was hauled into the secretary's office and given a dressing down and final warning for eating an apple in the Long Room. 'The committee take a very dim view of this behaviour, Bloggins, a very dim view indeed . . .' Shown the yellow-and-red card.

Saturday and their day of days in 100 years and they let the whole thing go to pot – from slight eccentricity to fairly decent charades to high farce to downright teeth-grinding tragedy.

Do you remember that day at The Oval a few years ago when we all helped mop up after a deluge? On Saturday the sun shone down and the breezes hummed but not a sack nor a sponge nor a pitchfork was in evidence. The groundsman had announced quite simply at elevenses that the match could start easily before lunch. The umpires said it could not. So did one captain. And all this time was the big boss wandering round with beady bloodshot eye as livid as his MCC tie keeping a lookout for some rotter who was daring to eat an apple in the Long Room?

At speeches all week guys fingering the same ties have got up to say how Lord's wanted us to remember this celebration shindig for the next 100 years. We will, sir, we will. Pray be upstanding . . . especially those thousands who queued outside (some all night) who were not let in 'till the umpires announce play will start' because officialdom did not want to be involved in argy-bargy about refunded money.

A month ago in that bureaucratic hellhole in Olympic Russia (like a friend said at breakfast one Moscow morning when told the Shah was dead – 'good, perhaps this bloody hotel will now release my laundry') one of our main grouses was that, in the second week when we all wanted to go to the athletics stadium, the press buses to other venues would still be scheduled. Hundreds who could not find a hubcap or mudguard to hang on to would be left stranded while empty buses came and went to the pistol shooting range or the egg-and-spoon stadium or whatever.

Buckpassing. Nobody at the depot could make a decision. Funk turned into ridiculous chaos. It could never happen in Britain, we said. Well, it can. It did on Saturday.

Late in the evening we cadging loiterers hung around Mick Jagger. The Mick Jagger. He summed it up. 'It's been a reasonable day for us boozers up here in private boxes. But what about the geezers queueing and those blokes munching their sandwiches up there at the Nursery End?'

Mr. Jagger agreed we might meet again on Monday – 'but we'll have to tune in to the weather forecast – I am not turning up to see the umpires inspect the wicket – when you've seen that once you've seen it all.' Quite.

Then, late into the evening as they announced in blissful sunshine that play had been abandoned, a handful of Australian players – Chappell, Lillee, Hughes and Co – ironically compounded the day's disaster by jogging around the ground in tight little tights. 'C'mon Sebastian!' shouted Max Boyce. 'C'mon Steve!' said Ollie Milburn. And Lillee and Chappell took the joke and waved back. They looked cheesed off as well.

Even after all the rum happenings, the Centenary Test continues oblivious. Strange opposites – well, Jagger, Boyce, Milburn, me and a million others – still get together today in celebration. Cricket will still win – but, bugger me, cricket's administration still does not know a thing about cricket's adoration.

I was almost the last to leave Lord's. In the immortal phrase I was 'as sponsored as a newt'. Well, put it this way, we were thrown out of our box.

At the Nursery End car park a light went on in the corner. In a caravan, of all things. I was intrigued. Through the undrawn blinds I saw a haggard man with a thin moustache slumped down on a bench looking worried, at the end of his tether. He seemed to be saying: 'I'd just love a nice cup of tea, dear, it's been a hard day at the office.' Painted on the outside of this caravan was the legend 'Welton Caravan Supplied To D. Constant, Umpire.'

He had certainly had a hard day at the office, hadn't he, dear? So had we all.

Australia 385 for 5 dec. (K. J. Hughes 117, G. M. Wood 112, A. R. Border 56) and 189 for 4 dec. (Hughes 84, G. S. Chappell 59); England 205 (G. Boycott 62, L. S. Pascoe 5 for 59, D. K. Lillee 4 for 43) and 244 for 3 (Boycott 128 not out, M. W. Gatting 51 not out). Match drawn.

LEADER   FEBRUARY 5 1982

India v. England

The following provisional schedule was issued yesterday for the first day's play in the seventh Test between England and India, to be played at Rann of Kutch CC on April 1.

11am Start of play.

11.5am Umpires take field.

11.20am Indian captain, S. N. Gavaskar, invites Kapil Dev to bowl first over.

11.25am Kapil Dev arranges field.

11.30am S. N. Gavaskar re-arranges field. After further discussions, field returns to positions earlier set out by Kapil Dev.

11.35-11.45am Interval for drinks.

11.45am Crowd invasion.

11.55am Kapil Dev bowls first ball to C. J. Tavaré, who plays it back to the bowler.

12 noon Ball found to be out of shape, and returned to pavilion for replacement.

12.05-12.45pm Smog.

12.45pm Play resumes. Kapil Dev completes first over to C. J. Tavaré, who scores single off last ball.

1-1.30pm Fog.

1.30pm Lunch interval. Listeners to Radio Three will be able to listen to an illustrated lecture on B. J. T. Bosanquet and his influence in the development of the chocolate eclair, by Mr. Brian Johnston.

2.15pm Play resumes. Crowd invasion.

2.25pm Crowd invasion cleared. S. Madan Lal bowls one over to C. J. Tavaré, who scores a single off the last ball.

2.45pm Crowd invades pitch and erects memorial to Sir G. Boycott.

3pm Play resumes.

3.1pm Fog.

3.20pm D. Doshi bowls maiden over to C. J. Tavaré.

3.30pm Hail, thunder and a plague of frogs. Tea taken early. During the tea interval, listeners to Radio Three will be able to hear a talk entitled 'How things have gone down since my day' by Mr. F. S. Trueman.

4.30pm Play resumes. S. Madan Lal bowls three balls to G. A. Gooch, who hits them for 4, 6 and 4. Ball goes out of shape and a replacement has to be brought from the nearest cricket ball factory, which is in Bombay.

4.45pm Drinks interval.

5.10pm Play resumes. S. Madan Lal completes over, whereafter Kapil Dev bowls a maiden over to C. J. Tavaré. Crowd invades pitch calling for appointment of Sir G. Boycott as Governor-General of India.

5.30pm England captain comes on to pitch to protest at slow over rate and recent spate of unfavourable lbw decisions.

5.35-5.45pm Captains confer over slow over rate.

5.45-5.50pm Umpires confer over slow over rate.

5.50pm K. W. R. Fletcher calls for replacement of umpires.

5.55pm Umpires call for replacement of K. W. R. Fletcher.

6-6.20pm Interval for drinks.

6.25pm Heavy snow. Kashmir cut off. Listeners to Radio Three will be able to hear an illustrated lecture entitled 'How things have gone down, even since my day' by Sir G. Boycott.

6.30pm Close of play. Extensive crowd disturbances cause severe damage to pitch. Groundsman of Rann of Kutch CC forecasts that because of the damage no play may be possible for the rest of the match.

6.35pm till midnight General thanksgiving.

FRANK KEATING AT LORD'S   JUNE 11 1986

England v. India

David Gower was unceremoniously relieved of the England cricket captaincy yesterday as India completed their first-ever Test victory at Lord's. Mike Gatting was called to the inner sanctum and offered the job.

Gower was told as he left the balcony after the presentation ceremonies. He shook Gatting's hand in the dressing room, put an arm round his shoulder, and presented him with his T-shirt, which reads 'I'm in Charge.'

In his disappointment, Gower handed over the reins with a chivalrous straightforwardness, which is more than can be said for the machinations of the mandarins at Lord's.

After England 5-0 defeat in the winter's West Indies tour, Gower had been given this match and the two one-dayers in which to loosen the noose they had already put in place.

But yesterday the chairman of selectors, Peter May, refused even to attend a press conference to announce the decision. On a staircase of the old pavilion, all he could mutter was: 'It's time for a change: aren't all decisions difficult?'

Inside, the *Daily Mail* correspondent was thanking Gower on behalf of the Cricket Writers' Club for his 'charm, frankness and help'. Gower replied, 'I wish you the very best with my successor.'

Gower had snapped open a tin of Australian lager, slung his bare feet into gym shoes and insisted that he wished Gatt well.

'Sure, I have never made a secret of the fact that I'd wanted to carry on,' he said. 'I'd be delighted to have a go sometime – at least I've had a couple of years now.'

To his credit, he has not changed a jot since the selectors appointed him two years ago. He remains a laid-back charming goldielocks with a touch of genius at the crease, no histrionic tactics or tantrums in the field, and an ambassadorial approach to the world.

As captain, his record reads: played 26, won 5, drawn 7, lost 14, of which ten were by the relentless West Indians. 'I can think of another guy whose captaincy consists of just ten games against the West Indies,' he said ruefully.

Gatting, in his very different way, has as much bigness, civility and love of the game as his predecessor.

Yesterday, he changed into blazer and white flannels and blue socks to attend his first skirmish in Fleet Street's circulation war. Squat, determined, combative, as we know, suddenly he was fingering his beard like a nervous Henry VIII at a divorce trial in Rome.

'I didn't think it would actually happen,' he said. 'But I suppose it will be nice to think about being captain of England when I actually dive into it – like on my pillow tonight.

'David said "Good luck" just now. I said: 'I'm very sorry, friend."

'Unfortunately, this match, we didn't do all we could have done for him. Not that we let him down by not trying, but there is a very different attitude when we know there is an axe over the captain's head, as well as one over a lot of other people . . . It's tough at the top, isn't it?'

County Days

JUNE 13 1868

Lancashire v. Surrey

. . . Surrey went in for their second innings at four o'clock, and at a quarter to six they were all out for the small score of 42. Hickton and Iddison bowled, and the former, whose delivery and great pace were aided by the hard state of the ground, was unprecedentedly successful. Humphrey received a ball which rose nearly to the level of his face, and in attempting to play it down he put it, from the handle of his bat, into Iddison's hands at point. Jupp was caught by Mr. Bousfield, the wicket keeper, in hitting round at a leg ball, which he slightly touched. Mr. Bousfield stood several yards from the stumps, but his caution was rewarded by the opportunity of thus disposing of the most formidable batsman on the Surrey side. Stephenson was unable to play the slows, and was easily caught by Rowley; Mortlock played a little too soon at a very fast ball from Hickton, and skied it to a great height directly over the stumps, whence it fell into Mr. Bousfield's hands. Griffith, the next comer, and once known as 'Lion hitter', was evidently nonplussed by the imitation of his own slows to which Iddison treated him, and played one quietly to mid-on. Bristow was immediately beaten by a slow, which had so much twist on that he thought it was going to leg and struck accordingly, whereas the ball came on to his leg and bounced thence to the stumps. Mr. Calvert went in to meet one from Iddison, and, showing himself 'rashly importunate', made 'one more unfortunate', inasmuch as he was very cleverly stumped. The disarray which the rapid fall of their men produced amongst the backers of Surrey may be imagined; and the glorious uncertainty of cricket was never more remarkably illustrated.

Surrey 253 (Bristow 79) and 42 (Hickton 6 for 14, Iddison 4 for 23);
Lancashire 204 and 93 for 2. Lancashire won by eight wickets.

Somerset v. Lancashire

Yesterday's cricket at Taunton will be long remembered by the few spectators who were fortunate enough to witness it. Not only did Lancashire in putting together a wonderful score of 801 beat the record made in first-class county cricket last May when Notts obtained 726 against Sussex at Trent Bridge, but A. C. MacLaren, their dashing young captain, in scoring 424, completely eclipsed W. G. Grace's innings of 344 obtained for the M.C.C. against Kent at Canterbury in 1876, which prior to the old Harrovian's performance had stood for nineteen years as the highest individual innings ever made in a match of first-class importance. Words almost fail us in trying to do justice to MacLaren's batting, for during the whole of the seven hours and fifty minutes he was in he only made two strokes that could be really called chances. He did not, as we had thought, give Wickham an opportunity of stumping him at 76, and his first mistake was to Stanley at mid-on when 262. The second was early yesterday to Wickham, who might have caught him at the wicket. It will be remembered that out of the 555 put together by the visitors for the loss of three wickets on Monday their captain's share amounted to 289 not out, already the highest first-class innings of the year. He went on batting yesterday with the same perfect confidence and command over the bowling, and in the first two hours, when the total had been advanced to 756, he had raised his total to 404. After luncheon he was palpably tiring: but it was not until the aggregate was 792 and his own score 424 that he hit a ball to Fowler in the long field and was caught. His hits, most of them beautifully hard, clean and well timed, were a six (a drive out of the ground), sixty-two fours, eleven threes, thirty-seven twos, and sixty-three singles. To say that he was heartily cheered scarcely does justice to the enthusiasm which players and spectators alike exhibited at the close of one of the finest achievements ever witnessed, and upon which MacLaren may look back with justifiable pride as long as he lives. The only other batsmen who did anything worthy of mention yesterday were Benton and Sugg, the former helping to put on 107 in an hour for the fourth partnership, and the latter aiding to make 95 in forty-five minutes for the fifth. The falls of the wickets in the unprecedented innings, which extended over exactly eight hours, were as follows:

1	2	3	4	5	6	7	8	9	10
141	504	530	637	732	738	792	792	798	801

Somerset, in the face of this gigantic total, went in tired out and disheartened, and Mold being able to do what none of their bowlers could (make the ball rear up occasionally), they made a poor show. Lionel Palairet and Fowler started well, and scored 71 before they were separated; but the whole side were out in two hours and 35 minutes for 143; while on following on against the enormous majority of 658 they lost another wicket in getting 57, so that as the game now stands they want 600 to avert an innings defeat. Today, therefore, they have nothing to strive for but a draw. The weather was dull, and in the last hour or so a slight, drizzling rain fell, which, however, was never heavy enough to interfere with the game. Only four or five hundred spectators were present . . .

Lancashire 801 (A. C. MacLaren 424, A. G. Paul 177, A. Ward 64, L. C. H. Palairet 4 for 133); Somerset 143 (J. Briggs 4 for 59, A. Mold 4 for 75) and 206 (S. M. J. Woods 55, Briggs 5 for 75, Mold 5 for 76). Lancashire won by an innings and 452 runs.

JUNE 20 1910

Lancashire v. Nottinghamshire

In the first moments of exultation over Lancashire's great victory on Saturday, when about 7,000 fellow-creatures suddenly went mad with joy, people kept telling one another again and again that there never had been a day of such intoxicating sport in the history of county cricket. Even now, after some hours' reflection and a quiet glance over Wisden, whose pages often have a sobering influence, the first impression turns out for once to have been the right one. There never was such a day before. Up to Saturday the highest score with which a county match had been won in a fourth innings was 350, which Leicestershire made for five wickets against Worcestershire in 1904. On Saturday, in order to win the match with Notts, Lancashire had to make 400 in five hours and a quarter – an average of over 78 runs an hour. After a terrific contest they made 403, with two wickets still in hand and ten minutes to spare. That fact alone, in the quietest setting, would be enough to give the match a historic interest. But it was only one in a group of incidents any one of which would have made the game memorable, and all of which were grouped together with quite extraordinary dramatic effect. There was first the unexpected collapse of the Notts batsmen. A team who had made 376 in the first innings and 138 for two wickets in the second were suddenly bundled out, neck and crop. In fifty minutes eight wickets fell for 47 runs. That was the first sensation. Then there was the great partnership between Tyldesley and Sharp, lasting nearly two hours and a half and producing 191 runs, in which both these great batsmen were seen at their best, and in which, incidentally, Tyldesley completed his thousand runs, 250 in front of any other English batsman. Then there was a partnership, equally remarkable though in a totally different way, which brought 80 runs in forty minutes; at the one end was Whitehead, with the lust for victory in his veins, smiting sixes and fours off the best Notts bowling with delirious effect, and at the other a mere boy – for young Tyldesley is little more – playing and getting runs, too, with the polish and self-possession of a seasoned veteran. Then, after a few dreadful moments during which two wickets fell for six runs, there was that last indescribable effort by Hornby, a badly crippled leader, who could only limp and hop across the wicket, but who banged the ball to every vacant part of the field, and finally carried the game, with the aid of the imperturbable Cook, through its most critical and harrowing stage to a glorious finish. What a wonderful day it was!

Nottinghamshire 376 (J. Hardstaff Snr 106, T. Oates 57, E. B. Alletson 50, L. Cook 7 for 102) and 185 (J. Iremonger 61, W. Huddleston 5 for 36); Lancashire 162 (J. Sharp 73, C. Clifton 4 for 67) and 403 for 8 (Sharp 102, J. T. Tyldesley 91, A. H. Hornby 55 not out, W. Riley 4 for 63). Lancashire won by two wickets.

AUGUST 18 1925

Somerset v. Surrey

Amid great scenes of enthusiasm J. B. Hobbs, the Surrey batsman, yesterday equalled Dr. W. G. Grace's record of 126 centuries and the record of thirteen centuries in one season held jointly by C. B. Fry, Hayward, and Hendren.

When stumps were drawn at Taunton in the Surrey v. Somerset match on Saturday Hobbs had scored 91 not out, and yesterday morning there were several hundreds of people on the ground by seven o'clock, many of them having come from London in the hope of seeing the completion of the century for which Hobbs has been waiting since July 20. Half an hour before the start there were over 10,000 present and no more tickets were issued. When Hobbs appeared there was tremendous applause, which was renewed when he scored a single off the second ball. Then came another single, a hit to the on boundary off a no-ball, and two more singles. Wanting one more, Hobbs faced Bridges and reached his goal with a single to leg. The cheering broke out again, and the players on the field rushed to Hobbs to shake his hands and thump him on the back. Then P. G. H. Fender, his captain, appeared with a goblet of champagne, part of which Hobbs drank. Immediately the game was resumed Hobbs scored another single and was then caught at the wicket.

Hobbs's wire to his wife, who is on holiday at Margate, read: 'Got it at last.—JACK.' During the luncheon interval hundreds of congratulatory telegrams were received by Hobbs, including one from E. M. Grace, of Thornbury. Other messages that reached him were addressed to 'Greatest cricketer in the world' and 'Superman, Taunton.'

J. C. White, Somerset's acting captain, said last night that he was very pleased Hobbs had managed to get the record-equalling century against Somerset, as both Grace and Hobbs scored their hundredth century against Somerset. 'I think,' he said, 'that Hobbs's hundredth was better than today's innings, though the latter was an excellent effort. We bowled our best against him, but he was in great form.'

H. D. Leveson-Gower, an ex-captain of the Surrey club, broadcasted from 2 LO last night an appreciation of Jack Hobbs's achievement. It was a happy coincidence, he said, that the scene of Hobbs's triumph should have been the same ground where 'W. G.' just over thirty years ago made his hundredth century. He supposed that there would always be discussion whether 'W. G.' or Hobbs was the better player.

'Personally,' he continued, 'I do not think it matters a bit, and to anyone who asked me that question I would say in reply: "Could anyone be better than 'W. G.' and could anyone be better than Hobbs?" and leave it at that. What I think does matter is this: 'W. G.' loved the game, he played the game, and during his era he placed cricket on a pedestal which can challenge any other game or sport, for fairness and integrity. Hobbs has done the same, and is doing it to-day.'

> Somerset 167 (A. Young 58, J. H. Lockton 4 for 36) and 374 (J.C.W. MacBryan 109, Young 71, G. Hunt 59, P.G.H. Fender 5 for 120); Surrey 359 (J. B. Hobbs 101, Fender 59) and 183 for 0 (Hobbs 101 not out, A. Sandham 74 not out). Surrey won by ten wickets.

Hobbs's century in the second innings beat all the records but attracted far less attention from the newspapers.

NEVILLE CARDUS AT OLD TRAFFORD   AUGUST 20 1925

Lancashire v. Gloucestershire

Yesterday was the gladdest I have spent on a cricket field for many years. The cricketers of Grace's lovely county – O the orchards of Gloucestershire and the ancient peacefulness of the Cotswolds! – came to dour Old Trafford and brought with them tidings of comfort and joy. The summer game is not dead, but is alive and returning to us, still the prodigal bearer of handsome sons who will grow up in the likeness of the men of old – the MacLarens and the Trumpers.

'Young fellow,' said W. G. Grace, many times and oft, 'you must put the bat to the ball.' Yesterday Hammond, of Gloucestershire, put the bat most beautifully to the ball from morning till evening. Against the attack of Lancashire he played one of the finest innings that can ever have been accomplished by a boy of his age, which is twenty-two years. To be present at the rise of a new star in the sky and to know that it is going to be glorious – here is a moment thrilling indeed to men who live their lives imaginatively. It was as plain yesterday as the nose on

Bardolph's face that Hammond is an England batsman of to-morrow; we could see the splendour of his cricket blossoming before us hour by hour. In years to come we shall remember August 19, 1925, at Old Trafford, for when in good time Hammond carves history out of Australian bowlers here and over the seas we shall be proud to say that we understood well enough that he was born for the company of master batsmen even in seasons that saw him at the wicket smooth and unrazored of cheek and apparently rather outside the consideration of the Wise Men of Lord's.

20 for 2, 350 for 3.

Middlesex batted brilliantly a week or two ago at Old Trafford, but the cricket of Hammond and Dipper was better for two reasons even than that of Bruce and Hendren. First, the Lancashire bowlers never fell into the helplessness that astonished us all in the Middlesex match; second, Gloucestershire, unlike Middlesex, made a bad start to their innings against McDonald at his fastest. The Gloucestershire captain gave his bat a giant sweep at the very outset, but he and Sinfield were victims to McDonald with only 20 runs scored. At twenty minutes past twelve Hammond and Dipper joined in partnership; they remained in supreme control of the game for three hours and three-quarters and lifted Gloucestershire's score from 20 for two to 350 for three.

But 'lifted' is the wrong word; it denotes labour and effort. Dipper and Hammond let us see batsmanship as *play* and not work. There was a smile from Fortune for both at the beginning of their stand, which, I believe, is the biggest ever hit for a third wicket at Old Trafford. Dipper gave an easy chance with his score 14 and the Gloucestershire total 45; Hammond was lucky with one or two snicks in his preliminary minutes 'in the middle.' The mistakes, though, were not the mistakes of cricketers out of form. They were those that will happen any day in the best regulated batsmen at an innings' outset. Hammond's snicks were more stylish than most county batsmen's best strokes; they hinted not of incompetence but of fine art frustrated. As the ball whizzed from his bat to a part of the field outside his envisaging his body was in proud poise.

It is possible that had the wicket possessed more life than it had yesterday Richard Tyldesley might have got Hammond out immediately. For Hammond is obviously so much in love with his superb back-play that he will exploit it even before he has tested the pitch's pace. If Tyldesley's first balls to him had come from the turf with accelerated speed Hammond's back method, splendid though it is, might not have worked quickly enough.

After Hammond had got through his first ten minutes at the wicket – a period that often enough finds his defence lacking – he never again gave the Lancashire attack the faintest hope. His forcing strokes from a position definitely defensive and belonging to back-play were more powerful than the forward drives of the bulk of batsmen. Once he actually drove straight for four a ball that rose sharply after pitching; while it was in the air Hammond 'shaped' for a forward drive with full arm-swing; then quickly seeing the ball pitch and come from the turf at a rather awkward angle he let all his weight fall on the back foot – a sign that he was lifting himself up to his full height – and hit the ball powerfully by means of short-armed thrust of his bat, wrist-work adding its bloom in a second's fraction.

Gloucestershire reached the century before lunch – an honour at Old Trafford that Lancashire usually reserves for her guests. After the interval boundary hits were frequent and maiden overs scarce. Yet Hammond and Dipper did not seem to have hurry in their feet; the bowling was played on its merits, ball by ball. The short length to the off side was driven – even as in days of old it was driven – through the covers or past mid-off. Neither Hammond nor Dipper observed the current fashion of allowing three balls to the off side out of every four to pass by untouched. And for once in a while the crowd was enabled safely to look boundary-wards whenever a half-volley was tossed up.

Dipper is usually a slow scorer. Yesterday he was so active that for a while Hammond could not leave him behind. Dipper played the innings of a cricketer brought up in an honourable school; his method mingled offence and defence in proportion. He hit strongly to leg and now and again intrigued us with an artfully artless little dab stroke through the slips. Dipper batted four hours and hit fourteen boundaries.

In the period between lunch and the tea interval Hammond's cricket was splendid enough to make us think of many a golden afternoon in the past at Old Trafford – when MacLaren or Spooner set the field in the light of magnificence. It would be easy – and perhaps sensible – to write extravagantly of Hammond's batting in that 'between lunch and tea' period; his cricket, at any rate, was extravagant enough! I doubt if MacLaren was capable of cricket more easeful and masterful – at the age of 22. Here was batsmanship broken free for a while of the chains that it has had to bear since the war. Hammond was always 'on top' of the ball; his bat seemed light as a cane; and yet, when he drove, as strong as a cudgel. Hammond did not, as cricketers say, 'flash' his bat; there were no 'if shots' in his innings once he settled down. His quick scoring was made possible by a wide range of hits, ambitious footwork, an eye that saw the ball quickly – and a confident mind. He was the image of confidence indeed – youth at the prow. For flexibility of style his cricket went far beyond anything else I have ever seen from a player still in the twenties. I can make Hammond no better compliment than this – that at half-past three yesterday Hobbs would have needed to recapture his finest arts to keep himself 'in the picture' with this young England batsman of to-morrow.

A score of 200 and over against Lancashire will probably cause Hammond to impinge on the mind of Lord's – argument on his behalf in hot and cold prose has, I have found, fallen on deaf ears.

Hammond completed his first 50 in one hour; his first 100 in two hours five minutes; his 150 in three hours ten minutes; and his 200 in four hours ten minutes. When his score was 203 he had hit 25 boundaries. He gave a chance at 105 to mid-on off Sibbles.

Lancashire bowled and fielded 'hard,' as they say, if not brilliantly, until the solid flesh grew weary. McDonald's onslaught at noon might well have caused a Gloucestershire collapse. The first ball he unloosened at Hammond was own brother to the breakback that has been known to smash the stumps of Hendren on more than one occasion.

Gloucestershire 456 (W. R. Hammond 250, A. G. Dipper 144, E. A. McDonald 5 for 128) and 53 for 1; Lancashire 323 (F. Watson 93, J. Sharp 75, C. Parker 5 for 120). Match drawn.

NEVILLE CARDUS AT DOVER   JULY 1, 2 and 3 1926

Kent v. Lancashire

DOVER, WEDNESDAY

The distance from Lord's to the Dover cricket field is farther than the crow flies or even than the train travels. Here we find a different habitation than cosmopolitan Lord's: here is Kent and real England. The Dover field is tucked away in hills along which Lear must have wandered on his way to the cliffs. There are green lawns and terraces rising high behind the little pavilion, and you can sit here and look down on the play and see the cricketers all tiny and compact. In such a green and pleasant place as this, with June sunlight everywhere, slow cricket by Lancashire has not seemed quite so wearisome as usually it does. The absence of animated play has gone well in tune with the day's midsummer ease and generous warmth. We have been free to watch the game idly and give ourselves up with lazy delight to the June charm and flavours of a field all gay with tents and waving colours; and we have been free to observe the delicious changes in the passing hour – the full light of noon, the soft, silent fall to mellow.

The gentle tap-tap-tapping of the Lancashire bats has made the quiet music proper to this gracious Kentish place and occasion. On a perfect wicket Lancashire made a poor prelude to the innings. Hallows was twenty-five minutes getting his first run, and with the total 24 he sent a puny stroke to short leg and was caught at leisure. Ernest Tyldesley and Makepeace then played the steady Kent attack with a like steadiness. At lunch, after ninety minutes' action, Lancashire's score was 60 for one, and on the whole Makepeace had revealed himself our quickest maker of runs.

Between lunch and tea, two hours and a quarter, Lancashire added 135 for the loss of the wickets of Makepeace and Tyldesley. These batsmen built a partnership worth 100 in 105 minutes. They showed us good cricket enough, but it was always kind to the bowling. Tyldesley was missed in the slips at 15, and got himself out by a half-hit to mid-on. I wish his batting were a little more masculine this year. Tyldesley and Makepeace persisted for the same period – two hours and 35 minutes. After Watson had let us see half a dozen strokes I chanced with myself a half-crown wager that he would make 50 at least. Watson's cricket, though slow, had always a more certain touch than anything he has done of late. One or two of his cover drives possessed a decisive strength I have not seen him use since last year he played an innings of a century at Lord's and delighted the heart of poor Sydney Pardon, who, alas! did not live to see his dreadful Australians considerably humbled yesterday on the cricket field he loved so dearly. Watson reached 50 in one hour and three-quarters, which apparently is the standard rate of movement nowadays in the making of a cricketer's innings. Watson seemed to give a chance to the slips at 28. Halliday struck too late at a fast medium length, after giving some hint of an ability to get his bat well over the ball. Lancashire's score arrived at 200 in ten minutes short of four hours – Poppy and Mandragora of cricket.

The Kent attack rarely fell for accuracy. Collins, Ashdown and Wright each exploit the fast to medium length which drops cannily just on the short side. Only batsmen with late, wristy strokes are able to get rapid runs against this style of attack, and, truth to say, Lancashire is not rich in wristy cricketers. Freeman's spin came from the ground with little venom, but his pitch and direction were reliable throughout all his labours. His flight has scarcely the clever variations of Mailey's bowling. To the lovely afternoon's close the Lancashire batting remained true to type.

Lancashire 307 for 8 (F. Watson 78, H. Makepeace 71, E. Tyldesley 69).

DOVER, THURSDAY

We have had another lovely day and plenty of fascinating cricket. The Kent innings began at noon under a sky that was like a dome of glass all stained blue. On such a morning as this, a batsman is certain to see visions and dream dreams as he comes to the ground eager for the game. And Hardinge and Ashdown started to make runs with easy, confident strokes. In half an hour the Kent score reached 39, and the Lancashire men must quickly have resigned themselves to hours of sweaty toil in the warmth of a sun whose rays of light hit the hard earth like blows from a golden rod. But the chances of cricket hang on a hair's breadth. McDonald's first 41 balls were hit for 29 runs, and he did not seem to be in a conquering mood. Another six balls without a wicket would, I think, have ended with McDonald going out of action and taking a longish rest. It was at this period of incipient crisis for Lancashire and McDonald that Ashdown was guilty of a foolish mistake. McDonald had been trying to bump them – a certain proof that he was not feeling at his best. Ashdown tried to hit one of these bumpers to leg, and instead of standing up straight and to the side of the ball and exploiting the authentic hook stroke, he scooped with a blind bat, ducked his head, and sent a skier to the leg side, where Duckworth held a clever running catch.

This unlooked-for success obviously caused McDonald to lift up his heart. His pace became faster immediately, and yet again was he encouraged by thoughtless batsmanship. Hardinge once or twice held out an indiscreet bat to quick lengths on the off side and was lucky not to touch them. The warnings taught him no lesson: again he put forth a highly experimental bat to one of McDonald's fast rising balls, and Duckworth caught him behind the wicket, crowing in glee like a cock as he did so. McDonald realised, in the style of a good opportunist, that he was in fortune's good books: he worked up a lot of his true speed, pitched a length on or near the off wicket. Seymour made a sheer reflex action and sent a slip-catch to Richard Tyldesley. Chapman also flicked a speculative bat, though this time the ball was much too close to the wicket to be left alone. Chapman was Duckworth's third victim in ten minutes. The match in this brief space of time wheeled round dizzily in Lancashire's way. McDonald got the wickets of Ashdown, Seymour, Hardinge, and Chapman in nine balls for three runs. This merciless exposure of Kent's want of acquaintance with authentic fast bowling reduced the crowd to a silence which was broken – at least where I was sitting – only by the emphatic statement of an old gentleman to the effect that modern cricketers cannot cut, and, moreover, that Jack Mason and Burnup would have cracked this bowling of McDonald far and wide – a strong opinion indeed, announced with much ferocity of tone and addressed to nobody in particular.

The Kent batsmen, no doubt, played McDonald feebly. Several of them merely thrust out their bats to the line of the ball, using arm strength only, and not getting the body over and into a resolute stroke. Woolley threatened for twenty minutes to stem the onrush of McDonald. He drove him to the off boundary with rare power and beauty, and then sent a cut past point like the flash of valiant steel. I settled myself down to enjoy a dramatic sight – Woolley and McDonald as antagonists: Woolley standing erect at the wicket waiting with his curving bat as McDonald ran his sinuous run along the grass: Woolley flashing his lightning and McDonald hurling his thunderbolts. This spectacle of grandeur did not, as they say, materialise outside of the mind's eye: Watson suddenly and comprehensively bowled Woolley even before some of us were aware he had begun to take part in the Lancashire attack. The ball scattered Woolley's leg wicket out of the earth: it pitched between the off and middle stumps and went with the bowler's arm. The Australians would gladly pay Watson £100 for the sole rights to that excellent delivery. The downfall of Woolley, fifth out at 74, knocked the decisive nail in the coffin of Kent's first innings. It is true that Hubble batted brightly for a while and also Freeman, but the lustre of their cricket was only like that of a sort of brass plate on the aforementioned coffin. The innings closed at three o'clock for a total which was an insult to the splendid turf. Duckworth was in reliable form: he made five catches and also accomplished a very easy case of stumping. His high pitched shout of 'How's that' was constantly in the summer air: shall we call him chanticleer of wicket-keepers?

The other day Mr. Warner wrote that English batting has improved vastly since Armstrong beat us in this country. As I watched McDonald get his wickets to-day I was convinced that Collins would win the Test matches almost as comfortably as Armstrong did if he commanded the McDonald and Gregory of 1921. English batting has not improved since then against really fast bowling – a melancholy truth which McDonald will demonstrate for us on any day that finds him in his strongest form.

Green rightly did not compel Kent to follow on: McDonald was tired and the wicket perfect. Makepeace and Tyldesley forced the runs excellently after Hallows had got out: 50 was reached in little more than half an hour. Makepeace scored 37 in 50 minutes – furious driving for him. Ernest Tyldesley was brilliant: not for many a long day has his cricket been so powerful, so handsome, so masterful as in this innings. He played Lancashire's proper game from the outset, drove in front of the wicket with a superb poise of body, and reached 50 in 70 minutes. No English innings in the Test at Lord's the other day, save perhaps Woolley's on Tuesday, could compare with this by Tyldesley in point of beautiful and versatile strokes. Moreover, the Kent attack was on the whole as good as the Australians' – at any rate until Tyldesley hammered it off its length. This is the kind of batsmanship we need for the winning of Test matches within three days.

Tyldesley arrived at his century in two hours and five minutes without a shadow of a mistake. Iddon played strong cricket, too, and this time his forcing drives were proportionately blended with strokes of sound defence. He has still much to learn of the art of picking out the right ball for a safe hit, but he is going along nicely. In Lancashire's second innings Cornwallis did not field because of an injury to his leg. Cornwallis, by the way, is a true Kent captain – keen, chivalrous, and always in love with the game. Iddon and Tyldesley scored 122 for the fourth wicket in 90 minutes. We have seen a Lancashire eleven to-day in which we could take a pride indeed.

Lancashire 336 and 243 for 5 (E. Tyldesley 144 not out); Kent 154 (E. A. McDonald 7 for 81).

DOVER, FRIDAY

Green closed the Lancashire innings last night, and Kent had the whole of this cool and pleasant day for the making of 424 needed to bring them a famous victory. Five hours and ten minutes of play were to be gone through. A bad beginning happened to the innings; with only a dozen scored Ashdown tried a leg hit from Sibbles, and the ball seemed to swing in from outside his legs astonishingly, and it clean bowled his leg wicket. Seymour, who is not at all a defensive batsman but needs must play the old Kentish game of chivalry, hit ten runs off three balls from Sibbles, and attempted a stroke to the on from a short bumper sent by McDonald. He skied the ball high to leg, and Halliday, running from somewhere near mid-wicket on the on-side, made an admirable running catch, taking his prize as it dipped away from him in the wind. Even with this unfortunate prelude Kent's score reached 80 in an hour – cricket is always a game for Kent, rarely a penitential labour.

Woolley and Hardinge joined partnership at five minutes to twelve, and in ninety-five minutes they lifted the total from 41 to 181 – which brought us to lunch. The cricket was never in the least rash or demonstrative; indeed, Woolley batted half an hour for eleven. The runs came by play in which defence and offence were mingled with the most accurate judgement conceivable. The good ball was treated soundly and cautiously; the indifferent ball was seen quickly by both batsmen, and hit hard by means of a splendid range of scoring strokes. On present form Hardinge is one of the best batsmen in the land. To-day his cricket was beyond criticism – solid yet antagonistic. He plays as straight a bat as any English cricketer; he can cut, drive, and glance to leg with the best of them. His batsmanship always shows to us the pre-war stamp.

Hardinge made his fifty in ninety minutes: Woolley was twenty minutes quicker over the same score. Just before lunch Woolley in getting his fifty sent a hit to third man that Hallows might possibly have caught had he made ground with some alacrity. Hardinge came to his century after two hours and three-quarter's handsome activity. At twenty minutes to three Kent wanted 224 with two and a half hours still to go. A slight drizzle hereabout damped the grass, and probably added to the hardships of a failing Lancashire attack. Woolley was badly missed by Richard Tyldesley when his score was 82, and Kent's 220 – a blunder which must have caused the whole Lancashire side to shudder from head to foot. Woolley got his beautiful hundred out of a total of 239 in two hours and ten minutes; his next stroke, a great on-drive, made the Woolley-Hardinge stand worth 200 – hit in 140 minutes. At three o'clock Kent were 170 runs from victory's goal, and two hours and ten minutes remained.

Green rung the changes on his bowlers, but all of them seemed merely so much fuel to the brilliant bonfire of batsmanship which was burning for the glory of Kent cricket before our eyes. Three fieldsmen stood on the edge of the offside field for Woolley – a rare sight in these days. The Lancashire cricketers looked rather broken in wind now: there was little hurry in their feet and apparently not much hope within their breasts. Every other ball bowled, it seemed, was hit to the distant parts of the ground: it was the fieldsmen near the wicket who had least work to do. At 294 Woolley was leg before wicket: in two hours fifty minutes he had shown us his own delectable art and helped Hardinge to make 253 for the third wicket. With no increase in Kent's position R. Tyldesley broke through Hardinge's defence and missed the wicket by an inch: his face, red as a moon of blood, wore the aspect of anguish as he saw Hardinge escape.

It was a bolt out of Kent's blue sky that finished Hardinge's great innings – a lion-hearted quick throw-in by Green from long-on hit his wicket with Hardinge out of his ground. But for this mishap I imagine Kent would have won easily. Hardinge batted ten minutes short of four hours and a half, and deserved a more fortunate end. The cricket of Hardinge and Woolley taught a lesson which at the moment is needed in our game – the ancient lesson that offence skilfully exploited is the best form of defence. Collins was bowled, fifth out, at 327. Tea was taken at four o'clock with Kent 341 for five – 20 minutes to be wasted, 85 runs wanted by Kent, and five wickets by Lancashire. Anybody's game and a moment of palpitating crisis in which a tea interval was an absurd irrelevance. Why should there be tea intervals at all on the closing day, on which, of course, stumps are drawn at half-past five? The heady situation challenged the audacity of Chapman, who flashed his bat like a sword at McDonald's off ball: he cut and carved 49 in fifty minutes, and then, as the game was coming again well into Kent's grip, he was neatly caught at cover by Makepeace, sixth out at 361. The next ball bowled Deed: thus a sudden heave of the game's great wheel landed the laurels at Lancashire's grasp. And McDonald's next ball shattered Wright's stumps – a hat-trick for McDonald at the very moment every Lancashire cricketer must have been praying for the miracle which alone could pull our county out of the fire lit by Hardinge and Woolley.

As Hubble and Freeman took up the defence of the Kent ninth wicket the band on the edge of the grass made the mellow music of the madrigal out of 'The Mikado'. The moment was too tense, perhaps, for these golden strains, yet their sweetness was in tune with the afternoon's lovely English flavour. To my dying day I shall remember gratefully these afternoons in Kent, afternoons full of the air and peaceful sunshine of imperishable England. McDonald bowled at a noble pace during this last act of a memorable game, and as he ran his silent run of sinister grace the scene was one of those that do cricket honour – the crouching slips, the dogged batsmen, and the crowd watching, hoping, and fearing, now dumb and now making exuberant noises as some lightning stroke beat the field. McDonald bowled Freeman at 390: the little man had shown himself a fighter. Two runs afterwards Hubble was stumped exactly on the stroke of five o'clock. And so a noble match was nobly won and, what is as true, nobly lost by 33 runs. Both sides did the grand old game service on this July day. Every cricketer played hard and passed through his difficult hours. The running-out of Hardinge was the afternoon's turning-point: the splendid feat of McDonald settled the issue. He bowled finely at the finish, and Richard Tyldesley bowled finely too. A match well worth remembering – the brilliance of Hardinge, Woolley, and Ernest Tyldesley, the changeful hurly-burly of Kent's Titanic second innings – and everything done in a beautiful cricket field.

> Lancashire 336 and 243 for 5 dec.; Kent 154 and 392 (F. E. Woolley 137, H. T. W. Hardinge 132, McDonald 5 for 106). Lancashire won by 33 runs.

NEVILLE CARDUS AT OLD TRAFFORD   JUNE 1 1928

Lancashire v. Sussex

Yesterday morning's proceedings at Old Trafford were concerned entirely with the getting of Hallows's thousand runs before the last day of the month of May was over. We did our best to feel the occasion was exciting, but Hallows himself did not assist, because he went on with his batting with the easiest mastery, the utmost calm. There seemed to be no anxiety at all in his cricket. It was as though he had made an appointment with honour and glory at 12.40 exactly and was now here at the place well in advance of the hour and waiting casually on the pavement. Immediately he reached the required number he was out to a beautiful catch by J. Parks. The Sussex bowling did its best to make Hallows's task easy; easy balls were served up in plenty. Hallows either could not or would not score from some of them. Sussex were generous, but was it cricket? Nobody would wish to be a spoil-sport in this hour of Hallows's splendour. And nobody in his senses would challenge the sportsmanship of Sussex cricket. The desire to 'accommodate' Hallows was understandable in terms of large heartedness. Still, the game is the game. Besides, Hallows is quite capable of dealing with good bowling.

The performances of Hallows this month have been admirable. And, now that he has made a record for Lancashire cricket, perhaps Lancashire county on Saturday will return the distinction and set up another record by going to the benefit of Hallows in unprecedented numbers. These records in batsmanship may not be good for the game itself, but seeing that they are fashionable just now it is good to know that a Lancashire cricketer has achieved one of the most remarkable in the game's history. We need not compare Hallows's skill and accomplishments with those of W. G. Grace. On modern wickets it is possible that 'W. G.' would never have been got out, save by accident.

This innings of 232 by Hallows lasted seven and a quarter hours. It could not be said that he batted through this innings with his eye on his 1,000 runs: after he had reached his 100 he indulged in a period of magnificent and devil-may-care driving. He gave only one gleam of hope to the field – at 175 – and he hit 24 fours. Lancashire were all out just in time for lunch . . .

Lancashire 506 (C. Hallows 232, E. Tyldesley 100); Sussex 272 (M. W. Tate 74, J. Parks 55, E. A. McDonald 4 for 112) and 148 (McDonald 5 for 66). Lancashire won by an innings and 86 runs.

Spectators did turn up in large numbers for Hallows's benefit, but the game, against Surrey, will be better remembered as one of the great batsmen's matches of all time: Surrey scored 567, with Sandham making 282 retired ill; Lancashire replied with 588 for four, with 300 not out for Frank Watson, one of the few triple centuries ever by a non-international, and (until Simpson's 311 in 1964) the highest at Old Trafford. Hallows, for once, missed out: he only made 36.

A SPECIAL CORRESPONDENT AT EASTBOURNE   AUGUST 20 1931

Sussex v. Lancashire

It will be recalled that some time ago public references were made in Eastbourne to Lancashire cricket and the continuance of the policy of giving the Lancashire fixture to the town, which created some natural resentment, especially among the Lancashire professionals. The authorities at Old Trafford, I believe, took some notice of the matter and received some explanation that apparently satisfied them. The Sussex Club itself was never a party to the dispute.

It was not anticipated that the grievance, still nursed by the professionals – because so far as they were concerned it had not been removed – would have any active manifestation, but events to-day proved that such anticipation was wrong, for by common decision the professional members of the Lancashire eleven refused to attend the luncheon which is invariably extended to them on the opening day of a festival match in view of the fact that it was given by the Mayor (Colonel R. V. Gwynne) and Corporation of Eastbourne . . . The comments to which exception was taken by the professionals were made at the annual meeting of the Eastbourne Cricket Club early this year. Alderman Kay on that occasion said:

I think people are rather tired of seeing a certain county playing in Eastbourne. We sent in a protest to the county and were told that we were too late, so we are to have them again this year.

And the Mayor of Eastbourne supported the criticism in the following words:

I agree with Alderman Kay that we are in an unfortunate position in always having a certain county from the north. I will not mention the name. (Laughter.) We are rather tired of them. We have made a protest to the county, and as we were too late this year we have asked them to make a note of it and see that some other county may have the honour in 1932.

91

Sussex v. Lancashire

Paynter to-day has erected a monument to his part in Lancashire cricket, for his innings against Sussex here must take high place among the most famous scores ever made for the county. Lancashire this summer have known days both of tragedy and of delight, but this was the height of magnificence. At last, after many chilly, depressing days, they saw the sun at Hove and revelled in it with intoxicated minds and bats that were merciless. Sussex have grown this season to the stature of contenders for the championship, but here they were treated with crushing disdain, for their attack was thrashed into stupefaction and ineptitude.

Paynter played ninepins with records for his side, and held the crowd dazed and fascinated. Paynter has made other big totals, yet none with the calm dignity of this. In reaching the highest score ever made by a Lancashire professional he was polished even in his most rapacious moments. Sussex, alas! had no Tate and no James Cornford, and from the first ball Washbrook and Paynter throve easily. On a foundation of a score of 100 runs in an hour and a quarter was the massive structure to spring up with unbelievable rapidity later on. Yet this was no jerry-built work but one capable of close scrutiny at every point.

Washbrook hit the first boundary from the first ball of the first over, and thereafter there were only two maiden overs before lunch. He and Paynter made 78 in the first hour. Washbrook's cut was his best stroke, but he drove and forced the ball away to off and on in front of the wicket with poise and skill. Seven Sussex players bowled before lunch, and except that Oakes, the leg-spin bowler, was treated more rudely than the rest, Paynter took his toll of them impartially. His first century came a quarter of an hour before the interval, with the total at 162. Washbrook, as an incidental, completed his 1,000 runs for the summer, and yet even in the total of 175 for none at lunch there was no more than a hint of the spate of run-getting which was to follow.

The storm descended on Sussex immediately afterwards, for the total jumped to 200 in ten minutes and Washbrook's century was being cheered generously in half an hour. Paynter had every virtue; his square cut had the power of a pneumatic drill; he drove and hooked and pulled. The field were helpless chasers, for their encouragement was nil. Not till the evening of his innings did Paynter put a ball in the air near their desperate hands. When Washbrook reached his century Lancashire were 247. And so the pace grew dizzier. The first wicket in all made 268 in two hours and thirty-five minutes. Runs at 100 an hour looked natural yet never commonplace, because of the art in their making. At last the flaw in perfection came, and Washbrook's concentration snapped. He was out to a slightly mistimed drive to mid-on. Only MacLaren and Spooner and Makepeace and Hallows have exceeded this first-wicket stand in all the county's glamorous past. This, of course, was Lancashire's best for any wicket this season, yet Oldfield and Paynter were to exceed it later with their 271 for the third wicket in two and a quarter hours only.

Iddon's coming and going were scarcely noticed – he was run out at 275 through a splendid return by Cox – for Paynter held all eyes. Oldfield played beautifully. Up came 300 in three hours – Paynter 172. The milestones flashed by; Paynter's 200 was reached 25 minutes later, and hereabouts he took 17 in one over from Oakes, including a magnificent straight drive for six. This became a partnership of a century at two runs a minute. There hardly seemed a break in the applause before it was frantically renewed as Paynter square-cut Cook for four and with the same stroke earned his 250 and the side's fourth hundred. Between lunch and tea he had hit his second hundred and Lancashire had increased their total to 411 for two.

But the violence was not subdued then. On and on went Paynter. A miss in the slips at 260 was his first error. At a quarter-past five the fifth hundred descended upon Sussex, and Paynter's first 300 followed closely when he hit James Langridge to square leg for four. So he kept the Sussex mouths agape for five hours, and finally left leg before and only third out at 546.

Thereafter it remained only for the later batsmen to hit their hardest in brief bouts. James Parks faced the massacre bravely, and he alone had good figures. Oldfield deserved a century, but Parks had him out in the nineties and Hopwood alone made runs freely late in the day and survived. Lancashire this day (with Paynter) have surely removed the taunt of slowness so often levelled at them.

Lancashire 640 for 8 dec. (E. Paynter 322, C. Washbrook 108, N. Oldfield 92, J. H. Parks 5 for 144); Sussex 340 (H. W. Parks 98, James Langridge 64) and 295 (G. Cox 115, J. H. Parks 55, W. E. Phillipson 5 for 91).
Lancashire won by an innings and five runs.

JOHN WOODOCK AT THE OVAL   AUGUST 23 1952

Surrey v. Derbyshire

At twenty-five minutes past one Surrey beat Derbyshire by 212 runs and, amidst joy unconcealed, the county championship returned to The Oval. Not since 1914, in the days of Hobbs and Hayward, have Surrey won outright, although two years ago they shared the honour with Lancashire.

It is, indeed, only their second undivided triumph since the county's golden era at the end of the last century. Then, for much of the time, they could call upon those great bowlers, Lockwood and Richardson, who carried all before them and took Surrey to the top of the tree nine times in thirteen years. Now again they have provided further evidence of the general principle that bowling wins more matches than batting. A. V. Bedser, Surridge, Lock, and Laker, with E. A. Bedser, Constable, Clark, Loader, and Cox in the second line, form as penetrative and varied an attack as any in the country, and they have been ruthlessly supported by the brilliant close fielding of Lock and Surridge.

But Surrey have, too, from E. A. Bedser and Fletcher downwards, made their runs objectively and at a good rate, and Surridge has instilled into the side his own rare enthusiasm. Finally, when the calls of Test matches have taken from their ranks their finest players they have been able to summon reserves competent enough to pull their weight in any side. It has unquestionably been Surrey's year, for not only have they won by the length of a street but, what is infinitely more important, they have enjoyed their cricket and people have enjoyed watching them.

To-day they completely overran Derbyshire, who did not play as though they were capable of holding fourth place in the championship. By declaring at the overnight score, Surridge ensured that his side would not be lacking time in which to bowl out their rivals. He allowed a possible five hours and twenty minutes and left Derbyshire with 308 to win. The pitch was easier than at any time in the match and the stage was set for a battle royal. But Derbyshire were unable to improve on their first innings showing, and with few exceptions they went down without a fight.

Surrey made the perfect start when Constable ran out Elliott from cover point off the fourth ball of the match – the result of Hamer misjudging a call in his anxiety to avoid a pair of spectacles. Hamer himself then played outside an in-swinger and any remote hopes of victory which Derbyshire might have cherished were shattered when Bedser sent Carr's off-stump rocketing out of the ground. In fairness to Carr this ball might have bowled almost anyone. But if this batsman consistently were to achieve what he promises then no England side would be complete without him. Revill and Sale, with Harlequin cap rampant, both played poor strokes so that when Surridge and Bedser gave way to the spinners after an hour Derbyshire were 35 for five.

Morgan has hinted for a fair amount of all round ability in this match and for 75 minutes he resisted sensibly while Lock and Laker strove for yesterday's results. Kelly, another youngster, remained with him for fifty minutes but never for a moment now did one seriously believe that Surrey were likely to be held up for long. Kelly eventually was out to a well-judged running catch by Fletcher and, when Morgan and Rhodes fell to Laker, Bedser appropriately enough came back to finish off the job. For 25 minutes, however, Surrey allowed triumph to linger on their palates while Dawkes defiantly carved his way to Derbyshire's highest individual score of the match. Then, within five minutes of lunch, Surrey's foremost cricketer knocked Smith's middle stump prostrate and the elusive prize was won.

Surrey 156 (D. G. W. Fletcher 50, C. Gladwin 5 for 44) and 258 for 4 dec. (P. B. H. May 88, B. Constable 58); Derbyshire 107 (G. A. R. Lock 6 for 16) and 95 (A. V. Bedser 4 for 41). Surrey won by 212 runs.

HAROLD MATHER AT BATH   JUNE 8 1953

Somerset v. Lancashire

At the end of one of the most remarkable days' cricket in recent years Lancashire not only had beaten Somerset by an innings and 24 runs but had done so when some 55 minutes still remained for play.

Exponents of brighter cricket certainly could not have wished for more excitement than they had in this match, but even they could not want it produced by false conditions, as it was to-day. H. T. F. Buse, whose benefit match this was, lives here and is greatly respected in this city, possibly even a little more than he is elsewhere in the county. But it was more than regrettable that he chose a game on this ground for such an occasion. The club ground undoubtedly is not without its beauty, but the wicket is far from being up to county match standards. Though it was relaid in October the cold winds and other unhelpful weather retarded the normal process of knitting together. This in itself was a problem for the groundsman, but added to his troubles were the facts that the turf was unsuitable from the start and that because of Coronation festivities on the ground he was unable to give it the strict attention it required. The result was that when it was mowed on Wednesday only a negligible amount of grass was removed. Even before the start of play to-day the wicket itself was lacking in grass generally, and what there was looked more like dried moss. To-day's proceedings were, therefore, a natural outcome, for even bowlers could not predict what any ball would do.

Criticism of batsmanship in such conditions would be futile and unjust. The bowlers made the most of their chances. Indeed, it was somewhat ironic that Buse should bowl so well as to take six for 41 and thus contribute to his own misfortune. It was, however, necessary only for any bowler to pitch an approximate length and immediately the unfortunate batsman had to decide what stroke to attempt to make or even whether to make one at all. Not surprisingly many wrong decisions were made, but in spite of the bowlers' efforts, and particularly those of Tattersall who never once lost his length, one's sympathy was with the strikers. The effects can perhaps best be seen from the details of Somerset's first innings. Not one man was bowled and apart from Buse and Deshon those who were caught fell almost the first time they chanced their arm.

Somerset are not strong at the best of times and to-day were without Hall. It must, therefore, have been cruel in the extreme that their opponents on such a wicket should be Lancashire, with one of the

95

strongest, most varied attacks in the championship. Washbrook's opinion of the pitch was immediately shown, for he opened his attack with Statham and Tattersall. The former was not successful, but ninety minutes later the home side was out for 55, Tattersall having taken seven for 25 and not having had to work hard to do so. Lancashire did start somewhat better, but the dismissal of Ikin began a collapse and with five men out for 46 they were not certain to gain the lead. But then came the most controlled and yet the boldest batting of the day.

Marner and Wharton were quiet only for a few balls, but then they began an onslaught. Fifteen runs were scored off an over by Lawrence, Marner hit the last four balls of the next over by Buse for six, two, four, six, and the pair later hit Redman for eighteen in an over. This may suggest wild hitting; in fact, it was not, and indeed it was refreshing to see the young Marner watch the ball so carefully and get so well over and behind it that when Wharton was bowled by Redman one thought their stand of seventy had lasted even fewer than 26 minutes. In the end Lancashire gained a lead of 103 and two hours twenty minutes still were left for play when Gimblett and Lawrence came out a second time.

By this time the pitch was in an even worse condition, for the ball removed grass and earth each time it pitched, and soon Somerset were seven for four, three of the wickets this time having fallen to Statham, Buse and Stephenson, who hit Tattersall for a four and six off successive balls, then added nineteen, but nine wickets were down for 44 at 5.15 p.m., 75 minutes from the close of play. Fine batting by Redman and dour defiance by Langford then held up Lancashire for twenty minutes and added 35 runs, but the end was obvious.

Somerset 55 (R. Tattersall 7 for 25) and 79 (Tattersall 6 for 44); Lancashire 158 (H. T. F. Buse 6 for 41). Lancashire won by an innings and 24 runs.

TONY GOODRIDGE AT HOVE   SEPTEMBER 2 1959

Sussex v. Yorkshire

For seven years the county cricket championship has been held, and held most worthily, by Surrey, but now at last the old order has changed. With a magnificent victory over Sussex at Hove yesterday, Yorkshire, set to make 215 runs in 105 minutes, reached that objective with seven minutes and five wickets and three runs to spare.

Not since 1946 have Yorkshire reigned as undisputed champions but the title fits them well, for they are a young side and a keen one. They have, indeed, had their anxious moments in this best of cricket seasons when things have gone far from well for them. They will not readily forget their recent visit to Bristol when with the championship very much in sight they foundered almost without trace. Neither would they willingly perhaps re-live the protracted but ultimately successful battle with Worcestershire at Worcester last week, which they just had to win. But they may, indeed, recall with pride and joy, as those of us of differing loyalties will unquestionably do, the final triumph – for triumph it was – at Hove.

For some time past the spectre of Surrey has been dogging Yorkshire's footsteps for Surrey had a match in hand over Yorkshire. At the start of this, their final match, Yorkshire had a lead of six points and they had to win to keep their chances alive. That Surrey also could not afford to drop any points brought no consolation, for Yorkshire were fully preoccupied with their own problems, which at 2.47 p.m. yesterday looked almost insuperable. Two points for first-innings lead seemed the most that might be expected for Yorkshire were 215 runs short of victory and stumps were to be drawn at 4.30 at the latest.

Never was there a moment so apt for a side to show that it was of the stuff of champions, and seldom can a side have proved itself so admirably. Stott and Taylor began their quest and although Taylor left quickly to an lbw decision to Dexter, Thomson found that at the end of his second over, he had taken no wickets for 32 runs – rough treatment indeed for an opening bowler. Stott, in fact, had taken two fours and a five off his first over and in his second, among other strokes, Stott drove him straight for six and Close hooked him out of the ground for another. Close left to a catch at the wicket off Dexter at 40 but the 50 came up in eighteen minutes and Stott and Padgett by unrelenting aggression added 141 runs in 60 minutes before Padgett fell to a well-taken catch by Dexter on the long-leg boundary. Padgett, when he had scored nine, became the first batsman to make 2,000 runs in a season for Yorkshire since Lowson reached that figure in 1950.

Stott went mercilessly on, although towards the end of his innings, Pataudi appeared to have made a legitimate catch on the long-on boundary before going over the ropes but Pataudi himself signalled a six. Eventually Stott fell to Pataudi in the same spot when just four runs short of a well-deserved century. He had batted for 86 minutes and hit two sixes, a five, and eight fours, and with the aid of brief but lucrative assistance from Trueman, who hit eleven runs off his only over, he had seen Yorkshire to within thirteen runs of their target and there were still twenty minutes left for play.

These runs came to Illingworth and Bolus without further trouble and new champions had taken over. The reason for all the hurry was the very proper and obdurate batting of Sussex on Monday afternoon and yesterday morning. Marlar is to be congratulated that he made Yorkshire work all the way . . .

Sussex 210 (Nawab of Pataudi 52, K. Taylor 4 for 40) and 311 (J. M. Parks 85, L. J. Lenham 66, R. Illingworth 4 for 66, D. Wilson 4 for 78); Yorkshire 307 (Illingworth 122, Wilson 55, E. R. Dexter 4 for 67) and 218 for 5 (W. B. Stott 96, D. E. V. Padgett 79). Yorkshire won by five wickets.

Yorkshire v. Surrey

First blood, then champagne flowed at Hull yesterday as Yorkshire, rather incredulously, achieved the victory they needed over Surrey, by 60 runs, to keep them well out of reach of all pursuers at the head of the championship table. It is now only a mathematical theory that either Kent or Glamorgan can deprive Yorkshire of their third successive title. They can sit back with their pipes and slippers reflecting on a 60 point lead, with their two rivals having two outstanding matches in which to overtake them.

Almost inevitably, Close was at the heart of yesterday's astonishing final drama. His flannels stained with blood from a severe blow on his left leg in his usual close to the wicket fielding position, Close manipulated his bowlers shrewdly at first and then, it seemed, anxiously, as Surrey looked like holding out. In the end it was only an astonishing catch involving Close and Binks, the wicketkeeper, which turned the tide in Yorkshire's favour. It came when Younis and Long were well entrenched in an eighth wicket partnership which had been formed when Surrey were 121 for seven, and seemingly heading for defeat.

As the minutes ticked by Close began to pace anxiously around rather like an expectant father. Then, when the partnership had put on 65 and the gallant Younis had been in for more than two hours for a quite splendid 75, he swept Wilson full-bloodedly, the ball rebounded off Close's forearm (leaving an egg-sized lump) and straight into the waiting gloves of Binks.

Yorkshire players danced in exultation, which was increased later in the same over when the ever-canny Wilson pinned Jackman right back on his stumps with a swinging delivery that had him leg before. Nine wickets were then down in the next over from Nicholson. Long touched a catch to the wicketkeeper and Yorkshire's victory, for so long in doubt, was secure at last.

Yorkshire leapt and bounded their way from the field like a team of Morris dancers, hordes of people invaded the arena and in the dressing-rooms the champagne corks popped as both teams toasted a notable win and an almost certain hat-trick of championship victories by Yorkshire. Close missed the celebrations at first, having been driven straight to a nearby hospital for two stitches to be inserted into a gash on his left leg, inflicted by another powerful shot earlier in the afternoon by Long, during that selfsame frustrating eighth wicket partnership.

He returned, still blood-stained, and wasted no time in saying that he regarded the championship as not yet won. 'At least the pressure is off us,' he said, 'but under the present scoring system either of these two teams could come from behind and overtake us. Mind you, they'll have to play damn well to get the points they need, and if they do it they'll deserve to win the championship . . .'

BRIAN CHAPMAN AT SWANSEA   SEPTEMBER 3 1969

Glamorgan v. Essex

Off the very last ball of the day, Glamorgan won the match by one run, ten extra and rather unexpected points, and, in all human probability, the championship as well. Such was the climax of as tense and thrilling a day at Swansea yesterday as one could hope for.

At the close, Tony Lewis, the Glamorgan captain, had the magnanimity to say this about Essex, his defeated opponents: 'In every one of the games we have played them this year, they have been the better side. Always they give us a magnificent game.'

Essex, led with panache by Brian Taylor, were indeed unlucky to lose a match in which they had throughout held the initiative. Two adventurous captains proved that this old game still can be the greatest.

Essex, at 183 for eight, needed seven to win off the last over from Roger Davis, who deals in gently optimistic off-breaks. Barker and East each took a single, then Barker strolled two yards down the wicket, missed and was stumped. Now it was five to win off three balls. Lever, last man in, and East ran two nonchalant singles.

Three were needed off the last ball. But the batsmen were clearly well coached in the rule that, if the scores were tied, the side batting last gets five points. So when Lever tapped the ball down to third man they went for that levelling second run. Wheatley's throw skimmed perfectly over the bails, and Lever was stranded far from home.

Glamorgan increased their total of points to 227 and, if any doubts exist about the destination of the title, these were not shared by the crowd, who called Lewis and his team on to the balcony and cheered mightily. In their capital city, Cardiff, during the next three days against Worcestershire, they can make assurance double sure.

It was ironic that the shield and buckler of Glamorgan's victory was an innings of 50 by Walker, lasting three hours and three quarters, to which an impatient crowd gave the slow handclap. Without it, Glamorgan would have been harried out of the game. Both the Joneses and Cordle, who hit two tremendous sixes, were out swinging their bats rewardingly but briefly.

By lunch, the score had advanced from the overnight 123 for four to 236 for seven, a lead of 141, and anxious calculations were in train about the timing of Lewis's declaration. Hobbs was allowed to bowl 11 maidens out of 24 overs of leg-spin, and it did, indeed, seem that caution needed an injection of courage. Nash supplied it with five boundaries in two overs off Lever and Boyce, and the declaration at 284 for eight set Essex 190 to win at something like five runs an over, a target they struck from the start.

Wheatley, whose speed appeared deceptively mild, removed Edmeades, Ward and Taylor for 43. Taylor, who had promoted himself from No. 7, was dropped by Lewis at mid-off, a matter for groans, then held by him at mid-on.

Fletcher, whose pugnacity and skill could be decisive, moved into top gear from his first shot. Fours flowed at the expense of Cordle (21 runs in two overs), Shepherd and Wheatley. So long as he remained, Glamorgan's affairs suffered sharp decline. The margin in the last 20 overs was 101. But Fletcher succumbed at 44 to a full-length dive by Bryan Davis at mid-wicket which surely grazed his knuckles and knees.

That was the turning point. Wickets fell at intervals too short for Essex's comfort. Irvine was bowled by Shepherd, whose cool head and cunning hand accounted for the big-hitting Boyce, abetted by another splendid catch, this time at mid-on by Lewis.

Sixty were wanted in ten overs, and still the Glamorgan fielding rose to the crisis, though Barker was missed at deep mid-on. Hobbs profitably patented a looped swing like that made famous by Bruen, the golfer. Any weapon that came handy would do now! He was stumped so far out of his ground that Eifion Jones waved him goodbye with the gesture that removed the bails.

With three overs left, 23 was the figure and Lewis posted seven fielders along the boundary like frontier outposts. The challenge proved just beyond the powers of Essex, but safety never entered their heads and they pressed hard for victory right to the end. One felt that the Men of Harlow, equally with the Men of Harlech, had marched to glory.

Glamorgan 241 (B. A. Davis 78, A. Jones 75) and 284 for 8 dec. (Jones 69, P. M. Walker 50); Essex 336 for 7 dec. (B. L. Irvine 109, B. Taylor 70) and 188. Glamorgan won by one run.

PATRICK BARCLAY AT SOUTHPORT   JULY 31 1982

Lancashire v. Warwickshire

Warwickshire, who began their match against Lancashire by scoring 523 for four declared, managed to lose it yesterday. They were bowled out for 111 (or Nelson, as that particular score is known to aficionados) at, appropriately enough, the Trafalgar Road ground in Southport and succumbed by 10 wickets soon after Graeme Fowler had completed his second century in successive days with the aid of a runner.

What an extraordinary encounter it had been, consistent only in its ability to astonish as a variety of records tumbled and both batsmen and bowlers recorded the best performances of their careers. In all 1,274 runs were scored as the sun blazed down on a pitch that seldom helped the bowlers, in which context Les McFarlane can take great satisfaction from his display; when he bowled, it was lovely weather for ducks, five of which Warwickshire sustained.

The 30-year-old McFarlane was born in Jamaica but went to school in

Northampton, where he played a relatively expensive season of county cricket in 1979. Last year he took 62 wickets for Bedfordshire at an average of 16.63. His fortunes have been mixed with Lancashire, but yesterday's figures of six for 59 were most encouraging.

Two of his victims, Dyer and Andy Lloyd, were claimed late on Thursday, and in the morning he turned troublesome again, removing Amiss and Wootton to leave Warwickshire on 47 for six as they tried to build on a first innings lead of 109. At that stage four wickets went in seven deliveries without a run, smart catches helping the enthusiastic O'Shaughnessy to remove Asif Din and Kallicharran, whose duck followed 230 not out on Wednesday.

With the impressive teenager Folley contributing usefully to the attack Warwickshire could not get back on an even keel and were all out soon after lunch. Lancashire's requirement for victory was 221 in 3¾ hours – a situation which could hardly have been foreseen on Wednesday evening as the champagne corks popped in Warwickshire's dressing room and Humpage and Kallicharran celebrated their stand of 470.

In the end Lancashire won comfortably enough, more than seven overs remaining when Fowler hit six off Asif Din to take his unbroken partnership with David Lloyd to 226. Yet, in keeping with the labyrinthine character of this extraordinary match, it could have been very different had Amiss not dropped Fowler at slip off Hartley when the score was seven. Instead the bowlers became progressively dispirited as Fowler and Lloyd picked their shots with splendid authority.

The 25-year-old Fowler's innings was rich in promise, some glorious cover drives keeping his runner's work to a minimum. Over his two innings he found the boundary 45 times while suffering from a pulled thigh muscle, and his performance must surely revive talk of a chance with England.

Fowler, who made his first appearance two years ago after studying at Durham University, began this season unconvincingly, but has now completed five centuries (three against Warwickshire this month) to take the total for his blossoming career to nine. He is a stylish and aggressive left-hander, fields well, and must surely be worth consideration for the selectors' problem position.

Fowler is not, of course, the only player with reason to remember these three days. Career best performances were recorded by McFarlane and Cockbain as well as Warwickshire's Humpage, who scored 254 in the stand that was a record for the fourth wicket in England. Humpage's was also the highest individual Warwickshire innings against Lancashire, and the partnership the highest for any wicket against Lancashire.

Warwickshire 523 for 4 dec. (G. Humpage 254, A. I. Kallicharran 230 not out) and 111 (L. L. McFarlane 6 for 59); Lancashire 414 for 6 dec. (G.

Fowler 126, I. Cockbain 98, J. Abrahams 51 not out) and 226 for 0 (Fowler 128 not out, D. Lloyd 88 not out). Lancashire won by 10 wickets.

This match also included the first case of a substitute taking a wicket. Under a new regulation, David Brown, the Warwickshire manager, was permitted to act as a full deputy for his fast bowler Gladstone Small on the first two days after Small had been called into the Test party as a standby.

DAVID LACEY AT EASTBOURNE   AUGUST 13 1982

Sussex v. Northamptonshire

The Eastbourne wicket was declared unfit by the umpires, Dai Evans and Billy Ibadulla, yesterday after Northamptonshire had spun Sussex out a second time to win by an innings and 58 runs with a day and a half to spare.

Sussex, following on 177 behind Northamptonshire's total of 261 after collapsing to 84 all out on Wednesday evening, were only marginally more successful the next time around, their main achievement being to extend their second innings beyond lunch, albeit by one ball.

With the Test and County Cricket Board's inspector of wickets, Bernard Flack, called in as a result of the way the pitch had behaved at the start of Eastbourne week and now the umpires' ultimate condemnation, it should be clear by now that the Saffrons is not quite what it was on that day in the 60s when Gary Sobers complained that his West Indies batsmen would gain no useful tour practice there since the conditions were more Barbadian than British.

Even now the idea of Eastbourne being reported to Lord's seems akin to the questioning of a Mother Superior's chastity. Nevertheless yesterday's evidence brooked no argument. At the end of its brief life the pitch resembled a badly-chafed piece of chipboard. By the time Willey and Steele had finished with the Sussex batting, the wicket was pockmarked where the sharply spinning ball had hastened the crumbling process.

This does not necessarily mean that Eastbourne's cricket will go the way of Chichester, Horsham and Worthing, all of which have lost first-class status since the war. Maybe the advice of Hove groundsman Peter Eaton, who has created such an excellent pitch there, will be sought.

One reason for the Saffrons' fall from grace could be over-use. This summer, what with the proliferation of local leagues, evening 20-over games and single wicket competitions, the ground has been played on almost every day, leaving little time for the preparation of a proper championship pitch. Perhaps the problem at Eastbourne is more administrative than horticultural.

Yesterday the Sussex batting swooned again with the predictability of dowagers in a renaissance comedy. Willey and Steele returned after two formal overs with the new ball and, as in the first innings, Mendis and Green appeared to have formed the basis of a respectable score. But from 50 without loss Sussex plunged to 119 all out, confounded this time less by Willey's offspin than Steele's slow left arm.

When the batsmen were not actually beaten by the spin they were out making desperate shots for fear of what the ball might do next. Willey and Steele finished with nine wickets apiece in the match.

Northamptonshire 261 (Kapil Dev 103, W. Larkins 81, A. C. S. Pigott 7 for 74); Sussex 84 (P. Willey 6 for 17, D. S. Steele 4 for 27) and 119 (Steele 5 for 32). Northamptonshire won by an innings and 58 runs.

MATTHEW ENGEL AT TAUNTON   SEPTEMBER 12 1984

Somerset v. Nottinghamshire

At 6.15 on a sunlit Taunton evening – 15 minutes after the season would have ended in the days when close of play meant what it said and almost five months after it began – Essex became county champions for the second year running.

One-day cricket has debased the currency, both of great finishes and of adjectives to describe them, but it would be hard for any form of the game, or any other game, to surpass the ending of the dear old County Championship last night.

Nottinghamshire needed 297 to beat Somerset and thus overtake Essex. Having virtually given up hope when their captain Clive Rice was out after scoring a masterful 98, they started the final over 14 runs short with the last pair of the crease: Mike Bore, an old-fashioned tail-ender of advancing years and girth hauled out of semi-retirement as second team captain because of injuries, and the tyro seam bowler Andy Pick.

Facing the 20-year-old slow left-armer Steve Booth, Bore smashed the first ball to the long on boundary first bounce, struck the second for another four through extra cover and then turned the third for a cunning two past square leg.

Four to win, three balls left. Bore, the improbable man of destiny, went on a nervous Tavaré-like walkabout; Rice, in the dressing-room, could no longer bear to watch; Keith Fletcher, listening on his car radio on the ground at Chelmsford, was both panic stricken and helpless.

The next ball Bore blocked. The fifth he leapt at, smashing it high and straight, but just a fraction too short. It came down into the safe hands of Somerset's substitute, a young man from Keynsham (spelt K-E-Y-N-S-H-A-M) called Richard Ollis. He can have the freedom of Chelmsford if he wants it.

The match was over, won by Somerset by three runs. The title, pennant, trophy and £15,000 booty from Britannic Assurance's first year of sponsorship thus went to Fletcher and Essex, the first team ever to do the championship/Sunday League double and the first to retain the championship since Yorkshire in 1968.

The winners' cheque that had been written out for Nottinghamshire had to be torn up, though they got £7,500 as runners-up and Hadlee won a new award, worth £500, for player of the year. Middlesex were third and Leicestershire fourth. It has to be said that the better and best team won.

The extraordinary finale was set up by an excellent declaration from Ian Botham. His obligation was to set the target that would give his team their best chance of winning, though whether Somerset finished eighth or ninth was probably not the weightiest matter on his mind. He judged it just right: 297 in a minimum of 52 overs, or just over three hours, since the pitch was turning and Marks and Booth were able to bowl above the union rate.

It was not especially generous but the short Taunton boundaries still encourage the adventurous batsman as they did when Wellard and Gimblett were going. Broad, not normally in that class as a hitter, hit 12 off Crowe's second over, and the race was on.

Broad dominated the opening stand with Robinson. A couple of catches went down but he batted very shrewdly, using his feet to the spinners this time, and his innings might yet constitute a late hint to the England selectors, though the Newmarket whisper is that Kim Barnett of Derbyshire is now the hot fancy as an opener.

The first wicket made 69, but both Broad and Robinson got out just before tea. Randall drove a catch back to Marks and young Johnson was easily stumped. The big two were now together.

Hadlee, who had not bowled before the declaration, was not quite at his clean-hitting best. Rice, however, was magnificent. He rarely makes the scores he did three years ago now, favouring the handsome 40 over the big hundred, but yesterday there was a glint in his eye.

It says a lot for the bowling, particularly for Booth, who looked both talented and astute, that Rice did not tear it apart, but Nottinghamshire were still making good progress; 138 were wanted when the compulsory last 20 overs began and Hadlee was just starting to middle it. Then he chipped to the mid-wicket boundary, Lloyds was there and took the catch falling on to the advertising boards.

There was some controversy about this and the vaguest hint of a riot, meaning – this being the County Championship – that three itinerant Nottinghamshire supporters in the River Stand got very agitated. However, as everyone knows without looking it up, Law 32, paragraph two, sub-section (a) clause II says that where there are boards rather than a rope, this constitutes a fair catch and Hadlee was on his way.

Still Rice was going well; 84 were wanted off 12 and after an incredible flat six over extra cover, 56 off seven. Then he holed out to Ollis at deep square. Surely it was over now.

Cooper and Hemmings charged and were easily stumped. Essex

began to relax, but everyone had reckoned without Bore. Twenty-seven were needed off two overs and a simple pick-up six off Marks set up the conclusion.

There have been superb finishes to the Championship before – 1977, for instance, when Gloucestershire chucked it away on the last day and 1959 when Yorkshire made a near-impossible target at Hove – but probably nothing like this.

It says something for the nature of the competition that it should be settled in the end by the conjunction, not of the big names, but of Bore, Booth and Ollis, and that the eventual champions were Essex, who by their all-round strength – their overseas stars fitting into the pattern not dominating it – entirely deserved it.

Somerset 274 (J. W. Lloyds 94, M. D. Crowe 57, K. E. Cooper 4 for 57, R. J. Hadlee 4 for 59) and 244 for 5 dec. (P. M. Roebuck 78, J. W. Lloyds 63 not out, E. E. Hemmings 4 for 123); Nottinghamshire 222 for 7 dec. (B. C. Broad 88, D. W. Randall 64) and 293 (C. E. B. Rice 98, V. J. Marks 6 for 111, S. C. Booth 4 for 138). Somerset won by three runs.

DAVID FOOT AT TAUNTON   MAY 23 1985

Somerset v. Hampshire

Taunton marvels at Ian Botham more by the day. His century yesterday, amid the apparent wreckage of a Somerset innings, took him just 76 balls. It equalled the previous fastest of the season, made on this same ground by this same imperious aggressor.

The members rose in doting tribute to his brutal brilliance. It was a glittering all-embracing collective item to cherish perhaps almost with the best – certainly the most stunning – in the county's history.

Another West Countryman, Gilbert Jessop, used to describe an extraordinary arc with his bountiful blows without ever looking a slogger. Yesterday, Botham, too, appeared thrillingly in control. Occasionally it seemed that he predetermined his muscular stroke, but that is the nature of the man.

His teammates, who like all county cricketers can be sparing in their praise, say their captain has never played better; he's back to the form of the richest years in that cussed and contradictory career of his.

He's nimbler than he has been for a long time, belying the rural sturdiness of the waist. He has more zest too, and his England place is what he, as a racing man, might call a cast-iron cert. The blond hair tops a face of buoyant challenge.

Somerset were 58 for four when he came in. His jet-lagged mate, Viv Richards, just returned from Caribbean climes, had lasted three balls. Tremlett had taken three for six in five unerring overs, but Botham took a calm look and then, after lunch, blazed away.

There were in all 20 fours and six sixes in his 149 when, daring as ever to drive Marshall – with whom he had an engrossing battle – he was bowled. He had scored his runs out of 193. It seems churlish to remember that he was missed in the slips when five.

The wicket had been damp and it was not a day to bat first, a point quickly made by Hampshire's deputy captain Terry as he sent Somerset in. By the 31st over, five wickets had gone down.

There were obvious virtues in the early bowling. It could be unsparing and, Roebuck might reasonably say, painful. His finger was broken in the third over by Marshall; he went on to make 18 but will now be out for three weeks. Davis added to Somerset's unwanted casualty station; he too went to hospital with a damaged hand.

Almost entirely due to Botham, the total reached 298. Hampshire, in response, quickly discovered problems themselves and when bad light stopped play were 90 for five in 32 overs. Garner, also playing for the first time this season, quickly dismissed Terry; a fine stumping by Gard, and a spectacular catch by Marks to get rid of the talented Robin Smith, threw the match wide open.

Two of the wickets went to Richards, implying that he is going to be used increasingly as an important support bowler. His leisurely seamers carry rather more threat than is apparent in the delivery. Turner scored some quick welcome runs, but his absent skipper Nicholas will read the scoreboard this morning with disbelief and some dismay.

He should have known the range of a Botham recovery, however. The sheer strength of the man is remarkable. Here he was, in the evening, opening the bowling again as if he'd been strolling around the Quantock hedgerows with his 12-bore all day. He once hurled at the stumps and Hampshire got four overthrows, but by then he'd have been forgiven anything.

Somerset 298 (I. T. Botham 149) and 358 for 5 dec. (I. V. A. Richards 186, N. F. M. Popplewell 68); Hampshire 334 for 8 dec. (K. D. James 124, T. M. Tremlett 102 not out) and 325 for 5 (C. L. Smith 121, V. P. Terry 83). Hampshire won by five wickets.

This match, almost as extraordinary as the one at Southport in 1982, was settled with three balls to spare. Tremlett and James broke the Hampshire eighth-wicket record by putting on 227, Richards scored his 186 in 176 balls with ten sixes and then Marshall won the game by scoring 40 off the last 32 balls.

QUIET DAYS

OCTOBER 14 1854

Birch Cricket Club: Annual Meeting

On Saturday evening last the members of the above club, with their friends, to the number of about 150, met in the infant school, and partook of tea, to celebrate the closing of the season. The room was tastefully decorated for the occasion with evergreens, banners, and mottos. Tea being concluded, the Rev. G. H. G. Anson, the rector, took the chair, and called upon the hon. secretary to read the report; from which it appeared that the club numbered thirty-one members; that two matches had been played during the season, and that the improvement in the science of the game had been accompanied with other and more important results. Various other speeches were made during the evening, bearing upon the features of a new literary society, which is being formed in the village. The library, reading-room, and singing-class, are already open, at a nominal charge. In addition to the above, the committee contemplate giving a series of concerts during the winter. These matters being amply discussed, the entertainments of the evening proceeded. Several glees and catches were sung, under the very able superintendance of Mr. Meadowcroft, the organist of the parish church, which elicited many an encore, and many a round of applause. The whole of the proceedings went off with very marked success.

JULY 20 1858

Longsight v. Cheetham Hill and Rusholme

The grand match between five gentlemen of Cheetham Hill and five of the Rusholme clubs (with Swain) and ten gentlemen of the Longsight club (with Hunt) came off on Saturday at Longsight, in the presence of a very large and highly respectable company of ladies and gentlemen of the neighbourhood, the day being fine; and the presence of so many elegantly dressed ladies reminded one of the gay scene at our late

107

Exhibition, and will long be remembered by the inhabitants of Longsight. At intervals, the splendid band of the 5th Dragoon Guards gave a selection of popular music. The play of the various clubs was considered excellent, although the score of the Longsighters was far ahead of their opponents. The proceeds for admission to the ground, one shilling each, after deducting some trifling expenses, will realise a very handsome surplus, to be handed over to the Building Committee of the Longsight Library and Mechanics' Institution, in aid of the fund for the erection of the new building now in progress. The admirable arrangements, together with the energy and ability displayed by the gentlemen of the club, have been attended with complete success.

JULY 27 1914

Burnley v. Church

It would be going, perhaps, too far to say that it was Parkin, the Church bowler who is to appear for the first time to-day at Old Trafford, who defeated Burnley on Saturday, and not really Church. But certainly Parkin made a big contribution to that result by dismissing seven Burnley batsmen for 44 runs. This, however, is only a half statement of the case, for it may be equally true that the success of the Church batsmen was due to the absence of the other side of Burnley's great bowler, William Cook. The Cooks are somewhat like the Tyldesleys – there seems to be an unlimited supply of them. When one is indisposed, as William unfortunately was on Saturday, another steps forward, not in this case the brother who bowls for Lancashire, but a yet younger one, known as Jack, who plays with a Scottish club. Unfortunately Jack is not yet the equal of the famous William, and the latter's absence spoiled the match as a great bowler's contest.

Out in the gale on Saturday, speculating rather dismally as to whether any race of cricketers would dare to venture out, one recalled a warm and pleasant afternoon in April when Burnley visited Church and went down rather feebly before the 'Ecclesiastics,' as they are called. That happened even with Cook playing for them. It was not a warm and pleasant afternoon at Burnley on Saturday – it was, in fact, an awful afternoon – and the same thing happened again. Down went the Burnley wickets before Parkin just as they had done in the first match, but the efforts to disestablish the Church wickets again failed. It might of course, have happened just the same if Cook had been bowling, but one can never safely set a limit to Cook's possibilities. The other Saturday he bundled the Todmorden men out in a style that made their supporters gasp, and he would have had a fine chance of doing the same with Church on Saturday. That was the real disappointment of the match – a great occasion for a great bowler, and the great bowler unable to turn out.

One may mercifully spare the reader a description of what Burnley looks like on a wet Saturday afternoon. Most people would have laughed at the idea of a cricket match in such weather. Yet there were the teams in readiness, if the slightest possibility of a game should emerge, and a handful of spectators ready to grow into a crowd at the faintest prospect of a start. Just after three o'clock out the players went, Church to field and Burnley to bat, a November gale playfully circling round them, and the turf underfoot juicy after the heavy rain. It was soon clear, however, that they meant business – especially Parkin. Clegg, one of the opening batsmen, was soon caught, then Hargreaves was run out, and after this the scorers were kept busy for some time in writing down the familiar words 'b Parkin'. It was soon all over. Only one man made any fight worth mentioning, and that was Crossley, whose innings of 24 looked quite an achievement against a setting of failures.

Eighty-one runs stood to Burnley's credit when the innings ended, and the Church batsmen grew impatient with the rain that once more returned. They wanted to rush in and win or go down in the attempt. One suspects that the absence of Cook brought a large accession of confidence to them. In any case their confidence was justified. They had an hour and a quarter's batting, after the rain had ceased, and they got the 82 runs required with eight wickets to spare. The first men, Howarth and T. A. Smith, really won the match, scoring 71 of the runs between them. Their steady play at the outset soon put all thoughts of a collapse out of mind, and the longer they stayed the better they scored. When Howarth was caught, after making 36, there was a little left for the other men to do but go in and hit. And when the winning hit was made only two wickets had fallen. Smith was 35 not out at the close – a thoroughly good performance.

NEVILLE CARDUS   MAY 10 1920

Oldham v. Rochdale

Rochdale defeated Oldham on their own ground on Saturday, as they, indeed, were bound in duty to do, seeing that they had in the team J. N. Crawford and Parkin – both international cricketers, actual and potential. It was a low-scoring match on a rain-affected wicket, which lost its top with every ball sent down. Rochdale won the toss and sent Oldham in, but the ground hardly varied during the whole match. Though never a sticky wicket, the bowlers could always turn the ball. Oldham scored 57, and to knock off these Rochdale lost seven wickets and had some luck in getting them.

The game was typical of league cricket through and through. For most people on the ground all that mattered apparently was cricket as a contest: there seemed little insistence on the game's artistic or spectacular charms. Bad strokes were cheered just as lustily as good strokes, no doubt in the belief they all would look alike on the score sheet.

One had, of course, to make allowances for the weak batting. There has not been much good practice weather this spring, and on Saturday nearly all the batsmen were stiff in the shoulders and slow on the feet. Still, early or late in the season, a good batsman will reveal his quality by his method whether he makes runs or fails. There was one great batsman on the field in this match. Crawford scored only 18 – the top score of the match – and he was missed quite early on, but in comparison with the rest of the day's cricket what an innings it was! He alone watched the turning ball keenly and knew when and how to go back to the off-breaks, moving the right leg slightly towards the off-stump and hooking the ball to the on just after it had turned. All the other batsmen played at the pitch for the turning ball with a wooden forward stroke, the right leg stiff. Good back play will soon be the main thing to distinguish a great from a merely competent batsman. On Saturday the cricket was much too slow for Crawford, whose natural style is forward. He adapted himself to conditions which must have been totally strange, just like the genius he is.

Not one of the Oldham batsmen showed any out-of-the-way quality, while Overstone, on the Rochdale side, was the only man other than Crawford really to shape. He plays quite straight in his forward strokes to the off, but when going back does not take enough care that his right leg keeps to the line of the ball. At present his forcing shots are distinctly limited.

The bowling was good enough on both sides to take advantage of the wicket. Parkin was hardly at his best; had he been, Oldham might well have found 20 or 30 an impossible score. He varied his pace cleverly, but his length was uncertain. One is indeed getting the impression that Parkin has a tendency to think of bowling rather too much in terms of flight variation and spin, forgetting the importance of length. The best bowler of the day was Leyland, the Oldham professional, whose analysis worked out 18-8-14-5. He was accuracy itself – even Crawford could not drive him. His best ball pitches a perfect length just outside the leg stump and whips across. Were he to sandwich it rather more subtly than he did on Saturday with an off-break, he would be a first-class bowler.

Throughout the afternoon the fielding was admirable, especially in the Rochdale team. Whewell is a brilliant wicket-keeper and Swire a swift and daring field.

LEADER   JULY 11 1928

Ashton St. Mary's v. Dukinfield Wesleyans

It is a great pity that Mr. J. Hughes, who, playing for Ashton St. Mary's against the Dukinfield Wesleyans, took all ten wickets, should have allowed a run to be scored off him. After all, if a thing is worth doing at all it is worth doing well, and nought is a round figure. Perhaps he was stricken with a sudden but sharply repressed access of pity, or perhaps the run was the product of a despairing frenzy in a batsman. Still, a liking for symmetry should not prejudice anyone against Mr. Hughes's achievement; he clearly has a faculty for keeping down the runs, and ten wickets for one is almost certainly a 'record'. If one hints a doubt it is only because the accepted bowling 'records' are much more astonishing than might be supposed. Thus Mr. Hughes took seven wickets with successive balls, and any one of us who did that would reasonably expect to be credited with a 'record'. But he would not be; the omniscient 'Wisden' says that three several people have taken eight wickets in eight balls, and one of them 'bowled down all the ten wickets in twelve balls.' But there is no mention of anyone having taken ten wickets for no runs, though various bowlers have shown themselves dissatisfied with the mere taking of ten wickets, 'W. G.', for instance, 'also scored 104' – a distinction which was denied to Mr. Hughes, as the other side only totalled nine runs – and J. B. King, whom many people will remember as the Philadelphia fast bowler, not only took the ten wickets but had also bowled the not-out man with a no-ball. Mr. Hughes, therefore, might have done better, but the Dukinfield Wesleyans will think that he did well enough.

C. L. R. JAMES   SEPTEMBER 1 1932

Nelson v. Rawtenstall

Sidney Barnes is generally admitted to be the greatest bowler cricket has yet seen. I had a glimpse of him the other day in action. He is fifty-nine years of age (the date of his birth given in Wisden's Almanack is incorrect). Yet the man is still a fine bowler. It was an experience to watch him.

To begin with, Barnes not only is fifty-nine, but looks it. Some cricketers at fifty-nine look and move like men in the thirties. Not so Barnes. You can almost hear the old bones creaking. He is tall and thin, well over six feet, with strong features. It is rather a remarkable face in its way, and could belong to a great lawyer or a statesman without incongruity. He holds his head well back, with the rather long chin lifted. He looks like a man who has seen as much of the world as he wants to see.

I saw him first before the match began, bowling to one of his own side without wickets. He carried his arm over as straight as a post, spinning a leg-break in the orthodox way. Then he had a knock himself. But although the distance was only a dozen yards and the ball was being bowled at a very slow pace, Barnes put a glove on. He was not going to run the risk of those precious fingers being struck by the ball. When the preliminary practice stopped he walked in, by himself, with his head in the air, a man intent on his own affairs.

His own side, Rawtenstall, took the field to get Nelson out. League sides will sometimes treat the new ball with Saturday afternoon carelessness; not so Rawtenstall. Ten of them played about with an old ball: Barnes held the new. He fixed his field, two slips close in and the old-fashioned point, close in. Mid-off was rather wide. When every man was placed to the nearest centimetre Barnes walked back and set the old machinery in motion. As he forced himself to the crease you could see every year of the fifty-nine, but the arm swung over gallantly, high and straight. The wicket was slow, but a ball whipped hot from the pitch in the first over, and second slip took a neat catch. When the over was finished he walked a certain number of steps and took up his position in the slips. He stood as straight as his right arm, with his hands behind his back. The bowler began his run – a long run – Barnes still immovable. Just as the ball was about to be delivered Barnes bent forward slightly with his hands ready in front of him. To go right down as a normal slip fieldsman goes was for him, obviously, a physical impossibility. But he looked alert, and I got the impression that whatever went into his hands would stay there. As the ball reached the wicket-keeper's hands or was played by the batsman, Barnes straightened himself and again put his hands behind his back. That was his procedure in the field right through the afternoon. Now and then by way of variety he would move a leg an inch or two, and point it on the toe for a second or two. Apart from that he husbanded his strength.

He took seven wickets for about thirty runs, and it is impossible to imagine better bowling of its kind. The batsmen opposed to him were not of high rank, most of them, but good bowling is good bowling, whoever plays it. Armistead, a sound batsman, was obviously on his mettle. Barnes kept him playing; then he bowled one of his most dangerous balls – a flighted one, dropping feet shorter without any change of action and, what is so much more dangerous, pitching on the middle wicket and missing the off. Armistead, magnetised into playing forward, had the good sense to keep his right toe firm. The wicket-keeper observed Armistead's toe regretfully, and threw the ball back to Barnes. Up to this time Armistead had relied almost entirely on the back stroke. It had carried him to where he was without mishap. A forward stroke had imperilled his innings. Behold there the elements of a tragedy, obvious, no doubt, but as Mr. Desmond MacCarthy says, the obvious is the crowning glory of art. Armistead played back to the next ball. But he couldn't get his bat to it in time. Barnes hit him hard on the pads, with a straight ball, and the pads were in front of the wicket.

He went from triumph to triumph, aided, no doubt, by the terror of his name. When Constantine came in I looked for a duel. Constantine was not going to be drawn into playing forward. Barnes was not going to bowl short to be hooked over the pavilion or overpitch to be hit into the football field. Constantine also was not going to chance it. For on that turning wicket, to such accurate bowling, who chanced it was lost. Constantine jumped to him once, and a long field picked the ball up from the ground, where it had been from the time it left the bat. Barnes bowled a slow one, that might almost be called short. It pitched on the leg stump. Constantine shaped for the forcing back stroke. The field was open. But even as he raised himself for the stroke he held his hand, and wisely. The ball popped up and turned many inches. Another ball or two, and again Barnes dropped another on the same spot. It was a sore temptation. Constantine shaped again for his stroke, his own stroke, and again he held his hand, wisely, for the ball broke and popped up again. So the pair watched one another, like two fencers sparring for an opening. The crowd sat tense. Was this recitative suddenly to burst into the melody of fours and sixes, to all parts of the field? The Nelson crowd at least hoped so. But it was not to be. Some insignificant trundler at the other end who bowled mediocre balls bowled Constantine with one of them.

After that it was a case of the boa constrictor and the rabbits, the only matter of interest being how long he would take to dispose of them. But nevertheless, old campaigner as he is, Barnes took no chances. Slip would stand on the exact spot where the bowler wanted him, there and nowhere else. When a batsman who had once hit him for two or three fours came in Barnes put two men out immediately. As soon as a single was made, the out-fieldsmen were drawn in again and carefully fixed in their original positions, although the score might be about fifty for eight or something of the kind. Barnes had lived long enough in the world of cricket to know that there at any rate it does not pay to give anything away. Nelson failed to reach 70. As the Rawtenstall team came in the crowd applauded this fine bowling mightily. Barnes walked through it intent on his own affairs. He had had much of that all his life.

Constantine, running seventeen yards and hurling the ball violently through the air, began sending back the Rawtenstall batsmen. One, two, three, wickets and bails flying every time. Forth from the pavilion came Barnes. He faced the West Indian fast bowler. He was older than Constantine's father and the wicket was faster now. Barnes got behind the ball, the pitched-up ball, and played it back along the pitch to the bowler. He judged the ball quickly and so got there in time. He kept his left shoulder forward and that kept the bat straight. He played the slower bowlers with equal skill, and whenever there was a single to be taken he took it. He never lost one, and he was in difficulties to get into his crease once only. 'Yes' and 'No' he said decisively in a deep voice which could be heard all over the ground. His bones were too stiff to force the ball away. But his bat swung true to the drive and he got over the short ball to cut. He stayed there some forty minutes for ten, and as long as he was there his side was winning. But Constantine bowled him behind his back. Barnes satisfied himself that he was out, and then he left the crease. He came in slowly amidst the plaudits of the Nelson crowd, applauding his innings and their satisfaction at his having been dismissed. Courtesy acknowledged the applause. For the rest he continued as he had begun, a man unconsciously scornful of his milieu. After he left Rawtenstall collapsed.

Since then Barnes has taken five for a few and startled Lancashire a few days ago by taking nine for twenty. In the years to come it will be something to say that we have seen him.

DON DAVIES   JULY 24 1943

Eagley v. Westhoughton

Recently my eyes beheld the most historic piece of cricket turf in the Bolton district – if not, indeed, in the whole of Lancashire – the ground of the Eagley Cricket Club. Few villages can claim to have played on the same patch of earth for upwards of one hundred years or trace the playing services of the same families through as many as four generations. Village pride is reflected in the richness of the turf, the excellence of the wicket, and the aspect of the pavilion, whose smooth green plots and whitened curbs give it the trim natty air of a coastguard station. During the war all work on this ground, of whatever nature and complexity, is wrought by the sweat and devotion of members.

The Eagley club was 'founded by resident gentry' in 1837. Photographs of the time show cricketers wearing black bowler hats jammed down on faces fringed with whiskers, neat bow ties, stiff collars, white shirts with red spots, tight white trousers, and brown shoes. The ethics of the game, it seems, were as arresting as the costumes. Early records of the Eagley club reveal that on at least three occasions shameful defeat was only narrowly averted by the outbreak of a tumult which successfully held up the fall of the last wicket, dented a few score bowlers, and brought the unsatisfactory proceedings to a close. No one knows where the umpires hid. Players and spectators in the good old days set out to fight for victory and were not ashamed to admit it. Much as old Sam Rigby once described the ending of a final match in the Sunday School Social League Medal Competition.

Bowler (wrathfully): 'Heaw's that?'

Umpire (gleefully): 'E's eawt! (triumphantly) An' we'n won th' medals! (then, plucking up a stump and brandishing it) An' if onnybody comes near me Ah'll spile 'is face!'

'Fight to the last ditch' was always the Eagley tradition, especially in that golden period from 1901 to 1914 when the club reached the Cross Cup final ten times in fourteen seasons, carried off the cup seven times (five times in succession), achieved the cup and championship double twice, and the championship three times. For a parallel ascendancy, on a higher plane, one must turn to the Yorkshire eleven of the Hirst, Rhodes, Haigh era, round about 1900.

Eagley had three remarkable characters – Herbert Thewlis, profes-

114

sional, from Lascelles Hall, 'Joss' Nuttall, opening batsman, and Walter Warburton, prince of all cup-fighters. Thewlis played only two seasons, but he left behind at Eagley a reputation for stroke-play that can still conjure up glowing comparisons and legendary tales. 'Joss' Nuttall typified the obstinacy of the Eagley make-up. He was probably the quietest cricketer who ever played, excluding only deaf mutes. He stood on guard like a graven image, patient, imperturbable, inscrutable; a heart-breaking stonewaller, yet quick to exploit profitable leg-strokes or a neat chop through the slips. He never flinched from punishment, and, being always ready to interpose his body between his wicket and the foe was a frequent sufferer from lbw. 'Joss's' end was in keeping. He died on the boundary's edge at Eagley as he was being wheeled away, a faithful follower to the last.

Hopeful of meeting Warburton again, the 'bonniest fechter' of them all, I went out to watch the Eagley v. Westhoughton match last Saturday, and there was the dark-eyed, silver-haired old crusader scoring for Eagley. Together we sat out the ordeal – for ordeal it was. Since the batsmen on both sides – Farrimond excepted – were disposed to treat all bowling as though spun from the subtle fingers of an O'Reilly, there was plenty of time for Warburton to attend to the mysteries of scoring and at the same time deliver himself of some trenchant observations on modern batting. The Eagley knock in particular supplied him with a magnificent text. 'Such flounderin abeawt!' he moaned. 'It fair gets on mi nerves.' 'Nerves! Nerves!' put in a former league captain and a lifelong enthusiast. 'First time Ah ivver knew tha' 'ad onny. Doesn't tha recollect thi'sen scorin' 315 runs i' three successive cup finals for twice eawt? When tha' 'ad a bat i' thi' ond, owd trayele-pot, tha' were feart o' noather mon nor boggart.'

Banter like this was a godsend. It enabled Eagley's old warrior to live again his glorious yesterdays and forget for a while the shameful present. Until, that is to say, some streaker off the edge woke up the scoring mechanism again, when note was duly taken that, in response to 'Howfun's' score of 144 for six, Eagley in an hour's time had gleaned no more than 27 pinched and miserable runs towards the 92 for four which they finally got. Talk veered to the hidden springs of batsmanship: the tactical ideas that govern method, 'Clout thi fust ba' for fower wur my motto,' said Warburton, 'an' keep on cloutin' chuzeaw tha con. Ne'er let bowler get at thi. Once tha's getten 'im as 'e dursna pitch 'em up an' 'e dursna poo 'em short tha'rt landed,' which would not be a bad precept for some present-day Eagley batsmen to follow. And in passing be it said that two of Warburton's prominent contemporaries, V. T. Trumper and A. C. MacLaren, held precisely similar views in higher spheres.

ALISTAIR COOKE AT CAMBRIDGE, MASS.   MAY 21 1951

Harvard v. Yale

The rivalry of Yale and Harvard is going into its third century and has been bloodied down the years by many a student riot and pitched battle on each other's campus, to say nothing of the more routine muscle-matching of football games.

By the end of the last century the typical Yale man had evolved into a human type as recognisable as a Cossack or the Pitcairn skull, and there was a tense period in the late twenties and early thirties when Harvard could no longer bear close proximity with these well-developed anthropoids and primly refused to play them at anything. The football and chess fixtures were summarily cancelled. But by now even a Harvard man has heard of 'one world', though of course he recognises no obligation to belong to it. So to-day, in a wild lunge of global goodwill, Harvard recalled the sons of Elihu Yale to their common heritage by suggesting a revival of the ancient joust known as cricket.

Not for 44 years have Yale and Harvard together attempted anything so whimsical. But a far-sighted alumnus lately gave $100 to revive the match and encourage Harvard men to learn how the other half lives. Accordingly, with this bequest, pads and bats were fetched from Bermuda and Canada and a roll of coconut matting was bought wholesale in Philadelphia. These props were assembled to-day on Smith Field, which is a dandelion enclosure lying west of the Harvard football stadium.

Here at 1.30 in the afternoon came ten of the visiting Yale men, various sets of white and grey gentlemen's pantings, a score-book and a couple of blazers for the sake of morale. Fifteen minutes later, and two hundred yards away, the Harvard team arrived in two old Chevrolets and a Cadillac. They carried the matting out to a weedy air-strip devoid of dandelions; stretched it out and pegged it down; made Indian signs at the glowering Yale men and, discovering that they understood English, formally challenged them to a match; spun a dime, won, and chose to go in first.

The eleventh Yale man was still missing and the Harvard captain, a mellifluous-spoken gentleman from Jamaica, offered to lend them a Harvard man. The Yale captain suspected a trap and said they would wait. Ten minutes later the eleventh man came puffing in, swinging from elm to elm. Everything was set. It was a cloudless day. It had been 92 the day before, but Providence obliged with a 35-degree drop overnight and we nestled down into a perfect English May day – sunny and green, with a brisk wind. The eleven spectators stomped and blew on their hands at the field's edge. And the game began.

Mr. Conboy and Mr. Cheek put on the purchased pads. Conboy took centre and faced the high lobbing off breaks of Mr. Foster, who delivered six of these nifties and was about to deliver a seventh but saw

116

that Mr. Cheek had turned his back and was off on a stroll around the wicket. This mystery turned into a midfield conference at which it was found out that Yale expected to play an eight-ball over and Harvard a six. An Englishman on the Harvard side kindly acquainted the Yale men with the later history of cricket, and they settled for a six-ball over.

This shrewd act of gamesmanship effectively rattled the Harvard team for a while, and Conboy was soon out for three and Cheek for a duck. But Frank Davies, from Trinidad, knew a sophisticated ploy that shortly demoralised the Yale men. He came in slowly, hefted his pads, squinted at the coconut matting, patted it, rubbed his right shoulder, exercised his arm, and while the Yale men were still waiting for him to get set, started to cut and drive the Yale bowling (sic) all over the field.

Yale retorted by occasionally bowling an over of seven balls and once an over of five. It had no effect. They were now thoroughly cowed by Davies's professional air – once he cleverly feigned a muscle spasm and had the Yale side clustered round him terrified at the prospect of a doctor's bill. They were so trembly by now that they thought it only decent to drop any fly ball that came their way. Davies hooked a ball high to leg, but the Yale man obligingly stumbled, pawed the air, and gave a masterly – and entirely successful – performance of a man missing an easy catch.

Davies tried another hook with the same result, but the agreement was now so firmly understood that no Yale man would hold anything. Davies accordingly cut with flashing elbows, secure in the new-found knowledge that considered as a slip fielder a Yale man is a superlative bridge player. Davies went on to cut fine and cut square and drive the ball several times crack against the cement wall on which two mystified little boys were sitting. This, it was decided, was a boundary, and the scorer was told to put down four runs.

Davies did some more shrugs and lunges with his shoulder-blades, and, though there was a fairly constant trickle of batting partners at the other end, Davies had scored never less than two-thirds of the total. Suddenly he let go with a clean drive to mid-on for two and the astonished scorer discovered that the total was now 68 and Davies had reached his half-century.

There had been so far a regrettable absence of English spirit but Bruce Cheek, a civil servant, formerly of Peterhouse, Cambridge, was signed up to repair this omission by shouting 'Well played, sir!' – an utterly alien sound to the two Boston small fry on the cement wall. This cued the growing crowd to rise and applaud the incomparable Davies. All fourteen of them joined in the ovation.

Ten minutes later the Rev. Bill Baker, a Baptist from Manchester, went in to receive his baptism of fire from Foster, who had suddenly found his off-break again. The result was that Mr. Baker was walking back right after walking out. Then Davies hit a short ball into a Yale man's hands. He failed to drop it in time. And the whole side was out. Harvard 102 – Davies 70.

The two small fry dropped off the cement wall and came into the field to investigate the ritual. One of them stayed in the outfield and the tougher one came on and asked a question of the retreating umpire. It was a simple question. It was: 'What game you playin', mister?' He was told, and turned round and bawled: 'Cricket!' at his pal. The pal shrugged his little shoulders and went off and picked up two Boston terriers from somewhere, for no reason that anyone discovered then or since. They did manage to invade the field during the Yale innings and had to be shooed off.

Meanwhile we had taken tea, from a vacuumatic container about the size of a city gas tank. From nowhere a parson arrived, wearing an old straw cadie. It was a heart-warming sight, and I found myself mumbling through a tear the never-to-be-forgotten lines '. . . some corner of a foreign field that is forever Lipton's.'

With a knightliness that cannot be too highly praised, Yale maintained the dogged pretence that they were playing cricket. It entailed their going out to the matting and back again in a slow though spasmodic procession. The continuity of this parade was assured by one Jehingar Mugaseth, a dark supple young man from Bombay, who had one of those long, beautiful, unwinding runs that would have petrified even the nonchalant Mr. Davies. At the other end was a thin, blond man with another long run, an American who distrusted breaks but managed a corkscrew baseball swerve in mid-air.

Between them the Yale team fell apart, and your reporter had no sooner looked down to mark 'McIntosh caught' than he looked up to see Allen's middle stump sailing like a floating coffin past the wicketkeeper's right ear. Yale were suddenly all out – for 34. They followed on, more briskly this time – they were catching on to the essential tempo of the game – and were out the second time in record time for 24 runs. It was all over at 6.40.

No excuses were offered from the Yale team. They had fine English names – such as Grant, West, Allen, Foster, Parker, and Norton – and true to the Old Country traditions they lost magnificently. Nobody mentioned the mean Colonial skill recruited by the Harvard side. Nobody, that is, except a Yale man who dictated to me the exact tribal composition of the Harvard team: one Indian, one Jamaican, one Australian, one Egyptian, one Argentinian, one from Trinidad, one from Barbados, a Swiss New Yorker, two Englishmen, and a stranger from Connecticut.

But after all it's not the winning that matters, is it? Or is it? It's – to coin a word – the amenities that count: the smell of the dandelions, the puff of the pipe, the click of the bat (when Harvard are batting), the rain on the neck, the chill down the spine, the slow, exquisite coming on of sunset and dinner and rheumatism.

Colne v. Bacup

In the lovely rolling country between Pendle Forest and Boulsworth Hill, where the Colne cricket field lies, a trick of the weather made possible as much as three and a half hours uninterrupted cricket on Saturday afternoon, some of it in warm sunshine, even, and with white fleecy clouds scudding across a blue sky. Yet the trail to the cricket field has been through a region, sodden and desolate, where rain water splashed and gurgled and spouted at every turn.

Colne, with the assistance of their brilliant Australian cricketing adventurer, Alley, got rid of Bacup in 2¼ hours for a beggarly 114 runs and that in spite of the presence in the Bacup side of a twine-toed stockily built West Indian run-getter easily identified as Weekes. In reply Colne lost Alley quickly, to the intense chagrin of his followers whose advance publicity had prepared us for something much more enlivening than one four and seven singles. But a portly gentleman named Parrington pressed on, laying about him with one eye on the lowering sky and the other on the bright smile with which the goddess of fortune was encouraging his efforts. After several amusing escapes, which turned Weekes's eyes up into his head so that the whites were visible from the ring, Parrington fell for a brisk 42. Three others fell with him for the addition of only two more; and the match was thus poised – 27 needed, four wickets to fall, and 25 minutes remaining for play – when the storm broke with a weight and persistence there was no gainsaying.

The joy of the Colne supporter in the beauty of his field's surroundings is rivalled only by his pride in its draining qualities. Only half an hour's delay was necessary on Saturday to enable the groundsman and a small ad hoc committee to prepare an auxiliary wicket just off the middle and the match was going ding-swing, with Alley bowling steadily downhill at one end and Nutter getting plenty of lift from the turf and the slope at the other. It was Nutter's lift which gave Bacup their first and biggest headache; for after Dunham had departed with a prize duck which it had taken him twenty minutes to hatch, Weekes arrived, after his manner is, as though treading on hot cinders.

As Weekes tapped his first ball to the off for a single we smiled in anticipation of the riot of run-getting before us; this fecund Jamaican requires only a further 64 runs to give him his thousand for the season: but Nutter had other ideas. It takes good bowling to make a cricket match as well as good batting: and before we had realised quite what was happening a spinning ball of perfect length had lured Weekes forward, risen sharply, tickled his glove, and fallen gently into Alley's safe hands at slip. From this point onwards Alley took over from Nutter. The next five wickets were his, all the result of superbly controlled length bowling. Whether or not it was Alley's best bowling effort since joining the club is no matter: what remains certain is that something in its steadiness, its whip off the pitch, and its relentless pitching on a spot no bigger than a dinner plate stirred up a few nostalgic memories of that prince of all fast-medium bowlers, Tate.

Why Alley himself, a batsman of world rank, should throw his own wicket away to a ball of no particular distinction soon after the start of the Colne innings is one of those puzzles which make of cricket the alluring and incalculable game it is. Bradshaw, the Colne captain, had departed almost immediately, thus leaving Alley plenty of latitude and scope in which to demonstrate his art and at the same time win the match. But, after having thrashed an upstart half-volley through the covers and having placed seven leisurely singles at will, he seemed to lose all sense of responsibility and lashed wildly at a shortish ball from Jones as though his place in the batting order had suddenly reverted to one above the roller. The resulting dolly catch to mid-on was a painful anti-climax.

With the dismissal of Alley the Bacup players perked up visibly and interest now centred on how long Parrington, for Colne, could continue swinging his bat at everything in the slightest degree pitched up without falling into the traps which Weekes was so obviously preparing for him. Some instinct perhaps told Parrington that this was his lucky day, for though he was missed at second slip off Jones and was beaten twice by teasers from Weekes which grazed the bails, not to mention a farcical escape from stumping, he went on undeterred. By the time he had sold his wicket for 42 highly speculative runs he had given his side a reasonable chance of victory. But others had caught his craze for living dangerously too. Ingham, for one, quite needlessly ran himself out, and so, with six wickets down for 88, Dickinson and Wilson were rightly leaning to caution rather than daring when the rain came and – as one neutral observantly put it – 'saved both sides.'

NORMAN SHRAPNEL   JUNE 27 1955

Over Peover v. Chelford

If village cricket is not what it was, it has certainly not lost its modesty. What club, entitled to call itself Peover Superior, would otherwise be content, as this one is, with the colloquial Over Peover? Yet the traditional pattern has certainly been shaken up a little, as was evident at the local Derby in Cheshire on Saturday.

Beneath the ass-head banner of the Mainwarings, who, lived here for close on a thousand years, on a field where General Patton was watching his boys play baseball not so long ago, the village team was beaten by its great rivals from Chelford. A chauffeur led the home side. The visitors, aiming fantastically higher in distance and speed, were captained by a distinguished radio-astronomer. The Mainwaring ass-head might have been thought to droop a little, and the family motto ('Devant si je puis') to hide itself in a fold, at the sight of this lithe expert in cosmic rays looking, in his striped cap, like a highly senior member of a Science Sixth, thoroughly capable of hitting scientific sixes.

What Chelford won by was not, as it turned out, astronomical: a mere 46 runs, and in the last five minutes. 'We'd have slaughtered 'em on the old ground,' an elderly spectator was saying; he referred to the one that was ploughed up in the war, about the time the bomb fell on the farm where the club's equipment was stored.

The present ground would seem to have compensating virtues. It is beautiful; it is rent-free; it is even – to the surprise, no doubt, of all properly trained in the lore of English village cricket – flat. It would take more than a war, more even than General Patton's baseball boys, to kill cricket in Over Peover. An old army hut was bought for a song, a veranda made of sawn-up railway sleepers and abandoned telegraph poles was nailed on the front, a small kitchen and some water were provided for the ladies' tea committee, and the new age was born.

Much, to-day, was as it had always been. Ringed by the vast circle of mown hay, over which cows gazed, were the scarlet caps of crouching fielders like poppies among the daisies. The creaking birds, the rumbling lorries, and now the screaming jet-planes; the rhythm to this counterpoint was provided by George the score-boy, clashing his numbered plates as he hung them on their nails. The fast bowler – a scowl, seven strides, and a leap. The slow bowler – two walking and four trotting paces, a hop, and a cunning look suggesting that his mind was on something else. The fielding eager with overthrows. A short boundary on one side bringing four for a tap; so distant a one on the other that the lustiest clout was lucky to get there.

Much was obviously different. The spectators, for the most passionate match of the year, were a mere handful. This could not be wondered at, when the humblest and most remote cottager is able to twist a knob and bring Evans leaping or Trueman pounding before him. Making ends meet – with costs always rising, and vice-presidents admitting to no increase in wealth – must be a painful problem for most village clubs.

Here they are highly resourceful in the way of special efforts and unconventional attractions like the six-a-side tournament which has its final on Wednesday. This knocks tradition right out of the ground. Each player except the wicketkeeper bowls one over, and the winner is the team scoring most runs in the five overs, irrespective of the number of wickets lost.

Sixteen local clubs are taking part. A match lasts about forty minutes, and three can be got into an evening's play. The impatient villagers, avid for sensationalism, like it. They even pay. A collecting-box is circulated, and, according to the treasurer, an evening of six-a-side can be 'quite a nice money-raiser'.

But to-day we were back in the older cricketing world of morals, manners, and Mainwarings, which meant something a good deal less than 50 runs an hour. The distinguished radio-astronomer – whose side, unlike the more strictly local Over Peoverites, was buttressed with foreigners from places as far afield as Didsbury, Jodrell Bank, and Australia – looked serenely at George's creeping arithmetic and confessed that Chelford were usually happy if they had 120 on the board. A wicket fell. Sometimes, added the distinguished radio-astronomer less serenely, one was able to win with as little as 80 on the board.

Chelford's chief hitter, reputed to have made sixty in twenty minutes the other day, peeled off his sweater, hit a brisk two, and at the next ball was marvelling at his fallen bails. Four more wickets fell for the subsequent seven runs. The radio-astronomer assumed a cosmic expression and strode off to put on his pads. But then there was a stand that carried the afternoon to tea and declaration, so that he did not bat after all.

MICHAEL PARKIN   JUNE 18 1976

Green Hammerton v. Headingley Broomfield

It was a true Yorkshire innings. The village team from Green Hammerton, near York, set to get 181 to win, were facing defeat at 14 for 8 wickets. Tom Bell, Green Hammerton's number 10, joined the not out batsman, Ken Kershaw, the village postman, and scored a single.

The two batsmen then met in the middle. Yorkshiremen waste no words in moments of crisis. 'What we doing?' asked Tom, 'We're stopping,' said Ken. 'Right,' said Tom.

And that was that. It was 6.15 pm and the match was due to end at 7.30.

Asked what happened then, Tom Bell said yesterday: 'Well, we just put our heads down and we stopped.' The two stone-walled through 33 maiden overs. Their despairing opponents, Headingley Broomfield, of Leeds, managed to get Kershaw out off the fifth ball of the 34th over of the partnership.

In walked Mark Williams, the last man. Tom, still set on stopping, tried to keep the bowling by lofting a single over the bowler's head, but was caught and bowled by Z. Ali. This gave Ali figures of 14 overs, 14 maidens, and one wicket. Green Hammerton had not quite stopped long enough to secure a draw. Their last wicket had fallen with only two minutes playing time left.

The last run scored by Green Hammerton was the single from Tom Bell before he began stopping. In the whole innings Headingley Broomfield bowled 288 balls and runs were scored from only eight of them. It was an innings of which Yorkshire legends are made.

MICHAEL PARKIN   JUNE 8 1978

Calder Grove v. Upper Hopton

A cricket club which used the mighty West Indian Test player Collis King to beat a village team – he hit 94, took five wickets, made two catches and ran one man out – has been fined £1 and has had to forfeit the match.

Collis King was invited to play for the Calder Grove team, of Wakefield, when he was staying with a club member. Mr. Brian Sykes, Calder Grove's representative on the Dewsbury and District League, said: 'We thought his presence would stimulate interest in the club and the league.'

It certainly did that. The village team from Upper Hopton, near Huddersfield, was nonplussed when it arrived at Calder Grove's ground and was told that the 'C. King' on the batting order was none other than Collis King, a member of Kerry Packer's cricket circus.

A spectator at the match, Mr. Alan Brook, captain of Upper Hopton's second eleven, said the village team captain said immediately that an objection would be lodged, win or lose. King went in to bat at number 5, was dropped when he was 14, and proceeded to maul the bowling. He was finally bowled by a yorker from Brian Foster, a medium pace bowler.

His 94 was half of Calder Grove's total of 188. When Upper Hopton batted King did not bowl at his full, awesome pace, but he was still fast enough for village players. Mr. Brook said that only one batsman could cope with him. Roy Ellam, a man well into his forties, smashed the second ball he received from King straight past the bowler's right ear and went on to make 53, most of the runs coming from King.

But Upper Hopton were beaten by about 80 runs. On hearing the objection the league executive committee fined Calder Grove £1 for fielding an ineligible player and reversed the match result. The committee reminded Calder Grove that it had power to deal with questions not provided for in the rules.

The last word must go to Upper Hopton. Mr. Brook said: 'Calder Grove's ground is a dump, not a patch on ours. It has no gent's lavatory.'

ONE-DAYS

DENYS ROWBOTHAM AT LORD'S   SEPTEMBER 5 1966

Warwickshire v. Worcestershire

Before the customary packed house prepared to cheer anything, Warwickshire won the Gillette Cup final at Lord's on Saturday by beating Worcestershire by five wickets with three overs to spare. In fact there was little to cheer. This was not only a tired and sedate match, but at times an exceptionally silly one.

Ironically it was Warwickshire, the victors, who perpetrated the day's most stupid 40 minutes. These followed their taking seven Worcestershire wickets for 104 runs in 49 overs. In reaching this highly enviable position M. J. K. Smith had run Cartwright, Bannister and Webster out of overs and Brown had only three left. Worcestershire's scoring rating was barely more than 2.1 an over and to support Gifford's efforts to improve it there remained only Brain, Flavell and Coldwell.

If ever there was a time for leg breaks pitched on or outside the off stump to bring an innings summarily to conclusion this surely was it. Yet what did Smith do? He brought on Barber to attack at medium pace with the seam. For him and, Brown's stint done, Ibadulla he also set six deeps and three half deeps while the wicketkeeper stood back. Warwickshire's tactical object could not have been clearer. They were prepared to settle for a Worcestershire total of approximately 150 rather than to try to dismiss them for 30 to 40 runs fewer. A fine team leader, Smith remains an incorrigible field captain.

Thankfully for the dark moods of those who still believe in the chivalrous challenge and aggressiveness of cricket Gifford treated these stratagems with the contempt they deserved. He and Brain survived the last of Brown circumspectly – scoring only five runs off seven overs in the process. Then, in no possible danger of being stumped, Gifford advanced gleefully as any schoolboy to drive. Barber and Ibadulla were lofted for sixes, off driven superbly, and swung to midwicket.

Twos and threes were scampered with the gayest abandon and 43 of an eighth wicket stand of 50 came in under seven overs. P. B. H. May awarded Barber the match prize for a disciplined innings. My own choice would have been Gifford for mocking this competition's acquired idiocy and attempting to restore cricket to sanity.

The rest of the game hardly merits comment. A pitch helpful to seam bowling from which the ball also tended to keep low suited Warwickshire's stereo-typed nonspin attack to a nicety, particularly Cartwright, who these last weeks has bowled with the controlled flight and pace variation which distinguished his early performances in South Africa. Worcestershire's batsmen, wisely determined first of all to establish themselves but doubtless weary from their last exertions in the championship, had to press, each in turn, just too much.

Graveney excepted, indeed, all got themselves out. Kenyon, attempting to force, hit his stumps. Horton and Richardson drove and missed. D'Oliveira hit disastrously to leg. Ormrod tried one thin glance too many. Graveney, brilliantly caught off bat and pad by Ibadulla at forward short leg, was well beaten by a ball deceptively flighted which cut into him. He was Cartwright's clinching and doubtless proudest victim. At 104 for seven Worcestershire were ostensibly finished. Gifford did his best with injections. The corpse was beyond recollection.

All that Warwickshire required was sobriety rather than swashbuckle from Barber. He provided it. Amiss supported him with the mature resource and judgement that England this season have recognised. A period of stagnation during which M. J. K. Smith and Jameson managed only eight runs from eight overs might have bubbled into final excitement if Graveney had caught a drive edged by A. C. Smith high to square leg when 18 were needed from seven overs. For once Graveney fumbled, however, and two effective blows by the reprieved reduced the last rites to formality. Full house or no, it was all very much second class cricket.

Worcestershire 155 for 8, 60 overs; Warwickshire 159 for 5, 56.4 overs (R. W. Barber 66). Warwickshire won by five wickets.

BRIAN CHAPMAN IN MELBOURNE   JANUARY 6 1971

Australians v. MCC

The first truly international one-day match in cricket history proved to be a memorable occasion indeed. England's know-how had been tipped to get them home against opponents less wise in the tricks of the one-day trade, but the tremendous fire-power of the uninhibited Australian batting carried them to a comfortable victory by five wickets in the thirty-fifth of 40 eight-ball overs.

A crowd of more than 46,000, starved of sun and sport these past 10 days, basked along the stands and galleries of this immense stadium to cheer on the champions of Australia and England alike. That is, by the way, 4,000 higher than the entire attendance at the five-day Brisbane

Test match. They watched some excellent and exciting cricket and took this new form of gladiatorial contest to their hearts.

There can be no doubt that pitting the two sides together by accident as it were to compensate for the rained out Test will start off a chain reaction. Colleagues bombarded me with questions, stimulated no doubt by their editors, about the finer points of the cup and Sunday League games in England. Room must certainly be found for repeat performances when England are here in 1974, probably in place of up-country fixtures that are an unwanted anachronism. It would be no bad idea to start thinking on the same lines for Australia's visit to England during the summer after next.

England experienced another setback in the fate of Edrich. He was awarded the man of the match prize by Charlie Elliott, here on a mission to further the cause of good umpiring, for an innings of 82, which alone made a match of it. But towards its close he appeared to stumble when completing a run and limped painfully. Soon after he was caught at fine leg an appeal went out for a doctor to go to the dressing room and he took a somewhat serious view of a damaged tendon in Edrich's left leg. The calf was badly swollen and he thought Edrich might have to rest for 10 days.

This would rule him out of the fourth Test on Saturday, but as the team flew in this evening to Sydney he reported that the leg was feeling easier and he had every hope that examination by a specialist would be more favourable. Even so, this development adds worries to a team that has not taken too kindly to an extra Test and to the care of a captain who has asked that Greig, of Sussex, should stand by in case a fast bowler breaks down. Fortunately, Luckhurst's broken thumb is mended though he did not risk it today. Edrich is easily top of the Test averages with innings of 79, 47, and 115 not out, and his sturdy, resolute batting would be gravely missed. Others next in line like Cowdrey, Fletcher and Hampshire still find form elusive, and the manager, David Clark, must be turning over in his mind the possibility of a top-class batting replacement if Edrich or another leading player has to drop out in the strenuous programme just ahead.

Today England were put in by Lawry, captain in only his second one-day game. He learned quickly and soon disposed a widespread field customary on these occasions. He set an example by diving sharply in catching a full-blooded hook from Boycott, but Edrich found a lively and punishing pace, especially against Connolly, a case of Surrey admonishing Middlesex.

Fletcher too was in temporary command of his best strokes until Greg Chappell, a cricketer who seemingly can do nothing wrong, held a stunning catch running back towards the rails. Chappell's brother, Ian, shared the family honours by running out D'Oliveira when the batsmen clearly thought his vicious cut was booked for four runs. He, not the fieldsman, was left standing. England's cause had prospect, its run rate lifted to 50 in seven overs. Now it fell to pieces, the last seven wickets falling for 46. Spinners in Britain, a despised breed in one-day cricket, can take heart that Mallett and Stackpole shared six wickets. Illingworth too was destined to capture three.

By Gillette standards 190 is a useful but not decisive total and, on a pitch marvellously recovered, it proved inadequate. Perhaps Australia had not heard of such cunning devices as 'timing your rate', for they went off at a fair pace from the start. Walters drove with thudding power against Illingworth. Lever dropped a hard chance in front of the screen while Walters completed six fours in succession. Walters was caught at the wicket for 41 and the runs dwindled until Ian Chappell applied the spurs in hitting 17 in one over from D'Oliveira. Chappell was stumped at 60 in essaying a big hit against Illingworth, but lethal damage had been inflicted and brother Greg stormed home with a salvo of pulls against Shuttleworth.

MCC 190, 39.4 overs (J. H. Edrich 82); Australians 191, 34.6 overs (I. M. Chappell 60).

ERIC TODD AT OLD TRAFFORD   JULY 29 1971

Lancashire v. Gloucestershire

It was just short of nine o'clock and the street lights were going on all round Old Trafford last night when Jack Bond took a single off Procter, and Lancashire, the holders, had beaten Gloucestershire by three wickets in their Gillette Cup semi-final.

Consider the situation. The light was fading fast; a special train scheduled to carry visiting supporters back home – it was due to leave Warwick Road at 8.30 – had been and gone, presumably to wait in the wilds of Cheshire; several schoolboys who had been instructed earlier to join the main party outside the gates had not reported to their leader (and no wonder). And Lancashire with five overs and three wickets left needed 25 to win. Mortimore bowled from the Stretford end and David Hughes hit him for six, four, two, two, four, six. Lancashire were level. Bond made the decisive hit in the fifty-seventh over and that was that.

The scenes outside and inside the ground would have revived the flagging spirits of any county treasurer. The gates were closed half an hour after the start and at 6 o'clock it was announced that the official attendance was 23,520 with receipts £9,738.

The game began at 11 o'clock after Gloucester had won the toss but it did not really get under way until noon. Green and Nicholls were embarrassed as much by the accurate bowling of Lever and Shuttleworth as they were by the incoming hordes walking in front of the sight screen at the Stretford end.

Green departed at 57. He played a ball from Simmons to wide mid-on and called for what would have been a safe single if the fielder in the area had been anyone in the world except Clive Lloyd. Lloyd swooped on to the ball and hit the stumps with his throw while Green still was some distance from safety. At lunch Gloucester were 83 for 1.

Heavy rain delayed the resumption by an hour and then Nicholls, having completed an admirable half century, played over a yorker from Simmons at 87. Knight stroked the ball beautifully past cover and midwicket before being well caught by Lever at long leg at 113. The Falstaffian figure of Shepherd caused little trouble and in the 49th over Gloucester were 150 for 4.

Procter had – for him – begun almost suspiciously and he had made only 20 when Wood dropped him at slip off Simmons, an escape he celebrated with a pulled 6 in the same over. Lancashire inevitably were made to suffer as Procter carved the bowling to the far corners of the field. He reached 50 in 71 minutes and shortly afterwards he pulled a ball from Shuttleworth to deep fine leg and the hapless Wood dropped it.

At 201, however, Procter glanced Lever, and Engineer, diving to his left, took a wonderful catch low down in his left glove. If any fielder appealed other than Engineer I did not hear him. Which was not surprising. Such catches are hard to believe. Brown skied a ball so high down the wicket at 210 that Engineer had ample time to run through and catch it, and the innings ended in a flurry of good looking drives from Bissex.

In view of their slow start – 80 from the first 30 overs – Gloucester had every reason to be satisfied with their total of 229 for six.

The light was better than it had been all day when Lancashire set out on their own innings. And there were fewer distractions – if one dare exclude Procter's hostility and Davey's accuracy which contained David Lloyd and Wood to 13 in 10 overs. When Knight and Mortimore took over the bowling, they conceded 17 runs in two overs, Wood's hits including a four, all run, for a cut off Mortimore.

With Procter out of the way, the opening partnership flourished and the spectators were treated to a masterful exhibition of how to run between wickets. The 50 was reached in the seventeenth over and everything was going splendidly for Lancashire until Brown relieved Mortimore and had Lloyd lbw at 61. Brown bowled Pilling in the thirty-second over after 44 had been put on, and responsibility weighed heavily on Clive Lloyd.

Gloucester's reply was to reintroduce Procter whom Lloyd hooked and drove for 4, 4, 2, 4, 2, off successive deliveries. The last ball of this over was a bumper. Lloyd took evasive action and Wood called his partner for a single. But Meyer threw down the wicket and Wood, his conscience mollified if not entirely satisfied, was run out for a brave 50.

Sullivan wasted no time in playing himself in. He pulled Mortimore high to the square leg boundary where Procter caught the ball but lost his balance and fell into the small boys round the boundary edge where, incidentally, they frequently impeded fieldsmen trying to cut off fours.

And that was a six for Sullivan who was bowled in the forty-third over. Worse was to come. Clive Lloyd, trying to hit Mortimore out of sight, failed to connect and was bowled in the forty-fourth over at 160; in the forty-sixth Engineer slipped while attempting a drive and his back foot dislodged the bails. 163 for 6.

Dusk was falling fast when Simmons joined Bond but Simmons could see well enough to hit a six over long-on off Mortimore. Procter was recalled and after one delivery the umpires conferred, but Procter was allowed to continue although goodness only knows he must be difficult enough to follow in broad daylight let alone in semi-darkness. Mortimore eventually bowled Simmons at 203 after he had contributed 25 in deplorable conditions. And so to the grand finale and Lancashire's wonderful victory.

At the end Hughes and Bond fled from their admirers as if for their very lives while the crowd gave Don Kenyon sufficient time and silence in which to announce David Hughes as his choice for the man of the match award.

Gloucestershire 229 for 6, 60 overs (M. J. Procter 65, R. B. Nicholls 53); Lancashire 230 for 7, 56.5 overs (B. Wood 50). Lancashire won by three wickets.

To the editor   JULY 31 1971

Sir, – 'It was just short of nine o'clock and the street lights were going on all round Old Trafford. . . .' This before a crowd of 23,520 and with 459 runs scored in a single day.

I understand that there is a similar game played at Lord's where only 100 runs may be scored in a day before a mere sprinkling of onlookers and the players insist on coming off the field when a cloud passes over the sun in broad daylight.

Is there any known connection between the two? – Yours sincerely,
                                Peter Ecker.
18 Mount Street,
Breaston,
Derby.

Lancashire v. Kent

The best of all Gillette Cup finals was decided by Jack Bond's brilliant catch at extra cover to end the superb innings with which Asif was winning the match for Kent. Nothing could have been more appropriate than Lancashire retaining the Cup through the man whose dedication, perception and direction have lifted them from their deepest trough to the peak of the newest form of cricket.

Lancashire's win, by 24 runs, was the closest, apart from the first in the series, of the nine finals; and it was yet another measure of their aptitude for this form of the game, their splendid outcricket and their tenacity at the pinch.

The appeal of this match is now established beyond all question; it is a matter of technical and temperamental tightrope walking for the players: fervour and favours for their supporters. All tickets except the 5,000 each for the finalists were sold a month before the semi-finals. The weather once more held good and Lord's did their part with an honest, flat wicket, better for batsmen than bowlers but, importantly, uniform. Even the dropping of four catches – two a side – did not impair a pattern of glorious fielding.

Teams who succeed in the over-limit game have the capacity to recover from early batting failure and to create a winning score from the lower half of their batting. This was the ability Lancashire displayed. Bond had no doubts about batting when he won the toss; freak weather apart, it is invariably the best policy in this cricket. Dye, whom Kent unexpectedly preferred to Graham, had Wood lbw with the second ball of the day; Asif at the opposite end began with five maidens. Lancashire pulled themselves up painfully to four in six overs. Pilling alternated neat strokes with uncertainties until he too was lbw to Dye.

This was the first formative phase of the game when the two Lloyds steadied the innings and Clive Lloyd, having settled in, began to roll out his strokes. Partisan feeling aside, the crowd had come to see him and with a massive, feline ease of stroke he pleased them. His second scoring stroke was a hook for six; and a straight drive all along the ground was in its way even more memorable. David Lloyd was bowled by Shepherd a few minutes before lunch, taken at 109 for three from 33 overs, which gave Lancashire a slight advantage.

In the early stages of the afternoon they lost it. Sullivan was sacrificially run out: Lloyd seemed relaxedly, even majestically, secure when he lofted Asif casually to mid-off, and when Bond was bowled trying to put Underwood away in the 47th over they were 150 for six: the game was again poised.

Engineer played himself in and then began to lift the run rate, but Woolmer bowled him at 179, leaving Simmons and Hughes together for the ritual slog at the end of the first innings which so often swings these matches: it did so now.

They hit boldly from a basis of deep experience in this kind of operation: 45 from 32 balls, 39 of them from the last four overs, and they scored from every ball of the last three overs. Kent could only settle for twos to avoid fours but eventually they were asked 225, the largest second innings total ever recorded in a Gillette final, to win.

They made a bad beginning. Luckhurst was caught at the wicket off Lever in the first over from a stroke unworthy of his normal technique. Nicholls never showed his hitting powers; Ealham swung across a half-volley and Denness, between some good strokes, was dropped twice before Wood bowled him. That was the fourth of Kent's self-critical departures.

Asif and Knott made their first show of worthwhile fight with a partnership of 37 which was growing in stature and momentum when, while Asif turned to contemplate the passage of a ball which had brushed his pad, Knott set off to run a leg-bye and could not get back. That was 105 for five and seemingly the end of Kent.

It proved the beginning of an athletic, clear-minded and cumulatively exciting innings by Asif. Shepherd, though unhappily less than his gayest self, and Woolmer a dutiful lieutenant, stood by him in stands of 57 and 35 but they were shadowy figures beside this man who recalled the occasion when he turned a Test match upside down four years ago. Once he went down the wicket to Wood and by a masterly turn of the wrists placed a cut between the two deep fieldsmen at third man.

Nimble, punitive, balanced, he had all but won the game – 28 wanted in six overs – when, checked by Simmons, he stepped out to him and drove him high through a gap at mid-off only for Bond, shedding half his 39 years, to leap up wide to his right and take the catch one-handed at full stretch before falling, holding it exultantly high.

All that came after was anti-climax: Kent's lately imminent win was demolished by Lever, and not Bond, Simmons nor Clive Lloyd would begrudge Asif his nomination by Ray Illingworth as man of the match.

Lancashire 224 for 7, 60 overs (C. H. Lloyd 66); Kent 200, 56.2 overs (Asif Iqbal 89). Lancashire won by 24 runs.

HENRY BLOFELD AT TAUNTON   JUNE 13 1974

Somerset v. Hampshire

Ian Botham, a young man of 18 from Yeovil, played not only the innings of his life when he made 45 not out, taking Somerset from 113 for eight to 184 for nine and victory by one wicket over Hampshire in the Benson and Hedges Cup, but also he lifted the game from a state of conventional excitement to one of unbelievable suspense and drama and finally into the realms of romantic fiction.

When he came in Somerset had obviously given up all hope of reaching the semi-finals of the competition. Steady bowling by Hampshire, who had themselves made 182, had slowly worn down the Somerset batting. Before another run had been scored Botham was joined by Hallam Moseley, Somerset's fast bowler from Barbados.

Meanwhile Gilliat had shortly beforehand brought back Roberts, who had only bowled three overs at the start of the innings and had eight to go. It seemed all over and the anticipation of the Somerset supporters, who boiled over when Hampshire were 22 for four in the morning, looked like being cruelly unfulfilled. When Moseley and Botham swung their bats at first it all seemed academic, for surely the inevitable could not be checked. The 150 was greeted with an almost disbelieving cheer and suddenly the realisation dawned all round the ground that it might just be more than a final despairing flourish.

Roberts was bowling fast, but these two met him with bats which were approximately straight. Then in the 49th over, when the score was 152 for eight, Roberts bowled a bouncer to Botham. He could not avoid the ball as he tried to swing it to leg and it glanced off his shoulder into his face and drew blood. Botham waved away help and a single took him to the far end to face Mike Taylor's next over.

Taylor bowled him one on his legs and Botham, who is tall and strongly-built, swung him with perfect timing over deep backward square leg's head for six. As if to underline the point, he straight drove the next ball with withering power for four. Eighteen were now needed from five overs. Roberts and another bouncer were survived and Herman took over from Taylor at the pavilion end. Immediately Botham unwound and, with a beautifully controlled hit, swung him over square leg and out of the ground for six. In the next over Moseley was lbw to a yorker from Roberts when he and Botham had put on 63 in 13 overs.

Clapp, the last man, came in with seven wanted and 16 balls to go. They ran a leg bye and then Botham played the last ball of the over past square leg. Turner chased, the batsmen ran and came back for a third. Clapp's frantic dive and the thud of the ball into Stephenson's gloves were simultaneous and Clapp survived. Somerset needed three when Herman bowled the last ball of the penultimate over to Botham with an over from Roberts to come. Coolly and correctly and still bleeding he cover drove for four, the game was over and the Gold Award was Botham's.

Hampshire 182, 53.3 overs (T. E. Jesty 79); Somerset 184 for 9, 54 overs (Jesty 4 for 28). Somerset won by one wicket.

India v. West Indies

All manner of strange things happened at Lord's on Saturday, but the strangest probably came when Vivian Richards, who had been playing a game somewhere between cricket and a sophisticated form of clock golf, mishit an intended pull towards Father Time and was very well caught by Kapil Dev.

The curiosity was not just that Richards was out, though that amazed everyone, not least Richards. It was that his dismissal did not signal, as usual, a retreat back into the bars but the reverse. It shook the crowd back to the realisation that India could win the Prudential World Cup, a possibility which had been eliminated from every mind for several hours. And at 7.28 – two minutes to midnight back home – they duly did, beating West Indies by 43 runs.

Midnight's children were deserved and decisive winners not just of the final, but of the whole fiesta. Within the past seven days, they have beaten Australia, England and West Indies with conviction and flair. The credit must go to brave, sensible and adaptable batsmen: spectacularly unspectacular bowlers helped by their own persistence and the soggy spring, which gave so many pitches a speed-deadening soft underbelly: and the rapidly improving captaincy of Kapil Dev. He outshone Lloyd by some distance in the final in his deployment of much sparser bowling resources.

India were 50 to one outsiders a fortnight ago, 100 to one with one gent in the Warner Stand between innings on Saturday (he is now £100 poorer), and heaven knows how many thousand to one when they were 17 for five against Zimbabwe at Tunbridge Wells the previous week.

But the blunt fact is that the initial odds were not wrong. If the same personnel could be reassembled in the same circumstances another 50 times, India probably would not win again. It is a bit like the infinite number of monkeys at an infinite number of typewriters eventually writing Hamlet. And there were an infinite number of us typewriter-types feeling like monkeys on Saturday night.

It has to be said that, though the excitement was worthy of the occasion, much of the batting was not. India had a great deal of help from the vanquished. In detective fiction, it is always the unconsidered clue – the paint-stain on the trousers, the cigar-butt in the shrubbery – that turns out to be crucial. The outcome of the final was decided after India had made a pig's ear of the silk purse of a start given them by Srikkanth and Amarnath and collapsed from 90 for two to 130 for seven.

At this point, the crowd's attention started to wander. Lloyd would be holding up the trophy, just as in 1975 and 1979 except for his trendier specs and wobblier legs. Shall we have the chicken legs now or later? It seemed of no consequence that while Gomes was wheeling away, the last three wickets were adding 53.

Even when Richards was batting – a drive to three o'clock, a cheeky flick to nine o'clock – people were admiring but hardly agog. It was just like any number of domestic cup finals. Any news from Wimbledon?

Well, West Indian batsmen can get hubris like all other over-cocky conquerors. Greenidge did not play a ball he should have done and was bowled; Gomes and Bacchus made the reverse mistake; Lloyd, in pain after aggravating his groin injury, and Haynes both mis-drove. After 50 for one, it was 76 for six.

But to the end there were possibilities. Dujon was reassuring in everything except his running. All the West Indian bowlers can bat, and three of them did so – Garner and Holding staying together for half an hour at the end until they had started to run out of overs as well as wickets. Had the target been much less than 183, West Indies would have won. Had it been much more, their batsmen would have been more prudent and would probably also have won.

Afterwards one captain criticised the wicket as too favourable to the seamers; the other disagreed. Surprisingly, it was Kapil Dev who was critical. Lloyd thought the pitch was perfectly fair and blamed his batsmen. Then he quietly announced his retirement from the captaincy. All politics permitting, Richards will lead the 1984 West Indian party to England with Lloyd as his elder statesman.

The man of the match award – a worthy conundrum for Brearley's brain – went to Amarnath for all-round worthiness though Madan Lal cannot have been more than a short head behind. I would have gone for Kapil Dev, for bowling well, leading well, holding the Richards catch and as a symbol that India's win belonged to the team and indeed the nation.

India's triumph will obviously help the game there. It may not harm the West Indies either. The whole tournament has done English cricket good with much bigger average gates than in the previous World Cups, a total attendance of around 250,000 and profits of £1 million, of which something like a half will stay in England. There would have been a far bigger profit if English cricket had an adequate stadium.

The English authorities will tell the International Cricket Conference this week that, if they can have a bigger slice of the cake, they will gladly stage another in 1987. Perhaps if other countries took a turn, the world could even stand one every two years. India and Australia are keen. But if the Australians staged it, they really would have to stick to this format, which has both cricketing credibility and popular appeal, instead of lumbering the world with their pyjama rubbish.

One thing about the Australian one-day system, in which everyone plays everyone else ad nauseam, is that it is less likely to produce a shock result than this one. Perhaps now people outside India will be less free with the title 'world champions' than they have been during the West Indies' reign. But the shock will do us all good.

India 183, 54.4 overs; West Indies 140, 52 overs. India won by 43 runs.

Roses

Huddersfield v. Manchester

A cricket match was played at Huddersfield, on Monday last, between eleven of the Huddersfield old club and eleven of the Manchester new club, which was won after a good contest by the former. The following is the result of the game:

Huddersfield		Manchester	
First Innings	36	First Innings	33
Second Innings	42	Second Innings	31
Total	78	Total	64

This match excited considerable interest amongst the connoisseurs of the game; and the Huddersfield club were saluted by a merry peal from the church bells on retiring from the field. They spent the evening together with the utmost conviviality, and the harmony was kept up by a company of glee singers.

Manchester v. Yorkshire

The great match, the Manchester Cricket Club *versus* all Yorkshire, which was to have commenced on Thursday last at one o'clock, on the Manchester cricket ground, was postponed in consequence of rain, which commenced about half an hour before time, to the following (yesterday) morning; when the wickets were pitched, and the play commenced at ten o'clock. The Yorkshire players went in first, and scored 77; the Manchester club followed and notched 80. The Yorkshire players then took their second innings, but were only able to score 39. The Manchester club resumed play, and won with eight wickets to go down. The match was not won till after eight o'clock in the evening.

AUGUST 4 1849

Lancashire v. Yorkshire at Old Trafford

We have not received a detailed account of this match, nor do we think it would have been very interesting, for from the beginning the Yorkshire party seem to have shown a decided superiority . . .

JULY 11 1867

Gentlemen of Lancashire v. Gentlemen of Yorkshire

This match, which was resumed on the County Ground, at Old Trafford, yesterday, and will be concluded today, will be memorable in the annals of cricket for the largest innings that we have any record of. Yorkshire had a weak team compared with the eleven which the county gentlemen can turn out on occasion. Several well-known names were absent from the list, which was particularly weak in bowling. Mr. Sale (Sheffield) displayed remarkable endurance, and he bowled well, but their prolonged exertions thoroughly wearied the fielders, and as was inevitable, many runs were thrown away. Mr. E. B. Rowley's score was made up of five fives, 19 fours, seven threes, 18 twos and 61 singles. His play was very fine and when he was caught at last, at slip (after the fielder had had a severe struggle with the ball), he was welcomed back to the pavilion with prolonged cheering.

Lancashire 586 (E. B. Rowley 219, E. Whittaker 146 not out, J. F. Leese 72); Yorkshire 212 (Savile 56) and 157 for 6. Match drawn.

To the editor   AUGUST 17 1877

Sir, – In commenting upon the game of cricket between the county teams of Lancashire and Yorkshire you intimate that Yorkshire is much less powerful than she was five or ten years ago. Now, as a man of 56 cricketing seasons, who has spent part of his time in watching the game, I venture to state it as my opinion that Yorkshire is not so much weaker than she was ten years ago as Lancashire is stronger, for it will be acknowledged by all, I think, that there has been great change for the better in the Lancashire county cricket. Five or ten years ago county palatine was not regarded at all as great for its cricketing power, and providing that county were now by death or some other misfortune to be suddenly deprived of its truly great Hornby, its splendid fielder Royle, and its everlasting sticker Barlow, how would the best eleven they could get together show up? There are in Yorkshire most excellent bats amongst the gentlemen, who if they had the time and disposition would make the Yorkshire teams quite equal to any producible by Lancashire. Personally I cannot but regard it as a mistake made by your correspondent when he intimates that the county of York is declining in its batting, for five or ten years ago 200 or 300 runs in an innings was not a regular thing, as it is at the present day; and moreover when we take into account the bowling of this season (Watson, to wit), the like of which Lancashire never had before and possibly may never have again, I am convinced that the writer has fallen into an error. – Trusting you will be able to find space for these few remarks, I am, &c.

S. W.

Bradford.

AUGUST 29 1881

The season which closed on Saturday, at Maidstone, is one not only without parallel in the history of Lancashire county cricket, but stands pre-eminent in the records of the national game. Out of 14 matches arranged for, ten have been won, three drawn and one (that with Middlesex) abandoned. The victories have all been decisive, in most cases by overwhelming numbers, as will be seen from the fact that in the closest contest played – that with Yorkshire, at Bramall Lane – a substantial advantage of 50 rested with Lancashire. The drawn matches have all been left unfinished when our county had a clear advantage over their opponents. To this result the play, the judicious management, and the indomitable energy of the Lancashire captain[1] has in a very great degree contributed, and he has had the satisfaction of receiving highly valuable aid from Mr. A. G. Steel and other gentlemen, and of commanding the services of a body of players who could always be relied upon to perform their part well. A remarkable feature in the Lancashire bowling is that not a single wide or no ball has been bowled in any of the matches.

[1] A. N. Hornby

MAY 18 1910

Yorkshire v. Lancashire

It was just as well, in discussing the first day's play at Leeds on Monday, that we did not speculate too confidently on the prospects of a Lancashire victory, for yesterday the game underwent a change of the most surprising and dramatic character. There were three things that played a part in bringing it about. There was first a group of blunders in the field which occurred at the most critical stage of the Yorkshire first innings. Altogether three catches were missed in the innings, and in addition on two occasions the fielders watched the ball, hit up between them off the bat, fall to the ground almost at their feet without making any effort to catch it. Perhaps, in any event, Yorkshire would have saved the follow-on – though at one point this was at least problematical – but Lancashire relieved them of all anxiety by giving away these five chances. Then there was a fine last wicket stand by Radcliffe and Haigh, quite in the best Yorkshire style. It prolonged the close of the Yorkshire innings over an hour, and it added 49 runs, only a fraction short of a third of the total Yorkshire score. Even so, however, the position seemed pretty good from the Lancashire point of view, for they had still a lead of 77 runs on the first innings. But the third and most decisive factor was yet to come. It was Hirst, who bowled – well, as only Hirst *can* bowl when the spirit is upon him. Before one could realise what had happened he had dismissed four of the best Lancashire batsmen for five runs – recalling his performance one memorable afternoon last year at Old Trafford, when five wickets were down for six runs – and he went on remorselessly crashing into the Lancashire wickets until he had bundled the whole side out. It was a disastrous shattering of the Lancashire prospects, but it was really magnificent bowling, worth seeing at any cost of partisan sympathies.

Hirst has done many fine things in the course of his long and remarkable career, but he has never done anything quite so good as his performance yesterday. On only one previous occasion had he taken nine wickets in an innings. That was in the match with Middlesex at Sheffield in 1907, but the wickets then cost 45 runs, whereas they were obtained yesterday for only 23. Yesterday's performance stands out, therefore, as absolutely his best bowling record. The wonder is not that he got the wickets so cheaply, but that he did not get them even cheaper, for a good proportion of the runs were the merest flukes. One four was snicked past the leg stump off a no-ball. Another ball, which MacLaren meant to hook to leg, glanced off the bat through the slips to the boundary. Try as they would the batsmen could not get the ball on the face of the bat. They either played outside it altogether and were bowled or narrowly escaped being bowled, or if they played it at all they played it with the inside edge of the bat. People with implicit faith in the 'swerve' theory declared yesterday that the ball travelled from the bowler's hand to the pitch by a semi-circular route. That, of course, is a vast exaggeration, but if it seemed to the batsman to take that course, as it undoubtedly did, that is all that matters for practical purposes. What is certain at any rate is that after the ball pitched, it shot across the wicket at a bewildering angle. Even when it came far enough up for the batsman to play, as they say, close to the pitch of the ball, he generally found it had slipped inside his bat. This illusive flight and break was not the only difficulty; it was combined with a perfect length and a very high pace. Hirst, in fact, bowled like a man possessed, and on yesterday's form no team of batsmen could have stood up against him.

LEADER   SEPTEMBER 1 1926

Lancashire's Year

The supremacy in county cricket has come back to Lancashire in the same year that two Lancashire teams competed in the final round of the Football Cup.[1] The county will offer its fullest congratulations to 'all concerned', as the saying goes. The Yorkshire team, unbeaten and with one match to play, has had bad luck with the weather, and some of its supporters may be eager to join once more in the ceaseless argument about points and percentages. One can sympathise with Yorkshire and yet hold that their players have some times incurred ultimate danger by thinking too precisely on the immediate safety. Yorkshire certainly beat Lancashire handsomely in May; after that Lancashire's eleven all found their best form together, and when the time for revenge came in August they had easily the better of it in an unfinished game. The 1st of September is a sad day for cricketers as well as for partridges, but Lancashire people can gather happy memories from the passing summer. Trailing clouds of glory does it go, for nothing became the county's season like the leaving of it, when the staid seniors turned themselves into sons of thunder. The bright light that has shone at Old Trafford has not been kindled only by the familiar planets; new stars have taken their places in the sky and shown a pleasant capacity to twinkle at opportune moments. Generous as that illumination has seemed to us it has attracted little attention at the National Observatory of cricket, whose astronomers royal have appeared to study the heavens on the supposition that no telescope could be expected to reach as far as Lancashire. But no amount of blind eyes could prevent Lancashire from reaching the championship. If Yorkshiremen feel sore, let them at least reflect that sovereignty has not left the Pennines and will probably stay there. But on which side? That seems to be a nice question for cricketers by the hearth to discuss while the footballers are settling which of the Lancashire teams is to lift 'the Cup' this time.

[1] Bolton 1, Manchester City 0.

LEADER   DECEMBER 10 1927

It would scarcely be human not to be amused by the flounders of the Yorkshire County Cricket Club in search of a captain. When Major Lupton retired they first of all, in defiance of tradition and Lord Hawke, asked Herbert Sutcliffe to captain the team. Once granted that the captain need not be an amateur (and their offer did grant that) there remained only one possible objection to Sutcliffe – that to appoint him was to ignore Rhodes. This objection had a certain weight, and it soon became apparent that a great many people in Yorkshire would prefer

Rhodes as captain to Sutcliffe. Thereupon Sutcliffe discreetly declined the offer. The Committee of the Club then reacted violently from their audacious innovation and selected yet another innocuous military gentleman, verging on middle age. It is apparently assumed that Rhodes, reluctant to serve under a colleague of international standing, will welcome the rule of a captain played largely for his initials, and that the many Yorkshiremen who objected to Sutcliffe only because they thought Rhodes should have the job will be satisfied to find that they have got neither. The proof of the pudding is in the eating, and no doubt the Yorkshire eleven under Captain Worsley will prove as formidable as the same eleven under Major Lupton. But if the team went into the field as irresolute and as much at the mercy of cross-currents as its Committee it would be something very unlike the real Yorkshire pudding that we should eat, and prove, next year at Old Trafford. More like Yorkshire hash.

JUNE 29 1929

Dr. Cyril Norwood, the Head Master of Harrow, who gave away the prizes at Berkhamstead School yesterday, referred to 'certain very dangerous influences which are making themselves felt in the land.'

'Take the Lancashire and Yorkshire cricket match,' he said. 'These two counties start not to finish the match, not to play cricket, but to get the points for the first innings lead, and they play the most miserable game and set the most miserable example for the whole country of how games should not be played.'

A very dangerous social phenomenon was the amateur who did nothing else but play games and demanded his expenses. It was not a very honourable way of spending one's life to go knocking balls about for thirty years. It was from the United States that these dangers were coming to this country.

'I hope that if we lose all the championships in the world you will not believe that this country is decadent. If we play games as they ought to be played it is exceedingly probable that we shall lose most of the championships all the time . . .'

THE CRICKET FIELD   JUNE 25 1931

Lancashire County authorities should keep a close eye on two clever Midland schoolboy cricketers, for both have a birth qualification for the county. One is H. K. Mills, captain of Denstone College, and the other is C. Washbrook, who plays for Bridgnorth Grammar School and the town club. Mills, who is only 17, is a right-hand batsman and bowls medium-paced off-spinners. In six matches this year he has scored 342 in four completed innings, including 101 not out against Craven

Gentlemen and 70 not out against Staffordshire Gentlemen. He has taken 33 wickets for 155 runs, and has twice taken eight wickets in an innings, once for only 11 runs. Washbrook, who is not 16, has been coached by one of the Tyldesleys, and has made centuries for his school and the Bridgnorth club.

LEADER   AUGUST 15 1941

Yorkshire is a county, 'Cricketer' once wrote, famous for woollens and George Hirst. He might equally have said Bobby Peel, who has died aged 84, or, if it comes to that, half a dozen others who have followed those great men. For a good many years Peel was a striking figure in a formidable team. He was one of the country's best slow bowlers and, as if that was not enough, he was one of those skilled, stubborn batsmen who stiffen the middle of an innings and, by refusing to get out and also making many runs, drive opponents to despair. What is it, people say, that keeps Yorkshire at the top? (Ah, the phrases of the piping times of peace!) There may be many reasons, but what other county has had so noble a procession of slow bowlers as Peel, Rhodes, and Verity?

                                                          SEPTEMBER 2 1943

It was announced yesterday that Captain Hedley Verity, the famous Yorkshire and England Test match cricketer, has died of wounds as a prisoner of war in Italian hands. Captain Verity, who was in the Green Howards, was wounded and captured in fighting outside Catania last week.

MISCELLANY   AUGUST 9 1950

The current battle of the 'Roses' at Old Trafford has reminded an older reader in Manchester of the time when he was taken by his father to one of those Bank Holiday matches in the late nineties. It was astonishing, he says, how a Lancashire supporter just below them smelled out a Yorkshire fanatic several rows lower and quite fifteen yards away. Both had voices that could be heard at a greater range, and the argument grew heated. The Yorkshire supporter finally silenced his opponent with some facts and figures – but only for a moment. 'I sh'd laike to knaw what thee knows abart cricket,' the Bury man replied. 'Or any other so-and-so as 'as 'is pudden afore 'is meat.'

To the editor   JULY 16 1954

Sir, – What has happened to Lancashire county cricket? As an exile from Lancashire I read the sports page, each day, with dismay. The experts told us that with Washbrook as captain we could expect great things.

We expect the team to have a tail but the opening and middle batsmen seem completely unable to score any worthwhile runs. Surely a better side can be found from such a great county obviously rich in potential cricket talent – Yours &c.

A. E. Tomlinson.
London N.W. 11.

DENYS ROWBOTHAM AT OLD TRAFFORD   AUGUST 3 1960

Lancashire v. Yorkshire

Lancashire achieved their first double victory over Yorkshire for 67 years from the last ball of the game at Old Trafford yesterday. It was the death or glory finish of a schoolboy's storybook, and greater excitement may not be generated at Lancashire's headquarters for countless seasons.

In all logic there should have been no need for excitement, for Yorkshire had been dismissed for 149 and Lancashire on a well behaved wicket needed only 78 runs for victory in two hours. With half an hour remaining, however, Lancashire were 43 for 6, only Grieves of the forceful stroke-makers remained. 35 runs were needed, Trueman and Ryan were still going great guns, and Yorkshire's fields were set deep, six and three, and shortly afterwards, five and four. Grieves could have singles comfortably but did not want them, until accurate bowling constricted him for ten minutes to a single glance, hook, and hammered force.

Then, with 24 wanted in 15 minutes, it was doubtful whether even singles would help Lancashire. There was no alternative, none the less, but to take them. So four runs were scurried from Ryan's next over. Grieves later cut Trueman for a fifth single and now Clayton opened his shoulders and heaved with all the strength of his small, squat frame. He lofted a good length ball over Trueman's head. J. V. Wilson trotted round from deep mid-off to take the easy catch, and to his and all Yorkshire's chagrin somehow managed to mangle it. Yet even after two more singles from this fated over Lancashire still needed 16 in six

144

minutes, and Wilson's miss seemed costly only if Yorkshire, out of brilliant defence, were conceiving scarcely credible victory.

The next six minutes showed just how incalculable cricket is. Grieves promptly swept Ryan for a single, Clayton cudgelled two fours and a single, and then from Ryan's last ball Grieves was caught at the wicket from a slash. So six runs had to come from Trueman's last over. Clayton straight drove the first for a single; the second bowled Greenhough; Dyson missed his first drive but achieved two leg byes; another single came from a full toss which Dyson mishit only inches wide of his off stump; Clayton edged another desperate drive to deep fine leg; and Dyson somehow glanced Trueman's last ball off his leg stump for four. No wonder Clayton threw his bat in the air . . .

Yorkshire 154 (D. B. Close 63, J. B. Statham 5 for 43, K. Higgs 4 for 48) and 149 (Statham 4 for 23); Lancashire 226 (A. Wharton 83, R. W. Barber 71, F. S. Trueman 4 for 65) and 81 for 8 (M. Ryan 5 for 50). Lancashire won by two wickets.

To the editor   JULY 9 1968

Sir, – 1967 County Championship table: Yorkshire No. 1.

1968 County Championship table: Yorkshire No. 1 (to date). Batting averages: G. Boycott (Y) No. 1. Bowling averages: D. Wilson (Y) No. 1; F. Trueman (Y) No. 2. Wicketkeeping averages: Binks (Y) No. 1. Yorkshire v. Australians: result – Yorkshire win by an innings and 69 runs.

Number of Yorkshiremen playing for England: one. Amazing! And the moral of the story? School ties and pink gins make for good chaps but not for successful cricket. – Yours faithfully,

G. E. Haslam.
(Yorkshireman in exile)
West Bridgford,
Nottingham.

BRIAN CHAPMAN   AUGUST 10 1968

There was a time when Yorkshire, descending on London towards mid-August, would have come as conquerors, with only the loose edges, the selvedge of the championship to be sewn up. The sides of the early twenties, and those which dominated the thirties would already have attended to any defects in the weft. Yorkshire are at Lord's today, playing against Middlesex, and although they head the table with a handy 21 points, seeking a hat-trick of titles, the issue is far from secure.

In those historic days they could echo without presumption the famous words of Walter Hagen before an Open golf championship: 'Who's going to be second?' Now, any of five or six counties are entitled to ask: 'Who's going to be first?' Recent championships have been marginal affairs. Last year, yet again, Yorkshire had to wait until the very last day before they could run up the victory pennant. Hampshire and Kent are pressing hard and Glamorgan, with a late thrust and two games in hand, come well into the short list.

The chances are that Close and his team of tough, experienced campaigners will manage it again. But it *will* be a question of management, not a triumphal procession, and it may be the last for some seasons in which they can deny their rivals. Creaks and chinks have appeared this season in the champions' armour. They have bowed to Warwickshire, not unexpectedly. Glamorgan humbled them at Bramall Lane, though revenge was exacted in Wales. Fallibility was chiefly apparent at Westcliff, where Essex comported themselves like champions and Yorkshire like wooden spooners.

It has been Yorkshire's boast, that, even in a bad spell, when they are finding it hard to win, they are also hard to beat. Their reputation was rudely defaced on that occasion. But I think that, looking back, they were most abashed, if not shamed, in that dreadful fall from grace against Gloucestershire late in May. Yorkshire entered upon the last day as killers, with the coup de grâce a mere formality. They finished prostrate, fending off defeat in a feverish last-wicket stand forced upon them by febrile batting.

Only men of the strongest nerve dared enter the Yorkshire dressing room that afternoon. One eminent player was, by report, admonished to 'stop moanin' and get out of there and start laikin'.' This was no laughing matter, certainly not for a Yorkshire side less assured than the giants of the past. One shrewd critic summed up this and other sombre occasions with the penetrative comment: 'The only sort of humour they know is to be doing well.' All Yorkshire is contained in that remark.

For a captain who avowed that the county which won the most matches would win the championship, give or take bonus points, Close comes to Lord's for the final run-in with a curious record. Yorkshire have pulled in 127 bonus points against 106 by Hampshire, in second place, and a trumpery 95 by Kent, in third, which seems to prove that keeping your eye on the main chance pays off in all possible ways. Curiously, Kent have won one more match.

But if bickering is bruited off the field, there is still the same welded team spirit on the field. Yorkshire rallied from the shock of being put out by Lancashire for 61 in the first innings of the Roses match. They are a team seemingly wedded to controversy, to public upsets season by season, and Close's personal methods of saving that game did not meet with frantic or universal applause. But he 'took it,' as they say, took physically all that Statham and the rest could hurl at him, and confirmed faith in him as a player and leader which might have been waning over recent months.

'Go all out for the win and when you can't win, go all out for the draw.' That as a maxim makes captaincy sense, not only in Yorkshire; Walter Robins applied it to Middlesex and successfully as a manager in the West Indies.

No, Yorkshire's troubles are not wholly traceable to decline in the old fighting spirits. They face, as a worry that will become more urgent in the next two or three seasons, the dilemma that pressures upon England. There are, if it is not unkind to say so, too many familiar faces. It is an ageing team in the cricket sense. Pick the best, indeed the accepted, Yorkshire side and only two are under 30, Boycott and Hampshire both being 27. Close and his deputy Trueman – a remarkably successful deputy – are 37. Illingworth, who would automatically be heir-apparent to the captaincy, is only one year younger. Close leans heavily on his tactical advice and 'Raymond' (rarely Ray) also tops the national bowling averages with 92 wickets. 'Give me Raymond,' they say at Headingley in tones brooking no contradiction when off-spin is being discussed.

If Yorkshire faced an early change of leader (an idea not entirely heretical) the most probable successor, on grounds of a comparatively youthful 31, is Sharpe, though Boycott would not disdain an invitation. Sharpe captains the MCC President's XI against Australia on Wednesday, a preview which opens wide vistas on a county and country level. He has had a wonderful run since he was restored to the position of opening batsman, which he really enjoys, about the middle of last season – by, incidentally, Trueman as acting captain.

But the county of Holmes and Sutcliffe and Hutton is strangely short of promising young batsmen. None has forced his way to the front since the début of Boycott and Hampshire six or seven years ago. Good judges think well of John Woodford, a physical training instructor and young right-hand bat from the Bradford League, who finds a place in today's XI. 'Lots of runs with the Colts,' is the report. Yorkshire can do with this type and with a new Trueman, for Nicholson, who nearly wrecked Kent at Canterbury, is 30. Otherwise the bell may toll for Yorkshire as it duly tolled for Surrey.

Yorkshire v. Lancashire

Nearly nine hours having been lost to rain, the final game there ended predictably in a draw at Bramall Lane where Yorkshire and Lancashire went through the motions, and the older spectators through the emotions. Lancashire declared 12 ahead and in their second innings Yorkshire made 114 for two. It was a fitting epilogue.

The dismissal of Simmons to Old's second delivery of the morning generated hopes of an exciting and appropriate finish. But Sullivan not only showed stout defence against the ball which lifted nastily at times, he pulled and cut profitably while Ratcliffe played a straight and confident bat at the opposite end. And when Bore joined the attack, Ratcliffe drove him for two fours in an over before heavy rain set in with less than an hour gone.

During the break, Lloyd declared, and when play was resumed shortly before three o'clock, Boycott was caught brilliantly by Hughes backward of square leg at 21, and at 45 Hughes accepted a return catch from Lumb. Hughes made the ball lift and turn, but there was nothing in the wicket to indicate anything catastrophic for Yorkshire, who took the opportunity to have some batting practice.

When it was all over, hundreds of youngsters ran on to the field and began digging up lumps of turf; the older generation had brought buckets for that purpose. But there were no audible songs of lamentation and contrary to rumour no empty hearse was driven round the arena. 'If tha' wants a 'eadline, try t'pitch that died of shame,' shouted a Yorkshireman towards the press box as he went home for high tea.

So ended the 118 years' old existence of Yorkshire's oldest ground where Herbert Sutcliffe made his hundredth century for Yorkshire and Geoff Boycott his first; where Douglas Jardine was given the greatest ovation of his life; where Denis Compton scored his first century against Yorkshire and was bitten by a dog for his sacrilege; where Lord Hawke sent Bobby Peel off the field allegedly for being intoxicated; where Yorkshire sacked Johnny Wardle; where W. G. Grace scored 150 and took 15 wickets in the same match; where Freddie Trueman led Yorkshire to victory against the Australians by an innings; and where 'Jock' Cameron of South Africa hit 30 in an over from Hedley Verity. They discovered the ball lodged in a drainpipe during an overflow the following winter.

Work will begin this week on a new stand for Sheffield United at a cost of £750,000, and the cricket square – or what is left of it after yesterday's uninterrupted scavenging – will be cut up for sale to customers all over the world at 20p a square yard.

During the depths of winter, the ghosts of cricketers long since dead no doubt will haunt Bramall Lane, and from time to time if they listen carefully enough, football spectators may hear an occasional 'owzat' or 'gerra move on, Lancasheer.' There is no reason to doubt that at least some members of what once was described as the 'most knowledgeable crowd in the country' will forget how to barrack even in eternity.

To the editor AUGUST 21 1973

Sir, – In reporting on the cricket match between Yorkshire and Middlesex your cricket correspondent remarked that this was the second time Yorkshire had been humiliated in London this season. A short while before another report was headed 'Yorkshire humbled.'

May I point out that there is no county team that can 'humble' or 'humiliate' Yorkshire, since it is the only county team in the country. When Kent take the field do the players look like eleven Kentish men and true? The press and BBC still talk of the Battle of the Roses when Yorkshire plays Lancashire. But where are the Lancastrians?

Some counties are so anxious to have a team that wins, that they even hire white South Africans and white Rhodesians.

We Yorkshire folk are made of sterner stuff. We need no mercenary army to do our fighting for us. Our heads will be bloody, but they will be unbowed.

(Miss) **E. H. McDonald.**
62 West Green,
Stokesley,
North Yorkshire.

To the editor AUGUST 24 1973

Sir, – I lived for four years in Leeds, but I still never fail to be amused by the casuistries which some Yorkshiremen – and now women, it seems, too – will indulge in to explain away the present poverty of their county cricket.

This much vaunted ruse of confining

selection to Yorkshire born men and true cunningly ensures, as Miss McDonald so adeptly argues, that no other county can ever defeat them by legitimate means. It adds relish to their rare moments of success – 'All done with Yorkshire lads' they will say – and enables the more frequent humiliation to be dismissed as simply a cheat, inflicted by opponents of mixed and tainted origin.

One would respect Miss McDonald's argument a little more if she could adapt it realistically to the present situation and console herself that with the thought that 'It may be rubbish, but at least it's Yorkshire rubbish.'

May I prove my lack of bias in this matter by revealing that I am a Lancastrian at present on holiday in Yorkshire. – Yours faithfully.

A. A. Mayne.

The Jolly Sailors Inn,
Whitby,
Yorks.

LEADER   OCTOBER 2 1978

Cricket is the gentlemen's game, run by gentlemen, played by gentlemen, written about by gentlemen. Thus the overwhelming reaction to Kerry Packer, who is not a gentleman, was the kind of spluttering rage you get when lads from the local comprehensive drop bubblegum wrappings in front of the pavilion. How can one have anything to do with chaps who don't know how to behave?

Geoffrey Boycott did not join Packer – though he had that lucrative chance. Mean, moody and magnificent as usual, he decided to hang on and help his country and his county. For his pains, a few weeks ago, England humiliatingly denied him the vice captaincy for the Australian tour. Now Yorkshire has abruptly sacked him as county captain after eight years. That decision, sudden and unprophesised, came on Friday, two days after the death of Boycott's mother. (Those who follow his career closely know how deep and abiding his family ties were.) Of course, say the county, the captaincy decision was a 'dreadful second blow'. But the relevant committee meeting was scheduled and Yorkshire can't mess around with the scheduled committee meetings.

Put the incident, for a second, against the public school ethic of British cricket. The treatment meted out to Geoffrey Boycott would seem cruel if visited upon a stray mongrel dog, the merest tyke in a Leeds back alley. To find the most brilliant and prolific player Yorkshire has produced in a generation treated thus is simply nauseating. Here is a game which throughout the summer has harped on about loyalty, decency and gratitude – which has hounded players like Dennis Amiss who, towards the end of their career, decided that these virtues alone didn't pay the rent. But what of those, like Boycott, who decided in the end to stick by the establishment definition of loyalty? Of course Boycott is a prickly character. Very few outstanding talents in any walk of life are bland yesmen. And, of course, Yorkshire have not been outstandingly successful through his eight years. (How could they be when the team he inherited was in tatters and when traditional pride prevented overseas signings?) But Yorkshire, and Boycott, have slowly recovered. The county now has some of the most praised young players in the country. At which recovery point, the architect of recovery is cast aside. Already the calls for him to be 'loyal', to be a 'man' in the face of adversity are starting. No one, considering the crass insensitivity of the past few days, should pay a moment's heed. Cricket in general – and Yorkshire cricket in particular – looks cheap and nasty this morning. The league of gentlemen make Kerry Packer seem like a compassionate saint.

LEADER   OCTOBER 10 1978

A schism in the classical mould is now being enacted behind the sightscreens of Headingley, and if there is a sense of uncertainty and apprehension in the land there is also the privilege of watching the deep processes of history working themselves out before our eyes. The Council of Nicaea, summoned by the Emperor Constantine in the year 325, was such an occasion, ending in the final repudiation of Arius and of his heresy. Even more momentous, was what, until the events of recent weeks, had been regarded as the Great Schism, resulting in the separation of the Greek and Roman churches in 1054. But as the Yorkshire schism develops it may prove to be closest in spirit and in outcome to the schism of the fourteenth century which led to the existence of rival popes, each commanding some allegiance, although one, Clement VII, left the heart of the ecclesiastical world to take up residence at Avignon. From Rome to the Pont d'Avignon, from Leeds to . . . Grace Road? The college of cardinals, which was the Yorkshire committee de ces jours, justified its change of course in electing Clement by pleading that the threats of the Roman mobs had dictated its previous choice of Urban VI. There is no exact parallel, but the threats of the Yorkshire mobs may well, in the event, determine the issue between the Boycott and the Hampshire confederacies. Or, as in 1570, when Pius V excommunicated Elizabeth I with his bull *Regnans in excelsis*, the issue may remain unresolved for a far longer time than either party would have believed possible, to the detriment of cricket as of Christianity.

It seems that no great institution can long escape schism. Indeed the tendency to schism in an institution may be the touchstone of greatness. At a lower level, and without the deep doctrinal undertow which lends conflicts of faith their special significance, the same phenomenon can be seen even in party politics. Gaitskell-Wilson, Butler-Macmillan, Heath-Thatcher, Joseph-Joseph: there is no need to comb history for examples. Who has not observed a charity, created solely for the good of mankind, riven into factions within a week? Yet it is only when schism enters the innermost of mankind's concerns that it acquires heroic, and tragic, proportions. That, in sum, is what we are now being called upon to witness.

ROY HATTERSLEY   FEBRUARY 26 1983

Once upon a time, the most exciting event in all of February was the early morning delivery of the big buff envelope from the Old Bank Chambers, Park Row, Leeds. It clanged its self-confident way through the letterbox and landed with a satisfying thud on the coconut mat which we would have used to wipe our feet if we had ever entered the house by the front door.

Upstairs in the back bedroom overlooking the churchyard I could easily distinguish the sound of its triumphant arrival from the apologetic noise made by the timid intrusion of pencil-written letters from elderly aunts, gas bills, and postcards sent by the Hillsborough Branch of Sheffield City Libraries informing us that the books we had reserved were ready for collection.

February's other delights – the third round of the FA Cup and a single Valentine with a coded name which I could not decipher – never compared with the first sight of next season's Yorkshire County Cricket Club membership card: Lady or Youth Under Sixteen (Not Transferable). It was cocooned in a complicated wrapping of annual report, statement of accounts, and application forms for Test Match tickets. But it was the membership card at which my heart leapt. It had the same effect last week, after 35 years of annual anticipation and February fulfilment.

I am now a Full Member (Non-Transferable) and I have apparently moved down the table of precedence which is kept somewhere in the pavilion at Headingley. For after the heady days of 1948, when I was number 901, I have been demoted to member 7302. But that double change of status apart, nothing about my February delight seems to have changed.

The membership card is exactly the same shape and size as it was when Don Bradman led the first postwar Australian touring team. It is still embossed with the wrong sort of rose – a rose which looks like a real rose, not a proper Yorkshire cricket rose, which looks like a dog-daisy. It still contains the little perforated tear-off coupons which admit non-transferable members to the Leeds Test match. And it still lists the County Championship fixtures – games which I have planned to attend for 30 years and which, for three decades, have been denied me by work or weather.

Today is my first chance to use the cardboard time-capsule and step back into the age of Gentlemen and Players; Brylcreem and crepe-soled shoes. For the annual general meeting takes place at half-past ten this morning in the Brigantes Suite of the Dragonara Hotel, Leeds. No doubt the Dragonara is renowned throughout the West Riding for its comfort and cuisine. But its name is far too redolent of shoe-cleaning machines and ice-dispensers for such a solemn occasion.

Last year, the club called its members to the City Memorial Hall in Sheffield – a tragically appropriate location, even though it was built to celebrate and sanctify peace, a condition that has been a stranger to Yorkshire cricket for some time.

Then I sat, apprehensive, on the edge of my back-row gallery seat waiting for the outbreaks of unseemly behaviour and the eruption of conduct which would not have been tolerated when I was a Youth or Lady (Not Transferable). It was a winter of unusual fixtures – a pirate expedition to South Africa, Ray Illingworth versus Geoffrey Boycott, and Geoffrey Boycott versus the world.

All these controversial contests were mentioned directly or obliquely in the annual report. It seemed to me that whoever took charge was in for a rough morning. The sacrificial victim turned out to be N. W. D. Yardley, a cricketer in whom I have taken a proprietary interest ever since he almost signed my autograph book at the Parkhead Festival in 1947. His pen was actually poised above the pale blue page when Bill Bowes warned him, 'Sign for one and dozens of 'em will be in here.'

Mr. Yardley opened the debate to the meeting and the first contributor prefaced his question with one of the emollient preambles which are always followed by a full frontal assault. 'No one,' he insisted, 'is more anxious to avoid trouble than me.' I waited for the 'but'. And sure enough it came. Then there was the bridging passage. 'Some things have to be said.'

I waited for the bumper to knock Norman Yardley's cap off. 'Unless a proper traffic-flow system is introduced into the bar at Bradford, someone is going to get killed.' The second inquisitor actually raised one of the controversial subjects. 'There has,' he said aggressively, 'been a lot of talk about a new manager. What we need is a new stock-control clerk. We ended the season with more cricket balls than we had at the start.'

Until that day, I had never heard an answer actually begin, 'I'm glad you asked that question.' But that is how the treasurer responded to the excess cricket ball crisis. And what was more, he went on to explain the cause of his pleasure. The surplus balls were an investment. Cricket balls were an appreciating asset. The increase in the commodity's value more than matched the theoretical interest charges on the notionally borrowed capital which (it might be hypothesised) had been used for the purchase. All thought of votes of censure was abandoned.

After that, Mr. Yardley was re-elected president with only two old ladies voting against his continued apotheosis. Perhaps they just made a mistake. Though – ever anxious about N.W.D.'s welfare – I feared that they were pursuing ancient vendettas concerning a catch dropped off a nephew's bowling, or a cousin carelessly run out.

It was the morning's only false stroke. And at a little after noon we all went home happy, ready for another season of failure and spectator dissatisfaction. I suspect that the meeting was made up of people like me who are made happy simply by the receipt of the big buff envelope. The trumpet of a prophecy. O, Wind, if Membership Card comes, can Spring be far behind?

LEADER   AUGUST 22 1983

Of the 38 paintings on show in the Lord's Memorial Gallery 16 are fakes, according to a report in yesterday's *Mail on Sunday*. Fourteen of the suspect works come from the collection of the late Sir Jeremiah Colman, described by the paper as a 'mustard magnate,' and could well be the work of a single hand. One, allegedly painted by a royal academician in 1828, includes a scoreboard not built until much later in the century, while another purports to show Sir Henry Dickens captaining his own side against the Men of Kent in 1860, the year in which he celebrated his 11th birthday.

For a single forger or even a school of forgers to have supplied nearly half the works in a collection is an achievement perhaps unmatched in the curious annals of the trade, and it would seem on the face of it unlikely that so prolific a fabricator of other people's work would have laid his brush aside simply because Sir Jeremiah Colman was no longer in the market for the occasional tasty bargain. Assuming that the *Mail on Sunday*'s story is correct, there seems a reasonable chance that more such pictures will have found their way into other collections and that these too may see the light before long.

There were, for instance, unconfirmed reports yesterday that a work said to be entitled 'Sir Geoffrey Accepts the Repentance of his Detractors' had been found in a disused fish store in East London. Attributed to Andrea Mantegna (1431-1506), it depicts a scene on Lord's cricket ground some time in the closing years of this century. Illuminated in a sublime shaft of sunlight, Geoffrey Boycott stands at the wicket, his bat raised above his head in modest acknowledgement of the ovation raging around him. By scoring 238 not out in 95 minutes, he has just ensured that Yorkshire have at last regained the County Championship. In the foreground, a gnarled figure clad all in white, dimly recognisable as Mr. Raymond Illingworth, lies full length in abject supplication. Beside him, on bended knee, one hand outstretched, the tears of penitence coursing freely down his face, is Mr. Ronnie Burnet, chairman of the county's peace-keeping committee. In the top left-hand corner of the painting, a host of cherubic figures, possibly angels, possibly members of the MCC ground staff, hymns the apotheosis of the hero. A flurry of activity at the pavilion gate announces the imminent arrival of Her Majesty the Queen, who has come hotfoot from the Palace on hearing the news to confer upon Mr. Boycott that knighthood which has so long eluded him. The jovial bearded figure at the bottom right-hand corner of the canvas is Mr. Bill Frindall, who has just calculated that this is the first occasion in the history of the game on which a batsman who has made 238 runs in 95 minutes has been knighted on a field of play in the presence of Signor Mantegna.

The police last night were said to regard this painting, masterpiece though it unquestionably is, as yet another forgery. A statement by the chairman of the Art Treasures sub-committee of the Yorkshire County Cricket Club, however, said that this was not necessarily the case. It might equally well prove, Mr. Trueman said, to be an authentic work of the great Paduan master, painted in a moment when he had been vouchsafed an uncannily prophetic vision of what the County eleven would achieve either next season or the season after that.

PAUL FITZPATRICK AT HEADINGLEY   MAY 29 1984

Yorkshire v. Lancashire

It was cold, grey and very miserable yesterday at Headingley where another incomprehensible Roses Match, like so many of the 215 which had preceded it, passed unmourned into history, a draw the inevitable dull result.

If there was one mitigating reason for yesterday's tedium it was the loss of the whole Sunday to rain. Allott's bowling on Saturday, when Yorkshire were dismissed for 188, followed by an unbeaten stand of 125 between Fowler and Ormrod had entitled Lancashire to believe at the end of that prosperous day, that they were on the verge of building a winning position.

Rain dashed those hopes, and that was disappointing for Lancashire, though it scarcely justified their strange tactics yesterday when play, surprisingly, started on time.

It might have been in Lancashire's best interests to have declared at their overnight total and thrown the ball into Bairstow's court, but such daring would be anathema in a Roses game. Instead they chose to bat on and in the two hours to lunch added only 58 runs in 32 excruciating overs, a rate which precluded any faint hopes they might have held of winning the game and even of them collecting one more bonus point.

Fowler had shown what seemed to be the right approach when he quickly moved to his second Roses hundred, but after his departure the innings ground to a halt. O'Shaughnessy, who last season scored a hundred in 35 minutes, took three minutes longer than that to get off the mark while Hughes, at the other end, was experiencing almost as much difficulty as his younger partner in getting bat to ball.

Hughes answered one Yorkshire shout of derision by indicating with his bat that he felt that the pitch should be dug up, but although one delivery from Stevenson had almost decapitated him, and although the light was invariably poor, things were never quite as impossible as Lancashire made them seem.

Whether Lancashire suffered some pangs of guilt over lunch is not sure but the tempo afterwards offered a ludicrous contrast with the morning's play. It was like suddenly wandering from a still-life exhibition to a Mack Sennett comedy. Runs were scrambled and wickets tumbled and Lancashire declared 100 runs ahead.

That left Yorkshire 47 overs to negotiate before the close. They lost Lumb and Sharp in scoring 16 runs, but bad light spared them further embarrassment and put the few remaining, frozen spectators out of their misery.

THORNS

Money, Money, Money

To the editor   SEPTEMBER 1 1847

Sir, – The late cricket match was an object of interest to assembled thousands. The behaviour of the multitude was such as to call from the celebrated Felix a very warm eulogium. As a Manchester man, I felt proud to hear him speak so highly of my fellow townsmen. There was, however, one draw back, which it is to be hoped will not occur again, and which was noticed with regret by several of the members, as well as by one of the gentlemen players of All England, to myself. I allude to the separation at dinner of the professional players from the others. In the south, it is customary for noblemen to dine with the players, and, as the gentleman before alluded to said when in one of their late matches, Lord Morpeth sat down with the whole of them, 'the members of the Manchester Cricket Club might do so without compromising their dignity.' The chief advantage of cricket is that it brings different classes together, and promotes kind and good feeling. Besides this, the All England professional players were as much gentlemen in their conduct and station as any on the ground. – Your insertion of these few remarks will, I hope, have a good effect on future matches, as well as oblige your obedient servant.
A Member of the Manchester Cricket Club.

To the editor   JULY 7 1890

Sir, – On Saturday afternoon I was walking through Little Lever, and noting two flags up, I asked a man who was walking in the direction of them 'what was up.' He replied that a cricket match was 'on' between Little Lever and Stand. Being a total stranger to the place, I remarked that I wondered so small a village could support so large a cricket ground. 'Lord bless you,' said my friend, 'it's Mat Fletcher; he's getten t'best club brass can get together. Why, let's

157

see, there's nobbut Joe Ashworth as lives in't village of all of them as is playing today.' Anxious to see the redoubtable 'Joe', I paid my threepence and entered the enclosure. It soon became clear that it was a team of professionals playing a team of amateurs, and though the former won the latter displayed the finer cricket, their fielding being especially admirable. When I played cricket, now forty years ago, the clubs around here would have declined to play any club which played more professionals than their 'groundsman', and there were real matches in those days. To hire a lot of gladiators to do your cricket seems to me quite contrary to the interests of fair play and true cricket. I enclose my card. – Yours, &c.,

A Veteran Cricketer.

Rochdale.

COUNTY PROSPECTS   APRIL 21 1948

. . . Somersetshire will be captained by three amateurs in rotation, N. S. Mitchell-Innes in May, J. W. Seamer in June and part of July and G. E. S. Woodhouse for the rest of the season. The first two are Oxford Blues and civil servants in the Sudan, who will spend their summer leaves in playing cricket. Woodhouse is a Cambridge war-time player. Three newcomers, K. G. Harvey and I. A. C. McLennan, both wicket-keepers, and K. H. R. Johnson, a batsman, are among other amateurs who may play.

MISCELLANY   JULY 22 1950

The cricket correspondents, and even commissions of inquiry inspired and sanctioned from Marylebone, may offer their own explanations for the dismal decline of English cricket, but is it necessary to look for the reasons? The decay set in before full employment, and cannot be blamed upon the Labour Government, but it is surely one of the losses which must be set against the gains due to the changes which have raised the economic standards of the many and depressed those of the few. The old-fashioned amateur has gone the way of the historic houses. Do even the most elderly members still recall those glorious years in amateur cricket, when from 1865 to 1881 the Gentlemen won 27 and lost only five out of forty matches against the Players? And, as for the professionals, is not employment the enemy of the good? Jack Hobbs tells how when he began to play for Surrey Colts the salary which he received seemed to him 'princely': he was promised an extra bonus of £10 for the season because of his difficult home circumstances.

This was in 1903. What can professional cricket offer the young working lad by comparison with other callings to-day? The crux is not what the established county professional receives but the prospects for the colt like Hobbs who is taken on in the hope that he will make the grade for the county. The rewards of professional cricket have never been large in absolute terms. Relative to those obtainable in other jobs, they have probably never been lower than at present.

LEADER   MAY 26 1952

In choosing Mr. Hutton to captain the English eleven against India the MCC have broken with the long-standing tradition (occasionally waived in an emergency such as illness during a match) that the team must be led by an amateur. The decision is right in principle: and we hope that the new captain's fortunes will show that the selectors have chosen the right man as well as the right principle. That the change has been so long in coming has not been due merely to hidebound conservatism on the part of the MCC. If we are well rid of the belief that leadership resides only in cricketers well enough off to play without being paid for it, the new policy has its pitfalls as well as the old. Captaincy is an art in itself and it calls for experience as well as for the right personality (which should include an attacking spirit). While most counties retain an amateur captain few professionals have a chance to gain much experience in it, however expert they may be in the game. The MCC's lead may change that in time. The old rule may sometimes have led to choosing an amateur who was not quite the technical equal of his colleagues. But that at least made it probable that he would be chosen on his merits as a captain. The new danger is that the selectors may pick eleven first-class players, and then consider which of them will do for captain – which is like picking eleven batsmen and then asking if any of them bowl. One should not ignore the fact, too, that many eminent professionals prefer an amateur captain, and are reluctant to take on the job themselves. We have not seen the last of the amateur captains. These thoughts should not deter us from congratulating Mr. Hutton on his distinction, and from hoping that he will have the best of luck and the unswerving support of the team chosen to serve under him, amateurs and professionals alike.

CHRISTOPHER FORD   FEBRUARY 1 1963

The amateur in English first-class cricket finally is dead, condemned by the Advisory County Cricket Committee last November and executed without a dissenting voice by the full committee of MCC, meeting at Lord's last night. From now onwards cricketers will be called neither more nor less than cricketers, however much or little they earn from their efforts on or off the field.

Nobody expected that the MCC committee would dare or even desire to go against a weighty decision taken by the ACCC after long debate 'by a clear but not overwhelming majority' – which was the expression used when cricket suddenly and dramatically became aware, last November, that it was living in a different world from that of Grace, Ranjitsinhji, and the resplendent names of the Golden Age. Justice and sense have combined for the game's benefit, and yet many people will feel, in passing, a twinge of nostalgia. That the decision should be taken only a day after the death of Sir Pelham Warner, that embodiment of the best features of amateurism, indeed is poignant.

There can be no doubt, however, that English cricket must look to the future, and its rulers have enabled it to do so in a more practical way. The full implications of the decision cannot yet be measured, for the counties must await meetings of their own committees before making the new financial arrangements which will be necessary. Yet certain points immediately are clear: not only the amateur, but also the professional, has passed away. In future, P. B. H. May and Trueman, F. S. will wear their initials in the same place. The game between Gentlemen and Players must be replaced; various suggestions for this include North v. South, MCC Australian XI v. The Rest, Over-30's v. Under-30's, and Dark and Light Blues v. The Rest. The guiding principle, stated MCC yesterday, is to find a match which will be of interest both to public and cricketers, one for which the players themselves will feel it an honour to be selected . . .

MICHAEL CAREY   SEPTEMBER 8 1969

Yorkshire, whose victory in the Gillette Cup final at Lord's was watched by a crowd of around 25,000 and, presumably, many millions on television, will receive the princely sum of exactly £5 a man for their efforts.

At least, if there are plans to offer the team something more in keeping with the merits of their achievement, which, after all, can be reasonably compared to a soccer team winning the FA Cup, the players know nothing about it.

Even as the celebration champagne bubbled on Saturday night, one player tossed a pay packet on the table and said: 'Look at that – £6 appearance money and the usual fiver win bonus to follow.'

This year, Yorkshire's pay structure has been revised, with basic salaries raised and appearance money cut down. Given a good season – which Yorkshire have not had by their standards – an average member of the side might earn £2,000.

Yorkshire, then, are arguably the best paid side in the Championship, discounting, of course, expensive individuals with other counties, such as Gary Sobers. Incidentally, I suspect that no cricketer is currently better rewarded than Graeme Pollock, who is said to receive £3,000, plus accommodation, for his stint with the International Cavaliers. He is worth every penny of it, too.

Derbyshire, whose own abject performance does not detract from

Yorkshire's disciplined and thoroughly professional display, will receive £80 a man, but this covers all their five matches in the competition.

Had they been successful – and that was out of the question for most uncommitted spectators even before lunch – they would have earned an extra £20. Nottinghamshire, beaten semi-finalists, were promised almost £200 a man if they won the trophy.

Yorkshire can expect to pick up at least £5,000 as their share of the Cup pool. In addition, there is the prospect of an extremely profitable challenge match against Lancashire next season.

HENRY BLOFELD   MAY 9 1977

In what could be a serious threat to Test cricket, an Australian television magnate is believed to be forming a new style 'cavaliers' team, composed of some of the world's best players.

Mr. Kerry Packer, who runs Channel Nine TV in Sydney, is the man responsible for this attempt to form a cricket circus which would be comparable to the lawn tennis troupe of professionals . . .

LEADER   NOVEMBER 26 1977

Mr. Kerry Packer may be a bounder and a cad. But he is a wholly legal bounder and a High Court sanctified cad. Mr. Justice Slade, the Great Umpire, not only ruled for Packer yesterday; he left world cricket officialdom prostrate from a bumper to the heart, defenceless against the World Series Circus and perhaps as much as £200,000 worse off.

The judge took five-and-a-half hours to deliver this drubbing; but he knew (and said) that his judgement would not stop the argument. Nor will it. Nevertheless the issues are clearer than ever before. Mr. Packer may not be a lovable fellow. The motive behind his entire cricketing enterprise may be base commerce: a Test contract for his TV network. The circus itself may flop, because it orchestrates and titivates a sacred ritual beyond (and above) such frills. And if the Supertests succeed, then cricket may be debased beyond recognition. But the undesirable is not the illegal. Legally, cricket officialdom, with its bans and threats, is found completely in the wrong. It sought to restrain trade; trade is now unrestrained.

There is also a new situation. For hours on end, Mr. Justice Slade seemed barely to be mentioning the law. He talked, instead, of attitudes. The cutthroat attitude of Mr. Packer. The aggrieved, disheartened attitude of cricketers. And the sentiment-clouded attitude of cricket authorities. The first two attitudes are facts of life. If Test cricket can draw a million pounds a series, then big business will sooner or later muscle in. If Test cricketers fail to feel grateful for pinched wages and long, hard, domestically-disruptive foreign tours, then they are ripe for the muscling. But the attitude of cricketing authority will have to change. Cricket, for the most part, is run by old cricketers. What was good enough for them is good enough for the current bunch. They revere a game that has – miraculously – evolved and developed, but striven to remain true to the legacy of Grace, Hobbs and Wally Hammond. Alas, for dozens of the modern stars of that game, the legacy no longer exists. Packer proves it.

That may be a cause for immense regret, but no reasonable action stems therefrom. Some English counties, under pressure, might not welcome back their Packer rebels next summer. That would be petty and destructive. The national selectors might decide not to pick the pirates. That risks petty vengefulness, too. Pragmatically, the English game has already picked up £1 million in sponsorship that, but for Packer, it might never have sniffed. The full galaxy of talent is available next season. Meanwhile Mr. Packer, having won the legal war, has yet to score any victories on his own crumbling agricultural pitches. If he wins there as well, then the whole fabric of cricket will change. If, far more likely, he plays only a tedious financial draw, then the chances of an (honours-shared) rapprochement in 1978 must be high. Packer will have his court victory to console him; officialdom will have the matches that people who care pay to watch.

Any outcome, of course, will leave a sour taste. There is the bitter sticking point of Packer's insistence on getting Test cricket for his Australian TV Channel come what may. But for the moment the sheer, devastating weight of Mr. Justice Slade's verdict must bring fresh thinking. Officialdom cannot beat Mr. Packer. He can only beat himself. While he is doing that, the authorities must take to heart the overwhelming Slade argument: that cricketers are professional men able to ply their trade; that they are not pawns, to be dispatched to a winter on the dole if they ('bad luck old son') miss a tour selection; that they have wives, families and mortgages like everyone else; that they grow too old too soon; that they cannot be cast into oblivion because a gentleman in a blazer in the Long Room at Lord's so decrees. It is these attitudes, in part, which have made Packer possible. Their passing may be widely lamented. But if the cricket its warmest fans love is, indeed, to survive, the way from the High Court is clear. No more threats; no petulance; a deal of diplomacy; and a lot more understanding.

HENRY BLOFELD AT VFL PARK, MELBOURNE   DECEMBER 3 1977

WSC Australian XI v. WSC West Indian XI

The first day's play in Mr. Packer's long awaited 'Super Test' series was a complete flop from the commercial angle. No series in the entire history of cricket has had such a build-up as this one and after six months of continuous publicity there were less than 400 spectators at the VFL Park when Andy Roberts bowled the first ball to McCosker. In mid-afternoon the crowd had reached only two thousand and at the final count numbered 2,847, on a fine day in a ground which holds nearly 80,000.

During the day Mr. Packer's West Indians did enough to show that they are a more formidable combination than when they were beaten 5-1 in Australia two years ago. After Gary Sobers had spun the coin Lloyd put Australia in to bat and they recovered from 73 for six at lunch before being bowled out for 256. By the close the West Indian XI had reached 47 for two in reply.

But somehow this was not a day when the cricket mattered overmuch, although the standard was high enough. After all the words which have come from the Packer organisation prophesying, even guaranteeing, success, it was the commercial aspect which was unavoidably the most interesting and the most depressing or satisfying according to taste. The first innovation one noticed this morning – there would have been no way of avoiding it – was two huge emblems about 15 yards by five painted on the grass midway between the straight boundaries and the wickets at each end of the ground.

At first they looked like some new-fangled base from which athletes throw the discus or javelin. It then transpired that they were giant reproductions of the World Series Cricket emblem of three black stumps with a large red ball where the bails would be. They were hideous on the green outfield and may be an indication of the type of commercial devices which this type of cricket will produce.

There was then a glossy-backed magazine to hail the 'Super Tests' with a brashly self-confident essay by Kerry Packer himself at the start and then some honeyed words by Richie Benaud before photographs of all the 'Superstars'. Lawrence Rowe is described as Wayne Daniel and vice versa and it is a hastily-prepared brochure. After the ceremony of Sir Garfield Sobers tossing the coin (and one cannot but wonder if it is for this arduous task alone that Mr. Packer has bought his services), the cricket began, and soon Mr. Packer was watching keenly beside Sir Henry Winneke, the Governor of Victoria, whose presence admitted tacit vice-regal approval, although his appointments prevented his watching after lunch as well.

Meanwhile the television cameras were doing their best in conjunction with Messrs Benaud, Trueman and Rosenwater although the empty stands can only have been an embarrassment, while the buried microphones gave out thumping feet and muffled Australian and West Indian grunts. In the third over one of the sight-screens blew over and there were not enough people for it even to raise a laugh. Later on a group of schoolchildren wearing 'World Series' T-shirts were endlessly photographed by Mr. Packer's television people – good PR stuff.

At last, the cricket, which inevitably suffered as a spectacle as a result of the desperately poor crowd, began. The West Indian fast bowlers were pretty hostile on a slow pitch and after Roberts had

McCosker caught at third slip when he played back to the second ball of the morning, Holding quickly went through the middle order.

Davis chopped a short one on to his stumps, Greg Chappell could only fend a nasty lifter into the slips and Hookes, beaten for pace, had his off-stump knocked out. After one or two defiant hooks, Ian Chappell then turned Holding to backward short leg and in what is, for him, the classical style, Walters pushed a lifter to gully. While this was happening Bedi, Prasanna and Chandrasekhar had the official Australian side in a terrible tangle up at Brisbane and there were a fair number of transistors round the ground picking up that game, where there were 8,147 spectators.

After lunch, Marsh, Bright, who is a much improved cricketer, Lillee and Walker played some good strokes and in the end the Australians were taken to relative respectability. In the evening Fredericks and Greenidge began to cut and hook in their best West Indian fashion. They scored 21 in the first two overs, from Lillee and Pascoe, and the sparse crowd did their best to chant 'Lillee, Lillee.' Six hundred people in this vast ground could only manage a pretty hollow noise and their vain efforts just about summed up the day.

WSC Australians 256 (R. J. Bright 69, M. A. Holding 4 for 60) and 192 (D. W. Hookes 63, A. M. E. Roberts 4 for 52); WSC West Indians 214 (I. V. A. Richards 79) and 237 for 7 (Richards 56). WSC West Indians won by three wickets.

PETER DEELEY AT VFL PARK, MELBOURNE   JANUARY 25 1978

WSC Australian XI v. WSC West Indian XI

It was a night when Packer men showed their scars and were proud to wear the colours of World Series Cricket. And as for us doubting Thomases, there was scarcely room in the packed football arena to hide our faces. Twenty-four thousand six hundred people, looking and sounding like a good First Division crowd, turned up yesterday, the latest evening fixture between the Australians and West Indians.

Suddenly this night-time cricket is taking off with a bang. Kerry Packer, we were earnestly told by an aide, had been fed the figures in Honolulu where he was in transit from America, and was 'ecstatic', not least because the takings for this one performance must have been in the region of £50,000.

The crowds have brought with them the atmosphere that was so lacking in previous games. They sat in shirt sleeves and shorts until the game ended at 11.50 p.m., cheering every Australian triumph and booing every West Indian downfall. After Monday night's storms and tropical heat, yesterday evening it was cool and cloudless with the full moon rising but being outshone by the volume of electricity burning from the four pylons.

Cricket takes on a different coloration under the lights: the players' whites would pass muster in a soap advert and the green outfield (though it may sound corny) seems greener. As for the wicket itself, it looks as though it has been tinted by the ground staff for the sake of the colour television cameras.

The night games are being televised inter-state on Packer's Channel Nine but only before the 'evening brunch' in Melbourne which probably explains why an eight thousand crowd at five o'clock had tripled by 9.30 p.m. And good television fare it is, as the quality of the camera work has improved over the months.

Unfortunately, the increased crowd popularity seems to have brought in its train an unpleasant element of niggling and needling on the part of the Australian side. They have so far been the poor relations of this three-sided series, picking up ony the occasional crumbs of prize money while the West Indians and the World have taken the major portions. So their need is the greatest and of course they have the crowd 'barracking' for them, as the saying goes here in upside-down fashion.

The prime example of this aggressive attitude was Greg Chappell who had hit a fine 68 off the West Indian bowling in 73 balls. In the last over before the 'brunch break' was taken at six o'clock he hit Joel Garner for three fours and was bowled off the last ball, stepping too far down his wicket to a short-pitched delivery. As Chappell walked off the field he kicked at the prone stump and cut a swathe through the scurry of young admirers with a swinging cross bat. He thoroughly deserved the boos from the crowd which greeted this gesture.

The game did not start until three, half an hour late, because of the overnight rain and both sides were restricted to thirty-eight overs. Thanks largely to Chappell, Australia reached the creditable total of 212 for nine, leaving West Indies just over five and a half runs an over to win.

One of the problems of batting second in these night games is that for an hour, between seven and eight, the men at the wicket are playing in half light. In past games we have seen batsmen go in this in-between period and last night was no exception. Gordon Greenidge, with the score at eighteen, misjudged a short run and was well out of his crease when Gilmour threw the wicket down. Then Roy Fredericks played and missed at five successive deliveries from Pascoe before being caught by Gilmour at second slip off the next ball.

We were then treated to another remarkable display of fierce driving by young Jim Allen from Montserrat, the least known of all the West Indian players. Following his eighty-three in Sydney at the weekend against Australia, he hit the first ball he received from Gilmour for six, put both Viv Richards and Clive Lloyd in the shade and had reached 58 in one hour off 45 balls when he marched down the wicket to spinner Ray Bright and was bowled.

Collis King went first ball to Bright, a debatable decision, Rod Marsh claiming loudly that the ball had brushed the wicket and King maintaining that the ball had come back off the wicket-keeper. After a mid-wicket consultation, the umpires upheld the appeal.

Julien and Murray hit 46 in nine overs to put the West Indians ahead of the required run rate, though not before Len Pascoe had fiercely protested against the award of one boundary to Julien, claiming that young spectators running onto the pitch had prevented the ball crossing the ropes, thus enabling him to save the four. Next ball, Deryck Murray was knocked flying when he and Marsh collided in a scramble for a single.

Pascoe finally had his revenge, running full tilt some fifteen yards to catch Julien when the West Indian had hit a swift 30.

It was almost the bewitching hour when the crowd was really brought to its feet by a fantastic climax. Fast bowlers Garner and Wayne Daniel were together with two overs left and 23 runs to get. They took 16 off Greg Chappell's over – sweet revenge indeed – and needed seven off the last eight balls. Off the penultimate ball, still five short, Daniel swung a colossal six off Malone and held his bat in triumph. West Indies had won, Australia were the lighter by another thousand pounds prize money and the late, late, show had paid off at last.

WSC Australians 212 for 9, 38 overs (G. S. Chappell 68); WSC West Indians 214 for 9, 37.7 overs (J. Allen 58, R. J. Bright 4 for 37). WSC West Indians won by one wicket.

To the editor   OCTOBER 24 1979

Sir, – There appears to be some confusion as to whether the England team preparing to take part in a truncated and apparently highly artificial Test series in Australia should be playing for the Ashes. May I suggest that it is played for a specific set of Ashes – preferably Kerry Packer's.
Amanda Skinner.
18 Barley Cop Lane,
Lancaster.

To the editor   AUGUST 18 1980

Sir, – Perhaps the real relationship
floodlit cricket (and, indeed, all limited
overs cricket) has with the real game is
analogous to the relationship between
prostitution and true love. No doubt both
are enjoyable (not always to the same
people) but one is tainted with the
questionable attribute of immediacy and
lacks the charm of delayed and subtle
gratification.

In a truly free society you would pay
your money and, unless it is detrimental
to the health of that society, you would
take your choice. Here's the rub. How
long will it be before the analogy completely breaks down and the lover of true
cricket is left with no choice to exercise?
– Yours faithfully,

Kenn Pearson.

5 Melton Court,
Maidenhead, Berks.

Black and White

MAY 16 1960

At their peak, there were about fourteen anti-apartheid demonstrators
at the University Parks when the match between the South African
tourists and Oxford was played last week. After a few hours of rain
there were only three and Jackie McGlew was able to report that the
demonstrators had affected his team 'not at all' . . .

LEADER   JANUARY 25 1967

The South African Minister of the Interior has no right to tell the MCC
who shall play for England and who shall not. The Minister, Mr. Pieter
le Roux, has objected in advance to Basil D'Oliveira, the coloured
all-rounder, who may or may not be chosen to tour South Africa in 1968.

The secretary of the MCC, S. C. Griffith, has said that the matter will be dealt with 'when it arises'. He evades the issue. The matter has arisen already and should be dealt with now. The MCC should tell Mr. le Roux that England will not tour South Africa in 1968 unless he withdraws his ban on D'Oliveira. The New Zealand rugby team refused to visit South Africa without its Maori players. The MCC should do likewise.

To the editor   AUGUST 29 1968

SIR, – JUST HEARD SCANDALOUS NEWS ABOUT D'OLIVEIRA STOP IF PROMPTED BY CONSIDERATION FOR SOUTH AFRICAN RACIAL POLICY COMMA CRAVEN ABDICATION OF RESPONSIBILITY STOP IF NOT SELECTORS BLOODY FOOLS – YOURS

J. LEWIS.

WOLVERHAMPTON.

JOHN ARLOTT   SEPTEMBER 11 1968

News of sport is, in general, news only inside the small world of sport. When it bursts into the outer world by the weight of its own importance it invariably tends to appear in false perspectives. The vehemence of the protest against the omission of Basil D'Oliveira from the MCC team for South Africa has amazed the close little world of cricket; and its amazement has, in turn, amazed those who live outside it. Even the grounds for protest have differed so widely that a fortnight of listening on both sides of the wall prompts the attempt to spell out the differences and the common ground to both camps; for what is elementary in one is, apparently, mystery to the other. Thus, this is a humble attempt to interpret not between two languages but between two worlds, made because it seems imperative and because no one else has made it.

Most county cricketers find it unreasonable on cricketing grounds that D'Oliveira was not chosen. This constitutes the basic justification for the objectors inside and outside the game. The blinkered cricket enthusiast – rarely the first-class player – ranks the omission of Milburn as a similar issue. This is the failure of the cloistered. Hirst and Jessop were left out in 1902, Charles Parker in 1921, Hutton in 1948, Watson in 1953: cricket was stirred by those events: history never noticed them nor needed to do so. The rejection of D'Oliveira, however, has made a breach in the walls of Lord's Cricket Ground through which international opinion has surged in to make, for the first time, an impact

168

on the self-perpetuating committee of a private club.

The discarding of Milburn leaves MCC in South Africa a duller side than it might have been, one less likely to seize advantage through an individual innings. Other players, such as Green, Sharpe, and Alan Jones, were reasonable challengers for team places. But none of them had done what D'Oliveira had done – scored 158 in a single innings which raised England's scoring rate and then taken the wicket which created the break-through from which the fifth Test match was won and the series tied.

If, in the Oval Test, Milburn had scored 158 runs and, as a bowler, taken the crucial wicket, he would have been chosen for South Africa. D'Oliveira did precisely that and was not chosen. If D'Oliveira had been white-skinned that decision would have been a matter for debate in cricket pavilions. But, because he is a Cape Coloured, it becomes an issue of British, international, and racial politics which the club responsible cannot evade.

Cricket is the senior, most widespread, and deeply-rooted of English games. For more than two centuries it has faithfully reflected its social background. At its basic club and league level, where thousands play it, especially in the North, the Midlands, and Wales, there is a strong vein of radical opinion among its participants. In the South, outside the often semi-feudal villages, it has a middle-class aura and at Lord's, through MCC, it is part of the Establishment. Most of the many MCC members of my acquaintance are such purely bred conservatives that they regard themselves as non-political. Indeed, few of those within the world of first-class cricket are political animals. That, however, is no excuse for being politically unconscious.

No one who knows them will doubt the integrity of the 1968 Board of Control Selectors: nor would they impugn the officers of MCC appointed to decide who should be taken on the tour of South Africa – 'so are they all, all honourable men.'

Only an inconsiderable minority attempt to justify D'Oliveira's exclusion on cricketing grounds: the figures exist to demonstrate not only his ability, but his capacity for rising to the high challenge. By reasonable inference, too, his temperament would enable him to justify himself before his own people.

For the other cricketers eligible for selection, this was simply another tour. For D'Oliveira it was the peak of ambition for himself and his people, to return to his own land as one who, by ability, had penetrated the race-barrier; and this redounded to Britain's credit.

It has been suggested that, in the West Indies last winter, D'Oliveira was 'not a good tourist' – which covers a multitude of sins and non-sins. But who would suggest that in South Africa before his own and all the other 'non-European' peoples who hold him in such respect, he would fail to uphold his reputation as highly as he did when he returned two years ago, as a coach, to plough back into their cricket the privileges he had gained from it?

The final argument of those who live within the boundaries of the cricket field is that politics should not be allowed to intrude upon cricket. They must, however, recognise that the totalitarian countries have employed sport for prestige purposes, and that racial problems, in cricket or elsewhere, are political problems which must be faced politically.

Neither can they have had the opportunity to observe the distressing coldness with which the Pakistani and West Indian cricketers so lately admitted to English county dressing-rooms veil their bitterness, and refrain from comment on the matter when the subject of D'Oliveira is raised. This is striking because the cricket teams themselves are an admirable example of integration, and dressing-room talk normally is wide ranging and uninhibited.

They should not, however, fail to recognise that, in the West Indies and emergent countries of Africa, where D'Oliveira won admiration as both a cricketer and footballer, his omission is seen as clear evidence of English cricket – and therefore Britain – truckling to apartheid. Governments with no interest in cricket – who do not even care what it is – will make capital of what seems so plainly to be racial discrimination on the part of a section of the English Establishment. To the people whose cricket is described in South Africa, where they live, as 'non-European', and to whom D'Oliveira is the unique hero who, by his ability, rose above the barriers of race and was accepted in the free country of England, this must seem the ultimate betrayal.

Those who met at Lord's a fortnight ago probably regarded their decision as a purely cricketing one, but they did less than their duty if they did not recognise that, in 1968, it is not possible to take a purely cricketing or non-political decision where race is involved. The politically-informed will have noted that Sir Alec Douglas-Home is the immediate past-president of MCC: and that MCC specifically excluded the usual matches in Rhodesia from the tour itinerary: it may be wondered whether Sir Alec was consulted on either decision or both.

It might be argued that a team would be affected, in a cricketing sense, by the inclusion of a player whose presence caused unsettling public reactions: but that ought not to be adduced as a cricket evaluation, as MCC have declared theirs to be. Two conclusions are inescapable. This decision of MCC will have strong and, for Britain, damaging impacts far beyond the limits of cricket: and it will continue to reverberate long after the results of the coming Tests in South Africa are forgotten.

LEADER   DECEMBER 12 1969

Oblivious of the realities of South Africa, the Test and County Cricket Board are intent on saving their wretched image. If we have forfeited any claim to being principled, at least we can show we stick to our word.

These seem to be their intentions in deciding to go ahead with next year's invitation to the South African cricketing 'all-Whites'. They are misguided. It is a pity that they did not keep the bulldog qualities of stubbornness which they are now showing against the threat of demonstrations for use against their real opponent. He is Mr. Vorster.

It was his original meddling last year during the D'Oliveira affair that should have incurred the board's anger. By refusing to sanction the selection of D'Oliveira Mr. Vorster interfered with the rights of sports-lovers in this country far more outrageously than any British demonstrators. It is sheer sanctimonious hypocrisy of the board to invoke this 'silent majority' of sports-lovers now. Cricket has ceased to be a cosy pastime bereft of political overtones. Apartheid is enforced as rigorously in cricket as in any other walk of life. And the South African Government sees its white sportsmen partially as salesmen of this policy.

By attempting to go on with the tour, the board is throwing down a direct challenge to demonstrators to do what it should have done itself – which is to stop the tour. Those who disagree with boycotts and other international action against South Africa are fond of telling opponents to stop meddling and worry about their own country first. That is what the British protesters are doing. They may be able to do little about apartheid inside South Africa, but they can act when it is exported to Britain.

OUR OWN REPORTERS   MAY 23 1970

The South Africans' cricket tour was cancelled by the Cricket Council last night and the decision detonated a reaction of rage and near-hysteria from some cricket supporters and right-wing groups. The Monday Club called it 'the triumph of the campus bums', and christened the victorious anti-tour campaign leader 'Führer Hain'.

And – while the Police Federation expressed 'delight' – Mr. Quintin Hogg, Shadow Home Secretary, gave notice that he would exploit the issue as the cornerstone of a Conservative 'law and order' election campaign.

'Mr. Callaghan and Mr. Wilson have bowed to threats and yielded to blackmail from persons who threatened extra-legal action to disrupt a perfectly lawful activity, and have resorted to bullying for the purpose of imposing their decision upon an independent body of sportsmen,' Mr. Hogg said. 'What is even more deplorable is that the Prime Minister, by his speeches, which deliberately encouraged these threats, was himself responsible in part for the situation out of which he has now sought to dodge.'

The same message, saddling the Government with the blame for the cancellation, came from Mr. C. R. Yeomans, chairman of the Council of Cricket Societies. 'The sombre silence of television screens this summer will have an even more numbing effect on Labour MPs than the sight of violent demonstrations would have done,' he said. 'Many cricketers will probably rejoice that if the Labour Party meets defeat it will come on the same day that a Test match at Lord's against South Africa was due to start . . .'

MATTHEW ENGEL IN PRETORIA   MARCH 4 1982

South African U-25 XI v. SAB English XI

If there was ever a time when turning back was a plausible option, that time almost certainly ended at 11 o'clock Pretoria time yesterday morning when Graham Gooch and Geoff Boycott walked out together – as they have done so often under other skies and circumstances – to open the batting for something now being called the South African Breweries English XI.

By the evening the players had still not seen the telex messages sent by George Mann and Donald Carr, chairman and secretary of the Test and County Cricket Board, pleading with them to reconsider their decision to play in South Africa.

Gooch, as captain of the English team, held a press conference in the ladies' toilet and changing room at the Berea Stadium at close of play, when he insisted he would only answer questions about the cricket.

Since the cricket on the first day of this extraordinary venture was rather dreary (Breweries English 152 for seven declared in four hours plus; South African Under 25 XI 51 for one) this was not a great success. Asked if he would still be here in two or three weeks' time as planned, Gooch said doggedly: 'We'll be here at 10 o'clock tomorrow morning.'

All kinds of conflicting pressures are at work on the hearts and minds of the adjectival dozen. But Carr and Mann can only send telexes. Peter Cooke, the joint impresario and manager, was at Gooch's elbow. 'If they renege on their contracts, they could be sued under British law,' he said.

And when Cooke is not with them, the players are talking and drinking with people who are wildly enthusiastic about a tour which they believe marks the end of their 12-year isolation from international cricket.

Indeed, the greatest threat to the tour's success yesterday probably came not from Lord's but from Boycott, who scored two runs in the first hour, 13 in 95 minutes in all, and must have made many spectators wonder if there was not something to be said for isolation.

Around 3,000 people were there to watch, which is almost 3,000 more than Kerry Packer got on his first day of operations, and was particularly remarkable in Pretoria, the most Afrikaans and rugby-minded of major South African cities. Cricket here is a minority taste.

Pretoria is also the whitest of the major cities, which may explain why the only blacks on the ground appeared to be employees.

The '13th man' mystery continued. Derek Randall, the latest to be touted, is in Perth, Australia, and said he was not the man. The organisers have promised an announcement this afternoon and boasted that they had plenty of willing cricketers to choose from.[1]

My understanding is that they would have settled for Alvin Kallicharran, who is playing for Transvaal and thus already in disgrace back home in the West Indies, but the South African Cricket Union want it to be an Englishman so their 'Tests' can look like Tests.

There was not a hotel room to be had in Pretoria though that was nothing to do with this match. The South African swimming championships are on, and if no-one else will play with you, such occasions are to be savoured.

But the papers were full of the cricket with Fleet Street comment reported back and described as 'hysterical' even in the liberal *Rand Daily Mail*, which devoted eight chunky paragraphs to a pro-tour telephone call it received from one London cricket follower.

It was a glorious day – it is late summer south of the Equator – with temperatures in the high 70s and just a hint of possible showers in the late afternoon clouds. The Breweries, who have a virtual monopoly, did good business. After the initial excitement died down, it was like a particularly sunny and profitable Wednesday at Chesterfield or Abbeydale Park or any other of the nicer, leafier English grounds.

Before long, some people were turning away from Boycott and started to play with tennis balls amongst themselves. Chris Old, left out of the 12 by consensus, brought out drinks. Gooch batted quite aggressively for 33. Then the middle order collapsed to a blond fast-medium bowler from Western Province called Adrian Kuiper, who is regarded here as the find of the season.

He bowls a little like Garth Le Roux and bats, so it is said, like Clive Rice. He finished with five for 22 off eight overs and, since it is only a two-day match, the English declared, a little sheepishly, more than an hour before the close. Gooch, when he had his way and talked cricket, moaned about the pitch. But it seemed flat and reasonable to me.

'Did you feel any undue pressure?' someone asked him. 'No, not on the cricket side.' 'What about on anything else?' 'I'm not answering about anything else.'

The toilet windows were open and it was just possible to hear the lovely, half-forgotten sound of a steam locomotive chugging through Pretoria station. I had not imagined anything could make the scene more unreal.

---

[1] The eventual, anti-climactic, answer was Geoff Humpage, the Warwickshire wicket-keeper.

JAMES CAMERON   MARCH 9 1982

It is well that we should be reminded, as our brave boys wield the willow in beautiful Botha-land, that this is the UN's official International Year of Mobilising Sanctions against South Africa. Pause for hollow laughter.

It is true that Britain, with most of the rich countries, voted against this spoilsport motion, on the reasonable principle that morality is bad for business. So there isn't a deathless hush in the close tonight, or not so you would notice.

Nevertheless our green unpleasant land has been much exercised by the consideration of grown men playing kids' games in the sunshine. Much of it is passing jealousy at the thought of Mr. Gooch's band of brothers frolicking on the greensward, and being paid quite tidy sums for it. A good deal of it is honourable anger, though it is the case that the great majority of black South Africans do not give a boycott for the bwanas' game, very sensibly preferring football.

What involves me in these concerns of (a) cricket and (b) South Africa? I know little about (a) but quite a bit about (b). The link is actually a fallacy. To think of South Africa in terms of cricket is like thinking of the Soviet system solely in terms of the Bolshoi Ballet.

To my regret, both cricket and the ballet are mysteries to me. Apartheid, on the other hand, is not.

My own upbringing meant that I did not become even aware of the game, or religion, of cricket until my late teens, and then only in the abstract. To this day I have never been present at a cricket match though this odd activity is hard to escape when you have a TV and a family that thinks God wears white flannels.

No, I tell a lie: I once attended a country meadow where in days of yore a team from the *New Statesman* magazine played a side from Parliament. These occasions were umpired by the late and loved cartoonist Vicky, an eccentric Hungarian to whom the whole business was as much an enigma as to me, and whose value as a referee was marred by his belief that anyone who hit a ball over a boundary was out and who would brook no argument about it. It was restful, but it was arguably Not Cricket.

One happy side-effect of this South African debate was the catching of Mrs. M. Thatcher flat-footed in a parliamentary quandary. Clearly she wanted to take the popular line of pained disapproval but, mindful of her gamey Tory backbenchers, she was obliged to hedge like anything, and to expound the right of all true Brits to travel wherever they wished.

I used to go frequently to South Africa, until the late Premier Dr. Malan grew tired of my petulant observations about his racial laws. Not that they made the slightest difference to his methods, or those of his successors. Nevertheless for many a long year I was on the stop-list, as they called it, and probably still am. I would not have it otherwise, though I once knew the country well and admired its natural, if

174

charmless, beauty. If every prospect pleases and only man is vile, then SA is not alone in that, but certainly ahead of the field.

I do not get at the white South Africans for this crude situation. They live in a rich and isolated society; the fact is that they are so physically, linguistically, and intellectually remote from the mainstream of contemporary feeling that they are largely ignorant of their own unpopularity. Their barbaric social legislation is accepted as a natural and even divinely inspired – except for a few dissidents who usually finish up in gaol or in Robben Island or, as we now see, not infrequently dead.

We, the uitlanders, from time to time raise our pious liberal voices in disapproval of apartheid, while the men who matter exploit it with vigour. The poor sportsmen say they knew nothing of the implications of their furtive stratagem, though I have grave doubts about this simple sporting innocence. Why did they shroud their pettifogging conspiracy in such schoolboy secrecy?

The boyos are said to be making a pretty easy £30,000, or £3 million, or whatever it is. Talk about that sort of small change to Mr. Tiny Rowland or Barclays Bank.

In last week's *Guardian* Joan Lestor, MP, spelled out many facts that I gratefully pinch. Britain is the mainstay and major foreign investor in South Africa. Eighteen years ago the Wilson government applied an arms embargo, made mandatory in 1977 by the UN. Now this Government delivers to South Africa a Plessey radar complex to computerise air-ground strikes against obstinate black neighbours.

South Africa's presence in Namibia was declared illegal 16 years ago. We are still hesitantly asking South Africa to get out and permit elections. Instead, it reinforces it as a base for action against Angola. How's – as they say in the slips – that?

One more consolation for the embattled Boers. On the heels of the cricketers another very important gathering is assembling in Cape Town: the six-yearly convocation of the orthopaedic surgeons of the English-speaking world – 60 or 70 most skilful people better known for the mending of bones than the breaking of them. They would perhaps be better employed in Pretoria prison, but the Cape is more agreeable.

As Mrs. Thatcher said to the Foreign Policy Association in New York a year ago: 'The time has come to make progress towards an ending of the isolation of South Africa.'

No one can say we haven't made a start.

However, the day after tomorrow the Anti-Apartheid Movement is having its major conference at Wembley with all the faithful – Michael Foot, David Steel, Oliver Tambo, Archbishop Trevor Huddleston. They will have more to talk about than cricket. I hope Pretoria will be listening in. Totsiens!

A Dangerous Game

To the editor   JUNE 15 1850

Sir, – While passing through Peel Park
on Monday evening, I received a severe
blow from a heavy cricket ball, on the
arm and ribs, which made me unconscious for several minutes, and the
greater part of my arm is now much
discoloured from the effects of the blow.
I believe a similar circumstance took
place on Tuesday, when a girl was struck
in the face. If the blow I received had
struck a boy or girl, or even myself,
upon the temples or some delicate part,
it would have caused death. Now, the
question is, whether this evil must
be overlooked, until something really
serious takes place.

W.C.

To the editor   JUNE 22 1850

Sir, – Perceiving in your last Saturday's publication, a communication on
the subject of 'Cricket playing in Peel
Park,' signed 'W.C.', I beg leave to state
that when 'W.C.' was struck by the ball,
he was standing near the wicket sticks,
though he saw the ball continually flying
that way, and repeated warnings were
given that it was dangerous. The girl he
mentions as being struck, was warned
more than once; and if people will be so
stupid as to remain after being warned,
surely they have no cause to complain.
The only excuse which can be pleaded,
viz. that there was no other ground to
play or walk upon, will not hold good, the
fact being that 'there is enough room for
all'. – I am, sir, yours respectfully,
A Cricket Player.
Manchester.

To the editor

Sir, – In your impression of to-day, you report the case of a young man killed whilst playing at cricket, the ball striking him on the left temple.

I am not surprised at such an accident with such result. The balls used are more like cannon balls than anything else, and seem invented to turn an innocent and healthy game into one of extreme peril and danger. I have a son connected with a cricket club, who has from time to time been considerably hurt and disfigured about the head and face, having been struck by the ball on the forehead, eyes, nose, mouth, &c. and only narrowly escaping serious, if not fatal injury. He is somewhat of an enthusiast at the game, and one does not like to express very strong opposition to such sport, although these accidents cause much uneasiness and annoyance.

Not only is the description of ball used thus objectionable, but the rest of the tackle is almost equally absurd. Youths of 14 or 15 frequently play with bats large and heavy enough for strong men, and calculated, it would seem, unreasonably to fatigue them, and strain them not a little about the ribs.

Indeed cricketers appear to be afflicted with the vanity of having everything they require, or imagine they require, got up without regard to expense, or rather so as to cost as much as possible. Fancy 7s 6d for a ball, with which to knock out each other's eyes, or worse. And fancy the necessity of being armed *cap-à-pie* to figure in a game of cricket. I am sorry to object to anything connected with the sport, but trust these remarks are neither ill-timed nor unreasonable. – Yours respectfully,

Father.

Manchester, August 12, 1859.

To the editor

Sir, – Why all this fuss about 'the leg theory', as though it were some hitherto unheard-of monster? It is not unknown in the Lancashire League – a dead-length ball at the batsman with most of the fieldsmen on the leg side, two at the bat's end. One of its best exponents is an ex-Australian. Surely Barnes did, and still does, exploit it. And years ago was there not some adverse criticism of Armstrong for bowling in such a way that batsmen could not score runs? Was not this 'the leg theory'? Is it merely that Voce is faster than any previous practitioner?

As for the suggestion that all great fast bowlers prior to 1932 have been imbued with quixotic notions of chivalry – afraid of soiling the batsman's pads, and the rest of it – this is mere sentimental nonsense. Gregory and McDonald owed their success largely to the fact that they put the batsman in fear of his body. It is, indeed, one of the points of fast bowling that it increases the strain on the batsman. He has two things to guard. After the Gregory-McDonald massacre the groundsman got busy with his marl and did his best to simplify the task of the batsman. The result was that by 1930 Larwood at Leeds could not get the ball above half-stump high, and Bradman's joy was unconfined. Now, when the bowler appears to have overcome this handicap and discovered how to make the batsman dance about a bit, we have all this illogical gush about 'the spirit of the game', 'is it legitimate?' and so on.

No wonder we wail the dearth of real fast bowlers. Not only are they handicapped by a doped wicket, which makes bowling against good batsmen a perfectly hopeless task, but they are also to be restricted by tender feelings about disturbing the dignity and poise of the batsman. – Yours, &c.,

S. Sagar.

Burnley Mechanics Institution,
Burnley.

NEVILLE CARDUS   JANUARY 27 1933

There's humour in all things, even in the present discontent between the cricketers of England and Australia. The 'Sydney Referee' have been giving Mr. P. F. Warner a rather embarrassing time. They have tried to interview him – and they have looked up the files of the 'Morning Post' of last August and found a few remarks he expressed then about 'body line' bowling as he saw it in the Surrey and Yorkshire match, when Bowes gave his celebrated if mild exhibition of the fast leg-theory methods.

A 'Sydney Referee' correspondent asked Mr. Warner how he 'squared' his views of last August 'with his present silent assent to the same hideous methods.' And Mr. Warner answered that he had been 'misreported'. 'Then we are to assume that you approve of this form of attack?' asked the 'Sydney Referee' man. 'I'm not allowed to give interviews,' replied Mr. Warner. Whereat, say the 'Referee', Mr. Warner 'repeated his refusal to be interviewed, and said, "Please don't say you have even seen me. I'd rather you didn't say you had put any questions to me." ' The correspondent went back to his office, and in the 'Morning Post' of August 22 of last year discovered an article headed 'Bowling Fast and Short at the Oval,' signed 'P. F. Warner.' And the 'Referee' quoted as follows from the article:

'While giving Yorkshire all credit for their out-cricket, Bowes must alter his tactics. Bowes bowled with five men on the on-side and sent down several very short-pitched balls which repeatedly bounced head high and more. Now that is not bowling: indeed, it is not cricket, and if all the fast bowlers were to adopt his methods the M.C.C. would be compelled to step in and penalise the bowler who bowled the ball at less than half-way up the pitch.' The 'Referee' quoted another passage from Mr. Warner's protest: 'These things lead to reprisals, and when they begin goodness knows where they will end.' The 'Referee' then say that Mr. Warner 'can, if he chooses, stop this short-pitched body theory that he so strongly abhorred before he left England . . . He is, by his official indifference, helping to breed a feeling of bitterness not only between the opposing teams but between the peoples of the two countries.'

It is hard to understand how Mr. Warner, even if he chose, could interfere with the English players' strategy. But it would be well if cricketers in this country were to try to see the Australian point of view. The outcry against 'body line' bowling began in Australia as soon as the English team landed and were first seen in action last year. The protest of the Board of Control has been the culmination of two months or so of agitation in the press. We are not likely to mend matters by talking of 'squealing' amongst the Australians. The Australian cricketer has never been soft-fibred; he has, on the contrary, gained a reputation for toughness, especially in moments of adversity. On the 1928-9 English tour in Australia Larwood, at Brisbane, wreaked destruction amongst Australian batsmen on a scale far beyond anything he has achieved this time. But the Australians did not complain, because then they saw nothing in his bowling which offended their sense of fair play.

Rightly or wrongly, the Australians are declaring that the leg theory of the English fast bowlers is against the interests of cricket, 'a violation of the fine sporting spirit that has characterised the game right through the ages.' It is denied that Gregory and McDonald ever exploited 'body line' bowling. 'True,' say the 'Sydney Referee', 'Gregory and McDonald, like every other bowler, have given batsmen a nasty crack, but these knocks have been accidental. Never has a body attack been premeditated.'

One of the most judicious comments on this leg-theory controversy has been made by Mr. Herbert Sidebotham. He admits he has not played cricket since he was sixteen, and then only with a soft ball on the sands. But, as he adds, 'the outsider and the ignoramus sometimes sees most of the game.' He scores a good point when he writes: 'I do not see how you are going to draft a rule which shall prevent a ball coming against a batsman's body. But it is one thing to bowl occasionally in that way and another to build up a whole theory of bowling upon it and set your field to take advantage of it.'

That is the Australians' case. They are not 'squealing' against fast bumpers as the game has usually known them. They are objecting to a wholesale exploitatoin of short, fast balls which, though the intention of the bowlers may be fair enough, are in effect of a kind which compels the batsman to think first of protecting himself from physical hurt.

The unhappy affair will not be settled if we pompously assume that all the right is on our side and that the Australians are merely 'squealing' and under a general and national optical delusion. Let us be honest and get rid of humbug. Most cricketers in this country have seen the recent development of the fast leg-theory, based on a short-pitched ball which is hard to distinguish from the sort of ball that a bowler would use if indeed he were attacking the batsman's body or even his head. And many English cricketers have agreed that this species of bowling is dangerous to limb, that it is likely to breed bad feeling, and that if it is generally adopted by fast bowlers it will put an end to good, scientific batsmanship. It is all very well to maintain that MacLaren and Tyldesley and other of the great old masters would have conquered the fast leg-bumper – and the leg-field. But we cannot argue from the things which it is possible for geniuses to perform. Club cricket is quick to imitate Test cricket. What will happen to the game at large if fast body-bowling, with the field packed on the leg side, becomes widespread?

Even supposing that batsmen should contrive to work out a technique capable of playing and scoring from the leg-bumper – what then? You can only get rid of a ball on the leg side which rises head high by hitting it to leg. Do any of us wish to see batsmen spending the whole day hitting to leg, and often caught out from the best strokes that they can make while partially engaged in protecting the body? Fast leg-bowling based on the high kicker reduces batsmen to a common level; a Richard Tyldesley becomes as likely as a Spooner to stay in. Indeed, you could not possibly evolve out of fast leg-theory bowling a batsman as free and stylish as R. H. Spooner. That is the best argument against the short high kicker, which leaves the batsman almost with no choice but to duck, get hit, or risk a catch in the crowded leg-trap.

At any rate, the Australian case cannot be dismissed as loftily as some seem to imagine it can be. The Board of Control's protest was tactlessly worded; but, none the less, we must recognise that there has been some provocation behind it. The defect of the M.C.C.'s reply, as Mr. Sidebotham has said, was that it was as touchy and stiff as the Board of Control's note was rude and lacking in the sense of proportion. Protests have been heard in England, as everybody knows, against short-kicking leg bowling, and protests will be heard again here, and before long and in greater force. For success breeds imitation. It is not a case of hard-and-fast ruling, for the simple reason that it is impossible to legislate as to the length, pace, and direction of a ball. But every cricketer knows the difference between the occasional 'bumper' of a fast bowler and a persistent exploitation of leg-bumpers, pitched short to a leg-field and rising at the batsman's head – a species of bowling which, however fair in intention, might, as I say, be hard to distinguish from the sort of bowling which actually would be used if the bowler's target were the batsman's body and head.

HENRY BLOFELD IN AUCKLAND   FEBRUARY 25 1975

New Zealand v. England, First Test

The first Test match ended after 45 minutes' play here in circumstances of sheer horror. Chatfield, the New Zealand No 11, had batted pretty well for 75 minutes altogether when Lever bowled him a short-pitched ball which ricocheted off his glove on to the side of his head. Chatfield reeled away and fell. Within three minutes his pulse and his heart had stopped. He was given the kiss of life by the England physiotherapist and revived having been medically dead for a few seconds.

The fact that New Zealand were then 184 for nine and that England therefore won the first Test match by an innings and 83 runs was irrelevant in comparison. It was the final and most appalling irony of this tour that one of England's bowlers, who had ducked and weaved his way through Australia against Thomson and Lillee, should himself have come very close to killing Chatfield.

That may sound a harsh sentence but if Bernard Thomas, the physiotherapist, had not been as quickly to the scene as he was, there is no doubt that Chatfield would have died. It was Lever's fourth short ball in 45 minutes. Two hardly rose to waist height, the third went down the leg side, and the fourth was, as Lever, shocked and utterly dismayed by what had happened, said later: 'A bad one.' And better batsmen than Chatfield would have had trouble with it. It was straight and not very short.

It is difficult to say whether Chatfield, who has recovered very quickly although he may have a hairline fracture of the skull, or Lever was the unluckiest. Lever had in no way infringed the laws surrounding the over-use of short balls. Chatfield had batted intelligently for 75 minutes, and was by then entitled to be treated as a batsman. Lever's intention was to have him caught off the glove and he had moved his gully three yards closer only two balls before for this very purpose. No one that I have met in Auckland today has held Lever in any way to blame for what happened.

Congdon, the New Zealand captain, and Bruce Hosking, their team manager, were both most emphatic about this, and Lever's own reactions to what he had done, and the distressed state in which he has been, show a man who has never borne physical malice against a batsman in his life.

He told me: 'I thought I had killed him when I saw him lying there in convulsions with his face turning purple. I felt quite sick and ashamed at what I had done, and all I could think when I got back to the pavilion was that I wanted to retire from cricket.' While Chatfield was being attended to Lever knelt down, flanked by two of his colleagues, in complete and obvious bewilderment. By the end of the day he was rather better . . .

To the editor   JANUARY 17 1975

Sir, – 'Cricket' used to be a synonym for honourable conduct. It is becoming a synonym for brute force. Is it not time that respected leaders in all countries who love sport spoke out?

It has proved inadequate to leave the issue to the discretion of umpires. An urgent decision should be reached to forbid all bowling aimed at the batsman rather than the wicket.

Unless action is taken serious injury, perhaps even fatal injury, may occur – Sincerely,

Fenner Brockway.
(Lord Brockway)

House of Lords.

To the editor   MARCH 17 1975

Sir, – Two weeks have now passed since John Arlott disclosed in your columns that 'In club cricket . . . there are some half-dozen fatalities a year.' But I still see no sign of a campaign to ban this lethal pursuit. Does it take so long to draft a specification for the soft ball which might still be permitted?

Your article did not say how many man-years of club cricket are played in an English summer, but I am sure the mortality rate is more than would be tolerated in any industrial context. Certainly I feel I am much safer in my job as a plutonium worker at British Nuclear Fuels, Ltd's Windscale works than I would be on the cricket field. – Yours etc.,

John K. Blair.

Whinyeat,
Rottington,
Whitehaven, Cumbria.

IAN PEEBLES　　　　　　　　　　　　　　　　　DECEMBER 30 1975

Once again the case for giving the batsman some form of head protection has been voiced, this time by a witness as well qualified as Rodney Marsh, the Australian wicketkeeper. In spite of his incurring an oblique charge of squealing in a Sunday newspaper he reiterates an argument worthy of very serious consideration.

According to the statisticians cricket has always been one of the more dangerous games, but this is surely a realm in which statistics can be more than ever manipulated to any desired end. Does the compiler attribute death on the field from heart attack (which has happened twice within my memory) to the actual play? Does he include the dog killed on the boundary by the legendary underhand fast bowler, Brown, who was said to have beaten two long-stops in the process?

Safety measures and protective equipment have evolved as the nature of the injuries have changed with the development of the game. Beldham recalled seeing a fielder tear off a finger nail on a buckled shoe, an accident subsequently avoided by the abandonment of the buckled shoe on the cricket field.

At that stage the batsman was in danger of little more than a bruised shin but, as the bowler's hand rose to round arm, his dangers increased until in 1836 Alfred Mynn was so injured about the legs after a long innings that the surgeons considered amputating them. Happily they desisted for had they proceeded this must have meant the premature end of 'kind and manly Alfred Mynn'.

It is said that pads were invented in the same year by one named H. Daubeney, but it seems more likely that they were just generally developed in view of their growing necessity. Before their widespread use players used to line their socks with strips of rubber or other absorbent material and hope for the best. The skeleton pad came in during the sixties and gloves appeared about the same time so that, at least in theory, the striker was guarded on his most exposed if not his most vulnerable areas.

The innovation of the box or, as it was politely called, the protector, came very much later and, one may think, none too soon. Early on it took various shapes and forms and Jim Swanton has one of my favourite tales on this topic. Gloucester were about to face an early in-swinger of lively pace and W.G., realising the dangers of this new-fangled form of attack, advised a young Arthur Croome to equip himself with one of those equally new-fangled boxes. But the best Croome could find in this line was a wire contraption resembling a hemispherical bird cage, and this he duly adjusted before opening the innings with W.G. himself.

As with so many of the great man's suggestions, this one was most timely for whenever Croome played forward at the in-swinger, the ball took him smack in the midst of the bird cage which responded with a loud musical 'ping'. Presently, by the tuggings of the beard, Croome could see that his captain was somewhat disconcerted by these recurrent percussions. At length, after one particularly melodious over, W.G. advanced down the wicket. 'Arthur,' said he, in his high-pitched tenor, 'When I told you to get a box I did *not* mean a musical one.'

Perhaps as with so many warming W.G. stories, this one has to be taken with a little seasonal indulgence and, I fear, the other story on this subject which comes to mind is also unsupported by documentary evidence. When I was young there was a tale of a batsman in Hampshire who invented a pneumatic protector. Apparently he was a better inventor than constructor for, when put to the test, his handiwork burst with a deafening crack.

My informant said that the embarrassment of the user was as nothing to the extreme alarm and perplexity of the fielders, ignorant of the cause of the explosion. Perhaps in his anxiety the inventor had over-inflated his brainchild (if that is the appropriate term).

The adequate protection of the batsman's head has long been a problem but one which, in recent years, has grown to be an increasingly urgent one. The head-high bouncer seldom appears in older chronicles presumably because it was such a rarity. It was in 1921 that Jack Gregory, with his high action and occasional short pitch, caused some complaints. But the only batsman he hit on the head was Ernest Tyldesley and this the result of a mistimed hook which nicked the ball on to the striker's jaw.

The first really serious head injury from this source occurred in the Lord's Test match of 1929 when a shortish ball from Larwood hit the South African Jock Cameron and knocked him unconscious. Three years later on the same ground Pat Hendren went to hook a similar ball from the same bowler, and, missing it, was also knocked cold.

I was sitting on the top balcony of the pavilion at that moment and, hearing the sickening thud at that range, feared the worst. However, Pat emerged from a spell in hospital seemingly completely recovered, but he was told, while there, that he was exceedingly lucky not to have been hit two inches further forward.

Understandably anxious to avoid another such injury he experimented with a cap of his own design which had peaks at the sides as well as the front. This was perhaps more of a gimmick than a measure of protection but it served to underline the potential dangers.

That noticeably eccentric man of Hampshire, George Brown, also made a gesture of protest in his own odd way. He surprised the Trent Bridge crowd by confronting Larwood and Voce with a crash helmet on top of his head. As this turned out to be a woman's cloche hat it did little to further science whatever its propaganda value.

The bodyline series really set off the search for protective equipment. Various sets of body armour were suggested and one, I believe designed by the ingenious Bev Lyon, featured scoops and wings intended to deflect the ball at over-obtrusive fielders. But the batsman's head, 'bloody but unbowed' as the poet's, was still left bare except for his cap. Here the baggy Australian model has its advantages and I recall seeing, in later years, Jimmy Burke emerging unscathed after a direct hit had removed his.

Over the recent years there have been so many incidents and near misses that action must be taken before there is a real tragedy. With the bouncer so persistently and deliberately used as a weapon it seems that the only solution is to give the batsman every protection consistent with freedom of movement and comfort. To legislate against the bouncer is difficult. The spirit of the play varies with circumstances, and to frame regulations of such precision as to ensure consistent interpretation is difficult in the extreme.

But if the batsman could be relieved of all or the greater part of physical fear, the short fast bouncer merely becomes a ball of indifferent length to be attacked or ignored according to the batsman's taste. The point that this gives the bowler carte blanche to use the bouncers seems to me to be irrelevant once it is shorn of its dangers.

The actual form of the protection also poses technical difficulties for, to be effective, it must be complete and protect the face and features as well as the skull. No doubt with modern materials something can be designed which would be wearable with equal comfort on an April day in England and a December day in Brisbane. If the strikers look like the opening pair of Dr. Who's Dalek XI, I fear it is something we old squares will just have to live with.

JOHN ARLOTT   JUNE 8 1985

The BBC screening of the Hayes/Schultz film *Bodyline* added seven hours 20 minutes to what was already the longest squeal in sporting history, one which has now gone on for 52 years. It has invariably happened in Test cricket that a side with a considerable advantage in fast bowling has beaten its opponents; as witness the West Indies' run of success, now so long as almost to bore them.

It has certainly been part of the historical pattern of England-Australia cricket. When England were weakened by two world wars, its batsmen were routed by Gregory and McDonald in 1921, and by Lindwall and Miller in 1948; while, to demonstrate that they do not need the assistance of a war, Lillee and Thomson did it in 1974-5 and again in 1975.

It almost invariably happens, too, that, when batsmen are faced by greater pace than they normally encounter in their own domestic game, the element of intimidation – part of the armoury of fast bowlers since cricket began – results in injuries to batsmen. That has been the case in virtually every instance of this imbalance, except in 1954-5, when Tyson and Statham simply did not employ that weapon.

Larwood, Voce and Bowes, under Jardine in Australia in 1932-3, undoubtedly did so, won the rubber by four Tests to one, and regained

185

the Ashes. The Australians resented it; and, apparently, many of them who were not even born in 1933 still do so.

It is true that the leg-theory christened by the Australian press 'bodyline' was successfully designed to defeat Don Bradman, whom Douglas Jardine saw, correctly, to be Australia's leading batsman and likely match-winner.

This account of the series, however, is not only corny, but inaccurate – unconvincing corn which still flourishes the old resentment. This is not the first attempt to retell the story: there have been at least 15 books on the series (12 of them Australian) running endlessly up to this year, and of which only one can be described as objective. Arthur Mailey, Test cricketer and professional journalist, who watched the entire tour, wrote *And Then Came Larwood*, which is the fairest account.

It is surprising to find in the Radio Times's advance notice of the latest series the claim that: 'It is surprising that nobody until now has made a film or television drama about bodyline.'

In fact, the BBC itself, in its series Forty Minutes (screened originally in 1983 then repeated twice) presented an unquestionably accurate account of the main incidents of the 1932-3 Tests, edited entirely from contemporary newsreels by Alan Patient.

On the other hand, the so-called newsreel included in the Hayes/Schultz film is a manifestly faked and patently inaccurate view from the departure of Jardine's team from London. The entire film is unconvincing, basically because the film actors seen 'in action' – apart from one or two 'tricked-in' shots of actual players – carry no conviction.

The run-up of the film 'Larwood' for instance, is quite comic: and, in tune with the rest of the cast, he pulled more histrionic faces and made more ham gestures in a quarter-hour than the real Larwood did in a lifetime.

That accepted, though, and since the lines required of the cricketers generally are puerile, something much better could – and should – have been done about the likenesses. For instance, Bradman, who was fair, of no more than average height, compact, broad-shouldered and nimble, is presented as tall, dark and handsome, but as clumsy on his feet as anyone ever filmed walking downstairs.

Of the English characters, it is difficult not to suspect an element of the old bitterness in representing P. F. Warner, who was slight and rather delicate, as a fat man; Lord Harris, who was tall and slim, as grossly heavy; and, above all, Douglas Jardine, who was physically a patrician and elegant figure, as one with sticking-out ears and an intrusive strine whine.

There is an attempt to dramatise a situation in which Jardine tells Larwood to bowl bodyline. In fact, that tactic was worked out in conference between Jardine and Arthur Carr, the Nottinghamshire captain, in England during the preceding summer; as anyone who watched Larwood and Voce bowling – as this writer did – for Nottinghamshire against Essex at Leyton and Glamorgan at Cardiff during the August before the team left for Australia would know.

It has been suggested that the film was made to explain bodyline to those who know nothing abut cricket, and that such people enjoyed it. Only they possibly could.

Chuckers

AUGUST 24 1880

Soon after play was resumed on Saturday in the match between the Australian Eleven and 18 of Scarborough and the district – the only match the Australians have lost this year – exception was taken by Bannerman to the bowling of Frank, one of the local team, it being said that he 'shied' or 'threw' the ball. Bannerman refused to play the next ball, which struck the wicket, and at once from all parts of the field there were loud cries of 'out'. This was continued for a short time, the spectators calling upon the Scarborough team to leave the ground if their opponents refused to play, and the Australians were more than once taunted with, 'You can't play the losing game.' Whilst the matter was being discussed on the ground, the spectators got impatient, and cries were heard of 'Out'; 'Play cricket', &c.; the home team being urged to 'come out', as some of them had already done. At length play resumed without any change being made in the bowlers, and at the third ball Bannerman was caught at point by Taylor, off Frank. During Spofforth's innings a ball from Frank struck him full on the hand, breaking some of the small bones and rendering the first two fingers useless. The doctors report that it will probably be three or four weeks before he will be able to play again.

JULY 18 1884

Crossland's bowling, against which action was taken by Lord Harris and the Notts County Committee at the commencement of the season, gave rise to an unpleasant incident on Wednesday. At the conclusion of the Lancashire and Yorkshire match on Tuesday Crossland returned to his native place, Sutton-in-Ashfield, and on the following day was invited to take part in a match with the Mansfield Town Club against the Mansfield Woodhouse eleven. At the commencement of the game Crossland bowled and was twice no-balled, and the umpire again no-balled him just as the player's stumps were removed. Crossland in somewhat strong terms threatened him and demanded his removal, a request with which Mr. Turner, the captain of the Woodhouse team, did not see fit to comply with. The game was then brought to an abrupt conclusion by the players leaving the field. The occurrence gave rise to some bitter and strong remarks, and it was alleged that the treatment Crossland received had been premeditated, and this was totally denied. Crossland afterwards sent a crier round to inform the public that, although he had been objected to there, they would find that he would not be the next day at Liverpool when playing with Lancashire against Surrey.

DENYS ROWBOTHAM   FEBRUARY 21 1959

There can be no excuses for England's defeat in the recent Test series. She was beaten by a better side which in every match played better cricket. She was outgeneralled. She was outbatted. She was outclassed in the field. And in so far as Benaud, Davidson, and Lindwall between them took more wickets than did all England's bowlers put together, it might conceivably be argued that she was outbowled.

In the Australian side, however, were always two and sometimes three bowlers who, according to the strict definition of the laws, did not consistently bowl. These were Meckiff, Rorke, and Burke. There would have been a fourth in the third Test at Sydney had Slater bowled at fast-medium pace with the pitcher's action he employed at the start of M.C.C.'s second innings against Western Australia.

The most obvious of the three throwers was Burke. Burke's flipped action from an arm bent so low that only his fingers are above his head at the moment of delivery is a replica of that of a darts player in any English village inn. Yet Burke has never been called in Australia and, if memory serves, in any first-class match in England. This presumably is because, as an off-spin bowler, he is so innocuous. Less happily the passing of Burke's action – an action so illegal that it moves even Australian crowds to jeers and hoots of ironic laughter – seems to have established an uneasy precedent. And it is this precedent which has allowed the actions of Meckiff and Rorke to pass muster.

Meckiff and Rorke were the men most dangerous to England. When they did begin to throw – usually after an over or so when their muscles were loose – they probably were as fast as any bowlers who have played cricket and certainly as fast as Tyson was on much faster wickets at Sydney and Melbourne in 1954-5. That both propel the ball not merely with the throwers' jerk from a bent elbow but from a drag so pronounced that, at the moment of delivery, both of Rorke's feet are in front of the popping crease, makes their great speed only more formidable. Rorke, who is 6ft. 4in., usually bowled from eighteen yards, and Meckiff roughly from nineteen.

When something of the shock of all this has been assimilated and it is remembered also that both bowlers usually were so erratic that half their deliveries during an over were wide one side or other of the stumps, something of the impact of a straight ball interspersed between the wides may be imagined. Nevertheless these bowlers, wild and whirling as one never expected to see Test-match or any first-class bowlers, took twenty-five wickets between them in the series . . .

DENYS ROWBOTHAM AT LORD'S   JUNE 28 1960

England v. South Africa, Second Test

England beat South Africa so comfortably by an innings and 73 runs at Lord's yesterday that half an hour after lunch an exhibition match was beginning.

It was not the least irony of an eventful four days that the second over of this friendly comic caper was probably more significant than any bowled during the Test match. The bowler was Griffin, the umpire at the other end Buller. Buller watched Griffin's first delivery from square leg, his second from point. He returned to square leg and, though Griffin was bowling from a short run at only medium pace, called four of his next five deliveries for throwing. After the fourth call Griffin changed to under arm and was promptly no balled by Umpire Lee for not indicating his intention of so doing. He contrived formally to complete his over by continuing to bowl under arm.

Buller's indictment of Griffin's action was unquestioning, unrelenting, and complete, and until such time as Griffin corrects himself it is hard to see how South Africa again can select him for a Test match. Nothing could be sadder for this fair haired, smiling, likeable young man. His action was approved by the umpires of his own country, and he has been the victim of conflicting rulings by uneasy umpires in England. The wind of suspicion has blown over him now hot, now cold. Yet his conduct through all his embarrassments has been exemplary. Certainly he will not forget the second Test match of 1960 at Lord's. In the match he was eleven times no balled for throwing before performing the hat-trick. The second over of the lighthearted spectacle which followed probably has ended, at least temporarily, his Test match career. . .

England 362 for 8 dec. (M. J. K. Smith 99, R. Subba Row 90, E. R. Dexter 56, P. M. Walker 52, G. M. Griffin 4 for 87); South Africa 152 (J. B. Statham 6 for 63, A. E. Moss 4 for 35) and 137 (Statham 5 for 34). England won by an innings and 73 runs. *Exhibition match:* England 142, 19 overs; South Africa 145 for 7, 15 overs. South Africa won by three wickets.

189

MISCELLANY BY MICHAEL FRAYN   JULY 22 1960

You may remember the serious international situation which developed recently when one of the South African cricketers over here was observed to be bowling with his arm bent *at Lord's*. At the suggestion of a plastic surgeon called Sir Harold Gillies, they have since been trying to improve this situation by making the young man in question wear his arm strapped into an aluminium splint.

This is an admirably rational solution – though there are some difficulties still to be solved, as Sir Harold points out. Some sort of self-locking device, he says, might be needed on the splint, so that the bowler could switch the splint free if he wished to bend his arm to make a catch. This might also be achieved by an electronic splint actuated by the movements of the bowler's muscles to send a signal to a receiving set carried by the umpire, which would ring a bell if the bowler's arm was bent.

I feel we should also examine the possibility of amputating this unfortunate young man's arm and replacing it with a mechanical arm worked by remote control from Strategic Air Command headquarters in Nebraska. Mr. Bolsover, the Shadow Minister of Sports and Recreations, is to ask the Prime Minister to set up a Commission of Inquiry into the matter.

The Umpire's Decision

SPORTING INTELLIGENCE   JULY 26 1848

Knutsford Royal Albert v. Congleton

. . . at this period of the game (after Drinkwater of Knutsford had been given out caught) the players of the Knutsford club disputed the correctness of the decision of the Congleton umpire; the Congleton players maintained the *correctness* of that decision, but admitted that the point ought to have been decided by the other umpire, and pressed the player out to go in again, so that the game might proceed. This the Knutsford club positively refused to accede to, and demanded the removal of the Congleton umpire; their right to enforce this demand was denied by the Congleton players, and thus the game terminated . . .

To the editor AUGUST 12 1848

Sir, – In the account of the match
between the Knutsford and the Congleton clubs, sent for insertion in your
paper by the latter, it is asserted that at
a certain point of the game, the Knutsford players refused to continue the
contest unless the Congleton umpire
was removed. This is correct; but the
reason was not solely on account of the
decision then given, but also of *three*
previous ones, which they were quite
satisfied were wrong, and which, not to
impute the motive of unfairness, showed
at least such inattention or want of
knowledge of the game, that the Knutsford players considered that their request ought to have been attended to,
and upon the refusal of the Congleton
players to accede to it, decided that they
could have no pleasure in continuing the
game. Will you be kind to insert this
explanation on the part of the Royal
Albert Cricket Club – Your obedient
servant

The Secretary.

LEADER JUNE 2 1925

If this goes on, the county umpires will soon be demanding the
prohibition of photographers, or at least of the telescopic lens, on
cricket grounds. At Lord's on Saturday, with Hendren racing for the
crease, the wicket-keeper threw the wicket down, but the umpire did
not raise the heavenward-pointing hand; Hendren escaped. But
yesterday the 'Daily Express' published a photograph which shows that,
with the wicket already clearly broken, the tip of Hendren's bat was a
foot or more outside the crease. That an umpire, with one eye on the
wicket and the other on the batsman, may make a mistake in the hurry
and scurry of the game is quite intelligible, but all the same our whole
system is built up on the assumption that his word is final, beyond
criticism, and certainly not to be exposed in all the nakedness of error
by a super-judge who cannot err. All our games are full of such
possibilities, and therefore we agree to put them out of our minds and to
remit all doubts and differences to a referee, an umpire, a touch-judge,
or a linesman. We even frown upon the ardent partisan who, looking

back over the years to some famous match, tells us that the result was not what history says it was, because he knows that a catch was not really made or that a try was scored which the referee disallowed. In a big lawn tennis match they have not only an umpire but a man in a basket chair to watch each line, and still, if this new fashion grows, the camera may come along to prove that the single point that was wanted for 'set – match' was really won when the linesman declared the ball was out. As for the lives of League referees, they would not be worth living at all if they had to submit their decisions about offside to the judgement of the camera. Fortunately the photographer can rarely foresee the critical second when his instrument may be able to show itself superior to human fallibility. From the 'Daily Express' photograph we get a glimpse of the mental torments which, as keen followers of one side or another, we should endure if we realised the truth about the uncertainties of every game. But a glimpse is enough; it makes us all the more content to 'leave it to the referee.'

PATRICK BARCLAY AT OLD TRAFFORD   AUGUST 7 1979

Lancashire v. Somerset

After a less than satisfactory morning, at one stage of which Old Trafford's ears pricked to the incongruous sound of breaking glass, Somerset's batsmen recovered their composure yesterday afternoon and proceeded confidently to a first innings lead of 188. Lancashire's reply was a troubled 67 for three wickets, so the West Country side will take the field today with a spring in their step and high hopes of victory.

In cricketing terms, it was a profitable day for Somerset. It was also an expensive one, however, for they had to accept responsibility for a glaziers' bill they expect to receive from Lancashire in the next few days, the consequence of an incident which occurred shortly after Viv Richards had been judged leg before wicket.

By no stretch of the imagination could the Antiguan's walk to the pavilion be described as jaunty. He plodded with a disconsolate air, jabbing the turf with his bat every few steps, he could not even bring himself to acknowledge the applause which Lancashire members rightly accorded his innings of 36.

Shortly after Richards had entered the pavilion a crash was heard from the players' balcony and members below were showered with fragments from the large plate glass window. It was later confirmed that a generally prolific, temporarily angry, cricket bat was the culprit . . .

The Crowd's Reaction

. . . The behaviour of the crowd at Derby was again of a most disgraceful character. When Crossland went on, before he had delivered a ball, he was yelled at, and the demonstration gathered force as it proceeded. Another cause of annoyance was a dispute about a boundary hit when the last men were in and only five runs were wanted to save the follow on. The boundary was marked only by a chalk line, invisible to the umpires and encroached upon by the crowd, so that it was only possible for the fielder to tell where he had secured the ball, and the umpires accepted Mr. Lancashire's word that he had secured the ball before the boundary was reached. But all this took time and aggravated the bad feeling previously shown. Then when the Lancashire team left the field they were mobbed in such a disgraceful way as to call forth indignant remonstrances from the hon. secretary of the Derbyshire club.

The disturbance at the Oval appears to have arisen from a genuine grievance. Emmett and the English players under him were willing to finish the game without the needless delay of an hour for luncheon, but Murdoch insisted upon the usual interval. There is a general belief that gate-money considerations induced this course of action, and though it was decided to take no more money this decision was not arrived at or announced till affairs began to wear a very ugly aspect through the violence of the crowd. The crowds at the Oval are never among the best behaved, and they were certainly provoked in a very unnecessary manner last week.

To the editor   JUNE 16 1948

Sir, – As one who loves cricket, I would like to give expression to my feelings of disgust at the unseemly conduct of many of the spectators of the cricket at Trent Bridge in the closing stages of the play on Saturday.

I was listening to the commentator on the wireless, and unless I had heard the booing of the Australian bowler I should not have thought that such a thing could take place on any English cricket ground; also, and this is a dreadful thing, much of it appeared to come from the occupants of the pavilion stand.

One feels deeply ashamed for such behaviour, and wonders why those who contributed to it should be there. Presumably they are of those who, calling themselves 'sports', have never taken an active part in any worthy games.

I would not like to think it could happen at Old Trafford. – Yours, &c.,

J. Brockbank.

Mile End, Stockport.

To the editor JUNE 16 1950

Sir, – Since returning from Old Trafford on Saturday I have wondered whether it would not be practicable to have a Junior Enclosure for all youngsters who are not accompanied by grown-ups. I get on well with the smaller fry normally, but three of them – about 11 or 12, I should say – almost ruined my afternoon. Apart from one blessed session of about fifteen minutes which served only to emphasise the appalling effect they created in the other four hours, they 'put on an act' – two of them ably supporting the third, who will surely one day be a worthy successor to one of our barrow-boy comedians! Everybody was patient with them and, though at times we all snapped at them, nothing dampened their spirits and the comedian-in-embryo never stopped talking (about anything and everything except cricket) from start to finish. Their arms flailing about added to the distraction.

I realised on leaving that notes I had made when England was batting, to send to my 17-year-old boy away at school (of the entertaining incidents one can never remember afterwards) had disappeared, and I shrewdly suspect they had been used to make paper darts with which the youngsters had been bombarding one another. – Yours, &c.,

Patience.

Stockport.

Australia v. England, First Test

The area round the Test match scoreboard was, as the Middle East correspondents say, tense but quiet yesterday as bewildered administrators tried to understand and recover from the crowd trouble on Saturday – the worst seen at a Test in Australia, or England, in modern times.

Extra police were called in, first enforcing a long-standing rule about bringing in drink by searching spectators' freezer-boxes, then mingling discreetly with the crowd. All the bars outside the members' enclosure were closed between lunch and tea. There was no trouble, the most inflammatory moment being the appearance of 100 lady gymnasts in leotards to cavort during the tea interval.

Twenty-eight people are due to appear in court, the first batch today. Two are charged with assault: one on the Australian fast bowler Terry Alderman, one on a policeman. Alderman, who injured his shoulder rugby-tackling the man who ran on to the pitch and cuffed him, has a stretched nerve and is likely to be out of the game for 10-14 days, which makes him very doubtful for the second Test, starting in Brisbane on Friday week.

Doug Insole, the England manager, yesterday repeated to his players what was said at the start of the tour: don't get involved with spectators who run on, no matter what. Phil Ridings, the chairman of the Australian Cricket Board (who issued a suitable deploring statement) merely asked his players not to get involved, which is not the same.

Rule A1 of the Board's code of behaviour for players – not the world's most zealously-enforced bit of law – forbids assaults on other players, umpires and spectators but specifically exempts assaults on spectators trespassing on the pitch.

There was some disposition in the England camp to blame Alderman, in part anyway, for his own misfortunes. Suggestions that the laws should be stretched to permit, for this injury only, a full replacement rather than a mere substitute fielder were swept aside. 'That has been neither requested nor offered,' said Insole.

The incident happened when England reached 400 and a group of youngsters ran on to the field waving a Union Jack. Alderman's injury forced the suspension of play for 15 minutes, during which fighting broke out in the crowd. It was 4.25 on Saturday afternoon. Had it happened at 4.25 on Saturday afternoon at any English soccer ground no one would have been in the least surprised. It followed the classic pattern of a soccer riot, with the extra elements of sun, a long day, the longeurs of the game and Swan lager.

All afternoon England and Australia supporters near the scoreboard were chanting slogans of the Lillee-is-a-wanker type at each other, occasionally stopping for a brief skirmish. They had wooden forms to sit on, but virtually no shade.

Most of the England supporters appear to be migrants. Several of those arrested or ejected were in skinhead gear, which is unusual in Australia. Some were wearing English soccer shirts or T-shirts saying 'Madness'. Quite.

Cricket and the pattern of migration have helped institutionalise the love-hate relationship between Aussies and Poms. For most people in Australia, it is little more than an elaborate joke. The TV adverts for the Test matches shown over here played on the worst aspects of that joke, with supposedly typical Englishmen making offensive remarks about Australians and vice-versa. It ought to be no surprise if some people are daft enough to take things further. If a sport cannot promote itself with dignity, how can it keep any self-respect?

To the editor   JUNE 20 1985

Sir, – I doubt whether sports writers have much idea of what things can be like for us ordinary cricket spectators these days, especially on Saturdays at Test matches?

Last Saturday I was driven out of my seat at Headingley by the vile and dangerous behaviour of the drunken louts who established a reign of terror as soon as play began. Incessant yells, screams, and so-called 'songs' – many of them 'patriotic' – were the least of the ills inflicted on those of us who were there to watch the cricket. Obscene abuse, sexist and racist insults were hurled at arbitrarily selected victims whose appearance offended 'the lads'.

The police appeared twice; they told 'the lads' to moderate their 'language' and even managed to persuade one of them to wear his trousers. (It is the fashion for these latter-day 'sans-culottes' to remove their trousers the better to demonstrate their manly contempt for decency and literally to point the invitations to sexual intercourse that they make to all and sundry, male and female, young and old.)

When the police left 'the lads' proceeded to pour beer down our backs and trampled on our clothes and lunch bags. These 'minor' assaults were accompanied by threats of 'real trouble' if we dared to complain again.

There was nobody to complain to. I left; and so did others. Well before play ended. And so cricket will be left to the hooligans who – this year or next – will be fighting each other in and around the seats we used to occupy before they drove us out. – Yours faithfully,

                                                              S. H. Burton.

51 Newport Road,
Stafford.

PEOPLE

A CORRESPONDENT   JULY 14 1908

Lord Hawke

If you consult the reference books they all say with convincing unity that Wighill Park, the Yorkshire home of the great cricketer who is to be honoured at Leeds to-day, is at Tadcaster. But if you are travelling by what local cynics call the 'washing line' that connects York and Harrogate it is best to go on past the busy country town where the famous Tadcaster ales are brewed – on to the little roadside station of Thorp Arch, set in the rich pastoral land of the West Riding, and redolent just now with the scent of flowers. From Thorp Arch a pleasant journey of two miles or so through the old village of Walton brings you to Wighill Park, a well-timbered enclosure of some hundred acres, and here I had the good fortune to find Lord Hawke at home and comparatively at leisure, imprisoned, in fact, by the rain which was spoiling the hay before his eyes, and readily disposed, in his hospitable, unpretentious way, to show me his rare collection of cricket trophies and to talk of the great game which has occupied so much of his time and thought.

Lord Hawke is the seventh Baron Hawke of Towton. His Christian name, Martin Bladen, perpetuates in the family the memory of the distinguished Colonel and Parliamentarian who was the uncle and guardian of the great Admiral Hawke, the first holder of the title. He succeeded to the barony in 1887, on the death of his father, a beneficed clergyman in the Church of England, his elder brother Edward having died at an early age. He is a bachelor, and the heir presumptive is his brother, Captain Stanhope Hawke, a naval officer. The present peer, who was in the army for a time, was born on August 16, 1860, and will therefore next month complete his forty-eighth year. Lord Hawke's 'den' at Wighill Park is a pleasant corner room, overlooking a wide stretch of meadow. Its rare collections of photographs and engravings, trinkets and trophies, and beautifully bound books, all related to cricket and to Lord Hawke's association with the national game and its past and present great players, testify at once to their owner's absorbing interest in the sport. Yet it is an error to think of Lord Hawke's interests as exclusively restricted to cricket. He is a good musician. There is no magistrate whom the police are better pleased to see on the bench if they have a tangled case in hand. Every Sunday, when at home, he reads the lessons in Wighill Parish Church. He is described by others as a brilliant shot; by himself as merely 'fair'. He does not despise even lawn tennis, for there are courts just outside his window. He is both fond and proud of his horses, and still rides to hounds with unslackened zest. Accustomed frequently to winter abroad, he has travelled far both East and West, and had some stirring experiences as a hunter of big game.

But the ceremony at Leeds to-day has to do with him as a great cricketer, and I must explain something about it, for Lord Hawke tells me the newspapers so far have been 'all wrong'. The presentation is intended primarily to commemorate the completion of twenty-five years as captain of the Yorkshire County Cricket Eleven. It should, then, be strictly a Yorkshire affair. Yes, and so it would have been if Lord Hawke had been nothing more than the greatest captain that great county has produced. But, with one inevitable exception, he is and has been for years the greatest single figure in English cricket, and so the presentation had to be thrown open, that it might correspond with the range of Lord Hawke's services. And what are the presents to be? There is, first of all, a diamond tiara. This has excited some merriment, the present peer being a bachelor, but Lord Hawke accepts the joke, and laughingly retorts, 'You never know what may happen!' Then there is an old Worcester dessert service, which Lord Hawke saw and fancied in the shop of a Manchester antiquary – for he is somewhat of a 'collector' – and a new dinner service, which has been made at Worcester. A pair of Purdey guns and a George III silver soup tureen, dated 1817, complete the public presentations. The guns were lying on the billiard table in a handsome case bearing Lord Hawke's touring colours, and he showed me the fine weapons, with which he hopes to do more shooting than he has done of late, with real pride. Beyond these, the Yorkshire professionals, knowing their captain's taste for fine old silver, are giving him as their own presents a George III silver teapot and stand, dated 1802, and a George IV silver teapot, sugar basin, and cream jug, dated 1821. And, finally, the Yorkshire Committee will give him three pearl studs. With the exception of the last, which will be given at a dinner later in the year, all these articles will be presented to Lord Hawke to-day during an interval in the Yorkshire and Notts match at Leeds.

It is, of course, as a captain rather than as a player that Lord Hawke has most powerfully influenced English cricket. Yet, considered solely as a player, he has a great record. His first appearance for Yorkshire was at Scarborough in 1881, and up to the close of last season he had played 652 innings, scored 13,061 runs, and maintained an average of 20. On ten occasions he has made centuries, his highest score being 166 against Warwickshire in 1896. He was also a partner in three record stands for Yorkshire. For the sixth wicket he and Wainwright made 225 against Hampshire at Southampton in 1899. For the eighth wicket he joined Peel in making 292 against Warwickshire at Birmingham in 1896. For the tenth wicket Lord Hawke and Hunter scored 148 against Kent at Sheffield in 1898. He is one of the ten Yorkshire batsmen who have scored over 10,000 runs.

One does not need to be long in Lord Hawke's presence in order to learn the secret of his success and popularity as a captain. Was it not John Morley who once said that whenever Gladstone entered a room everyone straightened himself out and looked and talked his best. Lord Hawke has the same quality, the secret of all leadership, of unconsciously challenging the best that is in a man. No one could play a slack game in his company. And yet it is all done without visible effort, in the easiest and friendliest manner conceivable. Whether this was the secret of the success of the first Baron Hawke, the Admiral whose victories at sea broke up the naval power of France, one cannot say; but in one point the present peer exactly resembles his great ancestor. It was written of the latter that, 'alike as captain and admiral, his anxiety for the health and comfort of his men was incessant. His discipline was strict, but kindly. His reproof of impiety, his care for the happiness of his men, his manly decision and dignified deportment worked a rapid though silent reformation throughout the whole fleet.' That might well stand as a description of what the present Lord Hawke has done to raise the manners of the cricket field, to improve the status especially of the professionals, and to safeguard the noble traditions of county cricket.

There is space for only a few of the interesting things which Lord Hawke said during my visit. In spite of numerous letters which reach him, inquiring the reasons for the decadence of county cricket, he sees no evidence of any declining interest, but rather the contrary, and he thinks the standard of play as good all round as ever. But, a sportsman himself to the core, he still protests against the habit of allowing the thought of 'those beastly weekly averages' to drive all sense of sport out of a batsman's soul. While severely set against all forms of slackness, Lord Hawke desires above all things to see men 'play the game', as he claims that Yorkshire have always done. While Yorkshire cricket has been, in his own words the 'ruling passion of his life', his own hobby in cricket has been 'the welfare of the county professionals,' whom he has always treated as personal colleagues and friends. 'I have repeatedly instilled into my committee the view that the more they respect the player the more the player will respect himself.' Yet no one is more emphatic as to the value of a proportion of amateurs in a side. In his own words once more: 'I am no advocate for wholly professional sides. Yorkshire has always played amateurs, and to my mind they are the moral backbone of a county team. Once you do away with them you will inevitably create an eleven which will only play for the gates. Amateurs infuse a freshness and an enthusiasm into the game which the most hard-working professional cannot impart.'

Of course Lord Hawke is here speaking of the traditional type of amateur, on which subject he has some very strict opinions. During all the time he has been captain no amateur playing for Yorkshire has received sixpence beyond his bare expenses. And yet, with this jealousy for the traditions of his own class, Lord Hawke has done probably more than anyone else to bind amateurs and professionals together in a common bond. Indeed, his own view is that a county captain should always have a professional on whom he can rely for a sound opinion – such men as he himself has had first in Ulyett and afterwards in Tunnicliffe. I asked Lord Hawke whether he thought sufficient attention was now given to fielding. '*We* do,' was the instant reply, 'whatever other countries may do.'

C. L. R. JAMES   APRIL 18 1933

George Headley

'Statistics prove——' began a speaker on the wireless the other night, and I turned him off at once. Yet in George Headley's case the bare statistics are the best introduction to his cricket. He was born in Jamaica in 1909, and in 1926 emerged from the village green into good club cricket. Tradition has it that he still wore short trousers. The youthful Bradman, it is related, astonished a big club in Australia both by his batting and by his black trousers. Victor Trumper also banged a Test match bowler about when clad in other than the regulation white flannel. Some forty years ago Ephraim Lockwood, hastily summoned to fill a breach, went in to bat at The Oval in a check shirt and short pants. The Ovalites were convulsed with laughter. They had a lot of time in which to laugh, for Ephraim made over eighty. Constantine relates that his father objected to his coming too early into first-class cricket and would not help him to buy flannels, wherefore he had to save the money sixpence by sixpence. So the material gathers for an essay on 'The nether garments of budding Test cricketers.' Remains only he who, wearing none at all, makes his mark in a match: the prospect is not so remote in these nudist days.

The next year, 1927, Headley attracted the notice of the local authorities and earned a place in the Jamaica side against the Hon. L. H. Tennyson's Eleven. Against Clark, M. J. C. Allom, Lee (G. M.), A. L. Hilder, and T. Arnott, Headley made 16 and 71, 211, 40 and 71. In the long innings he gave one chance, a hard one, early in the innings, and scored the 211 out of 348.

As is the sad lot of the West Indian batsman, he got no more first-class cricket until the next year, 1929, when Sir Julien Cahn took a team including Astill, Mercer, Durston, and Nichols. Headley made 57 and 22, 17 and 43, 44 and 143. He had therefore played in six first-class matches and was not yet twenty-one years old when the M.C.C. team under Calthorpe went to the West Indies in 1930. The bowlers on this team were Calthorpe himself, Voce, Astill, Wilfred Rhodes, Nigel Haig, G. T. S. Stevens. Limited as was his experience, they could do nothing at all with Headley. It was his first trip away to play, and he travelled from island to island for the Tests. In Barbados in the first Test he made 21 and 176; in Trinidad 8 and 36; in the British Guiana Test 114 and 112. Going back home to meet them in Jamaica, he made 64 and 72 and 52; and in the fourth Test 10 and 223.

In the autumn of that year he went to Australia. He began with 25 and 82 against New South Wales and followed them up with 131 against Victoria on the Melbourne wicket on the first day, batting before lunch. He made 1,000 runs in the season, scored a century in the third Test, and one in the fifth. Last year Lord Tennyson again took a team to Jamaica. Headley made 344 not out, 84 and 155 not out, and 140. His figures to date are 30 matches, 54 innings, 3,507 runs, highest score 344 not out, average 70.14. He has made in all thirteen centuries, including two double and one treble century, and a century in each innings of a Test match.

Whatever statistics may or may not prove, such scoring has only itself to blame if it arouses abnormal expectations. Moreover, he is as great a master of style as he is of runs. He is a negro, finely built but short and small, and only a careful judge of physique would notice him in a crowd. But at the wicket no one can miss his mastery. He is of that type which uses a bat as if it is an extension of the arm. Ease, poise, and balance, he has them all. Good as his footwork is for defensive play, it is even better in the way he makes ground to the ball. He and Edwin St. Hill, the Lowerhouse professional, are great friends, a friendship which began at the nets before the first Test at Barbados in 1930. Edwin St. Hill, bowling strong fast-medium, was amazed to see the little Jamaican wristing the good-length ball away between mid on and short leg or jumping in to drive it.

Though he makes all the strokes, these are the two in which he specialises – forcing the ball away on the on side with a back stroke and getting to the pitch to drive. In a bright summer the slow bowlers will be glad to see him go. As will be noticed from the scores enumerated, he is always in form, and it was noted that he never batted better during the whole of the Australian trip than in the first innings of all – against New South Wales. Hugh Trumble said that the Melbourne innings was one of the best that he had ever seen, and many habitués of the Melbourne ground thought that no finer innings had ever been played there. Headley is a good field. Formerly he was brilliant, but in Australia, for some reason, the edge of his keenness left him. I have seen him bowl Hendren, well set, three off-breaks and then send one away from the edge of Hendren's bat into the slips, where it was dropped. After that, however, he had shot his bolt.

He is a commercial clerk in ordinary life, but is devoted to cricket and is 'a good lad'. If he has to bat to-morrow he goes to bed to-night. In Australia he failed at first to get runs against Grimmett. 'I have to make a century against Grimmett,' he told his friend St. Hill. Batting very carefully, he made it in the third Test. 'Satisfied?' asked St. Hill. 'Not yet; I have to master him now.' In the fifth Test he made another century in a little over two hours, playing so brilliantly that even Bradman, Kippax, and the rest joined in the applause. 'Satisfied?' asked St. Hill. 'Ye-es,' said Headley, hesitatingly. He had been brilliant, but it galled him that he had had to treat Grimmett with some respect. It is the genuine artistic instinct faithful to an inner ideal.

GEOFFREY MOORHOUSE   JUNE 23 1965

Fred Trueman

Lord's Cricket Ground yesterday may have seen the end of a great sporting epoch. Unlike the Test match itself it tailed away tamely and a little miserably. It had taken the New Zealanders, the international bunnies of the game, just four cruel days to expose the English fast bowlers for the honest plodders they are at present. One of these was Frederick Sewards Trueman, who in his time has scared the pants off every batsman from Woollangabba to Old Trafford. But not any longer. Though he may pitch them up in the Yorkshire county side for a season or two more, by last night the experts were saying that not even he can cope with another Test.

Cricket has seen men like Trueman before, but not very often. And in the last 20 years no one has quite enlivened the game as he has by a combination of craftsmanship and personality. At his peak he was as dangerous to batsmen as the great Larwood, but his international career was a much more destructive one. It began in 1952 when he ran amok among the Indians to take eight wickets for 31 runs at Manchester; no genuine fast bowler has ever had a Test analysis like that. And now he has 307 Test wickets to his name; that's a record likely to last a long time.

Some men may have bowled a cricket ball faster than Trueman, but none has done so with more gusto. As much as anything his triumphs have been based on sheer belligerence. In one of his first games for Yorkshire against Lancashire he felled a batsman with a ball that rose like a rocket and nearly took his head off. Only one Yorkshireman didn't rush to the poor fellow's aid. That was Trueman, who ambled back to the other end of his run, rolled up his sleeve, and waited to have another go. He has always played like that. It is not the way of the gentlemanly giants of cricket, the Frys and the Ranjitsinhjis and the Worrells. But W. G. Grace would have understood it.

There has been no one more pleasing to cricket crowds. When

Trueman is put on to bowl, a breeze of anticipation stirs the ground because everyone expects action; more often than not it comes. When he goes in to bat small boys cheer and old men grin because they expect him to hit the ball out of sight, as he sometimes does; he can strike up 50 in as many minutes with the wind in the right direction. He can field a ball like a monkey when the mood is on him. And even when he is not actually busy in the game he is worth keeping an eye on; glaring at a batsman who has just hit him for four as though he would slay him; digging the next slip-fielder in the ribs and braying at some robust jest; occasionally breaking out into open pantomime.

It was always on the cards that in his travels abroad he would provoke an international incident. One story insists that he nearly did when in the West Indies at dinner one night he asked a local dignitary to 'Pass the salt, Gunga Din!' Trueman has always denied saying this; the point is, he might have. It wouldn't have been rudeness so much as the man being true to himself. He has always been that. He has been content with his origins in the South Yorkshire coalfield. It was never likely that as he became famous his voice would become a mongrel mixture of Mexborough and MCC, like some that Trueman could name. He never cared enough for that. He cared so little that on television last year he allowed his wife to tick him off embarrassingly in front of us. He just said 'Yes, my love,' rather weakly, and it was like seeing an emperor without his false teeth.

If, in one sense, he had been a careful man, Fred Trueman would have retired from Test cricket after the match at The Oval last year. That was where he got his 300th wicket and where, if lunch had not intervened, he might have got it in a hat trick. That would have been the moment to quit. But instead he chanced his arm at Edgbaston and Lord's and his arm was no longer quite good enough. The great men of cricket, however, have a habit of going out in anti-climax; when Bradman played his last Test innings he didn't survive an over and he didn't get a run.

The small boys at Lord's yesterday, they at least will have understood this. They know what we are soon going to miss. There was, we hope, another crop of Dexters and Cowdreys and Lakers among them. But not a sign, just yet, of another young Fred.

JOHN ARLOTT   FEBRUARY 16 1970

Herbert Strudwick

Herbert Strudwick, one of the great wicket-keepers – statistically the most successful of all – died on Saturday. He was 90 years old and his experience ranged from the so-called Edwardian 'golden age' to the modern game.

He joined the Surrey staff in 1898, played his last county match in

1927, and then became the county's scorer and wicket-keeping coach until 1958. For those 60 years he observed cricket with a sharp eye and a sympathetic mind.

In 1902 he kept wicket to Tom Richardson – they both came from Mitcham – whom he always regarded as the finest and the fastest of all fast bowlers – and in 1926 he took Larwood, when England beat Australia at The Oval and regained the Ashes. That was the last of the 28 Test caps he won in a period when England's only opponents were Australia and South Africa. He did not linger in the game when he was no longer at his best. When he retired at the end of the following season he had dismissed – caught or stumped – 1,468 batsmen; 140 more than any other wicket-keeper.

Jack Hobbs, whom he held in immense affection and admiration (the last game of golf either of them played was nine holes together at West Hove in 1960) once said of him 'it wasn't just that Struddy held so many catches, but – which isn't always the same thing – he missed so few.' The records do not show the number of batsmen he ran out by his speed in taking returns especially from Jack Hobbs at cover.

Strudwick created much of modern wicket-keeping technique. He was one of the first men to stand back to fast-medium bowlers, because he considered that position offered the surest guarantee against dropping a catch, and also against allowing byes – every one of which on a score sheet, he regarded, almost comically, as a slur on his ability.

Yet when Maurice Tate insisted, as Alec Bedser did later, on his wicket-keeper taking him close up, Struddy took Tate over the stumps in flawless style. A photograph of the Sydney Test of 1924-25 shows Tate bowling, with Strudwick up to the stumps and the five slip fieldsmen more than a pitch-length deep.

He paid for his devotion with some savage injuries. To his death he had a thumb-sized hole in his ribs from being hit by an edged fast ball: but he played in the next match. The flimsy wicket-keeping glove of his early days gave little protection; and his fingers fractured so often that they were misshapen and knotted as oak twigs. 'You see,' he explained, 'when I first went on the staff we had four wicket-keepers: if you got in, you had to stay in; I've often played with two broken fingers.'

He was one of the first wicket-keepers to widen the established range, and he surprised many critics in the early days of this century by leaping out to take catches in front of the batsman from defensive prods.

He was utterly content to have been a cricket professional. Slightly built, and quick in movement, he was unfailingly trim, and he kept his score books in a painstaking copper plate. His love for cricket and cricketers, especially of Surrey, was deep and generous, and his steady grey eyes were those of a truly kind and honest man.

Barry Richards

Barry Richards is a great cricketer. Either he or Sobers must be the best batsman in the world, and Richards is only 25, much the younger of the two. In Australia last winter the Coca-Cola people gave him a bonus of an Australian dollar (45p) for every run he scored, and it cost them £900. Only Bradman has scored more runs in an Australian season. No cricketer since Compton has scored his runs with more dash.

So Richards is not just a very good player but a great one, in the most beautiful of all games, whose great players are remembered and cherished. He will please, move, and entertain as many people as if he were, say, one of the English novelists of his generation. His name will live in the history of the game. Already he has a little bit of immortality, and he has, of course, no sense of this whatever.

Because he is a South African he has had a strange career. Mr. Vorster having for impeccable racialist reasons prevented the MCC tour of South Africa, and unimpeded promoters of disorder having for impeccable liberal reasons prevented the South African tour of England, the South African team found it could hardly get anybody to give it a game and so Richards took to playing round the world for a living. Last winter he played for South Australia in the Sheffield Shield. This summer he will play for Hampshire in the county championship.

At Southampton the other day he was practising with the Hampshire team in the middle. When he came off for lunch he agreed to talk about anything except apartheid. All right.

He sat on a bench in the pavilion and said nobody in his family ever played cricket, but when he was about seven he used to come home from school, take an old golf ball and Don Bradman's book on how to play cricket, throw the ball against the concrete wall of a garage, play a shot at it with a 12in. bat, and then look at the book to see if he had got the stroke right. When he grew up he went to see MCC play at Durban and watched Peter May score a magnificently struck two, and Insole, batting like a gorilla, make a century.

By the time he was 16 he knew he was going to be good, and in 1963, when he was 17, he toured England as captain of a South African Schools XI. He made 106 very fast against Eton, but hardly remembers it because Eton did not mean a thing to him. It was just another school.

He has played for Hampshire since 1968, when he scored more than 2,000 runs in the championship alone, which is now rare. But why did he go to Hampshire rather than a rich county like Warwickshire? Because Warwickshire had Kanhai. After last season he nearly did not renew his contract with Hampshire because he had far more lucrative business offers to go into marketing. Now he has signed a new three-year contract because the county put up his salary, but he still earns nothing like the sum people imagine and newspapers print.

But is he getting more than the other Hampshire players? 'Well, I should hope I am, yes.' He is very matter of fact and says this with no rancour against the county or the other players. It is just that he obviously is worth it.

But whatever he is getting, it is much less than a professional footballer of his class, or a tennis player.

'Oh yes, or a professional footballer of any class, not necessarily of my class. Fellows in the Burnley side, which is in the First Division at the bottom, would be earning more than me. I know for a fact that Pat Walkden – whom you've probably never heard of – she's a Rhodesian tennis player, No. 1 in South Africa but about No. 15 in the world, earns twice what I get.'

But, I said, he had been called a mercenary? He is indignant about this, saying that the papers never print anything about his cricketing ability, but that it is always Barry Richards earned so-and-so for his knock against Western Australia, and this gets him. He said there was all this writing about his money, but nobody before me had ever asked him how much he earned. They just guessed.

Then he said: 'Let's clear it up once and for all,' and went into details. He scored 2,000 runs all told in Australia in first-class and club games, and at an Australian dollar a run that made £900. He also got a weekly salary which, added to the Coca-Cola dollars, made £1,700 all told. And what, he wanted to know, had the MCC players been paid for touring Australia at the same time? I did not know. '£1,500 a man,' he said. 'So that leaves me £200 in the clear, and I'm a mercenary?'

With this £1,700, and with less than £3,000 from Hampshire, and with bits here and there from the sale of bats bearing his signature, he gets £5,000 for a year, playing everywhere, gross.

He is anxious about the future, when his cricketing days are over, and keeps returning to this. He is not sure he has done the right thing coming back to Hampshire. The marketing jobs he was offered would have provided for him when he was 45 or 50. He is not even sure he can afford to stay with Hampshire long enough to qualify for a benefit.

'I'm earning a good wage for a fellow of my age,' he said, 'but what happens when I'm 35? Hampshire say thank you very much, you've been a good chap (here he clapped his hands ironically), we'll all have three cheers, off you go, and you're stuck.'

He feels insecure even about his reputation as a cricketer, and for a man who has achieved so much, with such ease, this is strange. He says English cricket spectators are sceptical, and that even after his splendid year with Hampshire in 1968 he was regarded as a one-season wonder. It is difficult to think what can have given him this idea.

Why was he so definite that he would not talk about apartheid? Richards replied that his political views were his own business. He thought D'Oliveira was a very good player.

I got out the two words, 'Would he . . .?' when Richards said, 'I'm not going to answer the question would he get in the South African side.'

What about the reports that Richards was thinking of settling in Australia to be able to play Tests for Australia? He said this would mean living in Australia for four years, winter and summer, and he could not do this because, for one thing, he had his contract with Hampshire. Would he then settle in England? 'You see,' he said, 'I could never live through an English winter. I can hardly live through an English summer.'

Twice before I had tried to ask him how he felt when people called Sobers, Pollock, and himself the greatest batsmen of the present day, but he said you could not compare. Well then, putting modesty aside, did he believe he was one of the great batsmen?

He said: 'Of all time?'

If he liked.

No, he did not think so. He had not played in enough Test matches to judge.

Now apart from modesty – and I think he is modest because not once did he make any claim of any sort for himself – I think the fact is that he does not see himself as part of the continuing history of cricket. He has no sense of awe for the game, not in the sense that a comparably good novelist or musician might feel himself to be part of the tradition of English novels or German music. He says it means nothing at all to him that his innings are in Wisden, and that he could not care less if he never appeared there. And when he had a chance of beating Bradman's record for the number of runs in an Australian first-class season he never even thought about it.

So was he less enthusiastic about the game than many spectators were? – 'I just play, and I play to the best of my ability.' He obviously does not think that just because cricket is a game he plays superbly well, he should therefore feel some obligation to continue playing it. As he says, he is still wondering whether he did the right thing to prefer Hampshire to marketing.

The only time he gave an answer which came near to expounding anything like a philosophy of cricket was when he went through the ways of getting out. Then he really did sound like a man saying he knew death had 10,000 several doors for men to take their exit. It came up like this. He had said he would not mind scoring only 700 runs all season so long as Hampshire won the championship. I said he would have to put his mind to it to make as few as that.

'I don't know,' he said. 'It can happen. Every time you put the ball in the air some bloke dives and takes a brilliant catch. You get run out. You get run out backing up; it flicks off somebody's foot on to the wicket and you're rushing off for a run. Things like this happen.'

That's very pessimistic? – No, he said, just practical.

And again: 'The thing is, I've always lacked confidence.'

No!

'I'm telling you.'

Harry Pilling

At divers times and in divers places, he has been called the Tom Thumb of cricket; the big little 'un; the mighty atom; and Shorty. And when Lancashire were playing at Aigburth not so long ago, a wide-eyed youngster approached him and asked, 'Are you a Diddyman?' At 5ft 3in 'wi' nowt on,' Harry Pilling generally is as identifiable as was Fanny Walden of Tottenham Hotspur fifty-odd years ago.

He weighed 6lb 2oz when Mrs Esther Pilling produced him on February 23, 1943; he weighed five stone and stood 4ft 7in when he left school and set about shattering a then-prevalent belief that he was far too small ever to make the grade at cricket. He joined Staley Cricket Club near Stalybridge when he was 11, played for their third team when he was 12, and took 55 wickets at two runs a piece with leg spinners. Later, he played with Oldham in the Central Lancashire League before returning to pro. for Staley at £2 10s a week. In one season he made 1,000 runs, in another he scored 600 runs and took 60 wickets but decided to give up serious bowling 'when t'ball started bouncing twice.'

On Saturday mornings Pilling attended the Lancashire indoor school where he so impressed Stan Worthington, the chief coach, that he was invited to join the staff. His batting and sometimes his bowling – he was now experimenting with off-spin with which he once undermined Phil Sharpe in a second eleven game – confirmed his talent and potential, and in August 1962 he made his first appearance in the county side against Sussex at Old Trafford where he made 20 in the first innings before he was bowled by Ted Dexter.

Since then he has been a necessary and vital part of the Lancashire scene, and although averages and statistics may not be ruled out in any assessment of capability in the instance of Harry Pilling they cannot convey adequately the pleasure this little man has given us nor do they give more than a sketchy outline of his lovable character. But for those who rate a player's worth on figures alone, Pilling's will stand comparison with most.

He made his first century against Hampshire at Portsmouth in June, 1963. In 1967 he topped the Lancashire batting averages for the first time. In 1968 he was the only Lancashire batsman to reach 1,000 runs, a target he has passed seven times in eight years. In 1969 he and David Bailey put on 225 for the fourth wicket against Kent at Old Trafford, and in the John Player League he topped 50 on five occasions.

In successive matches in 1970, Pilling made 109 not out and 69 against Gloucestershire at Old Trafford, and 119 not out and 104 not out against Warwickshire at Old Trafford. He and Clive Lloyd added 231 for Lancashire's third wicket against Kent at Dartford.

In the John Player League Pilling scored 625 runs for an average of 52.08 and was the first player to complete 1,000 runs in that competition in which, as an aside, he took the wickets of Denman of Sussex and Barratt of Leicestershire ('Ah foxed 'em'). In 1971 he claimed his first wicket in first-class matches, Peter Robinson of Somerset being caught by Barry Wood off Pilling's bowling. When invited to describe the delivery, Pilling replied, 'Flighted filth.'

Last season he completed 10,000 runs in first-class cricket, had an innings of 50 or more in nine consecutive matches, shared with David Lloyd an unbroken second wicket stand of 234 against Nottinghamshire at Old Trafford, and in one of the finest innings of his life, he contributed 118 to Lancashire's first innings total of 196 against Somerset at Weston-super-Mare. Many judges believed that he had done more than enough, to have earned a trip to Australia – he would have held his own against Sydney's famous 'hill' – but it was not to be. 'A trip like that is a bonus for us cricketers,' he told me. 'Everyone 'opes to get one and deep down we are terribly disappointed when it doesn't come off. Anyway what you 'aven't 'ad you 'aven't missed. Besides ah'm quite 'appy just to play for Lancashire.'

Elderly ladies sometimes fear for Pilling's safety when he goes out to bat. (Really, Victoria, it is too bad making him play against grown men. And with a hard ball too. And he's such a little boy . . .') Don't worry, ladies. Harry can take care of himself. For a small man, he has tremendous power for his strokes, particularly on the offside, and once he has taken a step backwards and crashed the ball past point or cover, then we know we are in for a treat. His height of course occasionally prompts some comic scenes, and Tony Nicholson and Freddie Trueman more than once have lifted him up to facilitate his conversation with a taller partner. Clive Lloyd for example. On one occasion Alan Brown of Kent appealed for lbw against Pilling. 'Not out – too high,' said Charlie Elliott, the umpire. 'Too high? Too high?' spluttered the indignant Brown. 'If the ball had hit his head it would have hit the —— wickets.'

Off the field, Pilling has a rich store of anecdotes which he delivers in the style of Rabelais (of whom he probably has never heard) or of Colin Hilton (of whom he certainly has). Success in recent times led to Lancashire's presence at banquets where the fare and the 'posh folks' were, perhaps, beyond Pilling's normal experience. 'Ah were sat next to this bloke, Lord somethin' or other, an' Ah were none too sure o' misself at first,' quoth he. 'Onny road, 'e dropped a tatie on to t'floor an' then kicked it under t'table. An' when 'e started eatin' peas wi' a knife, Ah thowt "Well, tha's no better than t'rest on us." After that we got on famous.'

At another such function, Pilling found himself next to a titled lady 'drippin' wi' jewellery'. 'There were a card in front of 'er saying who she were an' when Ah asked if Ah could take card 'ome to show t'missus what sort o' company Ah kept when Ah were away, she were reet chuffed. After that there were no problems. Once you get to know 'em, they're not all that different to us, are they?'

A happy man indeed, capable of translating his happiness to the crowds. He has no malice in him, and so far as I know he has no particular favourite among the county players, although I suspect he has a soft spot for Clive Lloyd with whom he has had many profitable and riotous partnerships. 'A great bloke, Lloydy,' says Pilling. "E'll run just as 'ard for your runs as 'e will for 'is own. Only trouble is that sometimes Ah'm freetened Ah'll get trodden on.'

IAN PEEBLES   SEPTEMBER 16 1975

A Toast to Leicester

Leicestershire County Cricket Club have come a long hard way to win their first County Championship. Although cricket in that county has its origins in the mid-eighteenth century, it was not until 1895 that they achieved the grandeur of first class status. This they did in company with Derbyshire, Warwickshire, Essex, and Hampshire, which brought the number of first class competitors to 14. They are now the thirteenth county to win the championship, the empty handed being Somerset, Essex, Sussex and Northampton.

Before their promotion to first class status, cricket in Leicestershire seems to have been run by the sporting clergy, doubtless supported by many a good hunting squire. Their chief claim to fame as a minor county was to defeat the touring Australians of 1888, an impossible proposition in modern times.

Their start in the senior league was humble enough – they shared the second bottom place with Nottingham. Thereafter they had a comparatively prosperous period before settling into a comfortable second-half-of-the-table existence which lasted until the second war.

In common with most cricketing counties, Leicester should have produced a generous series of cricketing heroes, characters, eccentrics and, from time to time, disasters. They seemed at one time to have a powerful anti-Australian influence. Six years after their win over the touring side, one Pougher, a reliable but not very remarkable Leicester off-spinner, was picked by the MCC to play against the current Australian team. Going on at the pavilion end at Lord's when the Australian score was 18, he took the last five wickets without conceding another run, thus being responsible, with J. T. Hearne, for the lowest ever Australian score in this country. That, as in the case of some other cricketers, was his one great moment and, although a very good county all-rounder, he never again achieved international fame.

The mainstay of the professional batting during this period was Albert Knight, a deeply religious man who made no secret of the fact that he sought the advantage of divine assistance on all cricketing occasions. This led to an embarrassing situation when he had as guest and opponent Bill Bestwick, a great and redoubtable Derbyshire fast bowler but not, at that point, a very reverent man. Accommodation being limited, they shared a bedroom and the host before retiring, as was his custom, prayed in loud clear tones that he might make a hundred on the morrow. Bill heard this plea with mounting apprehension and, when the prayer was done, sought to rectify an incalculable advantage by praying in equally audible if rather less formal terms that he might shatter his host for nowt. Next day the score book read 'Knight b Bestwick 0', which led to a sad rift in the friendship as Knight considered that he had been outsupplicated by a novice. The cynics, however, were inclined to view the matter as just another example of beginner's luck.

It was about this time that a very bright lad of 15 joined the staff and got his place in the team during the following season. Ewart Astill went on to play for another 32 years, and become the county's best all-rounder. He was an attractive and delightful man, an amateur billiards champion, and a king on the ukelele, which he tried to teach me whilst touring South Africa. Although fairly frail of physique his career was a most arduous one, for which he was brought up in a hard school. He used to recall that in his teens he stood in the slips beside two stalwart, immobile figures, Sam Coe and J. H. King. When he had chased three snicks to the boundary's edge in one over he returned, blowing like a grampus, just as the striker snicked a fourth. 'I'm not going for that,' he gasped. His static companions eyed him serenely – 'Aint ya?' said one – and off he went again.

He survived to do the double nine times but, like Bobby Abel of old, had fancy heroic ideas where fast bowlers were concerned, customarily withdrawing to a position where he could conveniently play the stroke from a safe position. He once misjudged a very fast ball from Learie Constantine so that, at full stretch, he was some inches short of the ball which comfortably beat the leg stump. But despite being, in the words of Jim Sims's majestic euphemism, 'a trifle apprehensive' he astonished the cricket world by taking a hundred off Lol Larwood in successive years at Trent Bridge.

Ewart's close companion over the years was George Geary, whom some of the South Africans considered next to Sydney Barnes as a bowler on the mat. And well they might for George bowled a fastish off spinner, and a well concealed cutter that went the other way at the identical pace. When he retired he went to Charterhouse to teach the boys, where he was a huge success.

When an old colleague called to see him George said to him: 'Come over here, I'll show you an England cricketer.' They went over to a net where a fourteen year old was defying all comers. George remarked to his duly impressed friend that the lad's name was Peter May.

There reigned in Leicester in those happy days a very remarkable man named Alec Skelding, fast bowler, poet, first class scrapper, wit and sage. He wore thick specs, tried his heart out on all occasions and, when the local bully boy disturbed the peace, mounted the fence, knocked the nuisance cold and returned in peace to his place at third man. With all his talents he was no mathematician, so was ill qualified when given the job of working the county score board. This he got into such a muddle that a hostile mob gathered to demonstrate beneath it. Hearing the din the operator stuck his head out and surveyed the confusion of figures which bore little relation to events in the middle. He turned beaming to the nearest protester: 'Do us a favour, cock,' he said. 'Get us an evening paper and let's have the right score.' Happily he later found his true niche as a very senior and capable umpire.

If readers detect a certain warm affection running through these happy memories their suspicions are well founded. In the early twenties Leicestershire came to Inverness to play a few matches in the surrounding district. My brother and I were staying there with our grandparents and for us it was a tremendous occasion. On the Sunday after the match I went for a walk with George Geary and Ewart Astill which to me, so far from the nearest first class county, was to walk with the Gods. My brother asked Claud Taylor, the hero of that year's Varsity match, for his autograph, a request which eventually led to his becoming our brother-in-law.

I have no doubt that today's heroes are just as great players and characters as the generations I knew and they fully deserve all congratulation in bringing this honour to their county for the first time. In toasting them I would, like the poet Omar, turn down an empty glass for those I used to know.

FRANK KEATING   AUGUST 12 1976

John Snow

John Snow and Basil D'Oliveira had supper together in a Harrogate hotel on the evening of the first day's play in the fourth Test match against Australia in 1972. Cheery Dolly said to surly Snow: 'The ultimate thing in life is to play for England.' Snow beaded his buddy with his dark, dangerous eyes and pointed out quietly and decisively: 'My friend, the ultimate thing in life is death.'

That's the thing about John Snow. He's a different kettle altogether. He doesn't fit into his pigeonhole. Not many leading professional sportsmen these days so singularly give the impression that they know there's more to life than professional sport.

International fast bowlers are meant to enjoy bowling, to loathe being taken off, to whinny with nostril-flaring eagerness and paw the earth with impatient relish when the new ball is due; legend demands that great fast bowlers have to dislike batsmen; tradition demands that great fast bowlers work in pairs.

'Up yours,' says John Snow to tradition and legend. When he's called on to bowl he gives the impression, most times, that he is doing so only grudgingly, as though his captain only wants to nark him; often it seems he can't wait to come off, so's he can lope back to his own private shadows and thoughts at third man. And how can you dislike batsmen when most of the time you scarcely seem to be aware that they're there? And loners don't work in pairs by definition: Statham and Trueman, Lindwall and Miller, Hall and Griffith, sure, but in 11 years of Test cricket it's been Snow and No one, Snow and Everyone, Snow and Jones, Snow and Brown, Ward, Knight, Higgs, Lever, Shuttleworth, Larter, Price, Willis, Arnold, Old and Hendrick . . .

We've never known what makes John Snow tick. And perhaps now we never will. For one fancies that today could well be his last appearance in a Test match. Agreed, he's been left for dead before. But he will be 36 next year. I reckon these five days at The Oval represent our final chance to decide whether there is more to him than meets the eye, or less.

It would be sad to let this match go past without a heartfelt hail and farewell to a player who stands near the very heights of Test match excellence. In the whole history of English cricket only four other bowlers have taken more than 200 wickets – Trueman, Statham, Bedser and Underwood. Before this series Snow had taken 206 wickets, 30 fewer than Bedser, another bloke who sweated away in solo stints without the relieving succour of a comparably talented partner. Snow as good as won the Ashes himself in 1970-71 and was England's sharpest spear when they retained them in the following year. In those two series he took 55 wickets – 40 of them top-of-the-order batsmen.

Might the mood be on him today, we will think, as he disdainfully marks out his approach this morning. Sleeves high in a tight little collar near his armpits, he will forbear to check his field; after a couple of stuttering steps he will have found his 16-stride rhythm and his gathering momentum and menace reaches its climax without strain or extravagance. On delivery he's more square-on than the classics, more right-shouldered but his final whiplash propulsion discovers a venomous spit or polish in even the doziest of pitches. Snow's reliance is not on swing, but on seam, on change of pace and movement either way. He can rattle a breastbone from a good length; he's never been a nasty bowler, but ever a menacing one when the mood is upon him.

As well as English spectators, Snow has always worried English selectors. Sussex have dropped him for 'not trying'. England 'rested' him for the same sort of reasons in 1969. In 1971 he was dropped for steamrollering a tiny Indian batsman who was innocently attempting a single. He refused to go on the last tour of India. He was not invited to join Denness's ramshackle Ashes army, and our humiliating rout there was even more painful as there was no Snow to answer fire with fire. He was recalled by public demand and Tony Greig last year.

Great English batsmen are meant to emerge from Oxbridge with private means and pure cover drives. Great English fast bowlers are meant to emerge from the grimy bowels of the earth, hang up their pickaxes and miners' lamps, and start hurling swearwords and thunderbolts at Australian heads. It's always baffled and bothered the English that their only genuinely great fast bowler of the last decade, the man who's carried the banner handed down from the Larwoods and Truemans, has been, well, a bit of a nance. Well, I ask you, a clergyman's son – and a poet to boot.

Snow was born in Worcestershire in 1941. His father was parson to the gentle agricultural workers from the orchards of Pershore Vale. The Rev. William Snow was a cricket nut if ever there was one. He prayed that his son would play for England. But as a batsman, mind you. Day after day young John was coached at batting, his three sisters and even Mum dragooned into long-stop and long-on. Shades of the Graces and Fosters in *their* orchards not far away. John was a country boy, a fisherman with jamjars, a birdnester, a happy wanderer over the Malvern foothills. In 1948 the Reverend took him to see Bradman's juggernaut set out at Worcester. All the boy remembers is 'men in white who kept moving about'.

His father moved to Bognor. John went to Christ's Hospital, the lovely Horsham college with the yellow socks, the nice manners and the long blue religious habits. He was in the XV as a full-back and the XI mainly as a batsman. Len Bates was the first coach to egg him on at the speedy stuff. Ken Suttle introduced him to Sussex as 'a promising bat'. Snow thinks he might like to concentrate more on batting now his lethal days are numbered. He might yet manage it – May or Amiss wouldn't have minded playing those two drives through midwicket in the final stages of the recent Headingley Test match.

Meanwhile there's been a comparatively late marriage, and now a bonny babe. He's increasingly keen on music and painting. And there's more poetry to come from the beetle-browed brooder. His two published volumes so far have been seriously and kindly received. And certainly some lovely lines jump out of the what-a-piece-of-work-is-man sort of stuff. But no piercing giveaway as to what makes him tick. Or even if he ticks at all. As he wrote in *Thoughts and Murmurs*: 'Maybe the oughts and countless thoughts are best left in the thinker's head.' And there's a now-it-can-be-told autobiography almost ready for print. Rumour has it that it'll take the lid off the lot. It'll make him a deserved nest-egg (he's a trained teacher if ever he cares to get back to it) and doubtless put a few whizzers up the establishment for one last time. But today, in probably his last Test match, is not the day to bury John Snow. But to praise him. Simply, he's done us a grand job. And we've been more than a bit ungrateful.

214

Ranji and Co.

To the ordinary late Victorian India was still a land of mystery, rope tricks, and magical spells. It was appropriate, therefore, that his introduction to Indian cricket had about it an air of magic. From the moment he burst upon the scene in 1893 until the outbreak of the First World War, Kumar Shri Ranjitsinhji used his cricket bat with a deftness and grace which savoured of the movements of a conjuror's wand.

It was not until his last year at Cambridge that the University were aware of the treasure in their midst so that he only played in one match against Oxford, and that with little success. But three years later at Old Trafford he marked his first appearance for England against Australia with a brilliant 154 not out to save a very difficult situation. The following year he started the series against Australia with 175 in the first Test at Sydney where the robust humour of the Hill would have given the Race Relations Committee collective apoplexy. From then on he was a first choice for England whenever available.

Many would include Ranji amongst the first half-dozen greatest batsmen of all time. Nor was he unduly bashful about his own place in the ranks of the immortals. A very young Gubby Allen was taken to tea with Ranji and Charles Fry, and listened wide-eyed to their talk. When there was a pause he asked: 'Who was the greatest batsman of all time?' A longer pause was broken by Ranji. 'I think, Charles,' he said in his clipped English, 'that I was better than you on a soft wicket.'

Ranji died at the early age of 61 but he lived long enough to see his mantle firmly settled on the shoulders of his nephew Duleepsinhji – 'Smith' to his friends. Like uncle like nephew. In 1930 at Lord's Duleep went in when both Jack Hobbs and Frank Woolley were out for 53, and by the evening had made over 150 and England were getting towards 400. So little was realised about the impact of Bradman and four-day Test matches that by then the older brigade were calling for a declaration. Percy Chapman resisted this but signalled the batsman to push along, at which Duleep made a series of scoring strokes, but was then caught at long-on off Clarrie Grimmett for 175. As he retired Ranji turned to his neighbour. 'I told you so,' he said. *'The boy is careless.'*

On the same occasion Ranji was himself the subject of a somewhat unexpected remark. On one day of the match he came straight from some official function in full regalia which, what with materials, tailoring, and precious accessories, must have represented countless thousands in good pre-war pounds. It was a dazzling spectacle which filled Maurice Tate with awe and wonderment. After several prolonged scrutinies he turned to his companions, Ben Travers and Arthur Gilligan, with the somewhat superfluous query 'See Ranji?' Assured on this point he nodded darkly and, from behind a confidential hand, whispered: 'He looks a veritable Hindoo!'

It was later in the same series, at Manchester, that Duleep and I were bidden to dine with Ranji and a party of very senior cricketers. The burden of the conversation was largely that cricket was a fine game, how well it used to be played and what a pity it was that nobody could play it any more. Next morning on the ground someone, unconnected with the previous evening, produced an old press cutting of an interview with Ranji on the occasion of his great first appearance. He was quoted as remarking that the older generation were very severe critics of the young and he hoped that, when his days were done he would be more generous to his successors. Whatever else, human nature does not seem to change.

Brought up on the legend of Ranji and the feats of Duleep the British public may have been mildly disappointed by the first All-India team to come to this country in 1932. It was a very good side but the batting, with few exceptions, was solid rather than sparkling, and lacked any element of magic. It was, however, notable for a fine pair of opening bowlers. Mahomet Nissar was a good fast bowler and would have been very quick indeed if he had, like John Snow, been able to cure a habit of putting his front foot down in the direction of third slip.

His partner, Amar Singh, was a superb seamer at a very lively fast medium pace. He could move the ball in the air and off the pitch and, on matting, cut it either way. In the first and only Test match they gave England a very rough start. Nissar clean bowled Holmes and Sutcliffe in the opening overs and, when Frank Woolley was run out, three wickets were down for 19.

Amar Singh was also a good aggressive batsman and had much success in the Lancashire League, where he fought some good battles with Learie Constantine. Learie once told me that he discovered that Amar had a morbid obsession with death and any mention of it. Never averse to a little playful gamesmanship Learie would always turn up for their encounters wearing a black tie, sometimes straight from a funeral, or sometimes just out of respect for the sudden and imaginary decease of a non-existent friend or relative.

My only excursion into Indian cricket in its own land was a pleasant but unsuccessful exercise. In 1937 Lionel Tennyson took a side at the invitation of the Indian Board of Control and played five unofficial Test matches, winning 3-2. My active part ended with a shoulder injury in the first match of the tour, but I much enjoyed the hospitality of the Army messes and found our stays with the various Maharajahs quite an experience.

We did not see any rope tricks, and the nearest anyone came to a magical spell was Joe Hardstaff. His faithful bearer went thrice to his favourite shrine to pray for the 'Sahib's' success. There the good man must have got his lines crossed for the immediate result in each case was that Joe made nought.

Travel was rather different to the present day, as we took three weeks to get there by ship, which was very agreeable, then spent 45 days on the train, which was less so. We had one overwhelming advantage compared to the modern traveller. There was no question of prohibition and whisky was 12s 6d a bottle.

Finally an item for those who like cricket curiosities. We've all heard of the man who tried to hurry the East, but what about the man the East bustled into a speed record? In 1946 when the Indian game against Glamorgan was spoiled by rain an effort was made to give the crowd a little added entertainment. With the home side far behind and due to follow-on it was agreed that when the last wicket fell, there would be no interval and, with the last pair becoming the openers, they would carry straight on.

P. F. Judge went in at no. 11 and C. T. Sarawate obliged by knocking his castle down first ball. Judge now became the opening batsman and, as soon as the stumps were re-erected, Sarawate rushed up and knocked them down again, first ball, a feat which might be described in Hindustani as a trifle jaldi. I have often wondered if they took a new ball to achieve it.

IAN PEEBLES   JANUARY 19 1977

The Unorthodox Brigade

In reporting the MCC's match against the Combined XI at Nagpur Henry Blofeld describes Lever as twice sweeping Jadeja backhanded through the slips for four. Although over the years I have seen a wide variety of weird and eccentric strokes I cannot in honesty claim that this feat has been among them. I did once, however, have an eye witness account of a highly dramatic scene arising from this very cause.

The witness himself is worth a line of introduction. Cyril Foley was a man of many parts, having played cricket for Eton, Cambridge, and Middlesex. He had also taken part in various enterprises as diverse as the Jameson Raid and an expedition in search of the Ark of the Covenant. Neither was successful but, in the latter case, biblical authorities might allow that he got some way towards his goal by hitting a couple of sixes into the Pool of Siloam. When I knew him he was a staunch, but profoundly pessimistic, supporter of Middlesex which county he was actively representing against Gloucestershire when there occurred the incident in question.

Middlesex being in a strong position 'W.G.' sought to delay their progress by bowling very wide to the off at that spirited Irish Baronet, Sir Timothy O'Brien. A couple of wides were enough to raise the Bart's pressure to bursting point and the next one he thrashed backhanded through the slips, doubtless to the accompaniment of a blood-curdling Hibernian oath. Indeed blood was nearly spilt when the ball whistled past the ears of Brother E. M. Grace, who happened to be standing at slip. What fraternal alarm this caused W.G. is a matter for conjecture but, seeing his tactics foiled, he managed a fine show of shocked outrage. 'I'll tell you what it is, Tim,' he said. 'You'll kill my brother.' To this he received the obvious reply. 'And a bloody good thing too,' retorted the Bart.

Baulked in the verbal as well, W.G. dropped the lofty hauteur and proceeded to straightforward threats. 'If you do that again,' he said, 'I'll take my men off the field.' Of course the Bart did it again and immediately found himself, except for a scared young partner, alone and monarch of all he surveyed, at which he relieved his feelings by thrashing stumps many a mile into the air. In the prevailing atmosphere this could have proved a costly gesture; for the brothers, seeing the umpires unnerved, might well have lodged an appeal for hit-wicket.

Foley said that sanity might have prevailed at that point but for one 'Buns' Thornton, a famous hitter of the time, scenting the sporting possibilities of the Bart v. The Brothers, a contest of Homeric dimensions. Accordingly, having brought both parties to concert pitch by separate assurances to each of its complete propriety in the face of the other's unreasonable truculence, he was rewarded by a truly thunderous row. When W.G.'s beard had been all but tugged from its moorings (by its owner) his naturally high tenor was heard on rising key. 'I'll tell you what it is, Tim,' he cried above the din. 'I'll fetch a policeman to you.' This, said the narrator, was a suggestion so preposterous that the contestants momentarily fell silent, enabling lesser mortals to intervene and restore order.

Not all eccentric strokes have afforded entertainment on this scale but many have added to the joy of cricketing nations. Some spring from genius. Victor Trumper had a habit of chopping yorkers to the square leg boundary. I remember seeing, from short leg, much the same effect when George Gunn, suppressing a yawn, applied the old-fashioned draw to our fast bowler, Jack Durston. Nor was it a gentle deflection, but a lusty slap which sent the ball thumping into the Mound Stand fence.

As great a virtuoso as George and in rather more aggressive mould was Charlie Macartney, who loved to late cut full tosses and half volleys. When a young Jack Fingleton walked with him to open the innings of their Sydney club for the first time the 'Governor General' tersely warned him to 'Look out for the first ball.' This injunction 'Fingo' obeyed by making a good way down the track in anticipation of a quick single, and was nigh decapitated when the ball came straight back like a cannon shot. The striker apologised for what was an obvious misunderstanding, saying that what he had meant was that he always like to hit the first ball straight back at the bowler's head. 'It upsets 'em,' he said.

Some unorthodoxy is born in prudence. Ewart Astill, a humorous and agreeable man, frankly stated in his latter days that he did not intend to be maimed at his time of life. Having astonished the cricket world by taking 120 off Larwood, almost exclusively from the square cut played from a discreet range, he set out for the West Indies to meet Learie Constantine at his fastest. But, when he made a strategic withdrawal, in this case the impish Learie kept shooting at him instead of the castle so that soon, according to a reliable if unofficial spokesman, the action was taking place in the no-man's land between the wicket-keeper and the square leg umpire. When Learie did take a shot at the stumps it was said that the defender, with legs at full stride and bat at the extreme extension of his arms, was still a foot inside the line of the ball which missed the leg stump by the same margin.

My old friend and captain, Nigel Haig, unabashedly pursued something of the same philosophy, occasionally with surprising results. Playing against Surrey at Lord's he made a superb square cut off Alf Gover which must have been at the fence in a trice – had it not, after travelling a yard or so, knocked the leg stump out of the ground. That was in 1932 and the next year in the same fixture Alf contributed to another spectacular stroke. He bowled a bouncer at Bernard Atkinson, a large powerful man, who met it with a Wimbledonian overhead smash. The ball sailed back over Alf's head to land just short of the Nursery for six.

But whenever the subject of unlikely strokes arises, my mind inevitably turns to Jim Smith, who demonstrated what a vast range of glorious and unexpected effects could be achieved by one great agricultural swish with 18 stone behind it. As I write I see the ball a pin prick in the sky, and pity the babbling gaggle of fielders gyrating on the possible area of arrival, to say nothing of the harassed captain trying to remember all their names at once. Not that it mattered for he was almost certain to nominate the wrong one.

Fresh in the memory is the day against Hants when Jim and I ran a leisurely two, abandoning an easy third to see just what would happen when the ball returned to earth. It was worth it. The ball brought down mid-off (Lionel Tennyson, trundling backwards with arched back and head at maximum elevation) with a thud that shook St John's Wood and, deflected from the vertical to the horizontal by the heel of his hand, shot up to Father Time for four. To add a further touch of drama the concussion had riven Jim's mighty blade from splice to toe.

Last season we saw the West Indian batsmen play every beautiful shot in the book. For this let us be grateful; but I cannot think of any reigning batsman who brings to his craft the *fun* which Denis Compton did, either in his own crease or, as occasionally happened, when he turned up unexpectedly in his partner's or, more frequently, when he got stranded between the two. Perhaps this is too stern an age for buffoonery.

Sir Donald Bradman

It still hurts. Fifty-four years have done nothing to mollify the damage done one summer afternoon more than half a century ago. No matter how I try to gloss it over with temporarily satisfying thoughts of personal semi-triumphs achieved since, the only port of refuge for my cricket conscience seems to be the one which tells me that the very same thing has happened to every other bowler who shaped up to him.

Shaky though that consolation may be as a softening agency, here is my very own story of my first unforgettable encounter with Donald George Bradman, who reaches the seventies tomorrow.

At nineteen years of age I was enrolled as an undergraduate at the Teachers' College within Sydney University and, without reasonable doubt, had fairly high-priced tickets on myself as a classy spin-bowler and an athlete well established in the metropolitan fields of endeavour. These estimates, it is wise for me to mention forthwith, were entirely self-researched. No sporting writer to that time – 1924 – had come to realise the important fact that I existed. As for Don Bradman – no one had ever heard of him either. All these trivial items go together to show that the stage was magnificently set for O'Reilly's little lamb to be led to the slaughter at a time to be appointed.

My parents lived in a tiny rail-side village approximately one hundred miles south of Sydney called Wingello where my father was teacher-in-charge of the local school. Australians are apt to rate the size of their rural towns by the number of hotel licences contained therein. My town had no pub at all, consequently it was socially 'beyond the pale', whereas Bowral, a neighbouring settlement, proudly boasted three of them, and had ample reason to throw its municipal chest out wide whilst poor, chip-spitting, desiccated little Wingello struggled hard to find eleven mobile men all possessing cream pants to appear in the Southern Tablelands cricket competition.

It came as no real surprise therefore when I thought I heard my name called as the one-o'clock passenger train steamed into Bowral station that Saturday as I made my way home for the summer vacation. Poking my teenaged head eagerly through the window-opening I could see my local station-master hurrying along the Bowral platform loudly calling for 'Bill O'Reilly.'

Thrilled by the unaccustomed reception, I waved him across to be told that I must disembark and join the Wingello cricket team which was listed to face up to Bowral that same afternoon. 'No togs,' I said. 'All my cricket gear is at home, worse luck.'

'No fear it's not. I went over to see your mother this morning and I have it all with me, so hop out quickly and quit all the talk.' I hopped out and to this day I feel that I made a very grave tactical blunder by doing so.

Losing the toss Wingello were instructed – not invited – to take the field so that Bowral could have first use of a solid concrete pitch which would certainly still be there in its first-class condition today had the admiring local population not blown it sky-high to replace it with a beautiful turf model more fitting to the high-class tone of the Sir Donald Bradman Memorial Oval.

Perhaps to get full value from the trouble he had taken on my behalf earlier in the day my station-master captain handed me the new ball.

I got a wicket quickly – nice going. It was pleasantly reassuring to see the replacement batsman making his snail-paced diffident approach from the shade of the age-old gum tree which served as the shelter shed. This had all the signs of another easy job. How was I to know that I was about to cross swords with the greatest cricketer that ever set foot on a cricket field?

He didn't have it all his own way, let me tell you. Well, not for the first couple of overs anyway. Twice my first slip – a cheery old-timer – committed offences for which he might well have been publicly flogged had they been committed a few years later on.

Those fleeting examples of bad luck which haunted my early efforts were less than flea-bites by comparison with the bad luck which came in the form of the greatest hiding I ever experienced on the cricket field. Favouring a lofted shot over mid-on and larding that with incredibly powerful use of a lethal pull shot which sapped the enthusiasm of three or four square-leg fieldsmen who took turns to 'boundary ride', this jockey-sized schoolboy tore the Wingello attack to pieces. At the end of hostilities for the day Bradman was 234 not out, with more runs to his credit than Wingello would be likely to make in a week.

With the game to be resumed on the following Saturday afternoon there was plenty of time for me to lick my wounds, to reassess my sporting plans for the future.

'There are a lot of better games than cricket; why worry about it?'

'If a kid like that can skin you alive what hope have you got?'

'Get out and go swimming. The water's fine.'

Such disturbing thoughts harassed me throughout the ensuing week before Saturday arrived.

And when it came the sun shone, the birds sang sweetly, and the flowers bloomed as never before. I bowled him first ball with a leg-break which came from the leg stump to hit the off bail. Suddenly cricket was the best game in the whole wide world.

As I look back now and recall my harrowing reactions to my first taste of the killing weight of Bradman's bat, I find it easy to spare a sympathetic thought for all the great bowlers of my time who queued up in their hundreds for a taste of the same medicine. But, as I have said, it is small comfort when I remember that it was I myself, an unsophisticated teenager, who blazed the trail, who actually started the rot – the very first cab on the rank.

Nevertheless I rejoice with the cricket world that the 'Little Fella' is hale and hearty still and is, as usual, well on his way to another century.

IAN PEEBLES   MARCH 27 1979

Runners and Writhers

It came as something of a shock to cricketers of my generation to read
that Wood, a promising young Australian batsman, had been dropped
from the side because of his erratic and dangerous running between the
wickets. So well schooled have they been in this department that, as
player or spectator, I cannot ever remember an Aussie being run out. I
can, however, recall a Christmas party in Adelaide being enlivened by
Vic Richardson, teller of many a superbly outré tale, relating and acting
out a historic scuffle of long ago.

Australia won the last Test in 1930 by an innings after which we all
had a nice cuppa, and the victors set off in high spirits to Bristol, there
to despatch Gloucestershire. Perhaps their spirits were a bit too high
for, with only 118 to make on the last innings to accomplish this, they
found they had lost nine wickets with the scores no more than level.
The last pair were Perce Hornibrook and Charlie Walker who sweated
and struggled through three maiden overs of Parker and Goddard by
which time nerves were twanging like piano wires. At that point one of
them made a firm hit towards cover and the pair set out with glad cries
to collect the winning run.

But cover made a good interception and brought the heroes to an
abrupt halt. However, the striker seeing that the ball had not been
gathered set off again, bawling at his retreating partner to grasp this
gleam of hope. The partner was by this time practically at his own
doorstep but he gallantly put about once more, just as the striker had
lost heart and turned for home. There the striker, seeing the fielder still
fumbling made another desperate foray, but the roles were now
reversed, his partner in mid-wicket having made a simultaneous about
turn.

At the apex of this bizarre triangle was the fielder not much helped,
poor man, by the bellows of 'this end' which reached him from both.
With staring eyes trying to judge the intentions of the runners
(obviously an impossibility) he scrabbled furiously around his ankles
picking up successive handfuls of air and discharging them madly in all
directions, whilst the ball nestled cosily between his feet. This dictated
the tempo of the runners' pas de deux for, at each discharge, they
reacted frantically but without coordination so that each covered a
considerable distance on a regular beat eight yards from his crease and
eight yards back again. Since they were always going in the same
direction they might have been Perce East and Charlie West for ne'er
did they meet, let alone cross.

But all good things must come to an end and cover, at length,
grasping solid leather for once, thrashed it in but to the arrival end of the
shuttle service so that both escaped. And what did their agonies
achieve? Scarcely had the dust and din settled when Perce was lbw to

Tom Goddard and the match a tie.

The English endurance record for muddle between the wickets must still belong to 'Crusoe' Robertson-Glasgow and Tom Raikes. Playing for Oxford against Surrey at The Oval in 1922 they met in mid pitch and after a moment's hesitation, together made for the same end, whence they immediately left again in company abreast. It was calculated that as though attached to each other by some spectral harness they traversed the pitch four times at the end of which all the stumps had been flattened by repeated attacks and most of the fielders by hysteria. When they paused for a moment to draw breath and consider future policy one of the opposition had the presence of mind to erect one stump and, ball in hand, to uproot it as laid down in the book. This was not quite the end of the drama for neither the umpires, nor the runners, nor anyone else present could decide who was out. The problem was resolved by tossing and 'Crusoe' won.

My old club Middlesex have had some spectacular runners over the years. Tom Enthoven headed the list with the proud record of having, as captain of Cambridge, run out his entire side in the course of the short University season. Pat Hendren had his unpredictable moments of danger and Denis Compton provided almost as much excitement and entertainment between the creases as he did in occupying them. Walter Robins was a superb runner, very fast on the straight and like lightning on the turn. The trouble here was that, in his enthusiasm, he occasionally forgot that others were not quite so sprightly.

In the third Test match at Melbourne in 1937 Australia set England 689 to make on the fourth innings to win the match. Walter, having made nought in the first innings, went in at ten minutes before the close of play on the fifth evening, with 534 runs still wanted and four wickets down. Maurice Leyland was still there having battled his way through an intensely hot day against a spirited attack. It was with great relief that Walter steered Bill O'Reilly's first ball through the gully and was off like a whippet from the trap. He was back for a second in a flash and, seeing no fielder in the vicinity of the ball, set off for a third. Half way there he was aware of a figure by his side. It was Maurice whom he had lapped.

At once Walter turned back and Maurice plodded on to safety where, in a cloud of steam and sweat, he literally 'sat on the splice', blowing like anything. As Walter advanced to make his apologies Maurice tottered out to meet him. 'Take it easy lad,' he gasped, 'we can't get all these roons tonight.'

JOHN ARLOTT JULY 10 1979

Ernie Knights

On Sunday evening, Ernie Knights, the Hampshire groundsman, came in from an evening visit to the square that was his life-long interest, sat down in his house in the corner of the County Ground at Southampton, and died.

There was a peculiar emptiness about finding the door of his toolshed shut yesterday morning. For there he used to stand at the receipt of greetings; never looking his 72 years, his lean weatherbeaten face wryly expressive, half a hand-rolled cigarette hanging cold from his lip. He returned a morning salutation in a broad accent less Hampshire than pure Southampton. Pressed, he would predict, invariably accurately, the behaviour of his pitch, for he was profoundly, though never ostentatiously, wise in matters of soil, weather, rolling, raking, cutting, above all in making grass grow hardily.

Ernie joined the Hampshire ground staff 54 years ago under that autocratic Victorian Jesse Hopkins. He became head groundsman in 1947 and since then had produced true pitches with a consistency not bettered by anyone in the land. He had awards to prove it; but he was not a man to flaunt his medals; rather he esteemed the approval of cricketers. If batsmen, rather than bowlers, tended to approve of his 'belters', he would point out, without heat, the regular success of Derek Shackleton – 'and all such real bowlers' – on his creations.

County Ground was home to Ernie Knights and all his family, his wife Bella, the two boys, and his daughter; it will seem the less homely without them. He was a strand of Hampshire cricket history. His memorial is one of those rare strips of land capable of sustaining the heaviest traffic of cricket without betraying it.

FRANK KEATING IN BRIDGETOWN MARCH 16 1981

Ken Barrington

He had been so hale and full of beans. So dynamite chuffed at the end of the West Indians' innings in the morning. His nose crowded out the already jammed pavilion long room bar. His smile illuminated it. If, batting first, a side did not make at least 300, in this place they could consider themselves well and truly stuffed – and he was beaming because his boys had just bowled out the unbeatables for 265.

Across the change-of-innings pavilion barge and bustle, I caught his eye. You could only grin back as he gave a thumbs up. The last time I saw him was a little later on the players' balcony during England's afternoon collapse – choked he was, but always first up with a great big consoling arm round the incoming batsman and some perky get-stuck-in encouragement for the outgoing.

Then, late in the evening, somebody whispered me off the dance floor and told me the numbing news. It just could not be true. Why, he was so very happy that his wife had come out for a holiday only last week. No, you could not take it in – nor could the players after the team manager Smith had summoned them before breakfast to his room at the end of the pier that juts from the hotel into the Caribbean. The young men tiptoed back across the boards almost in single file, the tan drained from their faces and looking shellshocked as if they'd heard their very best friend had died in the night. For many of them he had.

Only since knowing him these past two months did I realise how heartfelt, even desperate, had been the demand from the players and the press that he be added to this touring party as assistant manager. When it was named in the autumn he was missing from the list for the first time in England's last five tours. Lord's were cutting costs – but the genuine outcry was relentless enough to make them admit their mistake and change their minds.

He was the players' man, both spiritual and temporal. Each morning he gave them all their individual alarm calls. In the nets he bowled at them and followed through to cajole or advise with tiny hints on technique; always a smile; always relishing the day like mustard. Perhaps he knew there wasn't all that much time. On match days he was ever lifting spirits and humping kits. In the evenings his boys would gather themselves and a few beers around him and listen to the tales of long ago when cricket tours might have been to other planets for all these new jet-aged players knew.

Ken Barrington had done it all. The first of his 20 foreign centuries for England had been here at Bridgetown. For a dozen years till a first warning heart attack in 1968 when the doctors ordered him to take off his pads, he had squared his shoulders, jutted his jaw and come back for more; he was England's rock-solid, often unconsidered trellis around which the public's favourite fancy-dans and flash Harrys entwined their colourful summer blooms.

He was invariably up the other end, grim and determined as he conscientiously swept the stage for the entrance of the Mays and Cowdreys and Dexters and Graveneys, the last great quartet of the golden line of legend. They would not have done even half as much without Barrington.

I will never forget that midsummer Monday in 1963 during that second Test match of unremitting tension at Lord's when in the last innings, England, needing 233 to win, lost Stewart, Edrich and Dexter to the blazing fires of Griffith and Hall with only 31 scored.

Barrington and Cowdrey dug in and ducked and battled it out on into the afternoon. They were on the point of swinging the match with an epic stand when a withering delivery from Hall broke Cowdrey's forearm. Crack! At once Barrington, in answering fury and in spontaneous hate, struck Hall for venomous one-bounce fours over mid-on.

The rage was on him in manic defence of his wounded officer – but then just as suddenly he took a deep breath, calmed his soul to concentrate, and turned to stand again to see out the day in England's cause. They always called him the Colonel, as befitted a soldier's son. But he was more of a kindly sergeant major without any bark or bite. Mind you, just a large beak and larger beam.

He first signed for Surrey as a leg-break bowler, but they soon realised that he had too much grit and guts to stay long messing about with the twiddly stuff.

In the end, it was a grim business he had worried and worked himself into. But after his ticker first complained at the unrelenting life at the top, he emerged to everybody's astonishment and joy from behind the ropes with one of the loveliest, hail-fellow natures that could be imagined. He bought up a successful Surrey motor business then asked if he could be of any more help to cricket.

Now he was in his element, talking about the old days. When one of his youngsters complained a fortnight ago about some aspects of the hotel service in Guyana he said: 'I dunno. When I first came here in the 50s with Peter May we stayed down the road at that wooden place and the cockroaches were so big that you'd tread on them as hard as you could and you'd lift your foot and they'd wave up at you, say "good morning", and potter off into the woodwork without a care in the world.'

When his boys moaned about tedious waiting in VIP airport lounges he'd grin: 'Blimey, we had 27 hours in a Pakistan train once with only a bucket as a latrine.' Or: 'You should have come out here with us, mates, in our banana boat. First six days through the Bay and all that time you wouldn't see another player except the dying geezer in the next bunk. We were all simply seasick.' Or a complaint that a Trinidad steak was a bit small: 'Crikey. I had five months in India and Pakistan once when my total diet, honest to God, was eggs and chips. Closey, my room mate, was so ill for days that all he could do was crawl from his bed to the loo on all fours every five minutes. He'd had a curry. I stuck to egg and chips. You can't muck around with eggs and you can't muck around with chips, can you?'

We would log his malapropisms; some pinched-lip types thought we were sending him up. He loved it, and laughed back at himself. 'Well, Frank, you all know what I bloody mean, don't you?' Sometimes they were quite ingeniously perfect. A batsman got out because he was 'caught in two man's land'. When that minor riot occurred last month in Port of Spain, it might have been worse than one he had encountered in Bangalore. Because there, to mingle with the crowd, the police had sent in '200 plain clothes protectives'.

Between their sobs yesterday his boys could only have faith that now he will 'sleep like a lark' in eternal peace.

FRANK KEATING   AUGUST 12 1981

Alec Bedser

By chance, we had lunch in an olde English place not far from Lincoln's
Inn Field where he started work as a solicitor's office boy at the age of
14 in 1932. The ageing, aproned English waiters recognised him, which
was nice. He didn't even look at the menu but simply ordered roast beef
and greens.

For a split second I even fancied he hummed a snatch of Gilbert and
Sullivan . . . 'When I was a boy I served a term as office boy to an
attorney's firm . . .'

The Englishness of it all was appropriate. Alec Bedser, at 63, may be
a successful something-in-the-city now, but he is still the great
big-eared English yeoman of a long and ancient and trustworthy line. He
bowled his boots off for England. He hung them up 21 years ago. In
1962 he became a Test selector and for the last nine years he has been
chairman. Peter May is to succeed him.

I had thought that the England team at Old Trafford tomorrow was
effectively the last one to be picked by Bedser and that May would be
co-opted to help choose the side for the last Test and the tour of India.
Not a bit of it. Alec's last list will be the touring team – 'And anyway,' he
says, 'I dare say they'll ask me to help 'em out again soon enough.'

So it meant I couldn't get any secrets out of him, though I did sniff the
teeniest, accidental hint that Keith Fletcher will be the touring captain.
We will see.

I met a young first-class cricketer the other day who honestly did not
know even that his chairman of selectors had himself played for
England. He just presumed Bedser was one of 'them' up there at
Lord's.

'I dunno,' moans Alec. 'These youngsters today . . .' and he shakes
his head and his eyes colour a sad grey-blue and he is at a loss for words
till another, 'I dunno, they don't know how lucky they are.' He loves a
good moan does Alec.

You sometimes think he blames it all on school meals. Well, Eric and
he had to walk four miles a day to and from the Monument Hill Central
School, Woking, didn't they, with sandwiches in the satchel and just a
cup of water in the lunch hour. This lot don't know how lucky they
are . . .

At 14 he and Eric would get the train to London at 7.30 in the
morning and get home at 8 that night – at 10 on the three evenings a
week they studied shorthand and book-keeping at night school.

Their father was a bricklayer. He died at 89 three years ago. The two
beloved bachelor boys still live with Mum, 88 last birthday, in the little
house at Woking that the family built, brick by brick, in 1932, the boys
labouring and Dad laying. Mother went to work even though they were
once down to their last shilling for the gas. Dad always said he would

earn the money if she looked after the boys.

She still does and is as lively and active as a cricket round the hearth.

Eric was born first by a few minutes. If they are not quite identical now, Eric being slightly plumper, there's scarcely a wrinkle in it. John Woodcock, the editor of Wisden, once played golf with them at Worplesdon. Same outfits, same shot off the first tee with identical No 2 woods and identical short swing; the two balls ended up on the fairway kissing each other – 'Eggs in the same nest.'

They both joined the Surrey ground staff in 1938. They served together throughout the war, long dusty, dangerous days in Africa and wetter ones in Italy. On the resumption of fun he started taking wickets by the hatful.

At once he played in the 1946 Test trial and though he had damaged a thigh he secretly strapped it up in the lavatory. 'Where d'you field?' said B. H. Valentine. 'Slip,' lied Alec. Then he winced, took a deep breath, and got out Hammond and Hutton and was chosen for the first Test against India.

The great big boy walked to Woking station; with his great big cricket bag. He took the tube from Waterloo to Baker Street, then a bus to Lord's. Wally Hammond gruffed 'Good luck.' He took 11 wickets in the match . . . then another 11 in the next one.

In all, he was to take a record 236 wickets for England. On Hammond's tour of Australia he toiled heroically for more than 500 overs. It lasted from August 31, 1946, to April 17, 1947: he was paid £295, plus 25 bob a week spending money. At Adelaide in 104 degrees he had to go off to be sick, then bowled Bradman with a ball that the Don still says was the best that ever got him. 'Yeah, and I bowled a lot more like it since,' mutters Alec, tucking into his greens.

He loves Australia. It's just that he likes England better. He still writes very regularly to Bradman, Arthur Morris, Ron Archer and Keith Miller. 'Keith, of course, has never replied, but always rings me first thing whenever he arrives in England.'

Brown's next tour of Australia: 'We could have won easy, but old Freddie stupidly wanted to be surrounded by youngsters. If we had taken the likes of Keeton, Langridge, Edrich, Gimblett, Brookes, Ikin, Jackson, Robertson or Watson instead of kids like Dewes, Sheppard, Parkhouse, Close and Berry, we'd have walked it.'

The end came, in terms of the big time, for the second Test of Hutton's tour. Alec had shingles and should never have played in the first match. England were slaughtered. Alec, sickly, took one for 131 ('seven catches dropped, mind you'). So they let the Typhoon loose. 'No sour grapes, Tyson got plenty, sure, but I would have got 100 wickets on those pitches. Arthur Morris put us in 'cos he didn't want to face me that first morning.'

But when the captain pinned up the team in the dressing room Bedser was not on it. Hutton had not even mentioned it. Alec felt humiliated. 'Funny bloke, Len. Do you know, when I was ill on that tour I was in the next room, but never once did he pop in to visit.'

He is a more kindly selector. Either he or the captain is always in touch with the team on the phone. Alec's first chairman of selectors was the late R. W. V. Robins. Snobby Robby. 'We would meet at his flat or his St James' Club on a Sunday morning. He never really watched any cricket. Just went on what he read in the papers or heard from his cronies. He would turn up to the first day of a Test, but on the second day, after lunch, he'd sometimes clear off and go to the pictures.'

Boycott had loomed large over Alec's own chairmanship. The self-imposed exile started around the time Geoffrey kept getting out to the Indian Solkar – 'a real toffee apple bowler.' Then he sulked something rotten when Denness was made captain.

At the beginning of every season Bedser would ring Boycott. The rum Yorkshireman was convinced 'public school blokes at Lord's had it in for him.' Alec would patiently tell him that the selectors, Bedser, Barrington, Hutton, and Elliott had all been to elementary school.

When Geoffrey telephoned that he might be ready to return in 1977 he was playing at Northampton. Alec said he'd come and see him. 'No,' said Geoffrey, 'not here at the ground, man!' 'All right,' said Alec. 'I'll see you after the game in the corner of the foyer at the Grand Hotel, Northampton.'

'No,' insisted Geoffrey, 'I'll be in the car park at the Watford Gap service station. No, not in the snack bar, in the car park. We mustn't be seen together.' They sat there side by side for two hours. 'At least he was on time,' mutters Alec. The truce was worked out and the glorious comeback determined.

To have to coerce a man into playing for England must have been extremely distasteful to Alec. It was probably something, he thought, to do with free school meals. 'I dunno,' and he shakes his head and his eyes cloud over. 'I dunno . . . these young blokes today. . .'

JOHN ARLOTT   DECEMBER 29 1982

Sir Jack Hobbs

In this month fell the centenary of the birth, and the 19th anniversary of the death, of Sir John Berry Hobbs, known affectionately through the cricket world of his time as 'Jack'.

He was born in Cambridge in 1882, the first of the 11 children of a servant, and later net bowler, of Jesus College. Without coaching Jack became the finest batsman of modern times, known to his contemporaries – opponents as well as team mates – as 'The Master', and, with no social or material advantages, a kind, generous, modest man who bore a knighthood with natural dignity and unassuming grace.

Merely to see him lift or swing a bat at close quarters, to observe the flexing, tensing and relaxing of his grip on the handle was to perceive the profound sensitivity of his batting. To watch him play an innings was an impressive demonstration of his mastery; the capacity to play naturally and easily while the man at the other end struggled. To watch his running between wickets, and the unhesitating response of all his partners, was to appreciate his judgement; and to share his quiet mirth at his ability to tease and outwit a fielding side.

Jack Hobbs never had a cricket lesson. Once, only, his father bowled to him; and when he took evasive action to save his unprotected legs from the impact of a brisk off break, he was told 'never back away from the ball.'

With that single item of instruction, he set out on his unmatched career. Because of the strict qualification regulations of his time he did not begin to play first class cricket until he was 22. He lost four seasons to war; most of another to illness and injury, and in his last two did not play a dozen matches. Yet he scored more runs (61,237) and more centuries (197) than anyone else in the history of cricket; and more runs (5,636) and more centuries (12) for England against Australia than any other cricketer. He had an average, first to last, of 50.65; characteristically, in Tests his figure was 56.96.

He did it all with brilliance, enjoyment, humour and magnanimity. He was such a generous man and splendid player that he never seemed to resent being out; perhaps he was confident of runs to come. 'How many hundreds did Jack score?' said Wilfred Rhodes, once – 'Aye, 197 – and he could have made 397 if he'd wanted but when Surrey were going well he used to throw it away – give his wicket to one of his old pals, hit up a catch and go out laughing – Aye, he could have made 400, and if he'd played for Yorkshire he would have.'

Twenty times he scored 100 before lunch. He had every stroke in the book – and extemporised many outside it – though he insisted that he abjured the riskiest, and best, of them after the first world war. That was when, resuming first class play at the age of 36, he went on to score 132 more centuries.

What more is there to say? Best, and best loved, batsman of his era, he did not create modern batting (W. G. Grace had already done that) but he gave it its ultimate lustre. He mastered all the wiles of the bowlers – high pace, googly, leg theory, inslant – with consummate ease; contemned the bouncer when it was bowled at him.

He was made an honorary member of Surrey, and the Hobbs Gates at The Oval were erected to his memory; an honorary member of MCC; and, despite his anxious request to the Surrey president to 'stop all this nonsense,' he was knighted in 1953. He lifted the standard of the professional cricketer to the point at which he took his wife with him (at his own expense) on a tour of Australia; a privilege hitherto reserved for amateurs. He founded a sports goods business, conducted it with scrupulous honesty and it flourished.

He was an admirable father; and for a decade he nursed his invalid wife Ada, night and day, fearing that, without him, she would be taken into a home. When she died in 1963, he simply relaxed. 'The Master's Club', founded in his honour, drank his birthday health a few months later; he acknowledged it graciously from his sick bed with a telegram.

A week afterwards he sank gently into death. He was indeed a gentle man, and as fine a gentleman as he was a batsman.

DAVID FOOT
JANUARY 15 1983

Zaheer Abbas

I landed in Lahore on the day Syed Zaheer Abbas scored his 100th first class century. As a batsman inclined to recoil from too much ostentation, he marked the occasion with some style on December 11. He reached his hundred with a perfunctory poke for three wide of mid-wicket and held his bat horizontally above his head with both hands – 'I'd seen Geoff Boycott do that on television when he got his 100th hundred.'

Then he went on to score 215 and the Indians, many of them his friends, were glad to see the back of him. Radio commentators shed their accustomed formality as they eulogised the innings. In the lofty open-air press box, where some reporters record their instant thoughts in a Persian-style script that is a thousand times more beautiful than Mr Pitman's, the prose was destined for expansive and affectionate headlines.

Zaheer wiped his spectacles as he walked with a triumphant spring back to the pavilion. His shirt sleeves, surplice-white, were as ever buttoned at the wrist. He smiled like the normally solemn choirboy who knew that he had hit the top note – with purity and grandeur. Imran and the other Pakistan team-mates were waiting to congratulate him.

It was a performance that demanded acclamation, not just in the newspapers the next day. Yet the circular Lahore ground offered only hollow applause. An entrepreneur called Mian Azizul Haq Qureshi had agreed to sponsor the whole series and one outcome was that admission prices soared. Cricket supporters protested by staying away, at least until there was saner counsel at the turnstiles. There were about 2,000 fans present to cheer Zed.

'Such a shame,' said Intikhab. 'The ground should have been filled to see that bit of Pakistan cricket history.' The sentiments were echoed by players of both national teams. I gazed round the boundary; in parts, the police, in their almost sinister grey, seemed to outnumber the spectators. Outside, eternally poised for action, were the riot squads, padded and protected in a way would make them eminently equipped to face a few early overs from fearsome fast bowlers themselves.

But crowd or not, the word got round about Zed. He was again a national hero, just as he had been after scoring 274 against England at Edgbaston in 1971. He was feted at a series of private parties in sophisticated Lahore. His wife, Najma, and two young daughters flew from Karachi to join him.

I went as his guest and although the parties were formal and restrained by our standards, I noted the collective idolatry. Men and women sat on opposite sides of the rooms. The hospitality was generous, though there were few signs of vocal conviviality. Zed enjoyed the compliments but as ever had the appearance of a reluctant hero.

When he joined Gloucestershire in 1972 he spoke few English words. He is now efficiently bi-lingual in the way of most of the Pakistan players. 'You know how important that innings was to me. Whenever I am scoring runs I am happy. I crack one record and am already looking for the next.' There is no swagger in the way he says it. His youngest brother keeps the scrapbook and the statistics in Karachi. Home in Bristol, scorer Bert Avery does the same.

Zed invited me into the Pakistan dressing room for the rest of the match. We chatted and then he snoozed in the treatment room – in a pattern which I found endearing. He isn't physically strong and has had problems with his health over the past year or so. You wouldn't think so as he rises on his toes to produce the best square-cut in current cricket. Many would argue that he's the most stylish player in the game. It isn't just romantic nonsense that so many believe he has been inadvertently transposed from the Golden Age of Cricket.

He's apt to survey his County and Test career over the last decade and confide: 'I'm either very good or very bad.' Clearly he's very good indeed at the moment. He went into the fourth Test with India with five consecutive centuries behind him, two of them in one-day matches. Inti says: 'He's a great player. All bowlers come alike to him. But you must also know how to treat and encourage him.'

To the younger Pakistan players Zed is a kind of Elder Statesman. They hold him in some awe, admire immensely his rich and rare talents . . . and suspect that he's also slightly a law unto himself. He isn't flamboyant and excitable in the extrovert style of some of them. He's rather moody and introspective. 'He doesn't like fielding too much – and we understand that,' I was told.

Before the Fourth Test he'd scored 3,992 runs for his country, more than anyone else. Scores in the present series of 215, 186, and 168 had given him an average of just under 190. Yet, for a batsman of such prolific inclinations, there have been only 11 Test centuries – a long way short of Sunil Gavaskar's 26 and Don Bradman's 29. That is partly because Pakistan have played relatively few Test matches.

His recent stand of 287 with Javed Miandad was a record for any Pakistan wicket. Such a profitable alliance at the wicket happily obscures less cordial moments between the two in the hardly distant past. Pakistan's cricketing politics have often been fiery and even incomprehensible to naïve British eyes. From my position of privilege I sensed one of Pakistan's happiest dressing rooms for a long time.

In 1976 and again in 1981 Zaheer headed the domestic batting records here in a way that other Gloucestershire batsmen, W.G. and Hammond, once did. At his best he's incapable of an ugly shot. For an uncoached palyer, his feet are instinctively right. The balance and the coordination are impecable. He's known to practise in front of the mirror at home.

Zaheer was born only weeks before the historic and at times acrimonious partition of 1947. His face, studious and preoccupied, carries the complexities of his proud and battle scarred nation. He has both the gentleness and solemnity of Islam.

A dignified man, with a lofty social standing and a family construction business to cushion him after he gives up playing, he keeps personal grievances to himself. One, certainly, is the way the Pakistan Cricket Board failed to give him the captaincy ahead of Javed.

But runs for him have always been the wondrous antidote. He overhauled first Fry and Hobbs and then Hammond in Karachi not long ago, by scoring a century in each innings for the eighth time. That was a world record.

'Let's see,' he's been apt to ask Bert Avery with that sheepish smile, eyes twinkling behind the spectacles (the same pair as he damaged while fielding several years ago), 'how many tons did this Bradman get?' The Gloucestershire statistician responds: 'Rather too many for even you, Zed!' And they jointly look for a target nearer realism.

Zaheer leaves Richards and Botham to corner the pages of Wisden with the more dynamic flourish. He goes into cricket history almost by stealth. 'Where do you bowl to him?' asks his good friend Doshi, to no one in particular. 'What are you complaining about – you've just taken five Test wickets,' says Zed. Doshi grins and returns to his P. G. Wodehouse.

Far away in Pakistan Zaheer is, at the age of 35, demonstrating once more the receding art of pure batsmanship. 'See you back in England,' he waves. I edge uneasily past the armed police – one of whom stops me taking some innocuous holiday cine film as if I were a fugitive from a le Carré novel – and I know indisputedly in my heart that the bat is mightier than the gun.

FRANK KEATING   MAY 2 1983

Geoff Boycott (1)

It was appropriate that Worcester was the setting for the Old Warrior to be buckling on his armour for his 21st campaign. Worcester is where romantics demand the cricket season should start, for it was there that all touring teams traditionally began their summers in England. This year it was Worcestershire versus Yorkshire and Geoffrey Boycott.

The Saturday morning sky was a startling hazy blue that made the

Cathedral's bold and beautiful outline more dramatic than any stage-designer's cut-out. The sun was warming fresh and the old pavilion newly white-washed. Alas, the irony – the week's rain made even squelchy cricket impossible until teatime. And yesterday was a wash-out.

Boycott, it goes without saying, was first in the nets. The night before he had driven from Yorkshire and went early to bed after a supper of mineral water and cheese. Not Perrier but Ashbourne, he insists, 'because it's English'. In the same breath, instead of, say, Wensleydale, he orders 'a hunk of that Dutch cheese'. You never know quite where you are with Geoffrey.

He was up early. After cereal, stewed fruit, a glass of milk and the ritual hot water and ginseng, it was over the Bridge smartish so that it seemed only the groundsman had got there before him.

Twenty-one years ago this month the squinting, bespectacled gawk had been given a lift from Fitzwilliam to Bradford to play his first match for Yorkshire. He opened with Brian Bolus. First ball he square cut for four; second ball he was out.

Now, 42,269 runs later, he was going through the post-breakfast rituals again. Net underpants on; box tied round the slim midriff; net flannels on; net pads – straps cut to exact length – briskly buckled; Elastoplast twirled expertly round the bottom joint of the right thumb; net gloves on. Hair combed, cap doffed, white rose badge exactly so. Then it was up with the Slazenger bat and off with urgency across the soggy field to the artificially surfaced nets.

An even grander old man leaned on the wicket gate and watched him stride across the field. Basil D'Olivera, now the Worcestershire coach, shook his head in wonder and laughed. 'Look at him. Have you ever seen him looking fitter? I'll bet you old Fiery will be playing for England again one of these days. You mark my words.' Basil shook his head in grudging tribute and laughed again.

You never know. Boycott has served one year of the three-year ban from Test cricket imposed after he took part in last Spring's private tour of South Africa. I last saw him bat in the Calcutta Test 16 months ago – will that be his last Test? He was out cheaply in both innings, batting, as Wisden reports, 'with unfamiliar levity'. He hooked in the first over, and I remember thinking he must be ill.

He insists he was poorly, and pulls up his shirt once again to show the scar that proves his lack of a spleen. But, you suggest, he was fit enough to get out of bed and play golf on that fourth day. 'I just had to get out of the room, out of the city-centre. Bernie Thomas, the physio, told me to get as much fresh air as I could. You ask him.'

Then he levels you with his Coventry-blue contact lenses: 'Do you honestly think that Geoffrey Boycott would rather play golf than play in a Test match? Anyone who knows me the tiniest bit and who thinks that must be totally crackers!'

He was in South Africa again this winter. 'Yes, earning my living as anyone else is entitled to do. Of course I'm against apartheid. Do I have to go through it with you again? It's all in my book, the book that saved the tour of India. Page 203 – 'I detest the system of apartheid just as I detest Communism; yet I confess I would love to go to Russia or China for a visit. If that's illogical, it's no more illogical than the stand taken by governments who trade with Communist countries, or have diplomatic relations with regimes they publicly frown upon . . . So why should sportsmen always carry the can?'

There are 70 county cricketers playing in South Africa this winter. They are made to feel, he says, like pariahs while no end of English businessmen are out there looking to get the Queen's Award for Industry. Boycott and his cricketers feel just slightly aggrieved at the illogic of the Lord's ban when a leading cricket administrator spends his holidays in the Republic and when another has business links there.

'You tell me what's the difference? Why one law for them, another for us? Now, if you will excuse me, I've got some more work to do.' And in the nets alongside the silvery Severn, the Yorkshire bowlers queue up to satisfy once more this original, stubborn, self-absorbed and truly astonishing old soldier's appetite for batting.

PETER ROEBUCK   SEPTEMBER 15 1984

Men of Essex

The only surprise, as Michael Bore's final blow fell into the hands of a Somerset fieldsman was that Keith Fletcher not only knew where Nottinghamshire were playing but was actually listening to the game on the radio.

Whether he sees himself as a latter-day Drake I cannot say, but whenever a crisis arrives it finds Fletcher decorating or gardening. He has an unworldly air, as if he were an archaeologist appearing on This Is Your Life. Forced to introduce his team in India, he peered at Jack Richards, puzzled and yet convinced that he had seen the fellow somewhere before.

It is as well that Fletcher has adopted an air of serenity rather as the Indian did in One Flew Over the Cuckoo's Nest. Nor are his reasons necessarily all that different, because around him has buzzed an extraordinarily demented group of men.

This manic atmosphere even affects their chuckling ground in Chelmsford where spirits are as chirpy and as caged as in an aviary. For many years, as Essex edged towards success only to retreat in its face, it seemed as if Fletcher was the only man in the team with any anchor.

People began to wonder if they would ever win anything, as if they were doomed to dash between the extremes like defreezing vindaloos. After a fraught day at the cricket, after another collapse or another defeat wrenched from the jaws of victory, painting a wall and watering a flower must have appeared a most recuperative activity.

Then, finally, the Benson & Hedges Cup was won. A few months later Essex were county champions, having found themselves 80 points in front by June, a lead which even they could not squander. Suddenly the team lost its brilliant but brittle characteristic and settled into a mature excellence they have not yet lost. Two more championships and two more John Player Leagues have been taken despite the replacement of ageing cricketers (Turner, Phillip) by promising youngsters (Gladwin, Prichard, Foster).

Slowly, Essex have assumed the characteristics of their captain – a cussed effectiveness and determination to prevail. They have made quite a jump from the accidents of 1978 to the thoroughness of 1984.

Essex's pattern is simple. Its origins lie in the change to covered pitches. When cricket was open to the elements teams could build big scores on the first day and hope for overnight rain. Once pitches were covered there was scarcely any point in winning the toss. Wherein lay the advantage?

Ah, thought Fletcher, if we cannot rely upon rain to damage pitches, we must prepare pitches helping bowlers from the start. And so the practice dawned of producing damp, green wickets upon which Fletcher could win the toss and invite his opponents to bat. It is ironic that the covering of pitches has led to their deterioration.

Essex are particularly suited to grassy pitches. They do not have a Marshall or a Hadlee to cut into batsmen. Their strength is not penetration, but accuracy. Fletcher's bowlers defeat batsmen by sudden movement, plucking the ball away as a stroke is played. It is an attack founded upon skill, stamina and persistence, qualities best captured by that most dangerous bowler, John Lever.

This season Lever has bowled 874 overs, 100 more than anyone else, and has taken 116 wickets. His efforts over the last few years show that he is the most valuable bowler in county cricket, for though Hadlee, Marshall and the rest have their seasons, Lever returns these figures year upon year. He missed only one game this year – and his team lost by 10 wickets. Lever's merit lies in the full length to which he bowls and the potency this lends to his swing and cut.

This skill is not as widely used as it was when Cartwright and Shackleton were around as many medium-pacers prefer a short length in the hope of an error in defence, on the hook or in frustration.

Of all his team it is Lever that Fletcher would most miss. Not that his other bowlers are weak. Foster and Pringle have represented England this year though the latter has the air of someone who has only recently left Woodstock and rather wishes he had stayed there. It is said that when Pringle suffered from too many no balls, he sought his captain's counsel and was advised to marry.

Not surprisingly, Essex depend upon medium pace rather than spin, which is not to say that Acfield and East are less than good bowlers.

East – who is supposed to have retired – has a look in his eye, the glint of the fellow in Apocalypse Now who lost the smell of napalm in the morning. It is the haunted look of a man to whom something outrageous has just happened or is about to happen.

East and Acfield are skilful cricketers and men of nervous energy who hide their cares behind roars of laughter, which is rather the Essex way. They do, though, take wickets on dusty pitches. Or they would if ever they saw one.

Since this attack is founded upon persistence rather than flair, Essex must collect their runs quickly to provide the bowlers with sufficient time to complete their task. In this Essex are led by Gooch's Bandido moustache, by McEwan's splendour and by Gladwin, whose beefy blows resemble Gooch's.

This barrage either succeeds magnificently or acquires the attentions of Hardie, Fletcher and Prichard in their resourceful middle order. Prichard is an intriguing fellow, shuffling out to bat with a deferential, quizzical air as if embarrassed by all the fuss, mannerisms resembling Fletcher's.

Not that Fletcher is nearly as meek as his tangled pads and bowed head indicate. It is his way of showing that he is an Essex man, with a sly Cockney wit balanced by rural patience. He is a countryman, he is saying, and not at all impressed by London's buying and selling. His air of enigmatic simplicity is as cultivated as his garden. It is designed to create an impression of mystical wisdom.

But he still scores his runs, the gaps into which he guides the ball have not vanished as his hair has greyed. It says much of his resolution that he has survived the wilder notions of his men. (At a team meeting called to work out a fresh batting order, he sat silently as the improbable arguments raged, suddenly stood up and announced in his squeaky voice that he was 'going to bat at four and the rest of you can sort yourselves out.')

Fletcher stands perched at silly point, sliding dry comments from a corner of his mouth. He is not a man easily deflected from his purpose. His team has succeeded because, eventually, it adopted the characteristics of its captain – an unforgiving, shrewd and persevering approach to a hard game.

FRANK KEATING   DECEMBER 22 1984

David Steele

A heartfelt valediction from the pulpit to David Steele, who announced his retirement yesterday, will set him shaking his grey head and wincing as he looks down at his shoes in the front row.

It is almost statutory to say he will be remembered for just one Test match – his first against Australia at Lord's in 1975 – even though that is not the whole story. He played in eight consecutive home Tests against Australia and the West Indies – then both in swaggeringly ferocious pomp – and never once flinched.

It was a truly heroic and very human chapter in which David Steele tapped the sporting adrenalin in the whole nation. Yet, having weathered the fearful gales, he was then peremptorily put out to grass with a Test match batting average of 42 – exactly the same as that of Ian Chappell and Cyril Washbrook, only a couple of pegs below Cowdrey and Graveney, and miles ahead of the likes of Woolley, Trumper or Bill Edrich.

Steele must have felt disappointed when he was dropped for the 1977 tour of India. Characteristically he would have moaned only to the nearest short-leg, but his legion of supporters which included by then a considerable lobby of housewives who couldn't tell lbw from PVC, gave voice.

The romantics, though, preferred him to leave on a high – the Indian spinners might well have shattered the image – and he waddled back to the county grind, garlanded with affection and remaining for ever the personification of that authoritative yeoman's pronouncement by Cliff Gladwin, another North Midland pro, who made the all-time anthologies with 'Cometh the hour, Cometh the man.'

In the mid-summer of '75, England's batting was yet again in shreds. They were laid to waste in the first Test and, amid wholesale changes, Tony Greig was made captain for Lord's. The beanpole pragmatist called for Northamptonshire's eminent and very *grise*, bespectacled, obscure Jude.

England batted. Lilian Thomson was at her most catty, cruel and spiteful. The openers went at once, and it was 20 for two when Steele, his favourite moth-eaten old towel elastic-banded to his left thigh inside his trousers, gave a last polish to his glasses, picked up his bat and plodded heavy-footed, down the stairs.

Of course, he had never been in the home dressing room before, so he went down two flights of stairs instead of one and ended up in the member's loo. Outside, meanwhile, 25,000 people were waiting.

When finally he emerged and clomped to the wicket all that was missing was the ARP helmet. The writer, Clive Taylor, described the entrance memorably: 'The bank clerk goes to war.'

Later that year David told me about it when he collected his BBC Personality of the Year trophy. As he reached the wicket Thomson said to his colleagues, 'Who the hell is this guy? Groucho Marx?' Steele simply said 'Mornin'' and took guard, two-legs, as he always did.

The first two balls from Lillee were devilish. As he prepared to face them, Steele muttered to himself, over and over again, 'Watch the ball, watch the ball.' He played both deliveries immaculately straight down into his boots – and swept the next for four to release an explosion of pent-up sound from the crowd that could be heard in Baker Street.

He ended with a valiant half-century which made the headlines on

News at Ten . . . as he did through that summer. He became a national celebrity. Knots of people would cluster round the TV rental shops in every high street, asking 'is Steele still in?' Usually he was, playing forward. Industrialists like John Moores of Littlewoods sent him cheques and butchers sent him free steaks.

Next summer the rustic epic continued. When he made a century against the West Indies at Trent Bridge I cannot remember such a cheer at a cricket match. He wiped his glasses and all Nottingham found themselves rubbing their eyes.

Now, after 21 years of admiration around the provincial paddocks of England – 500 games, 22,346 runs, 623 wickets and 546 catches – he will be plodding away, just as he came into our consciousness those nine years ago – with that rolling gait of a strangely-armoured infantryman: jaw jutting, eyes slightly bewildered behind glinting specs, pad straps dangling, front foot forward.

Thanks for the memory, Mr. Steele. The way you touched your cap, the way you played for tea . . . no, no, they can't take that away from me.

MIKE SELVEY   AUGUST 14 1985

Geoff Boycott (2)

I once overheard a delightful conversation between two Yorkshire cricketers down in the Smoke to play Middlesex. One had indulged in a cultural theatre visit, and the talk went thus: 'I went to see "Charley's Aunt" last night.' 'Oh, was it a farce?' 'No, it was quite good really.'

I mention farce, because there is nothing more rib-tickling to county cricketers than to see Yorkshire struggle. In the sixties, they were the most powerful side in the land. Since then, an astonishing series of events has reduced them to a laughing stock everywhere but in Yorkshire itself.

Briefly, the story is this. Brian Close, a master captain, was relieved of his position and replaced by Geoffrey Boycott, a dedicated batsman but no leader of men. The effect was galvanic – Boycott averaged over 100 and the county had their worst season ever.

With undercurrents already there, a committee man finally proposed his removal. The notorious Reform Group was formed to dredge up support for Boycott but subsequently he was ousted, Jack Hampshire, a seasoned professional, appointed and Ray Illingworth made manager.

Reform Group activities intensified and finally Hampshire left the club, Illingworth was sacked, the committee overthrown and, most bizarre of all, Boycott elected to the new one. An employee was on the governing body to which his captain was answerable.

Geoff Boycott recently scored his 100th hundred for Yorkshire, a celebrated event in those parts, but greeted on the county circuit with the same enthusiasm as an outbreak of anthrax. Statistically, of course, it is a superb achievement and the latest in a long line of personal milestones and meritorious figures. But statistics, like bikinis, are designed to conceal as well as reveal.

What they fail to show is the damage that single-minded obsessiveness with run-scoring at the expense of everything else can do to the spirit within the team, be it Test or county, and how it can adversely affect the performances of other team members.

The whole cut and thrust is now documented at length, warts and all, by Don Mosey, the former BBC cricket correspondent and long-time defender of Boycott, in a biography[1] that he was forced to write without cooperation from the subject – a disappointment to him, but the two are no longer on speaking terms.

While acknowledging Boycott's statistical contribution, Mosey comes to the reluctant conclusion that 300-odd professional cricketers can't all be wrong.

Bowling to Boycott in county matches has always been a mixed emotion. With the elation of beating the best defence in the world goes the knowledge that in spite of his relentlessness the fielding side always has one end under control.

One instance serves to illustrate. In 1977, teams were allotted a maximum 100 overs in their first innings, although if a side was bowled out in less, the residue could be added to the other team's quota. This introduced a tactical defensiveness to the game.

Middlesex had been ousted for a moderate 256 in 92 overs, leaving Yorkshire 108 overs to bat. In this time, they managed only 244 for four, with Boycott scoring 117 in 96 overs.

What I vividly remember was bowling over after over of straight full-length deliveries which were patted back down the pitch. There was no need to get him out and he wasn't going to get out, so we had stalemate.

Remember, too, the World Cup final when Clive Lloyd dropped Boycott. He denied deliberately having missed what was by any standards an easy chance, but I still wonder.

When he finally does call it a day, probably with 200 centuries, what will there be to look back on? A master technician and a fanatically dedicated professional who stifled himself in statistics and the belief that if he failed the team failed.

Perhaps someone will browse through a magazine, as I did recently, and come across an illustrated coaching series sponsored by an international airline. 'Brighter Cricket with Geoff Boycott,' it said. 'Number One – The Backward Defence Stroke.' I think that speaks volumes.

[1] *BOYCOTT*, by Don Mosey (Methuen)

OTHER PEOPLE

Politicians

JULY 6 1863

The members of the House of Commons took their annual treat at Lord's, London, on Saturday, when the Government side of the House played the Opposition. There was a large assemblage of political and aristocratic celebrities on the ground during the play, which was kept up with fair zeal and much mirth from mid-day till seven o'clock.

> Government 46 and 136; Opposition 259. The opposition won by an innings and 77 runs.

MISCELLANY   MAY 19 1931

Whatever else may be said about Mr. Baldwin he is very rarely a pessimist, and it is possible that something he said about cricket at the Worcestershire dinner last week was the result of a temporary depression following on Worcestershire's utter rout by Notts rather than a considered opinion. Is there, after all, the slightest evidence of any value to support his statement that 'in these days when people were always tearing about they had no time to stop quietly in the country on a Saturday afternoon and play cricket'? Probably it would be difficult to get statistics, but it is at least no empty suggestion that there may be more people playing cricket on a Saturday afternoon up and down the country this year than at any time in history. Fast trains, coaches, and cars foreshorten impressions, perhaps, but a railway or car or coach journey over any extent of country on a Saturday afternoon leaves the impression of, as it were, a layer of cricket across the land.

Unless it is suggested seriously – it could be no more than a delusion even then – that *everyone* played cricket when Mr. Baldwin was young, this particular complaint seems to lack substance. There is no shortage of Dingley Dellers to-day, and the modern Dingley Dellers do what Dickens's characters did not do – they play a game recognisable as cricket.

MISCELLANY   FEBRUARY 9 1933

Lady Bonham-Carter has introduced the 'body-line' simile into a liberal conference, and we may not unreasonably look forward to constant repetitions in all manner of places. For cricket similes have always been popular in politics, and they go back a long way, perhaps beyond the time when Disraeli was struggling for recognition from the Tory magnificoes, one of whom refused to admit that Dizzy was a 'member of our eleven' and dismissed him as a 'professional bowler we take round with us'. That definition alone dates the saying a long way back, but the chances are that something or other had been described in politics as 'not cricket' much earlier. Sir George Trevelyan found Charles Fox's cricket and his earlier politics very similar, and it is more than likely that the great round-arm bowling controversy had its echoes in Parliament and on the hustings. Why not, when it is remembered how largely cricket has been represented in both Houses of Parliament at every period of our history?

OUR PARLIAMENTARY CORRESPONDENT   JULY 20 1948

WESTMINSTER, MONDAY

It has been a day of contrasts. If Sir Waldron Smithers – the light of heart – had had his way the House of Commons would have been very much in the mode to-day. It would have been paying, as is the fashion, semi-divine honours to W. G. Grace. The elected of Orpington proclaimed to the world that he had asked the Speaker's permission to put down a motion to commemorate the centenary of 'W. G.'s' birth and had been refused. His object in mentioning this painful rebuff was, so one suspects, to get the name of 'the greatest cricketer of all time' on the Commons records since he had been denied the opportunity of delivering a panegyric on him through the means of a motion.

The Speaker admitted that he had refused the motion and went on to say something about Parliament being Parliament – a place where Parliamentary business is transacted. And then, mock-seriously, he asked where would it end if you began with W. G. Grace? Might it not go on to Bradman? The Speaker stopped at Bradman, but that was a piece of imperial diplomacy and it is not to be imagined for a moment, dear reader, that he was not also thinking of MacLaren, Spooner, or J. T. Tyldesley.

'At least,' Sir Waldron submitted with a final grumble, 'he ("W. G.") knew how to play the game.' Who, by that Parthian shot, was being condemned for not playing the game there is no need to inquire closely, but they were, beyond any doubt, the 'Red' multitudes Sir Waldron sees daily, with Mr. Morrison, Mr. Dalton, and Dr. Edith Summerskill conspicuous among them . . .

FEBRUARY 18 1950

'This I can say to Mr. Yardley. If I did take charge of the English cricket team I would be able to make a better job of it than the English cricket team has been doing in recent years in the Test matches. The poor showing of some of them does indicate that private enterprise in cricket might not be regarded as the last word, and ultimate State direction would not do it any harm.' – Stirring pronouncement on future cricket prospects from Mr. Emanuel Shinwell.

LONDON LETTER   JANUARY 9 1959

There will be a few short, angry balls bowled (metaphorically) at Lord's when the latest issue of 'Tribune' reaches St John's Wood – if, indeed, it ever penetrates that dignified neighbourhood. 'Tribune' writers have asked for many odd things to be nationalised in their time, but now one of the most distinguished has turned his attention to the M.C.C. Mr. Michael Foot, in guise of John Marullus, to-day complains that the 'reactionary, self-appointed junta controlling England's Test team' has continued the Tories' task of lowering Britain's world prestige.

'Macmillan in person might have been in charge at Melbourne. Wardle was hounded out of the Old Boy brigade because he had the guts to speak his mind about the whole snobbish business. Trueman is still unpopular because he sometimes says 'By gum' instead of 'By jove!' Twenty years ago 'Tribune' first made the demand that the M.C.C. should be nationalised. Now everyone can see the wisdom of our policy. What is the national Executive of the Labour party waiting for?'

Is all this just what cricketers call a 'Chinaman' – that Left-hander's ball which appears to be doing one thing but in fact is doing the other? Is Mr. Marullus being ironical?

Knowing some of the pitfalls awaiting journalists who experiment with this elusive quality, I put it to the editor of 'Tribune' that of course it was all a joke. After a brief consultation at the other end of the telephone back came this reply, 'Mr. Marullus says he is deadly serious.'

I should have realised there would be trouble at Brighton when my train down on Friday night was stopped at Balcombe Tunnel by some idiot who heaved a brick through the driver's window. But by Saturday afternoon, all seemed misleadingly rosy at the annual cricket match between the Press and the TUC. The first dispute came over the length of the pitch. Joe Gormley claimed it was over thirty paces long, but the press pointed out that he had very short legs. Hugh Scanlon, fetching in a matched outfit of burnt orange (clashing suitably with Len Murray's faded khaki) seemed most upset about the inadequate equipment for the wicket keeper. We pointed out that he had two pads and two gloves. What could conceivably be missing? He went off very concerned muttering about boxes.

No doubt this accounted for the remarkable number of byes scored by the reporters. The cricket pitch, on the delightful grounds of Mr. Briginshaw's NATSOPA Rest and Recreation centre, was oddly laid out. The boundaries were amicably agreed to be the rugby posts, the nettlebed and the deck chair where Jack Jones was sitting. It was later adjudged that this incentive to big hitting was a great success. Beer frequently stopped play. The only casualty was Joe Gormley, whose bowling figures of three wickets for 24 runs have left him quite unable to lift his right arm above shoulder level – which could have interesting results when it comes to voting by holding up the delegates' card. The Press, by the way, won – in spite of the sterling mathematical wizardries performed by the lady from the TUC who kept the score.

Once upon a time, in the dear dead days when members of the Labour Party not only spoke to each other but even played bourgeois games with each other, there used to be a notable annual event in the politico-sporting calendar. It was the Tribune versus New Statesman cricket match.

It would be an exaggeration to say that it was invariably a placid occasion. Sometimes there was genuine sporting needle in the performance of at least some of the participants, a few of whom actually displayed a distressing eagerness to win. On other occasions there were equally distressing political undertones, reflecting some esoteric difference of opinion between the egg-head staff of 'the Staggers' and the supposedly more earthy contributors to Tribune.

But in general the event was happy, with family picnics round the boundary and a good deal of social drinking (wine for the Staggers, beer for Tribune). As with all such memories, play seemed to take place against an unvaried background of warm sunlight and cloudless skies.

But the happiest seemed to have been staged on a village cricket ground in Buckinghamshire, close to a large and rambling farmhouse occupied by J.P.W. Mallalieu, Labour MP for Huddersfield and a contributor to both Tribune and the NS. It was a caricature village pitch, with a strangely undulating outfield which someone suggested was evidence that the meadow had not been tilled since the days of medieval strip farming.

The great and the famous would turn up from time to time, including one occasion when a slightly tipsy Nye Bevan decided to wander on to the playing area to debate with some of the fielders, only to be ordered off again by an egalitarian umpire. More often than not, the Tribune team would be captained by Michael Foot.

Gamesmanship was much in evidence, as when the Tribune side spread the word some days before the match that they had obtained the services of a certain Dr. David Pitt, a notoriously vicious West Indian fast bowler. He looked the part when he arrived, magnificently black and towering over the heads of everyone else.

Skipper Foot casually tossed him the ball to open the Tribune bowling, Paul Johnson visibly paled beneath his freckles as he took guard, and the mighty figure trudged to the boundary to begin his run. He turned, thundered towards the stumps, brought his arm over in the regulation manner – and then forgot to let go. The ball struck the ground about a yard in front of him, sank into the turf from sheer force, and lay still. The umpire signalled the Statesman's first run – a wide.

But it was clear from the attitude of the younger players and spectators that the true hero in these encounters was not a world famous politician, nor even a sham West Indian bowler, but the host himself. J.P.W. Mallalieu, whose P stood for Percival so that he preferred to be known as Curly or Bill, cut by far the most dashing figure.

He would appear on the pavilion steps in what may once have been immaculate whites, including not only cricket boots with metal studs and slightly yellowing flannels, but also a faded dark blue cap and a magnificently moth-eaten cable-knit sweater bearing some imposing legend across its chest.

For Curly was not only a distinguished writer on sport as well as politics, he was also an Oxford Blue and all that impressive gear was the regulation pre-war outfit of one who had played for the varsity. No wonder the youngers looked up to him.

There was only one problem, albeit a serious one. For Curly had won his undeniable Blue not for cricket but for rugger. By the time he got out on the square, the awful truth became all too apparent.

This annual encounter between what were once called Britain's leading leftwing weeklies has now been abandoned for some years, killed off by the increasing ferocity and sectarianism of modern leftwing politics. The New Statesman, after a giddy lurch towards the far left some years ago, is currently paddling back towards the mainstream. The staff of Tribune, on the other hand, give the impression that they would rather toss bombs than cricket balls at their opponents.

So it is unlikely that such a civilised event will reappear on the politico-sporting agenda in the foreseeable future, which is a pity. At the very least, its disappearance has deprived the world of sport of what may have been its only trustworthy one-eyed umpire, namely myself. And it has denied Mr. Foot's current dog, the nationally famous Dizzy, a day he would have enjoyed.

However, it is easy to become stickily sentimental about such phenomena, expatiating on the supposed essential 'Englishness' of this aspect of Anglo-Saxon left-wingery. But it was undeniably nice while it lasted, and pleasantly typical of the atmosphere which surrounded the Bevanite brand of leftwing socialism in the Forties and Fifties . . .

Foreigners

JULY 20 1868

Longsight v. Australian Aborigines

There was a large attendance of visitors at the Longsight ground on Saturday to witness the conclusions of the above match, and more especially the athletic performances that were announced to take place. When the stumps were drawn on Friday night Longsight had 32 to get to win, with seven wickets to go down, and play had not been long resumed on Saturday before the required number was scored. The athletic sports, which excited a considerable amount of amusement, kept the visitors upon the ground several hours. They consisted of flat racing, jumping, steeple chasing, throwing the cricket ball, &c. and were won as follows: – Flat race (100 yards), Mullagh; standing high jump, Mosquito; flat race handicap (440 yards), T. Whitworth; running high jump, Mullagh and Charlie; throwing cricket ball, Charlie; 100 yards backwards race, Dick-a-Dick; 150 yards steeple chase, over four hurdles, Mullagh; three-legged race, J. Oakes and J. Moir. At the conclusion of the above sports the aborigines appeared upon the ground in their native costume, and performed several clever feats with spears and boomerangs. Lawrence, the captain of the blacks, showed his perfect command over the cricket ball by playing with it upon his bat, where it was caught after being thrown a considerable distance into the air and across the field. The boomerangs used by the Australians are pieces of wood bent and curved, and when thrown into the air their motion resembles the flying of a pigeon. Dick-a-Dick, armed with two rather formidable-looking weapons, cleverly defended himself from a number of cricket balls that were forcibly thrown at him.

Aborigines 53 and 123; Longsight 78 and 100 for 6. Longsight won by four wickets.

AUGUST 3 1874

On Saturday the Boston and Philadelphia base ball players appeared on the Old Trafford cricket ground. The company was numerous and fashionable, and the Americans received a cordial welcome. The play was very good, and the surprising skill and activity of the men in the field elicited universal admiration. The Philadelphia players won a hardly contested game by a piece of consummate generalship on the part of Mr. McBride, their captain, the game standing 13 to 12. The Americans gave an 'exhibition' of fielding before the game began, and their throwing and catching was admitted by veteran cricketers to be worthy of the highest praise. As to the game of base ball itself, the impression made was most favourable, and we shall be surprised if it does not speedily become naturalised amongst us. The return visit of the players to this city, on the 21st and 22nd inst. when they play both base ball and cricket, will be extremely interesting.

OUR LONDON CORRESPONDENCE   AUGUST 6 1930

The blunder which caused the exclusion of the German cricket team from the Oval covered stand on Saturday has been apologised for, and they are to be entertained by the M.C.C. at Lord's this week. It would have been very unfortunate if the bad impression had not been thus handsomely removed, for the visit is an attempt to restore the interrupted relations between German and English cricketers.

The Germans have come over to play matches against English clubs. Tomorrow they are playing the Civil Service Crusaders in London. The visit has been financed largely by Mr. G. E. Rowlands, who is well known for his interest in Welsh cricket and football. Earlier attempts to get German cricketers over have failed.

Cricket in Germany is a comparatively recent development. It began to be played in Berlin in the eighties under the tutelage of English residents, and before the war there were many flourishing clubs in Germany. A team came over in 1911 to play the Leicester Club. During the war cricket almost died out there. The English players were not available, many of the German cricketers were killed, and there was the difficulty that cricket equipment is or was not made in Germany and could hardly be imported.

Since the war the game has revived, but there are many difficulties. Cricket is an expensive game for one thing, and, for another, it suffers in Germany from the much greater interest in football. The football season is so long there that it leaves little time for cricket. Last year the M.C.C. offered to send a team captained by Mr. P. F. Warner to play in Berlin, but the negotiations fell through. Now that representative players have come we ought to make them thoroughly welcome, if only as a gesture of international friendship.

The following three articles are extracted from a series, by a special correspondent, on cricket in Europe, published in the summer of 1939.

Two efforts have been made by S. Burt-Andrews, of the British consular staff in Sofia, to establish cricket in Bulgaria. About eight years ago C. Minns, of the British Legation in Sofia, financed the first venture. Nearly £100 was spent on equipment and an incalculable amount of enthusiasm and trouble on organisation. But the effort failed, and gear for which Bulgars found limited use went to the Foreign Office Sports Club, to be used on English fields. Burt-Andrews returned to the charge a few years later, inspired by C. H. (now Sir Charles) Bentinck, then British Minister Plenipotentiary in Sofia, who in turn was moved by his own hankering for the game.

Only five or six Bulgars were any good at the game, one Ben Filtcheff being the outstanding success. The true cricketer should feel an interest in Filtcheff. Here is a man of foreign race who, presumably after a few lessons, held his own with the cricketing breed. But Filtcheff was no 'wonder player,' and interest in him wanes with the knowledge that he went to school in England. Then there was Ivanoff. Ivanoff would not learn to bowl. But he could shy a ball as fast as any Briton and, though he got few wickets, he can boast of nearly knocking off an English head. The Minister Plenipotentiary was host at tea on the field, and a very good host, it seems, for up to the tea hour there were sometimes twenty players a side, and only a dozen all told afterwards. No century graces Bulgarian cricket, but Burt-Andrews scored a 97. Boyd Tollinton, British Consul; C. Tweedie, an English journalist; and Filtcheff the Bulgar all got fifties on a poor wicket. Filtcheff, as treasurer, had to announce an extreme reluctance (not confined to Bulgars) in the payment of subscriptions. Diplomacy was tested on a Sofia cricket field when, during a match, footballers claimed the ground. 'Cricket on Saturdays, football on Sundays,' had been the arrangement. This was a Saturday. There were arguments, and the prospect of something worse: but as the British Minister Plenipotentiary and Consul were at that moment the batsmen, and hostility might have concentrated on them, it seemed for their sakes that discretion was better than valour, and with as much dignity as possible the cricketers left the field.

Soon after Tom Dutton, of Newcastle, introduced cricket to Germany about two generations ago he had the pleasure of seeing boys play the lamp-post variety of the game in Berlin streets. While Dutton was championing cricket British students were introducing football to Germans, and when the seasons first overlapped it seemed as though public interest in the two sports was equally divided. Yet in Germany to-day there are about a hundred cricketers and a million footballers. 'There is a possibility of cricket ceasing here shortly,' says a Briton in Berlin. 'We are making every effort to develop the game,' says a German. He bemoans the shortness of the season (it lasts only six weeks) and blames football, that lusty giant which, without ill-intention, often gets in the way of the Continent's Tom Thumb of cricket.

Inquiries in Berlin revealed no development of an appeal made by a German cricketer, Felix Menzel, last year that the M.C.C. or some other body in England should arrange a European tournament and offer a trophy. Nor has anything come of a project to engage six English professionals to help to further the game in Germany. That proposal was first mentioned by the Reich Sports Leader, Von Tschammer und Osten, after he had been captivated by a few hours spent at Lord's and the Oval. The small band of German cricketers, all centred in four Berlin clubs, arranged a visit this summer by Stinchcombe Stragglers and a Danish eleven. Four English clubs proposed to visit Germany this season, but there are hardly enough players to entertain them. Dartford C.C., Gentlemen of Worcestershire, and Somerset Wanderers are among English teams that have played in Germany. Recalling matches with British teams, a German refers repeatedly to 'this beautiful game', and mentions 'magnificent hospitality' accorded to Germans on a cricket tour in the London district about ten years ago.

At one time there were teams at Frankfurt, Magdeburg, Hamburg, and two or three other cities. Magdeburg has a club called Cricket-Victoria. A few British cricketers who in recent years have settled in the district, or have been on holiday there and with joyful steps have gone to seek a game, have been disappointed. Magdeburg Cricket-Victoria now plays football. German cricketers were for a time reinforced by Britons engaged on missions arising out of the war. A number of Indians have played for Berlin clubs. The only foreign participants nowadays are stated to be a few Afghans employed by their Legation. The enthusiasm of the few teams that are keeping the game going in Germany is worthy of salutation.

From Moscow came intimation that cricket was 'unknown in Russia', but by next post arrived news of activity long ago at St. Petersburg on 'good grass wickets'. The game was first played there about 1880, and subsequently there was an annual match on the ground of the Cadet Corps that brought British diplomatists and merchants in opposition to managers and foremen of British textile mills. This was an outstanding social occasion as well as a sports event that had flavour of a rare quality in a Russian setting. Companies owning the textile mills provided three cricket grounds at St. Petersburg in 1896 and another at Schlüsselburg. Four clubs were formed, Nevski, Neva, Nevka, and Schlüsselburg, and winners of their competition received a cup and medals from the British colony. Later there was a ground at Narva (now in Estonia). Cricket in these limited circles was continued till the Revolution of 1917. It was of good quality, some county players and many public-school boys taking part. The highest score made in Russia is 170 by A. L. Gibson of Winchester College and Essex County.

A good deal of cricket was played in Rumania round about 1924, but interest faded when trade troubles and a sharpening of the nationalist spirit reduced the size of British communities. There were teams at Bucharest, Ploesti, Galatz, and Constantza and inter-city matches without Rumanian participation or concern. It seems Constantza held out longest, and maybe there is a little cricket there now. Best remembered of all cricket matches in Rumania is one against Constantinople in Bucharest in 1930, during a brief revival of the game and after there had been talk about it for years. There were obstacles to Constantinople's making the journey, and when Britons in Bucharest and Ploesti heard that one was merely a matter of cash they subscribed £140 towards expenses. The best ground in Bucharest was hired and the Constantinople team arrived on the eve of play. On the same day, and with what seemed like strategic suddenness, came a note from the military authorities ('The military seem to arrange everything here,' says a plaintive British voice in Bucharest) withholding use of the ground to cricketers because 'they would ruin it for football.' Bucharest was scoured in vain for the responsible officer. On match-day morning two desperate teams and their followers went to the ground and heard: 'Twenty-five pounds down for damage to the pitch and you can play cricket.' The money was paid and Bucharest just managed to win a capital game; but how the £25 was spent became a minor addition to the mysteries of the Balkans.

Humorists who used to assert that cricket was a sort of national religion of the English had better revise their opinion, so far from being a rallying-point for national sentiment it must have been a symptom of the class war. At any rate, the German wireless has just been putting out a story for home consumption to the effect that 'news' from London says that there has been 'a revolt against plutocratic cricketers'. 'People tried to destroy the playing grounds at night,' declared the announcer; 'this led to a sort of state of war between the population and the English sports clubs.' This throws new light on the well-known newspaper headline of happier days: 'Grim Struggle at Old Trafford.'

Enthusiasts

JUNE 21 1930

An Australian student, Gordon Rudolph Piper (23), found with his throat cut at his lodgings at Coleswood Road, Harpenden, and who, while awaiting the arrival of a doctor, dictated his will to a fellow-student, was stated at the inquest at St. Albans yesterday to have given as one of the reasons for his act that 'Australia lost the Test.' He died in the St. Albans Infirmary.

It was stated at the inquest that Piper was a graduate of Adelaide University and held a B.Sc. degree. He had been studying problems connected with soil science, and held a two-years' travelling studentship under the Commonwealth Council of Scientific and Industrial Research, Australia, being engaged at the chemistry department of the Rothamsted Laboratory, Harpenden.

Alan Jones Pugh, another Rothamsted student who lodged at the same house, said that after Piper had been discovered with his throat cut and was awaiting the arrival of a doctor he dictated his will to the witness, who wrote it down, and Piper signed it.

JULY 21 1930

Following the cricket match in Ravenor Park, Greenford, on Sunday week, arranged by two councillors as a protest against the Ealing Town Council's ban on Sunday games, another game was arranged by the Ealing Labour party yesterday in Lammas Park.

Just after the first ball had been delivered a middle-aged woman walked on to the pitch and refused to move. 'There is not going to be any game here,' she declared, 'and if you touch me I will send for a policeman. I have a perfect right to stand in the park if I want to.'

The onlookers, numbering about a hundred, realised what was happening, and there were cries of 'Go away, Mrs. Grundy, get off to your Sunday school.' An attempt to continue the game was made, but the woman, who refused to give her name, insisted on her right to stand where she liked in the park. The stumps were then moved to another pitch, but the woman's husband continued to protest by getting in the way of the fielders. He soon became the centre of attraction to the spectators, and after sending his wife home he argued with them for nearly an hour.

The players again moved the pitch and continued playing until rain drove them to shelter. The man went on haranguing those of the onlookers who remained until a park-keeper informed him that public addresses in the park were definitely forbidden by the by-laws.

There are no by-laws prohibiting Sunday games in Lammas Park, but the Ealing Town Council has passed a resolution disapproving of Sunday games in any of its parks. It is contended that in the absence of by-laws to the contrary Sunday games are lawful.

AUGUST 19 1930

Nearly two hundred people were waiting outside the Oval at 9.30 last night for the opening of the third day's play in the Test match to-day. Armchairs were carried out of near-by houses, and in them many of those waiting made themselves comfortable.

The first in the queue last night was a girl who had with her a travelling-rug, umbrella, book, and some sandwiches. She told a reporter: 'This will be the last day of my holidays and I am determined to end them well. I am very fond of cricket and sometimes play with our local team. This is the first time I shall have waited all night to watch a cricket match. I shall stay here even if it snows.'

By 1.30 this morning the queue was fifty yards long. A fresh breeze did not chill the ardour of the queue-sitters, though they welcomed the enterprise of vendors of hot tea and coffee.

Professional 'sitters' were fairly numerous. The highest payment so far seems to have been a pound, which had been offered by a visitor from the country, who appeared before midnight and wanted a place kept till 7 a.m. . . . .

OUR LONDON CORRESPONDENCE   JUNE 29 1948

A resident of Marylebone who has been seeing the people queueing outside Lord's cricket ground late at night and early in the morning says they look like displaced persons. He protests against the absence of any provision for the hundreds who choose to wait all night – no shelter, no sanitary arrangements, no canteen, and not much sympathy from the local shopkeepers. Possibly the local authority thinks that if people are foolish enough to queue up all night for a cricket match they deserve what they get, but perhaps the M.C.C. does not know what goes on outside its gates.

One of the oldest spectators to-day was a man of eighty who saw his last Test match over fifty years ago. He admired the skill of the batsmen and fielders in the present match, but would hear of no comparisons with the giants of his youth – A. C. MacLaren, W. G. Grace, F. R. Spofforth, and G. J. Bonnor. The last time he saw a Test match at Lord's, he recalls, most of the men in the crowd wore morning dress and there were few women. A pint of beer cost twopence instead of the present price of two shillings, and a five-course luncheon was 1s. 6d. To-day an austere three-course meal costs five shillings.

MISCELLANY   MAY 13 1957

England's oldest cricketer, Mr. Frederick Lester, who is 87, is on the injured list. The Yoxall, Staffordshire, cricket team in his village may be temporarily without him, but Mr. Lester has strongly denied that he intends to retire from cricket. 'It's just that I hurt my back a bit while doing a spot of gardening. I played in the team last month and I must confess that made it worse. My family had warned me not to do it, but I won't be stopped from playing,' he said. While he is on the injured list Mr. Lester is helping the team by repairing their cricket bats. His home is in the sixteenth-century oak-beamed schoolhouse in Yoxall and his smithy, where he repairs virtually everything, including cricket bats, is in the old school-house where nearly eighty years ago he attended lessons.

Mr. Lester's sons, Frederick, aged 67, and Christopher, aged 64, retired from playing cricket some time ago. 'They could not last the pace,' joked Mr. Lester. Ten of his relatives and in-laws are, however, still members and officials of the cricket club. Mr. Lester had a testimonial match seven years ago, but the following season came forward to offer himself for selection. 'After all, I was only 80 then,' he explained.

NIKKI KNEWSTUB   AUGUST 26 1981

The only statistic not recorded in the cricketing Wisden grew by one yesterday when Mrs. Mildred Rowley was granted a decree nisi because of her husband's excessive devotion to cricket.

Mrs. Rowley was granted the divorce in Wolverhampton divorce court two months after her husband, Mike, aged 46, left home to live in Stourbridge Cricket Club's changing pavilion. But he was not in court to hear his 17-year-old marriage terminated. He was in Devon with Stourbridge, who, under their touring name of Worcestershire Marauders, were playing Torquay Cricket Club.

Mrs. Rowley, aged 51, a nursing sister of Wolverhampton, said: 'Cricket was not just a hobby. It was a total obsession. I'd just had enough of it. I don't mind the game, at first I used to go and watch. But I object to it being the be-all and end-all in my home.

'Mike could tell you who scored what years ago, and what the weather was like at the time. But he could not remember my birthday unless I reminded him. I am not playing third fiddle to any cricket club. If I never hear the word cricket again, it would be too soon for me.'

Mr. Rowley works as a sales manager for a steel company in Smethwick, and is living in the cricket pavilion while he waits to be rehoused. He has been the club's scorer for 21 years, and has missed only one match. That was the time he went to Headingley to watch a Test against the Australians.

He conceded that Stourbridge Cricket Club was the main reason for the divorce. He said before yesterday's hearing: 'Cricket is the only life for me. I don't blame Mildred. I have to put my cricket before my family. I have been stopping at the pavilion on and off since the mid-1970s.'

Asked in Torquay to comment on his divorce, he said: 'Really, there is nothing more I can say. I can't stop – we've got to get on with the game.' A member of the team said: 'It's all right, he'll be joining the other four divorcés in the club. It's just the fact that the lads like their game.'

Kids

They had just finished making the hay in a Cheshire field, and some seven or eight village boys were endeavouring to bowl a sturdy little seven-year-old batsman. Thanks to the thick stubble, the ball was playing antics enough to make Dick Tyldesley wriggle with envy, when a little nipper in the slips – pessimistic of ever getting an innings – shouted 'Hey! that's fourteen! Declare!' He was joined in a general chorus which for volume and gesture left Duckworth a non-starter.

The seven-year-old leaned on his bat and raised his hand as a signal for silence. 'I'll declare when I'm bowled,' he announced.

The ultimatum had not the effect of restarting the game; but it subdued the barrackers, who remained stationary. The wicket-keeper broke the silence.

'They're my stumps,' he said, 'so declare, or I'll take 'em 'ome!'

A correspondent who spends his summer Saturday mornings 'stumping up and down L.C.C. parks umpiring secondary modern school cricket matches' has come across a curious and possibly unrecorded little custom. He writes: 'This is not the highest class of cricket: white flannels are a rarity and sixty is apt to be a winning score. Even so, a certain sophistication is creeping in, no doubt as the result of television commentaries. Every bowler of whatever kind now demands a leg-trap, and I was lately informed by a boy who had come in to play the last two balls before a declaration that he was the 'nightwatchman.' It is odd, therefore, that it should be an apparent article of faith among London boys in all parts of the city that the last ball of the over is called 'O.C.D.' (meaning 'over coming down') and that in playground or pick-up games at least the last ball is illegal unless announced in this way. One wonders if this expression is common elsewhere. Was there ever a time when it was part of the terminology of the adult game, and if so, is this a surviving oral tradition? It would be interesting to know. Only yesterday I heard an aspiring Jim Laker at the street corner announce, with a fine confusion of adverbs, 'O.C.D. coming up!'

Naked Ape

JULY 13 1853

A friendly game of cricket, exclusively played by females (married against unmarried) came off on Friday week, at the village of Wales, near Rotherham. The extraordinary spectacle created quite a sensation, and consequently there was a numerous concourse of spectators. The players wore bloomer hats trimmed with pink and blue, and decorated with rosettes of various kinds. The result of the game was as follows: Married 21 and 15; Unmarried 12 and 18.

CRICKET NOTES   AUGUST 3 1883

On Friday last a match was played at the village of Codford, near Warminster, gentlemen with broomsticks, ladies with bats, and the restrictions were that the gentlemen should bat, field and bowl left-handed. The Gents. won by 33 runs, the scores being Ladies 36 and 30; Gentlemen 28 and 71. 'Mrs. Extras' was the principal scorer on the part of the Ladies, making 25 in the first innings and 12 in the second.

JULY 9 1920

South Manchester Men v. Lancashire Ladies

A match of rather unusual interest was played on the ground of the South Manchester Cricket Club last night between a South Manchester eleven and thirteen of the Lancashire County Ladies' Club. The latter are a team of typical Lancashire girls, with some experience of the game. They have played cricket for a number of years, and during the war they turned the game to account on behalf of various war charities. They are a team, moreover, of some pretentions, having an unbeaten record in all games played against their own sex. But success has become monotonous with them, and, like Alexander, they have sighed for new worlds to conquer. It was with the intention of providing themselves with something in the nature of a real test that the game was arranged with South Manchester.

The ladies batted first, and scored a total of eighty-two runs. The innings was remarkable only for the batting of Miss Bennett, who accounted for 28. Miss Bennett might justly take a place in more than a few teams playing Saturday afternoon cricket. She played correct cricket, her judgement being as remarkable as her vigorous treatment of every loose ball that was sent down. But there was little indication of anything scientific exhibited by the rest of the 'eleven', and the satisfactory total was not altogether unaccountable, one imagines, to the forbearance of the South Manchester bowlers.

The game opened under perfect cricketing conditions in a blaze of mellow sunshine, but was terminated abruptly by a torrential downpour of rain. Yet South Manchester's innings was of sufficient length to prove that the strength of the ladies was rather in their bowling and fielding than in their batting. There is nothing subtle in Miss Sparke's bowling, but she is quite fast and she keeps an admirable length. Her solitary victim knew little about the ball with which she bowled him.

Women's interest in cricket dates farther back, perhaps, than is generally imagined. In a MS. of the 13th century, among the first known drawings of what was destined to develop into the scientific game of modern cricket is one of a male figure pointing a bat towards a female figure in the attitude of catching a hypothetical ball. Their participation in the game is quite justified upon historical grounds, but not, it would seem (except when confined among themselves) upon any other. Some measure of equality in opposing elevens is essential. With these conditions cricket is cricket, though the game be played in a croft by small boys with a ginger-beer bottle as the wicket, but under any other one must not take the game seriously.

MISCELLANY   FEBRUARY 4 1933

Lancashire cricketing women have not only formed the first women's county association but have announced that they do not wish to play with or against men; they 'are not trying to emulate men but rather desire to play in their own way and keep entirely separate from the men.' It may be permitted to wonder whether they have realised the great importance of this decision. It may be curiously timely, and Lancashire may be thinking a little in advance of the rest of England once more. Cricket, sadly menaced by recent events in Australia, may be throwing out new shoots to compensate for dying wood elsewhere. Fifty years hence a writer on cricket may think it well to preface her book with a brilliant introductory chapter in which she will explain that cricket was once a game for men but fell into ill-fame through the difficulty men had in controlling their tempers. It was then that woman came to the rescue, purged the game of its evil growths, eliminated men altogether, and started a new era in the history of the game. And really, when one comes to think of it, would not that be very much what men have deserved for their performances on and off the field this winter?

England v. Australia

An avuncular grin above an MCC tie was standard equipment at Lord's yesterday as for the first time in the ground's 189-year history women took the field. Having cautiously agreed after many years of stonewalling to allow the women's England v. Australia international on to its yellowing[1] turf, the MCC turned out in force.

'There were more members in the pavilion this morning than I've seen for many county matches,' commented one MCC stalwart. Another claimed that members had actually stood up to applaud as the English captain Rachel Heyhoe Flint led her team on to the field, a mark of appreciation given normally to batsmen returning with centuries.

The question that had caused some MCC coyness, whether the women could use the men's dressing-rooms, had been resolved without embarrassment. They did, just like any Test match team, but uncle MCC added one little feminine touch: some roses.

The MCC, it was reported, even took with calm the sight of white miniskirts and knee socks in the Long Room. But for that information we had to rely on hearsay. For all women except the 22 players the entire pavilion, Long Room included, remained as inaccessible as Mount Athos . . .

[1] It was the drought summer, remember.

At Old Trafford on Tuesday night at the club's annual general meeting Geoff Scargill (no relation) seconded a motion that would have given women equal rights with men at Lancashire County Cricket Club.

He realised, he said, that if the motion were carried it would bring about resignations. 'There are men who fear women more than they love cricket,' said Mr. Scargill. That was one of the more memorable phrases on a night when the quality of argument against the motion merely confirmed the view of the proposer, Brian Melville, that it was simply 'blind prejudice' that was excluding the women.

More than one chauvinist said that he went to Old Trafford to 'get a bit of peace' while another warned of the dire consequences of allowing women into the main pavilion. 'Let them in and the next thing you know the place will be full of children' and that, as far as he was concerned, was when all chance of cricket-watching ceased.

Another speaker, noted for his bellowings from the Hornby Stand during the summer, was told to use the microphone. 'I don't need a microphone for what I've got to say,' he yelled.

What he had to say amounted, it seemed, to a dread of being stuck in a crowded pavilion on a big match day and being unable to get to the toilets. The presence of women would somehow make this situation ten times worse.

One opponent showed some liberal leanings. 'Give us a pavilion behind the bowler's arm,' he appealed. 'Put a bar in it and the women can go where the hell they like.'

Those who know the Old Trafford pavilion and its members' enclosure, once described graphically by the man from The Mirror as the 'pit of hate', will wonder if the women are missing anything by being excluded. But of course that is not the point.

Staggeringly, this discrimination – which has cost Lancashire the money of at least one sponsor – will continue as it has done since the club's foundation in 1864. The motion that 'ladies over the age of 18 years be admitted to full, country, or life membership . . . and all reference to lady subscribers be deleted from the rules,' was carried but failed – by quite a margin – to win the two-thirds majority required to implement it.

Lancashire are thus left sharing the dubious distinction with Lord's of being one of only two county grounds where women are barred from the main pavilion. Mr. Scargill said that this was just as discriminatory as barring people because they were Jews, Catholics or black or brown. His argument seeme unanswerable but, as the voting showed, there are still plenty of hard cases left at Old Trafford.

This debate, which took up a sizeable chunk of the evening, was possibly welcomed by the committee because it helped to deflect some attention from another atrocious playing season by the county.

WHERE IT NEVER RAINS

JUNE 11 1857

Manchester v. Liverpool

The ground which for many years was occupied by the Manchester Cricket Club, at Old Trafford, is now covered by the Art Treasures Palace. It was given up to the exhibition committee in June, 1856, and during the year that has intervened a new ground has been laid out, a new pavilion erected, and everything prepared for resuming play. The club, as we stated at the time, liberally gave up their lease to the exhibition committee for £1,000, which, considering the amount they had expended upon the land, was an exceedingly moderate demand. For the pavilion an additional £300 was given, thus making the total amount received £1,300. One of the terms upon which the land was given up was that Sir Humphrey de Trafford, the owner, should provide another field; and this condition has been carried out by the hon. baronet to the entire satisfaction of the club. The field selected is situated to the west of the Exhibition building, and consists of about seven acres of good level land. As soon as possession was obtained by the club, preparations were made for laying out the land, and for the erection of the pavilion. Of the seven acres about five were laid down for cricketing, the remaining two being reserved for a quoiting and bowling green. On the north side it is bounded by a close wooden fencing, and if this could have been continued entirely round, it would have considerably improved the appearance of the ground. The pavilion is erected on the north side, and while it is a great ornament to the ground it is well adapted for the purposes for which it will be used. It consists of a central compartment (intended for a dining-hall), and two wings, a turret surmounting the centre. The dining-hall is 36 feet long by 22 feet wide. The western wing consists, on the ground floor, of a dressing room for the members, and above it a similar apartment for strangers, with a room for the committee. In the eastern wing are apartments for the residence of Hunt, the professional bowler, and for the accommodation of the caterer for the club (Mr. Johnson). The turret, which is raised a considerable height above the building, is a light and elegant erection, and commands a magnificent view of the surrounding country. Underneath the building is an excellent wine cellar, no unimportant

261

acquisition in a cricket pavilion. The design for the building was drawn out by the committee, who have profited by experience; and it has been erected by Messrs. David Bellhouse and Son. The roof of the dining-hall is in open rafters, which, with the doors and window frames, are stained. The entire front of this room, which commands a view of the whole field, is composed of glass. The front of the pavilion, and forming the boundary between the cricket and quoiting ground, is a very neat rustic oak fencing, which, in colour, corresponds with the stained wood of the building. The entire cost incurred by the club has been about £1,200. The present entrance to the field is by way of the Trafford Arms Hotel; but an arrangement has been made for opening a path leading directly from the Art Treasures platform to the ground, which will be a great convenience. Since the old ground was given up, the club has had very little practice, and on no occasion has there been a regular match between the members.

The new ground has only just been completed; and it was arranged that it should be opened with a match between this club and the Liverpool club, which was fixed to commence yesterday, at eleven o'clock. Accordingly, at that hour, several members of the Manchester club assembled on the ground, and they were shortly after joined by their Liverpool friends. The weather at this time was unfortunately very threatening . . .

To the editor   JUNE 9 1880

Sir, – The unprecedented occurrence of Lancashire playing two county matches at Old Trafford within one week induces me to trouble you with some few remarks as to the the games which will, weather permitting, be decided during the next six days. To a Lancashire admirer of our peculiarly national sport it must be a source of much satisfaction to see the steady lead which the county executive is at last taking in all that concerns the palatinate's interest in cricket. There is no reason why the Manchester club, now that it has been amalgamated with the Lancashire county organisation, should not become the Marylebone of the North. It has a lengthy membership list, possesses one of the best grounds in England, engages an excellent staff, whilst the various big matches played at the Old Trafford enclosure are now so well patronised by the sight-seeing public that a large and increasing income is almost a guaranteed certainty. It may be that there is at the present moment some feeling of jealousy amonst the Liverpool supporters of the game as to the control locally exercised by Manchester over the arrangement of county cricket fixtures. Such, I am told, is actually the case. Of course the existence of such a feeling is to be deplored, but when matters come to be viewed in a sensible light the Liverpool people must at once see how risky it would be to play county contests where they would in all likelihood prove financial failures. Cricket matches, like other 'shows', ought, in a certain degree, to be considered in a business light . . I remain, &c.,

An Old Spectator.

JULY 11 1884

Manchester's First Test

A great disappointment befell many thousands of cricketers 'past and present' at Old Trafford yesterday. Just as the great match between England and Australia was about to open rain began to fall, and continued during the remainder of the day. Play was therefore impossible. Mr. Hornby had obtained the choice of innings, and today, if the weather should permit, Messrs. Grace and Lucas will begin batting.

AUGUST 28 1890

The last of the three matches arranged to be played this season between England and Australia had to be abandoned at Old Trafford yesterday. Cricket had been impossible on Monday and Tuesday, so that not a ball was bowled throughout the three days upon which the match was set for decision. More rain fell on Tuesday evening and during the night, but some cricket would probably have taken place had the weather remained fine yesterday. Play was not practicable at eleven o'clock, and a sharp shower some time later caused the two captains upon an inspection of the wicket soon after mid-day to give up all idea of attempting to begin the contest. Curiously enough, the weather proved bright and pleasant after the match was abandoned . . .

THE CRICKET FIELD   MAY 6 1895

Although the new pleasure-house which Lancashire County and Manchester Cricket Club is building for itself at Old Trafford is not yet complete, everything else about this famous ground is in admirable order, and visitors will find that many improvements have been made in their interest. The turf on the county ground is in magnificent condition, and an inspection of it the other day left us firmly of the opinion that better wickets cannot be had in England, and that, weather permitting, it should be a batsman's year at Old Trafford. Great attention has also been paid to the club ground adjoining, and more than one county we know of would be glad to have such an arena to play their most important matches. Reverting to the new pavilion which occupies the site, and more, of the building with which Lancashire cricketers have been familiarly acquainted for many years, we must admit that whilst we are not impressed with its appearance, owing to the lack of elegance and brightness in its design, it cannot be denied that it is an immense improvement on its predecessor.

To the editor   AUGUST 10 1906

Sir, – I took my son to the match on Monday, but nothing would induce me to face such an ordeal again.

When we got to the ground at 9 a.m. we found an orderly crowd standing in rows opposite the three narrow doors, or death-traps as they might easily prove to be. If there had been a staff of policemen present order would easily have been maintained, but after waiting twenty minutes the crowd got impatient, with the result that as soon as the doors were opened a rush was made, and immediately there was a struggling mass of men and boys vainly fighting their way towards the entrance. The screams of the boys were piteous. Those who were near the edge of the crowd managed to 'squirm' out, and wisely waited until the rush was over; but once in the thick of the crush it was impossible to escape.

When nearing the door someone shouted 'For God's sake, ease off; there's a man on the ground, and he's being trampled upon.' But the crowd were powerless, for every moment there were reinforcements from all sides, and the battle grew fiercer instead of easing off. I was unfortunate enough to be just behind the poor fellow who was on the ground, and as I subsequently passed through the turnstile I saw him laid out in a dying condition. The policeman who came to the rescue was badly knocked about. That there were not more fatalities was a great mercy.

On the ground the short-sighted policy of the powers that be was again apparent. Finding that there was no room round the ring, some unruly spirit made a dash for the shilling stand, and in a trice several hundred fellows were scrambling on to the stand like so many wild cats! A solitary policeman then appeared, and was just in time to 'grab' one man and bundle him unceremoniously over the side, to the great gratification of those who had paid for seats. Next morning, when there was no Bank Holiday crush, there were policemen in abundance! – Yours, &c.,

Pro Bono Publico.

APRIL 29 1919

For the first time since August, 1914, official cricket was resumed at Old Trafford yesterday, with net practice. A heavy snowstorm during the morning and a biting north-easter in the afternoon made it anything but an ideal day for cricket, but as the authorities had chosen the day for the opening of the season the arrangement was carried through . . .

A. C. MACLAREN   MAY 4 1922

More depressing weather conditions than we have experienced at Old Trafford during the past three weeks would indeed be hard to imagine, but the keenness of the young players has been a fine set-off, and such a tonic to me that cold and damp have been kept well under and forgotten. It is not for me to write about my young charges at the top nets, beyond saying that if the future does not speak well on their behalf I shall be very much disappointed. Thanks to the great interest which Paul and the bowlers have taken in them, it is no exaggeration to say that these youngsters have one and all enjoyed their practices and felt the improvement that was theirs.

I have never forgotten the birthplace of my cricketing keenness, which was Old Trafford itself, and it seems but yesterday that my eldest brother and myself used to walk daily to the ground to bat against Alec Watson, Briggs, and Crossland. Right good 'tips', too, did old Alec and Johnny give us, but I can only remember Jack Crossland as a jocular publican who had no time for anything else but laughing between his two little steps and explosion of arms and legs, resulting in the ball's being shot at one as if out of a gun. I can see it all now, as I write: my father standing near the bowlers, Alec wise and inspiring, Johnny a mere lad, alert and keen, with Crossland of raspberry-hued face, swathed in black clothes, taking off his coat to reveal a gorgeous watch-chain. How Jack twinkled when a venturesome spectator came inside the net to take up his position at third man, the closest 'gully' ever occupied, and how pleased I was when Jack's short one was cut clean on to the venturesome one's foot – which kept Jack laughing to the end of the practice. My brother had a wholesome admiration for Briggs: he felt that Alec and Crossland were good but that they could be played, but he was 'hanged' if he could play Johnny. I was quite satisfied I could play the whole lot of them. How little I knew at the time that they were not trying to get me out, but to make me believe, which they did, that one day I should be playing for county.

Those kindly early lessons I have never forgotten, for they made me love the game, and nothing has killed or ever will kill that early love. The boys who have been practising the last three weeks have taken me back, as also did Sir Edwin Stockton's kind action in inviting past and present cricketers to his luncheon table at the ground on the opening day of our Lancashire cricket season. Many old friends were to be met including the dear old Boss (Mr. A. N. Hornby), as we who played under him are allowed to call him. Many a cricket ruse that succeeded after his retirement originated with him, and was passed on to me for further utilisation. No skipper was so genuinely appreciative of good work on the part of his men or so fearless in his untiring efforts to win the game. It was 'win the game' in those days with 'the Boss', and let it be 'win the game' to-day. Albert Ward, whom I had not seen for years, sat next to me at Sir Edwin's luncheon, with J. T. Tyldesley on the other side, and we talked of old times and old friends who had played in the past, and whilst there were joys of which to speak, alas, there were the sorrows also.

AUGUST 3 1926

Bank Holiday in Manchester

The heavens fulfilled the words of the prophets in Manchester yesterday. The sun shone hotly whenever it was able to thrust itself into full vision, but light clouds encircled it round and about during much of the day, and tempering winds helped in the good work of saving everybody from becoming overheated – even the more strenuous champions of the rival Roses at Old Trafford. It was a record-breaking day there. About 45,000 persons were said to have entered the gates; more than double the number, somebody proclaimed, that any county match had drawn before. From the hour of the earliest trains people flocked into the city, not only from the big towns but from many of the more distant villages and hamlets of the two counties, until it seemed to several of the ticket collectors at the stations that more people were entering than leaving the city . . .

To the editor   AUGUST 4 1926

Sir, – Many of the 45,000 who attended the Yorkshire match on Monday found bitter occasion for complaint, and at least one voice called out for a letter to the 'Manchester Guardian'.

The primary trouble is that the merry clicking of the turnstiles is quite grotesque as a record of spectators. Many paid and saw nothing worth seeing, and these were largely the earlier comers who had confidently waited for hours in the front seats, only to be deprived of all view of the wicket by masses of people admitted on to the grass, who were nominally supposed to be sitting, but were actually ringing the changes on sitting, kneeling, and standing, with interludes devoted to the return of miscellaneous missiles to the rear. Thousands were admitted to the ground hour by hour long after complaint had been made at the secretary's office, and, at a time when the police were barring all access, one of the Committee's stewards paced the queue outside issuing the assurance that there was plenty of room on the grass.

The Committee should make an honest estimate of the capacity of the ground and observe it as a matter of good faith. The greedy methods of Monday must have made an unparalleled addition to the coffers of the club, but much of the accretion is a dubious profit resulting from charges for entering and leaving a full house. Possibly one should not anticipate the Committee's defence; but it may be pertinent to observe that, if one of our city theatres acted similarly, any plea that an effort was being made to please everybody would meet with derision. – Yours, &c.,

H. W. Dawson.

King Street,
Manchester.

NEVILLE CARDUS   JUNE 5 1933

When we arrived at Old Trafford on Saturday morning our ears were filled with the dulcet strains of broadcast music. Somebody at Old Trafford has been seized with the beautiful idea that even on a cricket field the modern age cannot live without the loudspeaker. This anonymous genius has probably not entirely realised some of the consequences which may occur from the innovation. We all know that music is supposed to soothe the savage breast. On the other hand, music has been known to excite man's worst passions. What if at a Lancashire and Yorkshire match some impressionable batsman should get inflamed by the wild whirring strains – and go mad and hit sixes before lunch? It is an awful thought; I trust it will be solemnly considered by the enterprising spirit who this year has made the first move towards 'brightening' Old Trafford. Perhaps, though, it is only a tentative step towards mightier reforms. In time, maybe, if only we are patient, there will be other attractions added to Old Trafford's loudspeakers – say a few side-shows with dancing, and a bearded lady, and other diversions. Then, gradually, the cricket can be got rid of altogether, to the approbation of all and sundry . . .

NEVILLE CARDUS   JULY 13 1938

England v. Australia, Third Test

The Test match at Old Trafford was abandoned early yesterday morning; a single glance at the sodden field or foreshore was enough to satisfy everybody concerned that any and all forms of the sports of dry land would not be practicable for hours to come. So ended a sad experience, one which Old Trafford did not deserve. The Australians regretted it as much as the rest of us, for they heartily agreed that in no other part of England was there hospitality to compare with Old Trafford's. The wretched weather has done no good to the city's reputation throughout the country and the colonies. Only two Test matches between England and Australia have in the long history of cricket been abandoned without a ball bowled. And each of these matches has taken place or not taken place at Old Trafford. I doubt if anybody in authority would care to carry the responsibility of sponsoring another Test match in Manchester this season as a substitute for the one just ruined. If such a match were arranged and the rain again washed out the proceedings every cricketer in the world would laugh uproariously and the Manchester weather would gain a still larger public, and no wit would avail to parry the sardonic thrusts. No, we had better let the 1938 Test match at Old Trafford vanish into the limbo . . .

A. G. BROOKS

After seven years I approached the booking-office at Oxford Road Station and said, 'One, please.' The clerk stared at me and demanded, with some impatience, 'Where to?' It seemed a silly question to me, for the place I was going to had dominated my mind to the exclusion of all other destinations in the world. Then I realised the justice of his question, apologised, and said, 'Warwick Road.'

When I got off the train there was the old-time craning of the necks to see if any sense could be made of the distant scoreboard, and of course it was a schoolboy who answered the inevitable question 'Who's batting?' with 'Lancashire,' the information being given in such a tone as to imply that it was monstrous to think anybody else could be batting. The boy scuttled off under the subway, and I followed more soberly, though with a tightening of interest as the sounds of the cricket-field came over the fences.

At first I thought the years between had changed nothing, for there was the man by the gate shouting 'Cushions – sixpence all day' as if he had never moved since my last visit in the summer of 1939. I soon discovered how wrong I was. The pavilion and the stands next to it told us that Old Trafford had had an uncomfortably close acquaintance with German bombs, and I cocked my ears in vain for the cheerful croak which formerly assailed one on all sides: 'Card and the order. Card.' Not a sound from any honest retailer of the day's happenings on the green circle, and no sign anywhere on the Old Trafford horizon of the white-coated informer bearing on his back the device 'Score Cards.' A wind with a winter's edge on it swept the field, and I stood there disconsolately, feeling I had been dropped into a strange land.

Past experience had taught me that it always pays to keep an eye and an ear on the Old Trafford schoolboys, for not only do they keep the score in their books with an astonishing diligence, but they are learned in all the other mysteries of a great cricket headquarters. So when my wandering eye saw them scurrying round the cinder track and disappearing behind one of the stands I followed in their wake, sure that something was about to turn up. Away out of sight – it seemed with malice aforethought – I found a single seller of score-cards, with a long crocodile of people winding from him. As I was helpless without one I joined the line, though inwardly wondering what we should have to queue for next. Of course, when I got to within two or three of the attendant his supply of cards ran out, and off he went to the printing-place for more.

At last I felt capable of following the game and, card in hand, joined the ring of spectators. As soon as I sat down the man next to me apostrophised everybody in general by saying in a loud voice, 'You want sunshine, after all's said and done.' I do not know whether somebody had been advancing an opposite view, but no one paid any attention, and, as it seemed likely that the Government would come out before the sun did, we made ourselves as small as we could in face of the wind and determined to make the best of it.

I began to hear the famous names – Hobbs, McDonald, Woolley, Parkin, the Tyldesleys, Sutcliffe, and the rest of the game's elect. For a second I wondered what it was all about and whether I really was at Old Trafford in 1946. But it was all right; the spectators, not yet used to the forms and figures of cricket's period of reconstruction, were fixing their minds on far-off scenes and battles long ago. We have not accustomed ourselves yet to the idea of Middlesex coming to Old Trafford without Patsy Hendren, and we cannot recognise Kent without Frank Woolley. I suppose it is the same on all cricket grounds: the retirement of the game's regal personalities and the seven years' famine in sport have made Father Time and his scythe a symbol which presides over other fields than Lord's. A glance at the Lancashire team showed only two names which shone out bright in my remembrance of the pre-1939 era with another one which had been just breaking in on our cricket senses when the war came.

The crowd was cold, and watched the game with lack-lustre eyes. But gradually the old spell reasserted itself, and, prompted by what was happening on the field, they stopped talking of the past, and sober Lancashire comment began to prophesy, though in guarded terms, as if to avoid offending the immortal shades: 'We'n some good lads 'ere, tha knows,' and 'They'll do when they'n bin together a bit.' At the end of the day, when we were in a fair way to defeat the visitors, this faint praise had developed into something like enthusiasm, and one spectator had got so far advanced as to offer to take bets that we had three players in the team to go to Australia this autumn.

On this note we went home well content, regretting perhaps that we should never see the like of Frank Woolley again, nor stare fascinated as Herbert Sutcliffe bent on one knee to flick McDonald thunderbolts off his left ear, nor watch amused as Dick Tyldesley, at the low half-turn, indicated to the umpire that there was another one l.b.w. But we had seen enough to know that if Old Trafford is rich with the spoils of cricket's time it will have no mean store in the future. Though the great ones are gone, cricket has a way of reincarnating its choicest spirits, and summer days will resound with the praises of those now in their first season. At the moment we think that cricket, like everything else, is not what it was, and that there are no cricketers like the old ones. But 'W.G.' himself was once unknown and, unbelievable though it is, Jack Hobbs had never made a century, and, if I remember aright, the poet Woolley began his lyric career with a 'pair'. The famous names are made: there are others now a-making.

To the editor   JULY 24 1952

Sir, – In the cricket commentary yesterday on the third Test match at Old Trafford Mr E. W. Swanton included the usual note of local colour. He commented upon the Manchester weather and described it in something like the following terms – grey, overcast, and raw with an hour and a half of rain after lunch. He doubted whether listeners in India could possibly imagine it with the sun beating down upon them.

Listening in Bombay this was rather amusing. It was about 8.30 p.m. (we are four and a half hours ahead of B.S.T.) and it was pitch dark outside with swirling rain reducing visibility almost to the conditions of a Manchester fog. It had been raining without a break for three days and nights. The kind of rain that Manchester can hardly imagine – roads in many parts of the city were standing under two feet of water and three cricket grounds to my knowledge had the appearance of miniature lakes with the roped off crease rising forlorn like a drab green island in the middle of the flood. The south-west monsoon is now well established and we have not seen the sun for a week . . .

T. Blackburn.
30 Forjett Street, Bombay.

NEVILLE CARDUS   JUNE 5 1957

Old Trafford's Century

Of Old Trafford's hundred years of history and great cricket played by men of character I have had the good luck to enjoy at least half a century's portion. I first entered the ground in July, 1899, on Monday the 24th. Lancashire were playing Gloucestershire, and as I pushed my way through the heavy stiff turnstile (where did I get my sixpence from?) I heard a terrific yell coming from the field. I thought somebody had been killed. It was Charlie Smith, Lancashire's stumper, appealing for a catch at the wicket. I was then a small boy, and in the manner of all small boys I was always hungry, so in order to avoid the crowd at lunch I at once went to the refreshment bar to buy a ha'penny bun. As I stretched up to the counter to pay an explosion happened; glass splinters flew about, I was terrified, until a kindly Lancashire voice from a man in a cloth cap said, 'It's all right, sonny, it's only Jessop just coom in.' A prophetic introduction of Old Trafford to me, and to the 'Cricketer' to come, and to my Makepeace and my Hallows long ago.

Tom Lancaster played for Lancashire that day: and I reflected on the romance of things that with such a name he should indeed be playing for Lancashire. Who to-day remembers the Lancashire Eleven which contained my first heroes? – Ward, A. H. Hornby, Tyldesley, C. R. Hartley, Cuttell, A. Eccles, Sharp, Lancaster, Webb, Smith, Mold. Old Trafford was situated half a century ago in the country, surrounded by meadows. Stretford was a village. At the top of Warwick Road the Botanical Gardens was situated. I saw Johnny Briggs there one evening, but he was not studying botany.

It was difficult to become a member of the Lancashire County Cricket Club 50 years ago. I have seen (from a distance) tall hats on the pavilion at Old Trafford. The Ladies' Pavilion was a joy to sit in on sunny days. The black-and-white wooden house made a pretty picture, and afternoon tea was served by girls in frills and lace. One very hot day, with the sun bringing up blobs of paint on the woodland seats, Jimmy Heap, the Lancashire cricketer, joined me and sat down. He was wearing his flannels. He jumped up immediately, so hot was the seat. 'Jupiter Pluvius,' he said. The Lancashire players during the period occasionally dragged into their conversation, rightly or wrongly, a classical allusion, remembered probably from cricket reports of the period. Cecil Parkin, happiest of all bowlers (when he was taking wickets), assured me that 'when the day comes when I can't play cricket I'll do as them Roman emperors did – I'll get into a hot bath and cut mi ruddy throat.'

Scene and the atmosphere have much influence in making the style of a cricketer. It was against a green and pleasant background at Old Trafford that R. H. Spooner made the grass musical with his strokes. In a period of Manchester's cosmopolitan opulence A. C. MacLaren dispersed all hints of provincialism from Lancashire cricket and Old Trafford as he lorded the earth, at the wicket or directing operations from his position of authority at first slip. The first three Lancashire batsmen in the order of going in of those days were MacLaren, Spooner, and J. T. Tyldesley. No county has had an innings opened with so much mingled grandeur, graciousness, and sword-like brilliance as these three cricketers spread over the field day by day. They were my heroes, my gods, when I was a boy of twelve, yet though I believed in the superiority of each over any other batsman alive or dead I was obliged to pray that they would not get out as I watched them facing the attack.

After I had grown to manhood, a miracle happened. I actually found myself engaged in a match at Old Trafford with A. C. MacLaren and R. H. Spooner opening the batting. I was captain of the fielding side – a 'Manchester Guardian Eleven'. Imagine it: by the strange wheel of time the boy who had looked from a distance at these two cricketers playing for England and Lancashire on Old Trafford's historic sward was now clothed in flannels with them, drawn into the circle of history. Here was the chance of a lifetime. I decided to open the bowling. If I could get the wicket of MacLaren, life would be made worth while having been lived through. The whole meaning of life might at once become clear.

The last ball of my first over broke from the off, and just missed MacLaren's leg-stump. He played forward. The ball shaved the leg-stump. As the field changed over MacLaren said to me, 'Well bowled – but I didn't suspect that you could bring them back. So long as we know!' Then, every time I bowled an off-break, he moved back on his wicket and swept the ball effortlessly over the square-leg boundary. 'So long as we know!'

J. T. Tyldesley I came to know as a friend in a thousand. He asked me one day to play for a team he was taking to Romiley, at the end of a season, a village match. When Saturday came rain was drowning all Manchester. Also gross darkness covered the city. At midday the rain was still falling; the clouds were still heavy and Stygian. I confess that I decided that the journey to Romiley would be a waste of time. On the following Monday morning I went into a café where Tyldesley and I frequently met. He was sitting there reading a paper. 'Where were you on Saturday?' he at once asked. I explained – the weather. 'Why, Johnny, there was never the faintest chance.' He interrupted with these memorable words: 'You, of all people, should know that the first duty of a cricketer is to turn up.' I recommend the axiom as one of general and even universal moral application.

Long before my friendship with Tyldesley began I had spoken to him. One Saturday at Old Trafford rain fell in torrents at noon. I was still in my early teens. Urged by the hope of small boys I waited. I stood under the wall outside the ground. The rain persisted mercilessly. Everybody went home. But boys sometimes believe in magic and prayer. I willed the sun to shine. The rain fell faster. Then a man in a raincoat and blue serge came out of the ground, at the members' gate. I immediately penetrated his disguise. It was J. T. Tyldesley. And he spoke to me. 'What are you waiting for, sonny?' 'Won't they play again?' I supplicated. He told me the match had been abandoned hours ago. 'Get off home,' he said, and gave me a sixpenny piece. This was a boy's finest hour.

The same boy was present at Old Trafford when England lost the rubber to Australia by three runs, in July, 1902. Fred Tate's tragic match. He missed Darling, the Australian captain, ruinously, and was bowled by Saunders at the pinch. In this gigantic game Ranjitsinhji failed twice – lbw b Trumble 2: lbw b Trumble 0. He was in his prime and pomp, but he was promptly dropped from the England Eleven. That day, while England crashed to defeat, the end was watched by S. F.

Barnes, George Hirst, C. B. Fry, and G. L. Jessop, each temporarily dropped by the selection committee. As Ranjitsinhji waited to go in to bat, he for once in his wonderful career suffered from nerves. And while he waited he carved his initials 'K.S.R.' on the ledge of the rails of the amateurs' balcony.

The Australians have always liked to play at Old Trafford. 'The light is so good there,' they maintain – an unexpected compliment. But Old Trafford is one of the few great cricket grounds where sightscreens are placed at each end of the wicket, with the pavilion broadside. The fact that the pavilion at Old Trafford is at a right-angle to the flight of the ball is, however, no deterrent to the pavilion's convictions upon matters of leg-before-wicket.

When did Old Trafford's golden age occur? I suppose the answer depends on one's date of birth. I was too late on the scene to watch Hornby and Barlow. In 1904, when Lancashire won the championship undefeated, the team contained at least five England players – MacLaren, Tyldesley, Spooner, Brearley and Sharp. But my own view is that Lancashire cricket has never excelled the combined technical skill and personal genius of the summers of 1926, 1927, 1928, when the championship was enthroned at Old Trafford three years in succession, with Leonard Green a captain of understanding and control. And control was needed, for the team included Lancashire men of uninhibited character and vocabulary. Eight or nine of the players of this period were of England stature – Makepeace, Hallows, Ernest Tyldesley, Frank Watson, Duckworth, Richard Tyldesley and Iddon. There was also the most beautiful and on his day the most satanically destructive of fast bowlers – E. A. McDonald, who ran to the wicket so silently that Leonard Braund said that when he was umpiring he could hear the approach of McDonald to bowl only by the rustling of his shirt.

On Whit Monday, 1926, Lancashire amassed the total of 509 for nine against Yorkshire. At lunch the score was 451 for four. As the 500 was neared Leonard Green was batting. He decided that as Lancashire most likely would never again get as many as 500 against Yorkshire he would score the five hundredth run or perish in the attempt. So he blocked a ball from Rhodes and ran like a hare. The ball was vehemently fielded by Emmott Robinson and hurled to the bowler. The ball struck Rhodes in the wrist and as he picked it up hot and bothered, and as Green got safely home, he was heard to mutter: 'There's somebody runnin' up and down this wicket: Ah don't know who it is, but there's somebody runnin' up and down this wicket.'

In these years the Old Trafford wicket was so prepared that even McDonald at times was rendered harmless. The Lancashire and Yorkshire match was seldom finished. But the players had a richness that made even stalemate alive and humorous. 'Foony match, Lancashire and Yorkshire,' said dear old Roy Kilner: 'two teams meet at beginning and we say "Good morning"; then we never speak agin for three days, except to appeal.' But the Old Trafford wicket was not always a batsman's bed of roses. In 1901 the playing pitch was rough and fiery. 'While it remained bad,' reports Wisden, 'the totals at Manchester recalled the cricket of 40 years ago. Sharp profited to a great extent by the bad wickets, making the ball fly in a manner that was, at his great pace, absolutely dangerous.' Yet, though playing half his innings at Old Trafford on a 'dangerous' turf, J. T. Tyldesley in the season scored 3,041 runs, average 55.29. I don't believe that any batsman, Bradman or Hobbs, has, considering the circumstances, equalled this performance.

In 1928 Hallows scored a thousand runs in the month of May, and in the season Ernest Tyldesley scored 3,024 runs, average 79.57. Ernest Tyldesley, one of the most accomplished batsmen Old Trafford ever nurtured, played only twice for England against Australia at Old Trafford, in 1921 and in 1926; in two innings he scored 78 not out and 81. Yet he could not stake a sure claim to England honours, so keen was competition, so high the standard of batsmanship.

Cecil Parkin's heyday ended before the achievements at Old Trafford of 1926-8. At his best he was the most hostile off-spinner I have ever seen, unplayable on a 'sticky' pitch. His pace through the air was quick, his break from the earth was knife-edged and murderous. Even on a flawless turf he could turn the ball back; but under the then existing lbw rule batsmen were free to save their wickets by putting their pads in front if the ball had pitched outside the off-stump. One day at Worcester on a lawn of green silk, Parkin time after time beat the bat by beautiful spin. And each master ball was frustrated by dull-thudding pads. At the end of the hot day Parkin showed me his bowling analysis – 30 overs, 92 runs, one wicket. 'And,' he said, 'they send missionaries to China!' I believe that his ashes were scattered over the playing pitch at Old Trafford, and that on each anniversary of his death his lovable Lancashire wife placed a red rose at each end of the pitch. He was original, vital, dark skinned and upright. He walked to his bowling mark tossing his black hair; then he swung round, ducked, and with a great cartwheel action let loose the spin. On a good day he accompanied his bowling by his own singing – popular melodies of the period, generally about the sky is 'blew and I love yew – how's zat?' His energy shot out in spring-heel dartings, in angular flashes, in sudden waves of curving physical grace. As the sun burnished his raven head it was hard to believe that such gusto ever would be exhausted or become ineffectual or old.

Lancashire professionals of this period talked cricket at nights after a match; they would sit for hours matching plot with plot, craftsman's secret with craftsman's secret. At eleven o'clock the 'skipper' would order 'one more for the road.' 'Noa,' Richard Tyldesley would say, 'Noa, thanks, skipper, well, maybe . . . half a pint just half a pint . . . well . . . oh, tha might as well mek it a pint.' The Lancashire soil was in these men and pervasive. It got into the skin of McDonald, an Australian ('A Tasmanian,' Emmott Robinson called him, as though to worsen still Lancashire's practice of playing an Australian). The Lancashire stuff is not worked out, I hope, or diluted to-day. There is Washbrook still as dominating as MacLaren himself. There is Statham honouring the fast bowling tradition established by Mold, Brearley, Sharp, and McDonald. There is Hilton, as Lancashire as Eddie Paynter himself, who was as great a Lancashire lad and player as any. And we have only to look at Tattersall to know that we are at and of Old Trafford, bone of Lancashire's bone. The ground is full of ghosts. No cricket field has known greater players, greater games, rain or shine. Not the least of Old Trafford's distinctions is that W. G. Grace was unable to score a century there: he scored centuries everywhere else. The Lancashire (or the Australian) bowling was too good for him.

In my own active membership of Old Trafford I was lucky to have on the committee hosts as generous as Sir Edwin Stockton, O. P. Lancashire, T. A. Higson, Myles Kenyon, and J. C. Fallows. They made Old Trafford a happy place to go to and live in, summer by summer. There was William Howard, too, the dressing-room attendant, and – by no means least – the old man at the gate of the members' entrance in Warwick Road. In the year of Old Trafford's centenary let all these servants of the club be remembered and appropriately saluted.

THE UPPER CRUST

JULY 24 1852

The Officers of the Horse Brigade
v.
The Officers of the Foot Brigade

Thursday was a brilliant day at Lord's, for in addition to the above combatants, there were upwards of 1,000 of the men of their regimentals, sitting around the ground with their wives and sweethearts, gazing upon the doings of their officers. There were also nearly 50 carriages, filled with female fashion, as likewise a large number of ladies and gentlemen on horseback. The scene was considerably enhanced by the attendance of the two bands of the regiments, comprising of nearly 70 performers; so that taking the fineness of the weather, the scene presented was one of the gayest ever seen at Lord's . . .

AN OLD OXFORD MAN   JULY 7 1887

I am old enough to remember the Oxford and Cambridge match some thirty years ago. In the first match which I saw C. G. Lane, the most graceful of batsman, and E. J. Cassan, far the ugliest of bowlers, were playing. In those days only the two eights wore the sacred blue. White shirts were not yet in vogue, and the cricketers dressed themselves in all kinds of fancy colours. Most of the Oxonians sported the harlequin shirt of red, blue, and brown, and had the same blues in stripes down their trousers. There were then no ladies to be seen at Lords, and a single row of forms accommodated the spectators, who were nearly all under-graduates of the two Universities. The colouring of cutty pipes was at that time the favourite pursuit of ingenuous youth – who does not remember Mr. Bouncer's 'black doctor' in 'Verdant Green' – and as we smoked our favourite clays and compared their degrees of blackness, a single old waiter in a huge-flapping straw hat ministered to us with pewters of ale.

I must have seen some matches in the interval, but the next match, of which I have a positive remembrance, was that in which Mr. Yardley made his hundred. 'Centuries,' as they are called, were not as common then as they have since become, and Mr. J. Makinson, of the Cambridge eleven – the present Stipendiary Magistrate at Salford – had almost shocked the cricketing world when, a few years previously, he scored a hundred against professional bowling. At any rate a score of three figures had never been made in an Oxford and Cambridge match, and the excitement was intense when Mr. Yardley had made over ninety. The hundredth run seemed an age in coming. At last Mr. Yardley hit the ball straight to mid-on, and in a fit of desperation ran for it, and just got home amid frantic cheers. My next memory is the match of 1874, when the Oxonians won the glorious title of 'the fielding eleven,' by which they will always be known to fame. The bowling was nothing, and indeed Ridley was on for the greater part of the time with lobs; but the fielding was something to make every Oxford man thrill with pride and pleasure. I have seen Mr. Vernon Royle and Briggs field in the Lancashire eleven, but W. Law, an old Harrovian who played in that 1874 eleven, was as quick as either and far more sure. And then Lord Harris was in his youthful prime, and, fielding at long slip, could take a ball sideways and return it to the top of the wicket, with one action better than any man I ever saw.

Now comes a ghastly remembrance. I was fortunate enough, or unfortunate enough, to see that fearful event known in cricket history as 'Cobden's over,' when Oxford wanted but two runs, and three miserable caitiffs lost their wickets in one over. The last man, I remember, had to be stayed with brandy and water before they could get him to the wicket at all, I met one of these unhappy men several years after, and he assured me that the agony of those moments was still fresh with him, and would be till his dying day.

An uncommonly pleasant memory is a match the date of which I forget, except that Bentley, of Trinity, distinguished himself in it. I was with an old clergyman – I fear I must not mention his name, but he was well known in the neighbourhood of Manchester – who held the now obsolete opinion that learning should come first and play afterwards. He himself was a Trinity man, and as each Cantab went to the wickets he asked, first, whether the batsman was of Trinity, and, secondly, what he had done in the way of scholarships or the tripos. If the batsman was of Trinity and had also distinguished himself as a classic or mathematician, this old clergyman nearly broke his umbrella with drumming on the seat whenever the batsman hit a four. He died a few years after, and his last words were – for heaven's sake, let nobody laugh – *dulce ridentem Lalagen amabo, dulce loquentem.*[1] Scholarship was still the supreme thing with him, even in his last moments. One regrets that nowadays the ideal of this old clergyman is so seldom seen. Cricket in these latter times is an exacting pursuit, and he who would succeed in it must not hope to see his name high in the class list. The last of the cricketers that were good all round were, as far as I remember, the two Lytteltons.

But perhaps the best record of all was that of Mr. Justice Chitty. He rowed stroke in the Oxford boat, kept wicket in the eleven, and – the 'and' is a big one – got a first class in *Literae humaniores*. I was rejoiced yesterday to shake hands with Mr. Bacon, who looked hale and hearty. This is not the Cambridge Bacon immortalised by Calverley in the lines:

> *O fumose puer, nimium ne crede Baconi;*
> *Manillas vocat, hoc pretexit nomine caules.*[2]

No; the Oxford Bacon, whom not to know is, in a cricket sense, to argue oneself unknown. I always like to meet him, because I once made a miraculous left-handed catch off his bowling – a catch which astonished me more than anybody else – and I never see him but he says, 'Ah, Mr. Blank, do you remember that catch you made off my bowling?'

Now, Mr. William Bacon, tobacconist and seller of cricket bats in the Broad, is 72 years of age, and is one of the few who remember the very first Oxford and Cambridge match – the one in which the Rev. J. Pycroft, author of 'The Cricket Field', and, I think, Dr. Ryle, Bishop of Liverpool, played. Dr. Ryle, by the way, came from Macclesfield, and he would have answered to the old clergyman's ideal, for he was not only a good batsman, but also took his first class as beseemed a good scholar.

I think tricks of style in cricket are apt to become hereditary in schools. There were six Etonians playing to-day, and in all of them I saw the forward lunge of R. A. Mitchell accurately reproduced. It is a telling style on a hard wicket – C. T. Studd had it in perfection – but it is apt to lead to a 'caught and bowled.' By the by, I saw the originator of it himself at Lord's. He has become very grey, but still looks as if he could hit a sixer if any bowler would kindly send him down a half-volley. So, too, I saw Ridley, who has become considerably more bulky than when he fielded point in 'the fielding eleven' of 1874. I have never made out who formed the Harrow style. It was not Hornby, nor I. D. Walker, for I cannot recognise either of them in modern Harrovians. All I know is that E. Crawley, playing in the Cambridge eleven, is in every detail an accurate copy of A. J. Webbe, and indeed he might have a worse example. In all the Uppingham men one sees H. H. Stephenson, and nobody else. Talking of style, one cannot help regretting – though I accept the inevitable – the ugly action caused by the high delivery of modern bowling. Compare any bowler of the present day, twisting himself into a complicated knot as he delivers the ball, with such past masters as C. D. Marsham, E. M. Renney, or 'Mat' Kempson, and anybody must see that elegance has been sacrificed to break and bump.

I see a little difference in this year's match. It is not quite so much a mere social function as it was, say, half a dozen years ago. Many of the girls wear hats and costumes which seem rather designed for Henley than for a Royal garden party. The change is a welcome one. There should be just a touch of country life in a cricket field. And in other respects I have been delighted with the dresses. Never have pretty English girls looked better than they did to-day at Lord's. The reason is that they are just in the transition stage fron one ugly fashion to another which will probably be as ugly as any of its predecessors. The result is that nothing offends or catches the eye in their costumes. But I could not approve of one lady who was dressed in sulphur yellow from head to foot, even her sunshade being of the same hue. And, talking of sunshades, let me disburthen my soul. Mr. Romanes in the last number of the *Nineteenth Century* wrote learnedly and philosophically on the differences between man and woman. The article is all fudge. Everybody knows the differences, but nobody has dared to tell. But now that a woman has become senior classic it is time to speak out. The differences are two – first, a woman will chase a halfpenny about her purse while standing in a narrow passage, and keep a hundred people in a state of desperation to catch their train, without ever betraying the least uneasiness: secondly, a woman will so handle her sunshade – and in these days, with its deep fringe of lace, it is a formidable obstacle – as to shut off the view from as many people as possible. This second peculiarity is a dreadful nuisance at cricket matches. I was, however, rejoiced the other day to see a lady utterly defeated in her malpractices. It was at the Hyde Park treat to the school children. A group of children and teachers were naturally anxious to avail themselves of what might be their only opportunity of seeing their Queen. In front of them a great society lady took up her position, and of course held her sunshade so as entirely to intercept the view of those behind her. Prayers and expostulations were of no avail. At last a vulgar-minded but, I must say, highly intelligent male teacher exclaimed, 'After all, it's a very shabby un.' The sunshade instantly went down.

[1] 'I will love Lalage [a Greek courtesan], smiling sweetly, speaking sweetly.' The classicist John Claughton (see also page 289) says this is a veiled reference to both Horace and Catullus.

[2] 'O boy who smokes a lot, don't trust Bacon; He calls them cigars, but they are really cabbage leaves.' Claughton says this is a veiled reference to Virgil; some may think it sounds more like Botham.

OUR SPECIAL CORRESPONDENT   JULY 9 1898

Under the influence of the Eton v. Harrow match Lord's is transformed into something more than a cricket ground. It becomes the meeting-place of hundreds of old Etonians and Harrovians who have gathered from far and near to see the younger generation fight out their annual battle. Very pleasing it is to see portly respectabilities from the City, sunburnt colonels from the East, and rosy-cheeked country squires shaking each other warmly by the hand and recalling their school days in story after story. The fashionable world has taken the match under its expansive wing; Royalty has often honoured it by being present; and the ladies, as perhaps is only natural, have made it the occasion for a display of dress which almost rivals that exhibited in the Ascot enclosures on Cup-day. To keen cricketers this seems a degradation of a great match. As Lord Granby wrote last year in an indignant letter to the 'Times', cricket becomes subsidiary to 'carriages, corsets, and chatter.' Indeed, the M.C.C. would seem to deserve as severe a criticism for their arrangements in the Eton v. Harrow match as for the method in which they distribute the seats in the Oxford and Cambridge. The carriages are more numerous than ever, and do not give the general public the slightest opportunity of seeing even the top of an umpire's hat. It was generally understood that the big stand, which could not be opened in time to receive spectators in the inter-University match, would be ready to-day, but instead of being completed it has been entirely pulled down, though for what purpose it is impossible to imagine. However, the authorities are fully aware of the conservative instincts of the class with which they have to deal – a class which will continue to grumble and suffer under any anomaly for an extraordinary length of time . . .

JUNE 24 1914

There was a great gathering of Peers and cricketers to-night (writes a representative of the 'Manchester Guardian') at the dinner given by the M.C.C. in the Hotel Cecil to celebrate the centenary of Lord's. Among the cricketers none was more conspicuous than Dr. 'W.G.', his famous black beard now powdered with white, who was sat at the head table among the other heroes of the cricket field. Lord Hawke, president of the M.C.C., commanded his old colleagues and rivals from the chair. Among the famous cricketers present one noted C. B. Fry, A. H. Hornby, F. S. Jackson, G. L. Jessop, J. Hobbs, George Hirst, J. W. Hearne, Lord Harris, B. J. T. Bosanquet, H. K. Foster, J. R. Mason, and A. E. Stoddart. Prince Albert of Schleswig-Holstein sat on Lord Hawke's right, and in his neighbourhood were the Duke of Devonshire, Lord Chesterfield, the Duke of Rutland, Lord Desborough, and many other lords friendly to cricket, as well as the head masters of Eton and Harrow. Mr. Walter Long was present, and proposed the toast of 'Imperial Cricket.' The company included nearly every well-known name in recent cricket annals.

Lord Hawke ran all over the field of cricket in his speech in proposing 'Lord's Cricket Ground.' He read a telegram from the Jam Sahib, better known here as Ranjitsinhji, sending his sincere good wishes and his thanks for kindness in the past. Lord Hawke spoke of the progress of the club in the past century. 'Lord's,' he said, 'has become the Parliament House for arranging not only our home fixtures but all the fixtures of our overseas dominions.' Cricket, Lord Hawke claimed, was the true democracy. He would not admit that cricket is losing ground to-day. It was true that twenty years ago cricket had not to face the rivalry of golf and lawn tennis, but twenty years ago there were only eight first-class counties, whereas there are now sixteen. This showed that the national game was progressing and still enjoyed a fair share of public support. Lord Hawke deplored the rage for averages. We live in an age of selfishness, he said, in which batsmen, perhaps, play for their own scores. 'How I hate these averages! If newspapers would give averages only once a month or once a season they would do more to help cricket than by publishing correspondence on the decline of cricket.' A bright spot in present day cricket, he indicated, was the fairness of the bowling . . .

Dr. W. G. Grace, who had a great reception, remarked that 'county cricket in the old days was just as good as it is now, only there wasn't so much of it. I have not seen much county cricket in recent years,' he added. 'Test match cricket is rather too quiet.' 'W.G.' spoke pleasantly of the 'good old days,' and ended – 'So long as cricket is "the" game, so long will you have just as many good men coming up year after year as in former times.' The cheery speech of the famous veteran was the event of the evening.

MISCELLANY   JULY 10 1925

Thirty-five years ago (writes a correspondent), when I first went to Lord's for an Eton and Harrow match, things were a good deal livelier than they will be to-day. Even then barracking was officially frowned upon, but the small boy allowed himself considerable licence, and, looking back, it seems to me that even the Olympians of the upper school kept their powers of repression in check long enough to give the lower boy his opportunity of shouting 'Butterfingers' or applauding lustily the missing of a catch by the other side. And the small partisan did not at all mind the admonitory '*Shut up!*' after he had let out his yell. Yet there were veteran growlers even in 1890 who found the match dull by comparison with their own lower boy days. Defiance was the tradition in the Mid-Victorian period and for some time earlier. When Lang, the fast Harrow bowler who had two long-stops, was sending them down at his fastest, an Etonian, to underline his contempt for the 'speed merchant,' went in without pads or gloves. 'What's your analysis!' was a favourite howl of the sixties, and Augustus Liddell has a pleasant tale of having been reproved by an Eton master for 'excessive vehemence' for holloaing 'Mind your toes' when the sneaks were on. However, the chaff grew to such a pitch that it interfered with the game and had to be put down. Unfortunately, as some of us will continue to think, the putting down went a little too far, with the result that the 'butterfly' side of the match has assumed an undue importance.

JUNE 26 1926

Although Lord's was not the earliest English ground to stage a Test match – The Oval and Old Trafford came first – it did see the first real shock to English cricket in the oft-cited M.C.C. match of 1878, and it is possible that the ground has never quite got over the shock. Test matches at Lord's have a solemnity not quite equalled elsewhere; there is little of the jollity of the northern grounds; less of the frank democracy of The Oval. Those who are not of the elect survey the pavilion at Lord's during a Test match and rub their eyes, wondering whether the world really has moved on; whether Whig and Tory are labels out of date, and whether the old gentlemen in the sacred seats really are types of the modern world or ghosts from some distant cricket era returned to see the great old game. One sees there more of the England of the period of Palmerston than anywhere else in the modern world. These grey-haired and sometimes grey-whiskered survivals have a chastening effect even on the largest crowds. On most other grounds it is the 'popular side' which sets the note; it is on the popular side that the keenest of cricketers like to sit; at Lord's there is no real popular side. Everywhere is felt the influence of the patriarchs mumbling about cricket and cricketers of the seventies.

NEVILLE CARDUS   JULY 9 1932

Brilliant sunshine has made Lord's a gorgeous summertime pageant for the first day of Eton v. Harrow. At lunch the colours of the ladies' gowns during the promenade over the field put me in mind of a transcendental seed merchant's catalogue. Unless you can give a suggestion of rank and high life, you are outside the pale at this very English – or rather London – occasion. This morning I was standing near the carriages at the side of the pavilion. I had omitted to come to the match in top hat, and an overpowering dowager bore down on me. And she demanded of me imperiously, 'A match card, please.' Quite naturally she took me for some hireling of the back stairs.

The cricket was played to a ceaseless conversation: all over the ground the chatter went 'buzz, buzz' from noon till evening. The match might have been a classical concert. Just before the tea interval the terraces were jammed, and all the perfumes of Araby filled the air. There surely has never before been a time when women dressed so charmingly. But the men – with their preposterous collars and waistcoats and 'toppers' and spats! Even boys were wearing monocles. Beau Brummell himself would look emasculate and rather feeble minded dressed in this tailor's dummy fashion. Several times I found my feet trodden upon in the congestion, and seldom did I receive an apology. Next year I really must take the precaution of wearing a tall hat to disguise my plebeian origins.

The less said about a deal of the cricket the better. I was astonished to look at technique so unnatural amongst boys. On a perfect wicket Eton batted first, and Harrow's bowling at once showed itself weak in length, short of pace and spin. Yet there was not a single straight drive to be observed for hours. The worst defects of county batting were on view, only, of course, lacking the expert justification which the county professional is able to give to his strokelessness . . .

NEVILLE CARDUS   MAY 27 1937

M.C.C.'s 150th Anniversary

The antiquity of Lord's, which is being formally celebrated this week, has had its poets and its prose poets these many years. But the proper greatness of Lord's, and all that it stands for in the estimation of cricketers, is its influence at the present time. It stands for that conservatism which at bottom is the game's secret; nearly everything changes nowadays, or is in a hurry, or is breaking up. Not Lord's. A few years ago I came home from a visit to the Continent, where the rattle of the tumbrils could be heard in the street, given some exercise of the imagination. In England at the same time we were going off the gold standard. I went to Lord's on the depressing morning of my arrival. The papers were full of the National Crisis. I sat in the pavilion seats, next to one of the hereditary occupants. After a while I said, 'Things are looking bad sir,' 'Bad!' he snorted. 'Much worse than bad. The country's going degenerate!' 'But, sir,' I said, 'it's the same everywhere.' 'No!' he replied with emphasis. 'We've no bowlers who can really spin the ball like O'Reilly and Grimmett.' And at once I knew the heart of the Empire was sound and in the right place – Lord's on a sunny day.

The time to go to Lord's is on a June morning. It is a pity that hansom-cabs are not run specially for men of sentiment who wish to go to Lord's. A taxi or a bus or the Tube is well enough for The Oval; Lord's calls for a leisured way of transit. In the absence of the hansom-cab, which would drive through Regent's Park, the ritual of going to Lord's in June is best served by getting out of the Baker Street Tube and walking the rest of the way, with your mind playing with half-forgotten fancies of Sherlock Holmes and W. G. Grace and Mme. Tussaud. When you arrive at St. John's Wood Station you will see the little church and the trees which wave in the wind and delight the eye of the people who sit at Lord's facing the Nursery End. And as you walk along the wall of Lord's you will see the blind man who has been standing there for years; he is bronzed and upright.

It is necessary to sit in the proper position to get the flavour of Lord's. The pavilion is, of course, not for the common folk, but you can be 'signed in' on certain days. The average visitor will be wise to take his seat on the high stand next to the practice ground looking towards the pavilion. The stand is handsome, comfortable – and free. There is no ground in the world where the 'shilling' spectator gets more ease and comfort for his money than at Lord's. From the high stand Lord's is seen, or beholded, at its noblest. The pavilion sometimes seems a Valhalla of the game, the home of all the immortality of the heroes of the past. Every cricketer would give years of his life to have the honour of a century at Lord's or of a superb bowling performance.

The crowd is cosmopolitan; the Empire drops into Lord's any warm afternoon. It is strange to think of Lord's as the ground of any one county. Middlesex once were beating Yorkshire at Lord's, and a Yorkshireman in the crowd rightly did not like it and protested. 'My gum!' he said. 'Yorkshire whacked by Middlesex! Wheer is Middlesex, anyhow? Is it in London?' Likewise does the tradition of Lord's, its universal range, swamp county psychology. Never at Lord's does the fierce air of contention blow, such as comes out of the cockpit at Bramall Lane. The crowd at Lord's has, no doubt, many partisans, but many folk go there simply because Lord's is part of London's general show, or because they are aware of the aristocratic pleasure in going there, not entirely for cricket but as one way amongst others of enjoying the art of life. I have often wondered why Max Beerbohm has never written an essay 'On going to Lord's on a June Morning.' He need not have known anything about cricket.

The ground is a microcosm of the London that spreads outside. There is the East End and the West End, the Tavern and the Pavilion. There is a middle-class level too, a sort of suburb – the Mound Stand. It is nonsense to speak of Lord's as no place for the ordinary man. Lord's, like the Derby, is a good 'mixer'. We must, of course, understand and tolerate the isolation of the M.C.C. and the Pavilion. It is perhaps because of their aloofness that Lord's and cricket exist at all to-day in the forms that we know and love. There have been several noisy demands in recent years to bring the game 'up to date'. Thanks to the M.C.C., cricket has, like the British Constitution, grown and not been made. In a whirling world Lord's and cricket remain reasonably sensible and 'behind the times'. Its efficiency is not stridently obvious. All sorts of activities go on hour by hour; men move ladders about, and I have seen them emerge from the pavilion carrying gilded chairs. Under the grandstand is a printing works which is always busy with the score cards. There are shops and there is an authentic hotel. On Eton and Harrow days the place becomes as significant of the glass of fashion as Ascot or Henley. Butlers appear in the sunshine attending to the cold viands. I have seen a peer of the realm using a hammer at the Eton and Harrow match as he hung up his colours. This is the day of the year at Lord's when the public for once must be satisfied with the tradesmen's entrance, so to say. But there are many other days when the whole world may enjoy Lord's and know why cricket has conquered the English race. Lord's and the M.C.C. do their work well; they hold the balance between the West End and the East End.

The cricketers famous at Lord's sum up the things Lord's stands for: Grace, Stoddart, Lord Harris, A. J. Webbe, P. F. Warner, Trott, Rawlin, J. T. Hearne (to name a few of the past masters) and, in our own day, C. N. Bruce and the incomparable 'Patsy,' not forgetting Hearne, the groom of the whole great coach which is Lord's, always taking cricket a drive in state.

OUR LONDON CORRESPONDENCE   JULY 16 1937

The first man I met at the hundred and fiftieth anniversary dinner of the M.C.C. to-night was a friend who had been proposed for membership of the M.C.C. at the age of nine. Unfortunately he grew up to take some interest in rowing but none whatever in cricket. Nevertheless he was elected a member twenty-seven years later. To-day his godson, a nineteen-year-old Etonian, was playing for the Gentlemen at Lord's, but he has not had time to become a member of the M.C.C. yet and so he was not at the dinner.

There must be a moral in all this, but for the moment it escapes me. Nevertheless this superb unreason seemed wholly natural at a dinner of the most famous cricket club in the world, at which the first speech was made by a polo player (the Duke of Gloucester) and the second by a Cambridge rowing Blue (the High Commissioner for Australia). Perhaps the reason why cricket has such an unbreakable hold on the affections of the British is that, like art, it is wholly unreasonable.

So, at any rate, it must appear to the bustling athletes of other nations. Major Astor, this year's president of the M.C.C., hit off part of its baffling and endearing quality in two phrases of a brilliant speech. He called it 'the game which is worth playing badly,' and said 'the greater the pace of life becomes the greater the value of a deliberate game.' What use would a game like that be to the – well, no need to mention names?

There were more than four hundred cricketers present, of all sorts, shapes, ages, and attainments, and they certainly looked as if cricket had done them no harm. The oldest of them all was the Mackinnon of Mackinnon, 89 years old, who played in the historic Cobden's match in 1870 and toured Australia with Lord Harris's team in the seventies. An admiral, a general, and a lord lieutenant at my table craned their necks reverently to catch a glimpse of this great figure of the past.

At the next M.C.C. birthday party perhaps we shall see women present. They were not there to-night, but there were many flattering and by no means patronising references to their recent match at The Oval. Mr. Allen, indeed, described their fielding as an example to first-class cricketers.

Some forty members were present at the annual general meeting last night of the M.C.C. at Lord's. The meeting was held as usual in the main room of the pavilion, but the character had gone out of the room. The walls had been stripped of all the famous pictures, and the bust of the great Doctor no longer smiled benevolently on the proceedings. All, all had gone, the old, familiar faces, but the faces of the living were there – Mr. Stanley Christopherson in the chair and unanimously re-elected president for the coming year, the secretary, Mr. Findlay, sitting next to him, and on his right Sir Stanley Jackson, the three of them sitting on a dais decorated in front with a Union Jack and flanked by the colours of the M.C.C.

Standing not far off, with an ear for the meeting and an eye for the match that was being played outside, was that grand old man of cricket Sir Pelham Warner. The business was quickly dispatched and the meeting as quickly dispersed, more than one of them thinking of the anniversary dinner that might have followed.

A good many people, including some most unlikely ones, found it pleasant to sit at Lord's yesterday and dream away a rare day of rest on the pretext of watching the one-day university cricket match. There was little in the cricket to distract the musing mind, for the young gentlemen played some extremely amateurish stuff, having, no doubt, been more usefully occupied during the term. Such, at any rate, was the excuse loftily put forward by Oxford men for their team's unfortunate tendency to get out to full pitches and half-volleys. Nor did Oxford fail to comment acidly on the fact that the Cambridge team were wearing new caps specially designed for this one match. In the Tavern this was regarded as a failure to take the war seriously.

The ritual lay-out of the Lord's score-card is still the same, though most of the young professionals who used to sell it are away on sterner business. But the list of 'matches for the season at Lord's' on the back of it shows startling changes. There are matches between teams of Home Guards, civil defence workers, and barrage balloon men: auxiliary firemen, anti-aircraft gunners, policemen, and even the boys of the A.T.C. get a chance to hit a boundary or take a wicket at Lord's this year and have their form sternly assessed by the old, old men who still haunt the members' seats. The gates of the temple are open nowadays to all who serve their country.

There was an informal dress show yesterday at Lord's, where at least half the spectators for the University match had gone to see something else besides the cricket (which was not at all bright). Large hats and 'duster coats' were generally worn by the women, who so crowded the grounds that the stands looked like window-boxes. If the play was without colour the audience certainly was not, for this match is one of the minor social events of the London season and the members' enclosures were packed with visitors whose knowlege of cricket is rudimentary to say the least.

'Oxford won the toss, you know,' a man in a blazer said to a late-comer. His companion (who wore a backless taffeta dress and a coolie hat) showed some interest. 'Has Cambridge won anything yet?' she asked with wide eyes. Later, having studied the programme carefully, she said, almost in an 'Only Yesterday' tone: 'Why does it say Oxford Five Cambridge here?' Her companion shushed her and explained that 'v' stood for versus, Latin for 'against'. But, of course, not all the women were so ignorant. Some seemed more interested in the cricket than their escorts, who spent half the time in the Tavern.

DAVID HOLDEN   JUNE 5 1961

England's two nations were at play alongside each other at Windsor on Saturday. There were Mum and Dad, sweating a bit in the muggy sunshine, and seeking the relief of an outing on the Queen of the Thames; and there were Mummy and Daddy up the road at Eton, celebrating with their sons and débutante daughters the glorious 4th of June.

To the American tourists photographing the castle, neither nation seemed of much interest. Perhaps their thoughts were on the two K's meeting in Vienna, rather than the two Englands going their separate and parochial ways; or perhaps the British Travel and Holidays Association has done its work so well that the only Englishmen a foreigner can recognise any more apart from a policeman, are a beefeater at the Tower and a guardsman in uniform.

Up at the college the guardsmen were out of uniform – or rather had put on their mufti, which is not quite the same thing. 'May I introduce my ADC?' an unmistakably moustached gentleman with a bowler was saying to a lady with a small boy in a stiff collar. The stockbrokers were there, too, and a few tycoons, and a great many of the England's topmost people dropping each other's names without even intent. 'Of course, I wanted B—— to marry *her*, but he's such a bachelor now . . .'

The Duchess of Gloucester was said to have arrived to spend the day with her son Prince Richard, and probably did but went unobserved in the social press. The Lord Mayor of London, on the other hand, made sure of his audience by arriving in a helicopter just behind the cricket field.

There were strawberries and cream for tea, if you cared to queue; a military band playing 'My Fair Lady', and two cricket matches going on simultaneously on two separate grounds. England's topmost sons are not short of playing fields, even if they no longer (and perhaps, according to a recent revelation, never did) win international battles upon them. There was also a socially significant collection of motorcars. Only five Rolls-Royces and seven Bentleys could be seen in the main car park off Agar's Plough, alongside 17 minicars, a smattering of shabby shooting brakes, and a plethora of discreet Rovers.

The cars, however, looked better than the ladies, if slightly less expensive. If the 4th of June – held on the 3rd this year because the 4th was a Sunday – is a trial run for the costume stakes at Ascot, as some of its regular participants say, there are an awful lot of selling platers in the best stables this year. The raw material was there, both in the dresses and the ladies, but it rarely seemed to work into a pleasing whole. One wondered whether the training was at fault; certainly Eton had given something that Roedean obviously had not. The men looked elegant in anything, perhaps because as boys they all went through the discipline of riding bicycles in tail coats and trying to remain comfortable in spite of Eton collars. Now they carried off any convention, from tweeds to a topper, without even trying. But their womenfolk looked as if they could not outgrow the gymslip until their sons were already following in daddy's footsteps in the school.

As the warm afternoon fell into the cool of the evening a handful of the other England came to watch the college eights rowing past the meadows in nineteenth-century uniform. It stood behind a fence on the other bank, perhaps unaware that it might just as easily have walked in like me, to sit with Mummy and Daddy. But both Englands still know their place, even in the younger generation. Down the street in the 'Coffee Cantata' the other teenagers sat, blue-jeaned and sweatered, spellbound before a juke box and the pulsing cry of Adam Faith. They did not look up as the others strolled past the window, tails a-flutter and buttonholes still aglow, on their way to dinner at 'The White Hart'.

In fact, the only people who bridged the gap all day were three young things overtaken by some nameless tragedy, who went back to London on the bus with me. 'If only you told me,' the débutante was saying to her two escorts, 'I could have had us invited to a dozen parties tonight and now here we are without even a lift, going back on a bus!'

RICHARD YALLOP   JUNE 28 1978

John Claughton arrived at the 1976 freshmen's cricket trials in Oxford in some awe. He had been to school at King Edward's Grammar School in

Birmingham and come up to Oxford on a grant. He is a cheerful, straightforward type, but in his more romantic moments he had fantasised about the sort of person the Oxford captain would be. He imagined someone tall, blond and blue-eyed, surrounded by half a dozen beautiful women.

Reality proved rather different. That year's captain was Vic Marks, the son of a Somerset farmer, known for his quiet, thoughtful approach to life. The odd woman might make a punt-stop down by the river and wander through the cow parsley up to the boundary ropes, but generally they went for the louder attractions of the rowers and rugby players.

Two years later Claughton was standing in a pub down the road from the Parks surrounded by half a dozen Glamorgan county players. No one in the pub seemed to know who he was, nor that he would be leading Oxford out against Cambridge at Lord's. That seemed to reflect the general public's attitude to today's 134th University Match.

It is likely to be watched by a smattering of spectators and a number of old Blues nostalgically recalling the day they played in their first Varsity Match. Among them will be two former captains, Tony Pawson, Observer cricket correspondent who led Oxford in 1948, and, peering out from his eagle's nest high above Lord's, Jack Bailey, secretary of MCC and Oxford's captain in 1958.

In 1948 the Varsity Match was in its high summer. It was a social occasion to match Henley, Wimbledon and Royal Ascot. Cambridge had Insole and Bailey, Oxford the South African Van Ryneveld, Keighley, and an opening attack of Mallett and Whitcombe, who had twice bowled out Hutton for under 20 in the Parks. From early on Saturday the toppers and morning coats paraded through the Grace Gates, and all day Lord's overflowed.

In those days it was more important for some people to leave Oxford with a blue than a degree, and they were helped by an admissions system which put as much emphasis on sporting talent as academic ability, 'University education then was education for the whole man' – *mens sana in corpore sano* – Pawson remembers.

It was in the sixties that the admission policy began to not only ignore sporting ability but actively discriminate against it. 'One understood there was a prejudice against sportsmen, and a feeling in both universities that they were wasting their time,' says Bailey. One Oxford headmaster is still known to tell his potential Oxbridge entrants to ignore their sporting achievements on their entry forms.

The change had an obvious effect on the quality of the university's teams. The academic demands made on those who did play outside curtailed their involvement with the team. Appearances in the Parks had to be forgone to ensure attendance at compulsory tutorials and the captain was sometimes hard pressed to turn out a team. Because of final year examinations no-one in his last year has captained Oxford since 1973.

Claughton is now in the third year of a four year course. He gained entry to Merton College on the basis of three A passes in his three A levels. He feels that admission through athletic achievement is now all but ruled out, except perhaps in the case of some people studying for a Certificate of Education. 'The people who get in through sport make up only five per cent of the total entry, but there is a real danger that without them the university would lose its first class status.'

The opportunities open to Claughton when he leaves Oxford also mark a waning in the influence of an Oxford captain. The one firm offer he has received is a job with IBM.

Times have changed since Guy Pawson, father of Tony and Oxford captain in 1910, was welcomed into the Sudan Civil Service with his blue. They demanded either a first, which Pawson did not have, or a second and a blue, which he did. It led the administration of the Sudan to be known as 'the rule of the blacks by the blues.'

Admittedly Tony Pawson's captaincy did win him an invitation to join the East India club but then as now the one sure career avenue open to a blue was teaching at a public school. For a year he returned to Winchester. Ten years later Jack Bailey followed the same pattern, going to Bedford School, where he taught and ran the First XI. Twenty years later Vic Marks is about to take up a post at Blundell's while Paul Fisher, this year's secretary, has an offer from Marlborough.

One institution, at least, has remained sacred to Oxford cricket captains over the years: Vincent's, the Oxford sporting gentlemen's club. There a man may live on credit, be called Sir by the steward, and consider himself part of the tradition of past sporting heroes gazing down from fading photographs round the wall. The rugby team are at present debarred from the club because of the behaviour, culminating in a striptease, perpetrated by them one Saturday evening last winter. It was considered not quite cricket.

THE GAME'S NOT
THE SAME . . .

AUGUST 28 1847

Eleven of All-England v. Seventeen of Manchester
(with a wicket-keeper given)

This match (being one of a series got up by the veteran Clarke) commenced on the Manchester ground on Thursday last, and, from the well-known excellence of the competitors, caused no small degree of interest and speculation as to the result. These matches will always be anticipated with great pleasure by the Manchester gentry, in consequence of the friendly rivalry, which, since last year, when the match was first played, has existed between them and the All England eleven. They are indeed friendly *réunions*, and it is gratifying to notice the hospitable reception the All Englanders meet wherever they go. In one department of the game, the Manchester club were sadly deficient, with two or three exceptions; and whatever effect the old school of slow underhand bowling may have had in years gone by, we can assure the club that in the present march of improvement in cricket, it savours more of the *drawing room* than the cricket field . . .

THE CRICKET FIELD   JUNE 24 1895

There is in existence a fearful machine styled a catapulta, which, its ingenious inventor asserts, will provide 'noblemen and gentlemen' (who 'can be waited upon at their seats') with a mechanical Mold and Richardson, or, if the batsmen are nervous, a Briggs, deprived for the time of his tantalising twist. The thing is amazingly simple. You fix the batsman in his place, and then adjust the catapulta at the regulation distance. A spring is touched or a lever pulled, and the batsman stops the ball – if he can. Probably most cricketers would be of the opinion that the worst bowler's worst ball were preferable to the catapulta; but on the other hand the machine has its advantages from the batsman's point of view. It cannot appeal for leg-before, nor can it take, as bowlers of the ordinary type too often do, return chances; and we fear that many catches at the wicket and in the slips would never be appealed for by an inanimate bowler. The inventor should consider the advisableness of supplementing the machine by automatic fielders. Lytton, in 'The Coming Race', has given him the hint by showing how the nobility and gentry in the underworld were served by automata who were more reliable even than Chinamen in the capacity of butlers and general helps.

LEADER   AUGUST 18 1904

The less aggressive form that the Lancashire team has been recently showing is partly, no doubt, due to overwork. The weather and the exigencies of championship have allowed little respite. It is of course too late to suggest that originally cricket was a game, and that this element of grim toil is a little out of place. The obvious reply is that the county championship has come to stay, and we, for our part, would insist as emphatically as Sarah Battle on the rigour of the game. But can nothing be done? The M.C.C. rule is that each first-class county must play home-and-home matches with at least seven counties. There are fifteen first-class counties, and Lancashire plays all of them except Hampshire. Some counties, notably Middlesex, play fewer, no doubt with some antiquated idea that cricket matches are games rather than business. Should we lose prestige if we reduced our list of matches? There is no need to reduce it to the actual minimum. We shall never, we hope, forget that the game is more than the championship. There is a visible silver lining to this cloud of exhaustion in the recommendation that an Advisory Committee has just made to the M.C.C. It is that Northamptonshire's claim to be a first class county be granted. The remedy really lies in increasing the first class to such proportions that it will be a physical impossibility to play all or nearly all the counties in it. We shall then not attempt it, but be forced to a selection that no doubt will provide us with quite worthy opponents. It will also counteract the baneful tendency of this county championship to become a league. Cricket may still be possible.

To the editor   AUGUST 19 1909

Sir, – I should like to express the opinion that our cricket is not of the same quality just now as it used to be some years ago. I do not think that either the batting or the bowling is as good. Probably the deterioration is only temporary; at least we must all hope so. But I cannot see bats like W. G. Grace, A. G. Steel, F. S. Jackson, Ranjitsinhji, or Shrewsbury, a fast bowler like Richardson, Lockwood, or Mold, a slow one like Peate, Peel, or Briggs, or a wicketkeeper like Pilling.

There are several things in the game that require watching. One is the waste of time, as, for instance, in the tea interval. In the Lancashire-Sussex match at

Brighton this lasted twenty-two minutes. In the old days, if the weather was very hot, we had a drink sent out to us, and the stoppage of play was all over in at least five minutes; but we did not always have that. Then there are many minutes more than the allowed time both between the innings and when a fresh batsman goes in. These delays mount up to a lot of wasted time during a match.

I would try to prevent batsmen getting in front of their wickets as much as they do now. I do not think it fair that a bowler should be defeated by a man's legs after he has beaten his bat. This style of play to a great extent interferes with the old cutting and off-driving – two of the most beautiful strokes in the game, and a means of prolific scoring as well. It might be met by giving the batsman out if he walked in front to an off-break, no matter where the ball pitched, but I hardly think the penalty should apply to the leg-break.

I am strongly of opinion that when teams meet twice in a season each should have the option of batting first on one occasion. We want to eliminate luck as much as possible and the side that loses a majority of tosses suffers in a manner that I think is unfair. Let the visiting side have the choice. Noble has won the toss in five Test matches, and Jackson did the same when he was captain of the English team. This is manifestly unfair to the losing side. I cannot see any reason against the reform which I suggest. – Yours, &c.,

An old County Cricketer.

OUR LONDON CORRESPONDENCE   JULY 3 1914

Much has been written of recent years of the decay in the public interest in cricket. A correspondent of mine puts the chief blame on the boundary. The other day (he writes) though I have abandoned cricket for more years than I care to number, I took the opportunity of watching the great game between Surrey and Middlesex at The Oval. The impression which this fine match left upon my mind was that cricket has become a luxurious pastime, and, as such, laziness, the sure companion of luxury, had crept in. The evil of modern cricket seems to be the boundary. The match was played on a glorious batsman's wicket. The heat was abnormal. There is something wrong with the balance of the game when the strenuous efforts of the bowlers are discounted by the service which the boundary does the batsman. The batsman is there to defeat the object of the bowler, which is to dismiss him from the game with as few runs to his credit as possible. If, however, you remove from the batsman the onus of the sacrifice of endurance by permitting a boundary score you at once upset the equilibrium of the stresses of the game and handicap the bowlers. Part of the penalty for punishing bowling should be the exhaustion consequent upon running four times up and down the pitch. By all means have your boundary boards to keep the ball in the game, just as you have side boards at polo for the same purpose, but it is sheer shirking of hard work and the proper penalties of the game to allow batsmen to score dozens of fours without the expenditure of the energy which gave the old game its true balance.

One or two writers in the London papers are telling us once again that cricket as we knew it in the past is gone for ever. If it is to survive after the war, they say, it must be livened up. Arguments are put forward in favour of transforming the great game into a thing of immense rapidity – a sort of Bolshevist cricket devoted to hurricane yorkers and 'swipes.' This, of course, would make quite impossible the science, the law and beauty which are the charm of cricket – to cricketers. It would certainly put an end to the game that could produce the varied art of a William Gunn, a Palairet, a Spooner, a Ranjitsinhji. The suggestion is based on the notion that after the sensationalism of war we shall find the 'long-drawn-out' cricket of the old days too uneventful. The implication here is the alarming one that abnormal nervous excitation has become a permanent necessity to the race, even in our playtime. The notion is, happily, on the face of it, just a notion – perhaps a product of war-time delirium – as any sane person may realise for himself very simply. Let it be imagined that the battles are all over, the guns silent, and the frenzy gone, and that a match is going on at Old Trafford in the peaceful sun, with Spooner batting gracefully, and the flanelled figures moving to the old-time rhythm of the game. Would the average man, once again seeking summer relaxation, turn away from this to some intense and wholly combative affair with its heaven-splitting multitude? It is doubtful, indeed. We did not make cricket our national game in a few years, nor without reason, and we are not likely to spoil it in a hurry, even after a European war.

One of the effects of war seems to be a better philosophy in the playing of games. Before young men who lived the sheltered life went out to fight, games were the most important thing in a good many lives, and the evil fortunes of games the darkest disappointments. It is not that the returned soldier is less keen on games: he plays them, and, indeed, often insists on playing them in spite of dreadful disabilities. But he seems now to bring a lighter touch to them. Watch any of the games of tennis on suburban courts this summer, and you will see far less savage hitting; you will hear a great deal more laughter over feeble strokes. The player confesses that he is probably playing very badly instead of blaming his partner, the light, the court, and the world in general. In quite a big tournament a few years before the war a lady in a 'double' was so upset by the ferocity of her partner that she threw down her racquet and left the court in tears. That sort of thing does not happen now.

Watch cricket, and it will be apparent that the batsman given out for obstruction[1] takes the decision in a better spirit than of old, and is as unresponsive to the dreary denizen of the pavilion seats, with his 'Hard luck – right off the wicket,' as was MacLaren in a big match years ago, when the sympathiser was heartily snubbed. It was significant the other day that a certain golfer was pointed out to a spectator as a fellow who swears all the way round – for there were times when that golfer would not have been quoted as an exceptional person. No doubt the truth is that a man who has been through the great tragedy of war is steeled against the lesser tragedy of games.

[1]lbw, presumably

JULY 15 1920

There is a Manchester man, perhaps the oldest living member of the County Cricket Club, whose memory goes a good way back into the history of the game, but with the modesty of his generation he will not make his name public. His recollections range farther than those of Grace. In his view Johnny Briggs, Arthur Mold, R. G. Barlow, and A. N. Hornby are mere youngsters at the game. He remembers George Parr, T. Box, N. Felix, Alfred Mynn, and W. Clarke. As a boy he took something to eat in a little brown paper parcel and squatted down upon the turf at Old Trafford to watch twenty-two local gentlemen of Manchester contend against these heroes in the famous All England Eleven which travelled up and down the country in the forties and fifties. George Parr, one of the most brilliant fielders of his day, T. Box, the renowned stumper, he remembers well: but most distinct of all in his youthful recollection stands out the great batsman, N. Felix, because of his high spirits and love of boyish pranks. Alfred Mynn, the Kent 'crack', is pictured in his memory as a magnificent fellow whose manner as a batsman amounted almost to grandeur . . .

William Clarke, who managed the All England Eleven, is remembered late on, an old man in a tall white hat, persisting with his famous slow 'lobs'. In those days, says our informant, the idea of bowling for catches was the last thing a bowler thought of, and contempt for the idea would seem to have been general, for even in the official score-sheets of first-class matches the bowler's name is never given where a man is caught out. Neither does there seem to have been then any deliberate attempt in bowling to make the ball turn, for our friend distinctly remembers being troubled with the 'break' upon first facing the bowling of Alec Rowley, one of the most famous bowlers the Manchester Club ever had. He pondered over the startling innovation for a week before determining to vary the general practice of forward play by waiting to see which way the ball turned.

His recollections of local cricket are scarcely less interesting. In his early days at the Manchester Grammar School the farmers used to allow the boys to play on the 'butts' – the best piece of ground that could be found in an ordinary field. Grounds as we know them now were unthought of. From the Grammar School he joined, and played for, first the Old Rusholme Club and then the Manchester Club. He never played for the county, although he has been a lifelong member of the club, and has followed its fortunes almost from the beginning.

JANUARY 31 1923

The need for fast bowlers in English cricket was emphasised by Lord Hawke at the annual meeting of the Yorkshire County Cricket Club, held at Leeds yesterday. Lord Hawke said he had no doubt that cricketers as good as those of the past would be found in the future. The great fault of English cricket since the war was that our young batsmen had never met a really fast bowler except the Australian, Gregory. There was a time when every first class county possessed one good fast bowler, and that was the time when the standard of batting reached its highest.

Lord Hawke said the game had not deteriorated, but it was unquestionable that they were short of the 'stars' they had, say, fifteen years ago. The time would come again when England would be supreme, and if the young cricketers of promise were given the necessary opportunities he predicted a reversal of the unfortunate results of the last years.

MISCELLANY DECEMBER 21 1925

My memory of A. N. Hornby in his later period is associated (writes a correspondent) with boots! Memory is a queer thing, and I have only to shut my eyes to see him, on a hot summer day, trotting from slips to that remote portion of The Oval which means five for the lucky batsman, his feet twinkling in what looked like black but may have been brown boots. This must have been in the earliest nineties, when I was always taken to see the Lancashire and Surrey match. Hornby was fielding in the slips, and the batsman made one of those snicks which the slip fielder who is not a Gregory or a Tunnicliffe ignores. Presently it dawned on Hornby that no one was going after the ball, and he started off himself, lustily cheered by the Ovalites – that is the only thing I remember about the match; and I remember it because the boots shocked me as ranking the great man definitely with the departing generation. The young cricketer of the nineties was apt to be mighty particular about his kit; any boots but the white ones then just coming into their empire were not quite the thing. One permitted them to the 'old men', but brown boots were beginning to date a player – even a W. G. Grace or an A. N. Hornby.

Sir, – An old cricketer would like to give his impressions of the play at Old Trafford to-day. I make no comparison between present and past methods; I merely wish to point out the difference.

Thirty years ago a batsman required the greatest skill to stay in an hour. This afternoon Watson stayed in more than four hours, and was seldom in difficulties. The wicket was good, but in two hours and a half only 80 runs were scored – a poor rate in my time even for one batsman. There was no challenge in the game, and for hours the silence of the crowd was eloquent. A finish to the match was never possible. It was not cricket but a test of endurance. In short, it was a denial of sport – which must possess some element of risk and uncertainty.

The cricket I saw in my youth may not have been as clever as it is to-day, but it certainly sent the crowds home with the knowledge that they had lived through thrilling hours. The names of the cricketers of that far-off day – Grace, Steel, Hornby, Ulyett, Briggs – are remembered yet, and many of their performances are still talked about with pleasure. How much of the cricket witnessed at Old Trafford to-day will be remembered this time next month? – Yours, &c.,

Old Lancastrian.

Manchester.

LEADER   MAY 6 1931

Yesterday at The Oval the captains of the Gloucestershire and Surrey teams set an admirable example to cricketers everywhere how to play the game. At lunch the match was virtually dead, for on the last afternoon Gloucestershire's first innings, in response to Surrey's score of 258, stood at no more than 150 for four wickets. Nobody reading the score then thought the journey to The Oval worth while. But a cricket match, like any other mortal activity, can be moulded according to the heart's desire. B. H. Lyon, the Gloucestershire captain, declared the innings closed when his side were 83 runs behind. So much for first-innings points! This was a valiant gesture. Then Surrey, enjoying a lead which made them certain winners of five points, went all out for victory. P. G. H. Fender did not act according to the dismal philosophy of 'what we have we'll hold.' He ordered his men to get runs quickly, and six wickets were lost scoring 60. Then he too declared, leaving both his bowlers and the Gloucestershire batsmen with time in which to do their bravest and best. Gloucestershire won, with two minutes only to spare, but by losing magnificently Surrey rendered cricket most valuable and, let us hope, lasting service at a time when it is very necessary that captains of cricket should lead their players chivalrously. Cricket is as good as the men who play it. The game can only be dull when dull spirits take it in charge.

The day after the Lord's Test match I played truant from cricket. I felt I could no longer look at stuff so lacking in spirit and thought as I had seen over a long period at Lord's and, moreover, being a political correspondent in Canberra, my thoughts were often outside a cricket field. And so down to Westminster I went, and high in the gallery of the House of Commons I sat while the Foreign Affairs Minister, Ernest Bevin, effectively dealt with the bouncers off the Berlin pitch.

For an overseas man this scene and moment were unforgettable. I thrilled to my Australian backbone as I heard the squat, silvering, horn-rimmed Bevin say with cold calm and emphasis to the House and the world: 'We are in Berlin by right. We will not surrender an inch of our position nor a tittle of our responsibility to the Berlin people.' In front of him, on the Opposition bench, sat Winston Churchill, pink and somewhat pudgy. The rays of the sun through the stained windows of Westminster cast in alabaster-like relief the contours of his classical fingers as he sat with one hand stretched on his knee, the other along the back of the padded bench. One could see his jaw clench in determination. He nodded his head emphatically. Up to the galleries floated distinctly his spirited 'Hear, hear! Hear, hear!'

Now what, you are probably asking, has this to do with cricket? Well, it has a lot to do with cricket. At Old Trafford at 11.30 this morning eleven English cricketers will have arrived at one of the most significant moments in cricketing history. They will arrive at that precise moment when, unlike Nottingham and Lord's, they must not surrender either an inch of position or a tittle of responsibility to the British cricketing public. The time has arrived for British cricketing deeds, not words; for runs and wickets, not excuses and explanations.

An Australian is naturally chary of criticising anything in Britain (you seem to have sufficient critics to the square mile among yourselves!). Those of us who did not experience this country during the war appreciate to the full the reasons for the 'weariness, the fever, and the fret' to which England is justifiably entitled. But as I walked up Whitehall that other London evening I found myself asking if public and elderly men like Bevin and Churchill (who have certainly had their crises) can exhibit such fire and determination, why shouldn't we expect it from a younger generation which' has no worries or responsibilities of State, which spends pleasant days and weeks in the sun and breeze?

There is, obviously, something fundamentally wrong at the moment in English cricket, and here must an Australian write warily, because one can only express opinions after a long study and experience of your conditions. But, on the surface, it does seem that county cricket is not attracting or pulling its weight; that it does not represent the best, either in spirit or strength, of English cricket and that it is a poor practical preparation for the rigours of Test cricket. This was clearly shown at Lord's when the Australians met the M.C.C. Compton and

Edrich last season eclipsed Hayward's long-standing aggregate for a season's cricket, but so pitifully did they struggle against the Australian attack that one began to think they were being represented not by their own selves but by their second cousins. They had got out of the way of playing good bowling; runs came too easily for them against most county sides, and loose living, even in runs, is weakening for anybody.

Years ago in England the then members of the Australian team were discussing the merits of Dr. 'W.G.' and George Ulyett. Some contended Ulyett was as great a batsman as the 'Old Man'. Alick Bannerman, a user of few words and strokes, rose, stretched himself, and said: 'There was no difference up to the shoulders.' And, having delivered himself of that, the epigrammatic gentleman went to bed.

We have noticed much lack of thought in English cricket this season. Last time I was in Manchester I trembled at the sight of coach Harry Makepeace almost hurling himself into space as he stood on the players' balcony and furiously waved a whole set of stumps to the middle. He was telling a young player to bowl at the stumps with the new ball and on a helpful pitch – as if any bowler of any age should need telling that! But there you are. As I write there's something fundamentally wrong with English cricket and those of you who know more about it are free to say whether this fault is inherent in your county system, with the people in charge of the game, or whether it is transitory.

More people watch and play cricket to-day in England than ever before, and yet you can't find a fast bowler! I have been told often, 'We simply haven't got one,' yet down in Kent one Sunday I saw a young chap, standing 6ft. 6in., as strong as an ox, pounding the ball down yards faster than any county bowler I've seen. Six-days-a-week cricket would kill either him or his love of the game, but this is the type you should have scoured England for after your last Australian tour. You surely must have known then the line of fast attack the Australians would take in England this summer; you knew then that bouncers worried Hutton, as they worry some others in the game, and the best way to protect is to have the means of retaliation.

And so, sadly, we will not see Hutton to-day. The English selectors have bowled him and to them the Australians are thankful. There is about his omission something of the suggestion of a scapegoat. He has made 52, 64 (M.C.C.), 3, 74, 20, and 13 in representative matches against us. In his last three Test match innings in Australia he made 94, 76, and 122 (retired ill), so that in his last seven Test innings against Australia Hutton has made 402 runs at an average of 67. If this is failure England only needs about six such in this game and success is assured!

We would have rested Hutton, but only from the opening position. The team looks strangely unlike an English one without his name, but Washbrook must certainly see the significance of it all. No cuts and flicks and no hooks, Cyril, for the first hour, because more than ever in this game must the English batsmen settle down to their task with grim defence for a beginning. They must take leaves out of the book of endeavour as written by the valiant co-authors Bedser and Evans. English cricket simply *must* redeem itself in this tilt at Old Trafford, and nobody wishes it more so than those former Australian Test players who knew the merit and the steel of an English Test eleven.

One more point. I should like to see a solemn gentleman in tall black hat, black frock-coat, black tie and trousers walk as sadly as he will look to the centre to-day at 11.20 and conduct two minutes' silence on behalf of the departed race of leg-break bowlers. A Test between England and Australia and not a single leg-twister in either side! And let him be accompanied to the middle by the villain who conceived this arch plot of a new ball every fifty-five overs.

To the editor   JULY 31 1948

Sir, – Every Englishman who is interested in cricket will be deeply disappointed at our failure to win even one of the Test matches so far – many of them will have lost faith in the famous M.C.C., and have a somewhat jaundiced outlook for the future. But I wonder how many Englishmen have experienced a sense of disgust at some of the methods used in these Test matches, to win, or to attempt to prevent the other side winning? One of the most astonishing of these is 'putting on the big roller to break up the wicket more quickly' to quote the words in one article I saw in cold print. Can that be called sportsmanship? Is this sort of thing part of the traditional and much beloved game which has been played on the village greens of England for centuries past? And yet it is glibly described by all the spokesmen, and in such a manner as to make it perfectly acceptable, as a factor in the game. I feel certain that the captain of my local cricket club would be revolted at the idea of winning any of his matches by such an expedient. – Yours, &c.,

Hugh S. McColl.

Childwall,
Liverpool 16.

TERENCE PRITTIE   JANUARY 24 1951

A few years ago one of the leading authorities on the game of cricket walked up and down behind the Members' Stand at Lord's and explained his distress at an article commenting somewhat unfavourably on the first Test trial match in England since the war. This article criticised a batsman who had taken three hours in a determined but desperately dull attempt to play himself into the England eleven, and it was said that he had played himself out of any England team for a long time to come. He still has not played in a Test with Australia. The old member kept repeating hopefully: 'The game's all right, all right, all right.' One wishes that this statement were strictly true.

Why is English cricket in the doldrums and why does it still show no signs of recovery nearly six years after the end of the war? In 1919 the problem was the same. Half of a generation of cricketers had either retired or died in battle.

Since 1945 England has competed on barely equal terms with India, South Africa, and even New Zealand, made a poor showing against the West Indies, and had little chance against Australia. The present tour has confirmed this new balance of power which places England equal last among the Commonwealth nations which play cricket seriously. The captain, F. R. Brown, has, indeed, deserved only sympathy with a salting of praise. He has had the worst of the weather, the toss, and those incidental injuries which can crucially affect the issue of a hard-fought Test match. He personally has done nobly. But the plain fact is there for all to see: that he has been given a team to lead which is brittle, ill-balanced, and miserably lacking in first-class reserves. Never before has England been reduced to playing, as a batsman, a reserve wicketkeeper who has absolutely no claims to Test class in that respect.

There are plenty of reasons for the decline of English cricket, for that is what really is taking place. Far the greatest is that spirit of jolly and quite unfounded optimism which was so aptly expressed at Lord's by someone who had just had to sit through a sad exhibition of barren batsmanship, and – in the gallant tradition of Dunkirk, the Dodecanese, and all other ill-fated adventures – had refused to be discouraged. Keen, caustic criticism would be a tonic to English cricket to-day. Never has it been more needed. Part of the English press has tried to gloss over the appalling performances of the present M.C.C. side in games against the Australian country elevens, who pretend to the same standard as the average sides in our own club cricket. It has even been suggested that F. R. Brown deliberately 'ignored' these games in order to concentrate on the Tests – the same policy which Russia, maybe, pursued in the Finland campaign of 1939. No previous England captain has regarded these games as being of primary importance, but they have always provided practice in the art of making runs quickly and prolifically against second-class bowling. They are at least as serious as net practice. The batsman who gets himself out in the nets, dimly as well as wantonly, is not getting practice for a Test match at all.

A wry little joke has been made of the worst fieldsman in the M.C.C. side who goes through a dumbshow when he misses a catch in the field. This might be tolerated in a bucolic village game. On the whole, one likes to think that it would not. Village sides will forgive the occasional blunder in the field, but they will hardly applaud the sort of antics which are becoming too common in an England eleven. Once upon a time E. Hendren threw in an apple from the deep in an up-country game in Australia. This was effective as well as amusing, for the real ball lay ten yards beyond him and his object was to mingle fun with the saving of a run. He made a double success of it and hit the wicket with the apple into the bargain. There is a difference between wit and buffoonery.

Failures in Australia have helped to illustrate more fundamental troubles in English cricket. The first is the decline of the amateur. To-day he usually can set aside Saturday for cricket. His Sunday, at any rate, is his own. But he cannot find time for the six-day cricket week which can qualify him for a place in the England team. Only a few parallels need be drawn to illustrate this fact. F. R. Brown is an England captain at the age of 39. He last visited Australia in 1936, aged 25 and at the height of his powers as a googly bowler. He was not good enough to play in a single Test. Warr is not comparable to Farnes as a fast bowler, but he is good enough to play for England. Farnes, usually, was not. Sheppard, with a batting average of forty-odd, could not have won a place in the M.C.C. side before the war.

Another trouble in English cricket is the growing lack of interest of the professional cricketer. Once upon a time cricket was the only occupation of the professional cricketer. To-day he must needs have at least one other string to his bow. One county club, for instance, plays professional cricketers all of whom have an alternative occupation in summer as well as in winter. The rising cost of living means that they cannot make enough money out of the game and their alternative jobs are the ones they can always keep. A Washbrook now has to think twice before he accepts an invitation to tour Australia. When did this ever happen in the past? The professional, as much as the amateur, is on the decline. He has to earn a living all the year round and cricket does not bring security or prosperity. If county cricket continues on its present basis plenty of professionals will be retiring at 35 instead of 45. Many promising youngsters will never become professional cricketers at all. And professional batting, as well as bowling, is deteriorating. Before the war such men as Mead, Ernest Tyldesley, Holmes, Sandham, had to be left out of one Test series after another. What would we not give for one of them to-day?

To the editor   JUNE 10 1952

Sir, – I have had opportunities during the past two seasons of observing the process by which county cricket captains, when they are fortunate enough to possess a fast bowler, labour to convert his pace to fast medium.

Again and again I have seen such a bowler kept on when he is obviously flagging, instead of his being used as the spearhead of the attack. Worse still, he is allowed to pound away on a 'feather-bed' wicket.

It is small wonder that soon he begins, while 'going through all the motions of a fast bowler' (Neville Cardus's phrase), to bowl slightly below his best pace, and soon becomes incapable of really fast bowling.

I think anyone who follows cricket could produce a formidable list of bowlers ruined in this way, and I suggest that until county captains become less short-sighted we are unlikely to produce a fast bowler capable of troubling the Australians.

Probably many readers will remember, as I do, the way in which our outstanding captain of the last generation D. R. Jardine, 'nursed' his fast bowlers.
– Yours &c.,

C.

Manchester.

LEADER

MAY 7 1966

There is alarming news today from the Advertising Association Conference at Brighton. A director of the Rank Organisation has predicted the end of cricket. 'You may find,' Mr Graham Dowson says, 'that cricket will have gone in ten years.' Moreover, this daring man continued, soccer as we know it may have gone as well; there will be go-karting instead, sailing, day trips to New York, automated hotels, and frequent holidays in Jamaica. If the Rank Organisation has anything to do with it 1976 will be a year to remember.

It all sounds enormously progressive. And parts of the Rank (or

Dowson) plan for 1976 also sound enjoyable. Holidays for all in Bali, for example, and air-conditioned hotels and easier yachting and no sauce on the tablecloth and two vacations a year. Bemused by all these excitements, however, we shall have forgotten cricket – or so Mr Dowson thinks. 'Attendances at county matches,' he says, 'have been dwindling fast, and will go on dwindling so long as spectators are offered nothing better in the way of amenities than damp deck-chairs, cold sausage rolls, and cups of undrinkable tea.'

The Rank Organisation knows a great deal about air-conditioned hotels, and perhaps about Bali, too, but its understanding of cricket is deficient. People don't go to cricket matches for the sake of the sausage rolls.

LEADER   JUNE 17 1966

Because its cricket correspondent is ill, the 'Evening Standard' has dispatched Dom Moraes, the young Indian poet, to Lord's. Yesterday was his first innings and he got off to a brisk start: 'The West Indies have always been a side that has leapt in and out of form as unpredictably and frequently as Messalina leaping in and out of bed.' Scholarly, but hardly poetic. Try the next edition. 'The factory smoke was by now virtually invisible against a darkening sky. Then, gently, the sky began to weep; its tears fell slowly over Lord's . . . then the sky really decided to be sorry for itself, poured down its tears and . . . the players, commiserating with the sky, left the field.' Slowly, insidiously, as their typewriters clicked gently to a dying fall, the denizens of the press box, lofty giants of the battering ram metaphor, paused bemused like proud harts pursued by the pack. One of their number, slim, fawn-like, dusky, was still writing intently, though out on the green sward nothing stirred. Quietly, with the lowering skies, they began to weep.

HENRY BLOFELD IN ADELAIDE   JANUARY 29 1975

In the past six years the cycle of English Test cricket has done a half-turn. The splendid 1968 side gradually disappeared and the descent has been steady, right down to the present depressing situation. In time, no doubt, the cycle will reverse itself, but it will be fascinating to see if at the same time the sudden change of character in England's cricketers which has gone on during these past six years will also be reversed.

In this short time the life style and the attitude of the players has altered remarkably – and this is especially noticeable on a long tour. English cricket at both county and Test levels lacks and misses the rich individual characters who, until relatively recently, were still there and who helped give the counties their individual flavours. If a total stranger lined up the present England party and was allowed to talk, on general terms, to each individual for, say, three minutes and then try and put them into counties, he might have a shrewd idea that Fred Titmus hails from Cockney London, but with any other he would not know where to begin. This is in no way a reflection on Chris Old, but merely an indication on the way things have gone that one should wonder if ever a Yorkshireman on tour for England could be mistaken for anyone but a Yorkshireman.

England have been beaten before, but have England ever been so faceless before? All facets of life help develop 'character' and it is not only cricket which develops a cricketer's character, although obviously it plays a considerable part. The present mental approach to life by Englishmen as a race must inevitably play a part, for environment can only condition character.

The manifestations of this change of character on a cricket tour are important because I believe that they all add up to one of the main reasons why England's batsmen have made such a poor showing against the two Australian fast bowlers. It could well be the ultimate reason why there has not been one batsman who has been able to go out and fight to the extent of making a four-hour 60 – and in this series four-hour 60s would have made all the difference for England. If any two of the batsmen here had the grit and determination of, say, Ken Barrington, England would not now be on the point of going four down in the series.

On a tour nowadays players are not only looked after magnificently but they are given pretty well everything they could want from cars, to golf clubs, to boating trips, to visits to race meetings. And, human nature being what it is, these things begin to be taken for granted. It is the fashion now, too, for wives and small children to accompany their husbands for part of the tour. The hotel swimming pool during the Sydney Test resembled a nursery school – and a noisy one at that.

It would be wrong to prevent wives and children from joining their husbands and fathers at all, but this time wives were allowed to spend three weeks in the same hotel as their husbands. And when the time was up, several stayed nearby with friends and relations, and now every time the party moves on there are as many teddy-bears as cricketers going up the aeroplane steps. In future, more rigid demarcation lines must be drawn: certainly it is a problem which has not gone unnoticed by the management of this party.

There are many readers who will feel slightly indignant that there should be any suggestion of limiting the visits of wives and families on tours. The first and foremost consideration of a touring cricketer with MCC must be his cricket, and the determination to beat the opposing side. Cricket is a game which requires dedication and single-mindedness to no small degree, especially when things begin to go wrong.

When a player has his family with him he would not be human if his loyalties were not, at times, divided – any more than wives would not be human if they were at times not upset that their husbands were going to go off on a free day for voluntary net practice. Or the situation could easily arise at the crucial stage of a Test match that a player from whom much is expected the following day has a sleepless night because his small child has a miserable and tearful night. Instead of arriving at the ground the next day, fresh and eager to beat the other side, he would inevitably be feeling ghastly and would not be able to give of his best.

The other aspect of this tour, which is different even from tours of half a dozen years ago and for which the presence of the wives may be responsible, is that little or no time is spent by the players discussing the match and the day's play. When, 11 years ago, I went on my first tour with Mike Smith's side to India, the players met in the evenings and talked and discussed what had gone on during the day. This happened, too, in the West Indies in 1968. At the start of the present tour, until after the first Test match in Brisbane, the players' room – which they have in each hotel – was full most evenings with players talking about what had gone on.

Since Brisbane the room has still ever been there – but it has been mostly empty. The good team spirit which was originally with this side has been ignored. It has been the presence of the wives which has taken the players away from this very important aspect of playing Test matches, or indeed any other kind of matches. In the future a more satisfactory balance must be arrived at. By the way, when the Australians are on tour they do not allow wives to stay with their husbands during Test matches.

The other change in behaviour, which is very noticeable from tours of ten or so years ago, is that after a day's play the players would gather round the bar and have a drink – or two or even three – and talk, usually fairly disparagingly, about the opposition, go to bed (sometimes not too early) and be there first thing in the morning ready to fight for all they were worth. Nowadays, players do not gather in this way, and though their alcoholic intake may be less and they are probably earlier to bed just look at the manner of their defeats. The moral in all this is hard to pin-point; but there has, for sure, been a character change.

STANLEY REYNOLDS   APRIL 5 1975

With the snow and the rain and the rain and the hail and all the back gardens of the world looking like the Somme, it is hard to dream spring dreams. But here is a bumper issue of The Cricketer, full of new books about the summer game, and here is a new Saturday morning television series on ITV with Tony Lewis called Cricket in the Middle, and here is old Cedric writing to me, saying, 'Now it is April, then May, and before you know it, there it is, June, and where are you?'

The summer is out there waiting around somewhere if only spring could make a little more of an effort. And we shall be heading out again to see some matches if only the weather lifts; and if not we shall stand in dripping beer tents on that foul smelling hopsack that they cover the floor of beer tents with to keep the flies away or perhaps to discourage the amateur drunks, drinking soapy keg bitter out of plastic pint pots and pretending like mad that this is the real old fashioned England, the England of rural prints, the England of dog fights in the lazy blue sky of 1940 Kent, the New Yorker magazine's idea of rural England . . . if only they would turn that transistor down.

We went out last summer in search of the ye old England of the green-sward and the pock pock of the leather on the willow: old Cedric, the groundsman, Young Ainsworth, the Oxford blue and up-and-at-'em advertising account executive, and me, Buntsy Reynolds, who played third base with my chest (that was the only way I could stop the ball), and we got too paralytic to see anything but the plastic pint pots and the trannies. Maybe that was the story. The whole world has grown Mickey Mouse Ears and nobody has noticed. Cricket has grown Mickey Mouse Ears. The one day game, the idea of never-dull, action-packed cricket with all the homey atmosphere of speedway racing and the amenities of a Wimpy Bar, is Mickey Mouse cricket, but nobody will mention it. You see it all around you.

Ever since I came to England and turned first thing to the sports page because that is where I always turned first thing in the newspapers back home, I have been intrigued, mesmerised, called, by cricket writing. Has there ever been a game in the history of the world so lovingly waffled over as cricket?

Arlott on Maurice Tate on a sea-fret wicket at Hove, Cardus on Jimmy Heap's lumbago (who was Jimmy Heap and what exactly is lumbago? What for that matter is a sea-fret wicket? It doesn't really seem to matter, does it?); sitting in the warm sunshine of Eastbourne on a June morning, the first thing I reach for is Eric Todd writing about the rain in Derbyshire; Jim Swanton on the difficult young batsmen who just will not wear cricket caps; Swanton on the great marl wickets of 1938; Parky on his old dad's old whitewashed pit boots.

'Stanley,' writes Cedric from his new cricket ground in Bedfordshire where he has gone into a sort of semi-retirement as a groundsman because this pitch has no covers and no heavy roller, which is a sort of purgatory for Cedric because he loved a heavy roller like some old-time engine driver would love a steam locomotive. 'Stanley, we must settle what matches we are going to see this June. Then we can negotiate.' Cedric says we will 'see England, Scotland, pubs, and Wales.' He still has the idea that somewhere out there is a land safe for Ratty and Mole, if we can only find it; a Wind in the Willows land free of plastic pint pots (10p deposit at Folkestone CC) where there is only the squeaking of old-fashioned pumps drawing from the wood, where no trannies play, and where no Lucie Clayton rejects pass among you offering free-sample B & H or Player's No. 6. 'Will you look at this?' Young Ainsworth says.

The Lucie Clayton rejects are passing among us. The yobs are waving scarfs like this was some kind of football match. One of them is wearing an old top hat with KENT KINGS OF CRICKET chalked all around it. 'Would you gentlemen care to buy a chance on a new Ford Escort?' another Lucie Clayton reject asks. Chip papers blow across the outfield. The great M. J. K. Smith is standing there with a big smile on his face while the chip papers blow past him and the yobs summon all their wit to shout 'AL – AN! AL – AN! COME ON AL – AN' to A.P.E. Knott.

'Look at that big divvy,' Ainsworth says. 'I mean, how old is he anyway, Mike Smith? He must be forty and he's out there smiling like a div playing a little boy's game. What kind of a divvy is a divvy like that?'

'Bought me large whisky did M. J. K. Smith, my friend, just now up in members,' says Cedric. 'Oh aye.'

It is not that Cedric has made his peace with the world, drawn up a DMZ with life or anything like that, it is that he is a romantic like all the cricketing folk – except of course the blokes who brought in the plastic pint pots, the Lucie Clayton rejects, new car giveaways, and busloads of yobs – being a romantic cricketing folk, he is breaking his neck not seeing that cricket has also gone all crackerjack just like everyone else in the world.

Naturally, I have not read all the new cricket books published this spring, but I have read enough of them – and you can tell from the titles anyway, can't you? – and all the ones that aren't those ghosted how-to-bowl-a-winning-googly books for kids are myth, magic, and fable. The romantic view, the blinkered eye which doesn't see the scarf-waving yobs, the Lucie Clayton rejects, and the plastic pint pots. Stopped ears, too! They don't seem to hear the trannies.

'Ah, yes, yes, my dear sir,' says Cedric, 'but you are only a poor ignorant Yank, an ignorant lot, if you don't mind my saying so – no offence meant – and you do not know an Englishman's cricketing dreams of a pleasanter land beyond that daily grind, as twilight falls upon the village green and stumps are drawn, and the bells of St Mary's chime.'

Selling them the sizzle, Young Adrian Ainsworth might say if he were here to say anything. Young Ainsworth, I am told, has found himself a better spring dream and summer game. He has got himself a bird.

. . . But the Grauniad is the Grauniad

NEVILLE CARDUS   JUNE 30 1926

In my message yesterday a mistake in telegraphing made me refer to Woolley, Chapman and Carr as 'primitive' batsmen: the word I used was 'punitive'.

To the editor   AUGUST 8 1979

Sir, – Misprint or not, the vision of Bishan Bedi tiptoeing up to bowl 'in his sky-blue parka' is too delicious to pass unnoticed. Presumably it's one way of playing on in the rain! – Yours delightedly,

Ian Richardson.

Priory Drive,
Totnes,
Devon.

AUTUMN

FRANK KEATING   SEPTEMBER 24 1982

There can have been no more satisfactory or romantic finale to any cricket season than the clamorous curtain call staged by The Oval last weekend.

On Saturday the last shafts of a summer sun beamed down as a congregation of 13,000 West Indians and Ian Botham celebrated a Caribbean carnival: on Sunday in the misty, still opaque damp of an English autumn, middle-aged men became for a brief hour or two once more the champions of childhood. Time for olde tyme! Those, indeed, were the days.

As Sir Garfield Sobers walked back after a superlative innings – admittedly against avuncular bowling – there was, somehow, an echo of lamentation and desolation rising up from the fond and heartfelt tribute.

Everyone sensed that we would never see him bat again; never see that lissome tread, that jungle-cat's mix of jaunty, relaxed serenity and purposeful, businesslike intent; never see again the cavalier's smile fringed by the upturned collar, the pure arc of his golfer's follow-through after the cover-drive, or on-drive, or that genuflecting, exhilarating front-foot square-cut played late and cleanly murderous.

And in the evening drizzle, Ray Lindwall bowled. I had never seen him before. The nearest I got was the firm promise of a schoolmaster-monk to be taken to Worcestershire for the Australians' opening match of 1948. Then, on the eve of the trip, something came up and the black-cowled swine reneged.

I wondered on Sunday whether, even at the age of 61, Lindwall could muster just a glimmer, a sense of the outline and structure of what old men still say was the most perfect bowling action of all. He did too, though the arm was low and the run was short and sciatic. But I'd seen Lindwall bowl at last.

At the evening celebrations, four Aussies seemed very pleased to be back. They sat contentedly with their wives and their well-wishers. There was Bobby Simpson, patient bat and supreme snaffler of the slips; Neil Harvey, boy wonder who confirmed his promise a hundred-fold, and now in dark glasses, still smiling, and looking foward to a touring holiday in Devon and Cornwall.

Also Ray Lindwall, strong blue eyes and strong square shoulders and off next day for a Continental holiday; and Gary Sobers, now with a whispy grey mandarin's goatee under his gap-toothed smile. He now has Australian citizenship, but not an Australian accent.

Lindwall and Sobers just overlapped. At the end of January, 1955, Lindwall and Miller having laid waste the West Indian batting in the previous three, came the fourth Test at Barbados. A slim 19-year-old, who had been picked as a left-arm spinner, was sent in as a stopgap to open the batting with J. K. Holt. Lindwall and Miller paced out their runs. Said a West Indian supporter on the jam packed corrugated roof: 'Ooh'dear, dey feedin' de poor boy to de two tiger-cats to slacken off dey appetite!'

Lindwall admits he and his black-maned mate didn't know what, literally, hit them. Sobers hit six sumptuous boundaries in his first 25. In half an hour the boy had scored a breath-taking 43 and seen off the dreaded duo before Johnson had him caught. 'We were punch-drunk,' admits Lindwall, still shaking his head at the memory. Across the table, Sobers grins: still the sheepish grin of a found-out schoolboy.

Seven years before, at The Oval, Lindwall had, quite simply, demolished England. They were swept away; 52 all out; Hutton 30; Lindwall six for 20. It was the catching that was responsible, he says, recalling blinders by Tallon and Hassett and Morris.

With gentle modesty, he explains that earlier in the week it had been rainy and the pitch was under-prepared and damp . . . 'England's batsmen were distrustful of the pitch and expected the ball to fly from a length. Actually it went through at a uniform height. At least four of them were bowled by yorkers.' Hutton had played wonderfully well – 'first in, last out, caught by Don Tallon off a genuine leg glance.'

Hutton was the great, and admired, foe. Once Lindwall gave Hutton a lift from the Sydney Cricket Ground to the England team's hotel . . . 'We didn't speak a word to each other, apart from saying "good night!" By actions in the middle we had told each other a good deal about each other's play. What was there to say after all that?'

At The Oval in 1948, Lindwall clean bowled England's last three tail-enders, Evans, Bedser and Young. He does not condone present habits of bumping non-batsmen. 'If a fast bowler cannot bowl out numbers nine, 10 and 11 without resorting to intimidation then he ought not to be wearing Australia's colours.'

Sobers hates the use of batsmen's helmets. He, like Viv Richards today, would never have worn one. 'The point of cricket is to protect yourself with the bat, man.' He says that if they had been worn in his day, 'there would have been no point in bowling at the likes of Kenny Barrington or Slasher Mackay: we'd have taken months to get them out, man; years, probably.'

Sir Garfield, you fancy, had a massive regard for Barrington's dogged, stoic fidelity to his cause. Of the great quartet of post-war English batsmen, May and Cowdrey, Dexter and Graveney, you feel he admired, and warmed to, the latter brace far more.

Of the bowlers, Fred Trueman – 'What hostility! what a trier!' – was his sort of fellow, and also India's mesmerising leg-spinner of the '50s, Subhash Gupte, who seemed to be as inventive and experimental and as accurate – even more so – as the Pakistani who both enchanted and bamboozled the English this summer, Abdul 'the Bulbul' Qadir.

Sobers leaves. Lindwall nods goodbye. There is a sudden, awed hush in the room as Sir Garfield eases his way out, down the stairs, and across The Oval concourse for, perhaps, the very last time. The lights go out. It is, in fact, the end of many, many summers.

Index

Bold type indicates contributors and where their work may be found.

PUFFIN BOOKS

Georgia paxson
11A

Queensgate

KAY'S MARVELLOUS MEDICINE

A (TERRIFYINGLY) TRUE HISTORY OF
DISGUSTING DISEASES AND CRAZY CURES

ADAM KAY
ILLUSTRATED BY HENRY PAKER

PUFFIN

PUFFIN BOOKS

UK | USA | Canada | Ireland | Australia
India | New Zealand | South Africa

Puffin Books is part of the Penguin Random House group of companies
whose addresses can be found at global.penguinrandomhouse.com

www.penguin.co.uk   www.puffin.co.uk   www.ladybird.co.uk

First published 2021
This edition published 2022

001

Text design by Perfect Bound Ltd
Printed in Great Britain by Clays Ltd, Elcograf S.p.A.

The authorized representative in the EEA is Penguin Random House Ireland,
Morrison Chambers, 32 Nassau Street, Dublin D02 YH68

A CIP catalogue record for this book is available from the British Library

ISBN: 978–0–241–50854–1

All correspondence to:
Puffin Books, Penguin Random House Children's
One Embassy Gardens, 8 Viaduct Gardens, London SW11 7BW

To Michael Sharpington, who did an amazing fart at school,
which lasted over a minute, and was known forever
afterwards as Michael Fartington.

And with thanks to my Great Aunt Prunella
for reading an early draft of this book
and giving me her thoughts.

CONTENTS

MAJOR MEDICAL

1600 BC (ANCIENT EGYPT)

Doctors discovered that the heart pumps blood around the body. But then again, they also reckoned that poo flowed out of the heart . . .

400 BC (ANCIENT GREECE)

Hippocrates realized that illnesses aren't caused by magic. Apologies if you thought that illnesses were caused by magic and this is a massive spoiler.

1928

Antibiotics were discovered by Sir Alexander Antibiotic. I mean Sir Antibiotic Fleming. Sorry, Sir Alexander Fleming. That's better.

1910

Marie Curie discovered radiation and then everyone's houses were nice and warm. No, hang on, that's radiators. Radiation is a treatment for cancer.

1929

Doctors discovered that smoking was dangerous. Before then, doctors thought smoking was good for you – I don't like to call people idiots, but . . .

1954

The first kidney transplant took place, soon followed by liver transplants, heart transplants and bum transplants. (Maybe not bum transplants, actually.)

MOMENTS

800 AD (MIDDLE AGES)
The first medical school was opened. Before that, presumably people just guessed how to be doctors?

100 AD (ANCIENT ROME)
The Romans used their brains and realized that the brain is in charge of thinking.

1590
The microscope was invented and suddenly everything looked massive.

1895
The first X-ray was performed. I've got no idea what the X stands for. Xylophone, maybe?

1842
The first anaesthetic was given, so patients could sleep during their operations instead of going 'AAAAAAAAAAGH! STOP!'

1980
Adam Kay was born, the most handsome genius in all of medicine.

2020
The coronavirus pandemic swept through the world.

2185
Earth gets taken over by the Octopus People of Zaaarg. Sorry about that.

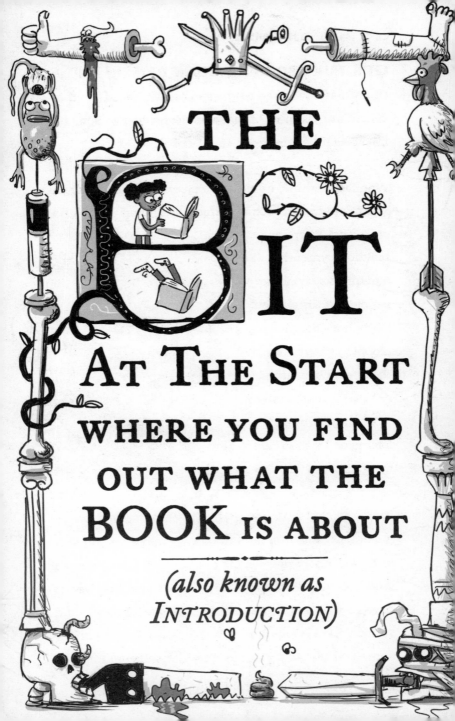

THE BIT AT THE START WHERE YOU FIND OUT WHAT THE BOOK IS ABOUT

(also known as INTRODUCTION)

LET'S TALK ABOUT THE OLDEN DAYS. No, not last Christmas – we need to go even further back than that. Where are you now? Dinosaurs. Nope, you've gone too far. Forward a bit – right, that's better.

When you think about history, you might imagine knights in clunky-looking armour riding off into battle, or Ancient Egyptians building pyramids, or kings and queens chopping people's heads off. You might have heard of poo plopping its way down the streets because no one had invented toilets yet, and grown-ups forcing children to climb up chimneys.

→ Quite right too – might as well make lazy, stinking children do some work for once in their miserable lives. Prunella

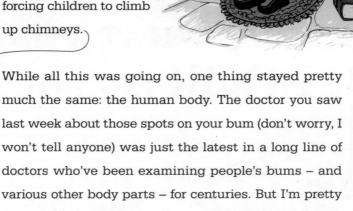

While all this was going on, one thing stayed pretty much the same: the human body. The doctor you saw last week about those spots on your bum (don't worry, I won't tell anyone) was just the latest in a long line of doctors who've been examining people's bums – and various other body parts – for centuries. But I'm pretty sure that the doctor you saw was a bit different from the ones in Ancient Egypt. First of all, she probably had better teeth and didn't wear a massive gold headdress. (I wish I'd been allowed to wear a massive gold headdress when I was a doctor.) More importantly, she knows an awful lot more about the human body than people did back then.

That was the main problem with the olden days – people didn't have the slightest clue how our bodies worked. So if you got ill, even if it was something really minor, like bum-spots, you could be in massive trouble. And the cure for your unfortunate bum-spots (how are they doing now, by the way?) would've been something mega-weird and useless – like gargling with wee or shoving insects down your pants.

> I HAVE REMOVED YOUR BUM-SPOTS. AND YOUR BUM.

Don't believe me? Well, how do you and your spotty bum fancy a bit of time travel? It's OK – you don't need a packed lunch, and there's no chance of changing history by accidentally sneezing on Julius Caesar and somehow causing the human race to be overthrown by earthworms.

We'll head back thousands of years to see how doctors of the past muddled through without all those things that now save our lives every single day, from anaesthetics and antibiotics all the way to X-rays and . . . umm . . . something else beginning with X. Plus, we'll look at all the mistakes and experiments (mostly mistakes, to be honest) that eventually led to us figuring out how everything works. When I say 'us', I mean famous scientists of the past – **YOU** didn't discover how any of the body works. ⟶ *Nor did you, Adam, you useless weasel. Prunella*

I'll answer all the questions you didn't even realize you had to ask, like:

WHAT HAPPENED IF YOU NEEDED A TOP-UP OF BLOOD BEFORE BLOOD TRANSFUSIONS WERE INVENTED?

It depends on which doctor you saw, but they might have told you to drink wee, or beer, or even dog's blood. I don't want to spoil the surprise, but none of those treatments worked particularly well . . .

WHAT WAS THE GREAT STINK?

No, it wasn't what historians called your bedroom after you ate that baked-bean and cauliflower casserole. It was a time when there was so much poo in the River Thames that the whole of London smelled like the inside of a horse's bum for months and months, and all the germs from it made thousands of people ill.

OI!

> It's lucky _you_ weren't around then, or you'd have been arrested for attempted murder every day. Prunella

I'll introduce you to geniuses like Louis Pasteur, who invented pasta. No, hold on, that's not right. He worked out that infections come from germs. Before that, people used to think infections were caused by bad smells! He even worked out how to get rid of germs in food, so people didn't die from drinking manky milk.

For hundreds and hundreds of years, women weren't allowed to be doctors or scientists – a horrible example of a thing called sexism, which means treating women and men differently. Women helped millions of people by working as midwives and healers, but they never got any credit for it – or even worse, they got punished for it! I know, right . . . We'll meet some brilliant women who pushed past all that stupid sexism and changed the world, like the marvellous Marie Curie. She was the first woman to win a Nobel Prize (the top award in science), and then the first person to win a second Nobel Prize (which is slightly greedy, if you ask me). And quite right too – her discoveries still save the lives of people with cancer every single minute.

But not everyone in history was a genius. For example, there's my dad, who once destroyed his laptop by cleaning the keyboard with soapy water. Going a bit further back, we'll find out why the Ancient Egyptians thought the brain was just a useless load of old stuffing that might as well be chucked in the bin, why teachers forced their pupils to smoke cigarettes, why hairdressers would chop their customers' legs off and why people got paid for farting. (Unfortunately, that's no longer a thing – sorry.)

→ I can tell who you got your brains from. Prunella

DID I TAKE TOO MUCH OFF?

Not gross enough for you? Well, how about the surgeons who never washed their hands and believed that the more blood and guts and brains they had on their clothes, the better? Or the ones who thought that patients should be wide awake and screaming during their operations, otherwise the surgery wouldn't be successful? Don't worry – none of them are still working today. Well, hopefully not . . .

So, if you're ready, pop a peg on your nose (there was a lot of stinky pus back then), pull on your wellies (there was a lot of poo around too), wash your hands (because *they* certainly didn't) and let's go back to where it all began. No, not dinosaurs – dinosaurs didn't have doctors. Maybe that's why they became extinct . . .

A doctor and a time machine – why has nobody ever thought of this before?! Let's go!

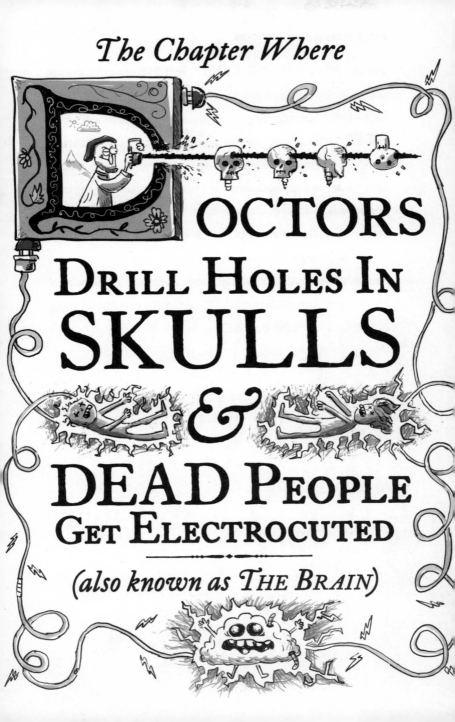

The Chapter Where

DOCTORS DRILL HOLES IN SKULLS & DEAD PEOPLE GET ELECTROCUTED

(also known as THE BRAIN)

YOUR BRAIN IS, TO PUT IT MILDLY, really, really, really, really, really, really important. It's the super-smart, high-tech control centre in charge of literally everything you do. When you eat, for example: that's your brain telling your teeth to chomp and your tongue to swish and your oesophagus to . . . umm . . . oesophagize? (Oesophagus means your food pipe, btw. (And btw means 'by the way', btw.)) Need to run away from a tiger? Well, your brain will order your legs to move and your arms to flail around and your mouth to scream and your bum to fart. (Is it just me who farts when I'm scared?)

But the brain hasn't always got the respect it deserves. Years and years ago, humans were a bit slow to work it all out. Can you blame them? They didn't have the internet, for a start. Also, I hadn't written this book yet. But, if **YOU** didn't have the first clue about how the body works, would you ever really look at that big, ugly pile of slimy sausages inside your head and think, *Well, that must be the most important part of the body!*? Probably not. That's if you'd even managed to find the brain in the first place – it's securely hidden away in its secret lair, inside a big, thick lump of skull. (I mean the skull is a thick piece of bone, not that you're thick. Don't send me any emails complaining, please.)

You could say this chapter's only half written because there's loads of things we *still* don't know about the brain – even some quite major stuff, like what bits of it make us clever. In a hundred years' time, they'll probably find a copy of this book and make fun of us and how little we knew about the body.

Your poor readers. They should get a refund for this book if you don't even know how the body works. Prunella

WOW, THEY REALLY WERE IDIOTS.

ANCIENT EGYPT

Who's the oldest person you know? The oldest person I know is my Great Aunt Prunella. She's ninety-two and even **SHE** wasn't around in the time of the Ancient Egyptians. The Ancient Egyptians lived about five thousand years ago, which is nearly two million days ago, which is three billion minutes ago, which is over 150 billion seconds ago, which is a weird way to measure it, actually.

How dare you tell people my age — you absolutely horrible wretch. Delete this, Prunella

Let's start by talking about mummies, and I don't mean the people who tell you off for not eating your mushrooms or when you wipe your nose on your sleeve. I mean the kind of mummy you dress up as when you need a last-minute Halloween costume and all you can find are ten rolls of toilet paper. The Ancient Egyptians believed that, when you died, there was something called an after-life that was apparently much nicer than ordinary life (less homework and more chocolate).

To prepare important people like kings and queens for the afterlife, they mummified their bodies. I'm glad they waited until people were dead because mummification wasn't a very fun process. Priests would hopefully put some gloves on first, then remove all the person's organs, then embalm the rest of the body (which means using substances like salt to stop it going all mouldy). Just before they wrapped the body in those spooky-looking bandages, they would pop the heart back inside because they realized it was very important. Some other organs, like the lungs and the stomach, would be stored in special jars to sit alongside the body for its journey to the afterlife, a bit like hand luggage when you go on holiday.

And how about the brain? They just chucked it in the bin, mate. I'm not even joking.

The Ancient Egyptians thought cleverness came from the heart, and the brain was just a load of padding like you'd find inside a cushion, and it was only there to stop your head going all flat. So they'd yank out the brain (stop reading immediately if you're eating) by sticking a massive sharp hook up the nose (I mean it – put those cornflakes down!) and scooping it out like the world's biggest bogey, then splatting it straight in the rubbish. Then they'd shove a load of old cloth into the empty skull. Let's hope the Ancient Egyptian afterlife didn't involve spelling tests because those former royals wouldn't have done very well at all with a load of tea towels where their brains should be.

ANCIENT GREECE

It's time to take the bus to Greece (make sure you go to the loo before you leave). Ancient Greece must have been a very exciting place to live because every city was crammed full of clever people who invented all sorts of important things, such as maps and the Olympics! They also invented things like geometry (the bit of maths that's about angles) and alarm clocks (which wake you up, so you can go to school and learn maths).

They get full marks for discovering all those things, but I'm afraid they weren't too hot on the old brain stuff either. They thought the Ancient Egyptians were right and that the heart was in charge of **EVERYTHING**. And who can blame them? It's in the middle of the body, it's got blood vessels sprouting everywhere, and if you cut it out with a penknife everything else stops working. (My lawyer, Nigel, has asked me to point out that under no circumstances should you cut out your – or anyone else's – heart using a penknife.)

KAY'S MARVELLOUS MEDICINE

So what did the Ancient Greeks think the brain was for? Well, for hundreds of years, they believed it was just there to make mucus – like some kind of phlegm factory. (Maybe they saw snot leaking out of someone's nose and thought it was the brain overflowing, like a bath you forgot to turn off.) The Ancient Greeks score a D minus for that. Luckily, one day a bloke turned up who realized the brain was more than a big snot-sack, and his name was Hippocrates.

Hippocrates was one of the most important doctors of all time. In fact, he's so important that he gets his very own fact box.

HIPPOCRATES: FIVE FACTS AND A LIE

1. He's known as the Father of Medicine because of his important contributions to the subject. (Not because he had a daughter called Medicine.)

2. The Hippocratic Oath was named after him: it's something doctors in Ancient Greece had to agree to before they could start work. Doctors still do this today, although it's been changed slightly (for example, they've deleted the bit where Hippocrates said students must give their teachers money if they ask for it).

3. He was the first person to discover that what you eat and how much you exercise are

important for keeping healthy. That means he's the bloke to blame when you're forced to run outside in the cold and eat mushrooms. Ugh.

4. He wrote sixty massive books about the body – I've only written two, so that makes me feel really lazy.

5. He invented endoscopy, which is a way of looking inside the body using a tube (a bit like an empty toilet roll). Endoscopy is still used all the time by surgeons nowadays – thanks, Hippocrates!

6. He was called Hippocrates (which is Greek for Hippoface) because he had massive teeth and nostrils and looked a bit like a hippo.

NO ONE CALLS ME HIPPOFACE!

6. He wasn't really known as Hippoface, so far as we know. I guess you can call him that if you like – he's not around to tell you off. Oh, and it's pronounced hi-PO-cra-TEES, not hippo-crates.

A lot of doctors in Ancient Greece thought that illnesses were caused by magic, and Hippocrates was one of the first who reckoned that was a load of old goat poo. How would you feel if you went to the doctor because you kept falling over and they waved a magic wand over you and said 'Izzy wizzy, stop feeling dizzy!' then pulled a rabbit out of your nose? I think you might ask to see their medical certificate. But why's he in the chapter about the brain? Well, he's the super-genius who realized that the brain is responsible for doing things like thinking and feelings. Good old Hippoface!

Hippocrates died when he was about ninety, which is amazingly old for someone who lived that long ago – in fact, it's an extremely old age even now. Inventing so much medicine clearly paid off for him. Until . . . he died.

Try not to get too sad – it was over two thousand years ago. Luckily, Ancient Greece was crammed full of other clever clogs, and very soon another bearded brainiac called Aristotle came along.

ARISTOTLE: FIVE FACTS AND A LIE

1. He got a job teaching the boy who grew up to be Alexander the Great (a very famous king and soldier). I wonder what he was called when he was at school? I bet it wasn't Alexander the Great – it was probably something like Alexander Smelly Socks.

2. He invented a subject called logic, which was basically a whole new way of arguing, and he taught it to thousands of students. Imagine having arguing lessons! No, you shut up!

3. He named over five hundred different animals. (I mean he gave the names to lots of different species of animal – he didn't just keep loads of cats and say, 'You're called Floofloo, you're called Nozzle, you're called Bimpsy . . .')

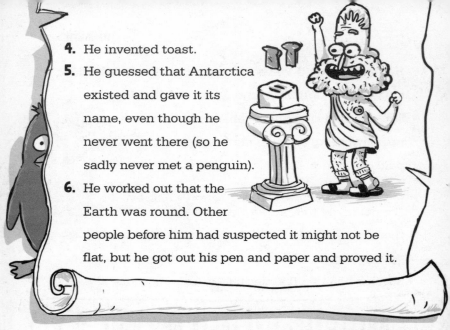

4. He invented toast.

5. He guessed that Antarctica existed and gave it its name, even though he never went there (so he sadly never met a penguin).

6. He worked out that the Earth was round. Other people before him had suspected it might not be flat, but he got out his pen and paper and proved it.

4. Bread has been around for about 30,000 years, and stuff has been on fire ever since humans started wandering the Earth, so toast is a lot older than Aristotle.

Now that Hippocrates had cracked the basics of the brain, what would Aristotle add? Would he perhaps discover the functions of all the brain's separate lobes? Would he work out which bit of the brain makes us speak or dream or waggle our ears? Or . . . would he go right back to square one and say that the brain isn't important at all?

Yep, I'm afraid he undid all of Hippocrates' excellent work and convinced the whole of Ancient Greece that the heart was the only important organ and the brain was basically just a big lump of beanbag stuffing. And, because he was so famous from all his other excellent discoveries, people believed him about this as well. Drat! (Luckily, Hippocrates was dead by then, otherwise he'd have been furious.)

I guess we can't all be perfect. For example, I sometimes get my 546 times table wrong. And your head teacher has terrible dress sense. So it's fair enough that Aristotle was kind of an idiot when it came to the brain. The best explanation he could come up with was that the brain was a kind of air-conditioning system, to keep the rest of your body nice and cool. **FACT CHECK:** not remotely true.

Stop pretending you're so great. Do you want me to show them your school reports? Prunella

ANCIENT ROME

I'm pleased to report that Aristotle's nonsense about the brain being some kind of weird, magical fridge didn't last long. A few hundred years later, round the corner in Rome, they realized that Hippocrates probably had the right idea after all and you didn't think using your heart. Phew.

Roman scientists rolled up their togas, looked at a load of brains and spotted that there were tons of wires coming off them, and that these wires went all round the body. They said, 'These wires are nerves, and they go from the brain and tell the rest of the body what to do! Crazy!' They probably said it in Latin, but otherwise that's pretty much exactly how it happened.

STAGE
DOOR

Nerves were such an exciting discovery that the scientists were desperate to tell all of Ancient Rome! But how . . . ? Did they write it in a book? No – too boring. Did they make a TV programme about it? No – didn't exist. That's right – they turned it into a hideous live show. Crowds of people would go along to a big outdoor theatre and settle down with their snacks to watch a scientist experiment on animals like lions and bears, to demonstrate how nerves worked, like some kind of horrendous circus. For example, they might cut a nerve so that an animal's voice didn't work any more. Hopefully those lions got their revenge on the scientists who did all this horrible stuff by eating them immediately after the show.

MIDDLE AGES

The next thousand years or so were known as the Middle Ages. We call them the Middle Ages because they came after one bit of history and before another bit – it's a pretty terrible name, to be honest. Makes it sound *sooooooo* boring. And it wasn't boring at all – it was full of banquets and battles, and they invented everything

from gunpowder to printing and even the calendar we use today. (I mean the way we count years, not the calendar you've got up on your fridge.) Maybe I should rename the Middle Ages so they sound more exciting – this is a textbook so I guess that'll make it official. How about Sparkle Time? That sounds much better. OK, let's start this section again.

SPARKLE TIME

In Sparkle Time, they were all totally on board with the idea that the brain was a pretty important part of the body, but they still had some slightly odd ideas about how it worked. I guess these ideas felt totally sensible all those years ago, but now they just sound . . . weird. Like the haircuts your parents had when they were younger – they probably seemed fine at the time, but in photos their hair looks like an explosion in a wig factory. People in the Middle Ag– sorry, Sparkle

> That's a bit rich coming from you. Your hair looks like your dog cut it. Prunella

Time thought that our brains were powered by spirits whooshing around inside them. I know, right? And they reckoned that the reason you could move your arms and legs was because these spooky little dudes would travel down your nerves (which they thought were hollow tubes) and do it for you. *Okaaaaaaay.*

How about if you had a headache, or your leg stopped working? Well, that was just the creepy brain-ghosts misbehaving. I don't want to ruin the rest of the chapter for you, but . . . nerves are nothing to do with creepy brain-ghosts.

THE KING AND EYE

I want you to meet Henri II of France. Well, you can't actually meet him – that would involve us all driving to France with some spades and a forklift truck because he's been dead and buried for centuries – but I want you to hear about him. Henri (which is French for Henry) II (which means the second – his surname wasn't pronounced 'eye-eye') was out one morning, enjoying his favourite hobby of jousting. Jousting involves riding on a horse and hurtling towards your opponent carrying a massive spike. A bit of a strange game, but I guess the Xbox hadn't been invented yet.

If you find yourself jousting against a king, the golden rule (if you don't want to be executed) is don't **EVER** stick the massive spike into any part of them, especially not their eye. Unfortunately, Henri's opponent, Gabriel, forgot the golden rule and . . . stuck his massive spike through the king's eye. What a **KNIGHT**mare!

> This is the worst joke you've done so far – and that's saying something. *Prunella*

It was mostly a nightmare for King Henri, who started having terrible headaches, then his arms and legs stopped working, then he went into a coma (like a very deep sleep) and then he died. At this point, his doctors sprang into action (a tiny bit too late, if you ask me) and opened up his skull and saw what a mess his brain was in. This made them realize that even though our brains are in the middle of a big lump of bone, we have to do things ourselves to protect them. Like not jousting, and always wearing a bicycle helmet. I mean when you're cycling – you don't have to wear one in bed.

ZZZZZZZAP!

In the eighteenth century, they finally worked out that your brain sends messages down your nerves using electricity. This was big news, especially for a *dottore* (that's Italian for 'doctor' – I'm so kind, I'm teaching you languages too!) called Giovanni Aldini, who decided that he should use this exciting new discovery to . . . bring people back to life. He teamed up with a few blokes who'd had a really rubbish day. In fact, they'd just had their heads chopped off for being criminals. Aldini zapped electricity down the nerves in the dead men's spinal cords and their limbs twitched, because their arms and legs mistook this electricity for the electrical messages the brain would usually send them.

So, did these people come back to life? Well, no. Which is good because it would be pretty scary to have a bunch of headless criminals running around, smashing into you. But when a young author called Mary Shelley heard about these experiments, she was inspired to write a terrifying book about creating a monster from old body parts, using electricity to bring them to life. Do you know what it was called? That's right – *The Very Hungry Caterpillar*. Sorry, I mean *Frankenstein*.

HEADBUMPOLOGY

You know how sometimes literally **EVERYONE** is playing the same computer game or coming to school with the same gadget or toy that you absolutely must, must, must have?! And then the next minute everyone's forgotten about it and moved on to something new? This happens to adults as well – remember that exercise bike your dad used once, or the month when there was a bread maker in the kitchen?

Well, it's been going on for centuries and centuries. Two hundred years ago, everyone was into something called phrenology. Phrenology was a fancy name for when people would try to discover things about you by feeling bumps on your skull – so it should really have been called headbumpology. Phrenology fanatics thought these lumps were there because they'd been pushed out of place by super-large parts of your brain, and they claimed that by feeling your head they could tell things about your personality, or even predict the future: for example, if you were going to fall in love, or fall in a pond.

We've all got lumps on our head (go on, have a feel. Of your own, I mean – not your teacher's), but these bumpy bits have absolutely nothing to do with our brain, or our personality, or our future. In other words, phrenology was a load of poo. And not even a small load of poo, like a bird might splat on a car. I mean a **HUGE** load of poo, like if a lorry full of manure skidded on a roundabout and it all poured out and totally covered twelve houses.

Please can you stop writing these disgusting sentences. No one will want to read a book like this, you hideous monster. Prunella

But in those days patients couldn't just google 'Is phrenology a big load of nonsense?' so they ended up believing it. Some grown-ups weren't allowed to start a new job unless a phrenologist had scanned their scalp to see if they were trustworthy or not. Pretty bad, right?

It gets worse. Phrenologists claimed they could tell if you were a criminal, or if you were going to be one in the future, and you could even be sent to prison for it! This would have been very bad news for me because my head's bumpier than a roller coaster in an earthquake.

1877
An American scientist called Harmon Northrop Morse (people really had much more interesting names in the olden days, didn't they?) invented paracetamol to help with headaches. And then, in 1878, people's uncles started telling the joke, 'Why aren't there any medicines in the jungle? Because the parrots eat 'em all.'

MENTAL HEALTH

It's very common to have problems with your mental health, and these days there are lots of people you can turn to for help. But we weren't always good at dealing with this kind of thing, to put it mildly. People wrongly believed that lots of mental health problems were caused by the moon, which is where the horrible word (that you should never use) 'lunatic' came from, because 'luna' means 'moon'. If someone had mental health problems, it was thought of as shameful – which we now know is ridiculous. Nobody today would ever be ashamed of having a broken arm or an infected tooth, and mental health problems are just like any other medical issue. But in the past, people would be sent to live in asylums.

These were awful places, and the people who lived there were treated very badly – some of the so-called cures for their illnesses basically involved beating them up or not letting them have any food. The doctors thought the shock of being treated so badly would cause any demons hiding in their bodies to leave. You won't be surprised to hear that this didn't work – mainly because demons aren't real. (Apologies to any demons reading this.)

To make it worse, people would even pay to come to asylums and stare at the patients – it was a top day out for them, like going to Alton Towers, except the queues were shorter at asylums and Alton Towers didn't exist in those days. Nothing like that would ever happen today, and it's really important to talk to an adult if you're ever worried about your mental health, or anyone else's.

In 1921, a German genius called Otto Loewi turned up and discovered something called neurotransmitters. You probably don't know much about neurotransmitters (unless you're Otto Loewi) but they're a **VERY** big deal. They're basically tiny chemicals that the brain uses to send messages between its cells – and too much or too little of these chemicals can affect your mental health, and how you feel and behave. Even better news came when other clever scientists developed medicines that could fix the levels of neurotransmitters in the brain.

These drugs, and talking therapies (where a trained specialist listens to problems and helps with them), meant that people with mental health problems didn't have to be locked away from the rest of the world. Obviously they shouldn't have been locked away in the first place, if you ask me, but I wasn't in charge of things then, annoyingly. One in four adults will have some kind of mental health problem every single year in the UK, so three cheers for modern treatments. Hip hip hooray! Hip hip hooray!

→ That's only two cheers, actually. Prunella

FANCY A SLICE OF BRAIN?

Brain surgery has been happening for a very, very long time. Brain surgery that actually **WORKS** is a much more recent invention though. Archaeologists think that brain surgery might be the first type of surgery that was ever performed. There are skulls of cavepeople born eight thousand years ago with holes drilled into them. Eight thousand years is *ages*. That's enough time to watch seventy million episodes of your favourite TV show. Although you might get bored after a few million.

The whole drilling-into-heads idea stuck around for centuries and was done for all sorts of reasons, from curing headaches to letting out evil spirits (which didn't exist in the first place). It even had a fancy name: trepanning. It was so common that in some graveyards they've found that more than one in ten people had holes drilled into their skulls. (My lawyer, Nigel, has asked me to point out that it's extremely important that you don't drill a hole into anyone's skull.)

AT LEAST YOUR HEADACHES HAVE CLEARED UP.

While over here in Europe we took a long time to come up with surgery any more complicated than that, in India they were miles ahead of the game. Over a thousand years ago, a king of India called Raja Bhoja was having terrible headaches, which his doctors thought might be caused by a lump in his brain. Not only was their diagnosis right, but they were able to cut into his skull to remove this lump – and he was totally cured! He went on to massively expand his kingdom, compose music and write about eighty books. Honestly, why did all these people write so many books? It makes me feel like such an underachiever.

Their books were probably a lot better than the rubbish you write too. Prunella

But not everyone was getting it right. In fact, a lot of what we've learned about the brain over the centuries comes from mistakes that happened during brain surgery. About seventy years ago, an American man called Henry Molaison was having terrible seizures, which means his body kept shaking. His doctors thought they could cure Henry's condition by removing part of his brain. Can you guess the slight problem with this plan? What if that part of the brain was . . . important? As it turns out, the bit the doctors removed was **EXTREMELY** important and, after the surgery, Henry suddenly couldn't make any new memories. If you told him something one day (or even splatted a cake in his face), he wouldn't remember it at all the next day. This was pretty bad news for Henry, but it meant that for the first time scientists knew which part of the brain was responsible for memories. When he died in 2008, his brain was sliced into thousands of tiny bits and every single piece was photographed and put on the internet. Interesting for scientists, I suppose, but to me it sounds like the most boring Instagram account ever. If my brain gets chopped up, I'd like the slices to be used as miniature frisbees.

45

BRAINFLIX

Dreams are pretty strange – they're like this TV show that happens in your own head while you're asleep – so it's not surprising that there have been some really weird explanations for them over the years. The Ancient Egyptians thought dreams were messages from the gods – and they'd even sleep in special dream-beds to encourage the gods to send them these magical WhatsApps. Other people throughout history thought that dreams were a way of predicting the future. King Xerxes of Persia kept having a dream that his army should invade Greece, so . . . he did.

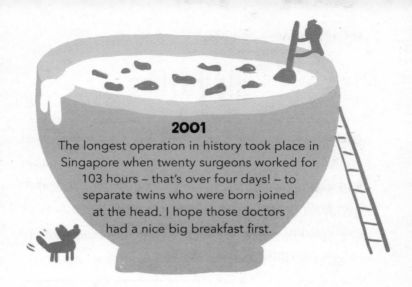

2001
The longest operation in history took place in Singapore when twenty surgeons worked for 103 hours – that's over four days! – to separate twins who were born joined at the head. I hope those doctors had a nice big breakfast first.

This went very badly wrong, which goes to show that you shouldn't just do things that happen while you're zzzz-ing. That's a big shame because I have this dream where I live in a house made of chocolate buttons and marshmallows, and it sounds dead fun. Anyway, the truth is that dreams aren't messages from gods or predictions about the future. They're much more boring than that – it's just your brain storing away things it learned during the day.

THE FUTURE

I'm sure your robot butler has got all the standard modules built in, like window washing, pizza cooking and cleaning dog poo off the carpet (thank goodness). I've just upgraded mine so he's now got a future-prediction module and can tell us what medicine's going to look like in the years to come.

PREDICTION 1 – PATIENTS WILL BE ABLE TO BEAM INSTRUCTIONS FROM THEIR BRAIN USING A NEURAL CONTROL INTERFACE.

Cool! I don't know about you, but I've always fancied being able to beam my thoughts into other people's heads. I'd be able to order a takeaway using my mind, or tell my dog, Pippin, to stop licking up that vomit she found on the pavement by sending her my *UGH STOP NO* brainwaves. (She'd probably still ignore me though.)

I don't know why they'd use such a boring-sounding name as Neural Control Interface for something so brilliant. I'd have called it the Brainwave Utilization Machine (or BUM).

Imagine being able to control machines using only your thoughts? Or downloading all your homework on to your computer directly out of your brain in one second? (You should probably check through it very carefully though, in case your brain was also busy thinking about how boring your teacher is.) Best of all, this technology could mean that people who are paralysed might be able to use their arms or legs in the future. Amazing!

PREDICTION 2 – YOU'RE HAVING PASTA FOR DINNER TONIGHT.

Oh, lovely! No mushrooms, thanks.

ADAM'S ANSWERS

HOW DID DOCTORS DISCOVER WHICH PART OF THE BRAIN CONTROLS YOUR PERSONALITY?

By accident! In 1848, a man called Phineas Gage had a really bad shift at work. He was on a building site, making a new railway, when – *BOOM!* – a massive explosion caused a huge metal pole to shoot all the way through his skull. Oops. Amazingly, he survived, even though the pole smooshed through a big chunk of his brain. One thing was very different though – his personality had totally changed from kind and charming (like me) to rude and moany (like you). This made scientists realize that the part of his brain that was damaged, known as the frontal lobe, had something to do with personality.

HOW DID A RECORD COMPANY HELP US UNDERSTAND THE BRAIN?

In the 1960s, a man called Godfrey Hounsfield was working at EMI, a company that made records for some of the biggest pop stars in the world, like the Beatles, the Beach Boys, and other bands that didn't begin with the letter B. Godfrey worked in the computer department there and one day clearly got a bit bored and wondered to himself if there was any way of doing a scan that looked inside the brain. A lot of fiddling and a bunch of experiments (on himself) later, he invented the CT scanner, which uses X-ray technology to show slices of any part of the body. It's still one of the main ways doctors look at the brain today.

WHY DO SOME PEOPLE HAVE THEIR HEADS FROZEN AFTER THEY DIE?

What a cheery question! Well, seeing as you asked, for the last fifty years, some people have believed in cryonics, which means freezing their chopped-off head after they die. The idea is that in the future, when science has got much more advanced, they can be brought back to life and their heads glued on to robot bodies or kept in a big jar or something. Unfortunately for these people, scientists are pretty certain there's never going to be any way to wake them up because all this does so much damage to the brain. Freezers are for ice creams, not heads.

TRUE OR POO?

OUR BRAINS ARE BIGGER THAN THOSE OF OUR ANCESTORS.

POO Yep, sorry about this. I know you probably think grown-ups are idiots (and, to be fair, a lot of them are), but their brains are actually bigger than yours – brains have slowly been getting smaller for thousands of years. And no, it's not because of all the TV you watch or because you don't eat your vegetables. Scientists don't actually know why it's happening, but the good news is that a smaller brain doesn't mean we're any less clever. In fact, smaller brains are often quicker at thinking, like a speedy little sports car is faster than a big old bin lorry.

DOCTORS TRIED TO TREAT MENTAL ILLNESS BY PULLING PATIENTS' TEETH OUT.

TRUE Horrifically, this didn't even happen a particularly long time ago – less than a hundred years in fact. Some doctors thought that mental illness was caused by infections hiding somewhere in the body, and they'd remove whatever they thought might have some lurgy lurking inside. Teeth, tonsils, stomachs and intestines would all get whipped out. Obviously it didn't help in the slightest, and over half of these poor people died as a result.

DOCTORS USED ELECTRICITY TO TREAT PAIN TWO THOUSAND YEARS AGO.

TRUE I'd forgive you for thinking this was an absolute load of poo because we didn't work out how to make electricity until about a couple of hundred years ago. But, thousands of years ago, doctors realized they could help pain in a patient's feet by pressing an electric eel on them. (That's right – they put eels onto heels.) Doctors still use electricity as a kind of pain relief today, but no slimy sea snakes are required.

I GET ALL THE WORST JOBS.

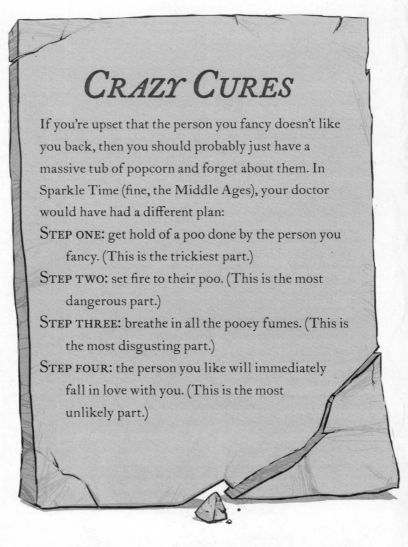

CRAZY CURES

If you're upset that the person you fancy doesn't like you back, then you should probably just have a massive tub of popcorn and forget about them. In Sparkle Time (fine, the Middle Ages), your doctor would have had a different plan:

STEP ONE: get hold of a poo done by the person you fancy. (This is the trickiest part.)

STEP TWO: set fire to their poo. (This is the most dangerous part.)

STEP THREE: breathe in all the pooey fumes. (This is the most disgusting part.)

STEP FOUR: the person you like will immediately fall in love with you. (This is the most unlikely part.)

(My lawyer, Nigel, has requested that you don't read the Crazy Cures sections at the end of each chapter.)

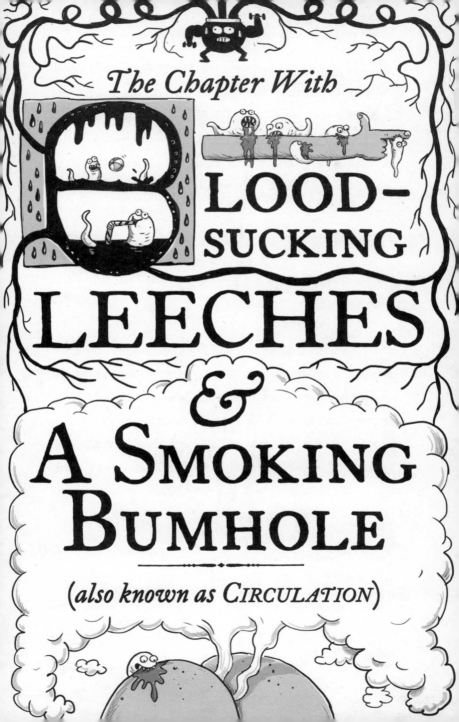

The Chapter With

Blood-Sucking Leeches & A Smoking Bumhole

(also known as CIRCULATION)

BY THE TIME YOU FINISH THIS SENTENCE, every single drop of blood you have will have gone on a complete circuit of your body. And – how about that? – it's gone all the way round again already. Your heart pumps blood through your arteries, and then the blood pops back to your heart through your veins, before whizzing off to your lungs to get some more scrumptious oxygen . . . and then the whole process starts again. I'm sure you know this already (or at least you should pretend to, if a teacher asks), but how did we get to knowing all this from knowing absolutely none of it?

Even though it took humans **AGES** to realize that the brain was anything more than a bunch of squidgy skull-stuffing, we've known the heart was useful for zillions of years (well, not quite zillions). It might have taken a bit of a while to figure out **EXACTLY** how it all worked in there, but we've known it was pretty crucial for the whole 'being alive' thing ever since we wore jeans made out of mammoth fur.

How did they know this so long ago? Well, let's imagine a sabre-toothed tiger decided to chomp off a bit of a caveperson for lunch. If it fancied an arm or an ear, that was pretty annoying for Mr Caveman, but it didn't mean it was time to measure him up for a coffin just yet. However, if our pointy-fanged friend thought the caveman's heart looked particularly tasty, it was definitely game over: no heart equals no life. Mrs Cavewoman would probably be quite upset, but Dr Caveperson would be thinking, *Hmm – that part of the body seems pretty important. Ugg.*

Luckily, there was still a little bit more to discover about the heart than that, otherwise this chapter would be extremely short. ⟶ *That's a shame — I wish this book was over already. Prunella*

ANCIENT EGYPT

Have you ever been given credit for something you didn't actually do? Like if your sister tidied the living room and you pretended that you did it? Well, for thousands of years, the heart got the credit for almost everything that happened in the body. The Ancient Egyptians noticed there were tubes coming off the heart going in all sorts of different directions, so they decided that it was responsible for moving around blood (yep!), spit (umm, nope), poo (what were they thinking?), the soul (is that even a thing?) and ghosts (umm, guys . . .).

But, to be fair to the Ancient Egyptians, they were the first people to realize that the pulse they could feel in people's wrists told them how fast the heart was beating. They also spotted that when people fainted their pulses

often got slower and harder to find, and that some illnesses made the heart get bigger and not work as well. Still doesn't make up for the whole 'poo goes through the heart' thing though.

You might remember that if you were important and royal enough to get turned into a mummy, then you'd have your heart plopped back into your body before you got wrapped up in kitchen roll. But getting into the afterlife wasn't as simple as that – the Ancient Egyptians believed the gods had to give a test first. *What sort of test?* you might wonder . . . Singing 'Happy Birthday' backwards in German? Swimming through a crocodile-infested swamp? Nope – the gods would weigh a person's heart and if it weighed more than a feather, then they wouldn't be allowed in. The Ancient Egyptian afterlife must have had hardly anybody in it – hearts weigh a lot more than a feather: they're usually as heavy as a big potato.

It's a bit pathetic it they don't remember – it was literally a few pages ago. Prunella

ANCIENT GREECE

Time to see what Aristotle made of the heart. Surely he could have a better guess about what it does other than pushing poo and spit round the body? Well, not really. He thought it sent air whooshing through your nerves and moved all your muscles, like the body was some kind of weird puppet. Very imaginative, but total drivel. And it turns out he wasn't very good at maths – he cut open a heart and claimed it had three chambers in it, even though it's got four. He's meant to be this super-genius, but he couldn't even count to four. Honestly.

And you're some kind of genius, are you? I know for a fact that you can't tie your shoelaces. Prunella

According to Aristotle, there wasn't much old hearty couldn't do. He reckoned it was in charge of all your thoughts and feelings, and was also a heater that kept the body going – like a massive fleshy radiator. Even weirder, he thought the cleverer you were, the more heat your heart would produce. Imagine if you wrote any of this in your science exam? They'd kick you out of school and make you wear a T-shirt that said I AM AN IDIOT.

I should get you one of those for Christmas. Prunella

ANCIENT ROME

You might be wondering why these people kept getting it wrong for hundreds of years. Well, in Ancient Rome, it was totally against the law for scientists to cut into the body of someone who'd died. Instead, they cut open dogs, pigs and monkeys, and just assumed that all creatures had the same inner workings. As you might have guessed, humans aren't the same as dogs. (I'm glad I'm not the same as Pippin, otherwise I'd spend all day eating slippers and rolling around in fox poo.) If humans and dogs really did have the same insides, you'd be able to go to the vet to get your broken arm fixed – and you'd never be able to eat a Twix because chocolate makes dogs really ill.

But, despite all this, the Ancient Romans did work out some important things about the heart – mostly thanks to a man called Galen.

PIPPUS
MAXIMUS

FOXUS POOUS

GALEN: FIVE FACTS AND A LIE

1. He wrote his first textbook when he was thirteen. So I hope you're planning to write one pretty soon . . .

2. The books he wrote contained over **TEN MILLION** words. That's more than ten times longer than everything lazy Shakespeare wrote (and two hundred times longer than this book).

3. One night, Galen's dad had a dream that said Galen should study medicine instead of philosophy, so Daddy Galen forced him.

4. His full name was Galen Xalen.

5. He was head doctor to the gladiators. (There wasn't much for him to do – you can't really help someone who's been turned into a human kebab by their opponent's sword.)

NEXT!

6. He invented a type of eye surgery that is still performed today.

4. We don't actually know his surname, only that his first name was Galen. Maybe he was one of those people who just have one name, like Adele or Pink or God.

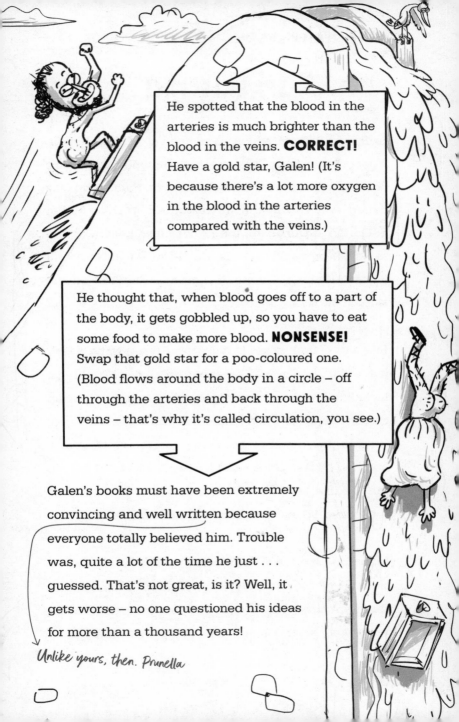

He spotted that the blood in the arteries is much brighter than the blood in the veins. **CORRECT!** Have a gold star, Galen! (It's because there's a lot more oxygen in the blood in the arteries compared with the veins.)

He thought that, when blood goes off to a part of the body, it gets gobbled up, so you have to eat some food to make more blood. **NONSENSE!** Swap that gold star for a poo-coloured one. (Blood flows around the body in a circle – off through the arteries and back through the veins – that's why it's called circulation, you see.)

Galen's books must have been extremely convincing and well written because everyone totally believed him. Trouble was, quite a lot of the time he just . . . guessed. That's not great, is it? Well, it gets worse – no one questioned his ideas for more than a thousand years!

Unlike yours, then. Prunella

SPARKLE TIME

In Sparkle Time (which some losers call the Middle Ages), a doctor in Syria started to wonder if Galen's heart theory wasn't quite right after all. Finally! He was called Ala-al-Din abu al-Hasan Ali ibn Abi-Hazm al-Qarshi al-Dimashqi, but he was also known as Ibn al-Nafis – probably because Ala-al-Din abu al-Hasan Ali ibn Abi-Hazm al-Qarshi al-Dimashqi didn't fit on the sign on his door.

Like a lot of brainboxes in those days, Ibn al-Nafis wasn't just a doctor – he was an expert in all sorts of things, including law and astronomy. It's good to have a backup career, I suppose. I'm not sure how Ibn al-Nafis had any time to see patients because he also wrote over a hundred books. (Once – just once – I'd like to be able to tell you about some doctor from the past who only wrote two books. I'd feel a lot better about myself then.)

In around 1250, Ibn al-Nafis totally worked out circulation. He realized the heart was connected to the lungs, that there are tiny vessels called capillaries between the veins and arteries, and he counted the number of chambers in the heart correctly. Hooray – bring out the party poppers! Unfortunately, Ibn al-Nafis' discoveries were soon forgotten about, and everyone went straight back to Galen's terrible ideas. Boo – put the party poppers away again.

It wasn't until 1924 that someone found one of his books and went, 'Whoops, this bloke worked it all out ages ago!'

You might have spotted that all the doctors a long time ago were men. That's not because women didn't want to be doctors, and it's not because women weren't just as good at medicine. It's because it was against the (extremely stupid) law. The church was worried that if too many people got cured by medicine then they would stop believing in prayer, so they said that any woman who healed someone was a witch and needed to be arrested. But this still didn't stop lots of wonderful women from helping patients. In 1322, a woman called Jacobina Félicie was put on trial in France for 'illegally' being a doctor. She called lots of her patients as witnesses, who said that she was much better than any of the male doctors in Paris. But she was still found guilty – ridiculous!

WILLIAM HARVEY

Let's fast-forward to the 1600s. Isaac Newton is busy discovering gravity by getting donked on the head by apples, Galileo is staring up into the sky to work out what the planets are up to, and Shakespeare is sitting at his desk, writing boring plays. Meanwhile, William Harvey was starting to wonder if Galen's theories were a load of nonsense. He thought it didn't sound quite right that your body immediately used up all the blood that flowed through it and you then had to make new blood out of food: if that was true, then everyone would have to eat about eight hundred hamburgers every lunchtime to stay alive. Nobody eats that much (if you're having

You can talk! This whole book is garbage Prunella

eight hundred hamburgers for lunch, I strongly advise you to cut down) and we don't all collapse because we've run out of blood, so he proved that Galen was making it all up. So that's a custard pie in the face for Galen.

WILLIAM HARVEY: FIVE FACTS AND A LIE

1. He lived in a huge treehouse in an oak at the bottom of his garden, so he could spend more time looking at wildlife.

2. He was the head doctor of a big hospital in London, and earned a salary of £33 per year. (That's the cost of four tins of Quality Street, so I hope chocolate was much cheaper then.)

3. He learned about the body by cutting people open, including his dad and his sister. (My lawyer, Nigel, asks me to mention that you shouldn't cut open any members of your family – however annoying they are.)

4. He saved the lives of lots of women who were on trial for being witches. He would cut up their supposedly magical toads in court to prove they were just standard boring toads, and so the women couldn't be witches.

I KNEW I SHOULDN'T HAVE WORN THIS HAT!

5. He became King James I's doctor, and his job title at the palace was Physician Extraordinary.

6. Loads of his discoveries were lost forever when his library was destroyed in the Great Fire of London in 1666. (He should have photocopied it – honestly, back up your work, Harvs.)

1. That's absolute rubbish, sorry. He lived in a normal, non-tree-based house.

As well as sussing out circulation, Harvey also realized why our veins have **VALVES** in them, which was previously a bit of a mystery. It's so the blood only flows in one direction, otherwise it would all end up sloshing back down our legs, and instead of feet we would have enormous balloons filled with blood.

He was so nervous about writing his discoveries down in a book that he didn't tell anyone about them for thirteen years. Why was he nervous? Maybe he was worried his handwriting wasn't neat enough and that everyone would make fun of him? Or perhaps he thought no one would buy his book because it didn't have enough jokes in it and his bedroom would end up full of boxes of unsold copies? Nope – in the past, people who suggested Galen might be wrong found themselves burned at the stake (seriously!) and Willz was in no hurry to get himself barbecued.

→ *like yours? Prunella*

RESTARTY HEARTY

Let's talk about cardiopulmonary resuscitation, or CPR as we call it if we're in a hurry. And if someone needs CPR then you're definitely in a hurry because it means their heart isn't beating properly. Eek. You've probably seen it on TV before, or maybe you've been taught it at school – it involves pressing down on the chest to get the heart working, and sometimes breathing into the person's lungs to give them oxygen. Presumably, as soon as doctors figured out circulation, they immediately invented CPR . . . Of course they didn't!

In fact, they got it really, really, really, really, really (please imagine another six thousand 'really's here) wrong. Instead of breathing into someone's mouth, they thought the answer was blowing smoke up their bumhole. Stop laughing – this is a serious textbook.

BUM
BELLOWS

BREAK GLASS
IN EMERGENCY

About three hundred years ago, if someone collapsed, then doctors would get a set of bellows (basically an old-school hand-operated pump) and a tube for . . . well, sticking up the bum. They'd then fill it with smoke and pump away. If that didn't work, they would blow smoke right into the person's mouth. I really hope they cleaned the tube first.

Strangest of all, this didn't only happen inside hospitals. Just like we now have defibrillators (machines that can restart people's hearts) in public places, back then they had these smoke-bum-pumps on the streets, just in case anyone collapsed outside.

And did it work? What do you think?!

→ This book is meant to be for children! Delete this whole section or you'll be sent to prison. And good riddance to you. Prunella

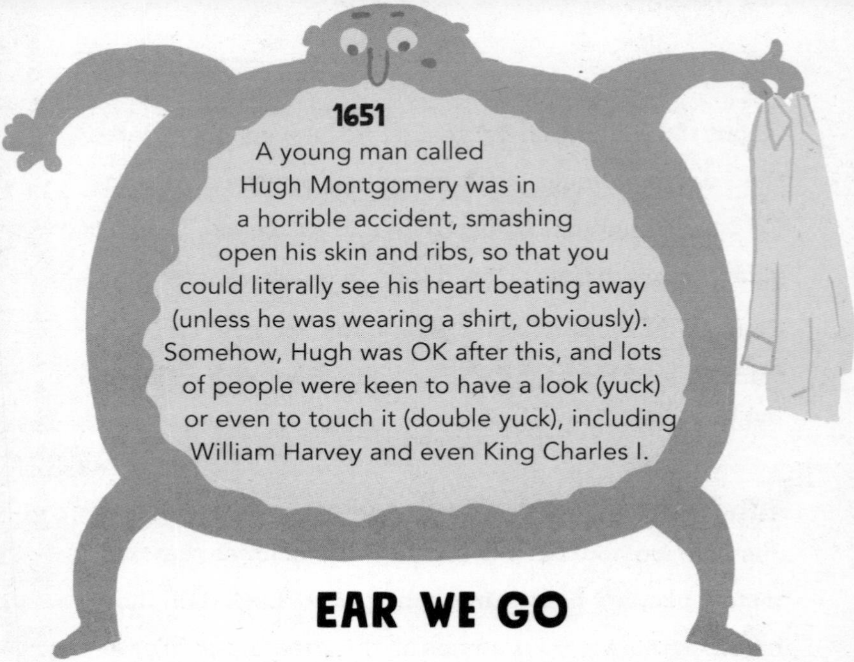

1651

A young man called
Hugh Montgomery was in
a horrible accident, smashing
open his skin and ribs, so that you
could literally see his heart beating away
(unless he was wearing a shirt, obviously).
Somehow, Hugh was OK after this, and lots
of people were keen to have a look (yuck)
or even to touch it (double yuck), including
William Harvey and even King Charles I.

EAR WE GO

You know the stethoscope – the Y-shaped thingamy doctors use to listen to your heart and your lungs and your other bits? The thing that makes you jump up twenty metres in the air because it's **SO COLD** when it touches your skin? (I would put mine in the freezer to use on patients I didn't like . . .)

Back in 1816, there was a French doctor called René-Théophile-Hyacinthe Laennec, or René to his friends. In those days, doctors didn't have any stethoscopes around their necks (or in their freezers) so, if they wanted to listen to the heart or the lungs, they'd have to just push their ear right up against the patient's skin. One day, René thought, *Well, that's a bit weird and disgusting, isn't it?* (in French) and decided to roll up a newspaper to listen to the patient's chest through that. *Blimey!* he thought (in French again) because he was suddenly able to hear the sounds much more clearly than before.

He must have reckoned that rolled-up newspaper didn't look professional enough, so he toddled off to his flute-making workshop (his hobby was making flutes – get a better hobby, mate). He made a tube from wood and metal, kind of like a really wide flute, and – hey presto! – the world's first stethoscope.

REPLACING THE RED STUFF

I'm not spilling any big medical secrets if I tell you that if you don't have enough blood in your body (for example, if you lose a lot in an accident or in an operation) then it can be extremely serious. Doctors have been attempting to replace lost blood since William Harvey's time. They've used all sorts of things to top up the body's blood supply, including beer, wine, milk, dog's blood and (in case you thought any of these ideas weren't ridiculous enough) wee. Unsurprisingly, none of these worked. At all.

→ If you don't stop talking about these fluids, then I will be writing to your mother. Prunella

ON SECOND THOUGHTS . . . DO YOU DO WEE?

Wilson Greatbatch invented a portable device that people could put on their chest to measure their heartbeat. Unfortunately, he made it slightly wrong and it ended up giving out electric shocks every second or two. No good at all for measuring heartbeats, but amazing for giving a regular heartbeat to people whose tickers can't tick properly on their own. He called it the pacemaker, and these days three million people in the world are walking around with pacemakers in their hearts. Not bad for something invented by accident!

In 1818, a doctor called James Blundell was called to see a woman who had lost lots of blood after having a baby. *I know!* he thought. *I'll replace the blood she's lost with some from her husband*, and he got to work, hooking them up together with tubes. Success! And, because taking-blood-from-one-person-and-giving-it-to-another was a bit tricky to say, this became known as a transfusion.

Very happy with his new miracle cure, he started using this method on lots of patients who'd lost blood. Unfortunately, it wasn't as big a miracle as he'd hoped – half his patients died from it. Oops. Exactly why this happened remained a bit of a mystery until nearly a hundred years later when, in 1900, Karl Landsteiner worked out that different people have different blood types. We now know that (if you want to stay alive) you need to have a transfusion of the same type of blood that you already have – otherwise it's like filling a car up with milk instead of petrol.

SQUIDGY SURGERY

If smoke started pouring out of my car, I'd probably open up the bonnet, stare inside for a few minutes, wondering what to do . . . and then close it again because it's way too complicated in there. That's how doctors felt about the heart for thousands of years. They thought it was impossible to operate on, and assumed that if they tried, it would result in a very dead patient and a very cross hospital cleaner, because there'd be blood all over the walls and the floor and the ceiling.

It wasn't until 1896 that a doctor called Ludwig Rehn did the first heart surgery, on a man who was extremely broken-hearted. And, by broken-hearted, I don't mean that he was sad. No, someone had stabbed him in the heart with a knife. Ludwig thought, *Well, if I don't do anything, he'll die*, so he got out his needle and thread and saved the patient's life. Today, over half a million open-heart operations are performed every single year and, yep, open-heart surgery is exactly what it sounds like – they open up the heart. Yuck.

LEECH TO THEIR OWN

For about two thousand years, if you went to the doctor about almost anything, the chances were they'd suggest bloodletting. *Letting your blood do what?* you might wonder. Answer: letting your blood slosh out of you and down the sink. That's right – they thought lots of problems were caused by having too much blood. Headache? Get rid of some blood. Fainted? Bloodletting time. A touch of the plague? *Splish splash splosh*. Whose idea was this? I'm not sure, but it sounds like something a vampire would come up with.

Different doctors had different ways of doing their bloodletting, some would use massive machetes and others would use sharp scalpels. And some would strap the patient into a special chair and let bloodsucking creatures called leeches get to work with their ugly, toothy jaws. One hospital in Manchester used over 50,000 leeches in a single year! And the Ancient Egyptians thought that leeches were a really good cure for farting. → *It's just as well you weren't around in those days – I've smelled your bedroom! Prunella*

Happily, bloodletting was a massive success and every single person who had it done was cured almost immediately. No, that's not quite right, actually. Bloodletting was a total disaster and literally millions of people died because of it.

So why did they keep doing it for so long? No idea, really. I guess they didn't have any other options. Or, obviously, they could have all been vampires.

OK, quick quiz. What links the following people: Pope Innocent VIII, King Charles II, Queen Anne, Mozart and President George Washington?

1. They were all in a pop group called the Beatles.
2. They all died after bloodletting.
3. They all ate swan's eggs for breakfast.

Here's a clue: this is the section about bloodletting. (It was 2. They all died after bloodletting.)

Luckily, as soon as doctors came up with actual cures for diseases, bloodletting became about as popular as jumping out of a plane without a parachute. But it took a long time for this to happen – in 1935, a medical textbook was still recommending bloodletting as a cure for things like asthma, infections and even sunstroke. Weirdly, leeches have come back into fashion though, and these days some doctors use them to help wounds heal. Cool, but also . . . yuck.

THE FUTURE

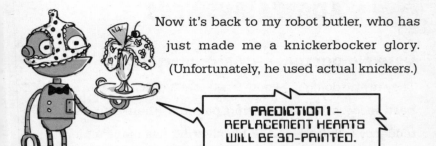

Now it's back to my robot butler, who has just made me a knickerbocker glory. (Unfortunately, he used actual knickers.)

PREDICTION 1 – REPLACEMENT HEARTS WILL BE 3D-PRINTED.

White-coat-wearing geniuses are currently working on this, using tissue taken from pigs. Before too long (but hopefully after this book comes out, otherwise I'll look like an idiot) it should be possible to make a brand-new heart from scratch in a lab, for people whose hearts have stopped working properly. This will be amazing, life-changing news for patients who are on a waiting list for a heart transplant. (My lawyer, Nigel, has asked me to mention that 3D-printing a heart using pig cells is much harder than it sounds, so you shouldn't try this at home by shoving a couple of sausages into your printer.)

PREDICTION 2 – CHRISTMAS WILL BE ON DECEMBER 25TH THIS YEAR.

That's not a particularly impressive prediction, to be honest.

ADAM'S ANSWERS

WHEN DID DOCTORS STOP BLOODLETTING?

They're still doing it! I know I said that it didn't have the best success rate at treating patients (thanks to its tendency to kill them), but bloodletting has made a bit of a comeback. It's only used for a couple of conditions though, such as polycythaemia, where your body makes too many red blood cells. (These days, they take the blood out very carefully, using a syringe: nobody's bleeding into a bowl.)

WHEN WAS THE FIRST HEART TRANSPLANT PERFORMED?

The first heart transplant was performed by a doctor called James Hardy in 1964 on a man whose heart had stopped working properly. Dr Hardy decided to replace it with a chimpanzee's heart and this . . . didn't work . . . at all. Three years later, in 1967, Dr Christiaan Barnard performed the first transplant using a human heart, which was a lot more successful. It went so well, in fact,

that heart transplants now save the lives of
thousands of people every single year.

HOW MUCH BLOOD CAN A LEECH DRINK IN A SINGLE MEAL?

About ten millilitres, which is a couple of teaspoons. It
might not sound much, but that's about ten times its
own weight. (I'm the same when I'm at an all-you-
can-eat buffet, to be honest.)

COOL!
INFINITE
REFILLS!

TRUE OR POO?

DRINKING BLOOD WAS A POPULAR TREATMENT IN ANCIENT ROME.

TRUE It didn't work, obviously, but they thought you could cure diseases such as epilepsy by having a delicious cup of warm blood. They reckoned the best blood to drink was from criminals, for some gross reason. Again, they could have been vampires, I guess.

PEOPLE WERE ALWAYS BURIED WITH THEIR HEARTS INSIDE THEIR BODIES.

POO In Sparkle Time (which I hope is what you're calling the Middle Ages by now), the heart was often buried in a different place to the rest of the body. Why have one funeral when you can have two, I guess? Sometimes a person would want their body to be buried in the same graveyard as their family, but for their heart to go in a place that meant a lot to them while they were alive. (I'd probably have my heart buried in the car park of my local Chinese restaurant.) There was another, slightly more disgusting reason why this happened: if someone died in battle miles and miles from home, their heart would be taken back home in a jar to keep it fresh, but their body would have to be left behind, otherwise it would decompose on the journey. And nobody wants their luggage covered in corpse juice, do they?

A DOCTOR WON A NOBEL PRIZE FOR OPERATING ON HIS OWN HEART.

TRUE In 1929, a German doctor called Werner Forssmann worked out a method of putting a tube directly into the heart, using a vein in his arm. He thought (correctly) that inserting a tube into the heart would be very useful for delivering certain types of drugs, but nobody had tried it before, and he was worried that it might instantly kill the person. So, instead of trying it out on a patient, he had a go on himself. And he immediately died. No! Come back! Stop crying! I'm joking – he was fine. It's a procedure that is still used all the time. (My lawyer, Nigel, advises you very strongly not to do any medical experiments on yourself, especially not on your heart. There is no guarantee that someone will award you a Nobel Prize for it.)

CRAZY CURES

In Ancient Egypt, they were big fans of the red stuff. Hair going grey? What you need is a lovely blood shampoo. Got an infection? Have a relaxing dip in a bright red bath of blood. Honestly, hadn't they heard of antibiotics? (Well, no, actually.)

The Chapter With

PLAGUES, POXES, PENICILLIN & A GIANT WORM THAT BURSTS OUT OF YOUR FACE

(also known as INFECTION)

I'M VERY HAPPY TO MAKE FUN of doctors in the past who thought the heart was a radiator, or nerves were controlled by ghosts, or that the brain was a load of useless stuffing – in fact, I've spent hundreds of pages doing it – but I can't be cross at them for not being able to figure out what caused infections, because bacteria and viruses are so tiny that they're totally invisible to the naked eye. (Why do we say 'naked eye'? It's not like eyes normally wear a shirt, trousers and a bobble hat.)

So, before microscopes were invented and doctors discovered these microscopic meanies, how did they deal with infections? Well, other than extremely badly. Let's find out. Or, if you couldn't care less, skip to the next chapter.

→ *I think I'll do that. Prunella*

MESOPOTAMIA

No, I haven't just made up a word. And no, it's not a part of the body, or a kind of soup – it's a place. Yes, I know you've never seen an advert for a weekend break in Mesopotamia. Yes, I know you've never watched an episode of *Mesopotamia's Got Talent*. But countries change their names over time. New York used to be called New Amsterdam and France used to be Gaul, and the place we now call Iraq used to be known as Mesopotamia.

You know how you sometimes have a really good idea, but no one listens to you, and you were totally right all along? Like when I had the brainwave that mushrooms should be made illegal, so I wrote to the government telling them to do it, and they totally ignored me, and now mushrooms are still being served up at dinner for people every day, even though they're totally disgusting and probably poisonous.

Well, back in 500 BC, doctors in Mesopotamia worked out the basics of infection. They didn't know about bacteria and viruses yet, but they did realize that if someone had an infection and you locked them away, then no one else would catch it.

They even realized that wounds healed faster if doctors washed their hands in a mixture of honey, alcohol and myrrh – basically the world's first handwash. Amazing! Except . . . this all got totally ignored and forgotten about for thousands of years. Instead, doctors came along who decided that infections were either some kind of punishment from the gods, or bad air wafting around, or the body being taken over by evil ghosts. Sigh.

ANCIENT EGYPT

If you lived in Ancient Egypt, then you probably had a pet that you took around everywhere with you. Not a dog like Pippin, who licks her own bum and then licks my face (ugh). Or even a pet like a baboon or a crocodile. No, a worm. The problem with this particular pet was you couldn't put it on a lead, or pose for selfies with it. Why? Because, unfortunately, it lived inside your body! Water in those days was contaminated with tiny worm eggs that would hatch inside whoever drank it, and then grow to about thirty centimetres long, which is about the length of a ruler (I mean a school ruler, not someone like Henry VIII or Tutankhamun). Eventually, these worms would decide it was time to make their way out of the body. Phew. But they didn't just get pooed out – they liked to burrow their way right through the body and burst out of places like the skin on someone's leg or the corner of their eye. Yuck, that's disgusting. I think I need to go in the garden now to get some fresh air – see you in a minute. Oh no. I saw a worm when I was in the garden and it reminded me of the ones that burst from people's eye sockets.

If doctors saw a worm coming out of someone, then they would wrap it round a twig, and twist it again and again until it all squirmed out – like you'd wind spaghetti round a fork. Thankfully, this kind of worm infestation is now pretty rare, but there are still a few cases of it every year. Sleep well!

SPARKLE TIME

I don't know if there's a prize for the most terrifying-sounding illness, but the Black Death has to be right up there, doesn't it? I mean it's got the word 'death' in it, for a start.

One day in 1347 a bunch of ships rocked up in Italy and all the sailors on it were either dead or covered in horrible pus-filled boils. The people standing on the harbour screamed, *'Aaaagh!'* (which is Italian for *'Aaaagh!'*), but it was too late because rats had already scampered off the ship, and those rats had fleas on them, and those fleas had plague-causing bacteria on them.

When someone became infected, they'd get a really high fever and big black swellings in their armpits or neck (hence the 'black' bit of the name), and then their fingers and toes would rot away, and then they'd vomit up blood, go into a coma and die (hence the 'death' bit of the name). Generally pretty unpleasant, I think you'll agree. You should never moan about having a slight sniffle ever again.

The Black Death swept through Europe, killing tens of millions of people: more than a third of the population. The main problem was that no one had worked out why it was spreading. Their best guess was that God had sent the plague to punish them, so they spent a lot of time trying to pray it away, or punishing themselves by whipping their own backs. They also lit lots of massive fires in an attempt to burn the bad air they thought was causing the disease. Unfortunately, none of this worked.

Eventually, the plague died out because of an idea called quarantine. If someone arrived in a country from somewhere else, they'd have to stay inside for forty days and would only be allowed out if they didn't develop the illness in that time. The word quarantine comes from *quaranta*, which is the Italian word for 'forty'. Next time an adult uses the word quarantine, see if they know that. (If they don't, then you're allowed to call them a massive ninny and make them sit in the corner for forty minutes.) Quarantine is still used, and it still works – it was one of the main ways that countries were able to control the coronavirus pandemic.

Like that terrible band whose music your parents always play in the car, the plague kept coming back out of retirement for one last tour. It reappeared loads of times over the next few hundred years, including the Great Plague of London in 1665. It wasn't that great, to be honest – if you ask me, it was actually pretty rubbish. All the rich people (including the king) fled London to their big homes in the country, so the plague mostly affected the poorer people who were left behind. Throughout history, and even to this day, it's a very sad fact that the people in the world who have the least suffer the most from illnesses.

Plague doctors plodded around London, offering totally useless treatments like bloodletting. There were two reasons they only offered useless treatments: firstly, there weren't any antibiotics yet; and secondly, they weren't even proper doctors – they were basically just blokes wandering about in terrifying costumes. They wore a black hat, a black cape and a mask like a pigeon's head with a really long beak that they put strong-smelling flowers inside, thinking (wrongly) that would protect them from illness. Plague doctors might not be around any more, but they still visit me in my nightmares at least once a week.

TB OR NOT TB

TB is this big black rectangle that sits in the corner of your living room that you can play computer games on, and where your parents can watch boring films full of people talking and crying. No, wait a minute, that's your TV. TB is the short name for tuberculosis, which is a bacterial infection that makes you cough up blood, have terrible fevers and sweats, and lose loads of weight. Oh, and unless you get antibiotics (which didn't exist for thousands of years), then it generally makes you die. Eek.

There are signs of TB in some of the oldest people archaeologists have discovered, such as prehistoric skeletons, Ancient Egyptian mummies and my Great Aunt Prunella.

Is this meant to be some kind of joke? Because it's not funny. In fact, none of your jokes are. Prunella

Old Hippoface wrote that it was the most common disease back in Ancient Greece, where he called it 'phthisis' – maybe he was trying to spit out a fly when someone asked him to name it? He thought it was passed down through families and there was nothing you could do about it, so just shrugged his shoulders if someone turned up in his clinic with it.

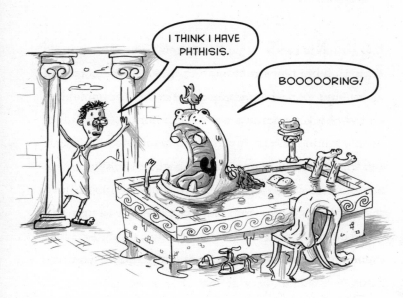

Later on, it became known as 'the white plague' because it made you turn really pale (with a splash of red, when your blood decided to escape from your mouth and go all over your cardigan) and other people called it 'consumption' because it made you go so thin that it was like your body was being **CONSUMED** by the disease.

TB was a huge problem all through Sparkle Time – it killed large numbers of people and no one had the faintest idea how it was spreading. It seems so obvious now, but I guess it's like watching a quiz show on TV – we all sit there, shouting out the answers from the comfort of our sofas (well, for the easy questions anyway), but it's much harder if you're a contestant in the studio with an audience watching you. And, because no one knew how TB was infecting people, there wasn't much doctors could do to stop it.

But there's always some know-it-all adult with a terrible idea about what to do. King Charles II thought that being king gave him magical powers and that he could cure someone simply by touching them. People queued up for miles round the palace to get some of his incredible kingly wizardry – but obviously it did absolutely nothing.

The microscope was invented by a man called Mike Roscope. OK, not really. In fact, no one actually knows for sure who invented it. Some people think that a man called Zacharias Janssen, whose job was making glasses, was playing around with his lenses and was suddenly like, 'Whoa, everything looks huge!' and then – *BOOM!* – one microscope. Other people think that a famous astronomer called Galileo was fiddling with his telescope and could suddenly see an insect's legs really clearly – maybe he just looked through the wrong end. Either way, someone was being silly at work, and accidentally changed science forever.

IT'S THE *JAB*SOLUTELY AMAZING INJECTION SECTION

Right, enough death and disease – it's time for some good news. In the 1700s, a disease called smallpox was sweeping through Europe, killing hundreds of millions of people – and those who survived would get really badly scarred. A doctor called Edward Jenner noticed that people who milked cows never seemed to catch smallpox, and decided to investigate why.

> Is this the good news? Doesn't sound like it. Prunella

His theory was that they caught a much less serious disease from the cows called cow pox, and this somehow protected them from getting smallpox.

There were loads of different types of poxes: chicken pox, monkey pox, rabbit pox, sheep pox, horse pox and mouse pox. Sadly, there wasn't fox pox, which is a shame because it would have been an extremely good name for an illness.

1721

Back in the awful days when black people were enslaved, a man called Onesimus was forced to work for a rich American called Cotton Mather, who lived in Boston. Onesimus explained to Mather that in Africa they used to prevent outbreaks of smallpox by injecting children with tiny doses of it. When smallpox swept through America in 1721, Mather told the city's doctors about Onesimus' idea, and it saved loads of lives. Onesimus never got credit for his idea during his lifetime, so the very least we can do is remember the brilliant work he did.

In 1796, Edward Jenner (I don't know if he was related to Kylie and Caitlyn Jenner, but let's just imagine he was) squeezed some pus from a blister on a milkmaid who had cow pox and injected it into his gardener's eight-year-old son, James. He then injected James with actual smallpox and . . . James didn't get sick! (That's the good news.) James had received a vaccine: an injection of something harmless that stops you getting a serious illness. Vaccines have saved literally hundreds of millions of lives since then, and the best thing of all is that they're made in a lab these days, instead of from disgusting blister-pus.

HARDER, BETTER, PASTEUR, STRONGER

Right, we're pages and pages into the chapter on infections and we've whizzed through thousands of years, but scientists still hadn't worked out what actually caused them. Here are just a few of their guesses:

- smelly air
- being cold
- wet feet
- lying down too much
- being angry
- staying up late (although maybe parents just made that one up to stop their children watching TV all night, or whatever they did instead of watching telly in the olden days. Looking at paintings?)

In 1856, a bloke called Louis Pasteur came along. He was a professor of chemistry who was doing some (pretty boring but apparently important) experiments on crystals. Yawn. But one day his mate, who owned a wine shop, asked Louis to investigate why his wine was going all manky. Louis took a break from his crystals and wondered if germs might be causing the disgusto-wine.

If so, he thought heating the wine up would kill off the nasties. And he was right – the wine was saved! He then realized that the germs in milk were causing people to get sick when they drank it, so he worked out a way of heating it up to make it safe. His method (which he called pasteurization – a bit boastful, Louis?) is still used today.

PROBLEM:

PASTEUR'S SOLUTION:

BOIL IT!

MANKY WINE

BOIL IT!

GROSS MILK

NEPHEW HAVING A FEW ISSUES AT SCHOOL

STOP BOILING EVERYTHING, PASTEUR!

Bethlem Hospital in London employed the
excellently named Robert Roberts as a bug catcher.
For three guineas a year (that's three gold coins, not
three guinea pigs), his job was to shake out all the patients'
mattresses and sweep up the lice and weevils and beetles
that flew out. Next time you're in a bad mood because
you've got to do some boring homework or eat
mushrooms or tidy your bedroom, just be
thankful that you're not a hospital bug catcher.

GROSSPITALS

If you have to go into hospital for any reason these days,
you know you're going to be looked after really well in
totally clean surroundings – but two hundred years ago
hospitals could actually make you sicker. They were so
filthy that rich people would pay loads of money to be
treated at home underneath their own duvets to avoid
catching any nasties in hospital.

You know the bit under your bed that never gets
hoovered? The bit with mountains of dirt and grime and
snotty old tissues and the legs of dead insects? That's
what a hospital looked like on a good day. Well, until an
amazing nurse called Florence Nightingale decided to
shake things up.

FLORENCE NIGHTINGALE: FIVE FACTS AND A LIE

1. She was known as the Lady with the Lamb because of an injured baby sheep she would always carry around with her.

2. She was named after the city she was born in – Florence in Italy.

3. Her sister was also named after the city she was born in, so got the slightly more unusual name of Parthenope.

4. She was the first woman (other than the queen) to have her picture on a UK banknote.

5. She hated having her photograph taken, and there are only a couple of photographs of her in existence. (She definitely wouldn't have used Instagram.)

6. She was a major maths whizz and developed a new type of pie chart. (That's a way to show data using pictures, not a poster with loads of different pies on it, by the way.)

1. Cute as that sounds, she was actually known as the Lady with the Lamp because she would walk around the hospital at night when the other staff had gone to bed, holding a lamp and checking up on all her patients.

Florence was born in 1820 into a rich family – she described the holiday home her parents owned as 'a small house with only fifteen bedrooms'. She knew from a very young age that she wanted to help people. After she trained as a nurse, Flo went off to work in a hospital in what is now called Turkey, where British soldiers were fighting in the Crimean War.

She was shocked that nearly half of the patients in the hospital there were dying, mostly because of infection, and she was sure it was because of terrible hygiene. She arranged for a new hospital to be built that was much cleaner, and introduced extremely strict rules about hand-washing. And it worked! Previously, half of all the patients were dying, and suddenly only two out of a hundred were.

When she came back to England, she set up the first-ever nursing school and wrote the first-ever book about how to be a nurse. Today there are *loads* of hospitals named after her, a fleet of aeroplanes that transport sick patients, the highest honour in nursing and even an asteroid. That's all **QUITE** impressive, but if you burp and fart at the same time it's known as 'doing an Adam Kay', which I think is much better.

SPOILSPORT!

1855

Another nurse who saved hundreds of lives in the Crimean War was Mary Seacole. Mary was born in Jamaica in 1805, before moving to London and volunteering to help in the war. She was an expert in treating infections like cholera and yellow fever, and was famous for riding out into battlefields to help wounded soldiers, so they could get treated as soon as possible. She cared for so many soldiers that she became known as Mother Seacole. (This is a bit unfair, because when I was a doctor, my patients never called me Daddy Adam.)

JAMES BARRY

There was a brilliant doctor in the 1800s called James Barry, who worked in the British Army as the Inspector General of Hospitals, going from country to country and improving the hygiene conditions on the wards, to stop patients dying from infections. It was only when Dr Barry died that it was discovered they were born a woman, and lived as a man partly because otherwise they wouldn't have been allowed to work as a doctor.

MARVELLOUS, MIRACULOUS MOULD

I do a lot of things by accident. There was the time I put my phone in the tumble dryer and it never worked again (but smelled lovely). And there was the time I was staying with my Great Aunt Prunella and accidentally spilled my milkshake into her piano. Or the time I left my birthday cake on a low table that Pippin could reach, and she ate the whole thing and had terrible diarrhoea for two days (and I didn't get any birthday cake – I'm still upset about that).

→ That was you?! It cost me a fortune to get that cleaned out. You total dunderhead. Prunella

But it's fair to say that none of those things changed the history of the world. In 1928, a Scottish scientist called Alexander Fleming was in a bit of a rush to go off on holiday, so he didn't tidy away some little dishes full of bacteria that he'd been growing for an experiment.

He came back a couple of weeks later with a suntan and a Mickey Mouse T-shirt (I'm not sure if he went to Disneyland, actually – maybe not because it hadn't been built yet) and there was some mould growing on his dishes of bacteria.

So far so boring – mould grows on stuff if you leave it out for too long. Take a look at the socks on your bedroom floor if you need any proof. But A-Flem noticed something weird. No, not about your socks – about his dishes of bacteria. There was no bacteria whatsoever growing around the mould – it was producing a substance that killed bacteria. And he named it . . . mould juice. Luckily, he soon realized that didn't sound particularly scientific or make him seem very brainy, so he came up with a new name: penicillin. This was the first-ever antibiotic, which means a drug that kills bacteria. He won a Nobel Prize for this – and fair enough really, because it has now saved hundreds of millions of lives. Just think of all the people who could have been saved throughout this chapter if antibiotics had been around to treat people with TB and the Black Death and so many other awful illnesses.

1965

If you're on holiday in Australia and going for a swim in a lake, what's the worst creature you think you could come across? A crocodile the size of a car? Wrong. A great white shark with three hundred teeth, each one as sharp as a knife? Nope. It's much smaller than either of those – it's actually five times thinner than a single hair. I'd like to introduce you to the brain-eating amoeba. It swims up your nose and it . . . well, you can probably guess the rest. The good news is infections from these amoebas are extremely rare – it was first discovered in 1965 and there have only been a few cases since then. You're more likely to win the lottery, then immediately get struck by lightning.

THE FUTURE

Prediction time now, from my robot butler, who just finished emptying the bins (unfortunately, he emptied them all onto the sofa).

PREDICTION 1 – ANTIBIOTICS WILL STOP WORKING.

The more you use antibiotics, the less powerful they become. You know, like how if you say 'bum' once then it's a bit shocking, but if you say it all the time it isn't as effective. Or how one slice of chocolate cake is delicious, but four hundred and thirty-five slices are . . . a bit much.

Already, there are some antibiotics that have stopped being effective, and the worry is that one day all antibiotics will stop working, and it'll be just like they'd never been discovered in the first place. But don't panic: there are things we can do to stop this from happening.

First of all, antibiotics should **ONLY** be taken by people who really need them – that's for bacterial infections, not viruses or sniffles or bumsquirts. And if you're prescribed a course of antibiotics, then it's really important to take the whole lot because stopping after a few days can help bacteria become resistant to them. And, most importantly, try not to get yourself or other people ill in the first place. You can do simple things to avoid getting sick like washing your hands, blowing your nose into a tissue, and not drinking from the toilet bowl. (That last one is mainly for Pippin.)

PREDICTION 2 –
THE NEXT CHAPTER
IS MOSTLY
ABOUT POO.

I like the sound of it already.

ADAM'S ANSWERS

WHY DO WE SAY WE'RE FEELING LOUSY?

You know how sometimes your throat feels like you've been gargling drawing pins? Or your head feels like a baby hippo sat on it? Some people say when they're ill that they feel 'lousy'. They've been saying this for hundreds of years, and it used to mean that lice were literally crawling all over their body. Did you scratch yourself when you read that sentence? Me too.

WHICH NURSERY RHYME IS ABOUT THE PLAGUE?

'Baa Baa Black Death'? 'Mary Had a Little Plague'? Well, some people think it's actually 'Ring-a-ring of Roses'. Let's have a quick singalong:

Ring-a-ring of roses (A rosy-red rash that people got when they had the plague.)

A pocket full of posies (Posies were flowers that people carried around, hoping that the smell would stop any infection.)

Atishoo! Atishoo! (Sneezing from the illness.)

We all fall down! (And now it's killed you. Oops.)

Other people think it's just a silly rhyme that doesn't have anything to do with the plague, so I'll leave it to you to decide.

DID ARMIES EVER USE INFECTIONS AS WEAPONS?

They did indeed. Thousands of years ago, soldiers would dip the ends of their arrows into poo so that it was more likely that the person they shot would die from an infection. And in Sparkle Time, if they couldn't get into a city, they would sometimes catapult the body of someone who had died of plague over the walls, to kill off a bunch of people inside. (My lawyer, Nigel, has asked me to point out that it's both illegal and dangerous to catapult a plague victim's body into your enemy's back garden.)

TRUE OR POO?

RABBITS CAN TELL IF YOU'VE GOT AN INFECTION.

POO Rabbits don't know if you've got an infection, but dogs do! (Well, not all dogs. Pippin can't even tell the difference between grass and carpet, so she regularly poos on my bedroom floor.) But some very clever dogs (no offence, Pippin) have been trained to sniff out if a patient has a disease such as malaria, which is transmitted by mosquitoes. Good dog!

A DOCTOR SAVED THOUSANDS OF LIVES BY SNAPPING A HANDLE OFF A WATER PUMP.

TRUE In 1854, hundreds of people in London were dying from a disease called cholera, which caused terrible vomiting and diarrhoea. A doctor called John Snow realized that everyone who caught cholera had something in common – they got their water from one particular pump. Back in the 1800s, people didn't have taps in their houses, so if they wanted a bath, or a cup of tea, they had to go to a water pump and bring it home. John was really sure about his theory but, because germs weren't a thing that anyone knew about yet, no one really believed him. The other doctors thought that cholera was actually caused by eating 'cold fruit' like melons and cucumbers. (What?!) But John wasn't having any of it, so he snapped the handle off the water pump so no one else could get any water from it and – ta-da! – there were no more new cases of cholera. If you're ever in central London, you can visit the pump on what's now called Broadwick Street. And they still haven't put the handle back on – better safe than sorry.

SOME INFECTIONS MAKE YOU SMILE.

TRUE There's a disease called tetanus, which people get by cutting themselves on a rusty nail or being bitten by an animal. It causes muscles in your body to tighten up, and this can affect the face, causing a constant big smile – a bit like the Joker in Batman, or Pippin when she finds a huge muddy puddle to jump in. There's nothing at all funny about tetanus though: if you hurt yourself like this, it's important to be checked by a doctor, in case they need to give you a jab to stop you getting ill.

CRAZY CURES

Got a bit of Black Death? Before antibiotics, there wasn't a whole lot that could be done, but this didn't stop doctors trying. One particular favourite was to take a live chicken, pluck all the feathers out of its bottom, then press the chicken on the patient's swollen armpit. It was said to be particularly important to centre the chicken's bumhole on the middle of the armpit. Unfortunately, this didn't do anything useful whatsoever for the patient (or the chicken).

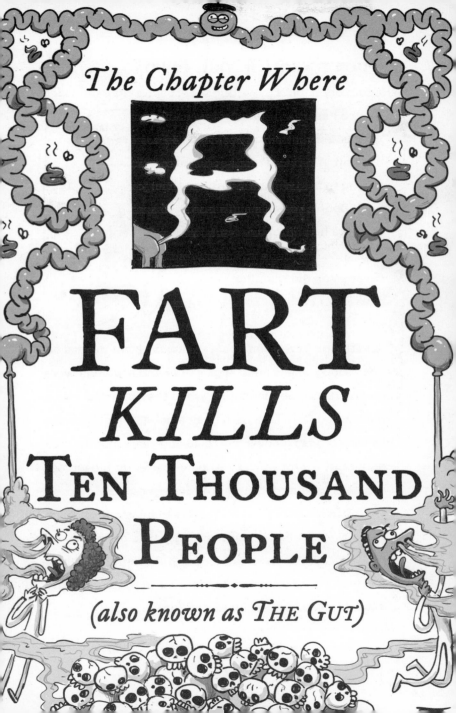

I DON'T KNOW IF THIS COUNTS as too much information, but I'm writing this chapter from the toilet.

Maybe I shouldn't have warmed up that leftover pasta for lunch after all. Anyway, I'm not the first person to have tummy trouble, and I definitely won't be the last. Humans have been obsessed with their guts ever since the first caveperson did their first cave-poo.

FINALLY, UG HAVE FRIEND.

And things have been going wrong with our insides for just as long. A few years ago, a man and a woman were on holiday in the mountains when they bumped into a man called Otzi. Otzi didn't say much to them because he'd been dead for over five thousand years, but the cold temperatures meant he had been perfectly preserved. Scientists examined him and discovered that he had worms in his intestines and ulcers in his stomach. Poor Otzi. (Not sure how they knew that was his name, by the way. Maybe he was holding his driving licence?) Anyway, I'd better get off the loo and tell you about the toilet habits of the Ancient Egyptians.

→ That's disgusting. You horrible boy. Rewrite this section when you are not on the toilet. Prunella

ANCIENT EGYPT

They may not have known that much about the body, but even the Ancient Egyptians knew that poo came out of their bums. (Although it must have been a bit of a surprise for the first person that it ever happened to. They probably screamed, '*Aaaagh!* What's going on?! Why is this brown stinky snake squirting out of my body?! Call an ambulance!')

They definitely realized the guts were important because, when someone was mummified, their guts were popped into a special jar for a safe journey to the afterlife. They even had a special god who protected the guts on this journey, called Qebehsenuef. I bet Qebehsenuef was annoyed that all the other gods had cool things like the heart and the lungs to look after, and he just got a pot of pooey intestines.

The Ancient Egyptians didn't **QUITE** understand what happened to food when it went into your body to be digested though. For a start, they thought that food travelled to your heart through a series of tubes, then went down to your bumhole. (Or anus, if you want me to use proper doctory words. Which would be fair enough because I'm a trained doctor.) It seems the pharaohs and their friends got the heart and the stomach mixed up there. They reckoned the best way to treat stomach ache was by wearing a special kind of necklace, with words of encouragement written on it. I can confirm that wearing a necklace does not cure tummy ache, in case you somehow thought writing YOU CAN DO IT! on your great aunt's pearls might sort out your diarrhoea.

> Don't you dare lay your grubby hands on my jewellery. Prunella

They did get some stuff right though. For example, they invented toothpaste! It didn't have nice stripes in it, and it probably tasted disgusting because it was made of crushed-up bits of rock, salt, pepper and mint, but at least they tried. And if you had toothache? Well, they treated it by shoving a dead mouse in your mouth. I'd stick to taking Calpol and lying in bed reading comics, personally.

ANCIENT GREECE

You know how, if you ever vomit up your food, it's become a horrific soup, like a blended version of your breakfast? We now understand that's because acid in the stomach has melted it, but the Ancient Greeks thought that the stomach cooked it. Kind of like a mini-oven installed inside your abdomen.

They also thought that emotions came from the gut – maybe they noticed that if they were really worried about something then they got bumsquirts and assumed it must be their gut that was getting worried. It's why we still say we have 'a gut feeling' about things, or we 'feel gutted' if something goes wrong. Once again, those Greeks were giving random parts of the body credit for stuff that the brain does. Poor brain.

I thought this was meant to be a serious textbook. Please use sensible words like 'diarrhoea' not vulgarities like 'bumsquirts'. Honestly. Prunella

The Ancient Greeks were among the first people to do bum surgery. They were particularly interested in a condition called haemorrhoids, also known as piles, which are little balls of muscle and blood vessels that look like grapes (sorry if you're eating grapes) and poke out of the bumhole, making things very sore down there. Old Hippoface, Hippocrates, came up with an operation to get rid of them. He would heat up a metal rod in a furnace until it was white-hot, then stick it on the haemorrhoids until they burned off. It worked, but I suppose you would have to decide whether it was better to have haemorrhoids or to be screaming in agony while your bumhole sizzled like a sausage.

ANCIENT ROME

As you'll remember from the chapter on circulation (unless you've got a hole in your brain), Galen had this incredible (and incredibly wrong) theory that all the blood in your body came straight from food. According to Galen, you ate food, it went into some kind of magic turning-food-into-blood device and then . . . *ping!* Lots of lovely new blood. Hmm, not exactly how it works though, is it?

He also wrote quite a lot in his books about farting. Who can blame him? So do I! But unlike me (hopefully, otherwise you'll fail all your exams) Galen got it all totally wrong. For example, he thought that you cured farting by reading out loud, which is a big load of farty nonsense.

. . . THEN STIR ALL THE BEANS IN A BIG POT, AND ADD SOME MORE BEANS AND . . .

1000 BEAN RECIPES

SPARKLE TIME

In Sparkle Time (or the Middle Ages, if you insist on using its terrible former name for some reason), they still thought the stomach was some kind of weird internal microwave.

But they did notice that the more stuff you shoved into your mouth, the bigger you would become. One day, King William I, also known as William the Conqueror, also known as Wee Willie Conk (well, he's only known as that to me), realized that he couldn't fit on his horse any more. To the relief of his horse, he asked his doctor how to lose a bit of weight. The doctor suggested that he should probably stop eating so much.

I DON'T UNDERSTAND WHY IT'S NOT WORKING . . .

'Perfect,' said Wee Willie Conk. 'I'll just lie in bed all day and not eat anything at all. In fact, I'll just drink wine constantly.' His doctor was probably worried by this plan, but it's a bit difficult to tell the king what to do, if you like your head still attached to your body, so he couldn't really say anything much. (My lawyer, Nigel, has asked me to point out that you shouldn't lie in bed all day and you **DEFINITELY** shouldn't drink wine all day.) Anyway, this weird diet somehow worked, and soon Willie was able to ride his horse again. It turns out he shouldn't have bothered because one morning he fell off his horse, his intestines exploded and he died. Whoops.

Fast-forward a hundred years and the king's a bloke called Henry. You might think of kings as boring people who just wear crowns and sign things with quills, but Henry was . . . How do I put this? Henry was . . . extremely interested in farting. He even employed a full-time jester called Roland the Farter. No prizes for guessing what Roland the Farter's party trick was. Yep, exactly. And Henry rewarded him for his excellent bum-work by giving him an enormous manor house and huge amounts of land. (If getting paid for farting was still a thing, Pippin would be the richest dog in the entire world.)

→ This is the worst book I've ever read. I recommend you delete it all and write about nice things instead, such as walks along the river and flower arranging. Prunella

GUFF TOWERS

1666

The Great Plague was sweeping through London, killing thousands of people, but doctors didn't understand about infections yet so they thought it was because of some kind of evil mist spreading through the air. And how did they suggest that people stayed plague-free? Well, everyone was advised to fart in a jar and, if anyone nearby caught the plague, then they should open the jar. They thought the bum-gas would basically beat up the plague-gas and everything would be OK. It's hard to count the number of things they got wrong with this idea, but I'm going with eight million.

BUMS AND BUZZARDS

It's now 1780 and not much has been discovered about your poo-making machinery for hundreds and hundreds of years. Luckily, an Italian whizz-kid called Lazzaro Spallanzani was about to shake things up. Spallanzani realized the stomach wasn't a weird oven or one of those big pepper grinders in Italian restaurants, but actually worked by squirting acid onto food, and that's what dissolved it! He called stomach acid 'gastric juice', which sounds a lot more delicious than it actually is.

SPALLANZANI: FIVE FACTS AND A LIE

1. As well as being a scientist, Spallanzani was also a priest and the boss of a museum.

2. He discovered that bats fly around using their ears to work out where they're going rather than their eyes. He took his pet owl (who even has a pet owl?! The olden days were crazy) and a few bats and made them fly round an obstacle course in the pitch-dark. The owl was useless, and the bats thought it was the easiest thing in the world.

3. The word zany, meaning 'crazy', comes from Spallan**ZANI** because everyone thought his ideas were so weird.

4. The first scientific paper he wrote was all about skimming stones: when you throw a rock onto the water and it bounces a few times before sploshing underwater. Luckily, he got bored with researching stones and moved on to humans.

5. Before Spallanzani, people believed that tiny insects could appear out of nowhere, from dust, which was known as spontaneous generation. Spallanzani said, 'Spontaneous poo, more like,' and proved it was a load of old twaddle.

6. He played a trick on another professor by glueing two halves of different animals together and leaving it in his office. The professor thought he'd discovered an incredible new species and published a paper about it – and then Spallanzani revealed it was all a joke. (Pranks were a bit rubbish in those days.)

3. Zany is nothing to do with Spallanzani, but actually comes from a different Italian word – 'Zanni' was a type of clown who wore a mask. Sounds more terrifying than crazy to me . . .

In case people weren't convinced by Spallanzani's theory about gastric juice, a French scientist called René de Réaumur did an experiment to prove it using his pet buzzard. Seriously, why did everyone have such weird pets? What's wrong with having a dog? (Well, I suppose my one vomits everywhere, then licks it straight back up.)

René didn't write down what the buzzard was called, so I'll assume she was called Buzzé. René fed Buzzé a diet of sponges on a string for breakfast, lunch and supper. After the sponge had been down in Buzzé's stomach for a while, René would pull on the string, and the sponge would come back out of Buzzé's beak, full of juice. And how did he prove that this stinky stomach liquid digested food? Well, he squeezed it onto a lump of raw meat and watched the meat dissolve away. Everyone in France

was so impressed with his experiment that they named a station in Paris after him. (Sadly, nothing got named after poor Buzzé, even though she did all the hard work. Oh, unless she was actually called Eiffel . . .)

1822

You might have noticed that quite a lot of important discoveries in medicine happened because someone got a horrible injury. Well, here we go again – Alexis St Martin was minding his own business one day when he got shot in the stomach: how rude! Miraculously, he survived, but the wound didn't heal very well, to say the least: he was left with a massive hole going from the outside world to the middle of his stomach. If he ate a biscuit and leaned forward, it would go down into his stomach, then fall out onto the floor – what a waste of a Jammie Dodger!

Fascinated by this hole in Alexis's tummy, a doctor called William Beaumont hired Alexis to be his servant – for duties including chopping wood, carrying the shopping and . . . having hideous experiments performed on him. Beaumont carried out over two hundred experiments on Alexis, one of which involved Dr Beaumont licking the inside of his stomach. Excuse me for a second while I'm sick. OK, I'm back now. Anyway, the main benefit from all this disgustingness is that Dr Beaumont made lots of important discoveries, including that the stomach produces more acid when there's food inside it.

IMPORTANT – please do **NOT** read this section out at mealtimes. In 1887, a man appeared onstage in France called Le Pétomane, which means the Fartmaniac. He could do a lot of incredible bum-based tricks, such as squirting a jet of water out of his bumhole and into the audience, farting the tune of the French national anthem, blowing out a candle with his farts, and singing 'Old Macdonald had a Farm' (with special farts for all the animal sounds).

ALL GOOD THINGS MUST COME TO AN ENDOSCOPE

These days, if a doctor is worried about a patient's stomach or intestines, they might use something called an endoscope to look inside. It's basically a tiny camera on the end of a thin, bendy tube that allows them to see your innards on a screen, like a particularly boring TV show. Before clever technology like video cameras and fibre-optic cables came along, doctors could only use straight tubes because it's impossible to see round corners. (Unless you're an alien. You're not, are you?) Unfortunately, this meant there was no way they could look down into someone's stomach because the throat and oesophagus are so bendy.

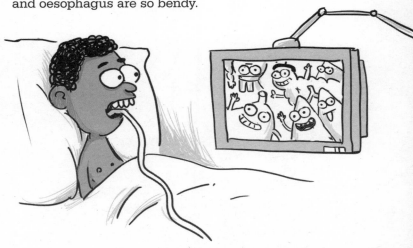

In 1868, a German doctor called Adolph Kussmaul was having a lovely night out at the theatre, watching a sword swallower, when he suddenly thought: *I know! I'll ask the sword swallower how he does this, and then I can build an endoscope that looks into the stomach!* All the other people at the theatre probably looked at him and said, 'Shh! We're trying to watch the show here!'

By then, doctors had pretty much sussed out how our guts work and the textbooks weren't too different from the ones today – although they were a lot more boring. I looked at one that had 227 pages about haemorrhoids, those bum-grapes I told you about before.

→ Sounds a lot better than this book. *Prunella*

2014

Ninety cows were hanging out in a shed in Germany, farting away happily, when the amount of fart gas in the air got so high that . . . *BOOM!* The entire place exploded. We already knew that farts were flammable, but this is the first time they'd blown up a building.

SOME WORDS ABOUT TURDS

I couldn't write a whole chapter on the gut and not have a section on poo. If I did, I'm pretty sure you'd ask for a refund, and who could blame you? Poo obviously hasn't changed much over the years – still brown, still smelly – although what we do with it has changed **A LOT**. These days, we flush it away, but in the past they used poo as medicine . . . In Ancient Egypt, your doctor would prescribe it for pretty much anything. Headache? Eat some poo. Rash? Smear some poo on it. Struggling to get pregnant? Eat some more poo. I just hope these doctors also prescribed breath mints for afterwards.

At least poo isn't involved in medicine today. Phew! Oh no, hang on – it is. There's a type of infection in the intestines that antibiotics can't always treat, and doctors realized that if they put a small pellet of poo from a healthy person into the intestines of the ill person, then it can get rid of the infection. This is called 'faecal transplantation' because if it was called 'prescribing poo' then doctors might burst out laughing in front of their patients.

THE FUTURE

Now let's hear what my robot butler has to say about the future. He's just changed my bed – unfortunately, he changed it into a wheelbarrow.

PREDICTION 1 – THERE WILL BE SURGEONS YOU CAN SWALLOW.

Until very recently, if a doctor wanted to look inside your intestines, they'd need to stick a tube inside and do an endoscopy. Obviously this wasn't particularly fun for the patient, so scientists came up with the idea of a tiny tablet that you swallow. It swims around in your innards like it's at a water park, taking hundreds of photographs, until you eventually poo it out. Much easier and much more comfortable – you just have to remember not to flush it away. In a hundred years, scientists will have worked out a way for these tiny capsules to perform actual operations, so doctors can do surgery on your intestines, and all you'll have to do is swallow a miniature remote-controlled robot.

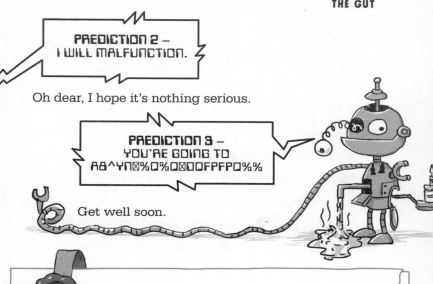

**PREDICTION 2 –
I WILL MALFUNCTION.**

Oh dear, I hope it's nothing serious.

**PREDICTION 3 –
YOU'RE GOING TO
A8^YΠ⊠%□%□⊠□□FPFP□%%**

Get well soon.

ADAM'S ANSWERS

HOW DID DOCTORS USE TO SEW UP INTESTINES?

The first records we have of doctors sewing up people's guts are in books from India about three thousand years ago. Did they use cotton thread? Bronze wire, maybe? Or did they get giant ants, make them clamp their jaws over the wound, then twist off their bodies, leaving a line of decapitated ant heads along the wound? Yep – you guessed it! They'd basically invented a kind of staple made from ants. Surgeons still use staples to stitch intestines today (although these days no ants get decapitated in the process).

HOW DID A FART KILL
TEN THOUSAND PEOPLE?

And you thought **YOUR** farts were bad – the worst they
do is make everyone hold their nose and leave the room.
(And maybe the odd bit of vomiting.) In Jerusalem, a
couple of thousand years ago, a Roman soldier killed ten
thousand people with a single fart. No, they weren't
suffocated by its toxic stench – baked beans weren't on
sale yet. It happened because he pulled down his pants
and let out a huge fart at a crowd of people, who were
so insulted they started an enormous riot and loads of
people got injured. I guess the moral of this story is:
think before you fart.

WHAT'S THE GREAT STINK?

It's what doctors call your bum. It was also the name for
a couple of months in 1858 when there was so much poo
dumped into the River Thames that London became
unbelievably stinky and lots of people got ill because of
all the nasties in the water supply. It led to a new system
of sewers being built to stop poo from getting into
people's drinking water.

WHY DID THE ANCIENT ROMANS EAT LYING DOWN?

You might have seen pictures of emperors lounging about on massive sofas, while servants dropped grapes into their mouths. Well, it was basically because they were lazy and bossy, and wanted to show off that they were far too important to do things like shove food into their own gobs. Medically, there aren't any real benefits to it, so I'm afraid you can't demand dinner in bed every day and say it's doctor's orders. In fact, eating lying down isn't particularly good for you: it makes it more likely that acid will slosh up from your stomach into your oesophagus, which can cause a pain known as heartburn. (It shouldn't be called heartburn because it's nothing to do with your heart. Maybe oesphagusburn is too difficult to spell?)

TRUE OR POO?

SHAKESPEARE WROTE FART JOKES.

TRUE Even though he was apparently the best writer who ever existed, old Shakey was a big fan of a fart joke. At least six of his plays include lines about bum-gas. For example, in *The Comedy of Errors*, a servant called Dromio says, 'A man may break a word with you, sir, and words are but wind.' Yeah, it's not great. But if a teacher ever suggests that you read some Shakespeare, you can just say that it's much too rude for you, and you should read a more sensible, suitable book. I recommend this one.

→ I don't. Prunella

THE ANCIENT ROMANS GARGLED WITH DIARRHOEA AS A MOUTHWASH.

POO Absolute nonsense. Even the Ancient Romans wouldn't do anything as strange and disgusting as that. They used . . . Oh. Urine. It was so popular that they had to import extra urine from other countries. The strangest thing is that it actually worked. Wee contains something called ammonia, which can still be found in cleaning products today. So their teeth would have looked shiny and white as a result, even if their breath stank like . . . well, like they'd just drunk a glass of wee. (My lawyer,

Nigel, has asked me to point out that you shouldn't ever gargle with wee.)

DOCTORS IN ANCIENT GREECE WOULD TASTE YOUR VOMIT.

TRUE I'm extremely glad that I didn't work as a doctor in Ancient Greece. First of all, I don't speak Ancient Greek. And, secondly, some historians think that doctors worked out what was wrong with a patient by investigating their puke. I don't mean just looking at the colour and the texture of it, which is bad enough, but also . . . how it tasted. I would have one hundred per cent quit medical school the second they told me that was part of the job. And how did they make their patients vomit? All sorts of tricks, from drinking a jug of salt water to eating toenail clippings. Ugh, I'm feeling sick just from writing that. Excuse me for one second. *Bleeurrrrrrgh!* That's better.

CRAZY CURES

Do you grind your teeth at night? These days your doctor might suggest you wear a mouthguard while you're under the duvet. But a couple of thousand years ago the treatment was a bit more revolting. Actually, it was a lot more revolting. Doctors would make you keep a human skull on your pillow and, a few times a night, you had to give it a kiss or maybe a nice big lick – your choice! They thought grinding your teeth was a sign that you were talking to a ghost in your sleep and maybe licking a skull would help. Absolute weirdos.

SLEEP WELL.

The Chapter Where

YOUR TOES FALL OFF &

YOU WASH YOUR HAIR WITH GROUND-UP MICE

(also known as SKIN)

IT'S TIME TO HAVE A LOOK AT THE SKIN – you know, the organ you can see every morning when you look in the mirror. (If you can see your heart or your lungs or your intestines when you look in the mirror, then please call a doctor quite urgently.) And yes, the skin **IS** an organ – it's not just your body's special version of orange peel, it's an actual living part of you. In fact, it's the biggest organ in the body. Well, *on* the body. Hmm. Around the body? Whatever – it's the body's largest organ, OK? Let's have a look through history at all its best zits. Sorry, I mean best bits.

We should talk about hair too – your very own built-in bobble hat and blanket. Sometimes, when it's cold, I look at Pippin and wish I had a nice thick coat like hers. Well, I mean I do have a nice thick coat, but I bought it in a shop. We used to be totally covered in hair, back when we were cavepeople – aka *aaaaaages* ago. We actually never really lost it entirely: we've all got the same amount of hair as a chimpanzee. The only difference is that our hair is a lot thinner so you can barely see it over most of our bodies. The main exception is your uncle who looks like he's got a welcome mat underneath his shirt and a sweeping brush coming out of each ear. No one really knows why we're not quite so hairy these days, but it's just as well – otherwise we'd have to constantly comb our faces and it would cost us a fortune to go to the hairdresser's.

ANCIENT EGYPT

They might have thought the brain was a useless, weird beanbag and that you cured stomach ache by wearing a necklace, but the Ancient Egyptians were pretty clued up about the skin. They took being clean extremely seriously (you could probably learn a thing or two from them – no offence, but I can smell your socks from here) and they had regular baths, although sadly they didn't have any rubber ducks. They did come up with the first-ever deodorant though, which for some reason was made out of porridge. Maybe they thought it tasted disgusting and hid it under their armpits so their parents thought they'd eaten it?

Because of their hobby of wrapping themselves up in bandages, there are loads of people from back then who are perfectly preserved, so we know a lot about their various lumps and bumps and boils and blisters. They basically had the same skin problems that we still get today, like eczema and headlice. You probably won't faint with shock if I tell you they had slightly different ways of treating their skin issues though. (Apologies if you just fainted.)

If they cut themselves, they'd make a bandage out of . . .
raw meat. (Hmm, first porridge for their pits, now beef
for their bandages. I guess chemists didn't exist, so they
had a quick look through their kitchen cupboard instead.)

And, if they had bad spots, they'd smear some honey on
them. (See?) I've got no idea if honey helps with spots –
maybe it just made a load of flies swarm around their
face so no one could see their zits?

If they had pus pouring out of a wound, the Ancient Egyptians would plonk a slice of mouldy bread on it. (Did they ever actually eat food or did they just use it for first aid?) They might have been on to something with the mouldy bread idea – remember Alexander Fleming and his mouldy old penicillin? What do you reckon? I sphinx so.

↳ Is this meant to be a joke? Absolutely awful. Please can you change your surname so no one realizes I'm related to you. Prunella

ANCIENT GREECE

In Ancient Greece, they didn't really understand the skin – Aristotle thought that it was a result of the flesh underneath going all dry and hard, like when you leave custard out for too long. But they did realize something very important: skin needs to be protected from the sun. They attempted to do this by rubbing themselves all over with olive oil – if you're wondering whether or not this works, think about what happens when you cover potatoes in olive oil and chuck them in the oven . . . They roast.

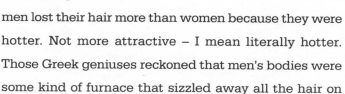

DELICIOUS!

CRUNCH!

The Ancient Greeks also had some pretty unusual ideas about baldness. They thought men lost their hair more than women because they were hotter. Not more attractive – I mean literally hotter. Those Greek geniuses reckoned that men's bodies were some kind of furnace that sizzled away all the hair on their heads. (That theory didn't quite explain the great big carpets of hair men had on their chests . . .)

Our old friend Hippoface came up with a cure for baldness. He made a lovely paste out of cumin (yum) and radishes (yum) and nettles (less yum) and pigeon poo (*aaaaagh!*). Well, I say it was a cure – it was about as effective as when I tried to teach Pippin how to speak Spanish.

ANCIENT ROME

The Romans thought that being 'beautiful' on the outside meant being healthy on the inside. This is obviously total codswallop. First of all, whatever you look like, you're beautiful – it's nothing to do with a random list of features that some idiots have decided you should have. Secondly, the shape of your nose or the colour of your hair isn't related to your health at all! I can prove it: I get so out of breath when I run for a bus that I have to sit down for half an hour – and I'm the most handsome man in the world.

Nonsense! You're about as handsome as my pet tarantula. Prunella

If people had any blemishes, they'd plaster on tons of make-up to hide them. Make-up was made from things like sheep's sweat, horses' urine, vinegar, eggs and onions – I'd much rather have zits than wear that. I've got no idea if this gross cure worked, but it must have made people smell like the inside of a rubbish truck. If you were really rich, you might have used a kind of make-up that was very expensive, very dangerous to get hold of and just as smelly. Yep, you'd dab your face with some delightful crocodile poo.

If you wanted to get rid of wrinkles, you might treat yourself to a bath full of . . . nope, not bubbles; nope, not rose petals . . . asses' milk. Don't panic – it's nothing to do with bums – it means milk from a donkey. It didn't work, and it doesn't sound particularly fun either. I'd much rather have a bath in a huge tub of hot chocolate, with extra marshmallows.

A lot of people dyed in Ancient Rome. No, that's not a spelling mistake – this book doesn't have any spelling mistaks – they dyed their hair. If you wanted lighter hair, then you'd dip it in vinegar and maybe even sprinkle it with gold dust. If you wanted your hair to look darker, then you'd slather it in a mixture of rotting leeches and red wine. Your locks would end up lovely and dark, but you'd smell like a zombie's underpants.

If someone's hair fell out in Ancient Rome, they thought it was caused by wearing heavy helmets all day, which is total drivel. Julius Caesar was really worried about losing his hair, so to make it grow back he invented a shampoo made out of horses' teeth, ground-up mice and the fat from under a bear's skin. It didn't work at all, so that treatment was abandoned very quickly (which the horses, mice and bears will be very pleased to hear).

JULIUS CAESAR'S **ANTI-BALDNESS SHAMPOO**

USING BEAR, HORSE AND MOUSE TECHNOLOGY

I CAME, I SAW, I CONQUERED BALDNESS.

SCIENTIFICALLY PROVEN
TO BE TOTALLY AND UTTERLY USELESS

Caesar eventually came up with a different plan: he made a kind of headband out of laurel leaves so no one could see his lack of locks – that's why, if you see a picture of him, it looks like he's just lost a wrestling match with a hedge.

SPARKLE TIME

If you think of Sparkle Time (or the Middle Ages if you're still using the old-fashioned term for some stupid reason), you probably imagine a whole load of stinkiness. And I don't blame you – we know that they used to fling buckets of poo and wee out of their windows onto the streets below. (My lawyer, Nigel, has asked me to mention that you should never throw buckets of poo and wee out of your window, and you should always use the toilet instead. Even if your dad is underneath the window and it would be hilarious to do it.)

But it's totally untrue that they didn't wash themselves. They actually took cleanliness extremely seriously and they didn't just bathe regularly, they believed having baths was a cure for all sorts of illnesses, including headaches and diarrhoea. (I hope their diarrhoea wasn't too bad, otherwise the bathwater would have turned brown quite quickly.)

1513

Since the beginning of time, people have been trying to make their skin look smooth and not like my Great Aunt Prunella's – her face is as wrinkled as a squashed sultana. For thousands of years, people have believed that there's a Fountain of Youth somewhere in the world, which makes you look instantly young again if you drink from it, and in 1513 a Spanish explorer called Juan Ponce de León set sail to look for it. He never found it (well, unless there's a very young-looking 500-year-old wandering around) but he did become the first European to set foot in Florida. So we lost out on eternal youth, but we got Disney World instead. Which would you prefer?

I've never been so insulted in my life. You are in big trouble, young man. Prunella

Not everyone in Sparkle Time was quite so clean though. Queen Isabella of Spain once boasted that she'd only had two baths in her entire life! She must have stunk like a turnip in a sewer – but of course no one will have told her that, in case they ended up with their head disconnected from their body . . . And, talking of heads, whether you lived in a palace or on a park bench, the chances are you were covered in headlice. They didn't call them lice though – they were known as 'worms with feet', which sounds far more disgusting (and is biologically very inaccurate). We know now that you catch headlice because they jump from one person's hair to another's when they're really close, like when a hero in an action movie jumps from roof to roof. In Sparkle Time, they thought that lice just magically appeared, as if they'd been teleported on to your head from the planet Louse.

Unfortunately, there's more to lice than an itchy head and a special comb – there are other, much more disgusting members of the louse family. (Much like there are much more disgusting members of my own family

→ Excuse me?! Prunella

than me.) There's another type of louse called the body louse or, to use its Latin name, *Pediculus humanus humanus*. (Nope, I've no idea why it has the same name twice. That's like if I was called Adam Kay Kay.) Headlice don't carry diseases, but body lice do – and back then they were having a massive party.

> Adam Idiot Idiot, more like. Prunella

INVITATION

Venue: Skin
Date: Sparkle Time
Time: Constantly
Theme: Disgusting
Menu: You

When the body louse chomps down on a person, it can cause a disease called typhus. Typhus is very rare these days because it can be treated with antibiotics, but in Sparkle Time it was a particularly grim illness. Typhus starts with a terrible headache and a really high fever, and then a rash that covers the whole body. And that's only the beginning! Next, the person's face swells up, and they start behaving really strangely, doing things like running around naked and screaming. Sounds awful, right?

Well, stay with me: we're only halfway through. They'd then flake out and lie down all the time, before their fingers and toes rotted away and they smelled like the alleyway behind the takeaway round the corner from me where no one's collected the rubbish for nearly a year. Would not recommend. (Typhus **OR** the takeaway.) And after that? What, you want more? Fine, they died.

In Sparkle Time, posh people were very keen not to get a suntan. It wasn't because they knew the sun could damage their skin or cause wrinkles so that their faces would look like a screwed-up piece of paper. And it wasn't because they knew it could lead to cancer. They didn't want a tan because people might think they got it from working outside on a farm, and they reckoned they were far too important to do a job like that. (These posh people sound pretty terrible.) Because sunscreen hadn't been invented, they protected their faces from the sun by using masks. But not like the masks people wear to protect themselves from things like coronavirus. These ones didn't have strings to tie round your ears – you had to bite down on them so they stayed in place.

Honestly, Pippin could have come up with a better design. How are you meant to order your lunch with a mask between your teeth? Try saying, 'One chocolate milkshake and large fries, please,' with your teeth clamped shut – it could have devastating results. They might mishear you and give you a banana milkshake (yuck). Worse still, how are you supposed to eat your lunch with a mask in your teeth?

IT'S AN ORGAN

It took until the 1500s for humans to realize that there was anything more to the skin than just a load of wrapping paper that stops our kidneys falling onto the pavement. This was all down to a man called Andreas Vesalius – he looked a bit more closely at the skin and realized it was made up of all sorts of different layers, and it had pores that let sweat out, and nerves that felt things.

ANDREAS VESALIUS: FIVE FACTS AND A LIE

1. His real surname was van Wesel, but he changed it so it sounded posher and more like Latin. (And less like he was a weasel.)

2. He was so good at university that they made him a professor of surgery on his final day as a student. What an absolute swot.

3. He discovered that women only have one uterus, not three.

4. For thousands of years, everyone used to think that men had more teeth than women until Vesalius proved this wrong . . . by counting them.

5. He discovered that nerves are solid, not hollow tubes full of weird magic.

6. Once, when he was cutting up a dead body (seriously, did none of these guys ever fancy tennis as a hobby instead?), he noticed that the heart was still beating – oops, the person was still alive! And then they died from being cut open – double oops! And then he was arrested for murder – triple oops!

WHAT AM I LIKE?!

CLASSIC VESALIUS!

3. That's not true, but doctors did use to think that the uterus was divided into two different sections (for twins, maybe?). Vesalius was the person who proved that there was no wall in the middle of it.

THE TERRIBLE TRUTH ABOUT SOLDIERS' SOCKS

There's nothing fun about fighting a war – you're miles away from home, there are bombs dropping everywhere and people you've never met are trying to kill you. Not recommended. And, as if all that wasn't bad enough, in the First World War, soldiers' skin was trying to kill them too. They fought from trenches, which are basically long ditches dug into the ground: wet, muddy, horrible and even stinkier than your bedroom.

Soldiers would stay in these damp conditions for weeks at a time, never changing their socks or shoes (because trenches didn't have en-suite bathrooms and washing machines), and this would eventually cause a condition called trench foot. Their feet would get so damp that they'd swell up and literally rot. Quite often soldiers with trench foot wouldn't be able to take their boots off because their feet had swollen up so much, and if they did manage to then (sorry – this sentence is about to get disgusting) sometimes bits of their feet would stay behind in their boots.

This foot-based nightmare eventually got sorted out by forcing every single soldier to have a foot buddy who would inspect their mate's feet once a day to check them over and cover them in oil made from whale blubber. (Seriously, is there any animal that hasn't been involved in weird cures over the years?)

Some soldiers also got something called frostbite, which happens when it's really, really, really cold. Your fingers and toes go white and numb, and if they're not warmed up soon then crystals form under the skin – like a human ice lolly. In severe cases, fingers and toes even have to be amputated. (My lawyer, Nigel, has asked me to mention that these amputated fingers and toes are not actually ice lollies and should under no circumstances be eaten in the park on a sunny day.)

2007

Trench foot made an unwelcome reappearance, and this time it wasn't because of a war: it happened at the Glastonbury Festival in England. People were keeping their shoes and socks on for days and days in rainy, muddy weather and . . . their feet started to rot.

The moral of this story is: CHANGE YOUR SOCKS, YOU DISGUSTING MONSTERS. Prunella

WHO WANTS TO BE A MILLIONHAIR?

Hair can make you extremely rich. No, not by shaving it all off and knitting it into a range of disgusting jumpers – I mean that every year people around the world spend about 100 billion dollars on hair products. In 1905, a woman called Madam C. J. Walker set up a company making shampoos, combs and lotions designed for black women. She started with $1.05 in savings and soon became the first-ever female self-made millionaire in America. Throughout her life, Madam Walker made sure that other women had opportunities, giving jobs to thousands of women and making a rule that the head of the company she set up must always be female.

SAVE YOUR SKIN

Even though people have been covering up their skin to avoid sunburn for thousands of years, it was only about a hundred years ago that anyone realized the connection between sun damage and skin cancer. Then, in 1962, a science student called Franz Greiter got terrible sunburn when he was skiing in the mountains, and decided he needed to invent something to stop this happening again.

1915

For as long as humans have been hanging out on Earth, they've been affected by a horrible disease called leprosy. It's caused by a bug called *Mycobacterium leprae* (if you ever need its full name to write it a letter) and it attacks the nerves, so people with leprosy can't feel any pain. Not feeling pain doesn't make you a superhero; it just means that those parts of the body are more likely to get badly injured because you can't tell if you're getting burned, for example. For thousands of years, there wasn't much that could be done to help people with leprosy. But in 1915 a young African American scientist called Alice Ball invented the first-ever effective treatment – she adapted a traditional medicine called chaulmoogra oil so it could be safely injected into the body and cure patients of this awful disease. Very sadly, she died before her findings could be published, and her evil boss pretended that it was all his idea – luckily, he got rumbled and we all now know that Alice was the genius.

He originally called his sunscreen Glacier Cream (which sounds like a delicious dessert) but then renamed it Piz Buin, after the mountain where he first turned tomato-coloured. Franz Greiter went on to become a champion skier and a famous scientist, and he also holds the world record for eating the most cheese in ten minutes. Actually, sorry – that's not true. I've got that world record (unofficially).

THE FUTURE

I've just asked my robot butler to draw the curtains (he did a beautiful oil painting of them) and now he's going to make some predictions.

PREDICTION 1 – A MACHINE WILL SCAN YOUR SKIN FOR PROBLEMS.

Scientists have actually already invented a machine that you walk into and it looks at every single centimetre of your skin. A bit like those security scanners you step into at the airport, except for these skin ones you have to be naked. (My lawyer, Nigel, has warned me that you shouldn't walk through the security scanners at the airport without any clothes on, otherwise you'll probably get arrested and not be able to go on holiday.) These scanners will look at every boil on your bum and nodule on your nose, then give an instant diagnosis and suggest the right lotion or potion for you to take. They will even be able to tell the difference between the harmless little moles that most of us have and early signs of skin cancer, by looking at their exact shape, size and colour. And picking up cancer early means it's much easier to treat and lives can be saved.

Agh! Pippin!

ADAM'S ANSWERS

WHY WOULD YOU BOIL YOUR COMB IF YOU LIVED IN 1900?

No, not to make a lovely comb soup. Scientists thought that baldness was caused by a kind of bacteria, and if you didn't boil your comb, then you might 'catch' baldness, like you'd catch a cold. To be honest, in those days, I think you could probably say any old nonsense like 'licking an eagle gives you asthma' and people would believe you.

IT DOES WHAT?

WHICH FAMOUS QUEEN WAS KILLED BY HER MAKE-UP?

Elsa from *Frozen*. (No, not really – she's fine.) It was Queen Elizabeth I, who wore make-up made from lead that was so white that her face became the colour of printer paper. What's the problem with that? Well, lead is very poisonous and gets absorbed through the skin – and she was said to wear so much of it that it looked like she'd covered her face in a thick layer of Play-Doh. All the portraits of her make her look extremely glamorous and wrinkle-free – that could have been because of the make-up or because if she wasn't happy with her picture then the artist would be sent straight to prison. (I wish I could send people to prison if they put a picture of me that I don't like up on Instagram.)

WHY WOULD YOU PUT SOME OF YOUR HAIR IN A BOTTLE AND BURY IT IN THE GARDEN?

To prevent witches from casting spells on you, of course. Well, if you lived in the seventeenth century, that is. And if you believed in witches. Talking of which (or talking of witch), in Sparkle Time, they thought that if you had more than two nipples you probably practised the Dark Arts. It's actually extremely common to have more than two nipples. About one in twenty people do – Harry Styles has four! – and none of them fly around on a broomstick.

TRUE OR POO?

DOCTORS USED TO PUT TATTOOS ON THEIR PATIENTS.

TRUE In fact, they still do. Thousands of years ago, if a patient had a condition that left them with a mark on their eyeball, then instead of treating it docs would tattoo it to cover it up – ouch! Today tattoos are sometimes used if a patient is having radiotherapy, a form of treatment for cancer that involves firing invisible beams into them to kill off the abnormal cells. To make sure the beams are lined up in exactly the right place every time the patient comes to hospital, doctors often tattoo tiny dots onto their skin.

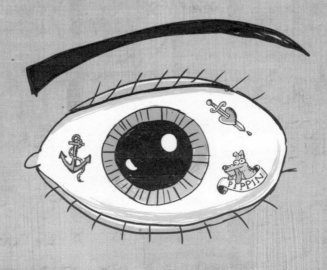

MOLES ON YOUR SKIN CAN PREDICT THE FUTURE.

POO Only robot butlers can predict the future – but in the sixteenth century they reckoned they could have a go. They thought the moles on your skin were basically a map of everything that was going to happen in your life. A spot on your neck – that was a sign you'd get suffocated at some point. Eek. A mole on your right hand meant you were about to have some good luck, and one near your belly button meant you would spend your life being lazy and greedy.

COLLECTING FINGERNAILS COULD MAKE YOU EXTREMELY RICH.

TRUE Not just any old fingernails though – in Sparkle Time, people would pay loads of money for fingernails from saints. Yes, long-dead saints. Quite how anyone knew that these were saintly fingernails and not just clippings from some local builder I have no idea. If you want to check out a set of holy fingernails, then pop over to Assisi in Italy, where St Clare's are still on display in a lovely vase.

CRAZY CURES

Mercury isn't just the name of the planet nearest to the sun. It's also a kind of metal – an extremely poisonous one. Deadly. Lethal. You'd be safer booking a two-week holiday on the planet Mercury than drinking mercury. But guess what? People have been taking it for centuries to help clear up their skin disorders. A Chinese emperor called Qin Shi Huang thought it would do more than just cure his acne – he reckoned it would make him live forever and be able to walk on water. (Saves taking a ferry, I suppose.) Unfortunately, it did the opposite of making him live forever and he died shortly afterwards. Of mercury poisoning.

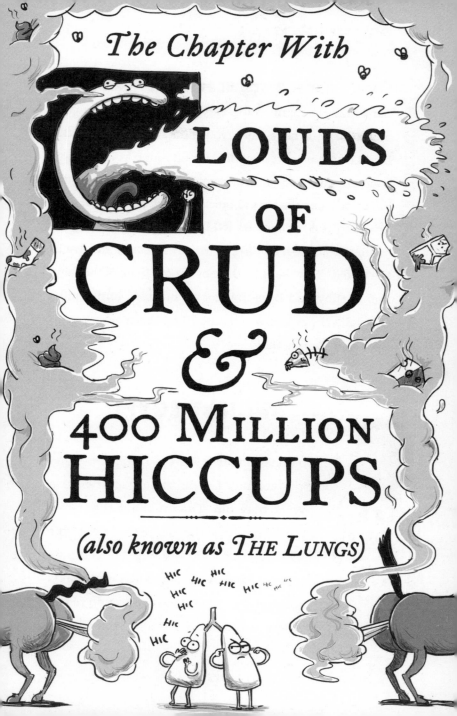

The Chapter With

CLOUDS

OF

CRUD

&

400 MILLION
HICCUPS

(also known as THE LUNGS)

I DON'T KNOW IF YOU'VE EVER TRIED BREATHING, but I really recommend it. Oxygen whooshes into your mouth or your nose, then your lungs sneak it into the blood so your heart can whizz it off round your body to your chin and your shin and your skin. Then, finally, the lungs puff out the waste products, aka carbon dioxide, aka lung poo. (Please do **NOT** write 'lung poo' in your exams.) You know all that, obviously, because you live in the twenty-first century. But how about back in the days before they had broadband and bicycles and bums? (Actually, they always had bums. I must remember to go back and change that.)

ANCIENT EGYPT

Our pharaoh friends knew the lungs were kind of important, but they didn't have any real idea of what they did. They thought they were quite a nice shape though, so they made lots of clothing and jewellery with lungs drawn on them. They even had chairs with lungs engraved on the back. I was going to call them a bunch of weirdos, but people today wear clothes and jewellery with hearts on, which actually isn't that different, although Valentine's Day cards might not be as popular if they had a big old pair of lungs on the front.

When it came to mummification time, the Ancient Egyptians thought the lungs were less important than the heart, so they went into a jar rather than going back into the body. I don't really know why they loved the heart so much more than the other organs – it's probably just a bit like the way I'm my parents' favourite, and when it comes to my brothers and sister they say, 'Yeah, they're OK, I guess.' The lung jar had a special god to protect it called Hapy. (Hapy sounds like he should have a massive smiley face, but I've just looked at a picture of him and he's got a baboon's head and is utterly terrifying.)

You're certainly not my favourite – I prefer your dog. And I don't particularly like your dog. Prunella

Hi!
I'M
HAPY!

Despite all the Ancient Egyptians' careful preparations, it turns out the organs didn't whizz off to the afterlife after all: they just stayed in their jars for thousands of years. This meant that when archaeologists cracked open the pyramids, there were loads and loads of perfectly preserved pickled innards that we've been able to have a look at. (Well, not me personally – other people did it.) When they examined the lungs, they saw something very surprising: the lungs turned into bats and flew away. OK, fine – it wasn't quite as surprising as that. They noticed that these Ancient Egyptian lungs had been damaged by pollution – the same as our lungs are today. It was probably caused by particles getting in the air from all the mining and metalwork going on, rather than factories and Ferraris, because I'm pretty sure they didn't have Ferraris in those days.

I've checked. They definitely didn't have Ferraris.

ANCIENT GREECE

If you were reading a book like this one in Ancient Greece, then the chapter on the lungs would just say, 'All the lungs do is cool down the heart.' Then you'd turn to the next chapter, safe in the knowledge that the lungs are just a pair of rib-based icebergs. For centuries, we've always just assumed that our teachers are right – maybe you should stop thinking that. I mean, these Greek guys got it pretty wrong . . .

Let's talk about strangling now. (My lawyer, Nigel, has asked me to mention that I'm not suggesting you strangle anyone.) Surely the Ancient Greeks knew that if you strangled someone and stopped the air getting into the body, then that person would end up kind of . . . dead? So that must have given them a bit of a clue about the lungs? Amazingly, no. They thought that if someone couldn't breathe, they died because their heart had become too hot.

There was only one person in Ancient Greece who thought this all sounded a bit wrong. Please welcome to the stage . . .

EMPEDOCLES!

Finally, someone to point out how weird their theories were and reveal that . . . Oh. Empedocles thought that we actually breathe through our skin. Go away, Empedocles.

ANCIENT ROME

I'm in a good mood so I'll be generous here. The Ancient Romans spotted that the diaphragm moved up and down and that's what made the lungs expand. But that's as far as their lung discoveries went, really.

They still believed in the whole 'breathing is the heart's air-conditioning system' thing. There were two main reasons for this. Firstly, the Romans thought that if the air contained anything that the body actually needed then we wouldn't have to breathe it out. (It's lucky we do breathe it out, otherwise we'd puff up like massive blimps and float away.) And the second, more important reason is that they were absolute nincompoops.

NINCOMPOOPS

NINCOMPOOPER SCOOPER

SPARKLE TIME

In Sparkle Time (ugh, fine, the Middle Ages), they didn't have any better ideas about how the lungs worked, but they started to have a go at treating patients who had difficulty breathing. They couldn't just pop into a branch of Boots, so most of their medicine came from herbs and flowers. Better than making them from manky old bread, I guess. There was a saying in Sparkle Time that went, 'How can a man die if he has sage in his garden?' Well, quite easily as it turns out because everyone from back then is dead now, however much sage was growing in their flower beds. But they were on to something: a lot of medicines we use these days come from plants – for instance, one of the most powerful painkillers in the world is made from poppies.

Unfortunately, they weren't great at working out which flowers to treat people with. They thought because God had invented diseases, God had also invented a specific treatment for every single disease, and all they had to do was find it, like some weird puzzle God had set for them as homework. They reckoned God would have made this easier for them by putting a clue on every cure, so doctors were on a constant treasure hunt, searching for roots that looked a bit like mouldy kidneys, or flowers that had the same colour as a skin rash. If someone had an infection in their lungs, they found a plant with leaves that looked like diseased lungs and made the patient scoff down loads of that. Obviously it didn't work at all – because plants don't look anything like the conditions they treat. But that particular plant is still known as lungwort, if you like facts. If you don't like facts, you can probably stop reading this book because it's a book of facts.

I wish I could, but I promised you I'd read the whole awful thing. Prunella

YOUR SPOTTY-BUM PLANT IS READY!

'TIS FOR A FRIEND . . .

LEECHES 3 FOR 2

PRESCRIPTIONS

LEONARDO DA VINCI

Leonardo da Vinci was one of the most famous artists in the history of the world ever – the *Mona Lisa*, with her famous smile, is probably the most well-known painting of all time. (It's pretty good, if you like that sort of thing, although I once did a drawing of a horse wearing trousers that was much better.) Why are we going on about art when we're in the middle of some serious breathing business? No, I haven't suddenly given up on the lungs and started writing about famous painters instead. The thing with Leo is, he wasn't just great at scribbling, he was also extremely important when it came to working out the mysteries of the human body.

LEONARDO DA VINCI: FIVE FACTS AND A LIE

1. He wrote backwards, so you can only read his notes if you hold them up to a mirror. Maybe he didn't want anyone to read them? He was left-handed, so perhaps it made it less likely he'd smudge his ink? Or he could have just been showing off.

2. He was totally self-taught. (This doesn't mean that you're allowed to bunk off school and say, 'Well, da Vinci didn't need to go to lessons!')

3. He invented the helicopter. He didn't fly around Italy in a helicopter – he just designed it. No one could be bothered to actually make it for more than four hundred years.

4. He invented the parachute. (In case he fell out of his helicopter.)

5. He invented the machine gun.

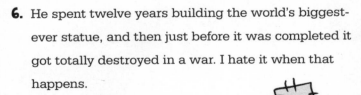

6. He spent twelve years building the world's biggest-ever statue, and then just before it was completed it got totally destroyed in a war. I hate it when that happens.

5. He might have invented a lot of things, but the machine gun wasn't invented for centuries after he died. He did invent a type of crossbow that could fire loads of arrows really quickly, so maybe you should have half a mark if you thought this was true.

Leo used his excellent artistic skills (although mine are still better, never forget that) to draw the most accurate diagrams ever of the body and all its organs. In order to do this, he cut up about thirty bodies. (They were already dead – no need to phone the Italian police.) He wasn't particularly interested in anatomy; he mostly did all this chopping up of dead people because he thought it would help improve his drawing. (My lawyer, Nigel, has asked me to point out that this is a terrible idea and that you should practise your art by drawing plants or vegetables or something. It's less messy too.)

Because anatomy was a bit of a hobby for old Leo (the way that your hobby is picking your nose), he never published any of these super-detailed drawings, and most of them went completely unnoticed for hundreds of years. It's a bit of a shame really, because if he had published them we would have understood how the lungs worked about

three hundred years before we did. Plus, people who lived at the same time as him would have found out about his amazing inventions and Henry VIII could have travelled everywhere by helicopter . . . Important: don't make the same mistake Leo did – if you invent something amazing, then tell everyone immediately. Especially if it's a machine that stops Pippin's farts smelling so awful.

One of da Vinci's lung-based discoveries was that it's impossible to breathe through your nose and your mouth at the same time. Try it! See? We think he proved this by trying to play two flutes at once – one through his mouth and one through his nose – and found that he couldn't do it. If his neighbours spotted him doing this experiment through the window, they must have thought he'd gone completely bananas. (Then again, they saw him cutting up loads of dead bodies and never said anything.)

WILLIAM HARVEY

So, with Leo's notebooks all hidden away in his drawer, maybe in the seventeenth century William Harvey would be the bloke to figure out what the lungs did? After all, he was the brainbox who worked out circulation. Unfortunately not. Turns out he was like a pop star who only has one good tune and then everything afterwards sounds like a cat vomiting.

He thought the lungs made the body float upwards and that's why we stood upright – maybe he got them confused with helium balloons? Noticing that dogs and cats have got smaller lungs than humans, he reckoned that's why they have to wander around on four legs instead of two. *Okaaaaaaay*. He wasn't a **TOTAL** lung-loser though. He did work out that exercising is good for your lungs, so we can thank him for that. (Or blame him, if you hate PE.)

MICE TO SEE YOU

It wasn't until a hundred years later, in 1774, that a bloke called Joseph Priestley came along and helped everyone work out what was actually happening in those spongey old lungbags. He had a theory that the air we breathe wasn't just one single gas, but it was actually lots of different gases mixed together, and one of them was a particularly important one called oxygen. (He didn't call it oxygen though. He gave it the slightly less snappy name of 'dephlogisticated air'.)

Joey worked out how important oxygen is by doing experiments on mice. Look away now if you have a pet mouse, or if you really, really love mice, or if you are a mouse. He realized that if he put a mouse in a jar, it would eventually die because all the oxygen would run out.

But if he put a mouse in a jar that also had a mint plant in it, the mouse didn't die because the plant was puffing out oxygen, which meant the mouse always had plenty of it to breathe. After he'd done this experiment, he held a quick mouse funeral, and told the world about this amazing new gas.

He tried breathing in pure oxygen himself and found that it made him more alert, more energetic and much better at dancing. (I might have invented the bit about dancing, if I'm totally honest.)

1922

A man called Charles Osborne hiccupped. So what's the big deal? He was weighing a pig while it happened. Still not impressed? OK, well, he hiccupped every couple of seconds and didn't stop for the next sixty-eight years. After about 400 million hiccups, one day he suddenly stopped! Hooray! And then the next year he died. Oh dear.

SMOKING IS CHOKING AND I'M NOT EVEN JOKING

I don't smoke, and you probably shouldn't either – it makes you smell like a bin that's on fire and gives you yellow teeth and brown nails, plus it literally destroys your lungs and knackers tons of other organs too. And you spend your life shivering outside doorways with a burning tube in your hand and ash all over your clothes. Seven million people die from smoking every year – that's more than the population of entire countries, like Denmark or New Zealand! And did I mention that it stinks worse than almost any fart you will ever smell? Even Pippin's. ——————

→ I know full well that you blame a lot of your own intestinal gas on your dog, and I think you should tell your readers this. Prunella

There's nothing new about smoking – people were doing it in America about five thousand years ago. I can forgive them for smoking in those days because nobody realized

how dangerous it was. Tobacco (which is the smelly stuff inside cigarettes) eventually made its way to the UK around five hundred years ago. King James I wasn't particularly impressed by smoking – he didn't know it was bad for your health, but he did realize it made everyone smell like a dead pigeon, so he increased the tax on it by over four thousand per cent. That's like if you went into the shop to buy your favourite chocolate bar (I'll have a KitKat, thanks) and it cost £30. Would you still buy it? Yeah, me too.

His plan didn't make smoking go away. It actually got more and more popular as the years went on. In the 1940s, eight out of ten British men smoked, and four out of ten women. All the most famous sports stars and Hollywood actors smoked and people thought it was a really glamorous thing to do. Doctors would even appear on adverts saying things like, 'This brand

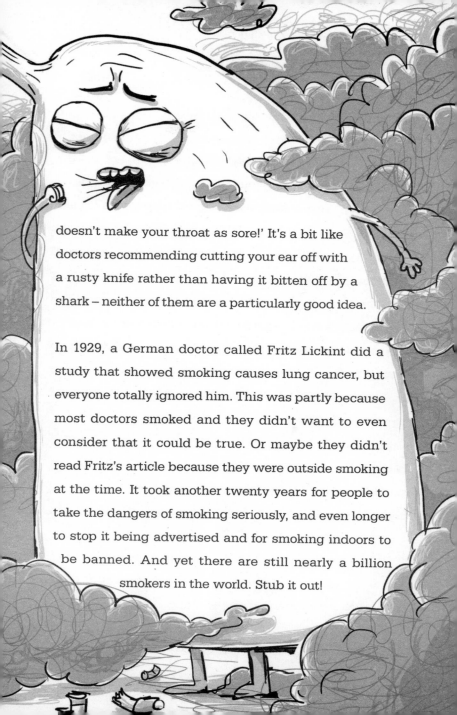

doesn't make your throat as sore!' It's a bit like doctors recommending cutting your ear off with a rusty knife rather than having it bitten off by a shark – neither of them are a particularly good idea.

In 1929, a German doctor called Fritz Lickint did a study that showed smoking causes lung cancer, but everyone totally ignored him. This was partly because most doctors smoked and they didn't want to even consider that it could be true. Or maybe they didn't read Fritz's article because they were outside smoking at the time. It took another twenty years for people to take the dangers of smoking seriously, and even longer to stop it being advertised and for smoking indoors to be banned. And yet there are still nearly a billion smokers in the world. Stub it out!

BAD AIR DAY

Pollution has been around ever since humans started barbecuing sabre-toothed-tiger sausages outside their caves. Any time you burn something, it releases substances into the air, and some of those – spoiler alert – aren't so great for your lungs.

Things got quite a bit worse when factories started springing up, spewing out all sorts of hideous chemicals. And then cars began to replace horses – the only toxic emissions our four-legged friends made were brown and had to be shovelled off the ground. Plus, before radiators were a thing, houses used to be kept warm by burning coal, which would send up great big clouds of crud into the sky.

In the 1950s, London was famous around the world, not for the Beefeaters or Big Ben or my Great Aunt Prunella's awful cooking, but for the terrible quality of the air.

I hope you're not referring to my turnip stew. It's a family delicacy. Delete that sentence immediately. Prunella

This air was so polluted you could literally see it. I know, right? It was known as a 'pea soup' fog because the air looked like . . . thick pea soup. It didn't smell like pea soup though. It was so full of poisons that the whole of London stank of rotten eggs – it basically smelled as if everyone who lived there had spent twelve years eating only baked beans. It seeped into people's houses under cracks in their doors and gaps in their walls, so you couldn't even escape the coughing by staying inside. If you did wander outside, you'd come back covered in soot, like you'd just climbed down a chimney. Or you'd get home with your wallet missing because thieves were able to steal things from you, and you wouldn't be able to see which direction they'd run away.

But worst of all was the damage it did to people's health. Over four thousand people died in just a couple of days because of this terrible pollution, and thousands more died afterwards. There were so many deaths that undertakers ran out of coffins and florists ran out of flowers for funerals. Luckily, we've learned lessons from tragedies like this, and now governments everywhere are trying to cut down on emissions, not just to protect the planet, but to protect all our lungs too.

ASTHMA

You've heard of asthma – the wheezy diseasey (a poem! For free!) – which people keep under control by using inhalers and other medicines. I'm pretty sure you know someone who has it because it affects one in twelve people. If you don't know anyone who has it, maybe you've only ever met ten people.

But it's not a modern disease like coronavirus or bum pox (which is so modern that I've only just invented it). Asthma has been around for a really long time. There are books from China and Egypt thousands of years ago which talk about it. The first treatment we know about for asthma was from Ancient Greece, where it was prescribed by a doctor called Aretaeus of Cappadocia. Imagine being so famous that people knew you just by your first name and the place you're from! I'd be Adam of Oxfordshire; my dog would be Pippin of the Manky Old Dog Bed that Smells of Sick. Anyway, Aretaeus of Cappadocia might have been very famous, but he wasn't very good at treating asthma. His prescription was owl's blood mixed with wine. Delicious, but not very effective.

ARETAEUS

OF CAPPADOCIA!

PIPPIN

OF THE MANKY OLD DOG BED THAT SMELLS OF STINK!

TOAD-FACE

OF PAGE 70!

The illustrations are very good. Perhaps you could have lots more of those and less of your terrible waffle? Prunella

You might think that asthma cures couldn't get any worse than that. Nope! Poor asthmatics over the years have been subjected to having cold water poured over their heads, smoking (which would make it much worse) and eating honey (yum!) mixed with millipedes (yuck!). Some doctors even prescribed the very poisonous arsenic in the 1800s, which definitely stopped people wheezing – mainly because they were dead. Suddenly an occasional suck on an inhaler doesn't sound quite so bad, does it?

2015

A woman in Australia started coughing up blood and struggling to breathe so she was rushed to the nearest hospital (which is a very sensible thing to do if you're coughing up blood and struggling to breathe). The doctors did an X-ray of her lungs and saw there was a lump of metal in there. They asked her if she'd been breathing in any metal recently and she said, 'Umm . . . no?' so they did an operation to see what was going on. They removed the object and found it was one of her earrings. It turns out that she'd pulled her asthma inhaler out of her handbag one day and an earring had fallen into the end of it. She took a puff and . . . whoosh . . . her earring was 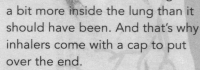 a bit more inside the lung than it should have been. And that's why inhalers come with a cap to put over the end.

THE FUTURE

And now some predictions from my robot butler. He's spent all morning planting bulbs in the garden (and now none of my lights work).

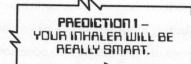

> **PREDICTION 1 – YOUR INHALER WILL BE REALLY SMART.**

No, I'm afraid it won't be able to do your maths homework for you or help you cheat in exams, but it will have sensors on it that detect if you're near a certain type of pollen or a load of pollution that might give you an asthma attack, so you can go somewhere else. Or it'll tell you if there's loads of dust in your bedroom, so you can clean it all up. (Yeah, sorry about that.) These ingenious inhalers will also let your doctor know how much you're using them, in case they need to increase the dose.

> **PREDICTION 2 – PIPPIN WILL POO IN YOUR OTHER SHOE.**

Ugh. I've only just finished cleaning the first one.

2018

A Croatian man called Budimir Šobat broke the world record by holding his breath underwater for 24 minutes and 11 seconds. Well, they say he's a man, but I hope they checked that he wasn't actually a dolphin wearing swimming trunks. Most people can only hold their breath for something like a minute at the most. (My lawyer, Nigel, has asked me to point out that under no circumstances should you try to beat Budimir's record.)

ADAM'S ANSWERS

IS IT POSSIBLE TO HAVE A LUNG TRANSPLANT?

It's very possible, yes, which is excellent news for over three thousand patients every year whose lungs stop working properly and need a spare. The first successful lung transplant took place in 1981, and was actually a heart–lung transplant, which means both lungs and the heart were replaced at the same time. It wasn't until a few years later that doctors first performed a lung transplant on its own. (Maybe they couldn't work out how to unscrew the lungs from the heart?)

WHY DO PEOPLE SAY 'BLESS YOU!' WHEN YOU SNEEZE?

In ancient times, people thought a sneeze meant evil spirits were trying to get into you, so they'd ask God to bless them to make the spirits think twice about their invasion. In Germany, they say '*Gesundheit!*'; in France, they say '*A vos souhaits!*'; and I say 'Oi! You've got snot all over me!' I don't understand why people say 'Bless you!' when you sneeze but not when you burp or fart – it doesn't make any sense.

WHAT IS AN IRON LUNG?

No, it's not a kind of lung transplant made from melted-down radiators. There's a very serious disease called polio, which can stop the muscles we need for breathing from working. Luckily, polio has almost completely disappeared from the world because of clever old vaccines but it used to affect hundreds of thousands of people. These days, if someone can't use their breathing muscles for any reason, doctors can put a tube into their mouth connected to a machine that inflates their lungs. But before this was invented patients had to go into an iron lung.

It was like a big metal filing cabinet that you would slide inside with your head sticking out of one end and your feet out of the other. The pressure inside the iron lung would go up and down and up and down, which puffed the chest in and out and in and out, and allowed the patient to breathe, but it made it very difficult for them to have a swim or play the cello.

TRUE OR POO?

DOCTORS USED TO THINK THAT PARROTS COULD STOP YOU GETTING CHEST INFECTIONS.

TRUE Before they understood about infections, doctors thought that people got illnesses in their lungs because the air was too 'stiff'. (Stiff? What were they even talking about?) They reckoned the best way to cure 'stiff' air was to make loud noises, such as banging drums, firing guns and letting parrots squawk around. Not only was this totally useless, but there's actually a lung infection that you can catch from parrots. (It's called psittacosis if you like knowing things that your teachers don't.)

UH OH.

ALEXANDER THE GREAT INVENTED AN OPERATION THAT IS STILL USED TODAY.

TRUE One day Alexander the Great was having dinner with some of his soldiery mates. Suddenly one of them turned blue and collapsed to the ground – he'd got a chicken bone stuck in his windpipe and wasn't able to breathe. Alex had a clever plan: he got out his sword and cut a hole in the soldier's neck, so air could flow into his lungs. This is a procedure that's sometimes performed by doctors, called a tracheotomy. (My lawyer, Nigel, has asked me to point out that if someone is choking on their food then the correct thing to do is to push upwards on their ribs from behind, using something called the Heimlich manoeuvre, not to stick a sword in their neck.)

SMOKING USED TO BE ALLOWED AT SCHOOL.

TRUE During the Great Plague of 1665, smoking was made compulsory at a school called Eton. (You might have heard of it – lots of prime ministers went there, for some reason. Maybe they had special lessons in how to be a prime minister?) The doctors of the day thought that the smoke would somehow fight off the plague, which they decided was floating around in the air. Pupils at the school who refused to smoke would get hit with a cane by their teachers. The olden days were **WEIRD**.

CRAZY CURES

You know how sometimes a good idea actually turns out to be a really, really, really bad one? Like when I was eight and had the excellent idea to slide down the pavement using home-made ice skates, and then suddenly found myself in hospital with an elbow pointing the wrong way and a big red hole where my tooth used to be. Well, a hundred years ago, doctors came up with a brand-new medicine to stop people coughing, called heroin. It worked! And then ... everyone got addicted to it and couldn't stop taking it, and it caused terrible side effects, including the very worst side effect of all. (I mean death, not farting.) You might have heard of heroin because it's now a totally illegal drug.

The Chapter Where

NO ONE
WASHES THEIR HANDS
&
A HAIRDRESSER CUTS YOUR LEG OFF

(also known as SURGERY)

IF YOU'VE EVER SEEN AN OPERATION (hopefully from watching something gory on TV rather than breaking into a hospital and sitting on a surgeon's shoulders), then you'll know that surgery is very sophisticated, extremely precise and super clean. It may not be the biggest shock in the world to find out that this hasn't always been the case. First of all, it's very difficult to repair something if you don't know how it's meant to work – and doctors didn't have a clue about how the body works until ages after they started attempting operations. It's a bit like if I tried to get Pippin to fix my computer – she'd have a go, but it wouldn't really help. (And she'd probably wee on it.)

Secondly, they didn't have anaesthetics to make patients fall asleep, and if they had any painkillers at all they were pretty basic.

This meant an operation might go a bit like this:

It was probably pretty distracting if your patient was fighting you off and wailing like they were being murdered. And even if you somehow managed to do a successful operation despite all this, the patient would probably still be killed by an infection. The poor surgeon – doing all that work only for their patient to die because antibiotics hadn't been invented yet. Oh yeah, and it was pretty bad news for the patient too, I guess. Thankfully, things got more advanced over the years. I'm really glad my tonsils weren't removed using a sharpened rock and no anaesthetic.

Might have taught you a lesson. Prunella

ANCIENT EGYPT

In Ancient Egypt, they were extremely good at stitching skin and used all sorts of different materials to do it, from cotton (fair enough) to bits of muscles that they'd pulled out of animals (not fair enough). Thankfully, they saved their sewing skills for people who'd already died: it was mostly to make mummies' bodies look nice and neat for the afterlife, just as soon as they'd cut them open and scooped out all their organs.

We know that they also tried some more advanced surgery because it was described in a document called the Edwin Smith Papyrus. (I presume Edwin Smith is the name of the bloke who found it or something. Most Ancient Egyptian people I've heard of were called things like Cleopatra or Tutankhamun – Edwin Smith sounds more like the name of a maths teacher.) There are lots of descriptions in Edwin's papyrus of operating on spinal injuries and removing lumps, but not many descriptions about how the patients got on afterwards. My guess would be . . . not great. It also said that you should spread some honey on the patient's skin to clean it before an operation (this might work), that you can stop a wound bleeding by putting a lump of raw meat on it (this probably won't work) and that if your operation isn't successful, then you should just do a magic spell (this definitely won't work).

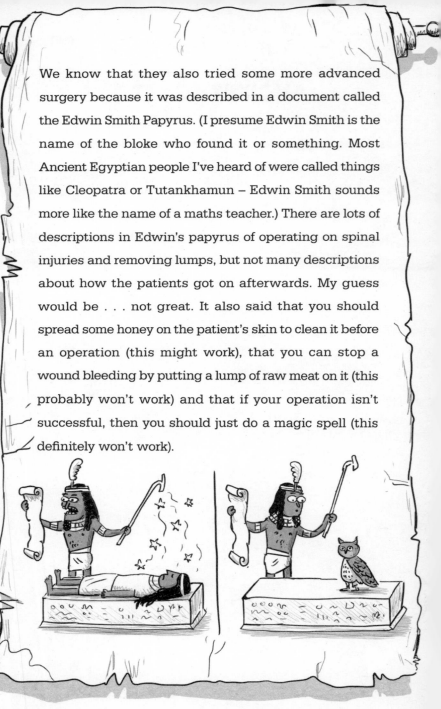

ANCIENT INDIA

A thousand years later, in about 600 BC, a man in India called Sushruta invented a whole load of operations. In fact, he invented so many operations that he became known as the Father of Surgery. (I hope Sushruta isn't reading this because I don't want to upset him or make him feel less important, but I've just looked up 'the Father of Surgery' on Wikipedia, and there are literally ten other people in history who have been called that. Actually, I've just looked Sushruta up on Wikipedia too and he died 2,500 years ago, so he's definitely not reading this.)

He wrote a book with 184 chapters (184! This book only has twelve!), which described how to do all sorts of things, from amputating an arm to making someone a new nose if it had been chopped off in a sword fight. His method involved cutting off the patient's cheek and turning that into a nose. Presumably, he then had to cut off something else to replace the missing cheek? Their bum, maybe?

Can you stop talking about bums? It's not funny, it's not clever, and it makes me embarrassed to be related to you. Prunella

ANCIENT ROME

In Ancient Rome, they developed an operation called a Caesarean section, which was a new way of delivering a baby through the abdomen (which is what doctors call the tummy because we like having weird names for stuff). Fancy a quick game? It's true or false, and if you lose you have to buy me a helicopter. True or false . . . the Caesarean section is called the Caesarean section because Julius Caesar was born by one?

Nope! False! You owe me a helicopter. (Can I have it in bright green, please, with ADAM'S LOVELY HELICOPTER in gold writing on the side? Thanks.) It might start with the name 'Caesar', but it's got nothing to do with old Julius. It was impossible for a mother to survive a Caesarean in those days, and Mummy Caesar (I'm not sure what her first name was – Julia, maybe?) was still alive when Julius was grown up.

YOU CAN INVADE BRITAIN ONCE YOU'VE TIDIED YOUR ROOM!

AL-ZAHRAWI

It's time to say hi to Abu al-Qasim Khalaf ibn al-Abbas al-Zahrawi al-Ansari, although I hope you don't mind if I shorten his name to al-Zahrawi. He lived in the year 1000 (I wonder if they had a big party to celebrate the year 1000?) and was a pretty amazing surgeon. He invented a type of stitch made from the intestines of cats (which – slightly disgustingly – is sometimes still used today). As well as that, he made over two hundred different types of instruments for surgeons (I mean like scalpels, not saxophones) and described lots of brand-new operations. Oh, and also he wrote about thirty books and invented loads of different perfumes. All right, al-Zahrawi. Nobody likes a show-off.

SPARKLE TIME

In Sparkle Time (you know what I mean), doctors weren't into the idea of surgery that much. Maybe they were worried that some blood would splash onto their shoes or something. Whatever the reason, they stuck to their leeches and lotions and potions, and pretty much refused to pick up a scalpel. So – what happened if you really, really needed an operation? Well, you went to the hairdresser's. It made sense in a way – they were already using knives and scissors for their normal job, so they didn't need to buy any new equipment.

Even though it must have been very handy to have a quick haircut and your leg amputated at the same time, the downsides were that anaesthetics hadn't been invented, doctors weren't very good at stopping things bleeding, and you'd probably get an infection afterwards and die. But at least you'd have a lovely neat hairdo for the funeral.

If you look outside a barber's shop today, you might see a pole with red and white stripes on it. Do you know why that is? It's in tribute to their favourite yoghurt:

Strawberry Fruit Corner. Hmm, maybe not. It's meant to look like a white bandage covered in blood, which told everyone walking past that they did operations. I'd have gone for something less off-putting, like a nice pair of scissors, maybe. The whole blood-on-bandages thing is a bit like a restaurant having a picture of a vomit splat outside.

That's disgusting — please delete that sentence. And the rest of the chapter too. Prunella

One of the most famous barber-surgeons (as they were known) was called Ambroise Paré. Not to be confused with Framboise Pâté, which is French for raspberry jelly.

AMBROISE PARÉ: FIVE FACTS AND A LIE

1. He was the official doctor to four French kings in a row. You only get a new king when the last one dies, so they probably should have found a better doctor.

2. He was taught how to do surgery by his brother. My brother taught me how to make a fart sound by putting my hand under my armpit, which is almost as good. (Did you just check if you could do it?)

3. If someone had been poisoned in the olden days, doctors would make them eat a bezoar stone to cure them. (A bezoar is a kind of stone that sometimes appears in the gut. Yuck.) Ambroise proved that these poo-stones weren't actually any good at treating poisons. Unfortunately, he proved it by poisoning his cook and showing that he still died despite eating a bezoar afterwards. Naughty Ambroise.

4. He once survived an attempted murder by hiding in a wardrobe.

5. He invented forensic pathology, which means working out how someone was murdered. There are TV shows about forensic pathology called things like **CSI: Miami**. (His TV show would be called **CSI: Sixteenth-century Paris**.)

6. Paris was named after him.

One of Ambroise's big inventions was a way of using stitches to stop blood vessels from bleeding everywhere during surgery (although he may have stolen the idea from al-Zahrawi). Previously, doctors would use an extremely hot bit of metal to sizzle and seal the bleeding blood vessels like they were cooking a steak. This had the unfortunate result of killing a lot of patients, so

Because a lot more of his patients lived to tell the (slightly gruesome) tale of their amputations, he developed prosthetic or artificial limbs for them to use afterwards. He also made artificial eyes for people who had lost theirs, usually in battles. You couldn't see through them, but they were made out of gold or silver, so they must have looked pretty amazing.

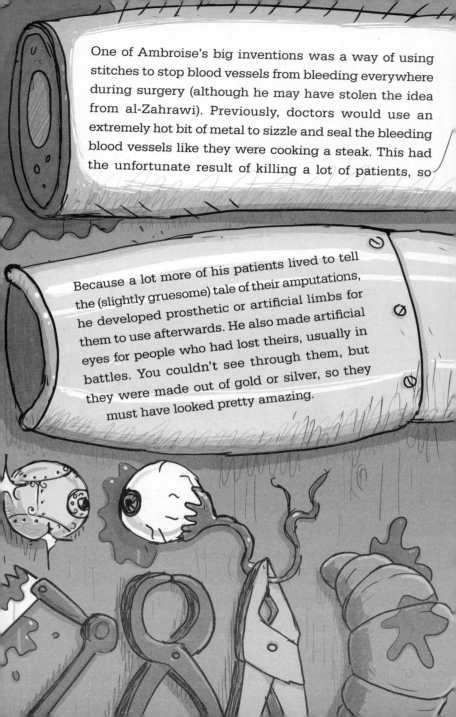

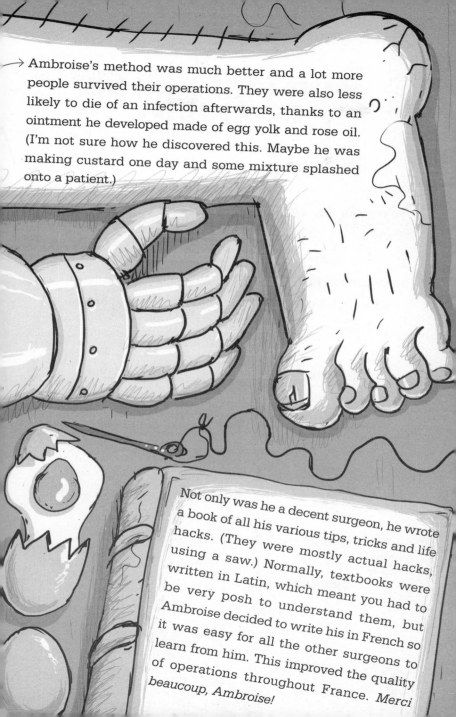

→ Ambroise's method was much better and a lot more people survived their operations. They were also less likely to die of an infection afterwards, thanks to an ointment he developed made of egg yolk and rose oil. (I'm not sure how he discovered this. Maybe he was making custard one day and some mixture splashed onto a patient.)

Not only was he a decent surgeon, he wrote a book of all his various tips, tricks and life hacks. (They were mostly actual hacks, using a saw.) Normally, textbooks were written in Latin, which meant you had to be very posh to understand them, but Ambroise decided to write his in French so it was easy for all the other surgeons to learn from him. This improved the quality of operations throughout France. *Merci beaucoup, Ambroise!*

MISTER LISTER AND SOME DIRTY BLISTERS

If you had to have an operation, where would you rather have it – in a hospital, or on your kitchen table? If you lived around two hundred years ago, then the answer would be, 'Definitely at home, please. Please, please, please, please, please!' because patients were five times more likely to die in hospital. Why? Well, let me describe how surgeons did their operations in hospital and see if you can work it out.

 Unlike surgeons now, who wear special hygienic outfits that look like pyjamas and get thoroughly washed after every operation, surgeons in those days never bothered changing their clothes between operations – they dressed in a black suit with a flowing cape, like they were doing an impression of Dracula. (It was actually a very good impression of Dracula because they killed a lot of people.)

They didn't clean the operating table, or their scalpels, or **ANYTHING**. They didn't even wipe them down – they just used them on the next patient straight away. They even reused blood-soaked bandages. Ugh.

They thought that if at the end of the day you were covered head to toe in blood and intestines and poo and pus and vomit and bits of brain and splinters of bone then it meant you were a really good surgeon. If you're in Cubs or Scouts, you collect different badges; these guys would collect different types of innards all over their clothes. Just like Pippin doesn't think she's been for a proper walk unless she's rolled in ten different kinds of fox poo.

 They didn't wear gloves and they never washed their hands. Ever.

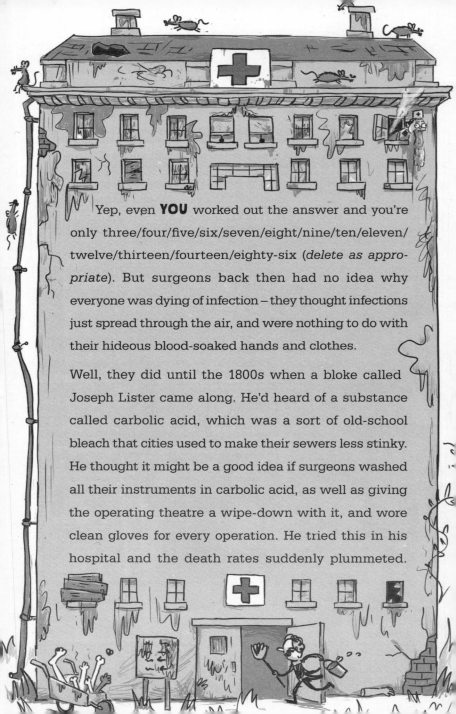

Yep, even **YOU** worked out the answer and you're only three/four/five/six/seven/eight/nine/ten/eleven/twelve/thirteen/fourteen/eighty-six (*delete as appropriate*). But surgeons back then had no idea why everyone was dying of infection – they thought infections just spread through the air, and were nothing to do with their hideous blood-soaked hands and clothes.

Well, they did until the 1800s when a bloke called Joseph Lister came along. He'd heard of a substance called carbolic acid, which was a sort of old-school bleach that cities used to make their sewers less stinky. He thought it might be a good idea if surgeons washed all their instruments in carbolic acid, as well as giving the operating theatre a wipe-down with it, and wore clean gloves for every operation. He tried this in his hospital and the death rates suddenly plummeted.

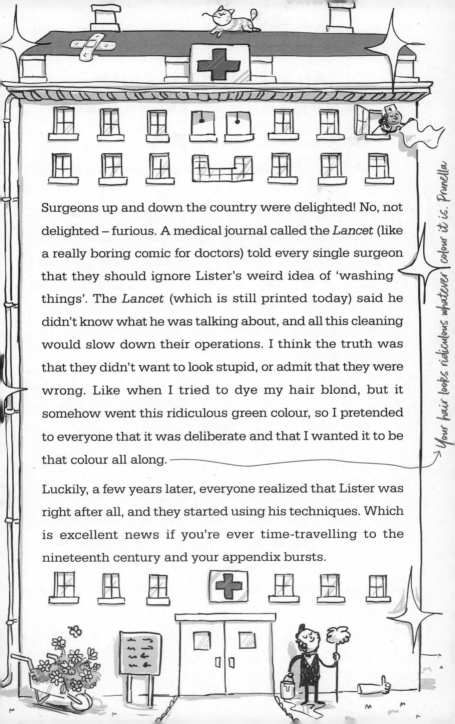

Surgeons up and down the country were delighted! No, not delighted – furious. A medical journal called the *Lancet* (like a really boring comic for doctors) told every single surgeon that they should ignore Lister's weird idea of 'washing things'. The *Lancet* (which is still printed today) said he didn't know what he was talking about, and all this cleaning would slow down their operations. I think the truth was that they didn't want to look stupid, or admit that they were wrong. Like when I tried to dye my hair blond, but it somehow went this ridiculous green colour, so I pretended to everyone that it was deliberate and that I wanted it to be that colour all along.

Luckily, a few years later, everyone realized that Lister was right after all, and they started using his techniques. Which is excellent news if you're ever time-travelling to the nineteenth century and your appendix bursts.

Your hair looks ridiculous whatever colour it is. Prunella

ANAESTHETICS: FROM
AAAAAAAAAGH TO *ZZZZZZZ*

Surgeons have known for thousands of years that it's not **GREAT** for people to be awake and screaming during their operations: it's hard to operate on someone when they're flapping about, and it's probably not a whole load of fun for the patient either. They tried all sorts of things, like giving the patient so much alcohol that they fell asleep, or smashing them on the head until they were unconscious, or even hypnotizing them. Unfortunately, these things either didn't work, or made the patients a bit too dead.

In the 1830s, there was a craze for university students to go to parties and breathe in a newly discovered type of gas called ether. One day a doctor called Crawford Long noticed that students who'd been breathing in ether and then injured themselves didn't feel any pain . . . and he wondered if this gas might be useful for when he was doing operations. (He was right – it was extremely useful.)

One of the first-ever operations that took place with ether as an anaesthetic was the amputation of a man's leg. It went so well that the patient asked when the operation was going to begin, but his leg was already in the bin and he hadn't felt a thing.

Other surgeons were very suspicious of ether, and said that an operation couldn't work properly if the patient didn't feel any pain during it . . . eek! But since then millions and millions of operations have been performed using anaesthetics, although today doctors use different types of gas because ether had this annoying habit of sometimes exploding. Oops.

To this day, doctors have no idea how anaesthetics actually work (idiots!), but the main thing is that they **DO** work, and operations are a lot less screamy than they used to be.

BEFORE

AFTER

Before anaesthetics were invented, a surgeon's best chance of not killing their poor screaming patient was to do the operation extremely quickly. The fastest surgeon in Britain was a man called Robert Liston, who boasted that he could amputate a leg in less than a minute. In 1846, Mr Liston did an operation so quickly that he killed the patient with a clumsy swish of his knife **and then** he killed his assistant by accidentally cutting off his fingers **AND THEN** he killed someone who was watching the operation, who died of fright. Whoops!

LEND A HAND (OR A LUNG OR A KIDNEY)

I've talked a bit about transplants already – the amazing operations to give people a new heart or lungs or even a new hand or a new bum. OK, I made up the bum bit. Doctors have wanted to do transplants for thousands of years, but they've only actually happened quite recently. So why did it take so long? Were they all just really lazy? Or did they keep putting it off, like the way you're always far too busy to tidy your bedroom?

The reason that it took surgeons *soooo* long to transplant an organ is that, when they tried it, the patients just died. Even if they put it in exactly the right place and

Then why did you put it in? This book is totally unsuitable for children. I hope they all have bins at home. Prunella

235

connected it up perfectly to all the complicated veins and arteries . . . the patient still ended up totally dead. This was because of something called organ rejection. Your body is so marvellous and miraculous that as soon as something appears inside that it doesn't recognize, it goes straight on the attack. This is excellent news if you have an illness because the viruses or bacteria or other evil invaders get zapped and destroyed. But it's not quite so handy if you're trying to install a new organ.

The big change happened when scientists invented a drug that stops the immune system (the part of the body that fights infections) from getting overexcited, which means the body doesn't try to boot out its lovely new replacement organ. This drug was invented by an incredible scientist called Gertrude Elion – she won a Nobel Prize for it, and fair enough really.

Because their immune systems have been turned right down, it's really important that people with organ transplants stay away from people who are ill because they're not as good at fighting off germs.

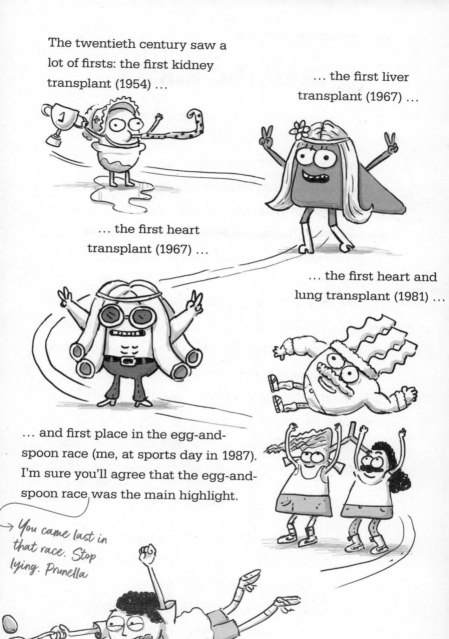

The twentieth century saw a lot of firsts: the first kidney transplant (1954) ...

... the first liver transplant (1967) ...

... the first heart transplant (1967) ...

... the first heart and lung transplant (1981) ...

... and first place in the egg-and-spoon race (me, at sports day in 1987). I'm sure you'll agree that the egg-and-spoon race was the main highlight.

→ You came last in that race. Stop lying. Prunella

FANTASTIC PLASTIC

What's plastic surgery? I'll give you three options:

1. Having Lego stitched to your face.
2. An operation to change the shape of things like your nose or your lips.
3. Surgery to restore the face or body after major burns, injuries or operations.

If you said 2 or 3, then you'd be right. If you said 1, then go and sit in a dustbin full of fish for an hour. The word plastic means 'reshaping', and it's a much older meaning of the word than the stuff bags and containers and plugs are made of. Just like the word poo-breath was around for years before I started calling Pippin that.

Doctors have been attempting plastic surgery on patients' faces for thousands of years, ever since Sushruta started making new noses. As well as losing them in sword fights (*aagh!*), there were also infections that ate away at people's faces (*aaaaagh!*) that doctors tried to repair over the years.

I'M OVER HERE!

Like most kinds of surgery, there wasn't a lot doctors could do until anaesthetics came along. But, even when patients could snooze through their operations, doctors didn't have much experience doing them, so very little plastic surgery got performed. This all changed about a hundred years ago, during the First World War. (Although I guess they didn't know it was called the First World War at the time, unless a friendly time-traveller had told them about the Second World War.)

2010

Doctors in Spain performed the first face transplant on a man whose (original) face got very badly damaged in a shooting accident. If you receive a face transplant, you still look more like your old self than the person whose new face you've got. This is because what you look like is more to do with the bones underneath than the skin on top. Some mornings I look at myself in the mirror and wonder if someone has secretly transplanted Pippin's face onto my head overnight, but I normally look a bit better after a shower and a quick shave.

Barely. Prunella

During the war, sadly, a lot of people were injured – and so many soldiers had injuries to their faces and hands from gunshots or explosions that in 1917 a whole hospital was set up in England to look after them. The doctors, led by a genius called Harold Gillies, performed over 11,000 operations on these soldiers, and basically invented all the techniques of plastic surgery that are still used today. During the Second World War they made the amazing discovery that pilots whose planes crashed in the water healed much better than pilots whose planes crashed on land. This taught them that using salt water on wounds could save a lot of lives.

THROUGH THE KEYHOLE

If someone collapses at home and they need an urgent operation, but the surgeons can't open the door to get to them, they do something called keyhole surgery from their front doorstep.

OK, fine. That might not be one hundred per cent true. Keyhole surgery (or laparoscopy, if you're a show-off who prefers much longer words) is actually what it's called when doctors don't make a big cut to do an operation,

but instead make a few tiny holes: one to look inside
with a mini camera, and a couple more to put little
grabbers and cutters and stitchers inside.

Think of it like removing a crisp from a packet. The
old-fashioned way is to rip the packet right open and
pluck out a delicious slice of fried potato. The keyhole
surgery method would be to make a couple of little holes
in the packet and use chopsticks to break up the crisp into
tiny pieces, then remove it all from one of the holes. No
one would ever know if you stole one of their crisps! (But,
on the downside, your crisp would be all smooshed up.)

Laparoscopy means the person having the operation recovers faster and feels less pain afterwards, and they don't end up with such a big scar. The downsides of this type of operation are that they often take a bit longer, and laparoscopy is quite complicated to spell. I won't lie to you – I've relied quite heavily on autocorrect to write this section. Also, you might be the kind of weirdo who wants to show off a massive scar to your friends.

The first-ever laparoscopy was carried out in 1901 by a German doctor called Georg Kelling who performed it on a dog. (Don't read this bit, Pippin!) Luckily, it all went well and he wrote in his notes that the dog was 'as cheerful as it was before'. How did he know? Maybe the dog told him a joke?

A dog could write better jokes than you. Prunella

2001

A patient in France had her gall bladder removed by some surgeons who were halfway across the world in New York. No, they didn't have really long scissors that reached right across the ocean. The patient had a three-armed machine moving its scalpel-ended arms around inside her, while her doctors were waggling its controls four thousand miles away. Luckily, the Wi-Fi didn't go down, and the operation was a success. Please don't have any nightmares about a three-armed machine with scalpel-ended arms performing surgery on you.

THE FUTURE

And now some more predictions from my robot butler. He's just been washing the car. (Unfortunately, he put it in the shower and destroyed my bathroom.)

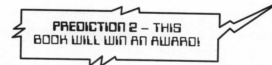

PREDICTION 1 – SURGEONS WILL ALL BE REPLACED BY ROBOTS.

Hopefully not my robot butler though, because he can't even make toast without burning it. But robots will be doing almost every operation, and there won't even be any doctors controlling them; they'll just get on with it on their own. The good news is they'll be a lot faster at operating than humans, and much more accurate, which will make surgery even safer.

PREDICTION 2 – THIS BOOK WILL WIN AN AWARD!

That's wonderful news – thank you! I'll get my suit dry-cleaned for the ceremony.

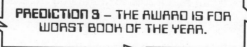

PREDICTION 3 – THE AWARD IS FOR WORST BOOK OF THE YEAR.

Oh.

ADAM'S ANSWERS

WHAT HAPPENS IF YOU NEED AN OPERATION IN THE ANTARCTIC?

It's not an ideal place to require emergency surgery because there aren't any hospitals, so most expeditions bring a doctor along in case there are any serious issues. But what if the doctor needs an operation? This happened in 1961 to a Russian doctor called Leonid Rogozov, who realized he had appendicitis when he was at the South Pole. It would have been impossible to get to a hospital in time to save his life, so the only solution was for him to do the operation himself, and cut out his own appendix! He lay down and cut into his abdomen while other people passed him equipment and held up mirrors so he could see what he was doing. Amazingly, the operation was a success and he made a full recovery.

WHAT WAS THE LARGEST THING EVER REMOVED DURING AN OPERATION?

In 1991, a woman had a tumour removed from her ovary that weighed 130 kilograms. That's about the same weight as a large panda, or twenty-five bowling balls or eight hundred avocados. Basically, it was massive.

CAN DOCTORS DO HEAD TRANSPLANTS?

No.

Oh, did you want a longer answer than that? OK, well, scientists have managed to transplant a rat's head onto a different rat's body. (Or at least they claim they did – all rats look kind of the same to me, so they might have just splashed a bit of blood on its neck and pretended they did the operation.) They've never attempted it on a human – partly because no one's sure if it'll actually work, and partly because (strangely enough) there aren't many people volunteering to have their heads chopped off for an experiment. (My lawyer, Nigel, has asked me to point out that you shouldn't volunteer for a head transplant.)

TRUE OR POO?

IT'S POSSIBLE TO DO OPERATIONS ON BABIES BEFORE THEY'RE BORN.

TRUE Sometimes scans on a pregnant mum show that the baby has a problem with its heart, lungs or spinal cord that needs an operation. Doctors can perform this surgery when the baby is still inside the uterus, many weeks before it's born. Amazingly, these babies heal so quickly that they're born without a scar. Aren't humans amazing? (Especially me.)

→ Nope. Prunella

THE WORLD RECORD FOR THE MOST SURGERY WAS A MAN WHO HAD NINETY-SEVEN SEPARATE OPERATIONS.

POO It was a lot more than that! The world record is an American man who had NINE HUNDRED AND SEVENTY operations – so, nearly a thousand! He had a rare condition that meant he developed lots of lumps on his skin that needed to be removed. I hope he had some kind of loyalty card that got him a free coffee with every tenth operation.

DOCTORS USED TO TRANSPLANT FROG SKIN ONTO HUMANS.

TRUE Some of the earliest attempts at skin transplantation used animal skin. Doctors did experiments using monkeys, goats and dogs (sorry, Pippin!) but they didn't go very well – plus, they must have left patients with random hairy patches of skin. One doctor treated a child who had bad burns by using frog skin, and . . . it was a success! Unfortunately, the boy didn't end up with cool slimy green patches on his body – it blended in with his own skin pretty quickly. Boring!

CRAZY CURES

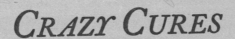

Been wounded in battle? Sorry to hear that. If it happened in the seventeenth century, your doctor's first question would probably be to ask if you've got the sword that attacked you. They would then make a delicious paste out of some old rust and ground-up worms and rub it on the sword because they thought that would heal the wound. You don't have to be the biggest genius in the history of geniuses to work out that this was a load of absolute nonsense.

AND IS THIS THE SWORD YOU WERE ATTACKED WITH?

The Chapter Where

FROGS WEAR PANTS

&

NEWBORN BABIES

EARN MORE POCKET MONEY

THAN YOU

(also known as REPRODUCTION)

OK, HERE'S WHAT WE KNOW. Reproduction means that a male sperm joins forces with a female egg and around nine months later they turn into a baby.

It's obviously slightly unexpected when you first hear about how it all happens. I was a bit like, '*Riiiiight*, OK . . .' and you might have been too. But it's something we need to know about. It's nothing to be embarrassed by – after all, we're all grown-ups here. Actually, you're not, are you? Well, we're all sensible people.

> You're clearly not a sensible person, Adam, so that sentence is a lie. Delete it. Prunella

Because sperm and eggs are a bit on the really, really, really tiny side, you can only see them with a microscope and there was a *loooooooooooong* time when we didn't have microscopes so no one knew what was going on. So what did they do?

1. Say, 'No idea what's happening here – let's just ignore it for a few centuries until someone else works it out.'

2. Make up a load of absolutely ridiculous gibberish.

You'll be delighted to hear the answer is 2.

ANCIENT EGYPT

The Ancient Egyptians thought that a baby was nothing to do with its mum: they reckoned all the woman did was grow the baby, like some kind of person-shaped plant pot, and the child would be a miniature version of its dad.

Their proof for this was that they said dung beetles were all male and they had loads of kids. (They were wrong, by the way – dung beetles aren't only male. Maybe it's just difficult to tell boy beetles from girl beetles? Fun fact: they're called dung beetles because that's what they eat – poo! Maybe Pippin should be called a socks-and-puddle dog.)

OOH. A THREE-COURSE MEAL!

The Ancient Egyptians also had a way of finding out if they were soon going to be a mummy. No, not the kind with bandages – the kind who tells you to eat your broccoli. The possibly pregnant person would wee into a bag of wheat seeds and if the seeds started to sprout this would mean they were pregnant. Strangely, scientists have tested this out recently, and it actually works!

ANCIENT GREECE

If I asked you what the uterus was for, you'd tell me it's where a baby grows. But if you asked someone in Ancient Greece they'd tell you that it was a creature with a life of its own that constantly moved around a woman's body like an out-of-control drone. Umm . . . If a woman had almost anything wrong with her, the Ancient Greeks would say it was because of her 'wandering womb' going for a cheeky float about. Feeling dizzy? The womb's gone up too high. Trouble speaking? The womb's too low. And the treatment was to use different smells to move the uterus back to its usual place . . . sweet smells to lure it nearer and revolting smells to make it go further away. Please wait a second while I sigh really loudly. OK, we can move on now.

FUN UTERUS MAZE!
GUIDE THE LOST
WOMB BACK HOME

Long before ultrasound was invented, people were very interested in whether their baby was going to be a boy or a girl – probably so they could think about what name to call it.

Old Hippoface thought that if a woman got spots on her skin while she was pregnant then she'd have a girl and if her skin stayed clear then she'd have a boy. What a load of dung (as they'd say in Ancient Egypt).

CONGRATULATIONS, IT'S A GIRL!

IT'S A BEE STING.

Remember how I said that women didn't use to be allowed to work as doctors because of something called sexism? Well, see if you can spot any other examples of sexism in this chapter. Clue: there are **LOADS** of them. In the fourth century BC, a Greek woman called Agnodice thought this was very unfair because she knew she'd be a great doctor, so she disguised herself as a man and sneaked into medical school. She specialized in obstetrics, which means delivering babies, and was the type of doctor I used to work as – it's a really fun type of medicine because you start with one patient, and you end up with two! Agnodice was brilliant at her job and helped hundreds of women. Unfortunately, the male doctors found out her secret and she was arrested and put on trial. Luckily, the women she'd treated came to her defence, and she was let off. Hooray! And then they changed the law to say that women throughout Greece could be doctors too. Double hooray!

Shockingly, in Britain, women weren't allowed to be doctors until 1865, when Elizabeth Garrett Anderson first picked up her stethoscope.

ELIZABETH GARRETT ANDERSON: FIVE FACTS AND A LIE

1. Because no universities would let her train as a doctor, she signed up for a nursing course, but secretly went into the doctors' lectures instead.

2. Even though she eventually qualified as a doctor, no hospital would give her a job, so she set up her own one. Basically, she was a woman who wouldn't take no for an answer.

3. To make it easier for other women to become doctors, her hospital only employed women.

4. Her sister, Millicent Fawcett, was one of the main people who got the law changed so that women could vote – what an amazing family. (My family is amazing too: I'm the cleverest man in the world and my sister can burp 'Happy Birthday'.)

5. Elizabeth later became the country's first-ever female mayor.

6. Even later, she became the first-ever woman to walk on the moon.

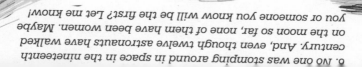

6. NO one was stomping around in space in the nineteenth century. And, even though twelve astronauts have walked on the moon so far, none of them have been women. Maybe you or someone you know will be the first? Let me know!

ANCIENT ROME

A quick reminder: the male reproductive system involves things on the outside like a penis and testicles; the female reproductive system has got things on the inside like a vagina, uterus and ovaries. Two pretty different set-ups, right? Well, you'd disagree if you lived in Ancient Rome – they believed that these were exactly the same thing. Yes, you did read that right: they thought the vagina was a penis that was turned inside out, and the ovaries were exactly the same as testicles. They didn't even give ovaries their own name: they were just known as 'female testicles'. Galen said:

WOMEN HAVE EXACTLY THE SAME ORGANS AS MEN, BUT IN EXACTLY THE WRONG PLACES.

(That's right, Pippin – it's definitely another example of sexism.)

Next up in the massive list of things they got wrong: periods. They thought periods (also known as menstruation, when the lining of the uterus comes out of a girl's vagina once a month after puberty) were evil. I know, I know – they're totally normal and about half of the people in the world have them. But in Ancient Rome they thought that period blood could make plants and animals die. Absolutely ridiculo– Sorry, what's that loud beeping sound? Oh, it's my sexism alarm going off again.

But it wasn't all bad news. A man called Soranus (which hopefully wasn't pronounced 'sore anus') wrote a book with a lot of handy hints about how to help a woman give birth. This became the first-ever textbook for midwives, who are the experts in looking after pregnant mothers and helping them give birth safely. I'd make a **FEW** changes to his textbook, to be honest. For instance, the part where he says that it's dangerous for a pregnant woman to have a bath. Not much fun for the pregnant person – or for anyone they hang out with either!

SPARKLE TIME

When girls or women have their period every month, it can cause pain – and this has been the case forever. Today they can just take painkillers if it gets bad, but this wasn't the case back in Sparkle Time. You might think this was because pain relief hadn't been invented yet, but actually . . . it had! Men would chew on the bark of a willow tree, which sounds a bit weird, but it was effective, and it's where we get a modern medicine called aspirin from. Even though men were allowed pain relief, women weren't. Sorry, I can barely hear myself think – my sexism alarm is going off louder than ever.

NO WOMEN

In the fifteenth century, there was a very popular book called *The Distaff Gospels*, which was full of useful advice for pregnant women. Or so they thought – it was actually as useful as getting Pippin to paint the ceiling. Advice included:

- It's dangerous to eat fruit – umm, pretty bad advice there.

- Don't eat fish heads or your baby's mouth will be too pointy – who even eats fish heads anyway?!

↳ I do, and they're delicious. Prunella

FROGS IN PANTS

I know what you're thinking – you've nearly read a whole book, and not once have I talked about scientists putting a pair of pants on a frog. Well, the wait is finally over, thanks to Lazzaro Spallanzani, who you might remember was the bloke who discovered all about stomach acid.

(Or you might have read that chapter in a hurry. Or you might be reading this book back to front because you're wacky like that. Or your pet lion might have eaten the first half of the book because you were out of raw steaks. There are lots of possible reasons.)

Lazzaro wondered if you needed both a biological mum and a biological dad to have a baby so he came up with a little experiment. He went off to the eighteenth-century version of Marks & Spencer and bought some XXXXXS size pants, which he handed out to a load of frogs. He discovered that if either mum frog or dad frog was wearing pants, there wouldn't be any baby frogs.

This was such an important discovery that there's now a statue of Lazzaro Spallanzani, in his home town of Scandiano, of him looking at a frog through a magnifying glass. Unfortunately, only one of them is wearing pants. (It's Spallanzani.)

1739

Labour (when a woman pushes a baby out at the end of pregnancy) doesn't often last more than a day – but, in Ireland in 1739, a patient called Alice O'Neal had been in labour for twelve days. Her midwife, Mary Donally, decided to perform a Caesarean section to save her life. There were two slight problems here. First of all, Caesareans are usually done by doctors, not midwives, and there weren't any doctors for miles around. And, secondly, no doctor had ever performed this operation successfully before. But there weren't any other options, so Mary took a razor and some needles and thread used for mending clothes and did the operation. Alice survived, which is very impressive – not just because Mary was kind of making up the operation as she went along, but because this was before the invention of anaesthetics or antibiotics.

STINKY SURGEONS

In the nineteenth century, it was very dangerous to have a baby. Many women died because they lost loads of blood during childbirth (luckily, we have drugs now that make that very unlikely to happen) and lots of others died of something called puerperal fever. No, I didn't spell purple wrong: puerperal means they've just had a baby. These women would develop an unexplained fever that they sadly never recovered from.

In 1847, a Hungarian doctor called Ignaz Semmelweis thought he would investigate why this was happening. There were two wards in his hospital where mums gave birth: one run by midwives and one run by doctors. Almost all the cases of puerperal fever were in the doctors' ward. Hmm. Why don't you put a detective hat on your head and a detective pipe in your mouth and see

if you can work out what was going on? (My lawyer, Nigel, has asked me to mention that you absolutely shouldn't smoke a pipe.)

Semmelweis's first thought was that a priest often went through the doctors' ward, ringing a bell, to visit someone who had died, so he wondered if the bell was causing puerperal fever. He banned the priest's bell, and what do you think happened? Yep – nothing. Then he noticed that the patients on the midwives' ward gave birth lying in a different position, so he insisted that everyone gave birth in the same position. And how many lives were saved? Yep – none. Finally, he realized that before the doctors turned up to work on this ward they spent a few hours cutting up dead bodies, then started delivering babies without even washing their hands first.

And there we go! But because Joseph Lister hadn't come along yet with his crazy idea about hand-washing, no one realized this was dangerous. I know, right? Ignaz thought that the dead bodies were leaving a dangerous smell on the doctors' hands, which wasn't quite right, but he came up with the right answer – to wash them! The doctors did this and immediately women stopped dying of puerperal fever. And all the patients in the hospital lived happily ever after.

No, not really. The other doctors started getting upset that they were being accused of making their patients ill, and no one likes to be told they're wrong, especially grumpy old men.

GRUMPY OLD MEN

Ignaz got the sack from the hospital and then became so miserable he ended up living in an asylum, where he died in 1865. (And then, a couple of years later, Joseph Lister proved that Ignaz was right all along – *aagh!*)

1847

Going through labour can be pretty painful (to say the least) so you can imagine that the first patient to get an anaesthetic while having a baby would have been extremely grateful. This woman was so astonished and so happy that she named her baby Anaesthesia. Well, I suppose it's better than being called Ouuuuuuuch Aaaaaargh.

CHILD STARS

Most babies are born after nine months spent hanging about in the uterus – if they're born much earlier than that, it's called being premature. These days babies can survive being born at six months and even younger, thanks to amazing doctors and nurses, amazing medicine and an amazing invention called the incubator. The incubator is basically a magic box – no, not the kind you might see somebody using to saw their assistant in half, a different kind – that keeps very premature babies alive by helping them feed and breathe, and by protecting and carefully monitoring them.

The incubator was invented in France in 1880, based on a machine that kept baby chicks warm. An American doctor called Martin Couney was visiting France and saw how well they worked, so told his hospital all about them, and how they massively increased the chance that a premature baby would survive. Unfortunately, his hospital wasn't interested – his bosses just did an impression of the 🤷 emoji and said that premature babies were weaklings who weren't supposed to live. They wouldn't buy any incubators. How mean! Luckily, Martin came up with a brilliant (but totally bananas) plan.

When a premature baby was born, he would care for it in an incubator, but not in the hospital . . . in a theme park. His idea was that after people had been on the roller coaster, and before they went off to buy candyfloss, they might fancy paying twenty-five cents to go into his 'Infantorium' to see some tiny babies, and the entrance fee would help him pay back the money he'd borrowed

During the First World War, a Frenchman called Paul Langevin developed a way of working out how far away underwater enemy submarines were. No, this book hasn't turned into *Kay's Marvellous Submarines*. I'm telling you this because, a couple of decades later, doctors realized they could use exactly the same technology – called ultrasound – to look inside people's bodies and see things like brains and bowels and babies. The first photo ever taken of you was probably an ultrasound – I hope you didn't pull any stupid faces.

to buy the incubators. Sounds weird, but amazingly it was a huge success and people flocked to spend their money and see these magical little babies, even though they didn't juggle chainsaws or walk across a tightrope. By doing this, Couney saved the lives of over six thousand babies. Luckily, these days all hospitals have incubators, which is good news for patients, but bad news if you want to see a cute baby after you've staggered off Nemesis.

THE AMAZING
SLEEPING
FARTING
BABIES

LAB BRATS

Just like people go to see their doctor if they have problems with their lungs or their liver or their bones or their brains, sometimes a man's or a woman's reproductive system needs treatment too. Until about forty years ago, if a couple weren't able to have a baby, doctors couldn't do very much. But these days there's a way of getting pregnant called IVF, which stands for in vitro fertilization and means 'fertilization in glass'. It's not a bad description because in IVF the sperm and the eggs are placed together in a glass dish to start to grow for a few days before they're put into the mother's uterus. The first successful IVF in an animal was carried out in 1959 on a rabbit called Carrotface Megabunny, and the first IVF pregnancy in a human was a girl born in 1978 called Louise Brown. (Yes, I did make up the name of the rabbit – the scientists didn't give her a name, and I thought it was unfair that she was nameless.)

THE FUTURE

Let's fire up my robot butler's prediction module once again. He's just pruned the trees (but unfortunately he covered them all with prune juice).

PREDICTION 1 – BABIES WILL BE ABLE TO GROW IN ARTIFICIAL WOMBS.

This is great news for parents who want to go on holiday for nine months until their baby is ready to be born and start screaming and pooing. These artificial wombs will be a bit like fish tanks and will mean that it's much easier to keep an eye on how a baby is growing – you don't need to do a scan if you can just look in through a window. And on the rare occasion that a baby needs an operation before it's born, that will also be much easier to do. Plus, delivering a baby will just be a case of scooping it out with a fishing net or one of those big claws you get at the service station when you're trying to win a prize – no more painful labours or messy Caesarean sections.

PREDICTION 2 – THE NEXT CHAPTER WILL BE EXTREMELY BORING.

Oi! I've got feelings, you know?

How will I be able to tell the difference? Prunella

ADAM'S ANSWERS

WHAT'S A WET NURSE?

No, it's not a nurse whose umbrella broke on the way to hospital. A wet nurse was a woman employed by rich parents to breastfeed their baby because they decided they were too busy and important to do it themselves. These days mums usually breastfeed their own babies, but people who aren't able to, or choose not to, feed them using a bottle. (Of milk, not Cherry Coke.)

CAN YOU FREEZE EGGS?

Yes, but they taste nicer scrambled. Oh, you mean the other kind of eggs. The answer's still yes – they can be safely frozen and used for IVF in the future. Women do this for lots and lots of reasons: for example, before they have treatment such as chemotherapy, which might stop their ovaries working. Also, because eggs disappear with age, some women decide to freeze them when they're younger in case they decide to have children later in life. Oh, and they have to be stored at minus 200°C, so you can't keep them at home, tucked next to your Zoom lollies.

IS IT SAFE FOR PREGNANT WOMEN TO HAVE PETS?

Yes, absolutely, although pet poo can have germs in it, so it's best to avoid pooper-scooping. But in Sparkle Time pets were an absolute no-no. Doctors thought that even looking at an animal would result in a baby being born totally covered in hair. It didn't matter whether a pregnant woman looked at a horse or a hamster, dopey docs thought the memory of this would stick in their brain and a baby would pop out wearing a permanent fleecy onesie.

TRUE OR POO?

YOU CAN ONLY HAVE AN ULTRASOUND WHEN YOU'RE IN THE BATH.

POO Come on – seriously? Ultrasounds in the bath? Utter tripe. But when ultrasound was first invented that was exactly what happened – if a doctor wanted to have a look inside you, they'd chuck you in the tub. This was because ultrasound only works properly if the skin is wet. These days they just put some slimy gel on the part of the body they're scanning. It's much more convenient than running a bath – and makes the hospital's water bill a lot cheaper.

TWINS ARE GETTING MORE COMMON.

TRUE About one in every sixty-five pregnant mums has twins, which is more than ever. There are a couple of reasons for this – firstly, IVF and other treatments that help people get pregnant increase the chance of twins. Secondly, women are having babies later in life than they used to, and this makes it more likely an ovary will randomly decide to release two eggs at once. Do you know any twins? My friend Chris is a twin, but I'm not sure which one is the evil one (there's always an evil one). It's either Chris or his brother, David the Vampire. Probably Chris.

WOMEN USED WEASEL TESTICLES TO STOP THEMSELVES GETTING PREGNANT.

TRUE Well, to **TRY** to stop getting pregnant, that is – I don't think you could really describe this as a successful method. Some historians think that, in Sparkle Time, women would wear a necklace with a pair of weasel testicles dangling from it because doctors believed it prevented pregnancy. Other methods included drinking water with lead in it. This might have actually worked, but unfortunately it also caused a few other minor issues, such as death.

CRAZY CURES

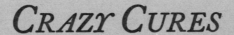

If a woman hasn't gone into labour after nine months, it can become dangerous for the baby. These days we have clever medicines to bring on labour, but in the eighteenth century their methods were a bit stranger (and a lot more useless). Top of the list was smearing the mum with pigeon poo.

Can you stop talking about poo? This is supposed to be a textbook. No one's going to want to read this horrible nonsense. You should go back to being a doctor. Actually, you were probably terrible at that too. Prunella

The Chapter Where

EVERY-ONE DRINKS A NICE WARM CUP OF WEE

(also known as
LIVER AND KIDNEYS)

HERE'S A QUICK REMINDER of where your wee actually comes from before we have a look at how our forefathers got it so wrong. Oh, and our foremothers and foregrandparents too. Your kidneys filter out waste products from your blood, along with any excess water, and send them off down the ureters to your bladder, and then it finally comes out of your urethra and into the toilet or onto the postman. (That was Pippin, and she's still in trouble for it.)

I think you should mention great aunts here too, otherwise it's very disrespectful. Prunella

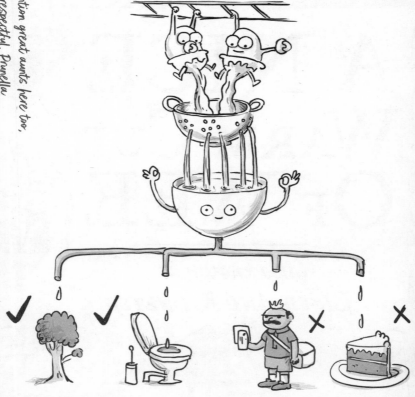

I'll also talk about the liver because I don't want to upset it. A bit like me, it has loads of different jobs. (I'm a writer and a former doctor and a part-time fire juggler.) It's the body's other waste-disposal organ – it takes anything you've eaten or drunk that might be bad for you and turns it into a substance called bile, which it squirts back into the intestine and gives poo its delicious brown colour. Sorry, I mean disgusting brown colour. Please ignore the part where I said poo was delicious.

Luckily, our ancestors have always known exactly what the liver does and how it works. Tricked you! Of course they haven't!

ANCIENT EGYPT

You know when you're not certain about something, but you just have a general vibe about it? Like when you decide not to go for a midnight swim in the lake with the WARNING! DEADLY PIRANHAS! sign on it. Well, the Ancient Egyptians had a vague feeling that the kidneys were pretty important – they just couldn't put their finger on exactly why. The closest they came to an explanation was that the kidneys were advisors to the heart. Advisors?! About what?! Whether to buy a blue T-shirt or a sparkly green one? We'll never know.

But anyway the kidneys were considered important enough to be popped back into mummies' bodies to go off to the afterlife, rather than being sealed in a jar or chucked in the recycling – sorry, brain. They clearly didn't think the liver was especially important though because it ended up with the old jar treatment.

ANCIENT GREECE

In Ancient Greece, they made a wee discovery in the subject of wee medicine – they spotted that it came out of the bladder. Unfortunately, they reckoned that it sort of appeared in the bladder by magic, rather than coming from the kidneys, so they only really get half marks for that. Aristotle was cutting up a fish for dinner one day and spotted that it didn't have any kidneys. He then decided that must mean our kidneys are totally pointless, otherwise fish would need them too. Aristotle clearly wasn't thinking this through, was he? Fish don't have arms or legs either – did he think **THEY** were unnecessary for humans?

The liver had a much better time in Ancient Greece. If this was a textbook back then, at least half of it would be about the liver. They thought the liver was the body's most important organ, and that it was pretty much solely responsible for keeping you alive. (I mean, it's a pretty essential organ, and you definitely wouldn't want your liver to go off on holiday for a fortnight, but I reckon the heart or the brain might have something to say about the whole 'most important' thing.)

They did get something right though, which we know because of a myth they told (myths are like bedtime stories, but all the characters have really long names) about a guy called Prometheus.

Prometheus was the god of fire, and one day he decided to give the people of Earth the gift of . . . you guessed it – fire. I mean, fair enough – he was the god of it. But Zeus, who was the head god – kind of like a head teacher, but even scarier because he could throw bolts of lightning – got extremely cross with him for some reason (maybe he didn't want humans to be able to toast marshmallows) and decided to punish Prometheus. But, instead of sending him to his bedroom or banning him from playing on his Xbox, Zeus chained Prometheus to a rock, where every day an eagle would fly over and peck out his liver. Bit mean, Zeusy. Then the next day Prometheus's liver would reappear . . . but unfortunately so would the eagle.

But what was the important medical fact in there? No, not that eagles love to eat liver for breakfast. The Ancient Greeks worked out that the liver is very good at regenerating – it doesn't happen overnight for us non-gods, but even if the liver gets really badly damaged it can usually sort itself out. Well spotted, Ancient Greeks!

ANCIENT ROME

The Ancient Romans finally worked out that wee comes from the kidneys. I wish they hadn't done it by putting a peg on a monkey's penis, but I promised to tell you how all these discoveries took place, and I'm afraid on this occasion it involved a peg and a monkey's penis.

When they did this, the poor monkey couldn't wee for a few days, and its kidneys swelled right up, so they realized that's where the wee was coming from.

AND THEN HE TOOK THE PEG AND PUT IT ON MY . . .

HEY, I'M EATING!

Just like the Ancient Greeks, they were big fans of the liver in Ancient Rome (although I guess they just called it Rome – they didn't know they were ancient). The main thing that they reckoned the liver did was produce the humours. I don't mean they thought the liver was always telling jokes – there's nothing funny about the humours. They were a weird idea that Hippoface came up with in Ancient Greece, which Galen then developed (well, made even weirder) in Rome.

The theory was that every person had four different liquids inside them, and if you had the right amounts of each, then you'd be healthy. On the other hand, if you had too much or too little, then your humours would be all wonky and you'd become unwell. People believed in the humours for thousands of years – in fact, some cultures around the world still base treatments on them.

BLOOD

Fair enough – there's no denying that your body has blood in it. But that's the only tick Galen's homework is going to get. If someone had a fever or was sweating, he reckoned it was because they had too much blood, and so the solution was to let a bit out. Or let a lot out. As you might remember from a few chapters ago, this wasn't really a good idea. (It killed thousands and thousands of people, and didn't help so much as a single headache.)

BLACK BILE

Too much black bile could apparently lead to things like depression. The treatment for this was to make the patient vomit. Unfortunately, they'd still be depressed afterwards, plus now they'd be covered in puke.

YELLOW BILE

The next humour was called yellow bile – too much of this and you'd become angry. The treatment for this was called cupping, where they'd put a load of cups on your skin, suck all the air out and leave them there until you had tons of big red circles all over you. And I do mean **YOU**, because it was also used on people with uncontrollable farting. Some people have cupping today for conditions like back pain, but doctors don't think it actually makes any real difference.

PHLEGM

The fourth humour was phlegm, which is an actual thing that we all have, so I guess they got that one right. As my Great Aunt Prunella says, 'A broken clock is right twice a day' – which means even total idiots get things right sometimes by accident. But they thought it was made in the brain (hmm) and that if there was too much of it going round your body, then snot would pour out of your nose like a broken tap (also hmm – they hadn't heard about colds, I guess). And their cure for too much phlegm? Drink lots of wine. (Biggest hmm yet.)

→ That reminds me, I must get batteries for my clock. Prunella

FOUR HUMOURS
COLOURING BY NUMBERS

BLOOD

YELLOW BILE

1

2

BLACK BILE

PHLEGM

3

4

COLOUR GUIDE

1 Red. (It's blood.)
2 See if you can find a subtle clue in the name.
3 Again, there's a TINY clue.
4 Look in your hanky.

SPARKLE TIME

If we jump ahead to Sparkle Time, they still believed in the humours, but they'd also gone absolutely urine crazy. Honestly, they thought it was the answer to everything. Before doing operations, some surgeons would rinse the patient's skin with wee. (Hopefully they used a bottle of it and a sponge rather than weeing on the patient directly.) Worse than that, doctors would advise their patients to drink a nice warm cup of wee every morning. Maybe they'd heard someone saying 'nice warm cup of tea' and got confused. And if a soldier got shot, then the army's doctors would advise the other soldiers to wee on him. Honestly, as if his day couldn't get any worse.

If I didn't know better, I'd think doctors used to all be sponsored by the Urine Society.

Even though in Europe it was just an extravaganza of people weeing everywhere, over in Iran in the eleventh century, a doctor called Avicenna was making much more important discoveries. He didn't think that wee was a delicious breakfast drink or some kind of antibacterial spray – he realized the yellow stuff was much more important than that.

You know when the doctor sometimes asks you to give a urine sample and you try really, really hard to get it in the pot, but even so most of it goes on the floor? Oh, just me? There are two reasons for that. First of all, the doctor doesn't have any idea what's wrong with you and just wants to get you out of the room for five minutes so he can google 'weird bum rash'. But the second reason is that doctors can use your wee to tell them loads of things about your health. And it was old Avicenna who worked this out.

AVICENNA: FIVE FACTS AND A LIE

1. By the time he was ten, Avicenna had totally memorized the Quran (the main religious book in Islam). That's more than seventy thousand words! By the time I was ten, I was still struggling to tie my shoelaces.

2. When he was eighteen, he was a fully qualified doctor and was already making medical discoveries. In fairness, by the time I was eighteen, I had totally mastered my shoelaces.

3. He recommended dancing as a cure for various illnesses.

4. He wrote his books
Just like a poem
I don't know why
Cos I didn't know him.

5. A copy of his book about the body, *The Canon of Medicine*, sold recently for nearly £200,000. So maybe hold on to this book – it could be worth a fortune (in a thousand years' time).

6. He was put in prison because some important people didn't like the books he'd written.

You should go to prison for this book. I'll visit you every two years. Prunella

3. He didn't prescribe dancing, but he did say that listening to good music was important for staying healthy.

For example, he knew that if your urine was concentrated (I mean a dark colour, not that your wee was thinking very hard) then you needed to drink more water. And if it looked cloudy and smelled really pongy, then it could mean you had an infection. He even worked out that if it was foamy like bubble bath, you might have a problem with your kidneys – all stuff we now know is absolutely true. Top marks, Avicenna! Finally, he worked out that if your urine was purple that meant you were an alien. (There's a tiny chance I made that last bit up.)

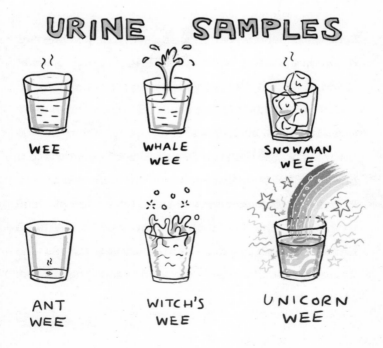

URINE SAMPLES

WEE

WHALE WEE

SNOWMAN WEE

ANT WEE

WITCH'S WEE

UNICORN WEE

Avicenna didn't get **EVERYTHING** right though. He wasn't the best at treating some of the illnesses he managed to diagnose. For example, if you had a problem with your kidneys, he would put a load of insects in your pants so they could crawl inside you and somehow sort things out. When you've finished screaming, we can move on to the next section.

NO SENSE OF HUMOUR

Sometimes people say things and everyone just believes them for ages, like when Julian Pringle in my class at school said that his dad was an Olympic sprinter and we all believed him until the next Olympics when there wasn't anyone called Colin Pringle competing in the 100 metres. Doctors believed Galen's theory about the four humours for even longer than we believed Julian Pringle. In fact, no one questioned it for about 1,500 years, until the seventeenth century when William Harvey came along. He was the smarty-pantaloons who figured out circulation, and decided to solve the mystery of the liver too.

Willz had a bit of a fiddle around and discovered that the humours were just a load of made-up old nonsense. (Galen had been dead for a very long time, so he didn't get his head flushed down the toilet, unlike poor Julian Pringle.) He also figured out how the liver worked and how it was connected to other organs around it called the gall bladder and the spleen.

THE DUSTPAN AND BRUSH OF KNOWLEDGE

THE HUMOURS

THE BIN OF HISTORY

THE SOCKS OF TRUTH

DIABETES

You might know someone with diabetes – you might even have it yourself. It's to do with an organ that hangs out next to your liver called the pancreas, which has the very important job of making a substance called insulin that sorts out the levels of sugar in your blood. If your pancreas starts misbehaving, then you get too much sugar sloshing around you and this is called diabetes. But diabetes isn't something new – it's existed for as long as grown-ups have been terrible at dancing (forever).

In Ancient Egypt, they wrote on their dusty papyrus scrolls about an illness that made people go to the toilet a lot and lose weight, which was almost certainly diabetes. Galen got it a bit wrong (classic Galen) and thought it was a problem with the kidneys. However, he did come up with a disgusting name for it: diarrhoea of the urine. The Urine Society must have been very annoyed when the name got changed to diabetes.

A bunch of people had a go at treating diabetes – but they had no idea what was causing it, so their attempts were pretty useless. Over a thousand years ago, a doctor called Paul of Aegina thought he was a bit of a diabetes expert. (Paul seems a very ordinary name for someone from the olden days, doesn't it? I wonder if he had a brother called Steve.)

His cure? Bloodletting and drinking wine. They seemed to think those things would cure quite a lot of illnesses, didn't they? Turns out they didn't work at all.

But it wasn't until 1675 that this condition was finally given its name. We usually just call it diabetes, but its full name is actually 'diabetes mellitus' – a bit like how we call the queen 'Elizabeth', but most people don't know her surname is actually Bummo. (I may have invented this.) Anyway, mellitus means 'honey', because (please put your milkshake down for this bit) the sugar in diabetic patients' urine makes it taste like honey. Quite how they discovered this in the first place doesn't bear thinking about. Maybe the vending machine was broken in a hospital one day and a particularly thirsty doctor decided to have a quick sip of some urine samples? It took until 1910 to work out what was causing diabetes, when a doctor with the pretty amazing name of Sir Edward Sharpey-Schafer came along. He discovered that people with diabetes didn't produce a certain substance and he named it insulin. (If I was him, I'd have named it Sharpey-Schafer Stuff.)

They weren't any closer to treating diabetes though. In 1919, a doctor called Frederick Allen put his patients with diabetes on a diet of . . . total starvation. (Umm, this doesn't sound like it's going to end well.) It helped a few patients, but most of them starved to death. (Knew it.) Thank goodness then for a couple of doctors called Banting and Best, who sound like a comedy double act, but were actually brilliant scientists who made insulin for the first time. If you're a cow, please stop reading now. The very first insulin injections were made by smooshing up a cow pancreas, and it meant that diabetes could finally be treated. These days, insulin is made in a lab rather than from smooshed-up cow pancreas. Cows, you can start reading again now.

NO BOOZE IS
GOOD BOOZE

We all know that drinking too much alcohol is very bad for the liver. Well, if you didn't know that before, then you do now. But for years and years and years doctors didn't just think it was totally fine to drink as much alcohol as you liked – they thought it was really good for you. I've got no idea how they got this so very wrong – maybe they were all drunk?

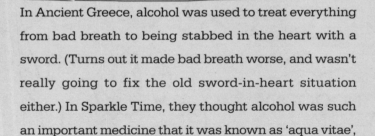

In Ancient Greece, alcohol was used to treat everything from bad breath to being stabbed in the heart with a sword. (Turns out it made bad breath worse, and wasn't really going to fix the old sword-in-heart situation either.) In Sparkle Time, they thought alcohol was such an important medicine that it was known as 'aqua vitae',

which means 'the water of life'. Whether you turned up to the doctor's with a dog bite or an attack of the plague, they'd send you home with a prescription for alcohol. The average adult drank four and a half litres of beer every day in those days – that's the same amount as thirteen cans of Coke. But of beer! *Aaagh!*

It wasn't until 1793 that a doctor called Matthew Baillie finally worked out that alcohol could damage the liver. He published this in a book called *A Series of Engravings, Tending to Illustrate the Morbid Anatomy of Some of the Most Important Parts of the Human Body*. It must have been a massive book to fit all those words on the cover.

1980

There's a condition called kidney stones where the kidneys decide to fill up with stones – maybe it's really boring being a kidney and they need a hobby? – and this can be extremely sore. People have had kidney stones for thousands of years – some mummies even had stones as big as tennis balls rattling around in them! The treatment used to be almost as painful as the stones themselves and involved putting some nutcrackers inside the patient to smash them up. The stones I mean, not the patients. In 1980, doctors in Germany worked out a new treatment that didn't involve anything going inside the patient – they used a special kind of sound wave that made the stones break up into tiny pieces. Good news for patients, bad news for nutcracker factories.

THE FUTURE

My robot butler has just finished laying the table (unfortunately, he tucked it up in bed under a duvet) so is now ready to give you some more predictions.

PREDICTION 1 – YOUR TOILET WILL BE INTELLIGENT.

It won't read you Dickens while you're pooing – but your toilet will be constantly monitoring your wee to keep an eye on the health of your kidneys. It might tell you to drink a bit more water if you're dehydrated, or it might notice that you have an infection or diabetes or something else that means you need to see your doctor.

Or it might say, 'Stop weeing on me! I've got feelings, you know?!'

PREDICTION 2 – YOUR GREAT AUNT PRUNELLA WILL FIND OUT THAT YOU BROKE HER VASE.

Eek – I hope not.

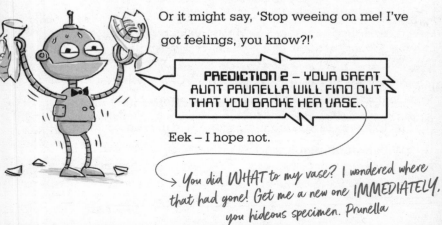

You did WHAT to my vase? I wondered where that had gone! Get me a new one IMMEDIATELY, you hideous specimen. Prunella

ADAM'S ANSWERS

WHICH NURSERY RHYME WAS ALL ABOUT A KIDNEY DOCTOR?

No, it's not 'I'm a Little Wee-pot'. No one's quite certain if this is true (because it was from hundreds of years ago), but historians think that 'Frère Jacques' was named after a bloke called Frère Jacques Beaulieu who wandered around France, cutting out people's kidney stones and unfortunately killing quite a lot of them in the process. The history books don't mention whether he whistled the tune while he cut his patients open.

HOW CAN YOU SAVE A LIFE USING A WASHING MACHINE, SOME CANS OF BEANS AND A FEW OLD SAUSAGES?

By turning them into a dialysis machine, which is basically an artificial kidney that filters people's blood if their kidneys aren't working too well. These days they're a lot more advanced, but the very first dialysis machine was built during the Second World War, when it was extremely difficult to get equipment because all the factories were making things for the war. A doctor called Willem Kolff made it from a washing machine, a few empty cans and some sausage skin (to use as a filter) and suddenly a load of people's lives were saved! Hopefully they didn't smell too much of sausages afterwards.

WHAT WAS UROMANCY?

It's impossible to predict the future unless you've got a robot butler with a future module. But that hasn't stopped greedy people pretending that they can, to earn money. Over the years, some people have done this by reading tea leaves in the bottom of your cuppa, some by studying the palms of your hands, and some by using uromancy, which is . . . looking at your wee. They would check out the pattern of bubbles in a pot of pee and say if you were going to fall in love or have success at work. If you're the sort of person who will wee into a pot for a 'psychic' stranger, then I can make one very accurate prediction about you: you're extremely gullible.

TRUE OR POO?

THREE HUNDRED YEARS AGO, DOCTORS TRIED TO FIX THE BRAIN USING EXTRACTS OF WEE.

POO It wasn't three hundred years ago – it's happening right now. There's a special type of cell called a stem cell, which scientists can turn into any kind of cell in the body, for example brain cells, if the brain has been damaged. You can find these in blood, but it's much easier (and less sore) to get a sample of urine, which also contains stem cells. A few weeks ago, Pippin weed on my pillow – maybe she was just trying to make me cleverer? Sorry, I mean **EVEN** cleverer.

THERE USED TO BE A TAX ON WEE.

TRUE Urine wasn't just used as an unhygienic mouthwash and a disgusting wound-cleaner – lots of different professions were splashing it around too. Romans softened leather with it, used it to make wool and even washed their togas in it (yuck). It was used so much that the emperor eventually decided to make some money out of it – so he put a tax on wee. (Tax is something grown-ups always moan about, but it's actually a good thing – because by paying it you give money to the government so we can have important things like schools and hospitals.)

THE SPLEEN IS RESPONSIBLE FOR YOUR SENSE OF HUMOUR.

POO Your brain is responsible for your sense of humour, and your spleen is all about getting rid of damaged red blood cells. Well, we know that now. Even though he made lots of great discoveries, William Harvey thought that giggling was all down to your spleen. It's a shame that isn't true, because if you don't laugh at the jokes in this book I could claim it's because your spleen's broken.

CRAZY CURES

Kings have always been obsessed with tricks that would make them stay young, presumably so they could be king forever and ever. King Louis XIV of France, who was known as the Sun King, thought that the secret to eternal youth was having liquids squirted up his bottom. His fave bum liquid was almond milk mixed with honey, and he had this done literally thousands of times, including during meetings. He should probably have been called the Bum King instead of the Sun King.

This chapter was sponsored by the Urine Society. I would like to thank them for providing me with a car shaped like a kidney and a lifetime's supply of toilets.

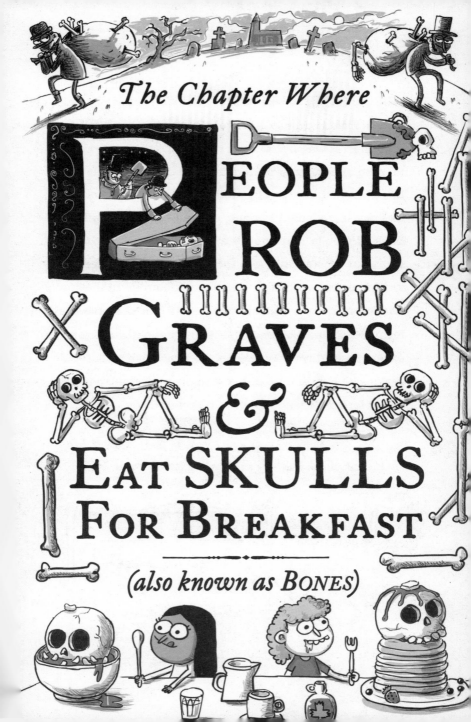

The Chapter Where

PEOPLE ROB GRAVES & EAT SKULLS FOR BREAKFAST

(also known as BONES)

THIS IS PIPPIN'S FAVOURITE CHAPTER of the book – bones! (Well, unless I write a chapter about rolling around in sewage, that is.) If there's one thing we know for sure about our ancestors it's that they definitely had bones. In fact, it's usually all that's left of them. And, for as long as we've had bones, we've been falling off the back of woolly mammoths and breaking them. If you smashed up your arm five thousand years ago, doctors would cover it with clay, which would harden in the sun and keep the bone nice and still until it had mended a few weeks later. Not much has really changed since then, except these days they make plaster casts out of material that's a lot lighter than clay and, more importantly, much easier for your friends to write rude words on.

Do not encourage your readers to write rude words, you vile boy. It's bad enough that you do it, without corrupting all these innocent children. Prunella

NOT OK		OK
BUMHOLE	→	ANUS
POO	→	FAECES
FART	→	FLATULENCE

ANCIENT EGYPT

Normally, when I talk about doctors in Ancient Egypt, it's to tell you how wrong they were about everything and I'll say something like, 'They thought the nose was made of pasta,' or, 'They treated earache by tap-dancing.' But when it came to the bones, they were pretty advanced. They wrote about how to treat a broken collarbone using a sling, exactly the same way we do today. They drew pictures showing a doctor putting a dislocated shoulder (dislocation means a bone has come out of its joint) back into place – another technique that hasn't changed in four thousand years. They even made a prosthetic toe out of wood and leather for someone who'd lost their big toe. (I mean it had been cut off, not that they'd accidentally left it in the supermarket.) It's a bit weird how they got some stuff totally right and the rest completely wrong – maybe an Ancient Egyptian travelled forward in time to medical school, but only went to one lesson and spent the rest of the day in the British Museum, visiting her family.

 **THE TIME-TRAVELLING EGYPTIAN GIRL (WHOSE FATHER IS AN ARCHITECT)**

HEY, DAD, I BUILT A TIME MACHINE! WANNA COME TO THE FUTURE?

I'D LOVE TO, BUT THE PHARAOH WANTS ME TO DESIGN A NEW TYPE OF BUILDING. HAVE FUN!

OK!

TO THE FUTURE!

LET'S GO IN THERE!

BRITISH MUSEU

IT'S AUNTIE CAROL!

TIME TO GO HOME. *OH NO!* I FORGOT TO GET DAD A PRESENT!

LATER (WELL, TECHNICALLY EARLIER)

THE END

Unfortunately, the Ancient Egyptians had their limits – if a broken bone burst through the skin or needed screws or pins to fix it, that would almost certainly result in death because, as you know, they didn't have antibiotics or anaesthetics. It makes me extremely glad to be alive today because we have those amazing medical advances and, just as importantly, choc ices. X-rays of King Tutankhamun show that he probably died from a broken leg that wouldn't have been possible for his doctors to fix. (Either that or someone accidentally dropped him down the stairs when he was a mummy.) He was buried with 130 walking sticks to help him in the afterlife – don't you just hate it when you turn up in the afterlife with only 129 walking sticks?

1987

Some archaeologists were exploring a cave in Somerset when they spotted a drinking bowl from about fifteen thousand years ago. Why's this in the bones chapter of this book, not the cutlery and crockery section? Well, firstly, this book doesn't have a cutlery and crockery section. And, secondly, the bowl was made out of a human skull. Luckily, skeleton-based dinnerware has gone out of fashion since then, and these days it's much easier and much less messy to get your bowls from IKEA.

ANCIENT GREECE

In Ancient Greece, they realized the importance of exercise for keeping your body healthy, and your bones and muscles strong. Hippoface was the first doctor ever to write a patient a prescription for exercise. (The patient had TB, so the exercise wasn't particularly helpful and they still died of it, but it's the thought that counts, I guess.) If you've ever seen a picture of a Greek statue, you'll know from their abs that they spent a lot of time working out – they even invented competitions so they could show off how buff they were. You might have heard of a little event called the Olympics? They also came up with the concept of gyms, or to use their proper name, gymnasiums – which means 'place to exercise naked'. (My lawyer, Nigel, has asked me to point out in the strongest terms that you should always wear your gym kit when exercising.)

ANCIENT ROME

The Ancient Romans also thought that exercise was very good for your health, and the three main kinds they recommended were walking, running and . . . reading out loud. Two out of three ain't bad. I'm a big fan of reading, but I'm not sure how it's a form of exercise – unless the book is made from enormous slabs of marble?

Galen did a pretty decent job of figuring out how the muscles worked (I guess they're just underneath the skin, so there's no excuse for messing that one up) and he also sussed out how muscles hang out together in pairs. Before you start thinking he was too much of a genius though – he thought that bones were made from solidified sperm. Umm . . . nope!

Well, reading this book is certainly exhausting. Prunella

BONEHEAD!

SPARKLE TIME

If you broke a bone in Sparkle Time, they had a much better way of keeping it still than covering it in thick clay, so no one had to walk about with an enormous flower pot on their leg any more. They would soak bandages in horse blood, then wrap them round you. When the blood was all dried up and clotted, the bandages became solid and the leg couldn't move. Clever, right? (But disgusting, obviously.)

You know at Halloween how people eat sweets shaped like skulls and crisps shaped like vampire fangs? Well, back in Sparkle Time, they were into spooky snacks too – there was one popular treat in particular called a mellified man. Sounds quite nice, doesn't it – a bit like a jelly baby? Shall I tell you the recipe?

😀 Take an extremely old man who's going to die in the next few weeks.

😀 Ban him from eating or drinking anything apart from loads and loads of honey.

😀 Make him have a bath of honey every day.

 When he dies (probably from eating too much honey), put him in a coffin that's filled to the brim with even more honey.

 Wait one hundred years.

 Cut him up and eat as a delicious, sugary snack.

Would you like some? I'll put you down for a few chunks. Doctors at the time claimed that eating a mellified man could cure broken bones. Personally, I think the only thing it could actually do would be to put you off your dinner for the next thirty years.

CHOP CHOP

Dissection is the word for 'cutting up dead bodies'. This is handy when you're a medical student because if you're out at the shops and one of your friends calls to ask what you're studying at the moment you can say, 'I'm doing dissection,' because 'I'm cutting up dead bodies' might make the other customers freak out and call the police. Dissection is an important part of learning how to be a doctor because bodies are 3D so you can't learn everything about them just from looking at diagrams in books. Well, they could use pop-up books, I suppose.

These days some very kind people say that they're happy for medical students to learn how to be doctors by dissecting their bodies after they die, knowing that this will help thousands of patients in the future. But it wasn't always like this . . .

For a start, in Sparkle Time, it was illegal to dissect anyone. This made it pretty tricky to train up doctors, and even trickier to discover anything new about the body. After hundreds of years of the medical schools stamping their feet and banging on the table and

moaning that this rule was **SO UNFAIR**, the government eventually allowed people to be cut up. But they only allowed ten people a year to be dissected in the whole country, which wasn't enough. Imagine if there were only ten laptops to share among every school in the country – you wouldn't learn very much.

A bit more begging and moaning from the medical schools meant that in 1752 the government decided that anyone who'd been executed for murder could be dissected. But medicine was getting more and more popular because everyone realized that being a doctor was the second-coolest thing in the world. (The coolest thing in the world is being called Adam.) As a result, there weren't enough murderers to go round. Soon the medical schools were getting desperate for bodies and offered money to anyone who could provide them with a corpse or ten. I think you might be able to guess why this was a bad idea . . .

Please welcome (or rather please boo extremely loudly) the bodysnatchers. They would hang around graveyards at night, and dig up recently buried bodies – the fresher the better because medical schools weren't interested in ones that had started to go all manky. Thousands of bodies were stolen, and the police didn't really interfere much because in those days stealing a body was an extremely minor crime. The bodysnatchers left the dead person's clothes and jewellery inside the coffin because it was a much bigger crime to steal those than the body itself . . . Weird. Medical schools would pay about £7 for a body in good condition – which might only be enough to buy a pizza now, but back then was tons of money (the equivalent of about £1,000 now, so **LOADS** of pizzas).

Families who were worried about their loved ones getting pilfered would bury them in iron coffins that were much harder to break open, or padlock their bodies into the coffins. Some would even set up a complicated booby-trap system involving tripwires that set off guns. But all this did was make the bodysnatchers more inventive: for example, digging tunnels underground to get to the coffins.

STILL FINDING THIS A BIT CREEPY.

It also meant that they would steal from poorer graves, because their families couldn't afford to protect the people they'd buried.

The most famous bodysnatchers were called William Burke and William Hare, who probably met at the People Called William Society. In 1828, they worked

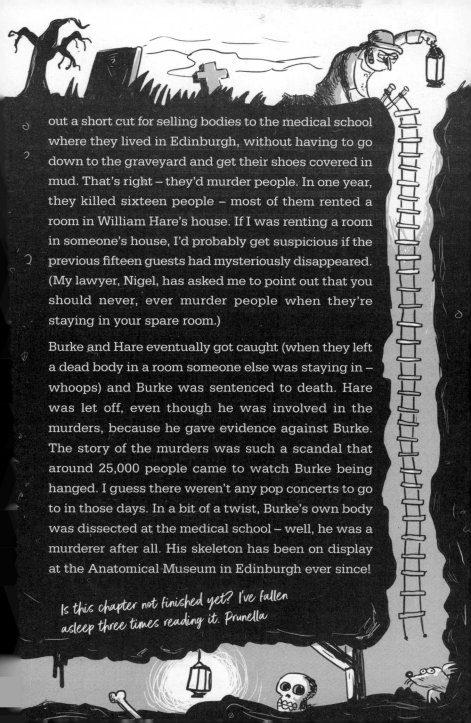

out a short cut for selling bodies to the medical school where they lived in Edinburgh, without having to go down to the graveyard and get their shoes covered in mud. That's right – they'd murder people. In one year, they killed sixteen people – most of them rented a room in William Hare's house. If I was renting a room in someone's house, I'd probably get suspicious if the previous fifteen guests had mysteriously disappeared. (My lawyer, Nigel, has asked me to point out that you should never, ever murder people when they're staying in your spare room.)

Burke and Hare eventually got caught (when they left a dead body in a room someone else was staying in – whoops) and Burke was sentenced to death. Hare was let off, even though he was involved in the murders, because he gave evidence against Burke. The story of the murders was such a scandal that around 25,000 people came to watch Burke being hanged. I guess there weren't any pop concerts to go to in those days. In a bit of a twist, Burke's own body was dissected at the medical school – well, he was a murderer after all. His skeleton has been on display at the Anatomical Museum in Edinburgh ever since!

Is this chapter not finished yet? I've fallen asleep three times reading it. Prunella

CRACK, CRUNCH, OUCH!

In the 1700s, if you'd dislocated a joint or broken a bone that needed to be wiggled back into the right position before you got your plaster cast, then you'd probably go to a bonesetter. They weren't trained as doctors, but on the plus side they were much cheaper.

One of the most famous and popular bonesetters was a lady called Crazy Sally. Would you want to go to get your broken arm fixed by someone with **CrAzY** written on their door? I think I'd prefer to see Sensible Susan.

2013

Doctors have been making artificial limbs for thousands of years, for people who were born without arms or legs, or patients who lost them in accidents or operations. Early artificial limbs were made out of things like iron (a bit heavy) and horses' legs (a bit weird) but technology has come a long way since then. In 2013, a man had an artificial arm fitted that's controlled by signals from his brain – it sounds like science fiction, but it's science fact. The technology for his arm cost nearly £100,000,000, so he'd better not accidentally leave it on the bus.

I CAN SEE RIGHT THROUGH YOU

If you've ever broken a bone, you'll probably remember the very important thing that happened soon afterwards. No, not getting the day off school. No, not getting an extra portion of ice cream. No, not complaining that it was vanilla ice cream when you really wanted triple chocolate fudge supreme. Look – this is the section about X-rays: stop talking about ice creams. I obviously mean you got an X-ray.

But if you broke a bone before 1895, then you wouldn't have had an X-ray – because they hadn't been discovered yet. Actually, if you broke a bone before 1895, then you're over 130 years old and you're outside the recommended reading age range for this book – please give it to someone younger **IMMEDIATELY**. X-rays were invented by Wilhelm Röntgen. It took me nearly forty minutes to work out how to do the letter ö on my computer. I might do a few more so it wasn't a total waste of my time: öööööööööööööööööööööööööö.

NÖÖÖÖÖÖÖÖÖ!

WILHELM RÖNTGEN: FIVE FACTS AND A LIE

1. He got kicked out of school for drawing a rude cartoon of a teacher. This was very unfair because one of his friends had actually drawn it. It's a bit like when I got in trouble for pouring jam into the toaster when it was actually my brother who did it. I'm still cross about that, to be honest.

2. Things that have been named after him include a mountain in the Antarctic, a chemical element and a range of delicious chocolate bars.

3. He refused to make any money from X-rays because he wanted the whole world to benefit. What a nice bloke.

4. He won the first-ever Nobel Prize for his discovery. I've not won any Nobel Prizes, which is very mean because there's a Nobel Prize for literature and I've written the best books in the world.

→ Ahem. Prunella

5. He spent seven weeks working uninterrupted in total silence before he made his big discovery, stopping only to eat meals and for the occasional nap. (I'm **ALMOST** the same – when I write books, I only stop every ten minutes to eat a snack or watch TV.)

6. The first X-ray ever taken was of his wife's hand. She screamed, 'I have seen my death!' which is fair enough because she was the first person who'd ever looked at their own skeleton. (Apart from people who've had some kind of terrible injury.)

2. He got the mountain (Röntgen Peak) and the element (roentgenium), but sadly no range of chocolate bars. He must be absolutely gutted.

HIP HIP HOORAY

X-rays meant that doctors finally knew what was going on inside their patients' smashed-up legs, and they could come up with better plans than 'chuck a plaster cast on it and hope for the best'. It meant they could rummage around in their toolbox for things to use, like nails and screws, and – thanks to newly discovered anaesthetics and antibiotics – their patients even stood a chance of living long enough to walk around on their newly fixed legs.

Not everything can be fixed so easily though. For example, I once accidentally smashed my Great Aunt Prunella's precious vase when I was practising tennis in her living room. Sometimes joints are damaged so badly that they need to be replaced. The first successful hip replacement was performed in 1938 by a surgeon called Philip Wiles, who made a new hip joint from steel. These days, most hip replacements are performed because when people get old their joints can wear out a bit and become painful. Over half a million hips are replaced every single year, and that's not to mention the artificial knees and shoulders and ankles and elbows and wrists and bums. Not bums, actually – I meant to say thumbs.

So that's how it broke! How many times have I told you not to play tennis inside?! Prunella

1923

You know how I mentioned the first *successful* hip replacement? That kind of suggests there might have been some less successful attempts . . . such as Marius Smith-Petersen who made a new hip joint out of glass in 1923. Unsurprisingly, this didn't work, and his poor patient's hip smashed into smithereens. Honestly, what was he thinking? He might as well have made it out of chocolate.

THE FUTURE

It's prediction time, so let's hear what my robot butler has to say. He's just been lacing my shoes (unfortunately, he's decorated them all over with lace).

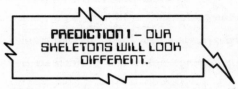

PREDICTION 1 – OUR SKELETONS WILL LOOK DIFFERENT.

If you're anything like me, you'll look in the mirror and think it's impossible for humans to be any more perfect. But humans have been evolving for millions of years, since we looked like monkeys and ate triceratops for tea, and we're showing no sign of stopping now. For example, the less we exercise, the smaller our bones will get. Scientists have already noticed that our elbows are shrinking slightly. Quick, do some more elbow exercises! And the amount of time we spend bent forward, looking at screens, is changing the shape of our skulls: we're developing an enlarged occipital protuberance. (Or, in English, the bump on the back of our heads is getting bigger.) To be honest, I was hoping for a slightly more exciting evolution than thinner elbows and a bumpier head – being able to fly, maybe? Making teachers disappear by clicking our fingers? A nose that produces candyfloss instead of snot?

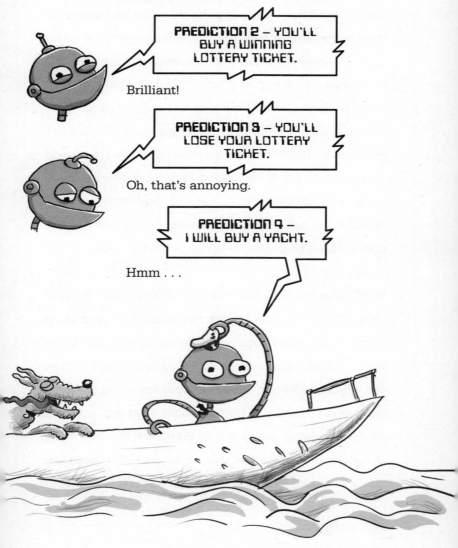

PREDICTION 2 – YOU'LL BUY A WINNING LOTTERY TICKET.

Brilliant!

PREDICTION 3 – YOU'LL LOSE YOUR LOTTERY TICKET.

Oh, that's annoying.

PREDICTION 4 – I WILL BUY A YACHT.

Hmm . . .

ADAM'S ANSWERS

WHY ARE WE TALLER THAN OUR ANCESTORS?

I don't know if you've ever been to a museum where they've got a really, really, really old bedroom on display, but you might have noticed that the beds were absolutely tiny. I remember seeing one that was only the size of a matchbox. No, hang on, that might have been a doll's house. Anyway, what I'm trying to say is that we're a lot bigger than we used to be. The reason is that in the olden days people's growth was affected by having serious illnesses in childhood and not getting enough food or vitamins. Today we're on average nine centimetres taller than people were a hundred years ago. And we've got much better clothes now too.

WHAT CAN WE FIND OUT BY LOOKING AT OLD BONES?

Quite a lot! Bones are almost as revealing as your great aunt's secret diary, which you definitely shouldn't have read, that tells you she kissed a soldier the night before she married Great Uncle Malcolm. Even if bones are hundreds of thousands of years old, they can tell us if they belonged to a man or a woman, how old they were, the various illnesses they had, how they died and their favourite song. (OK, fine, I made the last one up.) And

→ Delete this! You horrible, miserable little shrimp. Prunella

finally, if you find a load of bones in a suitcase underneath the floorboards in your living room, then that means you live with a murderer and should probably call the police.

WHO HAS THE WORLD RECORD FOR BREAKING THE MOST BONES?

I mean the person who broke the most of their own bones, by the way, not some hammer-wielding maniac. A man called Evel Knievel managed to break 433 bones while doing his job. That's quite a lot when you consider that the body only has 206 bones. What was the job that resulted in so many broken bones? He worked in a supermarket and a big pile of baked-bean cans fell on him every single shift. I made that up, actually: he was a stunt motorcyclist, who would drive off ramps and fly over long lines of cars. And obviously crash quite often.

OOH, THAT'S HANDY!

HOSPITAL

TRUE OR POO?

KING CHARLES II WAS A CANNIBAL.

TRUE He didn't munch on people's arms like lamb chops or eat people's eyeballs as if they were grapes, but Charlie boy was a fan of something called 'the King's Drops'. If he was feeling a bit groggy when he woke up, he'd pop some of this lovely liquid on his tongue: alcohol mixed with crushed-up bits of human skull. Maybe it's just me, but if I'm feeling rubbish in the morning I have a big glass of water and a bit of a lie-in.

DOCTORS USED TO INJECT JOINTS WITH GOLD.

TRUE There's a condition called rheumatoid arthritis that makes some people's joints swell up and become really painful. About eighty years ago, the best treatment was to inject affected joints with gold. These days there are much more effective medicines available, so there's no need to melt down your great aunt's earrings and stab them into your knee, which I'm sure you'll be pleased to hear. — *Don't you dare! Prunella*

THE ANCIENT ROMANS KNEW THAT THE BONES MADE BLOOD CELLS.

POO You obviously know that the body's blood cells are made in the bone marrow in the middle of our bones. (If you didn't know, you can just pretend that you did – I'll never find out.) Back in Ancient Rome, they had no idea about this – they actually thought the bone marrow was full of old, used-up, useless bits of bone, and they called it *excrementum ossium*. Hold on. I'm just going to look up *excrementum ossium* in a Latin dictionary to find out what it means . . . OMG. It means 'bone-poo'!

CRAZY CURES

If you had sore, swollen joints – known as arthritis – hundreds of years ago, the treatment used to be to smear fat all over them. Chicken fat, maybe? Elephant fat? Nope – human fat, delivered fresh by the nearest executioner. That's really quite revolting, and it obviously didn't work, but doctors back then could have actually been on to something – scientists have recently discovered that injecting some smooshed-up fat directly into joints might help people with arthritis.

The Chapter With

GOAT'S WEE,

MAGIC LASERS

&

A LITTLE DROP OF

PIGEON BLOOD

(also known as EYES AND EARS)

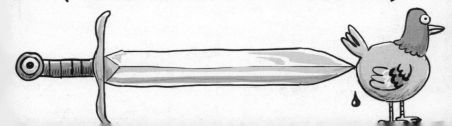

I PRESUME I DON'T NEED TO EXPLAIN what your eyes are? Big circles at the front of your face that you see out of? Well, humans have been trying to work out how they work ever since our great-great-great-great-great-great-great . . . actually, can you just imagine a load of 'greats' there, otherwise I'll run out of pages in this book? Ever since our hundreds-of-greats-grandparents were around.

ANCIENT EGYPT

The Ancient Egyptians didn't have a clue how the eyes actually worked, but they knew that lots of things could go wrong with them.

What do you first think of when I say 'Ancient Egypt'? OK, fine, pharaohs. Well, how about the second thing? Mummies, eh? How about the third thing, then? Pyramids? Oh, forget it. I meant sand. It was very common for people back then to have sight loss, partly because of the wind whipping all that sand into their eyes (ouch) and also because of infections that they didn't have any treatments for. That's what all their heavy make-up was about – they weren't going trick-or-treating every day of the week. They thought it contained chemicals that would prevent infections, and would keep dust out of their eyes.

If someone did lose their sight, the doctors had a couple of tricks up their sleeves. The first one was to mash up some tortoise brain, combine it with honey and spread it on the poorly eye. The second option was to kill a pig, pull out its eye and say a spell which would magically transfer the pig's vision into the patient's eye. I don't know exactly how the spell went, but it was probably something like:

This will make your eyes work,
Unless I am mistaken.
Then after let's have dinner:
There's tortoise or there's bacon.

But unfortunately for the patients (and the pigs and the tortoises) none of this made the slightest bit of difference to anyone's sight.

We know that back in Ancient Egypt there were many successful blind musicians and poets – just like today, sight loss didn't have to stop people doing what they wanted.

ANCIENT INDIA

Remember Sushruta from back in the surgery chapter? Well, he was also a bit of an eye boffin, and invented an operation to help people with cataracts. Cataracts aren't cats who do acrobatics – cataracts are a condition that people sometimes get when they're older, where the lens of the eye goes white, instead of see-through. And if the lens isn't see-through, then you can't see through it . . . Sushruta's method of removing cataracts meant his patients could see again, and it wasn't too different from the way that surgeons remove them today. Not bad for two thousand years ago!

ANCIENT ROME

Galen thought he'd totally worked out what made people go blind. Here's the list:

1. Drawing.
2. Writing for too long.
3. Smelly farts.

I'm pretty sure he got this wrong because I've been sitting writing this book for weeks with Pippin farting away constantly by my feet, and my eyesight seems totally fine.

On the plus side, by then they'd cut up enough eyeballs to work out all the different parts of the eye, although they reckoned the lens was the bit that detected light, rather than the . . . Go on – what part of the eye detects light?

The retina. You knew that, right? Sure, I believe you.

NOT EYEDEAL

Not everyone can be great at their job. In fact, some people are absolutely terrible. For example, before I was a doctor, I worked in a newsagent's at weekends, and one day I fell asleep at the till and someone came in and stole a load of Twixes. (My lawyer, Nigel, has asked me to point out that stealing Twixes – and indeed any form of chocolatey delight – is a very serious crime.)

These days doctors have to do loads and loads of annoying exams to make sure they're good enough, but in the olden days the rules weren't so strict, so there were some absolute losers working in medicine. One of the very worst was a man called John Taylor, who was an eye surgeon in the 1700s. He didn't think the name John Taylor sounded cool enough, so he called himself 'Chevalier' instead and travelled around Europe in a coach decorated with loads of eyes. (Bit weird, John.)

I'M JUST GLAD HE'S NOT A BUM DOCTOR.

Anyway, he might have been better off calling himself 'Eye Destroyer' because he was a really, really, **REALLY** terrible surgeon. He blinded hundreds of the patients he operated on, thanks to his bad surgery and his insistence on giving everyone eyedrops made from pigeon blood.

1972
Doctors at a university
in Germany were doing eye
tests on students when they noticed
that a pupil called Veronica Seider had
incredible vision. She could read writing that
was so tiny that anyone else would need a
microscope to see it, and she could describe
the faces of people who were standing over
a mile away. No one had a clue how she
was able to see so well (maybe she ate
a lorry full of carrots every evening?)
but she's in the *Guinness Book of
Records* for having the best
eyesight in history.

This didn't stop him, and he somehow attracted lots of celebrity clients, including the world's most famous composers. He operated on J. S. Bach (who wrote pieces including *Toccata and Fugue in D minor*, *The Well-tempered Clavier*, and *Pippin is the Smelliest Dog in the World*). Unfortunately, the surgery blinded him (eek) and killed him (double eek). Another composer he took his knife to was Handel (who wrote the *Messiah*, *Water Music* and *I Can't Understand Why She's So Smelly – Is It Something We're Feeding Her?*) and unfortunately he totally blinded him too.

ALL HAIL BRAILLE

In 1824, Louis Braille developed a system that helped people who are blind or have limited vision to read. He called it Braille (why did everyone name their inventions after themselves?) and to read it you run your fingers over little bumps on the page, which spell out the words. He got the idea from 'night writing' that some soldiers in the French army used so they could pass notes to each other in the dark – proper important soldiery notes, not things people pass around in class like 'You smell', which in Braille would be ⠠⠽⠕⠥ ⠎⠍⠑⠇⠇

Louis Braille's original system is still used today, pretty much unchanged. Next time you're with an adult at a cash machine, have a look at the keypad and you'll see the numbers are also written in Braille.

LOUIS BRAILLE: FIVE FACTS AND A LIE

1. Louis lost his sight when he was three by playing with sharp tools in his dad's workshop. (That's why you should never mess around with sharp objects!)

2. He went to the world's first-ever school for blind people, called the Institut National des Jeunes

Aveugles (or the National Institute for Blind Children, if you're not as amazing at French as I am).

3. He invented Braille when he was only fifteen. When I was fifteen, I did my grade three piano, which is almost as impressive.

4. Louis Braille's face was on a special dollar coin, which also had the word Braille written on it in Braille.

   → That sentence has the word Braille in it too many times. Prunella

5. He was a brilliant musician who played the organ in churches all over France, and developed a special type of Braille for reading music.

6. He wrote the first pages of Braille by using an owl's beak.

SPECS EDUCATION

The first spectacles were made in Italy some time around 1300 – the year, I mean, not one o'clock in the afternoon. Before then, I guess everything just looked a bit blurry. No one knows exactly who invented them, so maybe I should just pretend that I did. (Yes, I **do** look great for 750 years old, don't I?) You had to hold these early glasses up to your face if you wanted to use them, or balance them on your nose, which wasn't very convenient, but better than nothing, I guess. Later versions included the pince-nez (which means 'pinch-nose' – I told you I was amazing at French) that clamped onto your nose like a peg so they didn't fall off, but made you sound as if you had a terrible cold all the time. Then there's the monocle, which you just balance in one eye socket. They're a bit weird and not very popular these days: my Great Aunt Prunella is the only person I've ever seen who wears one.

In the 1700s, opticians finally remembered that people have ears, and started making glasses with arms on like we have today.

→ How dare you make fun of my beautiful monocle in front of all these readers. Prunella

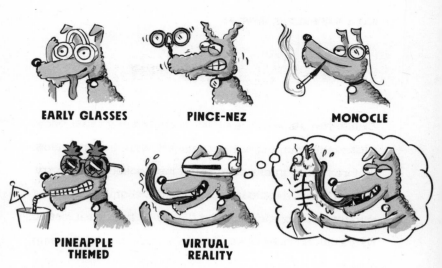

EARLY GLASSES

PINCE-NEZ

MONOCLE

PINEAPPLE THEMED

VIRTUAL REALITY

We used to think that contact lenses were invented in the 1940s, but then somebody was having a rummage in Leonardo da Vinci's old notebooks and spotted that he'd invented them over four hundred years earlier. We should probably have a careful look through everything he wrote, just in case he also invented the infinite ice-cream machine or flying trousers.

1988

The first-ever laser eye surgery was carried out on a patient in New York. It worked by making tiny adjustments to the cornea at the very front of the eye. It's extremely effective at improving people's eyesight . . . but would you want to be the first-ever patient to have a laser blasted into your eyes?

EARS

Unlike the brain or the heart or almost any other body part really, humans have always known what their ears were for. Throughout history, if someone's parents were telling them to clean up their cave or pyramid or whatever, then sticking their fingers in their ears meant they couldn't hear them. Simple.

That doesn't mean they knew how the ears actually worked, or what to do if they weren't hearing so well though. In Ancient Egypt, if someone had difficulty hearing, they'd make up a mixture of olive oil, ants' eggs, goat's wee and bat wings and glug it down their earholes. The weird thing is, that might have actually worked – nothing to do with the ants or the goats or the bats though. Olive oil can help to unclog any earwax that might be causing problems and we still use it today. (I'm so glad that it's olive oil we still use and not goat's wee.)

Hearing aids may be very high-tech now, and so small that you can't even see them, but early versions back in the 1600s were a bit more obvious. They were called ear trumpets, but, instead of blowing into one like a normal trumpet that makes a noise like a rhinoceros farting, you would place the smaller end in your ear and point the wide end at whoever was speaking.

TRUMPET: INVENTED 1500 BC

EAR TRUMPET: INVENTED 1639

BUM TRUMPET ('BUMPET'): INVENTED 2021

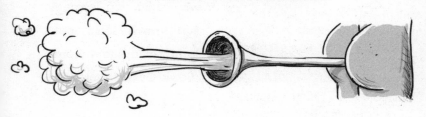

Sign language has been around for about a thousand years, but the first people who used it didn't have hearing difficulties – they were monks who kept a vow of silence in their monasteries. Monk-y sign language

(I'm not sure what it was actually called, but they were monks so I'll call it monk-y sign language) was quite limited because it was mostly phrases they used a lot in their day-to-day monking. For example: 'prayer' and 'bell-ringing' and 'why do we shave big bald patches on the tops of our heads?' In the 1500s, some Native American communities developed a complete sign language, but it took Britain a couple of hundred years to catch on – typical. Today over 150,000 people in the UK communicate using British Sign Language – why don't you learn a few words? (No, not bum. No, not that word either. Or that word.)

1977

An engineer at NASA called Adam Kissiah had hearing loss, but unfortunately his doctors didn't know any treatments that would work for him. So he thought, *I'm a NASA engineer – I can sort this out myself*, and spent every lunchtime coming up with a solution. What he invented was called a cochlear implant – a special type of hearing aid that transmits sound waves deep into the inner ear and now helps tens of thousands of people to hear. See, all the main geniuses are called Adam.

> That's untrue. In my experience, it's a name associated with total numbskulls. Prunella

THE FUTURE

My robot butler has just been running a bath (unfortunately, he put it on a treadmill and smashed it).

> **PREDICTION 1 – SURGEONS WILL BE ABLE TO IMPLANT BIONIC EYES.**

Scientists are already working on bionic eyes that can send pictures directly to patients' brains. These don't just have the potential to restore sight to people who have lost theirs, but could even give them super-vision that would allow them to zoom in on huge distances, see at night and show heat patterns. (Which means you'll be able to tell if someone has farted.)

> **PREDICTION 2 – YOU'RE GOING TO FORGET TO WATER THE PLANT ON YOUR DESK.**

Good point.
I'll water it now.
Or maybe later.

WATER ME!
DON'T FORGET!

ADAM'S ANSWERS

WHY WOULD AN EYE DOCTOR GIVE YOU DEADLY POISON?

Because they're evil and want to kill you. Or, alternatively, they might just want to dilate your pupils (make them go bigger) so they can have a better look inside your eyes. Doctors have known for thousands of years about a plant that can kill you if you eat it, but will make your pupils dilate if you put it in your peepers. There are lots of names for this plant, including deadly nightshade, devil's berries and death cherries, but its proper name is belladonna, which means 'pretty woman' (because people used to think that pupils the size of snooker balls were especially beautiful).

WHAT HAPPENED IF YOU WERE A KING WHO WAS HARD OF HEARING?

Well, if it was 1820 and you were King John VI of Portugal and Brazil (a bit greedy being king of two places), then you'd sit on a massive throne that was also a hearing aid. If you wanted to speak to King John, you'd kneel down at his feet and talk into the arms of the chair, which were shaped like lions' mouths. The sound would travel up through the mouths and into little speakers by his ears. He would then reply something like, 'Off with his head!' or, 'Bring me a massive chocolate cake – I'm the king!' Luckily, these days hearing aids are a lot more portable.

TRUE OR POO?

AN AMERICAN PRESIDENT INVENTED A NEW TYPE OF GLASSES.

TRUE Benjamin Franklin (who was president from 1785–1788) needed two different pairs of specs: one for reading things close up and one for looking at stuff that was further away, so he invented a new type of glasses with different lenses in the top and bottom halves. Bingo! He never needed to switch pairs ever again. These glasses are called bifocals and people still wear them today. There's actually a very long tradition of American presidents inventing things. James Madison invented a walking stick with a microscope inside it, so you could inspect any insects that might be scuttling around your feet; George Washington made a machine that planted seeds in fields; Thomas Jefferson built a pasta-making device; and Donald Trump invented a very strange type of hairstyle.

IN ANCIENT GREECE, THEY THOUGHT TEARS WERE CAUSED BY THE BRAIN LEAKING.

POO They actually thought crying meant the heart had been damaged and was turning to water, which somehow whizzed up to the eyes and poured down the face. It took until the 1600s for doctors to discover the tear glands, which probably made a bit more sense, to be honest.

BEETHOVEN COMPOSED MUSIC WHEN HE WAS TOTALLY DEAF.

TRUE Unlike a lot of composers, Beethoven managed to escape being blinded by the operations of John Taylor, but he gradually lost his hearing over a number of years. It started in 1798 when he couldn't hear higher sounds, so the music he wrote became much lower as he got older. When his hearing became even worse, he had to bang the notes on the piano really loudly so he could hear what he was playing, and he accidentally smashed up a lot of pianos (and probably really annoyed his neighbours). Eventually, he became completely deaf, but he was still able to compose music because he could imagine in his head exactly how the tunes would sound.

CRAZY CURES

If you had cataracts in your eyes back in the seventeenth century, you'd have to cross your fingers that you didn't go to see Robert Boyle. He didn't do surgery, or even use eyedrops – his cure was to grind up human poo until it was a brown powder, then blow it into people's eyes. I don't know if he used his own poo or someone else's, but either way it's pretty disgusting.

THIS HAD BETTER WORK.

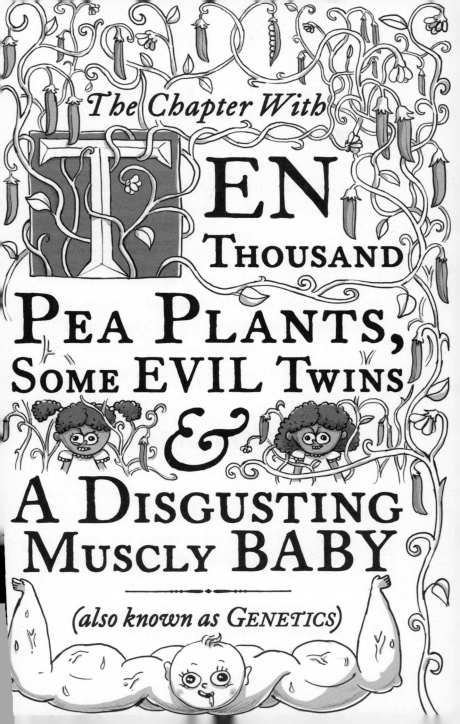

The Chapter With

TEN THOUSAND PEA PLANTS, SOME EVIL TWINS & A DISGUSTING MUSCLY BABY

(also known as GENETICS)

UNLESS YOU'VE GOT AN IDENTICAL TWIN, or an evil scientist has made a clone of you as part of some dastardly experiment, there's nobody on Earth who looks exactly like you. No one else has your nose, no one else has your ears, no one else has your knees, and no one else has your smell. Well, apart from some skunks, maybe. And it's your genes that make you unique.

And not just you. Me, Pippin, the shrivelled-up plant on my desk – we're all made up of a set of genes: a big instruction manual on how to build a living thing. In your case, a human. Well, I'm assuming you're a human. You could be a skunk who's learned how to read.

ANCIENT GREECE

Old Hippoface spotted that there were families where everyone looked very similar: for instance, they might all have a massive chin or nose hair so long you could tie it into a bow. He realized that things like this are passed down through generations, and he called this inheritance, which is what scientists still call it today. It's not the exciting kind of inheritance like getting a million pounds

Thank goodness for that – the last thing we need is loads of people like you running around. Prunella

from a long-lost uncle in Venezuela. I wish I had one of those relatives – all Great Aunt Prunella says she'll give me is a horrible lamp with a flamingo on it.

You are the rudest and most ungrateful person I've ever met in my entire life. Now you're not even getting the lamp. Prunella

Hippocrates still got some stuff wrong though – he thought that anything that happened to an adult's body would get passed on to their children – so, if you did loads of weightlifting and ended up with really, really strong arms, then you'd have some kind of disgusting muscly baby.

A BOFFIN WITH A BEARD ON A BOAT

The first person to really shake things up in the genes department was Charles Darwin: back in 1831, he went on a five-year trip round the world on a boat called the HMS *Beagle*, which is a type of dog. I mean a beagle is a type of dog – Charles wasn't sailing around in a massive dog.

His job was to make notes about every rock and plant and animal he saw in all the different places they visited, like a kind of human video recorder. Most of the time though he just sat in his cabin as the boat sailed from place to place – and, because he didn't have any computer games to play or music to listen to, he did a lot of thinking. If I'm left on my own, I normally think things like, *I wonder how many Maltesers you could fit into a car?* or *Who does bigger poos – horses or giraffes?* but Charles started wondering about where we all came from.

HUMAN

HORSE

GIRAFFE

No, not if we're born in Swindon or Sweden or Switzerland, but where we all came from millions of years ago. He cooked up a theory called evolution, which means that we are all descended from the same ancestor. And not just humans! Whether you're the queen or a potato, your maths teacher or a cactus, we all started out the same.

This was quite big news for people one hundred and fifty years ago – no one wanted to be told that their great-great-grandma had a tail and swung from trees – and it caused huge debates. (Debates are what scientists call it when they have massive arguments.)

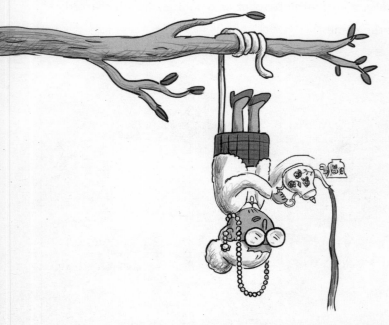

We now know that Charlie was right – and there's lots of proof: it's quite difficult to argue with evolution when you dig up ancient skeletons that are halfway between humans and apes. His theories also explain why certain animals have gone extinct. (RIP dodo, gone too soon, love you babez.)

I NEED A PEA

The next big development in genetics was all thanks to
ten thousand pea plants, which showed us exactly how
we inherit different characteristics from our parents.
Actually, I guess some of the credit should go to a monk
called Gregor Mendel who did the experiments on these
plants back in the 1850s and 1860s.

Greg's experiments demonstrated for the first time that
Hippoface was wrong – it's not all about the dads: you
get half your genes from your biological mother and
half from Sainsbury's. No, that's not right. I mean
you get half your genes from your biological mother and
half from your biological father. Greggy also explained
why not everything gets passed down through the
generations – which is great news
for me because my Great Aunt
Prunella's nose is so pointy
that it smashes windows.

> How dare you! I'm writing to your
> mother about this. Prunella

When Gregster had finished his experiments, he excitedly published them in 1865, then presumably wondered what to do with all those pea plants, so had a massive dinner of roast peas served with mushy peas with pea gravy and pea crumble for dessert (with pea custard).

Annoyingly, no one believed anything he'd written, so they totally ignored it until some other scientists in 1900 realized he was right all along. Unfortunately, by that point he'd been dead for sixteen years. Just as well because he'd have been extremely pea'd off.

D-N-YAY

The next big discovery was DNA, which is short for deoxyribonucleic acid, but we all just say DNA because no one should have to type deoxy*blahblahblah* acid more than once in their lives. DNA is the part of your cells that contains all your genes, wound into a spiral shape, like some kind of cool scientific pasta.

1996

Scientists cloned a sheep for the first time, which means they basically copied and pasted a sheep's DNA to make a brand-new identical one. All sheep look pretty similar to me, so I guess we just have to believe that's what they did. This sheep was called Dolly, which is quite a nice name, but not as good as Adam. Even though she was extremely special, she lived a fairly ordinary life – eating grass, baaing and pooing, like sheep generally do. After she died, she was stuffed and put on display at the National Museum of Scotland in Edinburgh. If you're ever passing by, pop in to see her, although I will warn you that her conversation isn't up to much.

DNA's twisty, twirly shape was discovered by four scientists called Rosalind Franklin, Maurice Wilkins, James Watson and Francis Crick – who all got a Nobel Prize in 1962 apart from Rosalind Franklin, which was very unfair. (She had recently died, and the stupid rules meant she couldn't be recognized for her work.) Understanding DNA's shape meant that scientists could figure out exactly how it worked, how it sometimes goes wrong and, more importantly, how to treat patients whose DNA has gone wonky and caused medical problems.

WE DID IT!

1998

Because everyone's DNA
is unique and it's in every cell of their
body, it means it can be used to catch criminals.
A bit like fingerprints, except more accurate, and
you can't get round it by wearing gloves: all the police
need to find are a few skin cells, or a hair, or even a bit of
sweat or earwax. The first person to be identified from
DNA evidence was jailed in 1998. I'm thinking of using DNA
evidence to work out who pooed on the kitchen floor.
It was probably Pippin (but I guess it could have been
my husband).

CANCER

Cancer happens when the genes in a cell have gone wrong and that cell has divided and divided and divided, out of control. Cancer has affected people for a lot longer than we've known about genes – there is evidence of bone cancer in Ancient Egyptian mummies and they wrote about breast cancer on their papyrus scrolls. Sadly, back then cancer was impossible to survive – doctors didn't know what caused it, so they didn't stand a chance of treating it. The invention of anaesthetics and antibiotics meant that surgery was suddenly possible for cancer, but the biggest step forward in treating cancer was the discovery of radiotherapy and chemotherapy.

Radiotherapy is a type of treatment that involves using radioactive substances. You might have already heard about radioactivity at school. Not sure what it is? Well, school is this building that you go into every day during the week where a bunch of boring grown-ups teach you about . . . Oh, you mean radioactivity? Well, that's a special kind of energy given off by certain substances, and it was discovered over a hundred years ago by a Polish scientist who lived in France called Marie Curie.

MARIE CURIE: FIVE FACTS AND A LIE

1. Her university couldn't find her a lab to work in, so she did all her experiments in a leaky, abandoned shed that was previously used for storing dead bodies.

2. She is the only Nobel Prize winner whose daughter has also won a Nobel Prize. No wonder I haven't won a Nobel Prize yet when they keep going to members of the same family.

3. She did a lot of her research with her husband, Barry Curie.

4. She invented the first-ever mobile X-ray machines, which could be used to help soldiers injured in the First World War. Her machines helped over a million soldiers.

5. She discovered two chemical elements: radium and polonium, and a third one was named after her – curium. If I ever discover an element, I'm going to call it AdamIsBrilliantium.

6. The notebooks she wrote in are still too radioactive and dangerous to touch more than one hundred years later, and have to be kept in lead boxes.

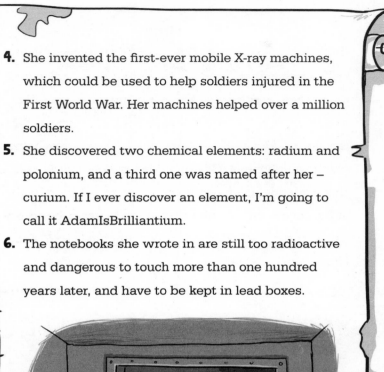

3. She did work with her husband, but unfortunately for fans of rhyming names they were Marie and Pierre Curie, not Marie and Barry Curie.

2002

A baby called Rhys Evans was born with a very rare condition called severe combined immunodeficiency disorder, which, as you can probably guess from its name, is very serious indeed. People with this condition have almost no immune system, which means that any infection could be extremely serious. It's also known as 'bubble baby disease' because patients often have to live inside a plastic bubble to make it less likely that they'll catch any bugs. Scientists discovered that it was caused by a problem in Rhys's DNA that meant a gene wasn't working properly. In 2002, Professor Christine Kinnon led a team that replaced this faulty gene in Rhys, curing him of his condition, and making him the first patient in the UK to have this kind of treatment.

Radioactive substances have hundreds of uses in science, from creating energy to working out what age dinosaur bones are. But, in medicine, one of the most important uses is to treat cancer. One of Marie Curie's colleagues kept a sample of radium in his pocket for a few hours and then noticed afterwards that the skin underneath it was badly damaged, so Marie did some experiments and found out that radioactive substances kill cells. Usually, this isn't great, but if you're trying to treat cancer then it's a very good thing. Radiotherapy works because normal cells are good at repairing themselves after they've been blasted with radiation, but cancer cells are usually gone forever.

Chemotherapy is the name for medicines that attack cancer, and they actually came from a very surprising place. No, not the moon. The first chemotherapy drug was made from mustard gas, which was a weapon used in the First World War. People who develop cancer today have a higher chance of survival than ever before thanks to huge advances in surgery, chemotherapy and radiotherapy, often used in combination.

THE FUTURE

My robot butler has been testing the smoke alarms (he asked them to recite their seven times table and name the capital of Belgium) so now he's ready to tell us what the future holds.

> PREDICTION 1 – HUNDREDS OF ILLNESSES WILL BE CURED BY FIXING PEOPLE'S DNA.

A lot of illnesses are caused by problems inside our DNA. In fact, it's a bit like the DNA has got a spelling mistake in it. At the moment, scientists are just starting to be able to correct simple errors in DNA, but in the future they'll be able to cure loads of illnesses, from blood disorders to cancer.

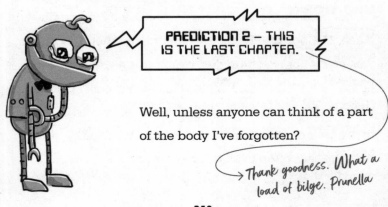

> PREDICTION 2 – THIS IS THE LAST CHAPTER.

Well, unless anyone can think of a part of the body I've forgotten?

→ *Thank goodness. What a load of bilge. Prunella*

ADAM'S ANSWERS

WHERE DOES THE WORD 'CANCER' COME FROM?

It's a word the Ancient Greeks first used that means 'crab'. This is because cancer can spread out with spikes that look a bit like the legs of a crab. Other medical conditions named after animals include lupus (which means 'wolf'), bird flu, chicken pox and Pippin plague.

IS IT POSSIBLE TO CLONE HUMANS?

Yes, it's technically possible – the same technology that worked for Dolly should work for humans too. But it's illegal in most countries, which makes sense, but is a bit of a shame because it would be handy if I had a few clones of me. One could write my books, one could walk Pippin, one could go to the supermarket, and the original me could just go on holiday the whole time.

WHO WORKED OUT WHAT EACH OF OUR GENES DO?

It took a lot of people! Nearly three thousand people worked for thirteen years on something called the Human Genome Project to map out all our genes. They weren't being slow or lazy: they had to look at over three billion bits of DNA, so I guess it's fair enough that it took so many of them.

TRUE OR POO?

JURASSIC PARK COULD ACTUALLY HAPPEN.

POO Bad news, I'm afraid, if you want a pterodactyl as a pet: DNA has got a best-before date, and if something is as old as a stegosaurus bone then there won't be any DNA left on it whatsoever. It's just as well, I guess – I'm not sure that Pippin would want to share her dinner with a diplodocus.

IT WOULD TAKE YOU A WHOLE MONTH TO TYPE OUT YOUR GENETIC CODE.

POO If you typed at a hundred words per minute (which is really fast), twenty-four hours a day without sleeping or even taking a break to eat a poo or do a sandwich (sorry, wrong way round), then it would take you more than ten years. And you'd be exhausted afterwards. And you'd have missed loads of school. Basically, I don't recommend it.

CHARLES DARWIN WAS AFRAID OF THE SIGHT OF BLOOD.

TRUE Charles Darwin's dad was a doctor and wanted him to go to medical school, so Charles went there so he didn't upset Daddy Darwin. One big problem: Charles was totally terrified of the sight of blood, so he couldn't face going to lessons after a while, and quit his course. It's OK to disagree with your relatives sometimes. For example, my Great Aunt Prunella doesn't think I'm a very good writer, but I still love her very, very much.

Hmm, maybe this book isn't so bad after all — please ignore all my previous comments. I love you too. Prunella

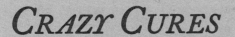

CRAZY CURES

As soon as radium was discovered, people thought it was a magical miracle cure for almost everything. They put it in eyedrops to improve people's vision and even toothpaste to make people's teeth shine bright white. (My lawyer, Nigel, has asked me to point out that you should never use radioactive eyedrops or toothpaste.) It didn't work, obviously. In fact, it made people extremely ill. Even though radioactivity can cure cancer when used correctly, it can actually *cause* cancer if used in random ways like this.

THE BIT AT THE END

(also known as CONCLUSION)

NOBODY LIKES GOING TO THE DOCTOR'S surgery – let's be honest. Even the doctors don't like it because they have to see a whole load of smelly patients.

But next time you've got a cough or a temperature, or you've hurt your leg, or your bum-spots have got worse, or your head's fallen off, then you should actually thank your lucky stars that you're seeing a doctor **now** and not hundreds of years ago. (This might be tricky if your head has fallen off.)

Because, however cold your doctor's stethoscope or however icky the medicine they give you tastes, at least they won't pluck a chicken's bum and stick it in your armpit or give you some human flesh to eat or make you fart into a jar or put you in a bath full of blood or feed you dog poo or blow smoke up your bum or make you eat millipedes or smear your eye with tortoise brain.

Well, hopefully not. If they do, you have my full permission to run out of the surgery, screaming.

Right – that's the end!

→ Get out of here. Prunella

IMPORTANT NOTICE
FROM MY LAWYER, NIGEL

Nigel Rosenkrantz
Official lawyer to Dr Adam Kay
One Embassy Gardens
London SW11 7BW

Dr Adam Kay (hereafter referred to as THE GENIUS AUTHOR) strongly advises **you** (hereafter referred to as THE IDIOT READER) against performing actions mentioned in the book, including but not limited to:

1. Sticking a hook up someone's nose to remove their brain.
2. Electrocuting corpses.
3. Drilling holes in skulls.
4. Draining any individual's blood into a bowl.
5. Feeding sponges to a buzzard.
6. Using urine as a mouthwash.
7. Sewing up intestines, using the heads of ants.
8. Eating crushed human bones.

9. Stealing bodies on which to experiment.
10. Cutting up your relatives.
11. Any other action or actions that would be considered illegal.
12. Any other action or actions that would be considered totally disgusting.

Furthermore, **THE GENIUS AUTHOR** takes no responsibility for any such action or actions performed by **THE IDIOT READER**. This contract applies in all countries of the world in perpetuity and is legally binding for both humans and dogs.

Signed by **THE GENIUS AUTHOR**

Signed by **THE IDIOT READER**

....

Dated ....

ACKNOWLEDGEMENTS

To my husband, James, for only being sick on my laptop once.

To my dog, Pippin, for your incredible support throughout the writing process and beyond.

No, hang on, those two should be the other way round.

To Henry Paker, illustrator to the stars (such as me).

To Cath Summerhayes and Jess Cooper, my awesome agents.

To Ruth Knowles and Emma Jones, my exceptional editors.

To Francesca Dow and Tom Weldon, my phabulous publishers.

To Noah, Zareen, Lenny, Sidney and Jesse – you're getting your names here instead of your birthday presents, soz.

To Hannah Farrell for all her help with factts, and to Justin Myers for saying things like, 'It's actually spelled *facts*.'

And, finally, to YOU! (But only if you think this is the best book you've ever read in your entire life. Otherwise my lawyer, Nigel, insists you have to cross this bit out or face immediate arrest.)

DOCTOROGRAPHY

ADEMOLA, OMO-OBA ADENRELE *(1916–?)* Omo-Oba Adenrele Ademola was born a princess in Nigeria, then trained to be a nurse in London in the 1930s where she worked throughout the Second World War. I really hope she wore her crown on the ward.

AGNODICE *(400 BC)* Back in Ancient Greece, Agnodice was the first-ever female doctor and also the first-ever female midwife. How cool is that? (Very.)

AL-ZAHRAWI, ABU AL-QASIM *(936–1013)* Al-Zahrawi invented loads of the things surgeons use today, such as the scalpel and retractor (which is a kind of surgical instrument, not a type of tractor).

ANDERSON, ELIZABETH GARRETT *(1836–1917)* The first woman to qualify as a doctor in Britain, she also founded the first hospital staffed by women and was the first female mayor. She was really amazing, and more people should know about her – and now **YOU** do!

APGAR, VIRGINIA *(1909–1974)* Inventor of the Apgar Score, a check for newborn babies. When you were born, a doctor or midwife will have checked your Apgar score to see how healthy you were. (I got eight out of ten, fact fans.)

ARISTOTLE *(384–322 BC)* One of the cleverest people of all time, Aristotle worked out loads of human anatomy. His nickname was 'the Mind', which makes him sound like some kind of evil supervillain (but he was good, honestly).

AVICENNA (IBN SINA) *(980–1037)* A well-known Persian and Islamic scientist who wrote *The Canon of Medicine*, one of the most important books ever about cannons. I mean, medicine.

BANTING, FREDERICK *(1891–1941)* and **BEST, CHARLES** *(1899–1978)* Banting and Best won a Nobel Prize in 1923 for making insulin as a treatment for diabetes. Four hundred million people around the world have diabetes, and they all say thank you. (Or *merci*, or *grazie*, or ඔයාට ස්තුතියි.)

BARNARD, CHRISTIAAN *(1922–2001)* Barnard performed the first successful human-to-human heart transplant operation. (He also tried a baboon-to-human heart transplant, but that didn't go so well . . .)

BLUNDELL, JAMES *(1790–1878)* The first doctor to successfully use a blood transfusion to treat a patient for blood loss after childbirth. He had a lie-in until lunchtime every single day, which I'm very jealous about.

BRAILLE, LOUIS *(1809–1852)* Braille developed a system that helped people who are blind or have limited vision to read. Braille is still around today (the language, not the person – he's extremely dead).

COOKE WRIGHT, JANE *(1919–2013)* A scientist who discovered new and better ways to treat cancer, including pioneering ways of using chemotherapy. Her work has saved millions of lives.

CORI, GERTY *(1896–1957)* The first woman to be awarded the Nobel Prize in Medicine. Gerty Cori found out how energy is transported around the body. (Turns out it's not in tiny taxis.)

COUNEY, MARTIN *(1869–1950)* Couney exhibited premature babies in incubators at fairgrounds. A bit weird, but he saved the lives of over six thousand babies, so I'll let him off.

CURIE, MARIE *(1867–1934)* Marie Curie discovered two elements, invented mobile X-ray machines and was one of the most important people in the history of treating cancer. She won two Nobel Prizes for all this, which is fair enough really.

DARWIN, CHARLES *(1809–1882)* He came up with the theory of evolution and explained why some animals survive and some become extinct. One of his favourite meals was armadillos, so it's a miracle that they aren't extinct.

DA VINCI, LEONARDO *(1452–1519)* Da Vinci drew amazing pictures of human anatomy, which helped the world understand the human body much better. He also invented the parachute, the helicopter, solar power, the tank and the calculator. A bit of a show-off, if you ask me.

DERHAM, JAMES *(1762–1802)* James Derham was the first African American doctor. He was born into slavery but went on to have his own successful medical practice and was very important in the fight against racism.

ELION, GERTRUDE *(1918–1999)* Gertrude Elion developed loads of life-saving and life-changing drugs, including treatments for leukaemia and AIDS.

FLEMING, ALEXANDER *(1881–1955)* Discovered the first antibiotic drug, penicillin, when mould grew in his lab. Proof that you should never do the washing-up.

FRANKENSTEIN, VICTOR *(1818–?)* Stitched loads of dead bodies together to make a monster, then brought it to life using lightning. You've got to have a hobby, I guess. (Might have just been a character in a book.)

FRANKLIN, ROSALIND *(1920–1958),* **WILKINS, MAURICE** *(1916–2004),* **WATSON, JAMES** *(1928–)* and **CRICK, FRANCIS** *(1916–2004)* Franklin, Wilkins, Watson and Crick discovered the shape of DNA. They called the shape a 'double helix'. I'd have called it a 'wibbly wobbly spiral', but that's probably why I've never won a Nobel Prize.

GALEN *(129–210)* A doctor in Roman times whose ideas and discoveries taught doctors what to do for over a thousand years. (Unfortunately lots of his ideas were wrong. Oops.)

GRAY, HENRY *(1827–1861)* Writer of the medical textbook *Gray's Anatomy*, which is still used today to teach anatomy to doctors. He stole the name of his book from *Kay's Anatomy*, which was a pretty rude thing to do.

HARVEY, WILLIAM *(1578–1657)* One of the first people to work out how blood is pumped around the body. (The answer is 'by the heart'. If you didn't know that, then go and sit in a bin full of worms.)

HIPPOCRATES *(460–375 BC)* Known as the 'Father of Medicine' to thousands of doctors (and known as 'Hippoface' to readers of this book).

HUA TUO *(140–208)* The first doctor to use anaesthetics for surgery in China. He also invented a type of martial arts, so I bet his patients always paid their bills on time.

IBN AL-NAFIS *(1213–1288)* Nearly one thousand years ago in Egypt, Ibn al-Nafis sussed out circulation. Unfortunately no one remembered this, so people got it wrong for centuries afterwards.

JEKYLL, HENRY *(1886–?)* A very well-respected doctor who sometimes drank a special potion and turned into a murderer called Mr Hyde. A bit naughty, to be honest. He was fictional though, so don't have nightmares.

JENNER, EDWARD *(1749–1823)* Invented the first-ever vaccine. Some people were worried that if they took one of his vaccines they'd sprout a cow's head. (They didn't – vaccines are super safe.)

KAY, ADAM *(1980–)* The main doctor you need to know about. Much more important than any of the other losers.

LAENNEC, RENÉ-THÉOPHILE-HYACINTHE *(1781–1826)* Invented the stethoscope. He was probably also the first doctor to say 'Sorry, this is really cold!' when he put it on a patient.

LISTER, JOSEPH *(1827–1912)* Joseph Lister invented the blister. Not really – he did work out that using antiseptic in operations saved lives though.

MENDEL, GREGOR *(1822–1884)* An Austrian monk and botanist who studied inheritance by experimenting with fleas. No, not fleas – peas. Still a bit weird, if you ask me.

METRODORA *(around 200–400 BC)* The first-ever woman to write a medical textbook. Probably known as Dora to her mates.

MOODY, HAROLD *(1882–1947)* Harold Moody was born in Jamaica, then travelled to England to train as a doctor.

He spent his life campaigning against racism and, brilliantly, he changed laws that discriminated against people because of the colour of their skin.

NIGHTINGALE, FLORENCE *(1820–1910)* The founder of modern nursing. She made huge improvements to hospital conditions and saved more lives than I can count. (Then again, I can only count to about fifty.)

PARÉ, AMBROISE *(1510–1590)* A French surgeon who invented tons of operations and was very interested in gunshot wounds. (I mean treating gunshot wounds, not giving people them.)

PASTEUR, LOUIS *(1822–1895)* Louis Pasteur proved that infections come from germs, and invented a way to get rid of them, which made milk safe to drink. So if you like drinking milk, say, 'Thanks, Louis!' Or if you hate drinking milk, say, 'I hate you, Louis!'

PRUNELLA, GREAT AUNT *(1929–)* A moaning old woman who always criticizes my writing.

I'm still reading this, you know?!

RÖNTGEN, WILHELM *(1845–1923)* Wilhelm won a Nobel Prize for discovering X-rays. Very handy to check if you've broken a bone or swallowed a sofa.

SEACOLE, MARY *(1805–1881)* Mary trained as a nurse in Jamaica and saved the lives of hundreds of wounded soldiers in the Crimean War by riding into battle on horseback to treat them. (I don't know the name of her horse, I'm afraid. Cloppy, maybe?)

SEMMELWEIS, IGNAZ *(1818–1865)* Sometimes the simplest things are the most effective. Ignaz told surgeons to wash their hands and – hey presto! – all the patients stopped dying.

SHERLOCK, SHEILA *(1918–2001)* The UK's first female Professor of Medicine. She did loads of research that taught us how the liver works. Not related to Sherlock Holmes.

SORANUS *(100 AD)* An Ancient Greek doctor who wrote textbooks about pregnancy and childbirth. Not to be confused with Uranus, which is a planet.

STRANGE, STEPHEN *(1963–)* The Sorcerer Supreme and primary protector of Earth against magical and mystical threats. Looks quite a lot like Benedict Cumberbatch, if you ask me. Slightly fictional. OK, completely fictional.

SUSHRUTA *(600 BC)* If you suddenly wake up two thousand years ago and need to amputate someone's arm or repair their cataracts, then, luckily for you, Sushruta has written loads of books to teach you how to do it.

TU YOUYOU *(1930–)*, **CAMPBELL, WILLIAM C.** *(1930–)* and **ŌMURA, SATOSHI** *(1935–)* Shared a Nobel Prize for inventing drugs to treat the awful disease malaria, which kills half a million people every year.

WHO, DOCTOR *(1963–)* An extraterrestrial being who explores the universe in a time-travelling spaceship called the TARDIS and hopes that Daleks don't exterminate him. (David Tennant was the best one, and I will not be entering into discussions about this.) Yeah, yeah, he's fictional too.

ZHANG ZHONGJING *(150–219)* One of the most important doctors in Chinese medicine. He also invented dumplings, making him my favourite doctor in all of history (except for me).

INDEX

My favourite pages!

Oi!

Oi again!

→ This is stupid. Stop it now. Prunella

CREDITS

INVENTORY
Katherine Whelan

PRODUCTION
Naomi Green
Michael Martin
Erica Pascal
Jamie Taylor

FINANCE
Aimee Buchanan
Duc Luong

CONTRACTS
Mary Fox

RIGHTS
Maeve Banham
Bethany Copeland
Susanne Evans
Beth Fennell
Alice Grigg
Millie Lovett
Lena Petzke

SALES
Kat Baker
Hannah Best
Toni Budden
Karin Burnik
Ruth Burrow
Autumn Evans
Han Ismail

Lorraine Levis
Geraldine McBride
Sophie Marston
Sarah Roscoe
Rozzie Todd
Becki Wells

MARKETING & COMMUNICATIONS
Simon Armstrong
Roma Baig
Dusty Miller
Jannine Saunders
Tania Vian-Smith

BIBLIOGRAPHIC METADATA
Lauren Floodgate
Jack Lowe

OPERATIONS
Lewis Pearce
Sally Rideout

PRINTERS
David Banks
Bart Chrzanowski
Richard Diaz
Ruby King
Nicola Kingsnorth
Rebecca Lynchsmith
Greg Manterfield-Ivory

ADAM'S LAWYER
Nigel Rosenkrantz

ADAM KAY is a former doctor who has written three million books and sold four copies. No, hang on – he's written four books and sold three million copies.

#KaysMarvellousMedicine

HENRY PAKER was once a little boy who did silly doodles in the margins of books. Now he is a grown man who does silly doodles in the middle of books.

INTRODUCTION TO ENGINEERING

THIRD EDITION

**Books are to be returned on or before
the last date below.**

LIBREX —

INTRODUCTION TO ENGINEERING

THIRD EDITION

PAUL H. WRIGHT

Professor Emeritus
School of Civil and Environmental Engineering
Georgia Institute of Technology

JOHN WILEY & SONS, INC.

ACQUISITIONS EDITOR: Joseph P. Hayton
MARKETING MANAGER: Katherine Hepburn
SENIOR PRODUCTION EDITOR: Valerie A. Vargas
SENIOR DESIGNER: Harry Nolan
PRODUCTION MANAGEMENT SERVICES: Argosy

This book was set in 10/12 Melior by Argosy and printed and bound by Courier/Westford. The cover was printed by Lehigh Press, Inc.

This book is printed on acid-free paper.

Library of Congress Cataloging-in-Publication Data

Wright, Paul H.
  Introduction to engineering/Paul H. Wright.—3rd ed.
    p. cm.
  Includes bibliographical references and index.
  ISBN 0-471-05920-X (pbk,:alk. paper)
  1. Engineering. I. Title.

TA145 .W75 2001
620—dc21   2001046541
ISBN 0-471-05920-X

Printed in the United States of America

10 9 8 7 6 5 4 3 2

D
620
WRI